# FORT HALL

Gateway to the Oregon Country

*By Frank C. Robertson*

A RAM IN THE THICKET

SOAPY SMITH:
King of the Frontier Con Men
(with Beth Kay Harris)

# FORT HALL

## Gateway to the Oregon Country

BY FRANK C. ROBERTSON

HASTINGS HOUSE
*Publishers*
NEW YORK

To KATHLEEN, JUNE and MABEL

the McNicholls girls who grew up in
Canada in the shadow of the fur trade,
and in Alaska

Published simultaneously in Canada
by S. J. Reginald Saunders, Publishers, Toronto 23.

Library of Congress Catalog Card Number: 63-19174

*Printed in the United States of America*

# Contents

Acknowledgments  7

Fort Hall and Frank Robertson  9
    by LeRoy R. Hafen

1   Introduction: The Land of Plenty Game  11

2   First Crossing of the Bar  20

3   The Fall of Astoria  35

4   The Prophet of Oregon  49

5   The Iceman Cometh  65

6   The Titans of the North  84

7   The Second Coming  97

8   The Fort on the Bottoms  108

9   Kelley in Oregon  121

10   The Playboy of the Mountains  133

11   The Explorations of Captain Bonneville  145

12   The Surrender of Fort Hall  161

13   The Social Chasm  169

14   "The Riddlings of Creation"  182

15   Oregon or the Grave  197

16   Brown's Hole  211

17   The Forks of the Trail  225

18   Indian Trouble  242

19   Hudson's Bay in Retreat   254

20   The Roaring Sixties   265

21   The Last of the Fur Trade   279

22   The Thundering Herds   288

Bibliography   304

Index   309

# List of Illustrations

*Between pages 160 and 161*

Nathaniel J. Wyeth, Dr. John McLoughlin, Hall J. Kelley, Peter Skene Ogden, Jason Lee, Francis Ermatinger, Captain B. L. E. Bonneville

Jack Edmo, prominent Fort Hall Indian

Indian tepee, Fort Hall bottoms

Tes Pokebro, well-known Fort Hall Indian

Old Fort Hall

Fort Hall, government trading post, 1878

Eagle Rock Bridge, Snake River; Utah & Northern locomotive

Overland Stage

Ezra Meeker, "Father of the Oregon Trail"

Discovery of old Fort Hall site, 1916. Ezra Meeker, Dr. W. Howard, Dr. Minnie Howard in foreground

Dutch John townsite, near Flaming Gorge Dam, Green River

Map of Fort Hall area   302–303

# ACKNOWLEDGMENTS

I am grateful to the following for aid and encouragement given me in the writing of this book: Kathleen Greaser, of San Mateo, California; Elva and Dr. William Olsen, of Pocatello, Idaho; Marie and Dr. Forrest Howard, of Santa Ana, California; Professor Thomas West and Mr. Nicholas Ifft of the *Idaho State Journal*, both Pocatello; Grace and Virgil Rice, of El Cerrito, California; Glen and Vera Robertson, of Visalia, California; Ersal, Ezra and James Corneilison, of Fort Hall, Idaho; Ted Faulkner and Art Bowman, of Chesterfield, Idaho; Agnes Just Reid, of Firth, Idaho; Beth Kay Harris and LeRoy and Ann Hafen, of Provo, Utah; Ralph Peters, of Dutch John, Utah; and Charles Kelly and Sam Weller, of Salt Lake City.

I also want to extend my thanks to Mr. Dale Morgan

7

and the staff of the Bancroft Library at Berkeley, California; to Mr. J. V. Root, of the Idaho Historical Society at Boise; to the staff of the Utah State Historical Society; and to the staff of the National Forest Service at Pocatello. To any others whom I may have overlooked, my apologies.

FRANK C. ROBERTSON

# FORT HALL and
# FRANK ROBERTSON

On that memorable day in 1834 when Nathaniel J. Wyeth, the Boston iceman turned fur trader, raised the American flag over the adobe walls of his trading post, a new era dawned in the history of the West. There on the "south branch of the Columbia" (now Snake River) he opened his bales of fur-trade goods, unbunged a keg of Mountain Man refreshment and christened the post Fort Hall.

To this place he had escorted, from the banks of the "Big Muddy" (Missouri River) the pioneer missionaries answering the Indian call for the white man's religion. And that missionary band was the precursor of the endless caravans of white-topped wagons which began to roll in 1841.

9

From the womb of those prairie schooners came the pioneers who subdued and peopled the Far West.

Into his popular treatment of Fort Hall, Frank Robertson has brought loving recollections of his boyhood land in Idaho, Oregon and Washington which for many years centered about Fort Hall. To it also he has brought a rich lifetime of writing in the field of his own West. In scores of previous volumes of lively fiction, many of which have been translated into foreign languages, he has recreated characters and scenes true to the time and place. His Sunday column, which has run in the *Provo Herald* since 1941, has endeared him to thousands of readers who regularly turn to the "Chopping Block" for fresh, original and courageous views on the current scene and significant problems.

A nationwide audience has read and continues to read the honest and graphic portrayal of the pioneering experiences of Frank's own family narrated in his autobiography, *A Ram in the Thicket. The Reader's Digest* had the wisdom to present for its millions of readers that same fascinating story. Mr. Robertson has served as President of Western Writers of America and also of the League of Utah Writers, and has been variously honored on numerous occasions.

It is good now to have my valued friend turn his fine talents to the story of historic Fort Hall.

Dr. LeRoy R. Hafen

Brigham Young University
    Provo, Utah.

# 1

Introduction:

# THE LAND OF PLENTY GAME

*I have built a fort on Snake, or Lewis, river which I named Fort Hall from the oldest gentleman in the concern. We manufactured a magnificent flag from unbleached sheeting, a little red flannel and a few blue patches, saluted it with damaged powder and wet it with villainous alcohol and it makes, I do assure you, a very respectable appearance amid the dry and desolate regions of Central America. Its bastions stand a terror to the skulking Indians and a beacon of safety to the fugitive hunter. It is manned by 12 men and has constantly loaded in the bastions 100 guns and rifles. After building the fort I sent messengers to the neighboring nations to induce them to come in and trade.*

The words are those of Nathaniel J. Wyeth, proper Bostonian, frontiersman and adventurous entrepreneur, written in 1834. To Americans back in the States, the raising

11

of the first United States flag in what Wyeth called "Central
America" and most of his countrymen thought of as the
Great American Desert meant little or nothing. Today we
know the central significance it had in the whole expan-
sionist movement to the Pacific; and even then the men
of the Hudson's Bay Company saw in the construction of
this fortified post on the banks of the Snake a real threat
to the British Empire. Their vision was a truer one than
that of the back-home Americans and they lost no time
in building their own fort not far away on the banks of
the Boise, their prime purpose in doing so being the forth-
right one of putting Fort Hall out of business. Eventually
they succeeded, to the extent of taking over Fort Hall themselves, but they could not change it from what it had become—a vital way point on the American emigrants' road
to Oregon. The Hudson's Bay men there did all in their
power to steer the Yankee movers toward California and
away from the Northwest. The partial success they achieved
assured our conquest of California. That it was only partial
also determined that the disputed Oregon country would
fall to the intruders from the lusty young republic that
just a few decades before had broken away from England.

It is one of the ironies of history that the sophisticated
and powerful Dr. John McLoughlin, head factor of Hudson's Bay in the Oregon country, was bested in the end
by the determination and the intuitive foresight of a Yankee
merchant-trader whose ambition outran his resources and
who soon retreated from the frontier, to all appearances
broken and defeated. The forces relentlessly at work were
bigger than the luckless Yankee; more importantly, they
were bigger even than the canny Scot who held all the high

cards in the game that was being played for the ownership of Oregon.

A prominent New York editor, speaking to a group of Western writers in Salt Lake City, once defended himself against the charge of being unable to comprehend the West by saying, "While it is true that I was born in Vermont, and have lived most of my life in New York City, my mother tells me I was conceived in Colorado." Similarly, it may be said that while Fort Hall was one of the most important outposts on the Western frontier, it was conceived in Salem, Massachusetts. Those who were involved in its conception had no idea that their actions would give birth to the fort on the Snake River. They knew only that some day they would go to Oregon to make their private fortunes and help to build a nation.

We shall trace separately the careers of a triumvirate gathered in Salem that was ultimately responsible for the building of Fort Hall. One of them, the idealist and visionary Hall Jackson Kelley, often called the "Prophet of Oregon," was never to see Fort Hall; actually, he saw Oregon only once, and then under bitterly disappointing circumstances. The second was Nathaniel Jarvis Wyeth, who saw plenty of Oregon and built the fort on the banks of the Snake. The third, Captain Benjamin Louis Eulalie de Bonneville, was to make Oregon widely known by relating his adventures in the vicinity of Fort Hall to Washington Irving, who thus came to write the first great romance of the West.

These three were accompanied and followed, first by hopeful scores, later by confident thousands, eager for pelts and furs, afire for gold and hungry for land. They were ready to contend for the country, both against the power of the Hudson's Bay Company, backed by British imperial might, and against the native tribes that occupied it. The careful British, interested primarily in exploiting the wealth represented by the fur-bearing creatures of its woods and streams, seemed to offer little threat to the Indians. The impetuous Americans, intent on grabbing everything in sight, were something else again.

Game abounded in the Fort Hall bottoms in 1834. Wyeth chose as the site of his fort the spot where a buffalo killed by his hunter fell and was skinned and dressed out. This place was, in fact, the "land of plenty game" for trappers and traders as well as for the Indians, although some twenty years earlier the Wilson Price Hunt party almost starved to death and in 1839 the men at Fort Hall had difficulty in getting enough to eat. There were good years and bad years, which the Indians took in stride; it was tougher on the whites.

The Indians who lived there, Bannacks and Shoshones, looked on calmly while Wyeth built his fort. These were peaceful Indians, especially the Shoshones. The only tribe they made war upon was the Blackfeet and then usually in self-defense. They were friendly and cooperative when the first traders and trappers came into their country and they remained so long after Fort Hall was built, although Wyeth was skeptical of them. Later on, they suffered exploitation, indignities and abuses until they retaliated in kind.

These Indians had little to gain by the coming of the white men. They were on friendly terms with their neighbors, excepting the warlike Blackfeet, and other tribes were at liberty to pass to and fro in their territory. The Fort Hall bottoms was their garden of Eden, and it was most fortunately situated. It was an area of more than 100,000 acres, covered with creeks and springs where the grass grew in abundance, and with a climate so mild that it afforded winter pasture in turn for buffalo, horses and cattle. The Indians called it *shawnt shawnip*, ("plenty game").

There were deer, antelope and mountain sheep, with fish and beaver in the streams. Old buffalo wallows are all over the area, and although this is about as far west as the great creatures usually got there were thousands of them. The Indians who lived there were not hoggish, and it was a favorite hunting ground for the Nez Percé and other horse Indians from the Northwest. There were occasionally bad times but as a rule the Indians lived well and had everything they needed to provide for their simple wants. Had their women not been frugal and industrious some of the winters might have been tough. But there were wild currants, chokecherries and service berries to be picked and dried, and there was that staple of Indian fare, the camas roots, to be dug. Snake River is a windy country, and the game had a habit of moving out at various seasons. This was particularly true of the buffalo, which traveled in herds.

Beyond the bottoms lay the desolate and dreary Snake River desert, where a man could die of thirst or starvation. In 1900 I crossed this desert in a covered wagon with my father. We followed the Oregon Short Line Railroad, making sixteen miles a day because the only water was at the railroad tanks, and they were placed that distance apart. Except for the train crews and an occasional lonesome hobo packing his blankets down the track, we saw no one. Ours was a trip of ease, though, compared to what the emigrants heading for Oregon and California had to go through. Here and there one may still see the wagon ruts worn into steep gullies and packed so hard that even the sagebrush, or wormwood as it was then called, refuses to grow. And I have seen some of the unmarked graves beside the way.

The old Oregon Trail was still being used by covered wagons as late as the beginning of the present century. I may not have seen the last wagon train, but I have an idea that I did. In 1901 I was living with my parents in Chesterfield, Idaho, only a mile or so from the old road. I was no stranger to a covered wagon for I had been moving around in one all my young life, but I was excited by seeing some thirty of them crawling along over the Portneuf meadows. Their destination, I learned, was the Grande Ronde Valley in eastern Oregon. In all the years that I lived there I never again saw a wagon train.

The exact location of old Fort Hall was in doubt for many years, for it had grown up to willows, and there were at least three other places within a radius of thirty miles that were at various times called Fort Hall. Today you may drive through a place on Highway 91 that is so named. It is an Indian Agency, and the number of Indians might lead you to imagine that it is not much different from what it was when the original fort was built, but if so you would be mistaken. Wyeth's Fort Hall was located some twelve miles west and a little north of the present Fort Hall Indian Agency. The ground surrounding it is at times covered by the water of the American Falls reservoir. All of the material used in the original fort was taken away to build other places. After it was finally abandoned by the Hudson's Bay Company in 1856 the old buildings were gradually obliterated, but there has always been a "Fort Hall" somewhere in the vicinity.

At the beginning of the century most people had lost interest in the old site, but fortunately there is always someone to see that the past is not forgotten. Here it was Dr. Minnie Howard of Pocatello, Idaho, affectionately known locally as Dr. Minnie, who has made a lifelong study of the history of Fort Hall and whose dream was to find the old site and erect a monument over it.

Then came Ezra Meeker, often called "the Daddy of the Oregon Trail," who stopped off in Pocatello on one of his many trips along the trail by ox team to find places for historical markers. He spoke to a group of Pocatello people, and in the audience was Dr. Minnie Howard. She invited Mr. Meeker home to dinner. The next day Dr. Minnie gathered a small group of people, including Mr. Meeker and an Indian named Jim Broncho, and drove out on the bottoms between Snake and Portneuf rivers. Finally, Mr. Meeker said, "This is the place." It was confirmed by Jim Broncho, and a stone marker has been erected there.

So now we know for certain that Nathaniel Wyeth built his Fort Hall on the banks of Snake River, some ten miles above the mouth of the Portneuf. The spot is dominated by Mt. Putnam, east of the Portneuf, and by Mt. Kinport on the west. From the top of a ridge on a clear day you can see the three Teton Peaks—a landmark for white travelers for a century and a half, and no one knows how long before that for the Indians. East of old Fort Hall is a long, low hill called Ferry Butte, where many thousands of westering Americans made their camps; it was known to every emigrant who followed the Oregon Trail. To the northwest, out on the desert, are three large buttes that also were landmarks, known as Big Butte and Twin Buttes. Beyond them stretches the formidable Snake River desert, with its lava beds, sagebrush, impassable gorges and rivers that disappear in the earth—fittingly called Big and Little Lost Rivers. Birch Creek, almost a river in size, likewise does a vanishing act in the desert.

In the early days five roads fanned out from Fort Hall like the spokes from the hub of a wagon wheel, leading east and west, north and south, and to the northwest. Over them rolled vehicles that carried precious human cargoes and flaunted the invisible banner of Manifest Destiny. For many years after it was acquired by the Hudson's Bay Company, Fort Hall was the padlock to the gate by which the British tried to stem the flood of American emigration to the Northwest. Our own statesmen were shortsighted enough to believe the land was barren and worthless, but the British were equally blind, measuring its value solely in terms of fur.

Truly, the streams were full of beaver then, and it remained good trapping ground long after the beaver had disappeared from most parts of the country. Later the land provided range for teeming herds of beef cattle, for vast wheat farms and prosperous homesteads. In the 1860s discovered gold added greatly to the nation's mineral wealth. In recent years huge deposits of phosphate have been found. Near the Craters of the Moon National Monument, where the tourist is well advised not to venture without a guide, is the government's atomic-energy plant at Arco. The land of plenty game is still in process of change.

I grew to manhood in the region around Fort Hall. It is a place and a land that I know and love. Its story, though, may be told only against the background of the whole Oregon country from the eighteenth century to the present.

# 2

# FIRST CROSSING OF THE BAR

NOT MUCH WAS KNOWN OF the Oregon country at the beginning of the nineteenth century. *Carver's Travels*, published in the latter part of the eighteenth, had mentioned "The river Oregon, or the river of the West," which was the first time the word Oregon appeared in print. People were still writing and talking about a great river, usually called the Buenaventura, which was supposed to flow from the Rocky Mountains into the Pacific Ocean. The Columbia was a mighty river, but until 1792 no sea-going vessel had ever entered it, and for a good reason.

The Columbia opens up into a broad estuary at its mouth, and the silt had formed a great bar separating it from the ocean. Sea captains did not believe that it was navigable. Great navigators such as Sir Francis Drake sailed past the mouth of the river without knowing that it was there. Best known of those who did so, perhaps, was Captain James Cook, who was later killed in the Sandwich Islands. Cook named Cape Flattery, but he missed the strait of Juan de Fuca, leading into Puget Sound; he did discover Nootka Sound off the coast of Vancouver Island in 1788.

As early as 1543 the Spaniard, Juan Cabrillo, had missed the Columbia, as did Drake in 1579; it was Drake who christened that part of the country New Albion. In 1592 a Greek pilot, Apostolus Valerianos (alias Juan de Fuca) found the Strait of Anian, which he claimed was the long-sought Northwest Passage.

In 1728 the Dane, Vitus Bering, employed by Peter the Great of Russia, discovered the Bering Sea, and in 1741 he established trading posts from Alaska to California, but he missed the Columbia. In 1775 Bruno Hecata and Bodega y Quadra, Spanish navigators, were in sight of the river but did not enter it.

1788 found Captain John Meares, British explorer, sailing up the coast to the Strait of Juan de Fuca, but again the Columbia was overlooked. The British established a post on Vancouver Island, but in 1789 they were expelled by a Spanish force under Estavan José Martinez, who took possession in the name of Spain.

It was inevitable that the United States, though a young nation, should have a go at it. Among the seafaring men of New England there was considerable interest in the Pacific Coast. They knew little, and cared less, about the interior. All they knew was that there were Indians there who might be induced to trade for trinkets furs which could be sold at great profit in China. There they could load up cargos of tea and other goods of the Orient which could be sold at substantial profit in Boston. Some of them were convinced that it would be even better than the African slave trade.

When Captain Cook sailed along the coast in 1788 he had on board his ships, the *Discovery* and the *Resolution*, two native-born Americans, Lieutenant John Gore, who succeeded to the command after Cook was killed, and John Ledyard, a man who deserves more credit than he ever received. Like Hall J. Kelley, Ledyard was something of a visionary, and like Kelley his plans were doomed to failure, but indirectly he had a great deal to do with making the Northwest known.

Returning to Boston, Ledyard told of the lush profits that could be made in the China trade, and created enough interest so that, in 1787, a group of practical businessmen met at the home of Dr. Charles Bullfinch in Bowdoin Square. Having verified Ledyard's claim that the Chinese were anxious to trade, a stock company was organized with a capitalization of $50,000, divided into fourteen shares. They purchased two ships, the *Columbia*, and the *Lady Washington*, the latter sloop under the command of Captain Robert Gray.

Ledyard was not included in the deal, and he chartered ship after ship of his own, only to have something happen to each of them before they could be put in trade. For year after weary year he traveled around the world trying to get financial backing. One of his temporary partners was American naval hero John Paul Jones.

In Paris, Ledyard won the friendship of Thomas Jefferson and Marquis de Lafayette, who gave him all the help possible, but always he encountered disheartening setbacks. As Kelley was to do later, Ledyard wrote voluminously, and for years he carried on a correspondence with Jefferson about the advantages of the Northwest Coast. Almost surely he influenced Jefferson to some extent in sending out the Lewis and Clark expedition, which gave us our first real claim on the country.

Ledyard's life was a tragic one. He proposed to walk across the country to become familiar with the interior and received Jefferson's encouragement, but the trip was never made. Instead, he tried walking across Siberia, and had almost accomplished the feat when he was arrested as a French spy on orders of Catherine the Great. His friends Jefferson and Lafayette got him released after he had served a term in prison, and he made his way to London. Here he undertook to lead an exploring party to Africa, but before he could start he sickened and died. He may have been our first real soldier of fortune, but history has almost forgotten him.

It took Captain Robert Gray nearly five years of sailing before he became the first man to bring a ship through the bar into the Columbia River, on May 11, 1792. As he commanded the *Columbia* at the time, he gave its name to the river, and claimed the country for the United States by right of discovery. During those five years he had several brushes with Spanish ships, and once he sailed around the Cape of Good Hope from Nootka Sound to Boston, thus becoming the first American sea captain to circumnavigate the world. It was while he was at Nootka Sound that Gray's belief about the Columbia was questioned, and his resentment caused him to sail south and across the bar. His burst of temper gave the United States an unsteady claim on the Northwest Coast.

Gray was none too soon, for the same year Lieutenant William Broughten of the British Navy sailed into the estuary, then up the river as far as the Cascades, and discovered Mt. Hood. Broughten maintained that Gray had only sailed inside some twenty-five miles and couldn't have known that he was in a river. Arguments about the respective claims by land and sea were to thunder through the halls of Congress and Parliament for fifty years.

Canada was pretty much controlled by two great fur companies, Hudson's Bay in the east and the Northwest Company in the west; so bitter were their feuds that many were killed, and they often resorted to kidnaping and robbery. Against the Americans, however, they presented a common front. In 1821 the two companies were merged under the title of the Hudson's Bay Company.

The Northwest Company was the first to see the possibilities of the fur trade in the Oregon country. In 1793 Sir Alexander Mackenzie led an expedition across the continent, opening up the Northwest to the fur trappers, but he didn't get as far south as the Columbia.

David Thompson, another Canadian, explored the country more thoroughly in 1807, but he was a little behind the American expedition under Meriwether Lewis and William Clark, who between 1804 and 1806 journeyed from St. Louis to the mouth of the Columbia and back, adding another stake to Gray's claim.

In 1810 the Winship brothers attempted a settlement at Oak Point on the lower Columbia but failed because the

Indians would not trade with them. Then in 1811 the wealthy John Jacob Astor, of New York, lured by tales of the fortunes to be made on the Northwest Coast, organized the John Jacob Astor Pacific Fur Company and sent out two expeditions, one by sea and one by land. The one by sea was the first to arrive at Astoria, and the American flag flew over the Oregon country.

The career of this German butcher boy needs no recounting here. He had but one motto: "Get ahead, give the least, and get the most. Get all you can, and keep what you get." He was so successful that he died leaving a fortune of $30,000,000. He had gone into the business often carrying his furs on his back.

He sold six million beaver pelts annually, most of them to be made into hats, and on those he shipped to England he made five dollars each, investing the returns in goods which enabled him to realize eight dollars of profit for every dollar invested. He sent cargos of fur to China, realizing a gain of $30,000 for every shipload. It was inevitable that his eyes should turn toward the Pacific Northwest.

At the beginning he took in as partners three former employees of the Northwest Fur Company; Alexander McKay, Duncan McDougal and Donald McKenzie. Also included was Wilson Price Hunt of New Jersey, who was to be principal agent on the Columbia River.

Hunt was to lead a party overland while the others were to go by sea on the ship, *Tonquin,* commanded by Lieutenant Jonathan Thorn, on leave from the United States Navy. Astor, of course, remained in New York.

The *Tonquin* was plagued with trouble from the start. Under the laws of the sea the captain was absolute master aboard his ship, and though Captain Thorn had been instructed by Astor to do everything possible to promote harmony and good will his first act was to antagonize his passengers who, as partners in the company which owned the ship, considered Thorn to be working for them. The four Scotsmen on board, McKay, McDougal, David Stuart and his nephew Robert, were no doubt clannish and rubbed the captain the wrong way. In the end he succeeded in proving that he could be just as stubborn as they were, but at the cost of many lives, including his own.

Thorn began by ordering them to extinguish their lights at eight o'clock, an affront to their dignity as partners in the company. The wordy war concluded when the captain threatened to put them in irons, and Duncan McDougal, as controversial a figure as Oregon ever produced, drew a pistol and challenged Thorn to try to carry out his threat. It was not a propitious beginning for a long voyage.

Astor had asked Captain Thorn to make special efforts to win friends in the Sandwich Islands, with the ultimate aim of setting up a base there, but his efforts were confined to carrying on his feud with the partners. He objected to their wearing kilts when they went ashore, and protested their cutting souvenirs from the trees at the place where Captain Cook had been killed. The natives gave a dance in honor of the Scotsmen, which further embittered Captain Thorn. All he could do was write letter after letter of complaint to Mr. Astor. David Stuart, he charged, was guilty of fraternizing with the crew.

At the mouth of the Columbia the bar was so rough that it was over the protests of the partners that Captain Thorn sent out five men under first mate Fox to make soundings. All were drowned. Still obdurate, he sent out five other men, and three of these were drowned, the remaining two managing to swim ashore.

When the *Tonquin* finally got inside, Thorn refused to waste time looking for a suitable site and dumped the passengers and supplies on shore at Baker Bay. When the Indians came on board to trade they looked like ragamuffins and Thorn refused to trade with them. The cargo was finally landed at what was to become Astoria, a site located by Duncan McDougal and David Stuart. There they made friends with Chief Comcomly of the Chinooks, who was soon to become Duncan McDougal's father-in-law.

Captain Thorn, with twenty-three men on board, sailed away to the north to trade with what he hoped would be a better class of Indians, taking along a native trader whose name, Washington Irving says, was Lamazee. (Hubert Howe Bancroft, who discounted everything Irving wrote, maintained that no Indian had a *zee* in his name.)

Thorn anchored at Clayoquot Sound on the west side of Vancouver Island, against the advice of the interpreter, who warned him that the Indians there were treacherous. While Alexander McKay went on shore to get acquainted Thorn broke out the trading goods, knives, axes, blankets, fishhooks and beads.

When the Indians came on board they were arrogant. Their chief, Nookamis, thinking Thorn was not impressed enough by a fine otter skin he held, shoved it in the captain's face. Angered, Thorn grabbed the pelt, rubbed the chief's face in it, then kicked him overboard and threw the remainder of the peltries into the sea. McKay, learning what had happened, urged the captain to set sail at once. He received the characteristic reply that when the captain wanted any advice he would ask for it; if the savages made any more trouble they would receive a dose of lead, Thorn vowed.

When a large number of seemingly humbled Indians came on board the next morning and asked to trade, Thorn overruled McKay's protest and began to bargain. By the time Thorn noticed that too many axes and knives were disappearing it was too late. The weapons came out from under furs and blankets and in a few minutes only five whites on board were left alive. Four of them, sailors, attempted to swim to shore but were captured and killed, leaving only Lewis, the ship's clerk, alive, and he was badly wounded. Captain Thorn was said to have accounted for one of the chiefs, but he was stabbed and thrown overboard.

The next morning the Indians came on board to loot the ship and suddenly the powder magazine exploded, killing more than a hundred of them, along with the injured Lewis.

Since the only survivor of the *Tonquin* was the interpreter, Lamazee, it is impossible to know exactly what happened. One account has Lamazee rushing back to Astoria with the news; another has him a prisoner of the Indians for two years. Irving has it that Lewis enticed the Indians aboard, then dropped a match into the powder magazine to blow up the ship and himself. The more realistic Bancroft believed that the Indians themselves accidentally may have fired the magazine. At any rate, John Jacob Astor could scarcely have found a man more unfitted for dealing with traders, trappers and Indians than Captain Thorn.

The loss of the *Tonquin* was a severe blow to the Pacific Fur Company.

However McDougal got the word, it was alarming. Fearful that the Indians along the Columbia would rise, McDougal called the chiefs together. Being mindful of their fear of smallpox he showed them a bottle and said, "In this bottle I hold the plague of smallpox. If I pull the cork it will come out and sweep you all from the earth. If you are peaceful and treat us well I will keep the cork in the bottle."

The bluff worked, and McDougal solidified his position by marrying the daughter of old one-eyed Chief Comcomly. These mixed marriages, encouraged by both the Hudson's Bay and the Northwest companies, had a great deal to do with the history of Oregon. Their effects were planned, but sometimes coincidence seemed to play an important part.

When the *Tonquin* sailed away from Astoria with Alexander McKay on board, his fourteen-year-old son Thomas had a cold and was left behind, thus escaping the fate of his father. Alexander McKay had left his wife, a part Ojibway woman who had received a good education at a convent in the East, at Fort William on Lake Superior. Young Thomas was sent back there, where his mother would marry Dr. John McLoughlin, who twelve years later was sent to head the Hudson's Bay Company on the Columbia. McLoughlin was the man to be accused by the Americans of doing most to keep them from getting past Fort Hall, and his stepson, Thomas McKay, was to become his chief trouble-shooter.

Meantime, McDougal and his men completed a large stone building at Astoria, and later they built and launched a small schooner called the *Dolly*, the first American-built vessel to be launched on the Pacific Coast. More trouble clouds were on the horizon, but John Jacob Astor and his associates were in business in Oregon.

Twenty-five hundred miles away in St. Louis, Wilson Price Hunt had begun one of the most hazardous overland journeys ever undertaken. The party was beset by difficulties all the way, for they had no trail to follow and little knowledge of the country except that gleaned from Indians, yet Hunt was fortunate in getting the services of a few experienced mountain men.

He had engaged as interpreter Pierre Dorion, son of the Dorion who had been interpreter for Lewis and Clark, and his Sioux wife, Marie, who aided Hunt much as Sacajawea had aided Lewis and Clark and who is known to history as "the Dorion woman."

Also accompanying Hunt to the vicinity of Fort Hall were Sacajawea and her husband, Touissant Charbonneau, and their son, returning to join her people, the Shoshones. It is not likely that Charbonneau, the man who collected $500 from Lewis and Clark for services his wife rendered, while she got nothing, was of any great help to Hunt. More valuable were four mountain men he had picked up whose names were to become famous in the lore of the West. They were John Day, Edward Robinson, John Hoback and Jacob Rezner. Both Day and Hoback have rivers named in their honor.

Some or all of these men had been with Andrew Henry, partner of Manuel Lisa, the year before. Henry had built a fort near present-day St. Anthony, Idaho, less than a hundred miles from where Fort Hall was later to be built. His party was the first to cross the Rocky Mountains and trap the headwaters of Snake River. It is possible that some of Henry's men had trapped down the Snake as far as the Fort Hall bottoms; if so, they were the first white men in that part of the country. However, this is only conjecture; there is no written record of it.

Henry abandoned his post and started east to meet his partner, Lisa, who was greatly concerned about him, and did not return to the mountains. Robinson, Hoback, and Rezner started down the Missouri in a bullboat but, encountering Hunt's party, were easily persuaded to turn back. Robinson had already lost his scalp to the Indians, and kept his head covered with a bandanna, but a little thing like that did not dismay a mountain man.

Robinson and his friends guided Hunt up the Yellowstone, keeping him from following the northward route of Lewis and Clark as he had intended. They crossed over Teton Pass at the foot of the famous landmarks, the Three Teton peaks, and on to Henry's abandoned fort, where Hunt paused to rest his horses and survey his prospects.

Among his men were a number of old *voyageurs* accustomed to traveling by boat, and here finally, after they had failed on a wilder river, was a broad, smooth stream. Hunt was persuaded to leave his horses in care of a Shoshone Indian, and his party set off downriver in five pirogues. He navigated Idaho and American Falls and in a few days reached the Fort Hall bottoms, and so was the first white man definitely known to have trod the ground on which Fort Hall was to be built.

From that time on the suffering of the Hunt party was unparalleled in the exploration of the West. The peaceful-looking Snake River was not what it seemed, for they entered a deep gorge between high, perpendicular walls where Shoshone Falls plunges over a precipice higher than Niagara, and Twin Falls, a few miles above, has never been navigated by any boat.

At the beginning of the gorge one of the pirogues was wrecked and a veteran voyageur named Antoine Chappine was drowned. They gave the name of Caldron Linn to the gorge, later changing it to the Devil's Scuttle Hole.

It quickly became apparent that they would have to travel by land, and Hunt divided his party into three, one on each side of the river, and the other heading due north toward the distant mountains. They were nearly out of food, and suffered agonies of thirst within sight of the river they were unable to reach.

It became a story of tracing and retracing their steps. The party under McLellin, which had gone north, was the more fortunate of the three, reaching the Nez Percé country ahead of Hunt. The only food of the other two was an occasional horse or dog they were able to buy from wandering Indian bands.

Hunt sent Ramsey Crooks and his men back to Fort Henry for the horses, but after a few days they turned back, preferring, if they were going to starve to death, to do it while going in the right direction. Hunt himself followed the north—later, the east—bank of the river, while Crooks kept to the south and west. Starvation was close to them all. Eventually, Hunt sighted Crooks's party across the river, exhausted and almost done for. Hunt finally succeeded in sending some horse meat over to them, although he had difficulty getting anyone to take it across the river. One man, becoming demented at the sight of food, jumped into the water and was drowned.

Both parties were stopped by Hell's Canyon, a gorge deeper than the Grand Canyon. Hunt turned back, got across the river and joined Crooks's starving men. Presently, they were reduced to one skeletonlike horse, the property of Pierre Dorion, who resolutely refused to allow it to be killed for food. On the animal's skinny back rode his pregnant Indian wife, and her two children, aged two and four. She had become a general favorite of the party; had it not been so the horse would have been eaten by the starving men in spite of Dorion's property rights. They finally got over the Blue mountains and were able to buy horse meat from the Indians. McLellin and his men were found awaiting them on the Walla Walla.

The troubles of the Dorion woman were by no means over. After the arrival of the party at Astoria a trapping party was sent back to the Boise under an Irishman named Read. One day the Dorion woman learned that the men had been attacked by Bannack Indians and were supposedly all killed. Taking a horse, she collected her children and fled for her life. She soon had to abandon the horse and, traveling by night and hiding by day, she again crossed the Blue mountains, under conditions similar to, or even worse than, those of her first trip across them. Undaunted, she finally reached the Walla Walla and safety.

Wilson Price Hunt and his bedraggled men finally reached Astoria and he promptly committed his greatest blunder. The year was 1812 and there were ominous rumors of war between the United States and England. Though Hunt was supposed to take charge, he left Duncan Mc-Dougal in command while he sailed away on a trading expedition to Nootka Sound. When he returned he found out that McDougal had sold out to his old employers, the Northwest Fur Company.

# 3

# THE FALL OF ASTORIA

In BLISSFUL IGNORANCE OF
what had happened to his two expeditions, John Jacob
Astor had chartered the *Beaver*, a vessel of 490 tons, under
Captain Sowle, and despatched it to Astoria. On board
were five clerks, fifteen American workmen, six Canadian
*voyageurs* and John Clarke, another partner in the company.

Captain Sowle was under orders to stop at the Sandwich Islands and take on board a number of skilled Kanaka
boatmen for service on the Columbia. The *Beaver* left
New York October 10, 1811, and reached Astoria the following May 6, after having fulfilled its mission in the islands.
Its arrival was hailed with joy by everyone except the traders
of the Northwest Fur Company. Duncan McDougal and
his new father-in-law, one-eyed Chief Comcomly, with a

large party of whites and Indians, met the *Beaver* and piloted it safely across the bar.

The Astor company was already being hard pressed by the British. Alexander Mackenzie of the Northwest Company had long since explored the region to the north by way of Fraser River, and David Thompson, another of its famous explorers, who had been trained as an employee of Hudson's Bay, arrived at Astoria in 1812 to represent the company. En route he had mapped seventy-eight company trading posts, and he had established Kullyspell House in what is now the panhandle of Idaho.

The rivalry between the Northwest and Hudson's Bay companies had been long and bitter. The HBC had been chartered by Charles II of England in 1670 and had enjoyed a virtual monopoly of the fur trade until the organization of the Northwest Fur Company in 1787. The latter firm, young and aggressive, had disregarded alleged royal rights and cut deeply into the business of the older company, particularly in the west. They were ruthless in their methods and seldom hesitated to use violence. Personal feuds developed that were long and bitter, and even Sir George Simpson, Governor General of Hudson's Bay, became involved in some of them.

In one of the great journals of the fur trade, Alexander Ross, an explorer and trader who entered the service of the Northwest Company, speaks cuttingly of their methods and personnel. He was familiar with Astor's company and comments that it deserved a better fate. He makes it clear that the one object of the Northwest Fur company was monopolization: "The Northwest company never has enough" . . . "It quarrels with its neighbors, and its vanity and extravagance are proverbial." Its methods, he adds, do not produce contentment.

The Northwest Fur Company was wealthy. Its headquarters were in Montreal, and it was powerful enough to influence public opinion. Most of the population were French-Canadians, many of them *voyageurs*, and they had no veneration for Hudson's Bay, because it was English. Ross states that the high officials of the Northwest Company were revered by these *voyageurs* as though they were Grand Lamas.

To Ross, the young officials of the company were dandies who wore fine clothes, rode fine horses and were usually followed by a dog. Often they strutted down the street throwing handfuls of coins to the children. He tells of one young swell who rode his horse into a pub and ordered bread and tea for the animal. While he was showing off the drums began to beat and the horse stampeded. During the uproar a mirror worth twenty-five guineas was broken, and the dandy paid for it with a laugh. Such goings-on were sorrowful indeed in the eyes of the thrifty Ross.

He states that the company officials at Fort William, on the shores of Lake Superior, lived just as regally. Here vanity and extravagance provided the keynote. The dandies showed off in gaily painted canoes and wore feathers in their hats. One custom Ross particularly deplored was that of the employers' allowing the help to deck themselves out in the fine regalia of the former. The sturdy Ross makes it clear that he became a Northwester only after he had laid down his own terms.

Clerks had charge of posts, and the *bourgeois* (the

Americans called them "bushaways") were superintendents of districts. Ross shows respect for the truly great bourgeois, but not for the aristocrats. These, he observes, can usually be seen loitering around the posts, smoking their pipes and playing with dogs and guns. They laugh and sing loudly, engage in long conversations with the real trappers, but seldom bother their heads about trade, know nothing about the country or the natives and never soil their delicate hands by touching a skin. He compares them to Chinese mandarins.

Such men obviously could not take care of themselves if they went among the Indians on their own resources. Ross tells of a company which marched into the Indian country armed with a small field piece. When hostile Indians appeared they fired the cannon, causing the Indians to fly in panic, which was no greater than that of the traders themselves when the piece exploded as it was fired.

More approvingly he writes of the quick response made by a *bourgeois* when a hostile Indian chief's knife was raised to strike down one of the white party's men. Realizing that they would all be killed once blood was shed, the *bourgeois* stepped forward and told the red man that if he was going to kill he should use a knife befitting the dignity of a chief, and handed over his own knife. So delighted was the latter by this bit of generosity that he lost the urge to kill and peace was restored.

There were many similar instances in which the *bourgeois* showed their mastery over the red men by understanding them. One of the most adroit of these was Peter Skene Ogden, a veritable field marshal under Hudson's Bay whose exploits we encounter again and again since he had much to do with Fort Hall. Ogden married a Flathead woman named Julia, and their daughter, Marie Julia, became known as the Princess of the Northwest. Many lives were saved by Ogden's skill in dealing with the Indians.

These, then, were the formidable gentry with whom Astor's men had to compete. It appears that at first Astor sought cooperation rather than competition, but that was not to the liking of the haughty Northwesters. After the destruction of the *Tonquin*, David Stuart and others did considerable exploring and trading with the Indians, but the venture wasn't panning out. They met opposition at every turn. The Northwest Company, which had no reluctance about locking horns with mighty Hudson's Bay Company, was not minded to compromise with the ill-equipped Americans.

When Wilson Price Hunt finally arrived at Astoria to assume his duties as Astor's representative he apparently had no stomach for immediately contesting the command with the small and irascible Duncan McDougal. This was the same McDougal who had threatened Captain Thorn with a pistol, had held the Indians at bay with a bottle he told them contained smallpox and had strengthened himself by marriage to the daughter of Chief Comcomly. At any rate, Hunt sailed away to the north, leaving McDougal in charge, and when he returned he found Astoria in possession of the Northwest Fur Company.

The War of 1812 had begun, and McDougal, on the pretext that British warships might capture Astoria, sold all the furs and supplies to the ever willing Northwest Company, making the deal October 29, 1813. Goods valued at $800,000 were sold for $80,000. Beaver worth five dollars apiece were sold for two dollars. Five-dollar land-otter skins went for fifty cents each, and sea otter worth sixty dollars each were sold for twelve dollars. Other skins, mink, lynx, raccoon, fox and bear, were thrown in as a bonus.

Soon after his return to Astoria Hunt sailed for the Sandwich Islands, where he got more bad news. McDougal had arrived ahead of him and sold goods at Astor's post there to the Northwest Fur Company as cheaply as he had at Astoria. In fact, McDougal now was back at work for Northwest, which had employed him before he signed on with Astor and the Pacific Fur Company. Astor wrote to Hunt: "Had our place and property been fairly captured I should have preferred it—I should not feel as if I were disgraced." All his plans and correspondence had been turned over to his rivals.

McDougal claimed that had he not sold out everything would have been captured by the British and the Pacific Fur Company would have got nothing. Perhaps he was right, but his action left his place in the history of Oregon a little insecure.

On November 30, 1813, the British sloop-of-war *Raccoon*, commanded by Captain Black, put in at Baker's Bay to capture Astoria, expecting considerable booty. At sight of the warship Chief Comcomly gathered 800 warriors to help his son-in-law defend Astoria, but to his disgust McDougal refused to fight. Comcomly expressed his displeasure by telling his men that his daughter had married a squaw rather than a warrior.

The Astoria venture had failed. Hunt sailed home from the Sandwich Islands, while discouraged David Stuart, McKenzie and Clarke headed overland for St. Louis.

The Americans were not permanently out of Oregon. A clause in the Treaty of Ghent provided: "All territories, places and possessions, whatsoever, taken by either party from the other, during the war, or which may be taken after the signing of this treaty, shall be restored without delay."

When the British took over Astoria they changed the name to Fort George, and for many years it was called Astoria by the Americans and Fort George by the British. On July 18, 1815, our Secretary of State notified the British government that the United States intended to occupy Astoria, as Mr. Astor planned to reestablish his trading post. It was a diplomatic bluff, for Astor's Pacific Fur Company was never again to become an important factor in the Northwest.

On August 19, 1818, the United States sloop-of-war *Ontario*, Captain James Biddle, sailed into Fort George and raised the Stars and Stripes over the fort, so it became Astoria again. That same year, the Treaty of 1818 provided for joint occupancy by the two nations of the territory west of the Rocky Mountains. That agreement was to last for ten years, when it was renewed with the provision that either nation might cancel it at will. Like most compromises, it satisfied nobody. Only a general feeling of forbearance, perhaps inspired by fear, prevented armed conflict. As the true value of the region began to be known, the Americans raised the war cry of "Fifty-four Forty or Fight!" and the British hung on with bulldog tenacity.

As long as fur was the only prize, the British had little to worry about, but it was their own man, Dr. John Mc-

Loughlin, who demonstrated the feasibility of raising all kinds of grain, fruits and vegetables; when the land-hungry Americans heard of it Oregon became a prize worth the seeking.

McLoughlin and Hudson's Bay Company naturally wanted to hold the country for the British and they had the advantage of controlling the sea and the Indians, but the Americans were soon to be moving overland by wagon. Presently Fort Hall was to come into existence at an ideal spot to divert westward emigration to California. It was strategically located for other reasons, and so helped to determine the future of the Northwest. The treaty of joint occupancy might keep both sides from using violence against each other, but it could not keep crafty men from thinking up slick tricks.

A somewhat similar struggle was going on to the south between the Spaniards and the Russians. The Russians, using some of the same methods as the British, had moved south as far as Baja California, trapping and trading along the coast as they went. They destroyed the seals and the sea otters, and the Spaniards were alarmed. The Russians established a large base, later to be called Fort Ross, on Russian River from which they hoped to dominate California. With the ranching Mexicans holding the interior, Fort Ross failed the Russians just as Fort Vancouver failed to hold Oregon for the British.

The first important development after the treaty for joint occupancy was the merger in 1821 of the two big British fur companies under the name of Hudson's Bay Company. It was not altogether a victory for Hudson's Bay, but it gave the new company greater power. Parliament approved the merger, and issued a twenty-one-year license, but with the stipulation that in the Oregon country trade was not to be monopolized to the exclusion of American citizens. However, monopoly was the very heart and soul of Hudson's Bay policy, and if they couldn't legally keep the Americans out they could do their extra-legal best to make it impossible for them to stay.

The great bulk of the fur was, and is, in Canada. Hudson's Bay husbanded its resources as a good farmer would cultivate his soil. When a district was trapped until there was danger that the beaver would become extinct, the trappers were moved out and the beaver allowed to propagate in peace. It was a fine example of conservation, and it kept the company prosperous for some three hundred years.

The American trappers were different. They were individualists; each man wanted to make his fortune now and let future generations look after themselves. They meant to trap as long as there was beaver left to be caught. When Hudson's Bay realized that the United States was going to get part of the Oregon country anyway, they modified their policy and set out deliberately to denude that part of what they thought of as its only source of wealth, fur. So they began to trap out everything they could south of the Columbia.

Sir George Simpson did not think the company was prospering as it should on the Columbia, and in 1824 he sent out Dr. John McLoughlin, a man he didn't like personally, to instill new life in the post. McLoughlin, now married to Alexander McKay's widow, acted with foresight and energy. As chief factor, one of his first acts was to abandon Fort George, or Astoria, and move the trading post seventy-five miles up the Columbia to a place he named Fort Vancouver, which then became the virtual capital of the Northwest Coast.

The move had not been a thoughtless one. Not only was it more conveniently situated for trade, with a better landing place for ships, but it also had a larger and richer area suitable for agriculture just across the river in the Williamette valley. Soon his polyglot employees, French-Canadians, Indians, half-breeds, Kanakas, Englishmen who mostly spoke with a Scottish burr, and a few Americans were busy tilling the fertile soil. It was a statesmanlike thing to do, but it was to lead to the defeat of the British and of Hudson's Bay Company, and even to the downfall of Dr. McLoughlin himself.

This thrifty man could not bear to see the fertile soil of Oregon going to waste, nor could he turn away anyone in need. As a British subject and a servant of Hudson's Bay he wanted the country settled by the British if he could bring it about. Yet he was constantly in hot water with his superior, Sir George Simpson, for his friendliness toward the Americans and was twice summoned to London to defend his actions.

That he acted in good faith against American interests is attested by the fact that after the acquisition of Fort Hall by the Company he used it as a base to discourage American emigration, and during the next ten years his agents turned back hundreds of settlers. This, even more than the fur trade, gave Fort Hall its primary importance.

It is interesting to speculate what the fate of the Oregon country would have been had someone else held McLoughlin's place. A Sir George Simpson might have held it for the British—probably at the cost of a war. A lesser man would have used brute force, and surely would have lost out after blood had been shed. During McLoughlin's twenty-year tenure there was a minimum of bloodshed, not only with the Indians, but between the British and the Americans. There were estimated to be 100,000 Indians in the territory under McLoughlin's control, and during those twenty years there was not what could be called an Indian war. It was an unparalleled record for the frontier.

No single man, with the possible exception of Brigham Young in Salt Lake City, ever wielded so much absolute power or used it more wisely, in the early West.

Only an employee of a private company, the doctor was universally referred to as Governor McLoughlin of Oregon, and his reign lasted from 1824 to 1846. He was feared and respected, and his rule was wise and firm. Like his Utah counterpart, he knew how to get along with Indians. Long before Brigham Young uttered his dictum, "It is cheaper to feed than to fight them," McLoughlin was putting the theory into practice. But he didn't hesitate to hang an Indian if the crime justified it.

McLoughlin lived like a king, and was indeed a benevolent despot. His hospitality was traditional, even to his enemies. This was never more clearly shown than in his relations with Jedediah Smith, the American explorer and trapper. Smith was one of the partners in the Rocky Mountain Fur Company, the only competition in the fur industry the Hudson's Bay company had cause to fear. McLoughlin's policy was to exclude competition in his territory, but in carrying out this policy he was rigidly correct, and was ever the gentleman in dealing with his company's rivals.

The Rocky Mountain Fur Company was supreme in United States territory east of the Rockies. The Snake River country and the Great Basin, centering around Fort Hall, comprised a sort of buffer between the British and the Americans. With a view to extending his company's operations Jed Smith moved across the Great Basin, along the Humboldt where Peter Skene Ogden of Hudson's Bay was already at work—in fact, the Humboldt was then called Ogden's River—and on into California.

Smith's adventures in California need not be recounted here, but he moved northward near the Oregon coast, trapping as he traveled, his destination Vancouver. There were eighteen men in his party, and they were clearly trapping in country claimed by Hudson's Bay. On the way they were attacked by Indians on the Umpqua; all but four of them were killed and their furs and other property were taken from them.

When Smith arrived at Fort Vancouver in 1828 with his three companions they were so disheartened by misfortune and fatigue that Smith refused McLoughlin's offer to send men back with him to recover his goods, though there was no more capable and courageous man on the frontier than Jedediah Smith. He simply thought it would be a waste of time to go back to the scene of the massacre to try to recover the stolen property, or to see if any of his men were left alive.

McLoughlin treated Smith with the utmost hospitality, but he wasn't minded to let the Indians get away with so brazen an act. "Where's Tom?" he demanded, and when his stepson, Thomas McKay, arrived he was sent out to head a party to reclaim Smith's property.

Of this venture McLoughlin said: "I divulged my plan to none, but gave written instructions to the officer in charge to be opened only when he reached the Umpqua, because if known before they got there the officers would talk of it among themselves, the men would hear it, and from them it would go to their Indian wives, who were spies on us, and our plan would be defeated."

Most of the Hudson's Bay men were married to Indian women who, though true to their husbands, still retained a sense of loyalty to their own people.

The plan was to have the Indians bring in furs to trade, count any bearing the mark of the American trappers, keep them separate and return them to their owners without the formality of paying the robbers for them. When those so branded denied having attacked Smith's party and claimed they had bought the furs from other Indians, they were told to look to them for payment.

No doubt they were telling the truth, for a small war ensued and the murderers were punished by the Indians who had bought the furs. McLoughlin could easily have let the Indians keep the fur or he could have retained them himself as payment for the expense he had been put to, and for the danger to his men. Instead, he turned them over to Jedediah Smith, and at Smith's request bought them for $3200, which was the full market price.

As a consequence of this generous treatment Jedediah Smith assured the doctor that the Rocky Mountain Fur Company would confine its operations to the region east of the Great Divide. When Smith recuperated and prepared to depart, McLoughlin, characteristically, sold him everything he needed except traps. In later days he freely supplied the early American settlers with milk, although he refused to sell them a cow.

The huge (six feet four) Dr. McLoughlin, whom the Indians called "White-headed Eagle," was said to have had a violent temper, a fact probably derived from his once having used a cane on a missionary, the Reverend Beaver, though he apologized after it was over. He was fair-minded and honorable, and more than any other man stood in the way of American expansion.

We must return to him later, again and again, for history now accords him the title, "The Father of Oregon." But now, to keep the issue straight, we must go back to New England and to that triumvirate of Kelley, Wyeth and Bonneville, beginning with Hall J. Kelley, for if McLoughlin was the Father of Oregon, Kelley was its prophet.

# 4

# THE PROPHET OF OREGON

HALL JACKSON KELLEY CON-
sidered himself to be the Messiah of Oregon, but he was
only its John the Baptist, crying in the wilderness. He inspired thousands who turned their eyes toward Oregon because of his burning message; most notable of whom were
the other two members of that Massachusetts triumvirate,
Nathaniel J. Wyeth and Captain Bonneville, who were
to open up the Snake River country for the Americans.

Not until forty years after his death in 1874 were the
fragments of his life pieced together by his biographer, F. W.
Powell, yet his writings were well known in his time. That
his accomplishments fell so far short of his dreams was in
part due to a trait in his character which caused Powell
to exclaim: "Oh, Polly Kelley, why did you not implant in
your son a sense of humor, a sense of relative values?"

Kelley was born at Northwood, New Hampshire, February 24, 1790. He was a descendant of John Kelley, one of the first settlers of Newbury, Mass. His grandfather was Samuel Kelley, of Salem, and his father, Benjamin Kelley, a native of Salem, was a physician who practiced in various places in New England.

The family moved to Gilmington when Kelley was ten years old. Though he began teaching school at Hallowell, Maine, when he was sixteen years old, he attended college at Middlebury, Vermont, where he graduated in 1813, with a degree of Bachelor of Arts, and August 16, 1820, Middlebury College awarded him the degree of Master of Arts. Harvard University conferred the same degree on him that year, though he was never a student there.

At his first graduation, fifteen of his twenty-nine fellow graduates entered the ministry, and with his strongly religious bent it is strange that he himself did not. However, he preferred to be a prophet rather than a mere preacher. His self-righteousness, his conceit and the total lack of a sense of humor that made him obnoxious to his associates would be unbelievable were it not for his own words. To understand him it is necessary to quote him:

"It is chiefly due to early parental instruction and training that my mind is what it is. . . . I came into active life serious minded, much inclined to consider my ways. . . . Before the years of manhood I resolved on a fearless obedience to the divine commands and to the present I have continued to desire and pray for understanding and skill for the possession of capabilities and substance to bless the suffering mortals about me.

". . . It was Mother who taught me never to take

the name of God in vain, never to be guilty of insulting the Almighty with the breath He gives. She impressed my mind with the profound and pious reverence for Jehovah, with a high and solemn veneration for the institutions of Christianity and so impressed it with the love of truth that not a single doubt of the Scriptures ever profaned the sanctuary of my heart.

"Her instructions and example inclined me to be diligent and persevering in business, faithful and patient in the discharge of duties, to be hospitable and merciful when the innocent hunger and thirst, to feed them and give them drink, and bless them that are persecuted, and finally by the grace of God I hope I have the love of my neighbor which meets the divine requisition and am disposed to do all in my power for Him, for the country, and for mankind in general, endure every evil coming upon me with patience and pious heroism."

He was a serious child who seldom participated in the play of other children. In his writings he states that he grew up coincident with the Napoleonic Wars, and early developed a taste for reading. Along with his religious reading he mentions: "Accounts of slaughter on fields encrimsoned with human blood, and plains bestrewed with human carnage of the armies of spiritual Gog and Magog, and of all the conquering princes and kings of the earth gathering to battle. . . . At once I left my juvenile plays and sports and turned to books and papers. I read at times through the day and even more than once through the night. When I took up a book I did not lay it down until I understood all that its pages could inform me."

From his own statement it seems he had a turn for

investigation. He tells of his interest in perpetual motion, and of going into a workshop to demonstrate its impossibility. Another time he constructed an orrery, a machine showing the pathways of the moon around the stars and the earth around the sun. While a junior he supplied one of the seniors, for a fee of five dollars, the solution for an eclipse of the sun, doing this on twenty-four hours' notice.

Kelley had ample opportunity to become informed about Oregon and the Northwest Coast. In addition to Captains Gray and Kendrick many other sea traders put in at Boston. There were so many of them, in fact, that the Indians of Oregon were already calling all Americans "Bostons." Tales of the great profits to be made there spread throughout all of New England.

Kelley says: "In the year 1817 the word came expressly to me to go and labor in the fields of philanthropic enterprise and promote the propogation of Christianity in the dark and cruel places about the shores of the Pacific." From that time on he considered himself to be divinely appointed to father civilization in the Oregon country. It took him years to get started, but he never deviated from his purpose.

Kelley was appointed Master of the West Reading School at Boston, September 29, 1818, and became Master of the Hawkins Grammar School June 17, 1820. He was transferred to the Mayhew School March 20, 1821, and here turbulence entered his life. He became involved in a quarrel with the head usher whom he wished dismissed. He had a sub-committee of the board with him, but when a special committee headed by Mayor Josiah Quincey investigated the case Kelley was informed that his services could be dispensed with, but that his salary for the remaining quarter would be paid.

There is no evidence of any serious reflection upon Kelley, and though he did no further teaching his interest in education did not cease. He was the man who introduced the blackboard and the monitorial desk into Boston schools. He met with favor as a writer of elementary textbooks. The first is supposed to have been *The Instructor's First Book*, though no copies of it can be found. It is presumed to be the same as his *The First Spelling Book, or Child's Instructor*, of which the eighth edition was printed in 1827. Other elementary textbooks followed.

With Reverend D. Chessman of Boston, Kelley organized the first Sabbath School in New England. He established the Boston Young Men's Education Society, and became its first secretary. He was interested in higher mathematics, and devised a new system of surveying which was adopted by government engineers. He claimed to have initiated a movement to found a Massachusetts Mechanical and Agriculture College, but the project was abandoned, and his name does not appear on the published documents concerning the movement.

Following his dismissal from the Boston school Kelley moved to Charlestown to engage in surveying, and thus he became interested in the Three Rivers Manufacturing Company. He put his money back into the company, made surveys and drew up a comprehensive plan for the plant, and for the development of the town of Three Rivers. The company failed, and Kelley lost heavily. He bought land there, however, when the affairs of the company were settled, and moved his family there in 1829, hoping for the ultimate prosperity of the village.

Kelley was far from being a failure in business. He was the owner of four "estates" which he had bought in localities where he thought there would be a rise in real-estate values. One of his purchases was a tract of twelve acres in Charlestown. In 1840 he said that the property would have been worth not less than $50,000 above the initial cost. He was doing well in surveying and railroad engineering when he gave it all up to follow the divine call to settle Oregon that had come to him back in 1817.

In 1829 Hall J. Kelley organized the American Society for the Encouragement of the Settlement of Oregon, which was finally incorporated in Boston, June 22, 1831, under special act of the Massachusetts legislature. It was the first organized effort to preserve the Northwest Coast for the United States.

Nathaniel Jarvis Wyeth and Captain Bonneville were members of the society. Bancroft opines that Kelley *was* the society. His activities had begun back in 1825, for in his *Colonization of Oregon*, published in 1852, Kelley listed his enormous expenses from 1825 until 1836, including loss of income from his profession at $2000 a year. Bancroft says succinctly, "He did not cease raving about it until he died."

During those years he was busy getting all the information he could from sailing masters or anyone else who had been to Oregon; he drew maps and made plans—and found an adversary, real or imagined, in the Hudson's Bay Company, which he claimed was doing everything possible to thwart his plans. He had early developed a persecution complex.

He claimed that he had 3000 people ready to start from St. Louis in 1828, but that the migration was defeated by the opposition of the press and the Hudson's Bay Company, to which he soon added another enemy, the American Fur company. In fact, anyone who would not accept his leadership—and that meant accepting his divine calling— was an enemy. Kelley seems to have had a lapse of memory, for in 1832 he was claiming that he had enlisted 500 people from all parts of the Union, considerably less than the figure he had mentioned in 1828.

Among his converts, Kelley claimed, was General Sam Houston, later the liberator of Texas. It is possible that Houston displayed some interest, for he was always ready to answer the call of adventure, but it is hard to imagine two less compatible characters than swashbuckling Sam and the Bible-quoting Kelley. The prophet's claim about Houston probably had no more validity than his belief that anyone who listened to him was bound to become a convert.

After the organization of his society Kelley was busier than ever. He lectured all over New England, and wrote pamphlets which he sent to anyone who might be interested. He published A *Manual of the Oregon Expedition,* or *General Circular,* giving full directions of organization, and A *Geographical Sketch of that part of North America Called Oregon.* Both came out in 1831.

In 1820 Congressman Floyd of Virginia had begun to agitate on behalf of Oregon and continued to do so until he retired from Congress in 1829 to become governor of

Virginia. In 1823 Floyd sponsored a bill for the occupation of the mouth of the Columbia, and Peter Little of Maryland stated in debate that eighty farmers and mechanics were eager and ready to go out there. The Floyd bill passed the House December 23, 1824, but failed in the Senate.

In 1828 Floyd presented a memorial from citizens of the United States, written by Hall J. Kelley, asking for a grant of land, and aid in founding a settlement on the northwest coast. In his memorial Kelley asked for a grant of twenty-five square miles in the Columbia River valley for the purpose of colonization, and petitioned the government to provide protection for the colony: military escort and transport, and the establishment of convenient military posts for the encouragement of emigration to the country.

In his *Geographical Sketch of Oregon* Kelley cited reasons why his petition should be granted. Those reasons contained sound logic which makes one wonder how they could have been ignored. The first, perhaps, was the one which doomed it. It stated that the occupation of Oregon by 3000 American settlers would secure it from possession by another country. Nobody would believe that Kelley could lead 3000 settlers out there; could that have been accepted, his other propositions were perfectly sound.

His second point was that a free and exclusive trade with the Indians would promote the commercial and manufacturing interests of the nation. The next was that the fisheries could be more extensively and profitably used. It would secure the friendship of the Indians, and prevent alliances between them and other nations.

He pointed out the advantage of a naval station at the mouth of the Columbia, or in the De Fuca straits, which would be of immense importance in protecting whale and other fisheries and the fur trade, and in the general control of the Pacific Ocean, where millions of dollars' worth of our property was afloat.

Next, it would conduce to free intercourse and more extensive trade relations with the East Indies, and stimulate the opening of communication between the Mississippi valley and the Gulf of Mexico, and the Pacific Ocean.

His final point he no doubt considered to be the clincher. The settlement of Oregon, he said, would benefit many of our seaports by ridding them of their excess population, who would be willing to go to a less restricted country.

It never occurred to him that the reason for the rejection of these really statesmanlike propositions was his own personality.

He was in Washington during much of 1830–31, trying vainly to get Congress to act. Though Congress would not pay even part of the expenses, he went ahead with his plans, proposing to raise a capital of $200,000, divided into $100 shares, each to entitle the holder to 160 acres of land in the new country. Two towns were projected, one at Gray's Bay on the north bank of the Columbia near its mouth, the other at the confluence of the Multnomah and the Columbia—the Multnomah being actually the Willamette River.

Gray's Bay was to be a seaport town and embrace five square miles. Not until Brigham Young founded Salt Lake City in 1847 was a town to be laid out so thoroughly. "Of the streets one 200 feet wide will run from the water in a northwest direction, bisecting at the distance of six squares an area of ten acres of parade or pleasure ground, which area is forever to remain open and unoccupied with buildings. The center of this street for the width of one hundred feet will be devoted to the purpose of a market. Streets crossing this at right angles are intended to be 100 feet wide, those parallel to it 50 feet wide. The squares are to be 400 feet on a side, each including 18 lots, 50 by 100 feet each. From the 100 feet streets and the public lands, no plant or tree is to be removed or destroyed without consent of the municipal authority.

"The commercial town at the junction of the Multnomah and Columbia rivers, will be about two miles square. A section of land adjoining the town will be surveyed into lots, 40 by 60 rods, of 40 acres each, making the number of these divisions equal to the whole of emigrants over 14 years of age, not including married women. Next to these will be other lots of 160 acres each, making up the complement of 200 acres to each immigrant. Lands for public uses, and to meet the demands of the stock (i.e. capital stock of the company) will be included in this last division. Roads as far as practicable will be laid out in straight lines, intersecting each other at right angles."

All this was planned by a man who as yet had never been west of Washington, D.C.

Kelley knew what kind of people he wanted with him. They must be of steady habits and must have some regular business or occupation. They were urged to continue their regular vocations until notified when the expedition was to start. Then they were to assemble at one of thirteen different points named in the Manual, and make their way to St. Louis, where the expedition was to start. Instructions as to equipment and organization were given in great detail in the Manual, which was widely circulated. Forty-seven agents combed eighteen states and the District of Columbia.

One of these agents was Nathaniel J. Wyeth, the future founder of Fort Hall. At first, Wyeth was enthusiastic about the project, but by the fall of 1831 his enthusiasm was waning. In a letter to his brother he questioned, as well he might, the wisdom of joining Kelley's party because it would include women and children and would be venturing into a wilderness where wagons were unknown.

In a letter to John Ball, dated February 10, 1832, Wyeth stated that he saw no probability of Kelley's party moving at that time, and doubted that he would ever move such a mass of people as he proposed. By that time Wyeth was convinced that Kelley was far more propagandist than he was colonizer. Wyeth would never risk the lives of women and children in such a hazardous venture. Two men could hardly be more incompatible than the daring yet cautious and careful Wyeth, and the reckless, sometimes irresponsible Kelley. Wyeth was a businessman who could see possible profits, while Kelley saw himself as an agent of the Lord who would build an empire. Destiny had cast them both in the role of noble failures. In 1832 few people had ever heard of Wyeth, but Kelley's name was widely known—too much so for his own good.

Many people were now taking note of Kelley's schemes and he was subjected to attack from all sides. It was represented in the leading magazines and newspapers that he was deceiving the people, that his plans were chimerical, that he was an idle schemer—in short, a madman.

The *New England Magazine* printed two articles by W. J. Snelling in its February and April, 1832, numbers bitterly attacking the scheme. Snelling claimed to have had experience as a fur trader. The immediate expedition was doomed anyway by the defection of Wyeth and others. Since Kelley's expedition could only have met with tragic failure, the divine Providence which he trusted so much may have been looking after him in a way he never could have foreseen.

Frederick G. Young, who did a paper on the Oregon Trail found in the report of the Public Archives Commission of 1902, philosophized: "Kelley wished to transplant a Massachusetts town to Oregon and make it the nucleus of a new state. He hoped to repeat the history of the Puritan colony of Massachusetts Bay. The New Englander of the Nineteenth century, however, was not ready to sacrifice himself for an idea as had his progenitor of the Seventeenth." Young was correct as to Kelley's hope, but questioning the man's courage was unfair.

The carefully planned towns on the Columbia were never to be built. Kelley never got his chance to challenge the Goliath of Fur, as Nat Wyeth was to do at Fort Hall and Fort William, and had he done so he would have been brushed off like a gnat from the beard of a mountain man, which was about what happened to Wyeth.

Like all true fanatics, Kelley never knew when he was beaten. His grandiose schemes blew away like dust, but his dreams remained intact, and he would not give up until he had seen Oregon.

What effect Hall Jackson Kelley had on the ultimate settlement of Oregon is still a moot question. A prophet he was; a practical man he was not, where his visions were concerned. Except on the Oregon question, which he felt

Providence had called upon him to settle, he was practical enough. He helped to establish the American school system, he was a capable surveyer and engineer, and he was the prince of pamphleteers. He also had a good Yankee eye for the dollar, but his personal efforts to carry out his schemes resulted in failure, and very nearly in disgrace.

Kelley's vision was greater than that of Daniel Webster who was thundering in the Senate that we should not extend our boundaries beyond the limits of the Louisiana Purchase, while Kelley was crying out that we should go all the way to the Pacific Ocean. When, as Secretary of State, the great Daniel negotiated the Webster-Ashburton Treaty in 1842 he was more interested in gaining a few square miles in Maine than he was in the whole Oregon country.

How many of the thousands of emigrants who poured across the nation in their covered wagons were influenced by Hall J. Kelley we shall never know, but there were many of them, for he never ceased to preach the glories of Oregon. He was talking and writing about the necessity of holding it long before statesmen began to fulminate about America's Manifest Destiny and scream, "Fifty-four Forty or Fight."

Kelley had the zeal of a crusader, yet he was not a missionary. There were men like the Lees, Whitman, Spalding and Father DeSmet who upheld the standard of the Cross. It was such as Jesse Applegate who turned the furrows. It was men like Nathaniel Wyeth who built the forts, like Captain Bonneville who had the fun, and like Ewing Young who had the adventures. Among them all Hall J. Kelley was a misfit who never found his proper niche.

When he began his crusade, events were shaping up to draw attention to Oregon. Four great nations, the United States, England, Spain and Russia, were laying claim to all or part of the territory. No other one man did more to create interest in the situation, but Kelley fought with words while others fought with guns, dollars, and the Holy Bible, all of them more easily measured than the value of a sentence.

Spain had been compelled by the Nootka Convention to give up her claims to exclusive rights north of 42°. In the squabble both Spain and England withdrew from Nootka Sound, but agreed that either might establish posts or settlements north of the 42nd parallel, provided that any proposed station should not be within 100 miles of one already established by the other party. Although the provisions of the Nootka Convention held until 1819, Spain was not a serious contender after that. Then, as the result of the agreement by which the United States acquired Florida and the boundary between Mexico and the Louisiana Purchase was confirmed, Spain relinquished all claim to territory north of the 42nd parallel.

Russia was moving south along the coast as far as Lower California, but did not attempt to push far into the interior. Except for the attempt of Captain John Sutter in the forties to build up a profitable trade with the Russians, that country was not a serious contender for Oregon (of course, if other nations should fall out, Russia was always ready to move in).

The treaty for joint occupancy by the United States and Great Britain, made in 1818 and ten years later renewed indefinitely, left Oregon without any government except that provided first by the Northwest Fur Company and, after the merger, by the Hudson's Bay Company. Neither of these was loath to assume the responsibility, and both were determined to hold the country at all cost. The trouble with them was that their fur caps came clear down over their eyes, and they could see nothing but fur.

The United States government was not much interested in the country, so American interests had to be upheld by such as Kelley, Wyeth and Bonneville. Few realized it when Fort Hall became the focal point of the contest, or that whoever held it owned the key to Oregon.

The British dominated the mouth of the Columbia, and Britannia ruled the waves. In 1824 came Dr. John McLoughlin, with his conviction that such settlement as was done should be by sea from England. The covered wagons had not begun to move—and only Hall J. Kelley was trying to get them rolling.

Russia, which in 1821 had asserted her claim to all the country as far south as the 51st parallel, in 1824 made a treaty with the United States in which she gave up her claim to territory south of 54°-40', the location of a Russian fort. Thus the possession of Oregon was left to two contesting powers—the United States and England.

Balboa had waded into the Pacific Ocean at the Isthmus of Panama and claimed all the shores the ocean might touch in the name of Spain. That claim and others like it were no longer valid. The fact of discovery alone did not spell the ability to hold territory. Permanent occupancy, except for conquest by war, afforded the most legitimate title. The British and Canadian trappers had a better idea of this than did the Americans, for they established permanent posts from which to trade, while the Americans were satisfied with the annual rendezvous, which was as portable as the sack of "possibles" on their backs.

As the end of the first term of joint occupancy drew near, a few responsible Americans began to take note that the whole Northwest Coast might slip away from us. As early as 1818–19 Thomas Hart Benton, then editor of the *St. Louis Inquirer*, was beginning to discuss the Oregon question and proposed a series of overland posts from the Missouri to the Columbia. Various impractical schemes were being proposed. One writer in the *American Farmer* of Baltimore, July 9, 1819, suggested Bactrian camels for transportation to the Pacific. Another, Robert Mills, also of Baltimore, somewhat ahead of his times, proposed the use of steam as the motive power for carriages, upon railroads across the mountains from the Yellowstone to the Columbia. Hall J. Kelley could see no obstacle to wagons, and Nat Wyeth was toying with the idea of an amphibian prairie schooner.

The indefinite extension of the agreement for joint occupation by the Convention of 1827, making it impossible for either the United States or Great Britain to establish government within the territory, was enough to discourage any would-be colonizer, but Kelley was no ordinary man. He had just begun to fight, and he went right ahead with his plan to take a large colony of emigrants overland by wagon.

# 5

# THE ICEMAN COMETH

IF THE OFFICIALS OF THE Northwest Fur Company or its successor, Hudson's Bay Company, having their hour of glory at captured Astoria, had heard that a new England schoolmaster named Hall J. Kelley had had a vision that he was going to drive them out of Oregon they would have rocked with laughter. The idea of a man armed only with a vision daring to contend with the mighty company passed the ridiculous. Yet in the long run this dreamer, this future Prophet of Oregon, was to be their Nemesis. He inspired emigration to Oregon, and he inspired Nathaniel Jarvis Wyeth, a dealer in ice in Salem, Massachusetts, to go out there and build Fort Hall.

Wyeth was only one of Kelley's many converts, and at first he had great confidence in the man. He had written to Kelley August 30, 1831, applying for a position for himself and his elder brother, Dr. Jacob Wyeth, in the expedition Kelley was organizing. But by October 5 the situation had changed, and Wyeth was busy organizing his own expedition, as shown by a letter to his brother Charles in New York detailing the obstacles his project was facing, of which financing was the most troublesome.

As Kelley's agent, he had thought the other man's plan was good, though he hadn't liked the idea of taking along women and children, but he had become thoroughly alarmed by Kelley's constant shift of dates and locations. It was becoming apparent to Wyeth, as it was to many others, that Kelley was long on theory but short on practice, but it had not shaken his own determination to reach Oregon.

Once committed to Oregon, Wyeth had familiarized himself to some extent with General Ashley's venture in the fur trade, that had begun in 1822 and resulted in the formation of the Rocky Mountain Fur Company, with which Wyeth was soon to brush shoulders.

The history of the fur trade in the Rockies is a long and thrilling one, and has little to do with this narrative except as it touched the men whose eyes were on Oregon, but some of those men were to play an important part in Wyeth's career. General Ashley had placed an advertisement in the *Missouri Republican* of March 20, 1822, calling for one hundred volunteers to ascend the Missouri to its source, there to be employed for one, two, or three years.

The roster of those men would include such famous frontier characters as Jedediah S. Smith, William L. Sublette and his brother Milton, Jim Bridger, David E. Jackson, Thomas Fitzpatrick, Robert Campbell and others too numerous to mention. Yet Wyeth did not hesitate to go into competition with them in the fur trade, though he intended to go farther west and he would not limit himself to fur. He proposed to establish permanent trading posts on the Columbia and go into competition with the powerful Hudson's Bay Company somewhat along the lines John Jacob Astor had tried.

He had a double-edged plan to obtain furs from the mountains and ship them to China in his own vessel, then buy silks and tea and other Oriental commodities and ship them back to Boston. He was also minded to enter the fishing industry, and his heart was set on establishing himself at the mouth of the Columbia. To this end he chartered the ship, *Sultana*, and sent it around Cape Horn to meet him when he reached Fort Vancouver.

It seemed a wild, impractical scheme but Wyeth, though no frontiersman, was a hard-headed businessman. Thomas Jefferson Farnham, the well-known traveler and journalist, rated Wyeth as the most capable businessman ever to enter the mountains. Others voiced the same opinion.

An estimate of his character was well expressed by the poet, James Russell Lowell, in a tribute to the memory of Captain Wyeth, from the archives of the Oregon Historical Society. It was sent to the Portland, Oregon, High School, from Cambridge, April 24, 1890, and said in part:

"Dear Miss H——
I feel as if I had a kind of birthright in your Portland, for it was a townsman of mine who first led an expedition thither across the plains and tried to establish a settlement there. I well remember his starting sixty years ago, and I knew him well in after years. He was a very remarkable person whose conversation

I valued highly. A born leader of men, he was fitly called *Captain* Nathaniel Wyeth as long as he lived. It was the weakness of his companions that forced him to let go his hold on that fair possession. I hope he is duly honored in your traditions. . . .

Very sincerely your friend, J. R. LOWELL."

Wyeth was wise to pull out of Kelley's company, which was never to travel. Only a mutual dream gave them temporary compatibility, though there were similarities in their background and upbringing. Both were proper Bostonians, but their temperaments were different, and Wyeth was much the younger man. This may have accounted for Kelley's patronizing manner and Wyeth's rebellion against the older man's vagaries. Kelley's ancestors were in the professions, while Wyeth's people had a leaning toward business. The lives of both centered around Cambridge.

The historian, Bancroft, says of Wyeth that "He was a thoroughly good man with bright open countenance, strong limbs, warm of heart, thoughtful and determined."

As much as Hall J. Kelley, he was an aristocrat with a tradition of trade and culture behind him. The Wyeth family had settled in Cambridge in 1645, and was one of the oldest families. Nathaniel was born there January 29, 1802; and he died there August 31, 1856. In 1751 his grandfather, Ebenezer, purchased through the state part of the present town of Mt. Auburn, and extending to Fresh Pond. His father, Jacob, 1764–1856, built a pleasure resort known as Fresh Pond Hotel. Jacob Wyeth married Elizabeth Jarvis, whose family were the owners of Jarvis Field, famous in Harvard's athletic annals. Jacob was a Harvard graduate, as was his eldest son, Dr. Jacob Wyeth.

Nathaniel was the fourth son, and though fitted for

college he did not finish the course: he wanted to go into business and could not spare the time. In his writings, however, he was as lucid as the average educated man of his day. He married his cousin, Elizabeth Jarvis Stone, in 1824, and before his first Oregon expedition built his home on a family estate where he resided until his death.

He began his business career as an assistant to his father in the management of Fresh Pond Hotel but, not liking the business, he entered the employment of Frederick Tudor who had just organized the first ice company in the United States. Besides catering to local demands this firm began shipping ice to foreign ports, even as far away as Calcutta, thus giving Nathaniel a familiarity with sea transportation at an early age. He resigned his position as manager of the company before starting to Oregon, but after his eventual failure there he again entered the ice business with Tudor, became the head of the firm in 1840, and remained an iceman until he died.

His business ventures were not confined to ice; he became interested in brick making and nurseries, among other undertakings. By all accounts he was intelligent and aggressive. Unlike Kelley, he did not consider himself perfectly pure and immaculate; in his journals he shows himself very human. Once he wrote of a Fourth of July celebration on Bear River: "I gave the men too much alcohol for peace and took a pretty hearty spree myself."

To offset his inexperience, Wyeth had the ability to learn and the courage to face the unknown, and he was a keen observer. He was aware that he would face fierce competition, but he did not realize that the golden years of the fur trade had been reached five years before he started, and that the supply of beaver was even then fast decreasing.

While Hall J. Kelley hemmed and hawed and exhorted Wyeth went calmly about his business of getting his company under way in the spring of 1832.

There had been no trapping on the Pacific coast prior to 1787, and after that it had been desultory, so Wyeth had small reason to fear a dearth of pelts. Fate was to take him by the hand and lead him into the one region where little trapping had as yet been done. That was the region around Fort Hall, but it was not until his second expedition that he was to build his fort there, and by that time Hudson's Bay was all set to freeze him out. So, too, were the veteran trappers of the Rocky Mountain Fur Company.

While Wyeth was getting ready, so was his friend Bonneville, whose expedition must be treated separately, though during the long trek the two parties were often in sight of each other, and exchanged visits along the way. Bonneville was much better equipped, but his and Wyeth's purposes were quite different. To Wyeth it was a serious business of looking over the country with a view to future operations. To Captain Bonneville it was more in the nature of a holiday.

Bonneville's accounts do not carry the prestige with historians they once did, and he was much less serious-minded than Wyeth, but he holds a high and honored place in the history of the West. Like Kelley he must be judged not by what he was, but by what he did.

Wyeth did not solicit the members of his family, with the possible exception of his elder brother, Dr. Jacob Wyeth, whom he had every reason to believe would be a valuable addition to his party, but he did not object to taking along his harum-scarum young cousin, John B. Wyeth. Another youthful kinsman, Thomas Livermore, did not arouse Nathaniel's enthusiasm, and it required all the persuasion of the youth's father to have him taken along. None of them finished the first journey.

Twenty-four men were finally chosen, including a gunsmith, a blacksmith, two carpenters, two fishermen and thirteen farmers and laborers. For some time before the departure they met every Saturday night at the home of Captain Wyeth for encouragement and instruction. None of them had a very good idea of what they were getting into. John Ball, one of the company, describes them as laborers and loafers such as Wyeth was able to pick up.

Out of this uncertain material a company was formed, and a stock company was organized to continue for five years. Each member at the outset was to deposit forty dollars with Wyeth, who assumed all expenses. Implicit obedience to him was promised. The proceeds were to be divided into fifty parts, of which Captain Wyeth was to have eight shares for taking charge of the business and furnishing the capital. Dr. Jacob Wyeth was to have two parts; the remaining forty parts to be divided equally among the rest of the company. When they came to start, twenty men left Boston with Wyeth, while Ball, Sinclair and two others joined the party at Baltimore.

Wyeth was aware that he would have many rivers to cross so he built a wagon-bed in the shape of a boat for which he had high hopes. When they came to a stream they would simply launch the wagon-bed and row the goods across. This strange contraption was highly amusing to young John B. Wyeth, who christened it the *Natwyethium*.

At this time few wheeled vehicles had got far beyond the Mississippi. William Sublette had dragged a small cannon into the Rockies, and this was the nearest thing to a wagon track Wyeth had to follow. His fellow traveler, Captain Bonneville, better equipped, had the honor of taking wagons farther west than anyone else had been able to do, leaving them at Fort Bonneville, on the Seedskeedee, or Green River.

Among Wyeth's prized possessions was a complete blacksmith shop, including an anvil. It and the *Natwyethium* were sources of endless merriment to gay young John B. Wyeth, who had a good laugh when the hybrid vessel tipped over in a river and the blacksmith shop was lost.

The trip was planned as carefully as was humanly possible. The party traveled by sea to Baltimore, having left Boston March 11, 1832. From Baltimore they took the railroad for sixty miles to the foot of the Allegheny mountains. They marched through the mountains to Pittsburgh, whence they traveled by boat to Independence, Missouri.

Here six men deserted; one among them, young Thomas Livermore, borrowed a horse which Wyeth had some trouble recovering. At Independence Wyeth made his first contact with the behemoths of the mountain fur trade. Preparing to leave for the mountains was William Sublette, senior partner of the firm that had bought out General Ashley the year before. He was a man of affairs and consequence whose ancestors had fought alongside Daniel Boone, and he knew the mountains as few other men knew them. His associates included such men as his partners, Smith, Jackson, Fitzpatrick and Bridger, all financially interested in the Rocky Mountain Fur Company.

Sublette was awaiting the arrival of Robert Campbell, an-other partner in the firm, and he agreed to take Wyeth along; but for that circumstance, Wyeth's party probably would have disintegrated.

Sublette took one startled look at the *Natwyethium* and advised Wyeth to get rid of it and his other vehicles. In place of them, he said, Wyeth should buy horses and packsaddles to carry his equipage. He also urged the East-erners to purchase oxen and sheep for food until they could reach the buffalo country.

Sublette saw no future rivalry with the young East-erner, and even had he done so it would not have disturbed him. Wyeth's mind was set on journeying to the mouth of the Columbia, in which Sublette had no interest. If Wyeth planned to do any trapping along the way it might be inter-esting to watch. Actually, Nat's merchant soul was intent on building a factory to pack salmon, which he had heard were plentiful in the Columbia, and these he intended to send back to Boston by sea.

Most of the business in the Rocky Mountains was con-ducted by such big firms as the Rocky Mountain and Ameri-can Fur companies, and by Choteau & Company of St. Louis, though there were others which sprang up and disappeared like fireflies both east and west of the Rockies. Some of the more enduring were the Bent Brothers, Drips & Fontenelle, Lancaster P. Lupton, and Vasquez & Sub-lette—the Sublette in this instance being Andrew, one of William's four brothers. Most of these companies played mountain politics for special advantage, which may have been the reason General Ashley, who had brought most of them to the fur country, preferred to sell out rather than

deal with them. William Sublette, for instance, was supposed to be in competition with Vasquez & Sublette, but
he could hardly be expected to work against his own
brother, so he owned stock in the rival company.

The venturesome young men Ashley had enlisted were
now veteran mountaineers, bound to be indifferent to
Wyeth and his fellow tenderfeet; but Wyeth, finding himself among these hardy men, learned from them rapidly.
It is doubtful, however, that his small, inexperienced band
cut much ice in the company which left Independence in
May, 1832.

After Robert Campbell joined the party it numbered
about eighty men and 300 horses, besides the oxen and
sheep destined for slaughter. William Sublette was in charge
and they were traveling over what would later be known
as the Oregon Trail.

They had adventures such as were common to most
early-day travelers. The Indians, with the exception of the
warlike Blackfeet far to the west, were usually peaceful,
though most of them were not averse to lifting a white scalp
if it could be done safely. Few of the mountain men wanted
any truck with the Blackfeet, who might strike anywhere.
Indeed, they did so on the night of July 1, firing about
forty shots into the camp and running off ten horses, four
of which belonged to Wyeth.

The Blackfeet were the particular pets of Hudson's
Bay, which had a monopoly of their business until the company, under the direction of Sir George Simpson, tried to
stamp out the traffic in spirits. The effort was unsuccessful,
for as one Blackfoot chief told Sir George, "We do not

need your blankets or your guns, for we can revert to the weapons and furs used by our forefathers. But at the end of a long season we need liquor to revive our spirits and get through the long winter and be ready for the spring hunt." Besides, the Indians could always obtain whisky from the Americans, who possessed no such scruples.

Wyeth's journal between May 3 and June 4 has been lost, but his cousin John gives a somewhat superficial account of events, and it appears that at about this time John and some of the others began to decide that the expedition was not exactly a picnic. The brush with the Blackfeet on the Sweetwater River in Wyoming and the knowledge that they were heading into hostile country had a cooling effect on youthful exuberance.

July 8, they reached the trappers' rendezvous at Pierre's Hole, a place in Idaho which is now known as Teton Basin, with the three lofty Teton Peaks towering above it. Here they ran into real trouble.

Although a great deal has been written about these mountain rendezvous, our picture would not be complete without saying something about their purpose and the difference between the methods of the American and the British trappers. Wyeth was with the Americans now, but he was soon going to be dealing with the British.

By this time the Rocky Mountain trappers had found it advantageous to abandon fixed trading posts, such as were used by the Hudson's Bay men, in favor of rendezvousing at a predetermined place where trappers could meet and exchange furs for goods that had been brought out from St. Louis on pack animals. Captain Bonneville was to learn the lesson when he tried to establish a permanent post which he called Fort Bonneville and the mountain men contemptuously dubbed Fort Nonsense.

Pierre's Hole was admirably situated for a rendezvous. The trading was only a part of it. Here the lonely trapper, often out by himself or with a single companion for months at a time, could enjoy the society of his fellowman. He could buy the guns, traps, and other things he needed and he could get gloriously drunk. He could gamble, engage in shooting matches, run races and wrestle. He might lose an eye or an ear in a fight, but it was all good, clean fun.

There were other forms of amusement besides tests of skill. Long unaccustomed to the sight of white women, the trapper had a keen eye for the dusky beauties of the mountains. Here liaisons, temporary or permanent, were formed. A man would do well to have a squaw with him on his journeys. She would not only be a bedfellow by night, but she could cook his food, mend his clothes, set up his shelter, tan his hides and pack his possibles. Above all, she kept him from being lonely.

Some of these unions lasted a night, some a year, while others might endure a lifetime. One trapper in Oregon had a standing offer of $700 for his woman, but she was never sold. With the Hudson's Bay men, marriages were usually legal and permanent and supplied one of the reasons for that company's fantastic success. With the mountain men, such relationships could be terminated at will by either party. One of the advantages of a lasting union was that the trapper would henceforth enjoy the friendship of his squaw's tribe, and so was much less likely to lose his hair.

From the woman's point of view, it was no less favorable. Indian women loved finery, and the trappers could provide what the men of her tribe could not. She was the envy of her sisters before whom she could strut and show off, and if she couldn't mate for a lifetime she usually was willing to settle for a night. If such goings-on were shocking to New Englander Wyeth, and we may assume they were, we can comfort ourselves with the knowledge that prim, sanctimonious Hall J. Kelley was not there.

At this rendezvous in Pierre's Hole occurred one of the more notable battles with the uninvited Blackfeet. The party with which Wyeth was connected was camped at one end of the basin, while a hundred men under Milton Sublette and Henry Fraeb, ninety trappers with the firm of Drips & Fontenelle, and a number of free trappers were camped lower down. There were also a hundred lodges of Nez Percé and eighty lodges of Flathead Indians, both tribes friendly to the Americans. There well may have been some Bannacks and Shoshones also, since this was at the very door of their territory.

A long file of Blackfeet was observed riding along a ridge, but at first it was assumed they were friendly Indians arriving for the rendezvous. Near-panic resulted when it was found out who they were. Because of one rash act it was never learned whether the initial intentions of the Blackfeet were peaceable or otherwise.

Some of them rode ahead and asked for a parley. Antoine Godin, a half-breed, and another man were sent out to talk. Godin, no lover of Blackfeet, told his companion that while he engaged the chief in talk the other man was to shoot him. It was a deed which Godin was later to atone for at Fort Hall, but the immediate consequence was that the Blackfeet went into camp near by and prepared to attack. Wyeth estimated that there were 600 of them.

In the ensuing battle six white men and seven of their Nez Percé allies were killed and several wounded, among them William Sublette, who had concluded his business and was planning to return to St. Louis. Twenty-six Blackfeet were known to have been killed, and there were probably more. Both sides fought hard.

Just when the battle was going against the defenders Milton Sublette and his men arrived from the other end of the valley and drove the Blackfeet back behind fortifications they had dug in the brush and timber, one of the few times that method of warfare was ever adopted by Indians. This was Wyeth's first experience with Indian warfare, and he acquitted himself well.

During the night the Blackfeet slipped away, and in the morning only a solitary grieving Blackfoot woman was found. She had refused to leave her dead husband. Admiring her spirit and loyalty, the trappers were for letting her live, but the still hot-under-the-collar Nez Percés put a permanent end to her grief.

In 1932, exactly one hundred years after the battle, the meadow on which the battle was fought was the property of my brother Chauncey. I have often walked over the old battleground, and the marks of the Blackfoot trenches were still visible in places. I had been told it was still possible to pick up relics of the fight, such as flint arrowheads, but I had no luck: too many souvenir hunters had been there before me. Somehow the scene of the battle became very

real and my imagination peopled the meadow with long
dead trappers and Indians.

At this time the timber consisted of nothing but willows
and an occasional alder tree. Where buffalo used to roam
only a few gentle dairy cows mooed plantively to remind
me that the milking machine was waiting in the shed. There
is nothing in the peaceful Mormon settlements of the
valley to remind one of the wild, free days of the rendezvous.

By the time they reached Pierre's Hole, Wyeth's patience with his men was being sorely tried, and they were
in almost open rebellion against him. A day or so before
the battle began the malcontents demanded a showdown
to decide what was to be done. Wyeth was agreeable to
the council, but he personally took charge of it and told
them bluntly that it was not a debating society; there was
only one issue and one leader. Those who wanted to turn
back were at liberty to do so, but those who continued must
accept his word as law.

While this may sound arbitrary, it was only evidence
that he was a man of force and determination. That his
men had little reason to complain is made clear by John
K. Townsend, one of the two scientists who accompanied
Wyeth on his second expedition. Wrote Townsend: "I am
much pleased in the manner in which Captain Wyeth
manages his men. He appears calculated to gain the good
will and sure obedience of such a company, adopts the
only sensible mode of accomplishing this end. They are
men accustomed to acting independently. They possess a
strong and indomitable spirit which will never succumb
to authority, and will be reconciled by kindness and familiarity. Captain Wyeth may frequently be seen sitting

on the ground surrounded by a knot of his independents consulting them as to the present arrangements and future movements, paying the utmost deference to the least among them."

The group of which Townsend wrote consisted of far different material from the tenderfeet of the first expedition. One of the chief malcontents was young John Wyeth, one of those who turned back at Pierre's Hole. He made his way to New Orleans, had some boyish escapades there and later at Cincinnati, and finally made his way back to Boston where he wrote a book, A *Brief History of a Long Journey*.

A certain Mr. James Waterhouse, who was dead set against pioneering the Oregon country, evinced an interest in John Wyeth's book, and indeed was a co-author, giving it a strange blend of careless youthful enthusiasm and stern disapproval. For John, the trip had begun as a lark which had gotten a little too rough, but he was never an enemy to his cousin, though Nathaniel called the book "a pack of white lies."

Another one who turned back was Dr. Jacob Wyeth, who did so for reasons of health. As a result of the Pierre's Hole council, Nathaniel Wyeth was left with only eleven men. Three of the departing ones hired out to trap for William Sublette, and two of them were killed by Indians as soon as they got across the first pass. The next year Wyeth found and buried their bleached bones. He was particularly distressed by the fate of a young man named More.

On July the 4th Wyeth threw in with Milton Sublette,

a mountain man no less capable than his elder brother
William and with whom the Easterner got along better.
From Pierre's Hole they followed a trail once used by
Andrew Henry and by Robinson, Hoback and Rezner, and
soon reached Snake River, which was also at various times
called the Saptian and the Lewis River.

Having fought their Indians they were now hardened
mountain men, ready to trap the not too elusive beaver.
They were in a country where not many mountain men had
penetrated, though it was well known to Hudson's Bay
people. Peter Skene Ogden had trapped there some time
after 1825. Previously, Donald McKenzie of Hudson's Bay
had explored and mapped the country and named the
streams, but Wyeth apparently was not familiar with the
map, so it is difficult to tell exactly where he went in pursuit
of beaver.

They did, however, proceed in a southwesterly direction along the south side of Snake River, trapping up its
tributaries, which would have included such streams as
Blackfoot and Portneuf rivers, and Wolverine, Lincoln,
Ross Fork and Bannack creeks. Their course would have
taken them close to the future site of Fort Hall in the
angle between Snake and Portneuf rivers.

On August 29 Wyeth and his men parted with Milton
Sublette. This was probably near the mouth of Raft River.
We can hazard a guess that the more experienced Sublette
followed the rim of the mountains farther south over
what was later to be called the California Trail, though
he didn't follow it any great distance. Wyeth kept closer
to the south bank of the Snake. The two parties came to-

gether September 28 near the mouth of the Boise. Wyeth was away from camp and much to his regret missed seeing Sublette, with whom he had become firm friends.

Wyeth says that Sublette went two creeks farther than he himself did, and saw a large stream running northwest. He was undecided whether this was a stream running into the Snake or into the Gulf of Mexico. Some have thought that Sublette reached the Humboldt, and that Wyeth came near to it, but it is more likely that Sublette crossed the Bruneau and Owyhee rivers, and it is logical to suppose that Wyeth had crossed the Snake, for the Boise runs into the Snake from the east.

It was time to move on. Wyeth found an Indian who agreed to guide him to Fort Walla Walla, then the farthest east of any Hudson's Bay post in Oregon. They reached Walla Walla October 14, and were kindly received by Factor Pierre Pambrun. A McLoughlin rather than a Simpson man, Pambrun would treat even a trade rival hospitably. There was little indication, however, that the bedraggled Wyeth party with its pitiful supply of furs would ever be a serious threat to Hudson's Bay.

Wyeth had been fairly successful in his trapping, but because he lacked horses to carry his harvest he had been obliged to cache the peltries along the trail to be reclaimed later. It was not an uncommon practice, although the furs sometimes spoiled before the owners could get back to them. They always had to be well hidden from the Indians.

Wyeth rested five days at Fort Walla Walla; then, leaving his horses behind, he set out for Fort Vancouver in a Hudson's Bay barge, arriving there October 29, to the great amazement of Dr. John McLoughlin. Seeing the approach of the barge with eleven strangers, McLoughlin ordered a salute to be fired from the fort. With the punctilio of a New England gentleman, Wyeth presented himself.

"Wyeth is my name. I am from Boston on a trading trip to the Columbia."

"Bless me!" exclaimed the doctor. "Welcome to Fort Vancouver."

The iceman from Boston had reached the end of his long journey and if he was astonished at his cordial reception by the "White-headed Eagle," he did not let it show. The Pacific Ocean lay only a few miles away, and he heard opportunity knocking at his door. He was invited to spend the winter, which would give him an opportunity to look over the country before he returned to Boston the next year to start his second expedition.

Having endured so much, he was to face his greatest disappointment at the end of the journey. McLoughlin gave him the news that his ship, the *Sultana*, which he had sent around the Horn, had been lost at sea.

At Fort Vancouver Wyeth discharged his men, leaving them free to enter the employ of Hudson's Bay if they wished. Some of them would stay and become honored pioneer citizens of Oregon.

# 6

# THE TITANS OF THE NORTH

THE NORTHWEST COAST COUN-
try extended roughly from the 42nd to the 54th parallel,
and from the Pacific to the crest of the Rocky Mountains.
Many nations vied for it. Their ships sailed up and down
the coast making "discoveries," often threatening each
other. The discoveries were too conflicting to have much
validity except as arguments for diplomats.

Had the Northwest Coast been appraised at its real
value wars doubtless would have been fought over it. But
the wars were fought in the East, and the Northwest was
only an incidental when the treaties were made.

In our own disputes with Great Britain over the Canadian boundary our statesmen were much more concerned
over that part east of Lake of the Woods than they were
over the part west of it. They didn't mind giving away a

few hundred miles of border in Oregon, but were prepared to fight for a few square miles of Maine.

Such seeming carelessness could only have been the result of the general belief that the area was a desert waste that could only be inhabited by savages, and whose only natural resource was fur. When that was gone the statesmen believed that it would revert to a natural wilderness. The banner of Manifest Destiny had not yet been unfurled.

The coast line was of course valuable, for whoever controlled it would be in a position to dominate trade with the Orient. Eventually, it became apparent that the country could be held only by permanent settlement. The claim of the United States to the Columbia was always disputed by Great Britain. Meares and Vancouver had been outside the estuary ahead of Gray, and Broughten and others had gone farther up the river. The War of 1812 had given England the river by right of conquest but the claim later was relinquished. The Northwest Company, and later Hudson's Bay, had penetrated the interior and were in command of it, although Lewis and Clark had been there first.

The whole result was confusion. Eventually, a few farsighted men perceived that the nation which controlled the Columbia River and its tributaries would control the entire Northwest Coast.

The Hudson's Bay Company was slow to admit that there could be anything of value except fur, but their methods were more comprehensive than those of the transitory Americans. Things began to change with the arrival of John McLoughlin, who was the first to see agricultural possibilities in the Northwest. A French-Canadian named

Etienne Lucier was grubstaked by McLoughlin and became the first farmer in Oregon. McLoughlin brought livestock, cattle, hogs and sheep—and even sheep dogs from Scotland. He planted trees, raised wheat and vegetables.

The Northwest is famous for its horticulture, but perhaps few have heard the legend that the apple industry of Oregon and Washington began in a London ballroom when a society lady playfully slipped the seeds from an apple she was eating into the pocket of a sea captain. He only discovered them when he was visiting McLoughlin at Vancouver and handed them to his host, who planted them and they grew into the first apple trees in Oregon.

John McLoughlin was born in 1784 at Riviere-du-Loup on the lower St. Lawrence, of Scottish ancestry, with strains of French and Irish in his blood. He obtained a medical education in Edinburgh, Scotland, his father having been a doctor. Returning to America, he became a surgeon for the Northwest Company at Fort William on the Kaninistiquia river on the shores of Lake Superior. By 1814 he was a partner in the business, in charge of the Rainy Lake district. McLoughlin went to London with Angus Bethune to secure better terms for the partners in the field, was there when the Northwest and Hudson's Bay companies were combined and became acquainted with Sir George Simpson, who was to become Governor General of Hudson's Bay Company and by far the most influential man in Canada.

George Simpson, born out of wedlock in 1787 at Loch Broom, Ross-shire, Scotland, was raised by a kinswoman and received a good education. He began his business career as a clerk in the London mercantile house of

Graham, Simpson, and Wedderburn. He was introduced to Hudson's Bay Company by Andrew Colville, and his advancement was rapid. A martinet and a driver who never let anything stand in his way, or in that of Hudson's Bay, he was a good hater, and he was ruthless.

In 1824 Simpson sent McLoughlin to Fort George, as factor in charge of the Columbia River district. McLoughlin promptly moved the post upriver and named it Fort Vancouver. It was on the north bank of the river. He may possibly have been acting on Simpson's orders.

Simpson had chosen McLoughlin because the Columbia district was running down, and he thought McLoughlin was the man to build it up; yet was never satisfied with him, and became more discontented as the years passed. He is said to have been kind to the poor, but he lacked all the broad humanitarian instincts that moved Dr. McLoughlin. He seldom lost sight of the fact that he was the biggest toad in his puddle.

Eventually, it was Simpson who drove McLoughlin out of the company by what McLoughlin considered persecution. It was galling to his pride to be called back to London and put on the carpet before the Board of Hudson's Bay Company like an erring child. Simpson's main charge against the doctor was that he was too friendly with the Americans. To Sir George, anyone who thought of anything except the interests of the company was an enemy.

Apparently, he had little liking for McLoughlin from the start, although both were aristocrats of equal heritage and standing. At Fort Vancouver McLoughlin lived like a feudal baron. The Indians called him White-headed Eagle; most others called him Governor McLoughlin. He

was a magnificent figure of a man who stood six feet four,
and his long white hair always hung down over his shoulders. He wore broadcloth coats and knee breeches and
silver buckles on his shoes. He exercised the power of life
or death—wisely and sparingly, it must be said—over his
subjects. He incurred the lifelong enmity of Hall J. Kelley,
yet Kelley had no just personal complaints.

That picture of Dr. McLoughlin is at wide variance
with the one Sir George Simpson left of him. On the way
from Fort William to the Columbia McLoughlin had two
days' start, yet Simpson caught up with him on River la
Biche and found him still in camp at seven o'clock in the
morning.

Simpson wrote gleefully of the encounter: "He was
such a figure as I should not like to meet in a Dark night
in one of the bye lanes in the neighborhood of London,
dressed in Clothes that had once been fashionable, but
now covered with a thousand patches of different Colors,
his hands evidently Shewing that he had not lost much
time at his Toilette, loaded with Arms and his own her-
culean diminsions forming a tout ensemble that would
convey a good idea of the highway men of former Days."

In a little private diary Simpson wrote an opinion
of McLoughlin under the heading of "No. 10," but without
mentioning his name.

"A very bustling, active man who can go through a
great deal of business but is wanting in system and regularity
and has not the talent of managing the few associates and
clerks under his authority; has a great deal of influence with
Indians and speaks the Soulteaux tolerably well. Very zeal-
ous in the discharge of his public duties and a man of strict

honor and integrity but a stickler for rights and priveleges and sets himself up for a righter of wrongs. Very anxious to obtain a lead among his colleagues with whom he has not too much influence owing to his ungovernable temper and turbulent disposition, and would be a troublesome man to the Comp'y if he had sufficient influence to form and tact to manage a party, in short, would be a Radical in any Country under any government and under any circumstances; and if he had not pacific people to deal with, would be eternally embroiled in 'affairs of honor' on the merest trifle arising—I conceive from the irritability of his temper more than a quarrelsome disposition—altogether a disagreeable man to do business with as it is impossible to go with him in all things and a difference of opinion amounts to a declaration of hostilities, yet a good-hearted man and a pleasant companion."

There were other highly placed men in the fur trade who had an even lower opinion of Simpson than Simpson had of McLoughlin. One of these was John McLean, who made his hatred plain in his two-volume, *Notes of a Twenty-five's Service in the Hudson's Bay Territory*. He accused Simpson of breaking promises of advancement, and described him as cold and callous, favored by fortune and guilty of favoritism; and said that he combined with "The prepossessing manners of a gentleman all the craft and subtlety of an intriguing courtier." Simpson's knighthood, McLean maintained, had been earned not by himself but by the Dease and Simpson Arctic expedition to which Sir George had contributed only about half an hour's desk planning.

Others accused McLean of bias, which was probably

true. However, Simpson was undoubtedly as arrogant as the usual aristocrat of his time.

Another writer who accused Sir George of blocking promotions and exploiting his subordinates' careers for his own personal interest was a kinsman, Alexander Simpson, in a biography of his brother Thomas Simpson, the Arctic explorer. From all accounts Sir George's unofficial title of "The Little Emperor" was well deserved.

He seems never to have let up on McLoughlin, and the chief cause of his dislike was McLoughlin's friendliness toward the Americans, particularly the settlers. His fury knew no bounds when he learned that McLoughlin had extended company credit to them to the amount of $30,000. Embittered by Simpson's unrelenting attacks, McLoughlin in 1845 gave up his $12,000-a-year position with the company and made application to become an American citizen. Unfortunately he got no more gratitude from the settlers he had helped than he did from Hudson's Bay Company— though today the descendants of those settlers venerate McLoughlin as the father of their state.

From all the evidence, we may deduce that McLoughlin was a true but kindly aristocrat. His dealings with Jedediah Smith, Nathaniel Wyeth, Ewing Young and Hall J. Kelley make that clear. Sir George Simpson, on the other hand, seems to have been a self-centered snob.

McLoughlin had surely lost caste with Simpson when he married a half-breed Ojibway woman, the widow of the Alexander McKay who had been killed in the *Tonquin* disaster. Her son Thomas was McLoughlin's chief trouble-shooter, especially around Forts Hall and Boise. He was also the man called upon to retrieve Jedediah Smith's goods after his dismaying encounter with the Indians on the Umpqua. Although Sir James Douglas was McLoughlin's official assistant, his stepson Tom was his shield and buckler.

McLoughlin and his Ojibway wife had four children, two boys and two girls, and it was his son John who was to drive the deepest wedge between him and Sir George Simpson when John was murdered at Stickeen, where he had been sent as factor.

McLoughlin demanded that the murderers be punished, but Simpson refused on the logical grounds that there was no legal government by which the culprits could be tried. Yet McLoughlin knew, as everybody else knew, that Hudson's Bay did occasionally hang an Indian. On two occasions McLoughlin himself had done so where there was no question of guilt.

Simpson claimed that young John McLoughlin was a drunken wastrel, and in no way suited to be the factor at Stickeen, or any other Hudson's Bay post. His view was that John had debauched the Indians and they had killed him. McLoughlin's view was that of a father who had lost a beloved son. After that there could only be distrust and hatred between the two men. Simpson was too well bred to express personal prejudice toward an associate, yet in his eyes Dr. McLoughlin was a squawman, regardless of the fact that his wife was an educated, cultured woman.

McLoughlin never forgave his superior. Simpson himself seemed to be of the opinion that a half-breed should never be trusted with the administrative duties of the lofty Hudson's Bay company. Another who shared this contemptuous view was the historian Bancroft who stated that it was a waste of time trying to teach McLoughlin's "half-breed mongrels." McLoughlin's two daughters certainly gave the lie to the historian, as we shall see.

Both men were completely loyal to the company, but McLoughlin could never forget his humanity and he was never petty, which can hardly be said of Sir George. Once he wrote to Donald Ross at Norway House calling attention to the officers' practice of sending preserved buffalo tongues to their friends in England. There were, he pointed out, penalties for giving furs as gifts, so if buffalo tongues had cash value there should be penalties for giving them away. Any property of the company was sacred.

The Little Emperor urged his employees to keep on good terms with the missionaries, "especially gentlemen of the Wesleyan Society." McLoughlin was equally friendly to them, but he drew no distinctions. Although claiming membership in the Church of England he had received Catholic training from his grandmother, a member of the powerful Fraser family, when he lived with her a few years as a child. He befriended the Methodist, Jason Lee, and other missionaries of the Willamette valley, though many of them were in time to turn and bite the hand that fed them.

He was equally friendly to the Catholics, and to the Presbyterian missions of Dr. Marcus Whitman and Reverend H. H. Spalding. He persuaded Jason Lee not to go among the treacherous Cayuses, and also did his best to dissuade Whitman from doing so; the rejection of the advice caused Whitman, his wife and others to lose their lives. The net result of his broadmindedness in helping all denominations to establish schools and missions and build churches was that the Protestants called him a Catholic, and the Catholics called him a Protestant.

Both Simpson and McLoughlin tried to end the liquor traffic with the Indians. At one time McLoughlin purchased an entire cargo of whisky to keep it from them. For a long time Hudson's Bay held the exclusive trade with the Blackfeet, but when Sir George tried to cut out the whisky he was told that they could always get it from the less finicky Americans. Faced with the urgency of profit, Sir George resorted to persuasion rather than embargo and boycott and held the trade. Perhaps it was because the British admittedly had better trade goods than the Americans, including better booze. Yet it was to their credit that both Simpson and McLoughlin restricted the liquor traffic as much as they could.

The matter of the HBC's trading in liquor with the Indians was thoroughly overhauled in the House of Commons in 1857. Sir George had little liking for the inquiry. He could point to the fact that he had always urged his employees to observe the Sabbath, and he had warned them of the iniquities of idleness, but his answers to queries about the use of liquor were said to have been evasive.

In the ten years 1847–1857, he stated, the average importation of spirituous liquors had been less than 5000 gallons a year, two-thirds of which was taken by the inhabitants of Red River, and the remaining third was for the servants of the company, with "An occasional dram to the Indians who are employed in transport with our own servants, or for the purchase of provisions in parts of the country where we cannot get them otherwise."

If there was a bit of hypocrisy in Sir George's defense it was small when compared with that of the American fur traders. The Americans, who had never tried to suppress the traffic in their own territory, once came down with a sudden attack of righteousness and protested to the government in Washington against the way the Hudson's Bay people were selling liquor to the Indians, endangering the peace and drawing trade away from the Americans. The complaint reached Viscount Palmerston of the British Ministry of Foreign Affairs, through the American legation in London. It was called to the attention of Earl Grey, Minister of Colonial Affairs, and Hudson's Bay was asked for an explanation.

Sir John Pelly, then Governor General of the company, issued a categorical denial, and stated that their efforts to control the traffic had been thwarted by the indifference of the American officials along the border. He admitted that after each season it was customary to hold "a regale" for all parties concerned, but claimed that the whisky was highly diluted. As a matter of fact, the regales could not be compared to the wild dissipation common in the rendezvous of the American trappers and traders. As for the peace, the Canadians had the best record. The object of the protest was to provoke an international incident that would lead to the suppression of the liquor trade north of the border—in which case that trade would just naturally come south. The well organized HBC was much more able and willing to cease dealing in whisky than were our own free traders, who were under obligation to no one but themselves.

The struggle for control of Oregon during the joint

occupancy never ceased, though it was conducted mostly by private citizens rather than by governments. In January, 1841, Simpson was knighted by the queen for his long services, and at the same time Pelly was made a baronet. Sir George made a trip into California and called upon the Mexican grandees at Monterey and Santa Barbara. He saw there a decaying government and a country which must inevitably fall into the hands of either the British or the Americans.

Already the company was entrenched at Yerba Buena, on San Francisco Bay. In his travels Simpson encountered that trusty cockney, Francis Ermatinger, who at that time had just been released as factor at Fort Hall and was on a scouting expedition from Canada to California. When Simpson met him there he was disguised as a Spanish *caballero*.

Hudson's Bay was reaching out. That winter Sir George sailed to Honolulu on the company ship *Cowlitz* to inspect the post there. He was royally entertained by the brown king of the Sandwich Islands.

In spite of Sir George's efforts, California showed no signs of falling into the hands of the British, and there came a time when the company perceived that it was not going to be able to hold any of the territory south of the Columbia. So steps were taken to leave what is now Oregon desolated and empty of what they thought of as its only resource, the beaver.

Peter Skene Ogden, the commando leader of the company, who may have covered more miles for the company than any other man, was entrusted with the task. He was sent up the Columbia with a large party on a roundabout mission. He crossed the Blue Mountains and the Great Basin into California, and thence proceeded north into Oregon to see about trapping out the country. McLeod, another veteran company man, moved southward for the same purpose. But events were moving too fast for them: the wagons and the plows had already reached Oregon.

Hudson's Bay had ignored colonization too long while they concentrated on the fur trade. Even Fort Vancouver on the north bank of the Columbia was no longer impregnable. Most of the settlers on the Willamette were Americans. McLoughlin, through his lieutenants Ermatinger and Grant at Fort Hall, was doggedly trying to hold the line and divert emigration to California, while he tried to get British emigrants brought in by sea, but it was a losing struggle.

The British government had left things too long in the hands of the great company which believed that trapping and farming were incompatible. A few weak efforts to colonize had been made around Puget Sound and Spokane, but when the Americans came it was like a thundering herd of buffalo, irresistible.

The company was having its own troubles. Every twenty-one years, its charter had to be renewed, and there were radical elements in Parliament who opposed its monopolistic tendencies. The grand old men of Hudson's Bay were finding themselves more and more on the defensive.

Marcus Whitman had broken the dam at Fort Hall in 1836. Before his tragic death in 1846, and McLoughlin's retirement, the trickle of wagons had become a flood.

# 7

## THE SECOND COMING

NATHANIEL WYETH SPENT A pleasant, and no doubt profitable, winter at Fort Vancouver as the guest of Dr. McLoughlin. Though the two men did not agree on the future of Oregon they got along very well.

Holman, in his book, *Dr. John McLoughlin*, gives a good description of the fort at that time. "Fort Vancouver was a parallelogram about seven hundred and fifty feet long and four hundred and fifty feet broad, enclosed by an upright picket wall of large and closely fitted beams, over twenty feet in height, secured by buttresses on the inside. Originally there was a bastion at each angle of the fort. In the earlier times there were two twelve pounders mounted in these bastions. In the center were some eighteen pounders; all these cannon from disuse became merely ornamental early in the thirties. . . . It was a very peaceful fort.

"The interior of the fort was divided into two courts, having about forty buildings, all of wood except the powder magazine which was constructed of brick and stone. In the center, facing the main entrance, stood the Hall in which were the dining room, smoking room and public sitting room, or bachelor's hall. Single men, clerks, strangers, and others make the bachelor's hall their place of resort. To these rooms artisans and servants were not admitted. The Hall was the only two-story house in the fort. The residence of Dr. McLoughlin was built after the model of a French-Canadian dwelling-house. It had a piazza with vines growing on it. There were flower beds in front of the house. The other buildings consisted of dwellings for officers and their families, a schoolhouse, a retail store, warehouses and shops.

"Fifty houses for artisans and servants were a short distance away. Population about 800."

Another account has it that the place was well fortified for the times, with a three-storied log tower at the northwest corner bristling with portholes and cannon. This also alludes to the governor's *two-story* residence where he and his assistant, James Douglas, dispensed hospitality. Ordinary trappers and their Indian wives had their quarters outside the compound.

While Wyeth was housed in the governor's mansion, he spent most of his evenings at Bachelor's Hall, which indicated that he was a hail fellow well met. During his stay at Vancouver he made a trip up the Willamette valley, one day destined to be the garden spot of Oregon. Already McLoughlin had shown what the country could produce,

but Wyeth, unlike Kelley, was interested in trade. In any
event, there can be little doubt that he saw the country
as future American territory, and he was storing up information for his next trip across the continent.

Wyeth enjoyed the hospitality of Dr. McLoughlin
until February 23, 1833, when he set out on his return
journey with just two of his men. He felt no resentment
toward those of his men who decided to remain in Oregon.
Two of those are worthy of note. One, the scholarly John
Ball, had been trained as a lawyer, but to the delight of
Dr. McLoughlin he consented to teach the children at the
fort through January and February of 1833. He tried farming during the summer of that year, then returned to the
East to practice law, but his account of the first expedition
is one of the best.

Ball was succeeded as teacher by Solomon Smith, another of Wyeth's men, who continued for eighteen months.
Later he taught the first organized school on French Prairie,
near the present town of Wheatland. He ran away with a
Clatsop Indian woman, the wife of McLoughlin's baker,
later married her and became a completely assimilated Ore-
gonian as well as a missionary.

Wyeth was accompanied as far as Fort Walla Walla
by Francis Ermatinger, the man who would one day take
over Fort Hall and make it a miniature Fort Vancouver.

From Walla Walla, Wyeth and his men angled northeast to the Hudson's Bay post at Fort Colville, thence eastward 175 miles to Flathead House, just south of Flathead
Lake in Montana. From there he crossed to the headwaters
of the Missouri, then back across the Continental Divide
to the headwaters of Salmon River. He was following pretty

much the route used by Chief Joseph of the Nez Percés half a century later in his courageous but futile attempt to reach Canada.

On the Salmon, to the surprise of both, he encountered his friend, peripatetic Captain B. E. L. Bonneville. The portly, bald-headed Frenchman and the lanky New Englander were as unlike as men could be, but they had once planned to go to Oregon together with Hall J. Kelley's still-born company, and it was only natural for them to speculate on new ventures.

It had always been in Bonneville's mind to explore California, and he proposed that they should return to the Columbia over the route which Wyeth knew, and from there conduct a joint expedition south into California. Wyeth toyed with the idea for a time, but gave it up to return home. His own plans were fixed and definite, and he was not the man to follow a will-of-the-wisp. The explorers parted company.

Wyeth did not bother to collect the furs he had cached, but started on his way; passing the Pierre's Hole battleground, he proceeded to Green River where the annual rendezvous was going on. En route, he buried the skeleton of the unfortunate young More and his companion who had been killed by Indians.

Remaining at the rendezvous a week, Wyeth left on July 24, striking across to the head of the Bighorn, down which he traveled to the Yellowstone, passing Fort Cass three miles below the mouth of the Bighorn.

For a time he was covering trail again with his friend Milton Sublette. At this time there could have been no doubt in Wyeth's mind as to the ultimate success of his enterprise, for he entered into an agreement with Sublette, as agent for the Rocky Mountain Fur Company, by which he agreed to bring out $3000 worth of goods the following spring. Wyeth, ever the careful businessman, insisted that an agreement be drawn up and signed by which the company agreed to forfeit $1600 if for any reason they refused to accept the goods. As it turned out, it was a wise proviso on Wyeth's part.

Traveling with Milton, Wyeth continued on down the Yellowstone to its junction with the Missouri, where at Fort Union they found William Sublette.

It is quite possible that William, who sometimes had to restrain the impulsive actions of his younger brothers, had a few choice words for Milton, but if so Wyeth knew nothing about it. There was a change of plan, however, and Milton remained at Fort Union instead of accompanying Wyeth as far as St. Louis. Though having no guide Wyeth decided to go downstream, and arrived at St. Louis October 9, 1833. He reached Cambridge on the 7th of November.

On his arrival back at Cambridge Wyeth busied himself organizing a new company and raising capital. His ideas had undergone some change, and he foresaw the eventual end of the fur business. He would continue to trade in furs as long as they lasted, furnishing supplies to the inland trappers and traders, but by way of the sea rather than overland. He saw his great opportunity in the salmon-packing industry, which would be profitable notwithstanding the expense of the long trip around the Horn. He was sure there would be other opportunities; none of them would be neglected.

He organized the Columbia River Fishing and Trading Company, and had little difficulty interesting the substantial citizens of Boston in the project. A capital of $20,000, later raised to $40,000, was quickly subscribed. Of this Wyeth took one-eighth. It was agreed that he should have complete control, with no risk other than his own investment.

A vessel, the *May Dacre*, was chartered and loaded with goods which Wyeth deemed would be beneficial in the trade. The possibilities of this ship's meeting the fate of the *Sultana* were remote, and Wyeth left nothing else to chance. The first trip had been exploratory, and now he was in a position to put his knowledge and experience to good use.

On this second expedition he would have a better class of men. On his return in 1833 Wyeth had picked up a bright Indian lad named Baptiste with the idea of educating him so that he might serve as interpreter. A captured Nez Percé boy had also pleaded to be taken along, and the arrival in the East of the two Indian lads created a sensation among the God-fearing people of Massachusetts, who yearned to save the souls of the heathen savages.

None was more stirred than Reverend Jason Lee, who only a short time before had been converted by his nephew, Daniel Lee. A tall, black-bearded, modest man with a knack for getting along with people, Jason Lee conceived the idea of starting missions in the Oregon country, and applied to Wyeth for permission to join his company. Along with him were his nephew Daniel and three other men with similar interests. Wyeth accepted them gladly.

About this time the entire East was excited about carrying the gospel to the Indians. Four young Flatheads, members of an unusually peaceful and thoughtful tribe, had come to St. Louis, saying they were in search of a book which they had heard would bring salvation to the Indians.

Among the orthodox this book was, of course, thought to be the Bible. There were others with different ideas. The Church of Jesus Christ of Latter-day Saints had been organized April 6, 1830, by its leader and prophet, Joseph Smith. Claiming to believe in the Bible, they had another sacred book, *The Book of Mormon*, which Smith had translated from golden plates by supernatural means. *The Book of Mormon* purported to be the history of an ancient people who had once inhabited the American continents, and of whom the Indians were the sole survivors.

Having heard of the questing young Flatheads, Joseph Smith had hastened to send Apostle Parley P. Pratt to the frontier to open an Indian mission. Everyone was intent on saving the souls of the redmen. They might be plundered of their land and their game, but their spiritual welfare would not be neglected.

Along with Jason Lee and his party, Wyeth was joined by two young scientists, John K. Townsend, who faithfully kept a journal of the trip, and Thomas Nuttall. The middle of March, 1834, found Wyeth back at Independence with fifty men, ready to pick up the goods for the Rocky Mountain Fur Company. Traveling with them would be Milton Sublette himself, with twenty-four hunters. It was a far cry from the bedraggled party he had started out with two years before.

Soon after getting under way they were passed by another party led by William Sublette, anxious to reach the mountains ahead of his rivals. Meanwhile, because of trouble with one of his legs, Milton Sublette was obliged to turn back, and the disease, probably cancer, caused his death a year later. Thus passed from the scene one of the most capable and admirable of the mountain men.

Wyeth's trip presented only the usual difficulties. The trail was well known, and most of his men experienced. Wyeth had every reason to feel optimistic. When he arrived at the Green River rendezvous he received a shock. It became painfully clear why William Sublette had been in such a tremendous hurry. Earlier, he had treated the Easterner with good-natured tolerance, but now he saw in him a possible trade rival to be put out of business. He had brought his own trade goods and refused to accept those his brother had ordered. Wyeth was left with $3000 worth of goods on his hands for which he had no market! No tenderfoot where business was concerned, he insisted on the forfeit money, and William reluctantly forked over the $1600 which Milton had agreed to pay if the goods were refused.

Wyeth had other complaints, which he enumerated in a letter to Milton Sublette. William refused to pay interest on the cash advances, his excuse being that the Rocky Mountain Fur Company had been sold to Thomas Fitzpatrick and James Bridger that year and the new company was known as Fitzpatrick, Sublette & Bridger.

In his letter to Milton, Wyeth does not accuse the Sublettes of intention to defraud him when the agreement was made, but puts the blame mostly on "Broken-hand" Tom Fitzpatrick, who seemed to be the real head of the company. Wyeth thought that Fitzpatrick had been bribed by William Sublette to break the contract because William had reached the rendezvous first with his own trade goods. He was learning that competition could be the death as well as the life of trade. The Rocky Mountain men also had some success in debauching Wyeth's followers and hiring them away from him, but Wyeth states that he was able to hire a sufficient number of their employees to make up for the desertions. He could fight fire with fire, and did.

The notice of dissolution of partnership contained a clause that all persons having claims against the company should notify them and receive payment. This Wyeth could not do in the short time provided, so the company was within its legal rights in refusing the goods, though it was bound by the forfeit. However, Wyeth was left with merchandise on his hands in a country completely dominated by his trade rivals.

Never a man to refuse a challenge or to give up easily, he gathered up his pack animals and plodded on over the familiar trail. He had seen the upper Snake River valley, and knew that it was still the most virgin fur country left in the West, and there were as many Indians there as anywhere. Here he would build a fort and dispose of his surplus goods.

He knew that Jed Smith had promised that he and his partners would not trap that country. Wyeth was not naive enough to believe that Smith's word would forever bind all his partners, but there were not many of them there yet. He must have known that Mackenzie, Ross and others had explored and mapped the country, and perhaps he knew that Peter Skene Ogden had trapped there for Hudson's

Bay as early as 1825, but they had not been active there two years before. He did, however, have a Hudson's Bay man as a traveling companion. Thomas McKay had accompanied him all the way from the rendezvous, doubtless pouring words of sympathy into his ear.

To Wyeth the Snake was known as Lewis River, but a tributary was known to Hudson's Bay men as the Portneuf, named in honor of a trapper who met his death there. Somewhere between the confluence of the Snake and the Portneuf were the lush meadows which the Indians called *Shawnt shawnip*, meaning "Plenty game." Here Wyeth had trapped successfully, and his furs were cached not far away. It would be an ideal place for a fort.

Keeping far to the north of what was to become the Oregon Trail, Wyeth struck the head of the Snake, following a route he knew. Somewhere, they struck the Blackfoot River and observed a great many buffalo. Present place names are sometimes hard to identify with the ones used by the early trappers, but since Wyeth knew approximately where he was going it is reasonably sure that he crossed Lincoln Creek and cut across the foothills forming the north slopes of Mt. Putnam, where he would have a good view of his destination.

Townsend relates that as they were coming down somebody noticed an Indian skulking on a ridge. "A Blackfoot, by God," Tom McKay yelled, and spurred in pursuit. Both he and the Indian disappeared. Townsend and his fellows followed, fearing that McKay would be led into an ambush, but they found that he had given up the chase. Assuming that McKay did see a Blackfoot, he was probably on one of the ridges above Ross Fork Creek.

The party must have proceeded on past present Fort Hall to the Fort Hall bottoms, which break away from the sagebrush plateau so gently as scarcely to be noticed. In the distance lay Ferry Butte, and there was plenty of game, for Paul Richardson, hunter for the party, killed a buffalo close to the bank of Snake River, and where they dressed it out was the site Wyeth chose for the building of Fort Hall. The date was July 15, 1834, and it would be a significant one in American history. Wyeth's own version of the founding of the fort, quoted at the beginning of this book, says he named it for "the oldest gentleman in the concern" (Mr. Henry Hall, of Boston; not one of the explorers, but one of Wyeth's financial backers).

As has been noted, McLoughlin's stepson, Thomas McKay, accompanied Wyeth from the Green River rendezvous. The troubleshooter's presence could hardly have been accidental. Hudson's Bay was keeping an eye on its competitors. John K. Townsend and Osborne Russell, a young trapper with Wyeth, were both keeping journals, and from them we know a great deal of what was going on. A party of horsemen was seen approaching from the west, and it turned out to be some of McKay's men coming to meet him.

They joined in the celebration of the opening of Fort Hall, but after Wyeth left for Fort Vancouver McKay's party was mysteriously lost sight of. The next that Wyeth heard of Tom McKay he had just built Fort Boise at the west end of the desert. It was never a profitable trading post, but it wasn't meant to be. Its purpose was to keep the Americans from becoming too strong at Fort Hall.

# 8

# THE FORT ON THE BOTTOMS

ONE OF THE BEST STUDIES OF
Fort Hall I have read was a paper written by Thomas Payne
West while he was a student at the University of Idaho in
1924. Mr. West's home is in Pocatello, Idaho, where he
has had the benefit of associating with Dr. Minnie Howard,
the region's leading authority on old Fort Hall. Tom West
had a strong personal reason for his interest. His father, a
Portneuf River rancher, once ran cattle on the Fort Hall
bottoms and Tom was a rider there, along with my brother.

From Dr. Minnie Howard he had the story of the finding of the old fort's location by Ezra Meeker and Jim
Broncho. So sure was Mr. Meeker of the site that he dug
around until he unearthed bits of old wagon parts, ox shoes
and other relics which proved conclusively the exact spot
where Wyeth built the original fort. Its position with rela-

tion to the two rivers at the time is still uncertain because in the course of more than a hundred years both streams have changed their channels many times.

That it was near the banks of Snake River is certain, and it is now washed by the waters of the great American Falls reservoir. When I was there in the spring of 1962 the water covered the road to the monument so that we were unable to reach the place. The monument is now some ten miles from the mouth of the Portneuf, which bends west from Pocatello. The distances vary in the old accounts. Quoting Mr. West: "An army officer who passed Fort Hall in 1849 says it was fifteen miles from the fort to where the Portneuf empties into the Snake, and about eleven miles to where the road (Oregon Trail) crosses the Portneuf. Frémont makes all these distances less. One thing to take into account when these distances were recorded is that there was always considerable drinking around such a place as Fort Hall, and when distances were estimated extravagantly the man giving the report may have been drunk.

"Much confusion arises as to the exact site of Fort Hall. . . . The main reason for this is to be found in the fact that a number of places in the vicinity of the original old 1834 Fort Hall later were designated by the same name. There have been at least four spots called 'Fort Hall,' and possibly more. Almost any spot of government activity in this vicinity seems to have carried the name with it."

Disregarding the other places for the moment, there is no doubt that the original fort was where Ezra Meeker said it was. Plans are being considered for building a replica of the old fort, but whether it will be at Pocatello, Fort Hall, or Blackfoot I do not know. Because of the possible rise of the reservoir it will not be built on its original site.

There was some timber available along the river bottom when the fort was built, and this was undoubtedly used at first. Later, adobes were used, and the old ruins were sometimes referred to as "The Dobies." A traveler speaks of the white walls of Fort Hall "gleaming in the sun," so presumably the adobes may have been whitewashed.

Paul Richardson killed his bull buffalo July 15, 1834, and Wyeth left for the Columbia August 6, so the days between must have been extremely busy ones. Townsend says that he was one of a party of twelve sent out to shoot buffalo for meat. Nuttall was along and so, according to Townsend, was a Mr. Ashworth, who probably went for the sport of the thing, for no other mention is made of him. There may have been other sportsmen with the group, for Townsend mentions a "Mr. Stewart" who accompanied McKay when the trouble shooter left for Vancouver on the 30th of July. This must have been William Drummond Stewart, the nobly born Scotsman who, enamored of the West, spent several years with the Rocky Mountain trappers and traders. The hunting party moved up the Blackfoot River, a good country for buffalo, and were successful in the hunt, but one of the members suffered a painful accident when his gun exploded, burning him painfully and nearly blinding him.

It is not likely that McKay's men did much voluntary work in helping Wyeth build the fort. There was considerable drinking and horse racing. One of these contests resulted in a collision, and a Canadian named Kanseau was killed. His was the first funeral ever held at Fort Hall.

With Wyeth all the way had been Reverend Jason

Lee and his four companions, who drove a bunch of cattle with them. The Canadian-born Lee played an important part in the history of Oregon, but his chief claim to fame may rest on the fact that on Sunday, July 27, 1834, at Fort Hall, he preached the first sermon west of the Rocky Mountains.

Townsend describes the services: "The next day being the Sabbath, our good missionary, Mr. Jason Lee, was requested to hold meeting with which he obligingly complied. A convenient, shady spot was selected in the forest adjacent, and the greater part of our men, as well as the whole of Mr. McKay's party company, including the Indians, attended. The usual forms of Methodist service, to which Mr. Lee is attached, were gone through, and were followed by a brief, but excellent and appropriate exhortation by that gentleman. The people were remarkably quiet and attentive and the Indians sat upon the ground like statues. Although not one of them could understand a word that was said, they nevertheless maintained the most strict and decorous silence, kneeling when the preacher knelt, and rising when he rose, evidently with a view of paying him and us a suitable respect, however much their own notions as to the proper and most acceptable forms of worship might have been opposed to ours."

Of this historic sermon Jason Lee said modestly, "We repaired to the grove about half past three for public worship. I did not attempt to preach but gave a short exhortation from the text, 'Whether therefore ye eat or drink, or whatsoever ye do, do all to the glory of God.'"

Such a meeting in the Rocky Mountains, Townsend comments, "is almost as unusual as the appearance of a herd of buffalo in the settlements." He adds, "Mr. Lee is a great favorite with the men." Lee, however, was known to have rebuked the men occasionally for their profanity and drunkenness.

It was the evening of that same day that the unfortunate Kanseau was killed. The body was wrapped in coarse linen, over which a buffalo robe was sewed, and was buried the next day about a hundred yards south of the fort, with a black cross at the head of the grave. Mr. Lee conducted the ordinary church ceremony. Then Catholic hymns were sung by the Canadians present. The Indians had their turn in the last of the three services, since Kanseau had an Indian wife and other Indian relatives present. Comments Townsend tersely, "He was at least well buried."

On Saturday evening Townsend, Nuttall and Wyeth had supper with Thomas McKay at his lodge. Townsend, throwing some light on McKay, writes: "Mr. McKay assures me that he had considerable difficulty in bringing his men to the state in which they are now. The free and fearless Indian was particularly difficult to subdue; but steady, determined perseverance, and bold measures, aided by a rigid self-example, made them as clay in his hand, and has finally reduced them to their present admirable condition. . . .

"After supper was concluded, we sat ourselves on a buffalo robe at the entrance of the lodge, to see the Indians at their devotions. . . .

"I think I was never more gratified by any exhibition in my life. The humble, subdued, and beseeching looks of the poor untutored beings who were calling upon their Heavenly Father to forgive their sins, and continue His mercies upon them, and the heartfelt sincerity which characterized the whole scene, was truly affecting, and very impressive."

On July 30, McKay and his party, accompanied by the missionaries, pulled out. The fort was usable by August 4, so that the twelve men to be left there could finish it, and the next morning Idaho's first patriotic exercises were held and the account by the pious Mr. Townsend indicates that he wished he had left with McKay and the missionaries. He writes: "August 5th. At sunrise this morning the 'star-spangled banner' was raised on the flag staff at the fort, and a salute was fired by the men, who, according to orders, assembled around it. All in camp were allowed free and uncontrolled use of liquor, and, as usual, the consequence was a scene of rioting, noise and fighting, during the whole day; some became so drunk that their senses fled them entirely, and they were therefore harmless; but by far the greater number were just sufficiently under the influence of the vile trash, to render them in their conduct disgusting and tigerlike. We had gouging, biting, fisticuffing, and 'stamping' in the most 'scientific' perfection; some even fired guns and pistols at each other, but these weapons were mostly harmless in the unsteady hands which employed them. Such scenes I never hope to witness again; they are absolutely sickening, and cause us to look upon our species with abhorrence and loathing. Night at last came, and cast her mantle over our besotted camp; the revel was over, and the men retired to their pallets peaceably, but not a few of them will bear evidence of the debauch of August 5th."

The "debauch" which so shocked the sensitive scientist

was a natural part of life in the mountains, and the mountain men, whether Hudson's Bay or not, recognized the
fact that after the hard, lonely months the men had to
blow off steam occasionally. Had Fort Hall been built in
New England its opening would no doubt have been celebrated more decorously, but this was the wilderness, and
the establishment of the fort meant that the Americans,
no matter how impermanently, had their feet planted on
the soil of Oregon. That the men were rough is indicated by
the fact that the guns inside the bastions were fixed so
that they could command both the inside and the outside
of the fort.

Wyeth left Fort Hall for the Columbia, hangovers
notwithstanding, on the morning of August 6. The usual
trail followed down Snake River, but Wyeth struck northwest across the desert past the three buttes which rise
abruptly from the flat plain. Two of them, very close together, are called the Twin Buttes; the other and larger one
twenty miles distant is known as Big Butte. This route led
him across the two Lost Rivers, one of which was known
for a long time as Godin's River. He crossed another stream
that has been called variously Malade, Wood, and Magic
River. He also crossed the Boise, not descending it to where
Tom McKay was already industriously building Fort Boise
as Hudson's Bay's answer to Fort Hall.

Actually, Wyeth's ownership of Fort Hall was to last
only a little more than two years, when he turned it over
to the HBC's Thomas McKay, who promptly installed the
gregarious and much-traveled English cockney, Francis Ermatinger, as factor. There was another flag-raising then.
The Star and Stripes were hauled down and replaced by the

flag of Hudson's Bay Company, which was to fly above the fort for twenty years. This flag was the British Red Ensign, carrying a red ground, the Union Jack in the upper left-hand corner, and the letters H. B. C. in the lower right-hand corner. When Francis Ermatinger was asked what the letters stood for he replied in his best cockney accent, " 'Ere Before Christ."

While Nathaniel J. Wyeth's claim to fame must rest on his having built Fort Hall he was not himself overly impressed with its importance; it was a place to dispose of the merchandise he had on his hands, though he had the idea of making it a permanent base which he could supply from the more important fort which he proposed to build on the Columbia. It was Fort William which loomed large in his mind. Leaving a man named Evans in charge of Fort Hall to pick up the furs he had cached and build up trade with the Indians, Wyeth was on his way to Fort Vancouver; he would impudently build Fort William under the very nose of John McLoughlin. When he returned to Fort Hall he placed it in charge of Captain Joseph Thing, whom he considered to be the ablest of his lieutenants.

No doubt Governor McLoughlin was surprised to see Wyeth back again, but he liked the New Englander and received him as hospitably as he had before. With the power to destroy Wyeth, in a financial sense, immediately he withheld his hand, content to let time and the natural power of Hudson's Bay do its work. Years later, it was McLoughlin's tolerance for men like Wyeth which led to his own undoing.

Wyeth's vessel, the *May Dacre*, arrived on the Columbia about the time he did with the badly needed supplies.

Part of the cargo was whisky for the Indian trade, and it is evidence of the good feeling between the two men that at McLoughlin's request Wyeth refrained from peddling the stuff to the Indians.

McLoughlin watched complacently while Wyeth built Fort William at Wappatoo, or Suave Island, within cannon shot of Fort Vancouver. It was a log building, modeled after the HBC fort. In addition to trade goods the *May Dacre* had brought Kanakas from the Sandwich Islands because of their skill in boating and fishing; Wyeth was in business.

It was somewhat reminiscent of the old trade war between Hudson's Bay and the Northwest Company, except that there was no violence. The HBC treated Wyeth with every consideration, even when they saw his boats passing right underneath their fort, but they intended to crush the upstart and dispose of him as they had Astor before him. Oregon was for the British; they watched him like hawks.

He had built Fort Hall in the interior; very well, they would build Fort Boise in a land where there wasn't enough business to support two trading posts. When he sent out trappers he would find that Hudson's Bay men had preceded them. The big company raised the price of fur to more than Wyeth could afford to pay, and they sold goods to the Indians for less money than similar goods had cost Wyeth. With studied contempt the company men called the Americans "Bostons," and taught the Indians to regard the Bostons as their enemy. Wyeth's dream of dealing in furs on the Columbia was fast vanishing.

Still, relations between the two forts were friendly.

Governor McLoughlin sent over presents of fresh fruits and vegetables, and many evenings Wyeth rowed his boat over to mingle with the jolly fellows at Bachelor's Hall. But back of this friendly façade each side tried to find out the other's plans and forestall them. In this Wyeth always got the worst of it. Whenever, for instance, he set out to trade with a band of Indians the grinning Hudson's Bay men were already there to greet him.

For Wyeth the winter was a harrowing one. The rains were worse than usual in that always rainy country. His shelter was inadequate, and his bales became soaked and ruined. He could not hire Indians to fish, and his Kanakas deserted. Back at Fort Hall things were not going well. A party of his men under Captain Thing was attacked and defeated on the way to Salmon River, by the Blackfeet.

Not only was Wyeth's personal fortune at stake but, worse for him as a man of honor, the credit of his Boston backers was involved. The salmon-packing industry on which he had counted so much would send the *May Dacre* back to Boston with half a cargo. He was in no position to buck Hudson's Bay with its hundreds of trained employees, and he found himself facing bankruptcy.

Once he complained to McLoughlin about his "hereditary" influence with the Indians. McLoughlin replied, "I had no hereditary influence. I made the Indians fear me. I compelled obedience, studied justice, cultivated confidence. It takes time, Mr. Wyeth."

Wyeth argued, "Your servants have intermarried with the tribes to hold the trade. Our policies are diametrically opposed. Yours is to perpetuate savagery; mine would be to fill the country with civilized people." It was dangerous talk to the husband of an Indian woman, but McLoughlin was patient. "If Oregon is ever settled," he said, "it will be by sea, from England."

But nothing could shake the mutual liking between the two men. "What more can I do for you, Mr. Wyeth —consistent with my duty to my company?" McLoughlin demanded. "Was I not glad to engage your lad, Solomon Smith, to teach our boys and girls? Did I not hail with joy your good missionary, Jason Lee, and help to establish him in the valley?"

This was true. McLoughlin had helped Lee in every way he could, even to the extent of making him a good-sized loan which some were unkind enough to say was a bribe to insure his friendship for the company. However, Lee at this time was interested only in saving souls of the Indians, not in bringing in American emigrants.

McLoughlin had a friendly interest in the tall, black-bearded Methodist missionary, although he was not himself a Methodist. For one thing, both of them had been born just across the Canadian border. McLoughlin had started a settlement at Champoeg, on the Willamette; he wanted his people instructed and he wanted the mission dependent on Fort Vancouver.

The Indians were ready for the reaping by Jason Lee's sickle. The inquiring Flatheads had been inspired in their search for the Great Spirit by Captain Clark of the Lewis and Clark expedition which they had befriended, and there was a great religious movement among them. A young clerk in the house of Chouteau in St. Louis had written a friend in the East about the Flathead men who had come there searching for a mysterious book, and it had gotten into the papers. Says Eva Emery Dye in *McLoughlin and Old Oregon*, "The Macedonian cry swept like a trumpet summons through the churches."

Baptiste and the Nez Percé youth Wyeth had taken home with him had further inspired Jason Lee to believe that his life's work lay among the Indians. He and the young men with him intended to stay. The Nez Percés also, Lee had heard, were anxious for the gospel.

At first Lee was intent on preaching among the Flatheads, but McLoughlin had persuaded him to stay on the Columbia. "Up there," he said, "we cannot protect you, but we have plenty of Indians right here. Besides the Indians there is a settlement of French-Canadians with their Indian wives and half-breed children. Those Canadians are your own countrymen, far from church and school. Then, too, I can assist you with my boats and my influence. Up there in the Flathead country you will be cut off from a base of supplies and from communication with the civilized world."

Jason Lee took a trip up the beautiful Willamette valley, and saw that it could be made into a veritable paradise; he also saw there all the Indians he could ask for. At that time Oregon had an estimated Indian population of 100,000. He returned to Fort William, got his supplies out of the *May Dacre*, and for a trifling sum engaged Indian boatmen to transport them to the site of the future mission. He was to stay there more than twenty years, until he was forced to retire with a broken heart. He was one of the noblest and most beloved of all the early pioneers of Oregon.

Wyeth was ruined by a man he liked so well that he

never expressed the slightest resentment. He knew that Mc-Loughlin held no malice and was simply doing what his duty to the company demanded. The Hudson's Bay man tried to remedy the situation. He said, "If you will come over to us, Wyeth, join us, then I will forward your credentials to the house in London."

It must have been a tempting offer, but it was further than Wyeth was prepared to go. He was an American, and he could not enter the service of a foreign country. He did not sell out at once but held on until 1836, making a number of trips back to Fort Hall and leaving Fort William in the custody of a trusted man, I. R. Walker (in some accounts called Courtney Walker).

He finally sold out to Hudson's Bay at a loss estimated at $30,000. He returned to Boston, but made a third trip to Vancouver in 1837 to settle his affairs. Only once more was he heard from in connection with Oregon, when he spoke out in defense of his great adversary, Dr. John Mc-Loughlin. The founder of Fort Hall failed financially, but he was a credit to his country.

# 9

## KELLEY IN OREGON

HALL J. KELLEY WAS NOT GO-
ing to give up without personally seeing Oregon. He had
been in the public eye a long time and he was absolutely
sure of himself. He had ridiculed those who thought it
criminal to take women and children into an uncharted
wasteland. They could travel comfortably in wagons, he
claimed. The sufferings of the thousands who came later
would give the lie to that belief.

At that time only two wheels had crossed the Continental Divide, and they were attached to a small cannon
which William Sublette had dragged as far as he could.
Bonneville and Wyeth had been going to take wagons,
and if they could do it it should be easy for the master.

Congress had lost interest, and that old devil's advocate, the Hudson's Bay Company, was still holding Oregon. Hall J. Kelley would tell them a thing or two when he got there. A few people still seemed to believe in him.

Instead of taking the route followed by Bonneville and Wyeth he would go by way of Mexico, mostly by water, and probably get there ahead of them. He left his family with his father, Dr. Kelley, and wangled free passages for himself and his men to New Orleans.

There his associates deserted him. Subject to Kelley's homilies, they had lost interest in taking civilization and Christianity to the savages. Two of them followed him into Mexico, but at a discreet distance; Kelley still had goods that were worth plundering. A passport was provided him and he set out for Vera Cruz. Here he ran into trouble. His goods, destined for Oregon, were seized for duties. Futilely, he pointed out that they were not dutiable since he was only taking them across Mexico. He met with the usual responses of *quien sabe* and *mañana*. Kelley's fiery and indignant oratory got him nothing. They knew even less about Oregon than some Congressmen.

After a period of vexation and what he called incredible hardships, the United States consul intervened and part of the goods were released. He went on his way, stopping at Jalapa and Mexico City. The trip, he says, was a succession of trials and catastrophes. The two men who had followed him caught up and robbed him of some of his remaining goods. But this incredible dreamer was seeing visions wherever he went.

He considered the feasibility of building a railroad from Mexico City to Vera Cruz. The flora and fauna, the geography of the country, the character of the government and the ignorance of the people impressed him greatly. There was a general lack of development abhorrent to his thrifty Yankee soul.

He conceived a plan which he broached to the officials of the Mexican government for the settling of immigrants from his own and other countries as soon as the northern emigration slackened. To the Mexicans he was a great impresario. Characteristically, he chose a place he had never seen for the proposed colony. Nothing ever came of it.

At Guadalajara he called upon Richard M. Jones, son-in-law of Joseph Lancaster, who had developed the Lancasterian system of instruction. Jones was conducting a state institute here using this method. Kelley, an authority on everything, urged him to adopt "the Philadelphia plan."

Kelley worked his way to San Blas on the Pacific Coast of Mexico, then went on to LaPaz on the gulf coast of Lower California. From there he went to Lorreto, also on the gulf coast. He was obliged to travel overland almost three-fourths the length of the peninsula. It could not have been an easy trip.

Kelley arrived in San Diego, California April 14, 1834, and in near-by Pueblo he met Ewing Young, no doubt the first real mountain man he had ever seen. The hardy Tennesseean, friend and associate of Kit Carson, was a veteran of the Santa Fe trade and he, too, had his mind set on Oregon. For a time their destinies were to intertwine.

While Young worked his way north, trapping around Tulare Lake in the San Joaquin valley, Kelley hied himself up the coast to the capital at Monterey and laid before Governor Figueroa a proposition to survey the Sacramento valley. Again it was a place he had never seen, but Kelley had vision.

Apparently the Mexican governor, a true grandee, was not overly impressed by the lean, talkative Yankee. The aristocratic Mexicans never took kindly to the Americans, particularly the mountain men. Both Jedediah Smith and Joe Walker had had their troubles with them. The Mexicans' viewpoint was the fewer Americans the better.

Undaunted, Kelley made a hasty survey of the Sacramento and made a map of it. Here he was joined by Ewing Young, who was practical if he was anything. On the eighth of July they set out for Oregon with a party of nine men, which may or may not have included the two principals. We are even less certain of their number when they arrived. Some of the chroniclers, such as Bancroft, Gray and Daniel Lee, hardly thought Kelley important enough to mention.

Two days after leaving San Jose the party was overtaken by what Kelley termed a band of marauders. Both Kelley and Young gave the number as nine, though four of them pulled out soon afterward. McLoughlin says they arrived at Vancouver with eight English and American "sail persons."

Ewing Young had an idea that there would be a good market for horses in Oregon, and he was the first to drive a band of them from California. Young had ninety-eight head, according to his own account, and the men who joined him had fifty-six more, some of which turned out to have been stolen. Two of these men had come to California with Joe Walker,whose exploits had been a source of considerable embarrassment to Captain Bonneville, Walker's employer.

The route chosen was up the Sacramento and down the Willamette or Multnomah River, a much easier route than Jed Smith had taken when he had met disaster on the Umpqua a few years earlier. The Indians they met were inclined to be friendly, but the Walker men would not have it so, and seven or eight were shot down in cold blood, Young's party taking part in the massacre. It is hard to imagine Hall J. Kelley shooting an Indian, and the party appears to have split up at this point.

Kelley became ill with malaria and might have died had he not stumbled onto a party of Hudson's Bay trappers under one La Framboise who treated him with simple mountain remedies. La Framboise found an Indian willing to take Kelley down the Umpqua some fifty miles in his canoe. From that point Rondeau, one of the trappers, took Kelley on to Fort Vancouver, which he reached October 27, 1834, still a very sick man.

Kelley had planned to reach Oregon triumphantly at the head of a large and well organized colony. Instead, he arrived as an ill, impoverished lonely old man—and Dr. McLoughlin, who had treated other American travelers hospitably, received him coldly. Kelley was not invited to the governor's mansion, or even inside the stockade, but was assigned an outside cabin and provided with food and medicine. Rondeau was given the task of nursing him back to health. Ewing Young was simply told to move on. Both men became lifelong enemies to Dr. McLoughlin.

McLoughlin's actions were prompted by the arrival of a ship from Monterey ahead of them, bearing a letter from Governor Figueroa accusing Young and Kelley of having stolen their horses. McLoughlin posted warnings in

French and English that the people were not to trade with them—an affront neither man would ever forget. At the same time McLoughlin wrote to Governor Figueroa demanding a bill of particulars, but communication by sea was slow, and it was a long time before the matter was cleared up and Kelley and Young were exonerated.

Ewing Young located a ranch on French Prairie and became a wealthy and respected citizen who was still to have a great influence on Oregon's future. Once Young sent to Fort Vancouver for supplies, which McLoughlin refused to sell to him, offering the goods as a gift. The independent old mountain man sent them back without a word of thanks, and the enmity grew.

Meanwhile, Kelley recuperated in his cabin, cared for by McLoughlin's man Rondeau, and of course wrote long letters vilifying his host and benefactor. The missionary, Jason Lee, who had known him in Boston, came to visit him. Kelley thought his visits were surreptitious, with Lee not wanting Hudson's Bay to know that he was on friendly terms with its arch enemy.

Nathaniel Wyeth had arrived on his second expedition, and though he came as an avowed competitor and had already started to build Fort William under McLoughlin's nose, relations between those two men remained as cordial as ever. Wyeth dined at McLoughlin's table, and was free to spend his evenings at Bachelor's Hall, which he frequently did.

He must have been astonished to learn that the man who had first interested him in Oregon was now at this very post, practically under protective custody and suspected of larceny. He couldn't refuse to see Kelley, even though his faith in him was gone. Two years on the frontier had shown him how fantastic Kelley's plans had been. The dream was good, but it required more than admonitions to carry it out.

Wyeth knew that he was risking his financial neck by trying to buck Hudson's Bay, but his weakness was his best shield. McLoughlin was amused at Wyeth's trying to trade in territory where all the cards were stacked against him. He had only to speak the word and the Bostons were done for. McLoughlin could have been more worried about Fort Hall, but even there he had taken steps. He wished for Wyeth everything that was good, except success, and he wasn't worried about that.

Hall J. Kelley was something different. McLoughlin had read his pamphlets and knew that he hoped to oust Hudson's Bay and build up what he called a godly, civilized country. Kelley never ceased to shout his defiance. Had he appeared with the horde he had planned to bring he would never have gotten beyond Fort Hall. McLoughlin would not have used violence, but there were other means. Kelley had arrived little better than a tramp, and the doctor would pay him no respect.

Wyeth was not the kind to run down an enemy, or turn his back on a friend, and we may be sure that he protested that Kelley could not have been a horse thief (he didn't know about Ewing Young). On the whole, under the circumstances, Wyeth knew that McLoughlin had treated Kelley well. He went to see Kelley, who complained that Wyeth treated him coldly.

It is not to be wondered at. Beyond a doubt Kelley would have upbraided him for having organized his own party instead of sticking by the original Kelley plan. Any argument would only have incensed him. He would have slandered Dr. McLoughlin and the doctor, too, was Wyeth's friend.

It is not hard to visualize the two men in that small cabin. Wyeth, tanned and bearded from his long trip overland, perhaps a little flushed with his success in being the first to establish posts in Hudson's Bay territory. Kelley, pale and weak from his illness, the fever of fanaticism still in his eyes, knowing that Wyeth was being entertained royally only a few yards away, while all he had to offer was a cup of tea and a hard wooden bench to sit on.

No doubt they came close to quarreling, for Kelley was never one to restrain his tongue, but Wyeth did not lose his temper, and the only feeling he expressed toward the Prophet was sorrow. Wyeth may have treated him coldly, but surely not condescendingly. Wyeth was not that kind of man, but it is certain that he did not espouse Kelley's cause.

Wyeth, like Jedediah Smith before him, realized that McLoughlin's first duty was to his company, and that he could not betray its interests. They also knew that he gave them every possible legitimate aid, and they were grateful for his hospitality. Kelley, on the other hand, never tried to conceal his bitter enmity, and in later years McLoughlin was to be accused of mistreating Kelley and other Americans.

Kelley professed great shock and indignation at seeing white men living with Indian women. McLoughlin himself was married to a half-breed—a genuine lady, from all accounts, but had Kelley ever met her he would have had only condemnatory words. He thought Hudson's Bay was debauching the Indians with whisky, while in fact McLoughlin was trying to put an end to the traffic—a campaign in which the American traders with the exception of Wyeth did not join.

Kelley, however, still had a few friends in Oregon who remembered his fancy promises, and when he was discharged from his private one-room hospital they urged him to lay out the land he had promised—land for which he had no vestige of a legal claim. He set aside a day for the purpose, but was discouraged by threatening letters, one from his late associate, Ewing Young. It became apparent even to Kelley that he could never carry out his plans, though he blamed everyone but himself. He was broke and tired.

Without instruments of any kind, he passed the waiting weeks trying to make a survey of the country from Fort Vancouver to the mouth of the Columbia, and in collecting information about the country and Hudson's Bay. He was still looking forward to an influx of American settlers. Putting on a bold front, he went to Dr. McLoughlin to beg free transportation to the Sandwich Islands on a company boat. Having no liking for an avowed enemy of the company on board one of its boats, McLoughlin refused him, though he did arrange for Kelley's fare on another boat, the *Dryad*, and gave him a draft for seven pounds besides. Unlike Ewing Young, Kelley was not too proud to accept charity.

He sailed away from Fort Vancouver March 15, 1835.

Remaining in the Sandwich Islands for a time, he took passage on the *Canton Packet* and arrived in Boston after a six months' voyage.

So the prophet of Oregon appeared and vanished from the land he had been divinely called to colonize. He made not a ripple on the country that was belatedly to do him honor as the man who had done most to create interest in settling the Northwest Coast. He was a man obsessed by a single idea, a visionary many years ahead of his time. One can only regret that his solitary trip to the country to which he had dedicated his life was filled with disillusionment and pain.

Hall J. Kelley returned home a broken, shattered man, physically and financially. He was heavily in debt and his family was never reunited with him, but he was far from through. His dreams died hard. In 1837 he again turned to surveying, establishing the routes for three railroads in Maine and making a report upon one of them. In 1839 he was planning a railroad thoroughfare that would unite the two oceans, and announced his intention to form a settlement at New Dungeness. Both projects, of course, failed.

Within a year Kelley was again writing on Oregon. His studies had given him considerable knowledge which might have been useful could he have spoken with less authority; but conceited and self-centered as he was, he considered everything he said absolute truth and that only his "enemies" would disagree with him. Important people were usually willing to give him a hearing, but his manner made them think less and less of him. Whatever he was interested in was of course the most important matter in the world.

He had no understanding of people, and his outlook was limited by his own false values.

One of the men he interested temporarily was Caleb Cushing, Chairman of the House Committee on Foreign Affairs. At Cushing's suggestion Kelley wrote a highly colored memoir of his experiences in Oregon and California which Cushing included in a supplement to his report on Oregon to the Twenty-Fifth Congress.

Encouraged by this, Kelley presented a memorial to Congress asking for a grant of land in Oregon on which he could found a colony, basing it on his work in attempting to settle the country and his claim that he was responsible for the first settlement. The grant was denied. In 1843 he petitioned Congress for permission to purchase land from the Indians on which to build his colony. This was referred to the committee on private land claims and promptly forgotten. After 1844 he gave up the idea of founding his own colony, and began a long fight to obtain compensation for the money he had spent and the years of effort he had put in.

Alienated from his family and practically friendless, Kelley retired to the town of Palmer, Massachusetts, where he became known as "the Hermit of Three Rivers" and was considered mentally deranged. Small boys stopped to jeer at the pathetic old man. He got nothing for the years he had put in and the money he had spent. He lived on until June 20, 1874.

Had it not been for certain fundamental handicaps, Hall J. Kelley might well have become the great man he considered himself to be. He was without humor, and took himself far too seriously. He was a fanatic about many things, including religion. He could not stand criticism and considered all who did not agree with him his enemies. Though wanting to manage people, he had no feeling for them as individuals. How much he might have accomplished had he not considered himself divinely appointed to a mission is problematical.

On the credit side, he certainly did more than any other man to arouse interest in Oregon and to set in motion the great tide of emigration which saved the three states of Oregon, Washington and Idaho for the United States. He was even responsible for the great missionary movement. His writings about the country before he saw it had an uncanny accuracy, and certainly the country had the potential he attributed to it. In that, he was certainly much wiser than the statesmen of his time.

Said Harvey W. Scott in an address before the Oregon Pioneer Association in 1890: "This strange eccentric man can almost be called the Prophet of Oregon, the father of migration to Oregon, the man who hastened the fulfillment of Oregon's destiny." The word "almost" should have been deleted. Hall J. Kelley *was* the Prophet of Oregon.

There are few more pathetic figures in our history. He was a great benefactor of mankind, and his reward was to be ridiculed and virtually forgotten.

# 10

# THE PLAYBOY OF THE MOUNTAINS

IT IS TIME TO RETURN TO THE third member of that triumvirate which had so much to do with the founding of Fort Hall. Thanks to his biographer, Washington Irving, and to his own flair for publicity, Captain Benjamin Louis Eulalie de Bonneville is far better known to history than his two more important associates.

This French-born adventurer began his career at West Point, his appointment being due to his friend, and the friend of America, Marquis de Lafayette. As an honor grad· uate his career seemed assured until he fell under the siren spell of Hall J. Kelley. Thenceforth, he too dreamed of Oregon and the fur trade, and he secured a three-year leave of absence from the army to explore the then little known West. For a long time rumor had it that he was actually on some secret mission for the government, but there is little to bear out this notion. No doubt the army hoped to profit from such information as he might gather, but his subsequent actions implied that he was an entirely free agent.

Like Wyeth, Bonneville had studied what was known of the fur trade. The ill-fated Astor venture was then history but Astor was still in the fur business under the name of the American Fur Company and its field operations east of the Rockies were under the command of able Ramsey Crooks, the man who had accompanied Wilson Price Hunt on his perilous overland journey. It was indeed in the mansion of John Jacob Astor in later years that Captain Bonneville related his incredible adventures to Washington Irving.

In Bonneville's time the activities of the American Fur Company were confined to the upper Missouri, and the competition of half a dozen other companies was severe. Foremost of the businessmen mountaineers was General William H. Ashley of Missouri, who had enlisted in his company a number of young men who were destined to make frontier history, among them Jedediah S. Smith, Jim Bridger and the Sublette brothers, William and Milton. The names of the first two are well known in Western lore, but in their day William Sublette was the most influential, and certainly the most financially successful.

Jed Smith did the most exploring on a grand scale, and would have done more had he not been killed by Indians at an early age. Jim Bridger knew his own part of the country as he knew the back of his hand. Campbell, Fitzpatrick, Jackson and the others were equally familiar with the country from the Mississippi to the crest of the Rockies, but few of them went much beyond that.

There were two good reasons: the Hudson's Bay Company and the warlike Blackfoot Indians. The neutral ground, then under joint occupancy by the United States and England, was the region around the upper Snake. There was, however, some poaching by both sides. Jim Bridger was there, and so was Peter Skene Ogden, the field marshal of Hudson's Bay. Bridger was the first man to float down Bear River in a bullboat, and so discovered the Great Salt Lake, though some of Ogden's men may have preceded him to the lake. Ogden himself was put on the carpet by his own company for trespassing on the American domain east of the Rockies.

General Ashley in person had crossed the Uintah Mountains and penetrated as far south as present-day Green River in Utah. Ashley sold out to his young men in 1825, and the new company was headed by William Sublette, who in turn sold out to Fitzpatrick, Jackson and Bridger. These three did business under the name of the Rocky Mountain Fur Company, and it was by all odds the most important company east of the Rockies.

That Bonneville was familiar with the American companies is clearly indicated by what Washington Irving said about them. "They keep no established posts. Everything there is regulated by resident partners; that is to say, partners who reside in the tramontane country, but who move about from place to place either with Indian tribes, whose traffic they wish to monopolize, or with main bodies of their own men, whom they employ in trading and trapping. In the meantime they detach bands, or 'brigades' as they are termed, of trappers in various directions, assigning to each a portion of country as a trapping or hunting ground. In the months of June and July, when there is an interval between the hunting seasons, a general rendezvous is held, at some designated place in the mountains, where the affairs of the past years are settled by the resident partners, and the plans for the following year arranged."

At such times, Irving went on, a convoy from the East, usually under the direction of one of the partners, would arrive with supplies and trade goods. The rendezvous were held at such places as Horse Creek, Ham's Fork, and Pierre's Hole. They not only served as places for trade and settlements of accounts and making deals for Indian women, but always wound up with a wild jamboree to which the trappers looked forward for an entire year.

Bonneville and Wyeth were both familiar with the practice, but since they were intent on battling the Hudson's Bay Company for trade in the Oregon country their idea was to set up permanent trading posts in the manner of their powerful competitor. Bonneville's plans were considerably more grandiose than Wyeth's. On the first of May, 1832, we find him leaving Fort Osage on the Missouri with a party of 110 men, most of whom had had experience in the mountains. At about the same time Wyeth was leaving Independence with William Sublette and Robert Campbell. Wyeth, as we have observed, was persuaded to give up his wagons and travel by pack train. Bonneville, better equipped and army-trained, stuck by his wagons. Until they reached the mountains it was not so difficult, except for the rain and mud, and the necessity for building bridges across flood-swept ravines.

Since Wyeth and Bonneville, now called "the Bald-headed Chief," were close enough to exchange occasional visits it can be assumed that Bonneville made pretty good time on his journey. It is noteworthy that Bonneville took his train of twenty wagons farther into the Rockies than wheels had ever gone before, though he abandoned them at Fort Bonneville on the Seedskeedee. He was the first to break road over what was to become the Oregon Trail.

The Frenchman marched with military precision, his wagons in two columns, with a rearguard and a vanguard. He had chosen two capable assistants in J. R. Walker and M. S. Cerré, both of whom had had considerable experience in the Santa Fe country. Joe Walker, whose exploits were to have much to do with Bonneville's fame and many of his troubles, had been a prisoner of the Mexicans, a veteran of several Indian wars and a Missouri sheriff, as well as a trader and trapper. Cerré, a man of only twenty-five, was thoroughly experienced and capable.

Irving's description of the trappers in the mountains divides them into two kinds, the American and the French. The Americans, he states, were mostly of old American stock from Kentucky, Tennessee and other southern states. The French were either from Canada or Creoles from Louisiana. The French are represented as being lighter, softer and more self-indulgent. "He must have his Indian wife, his lodge and his petty conveniences. He is gay and thoughtless, takes little heed of landmarks, depends on his leaders and companions to think for the common weal, and if left to himself is easily perplexed and lost.

"The American trapper stands by himself, and is peerless for the service of the wilderness. Drop him in the midst of a prairie, or in the heart of the mountains, and he is never at a loss. He notices every landmark and can retrace his route through the most monotonous plains, or the most perplexed labyrinths of the mountains; no danger or difficulty can appall him, and he scorns to complain under any privation. In equipping the two kinds of trappers, the Canadians and the Creoles are apt to prefer the light fusee; the American always grasps his rifle; he despises what he calls the 'shot-gun.' We give these estimates on the authority of a trader of long experience, and a foreigner by birth [Bonneville] 'I consider one American,' said he, 'equal to three Canadians in point of sagacity, aptness at resources, self-dependence, and fearlessness of spirit. In fact no one can compete with him as a stark tramper of the wilderness.' "

Considering the times and the nature of the two men in Mr. Astor's mansion, we might allow for a certain amount of patriotic exaggeration.

Bonneville had his troubles not only with rain and mud but with some Indian marauders in getting as far as he did. On the way he made friends with a Kansas chief named White Plume, who complained to him of the Indians' difficulties with the white settlers along the border. On the way Bonneville fell in with a Mr. Fontenelle, a famous trader known as a partisan, and they journeyed more or less together up the Platte, sharing each other's dangers and liquid refreshments. Here Bonneville was gaining experience at first hand, but when they parted Fontenelle decoyed some of Bonneville's Delaware Indians away from him.

Not liking the climate of Green River, Bonneville presently abandoned his wagons and pressed on for the

Salmon River country. At the rendezvous on Horse Creek he had encountered Vanderburgh and Drips, representing the American Fur Company, who were almost as ignorant of the mountains as he was. Vanderburgh was soon to be killed by Indians, but Drips was to make a name for himself in the Rockies.

Bonneville loaded the goods which he did not cache onto pack animals, and divided his party. One group, under a man named Mathieu, headed for Bear River, while Bonneville himself took a more northern route through Jackson's and Pierre's Holes for the headwaters of the Salmon.

Here we run into one of those conflicting accounts with which the West abounds. Bonneville states that on the way he was shocked to come upon the bodies of More and Foy, who had been killed by Indians, and says he buried them. Either he made a mistake or he didn't bury them very deeply, for a year later Wyeth claims that he found the two bodies and buried them, identifying them as men who had come out with him but had quit at Pierre's Hole to go to work for Sublette. Wyeth names More but not the other man, though other writers have called him Greeley.

On September 19, 1832, Bonneville reached Salmon River and was quickly engulfed in a snowstorm. A large party of Indians approached and Bonneville prepared to defend himself. They turned out to be Nez Percés far from their own country who had been hunting in the region around Fort Hall where buffalo were plentiful. Always friendly unless put upon, the Nez Percés gave Bonneville no trouble. He sent a few men under Cerré to join them in the hunt, and to trade for meat for the winter.

Bonneville says he made winter camp about five miles below the fork of the Salmon. It is more likely that his camp was on the Salmon just below its confluence with the Lemhi, near where the city of Salmon City now stands. He kept some twenty men with him at the cantonment, and sent out three brigades to try to support themselves on the buffalo. This was the farthermost western edge of the buffalo country, and since the Nez Percés had recently hunted the area they found the pickings were scarce.

Finding his own supplies short, Bonneville decided to cross the Bitter Roots to a place called Horse Prairie, in what is now Montana. In doing so he must have passed the birthplace of Sacajawea, the Shoshone heroine of the Lewis and Clark expedition. He invited his Nez Percé neighbors to accompany him on the hunt and was surprised at their refusal, though after religious rituals four of them did agree to go. Bonneville was still acting the playboy who wouldn't let anything interfere with his fun.

He was taking a greater chance than he realized, for Horse Prairie was in Blackfoot territory, which accounted for the Nez Percés' hesitancy. The Blackfeet were the fiercest of all tribes, and frequently made incursions into the Snake River country all the way from the Salmon to the Portneuf. Wyeth was to encounter them when he built Fort Hall, and afterward.

On Horse Prairie some of the Nez Percés reported seeing the smoke from a Blackfoot village, and the hunt didn't last long. Joe Walker, with a party of twenty men, had gone beyond Horse Prairie and encountered the Blackfeet, who contented themselves by stealing the white men's horses. When they got back to the cantonment on Salmon River

Cerré reported having found a wallet of fresh meat and a cord which he believed had been lost by a party of prowling Blackfeet.

During the winter Bonneville had two parties of visitors. One consisted of four employees of Hudson's Bay, the remnants of a band of Iroquois hunters led by a man named Pierre who had once given Alexander Ross considerable trouble and after whom Pierre's Hole had been named. The other visitors were a band of Pend' Oreilles, or Hanging Ear Indians, whose home was to the north of the Nez Percé lands. They, too, were friendly Indians.

Bonneville despatched fifty men southward to trap along Snake River, and some of them went into camp near the future site of Fort Hall, some ten miles from present Pocatello. Back on Salmon River the captain was surrounded by a cosmopolitan group of mountain men, Americans, French, half-breeds and Indians. The Indians, he says, were Nez Percés, Hanging Ears and Flatheads. Since this was the ancestral home of the Shoshones, Bannacks and Lemhis, there were probably some of them camped in the neighborhood. Since the Indians were all friendly and had plenty of horses life at the camp could not have been dull. Here Bonneville may have formed his opinion of the relative merits of the Americans and the French.

Inevitably the camp became overcrowded, and some of the Indians pulled out. Bonneville prudently cached most of his supplies before settling down to spend the winter with his Indian allies, since it was his purpose to obtain horses from them. On December 26 he and his Indian allies raised camp and entered a gorge of the Salmon river, leading out on the Snake River desert. They moved cautiously in hourly fear of an attack from the Blackfeet. They followed a stream which seems to have been Little Lost River, and then over to Big Lost River, then or soon to be known as Godin's River, after the half-breed who precipitated the battle of Pierre's Hole.

They were now out on the great lava beds of the Snake River desert, in sight of the three buttes which rise out of the desert to a considerable height, and which some early travelers mistook for the far higher and more majestic Teton Peaks. Here Bonneville encountered a party of Bannacks, a tribe closely allied with the Shoshones, though considerably more warlike. The Bannacks told Bonneville of the arrival of his men under Mathieu in the vicinity of the Fort Hall bottoms. Bonneville joined them there, and stories were exchanged.

Mathieu's party had passed Beer Springs, the present day Soda Springs, Idaho, and camped at the well known landmark of Sheep Rock, at the big bend where Bear River turns south to flow into Great Salt Lake. Later, they moved north to Twenty-four Mile Creek. The men had food for themselves but none for their horses, the country being under several feet of snow. One day some Shoshones who were wintering on the Portneuf came over and told the trappers about Warm Spring Mountain, some five miles distant, where they could winter their horses. The party then moved over to the Portneuf, passing over the site of a present-day hamlet known as Chesterfield where I grew to manhood, and where in 1914 I bet the government three years of my life that I could prove up on a homestead.

My brother-in-law, Ted Faulkner, owns a ranch on the Fort Hall Indian Reservation at the foot of Warm Spring

Mountain, and he assures me that horses can still winter out on that mountain, as the snow never gets too deep for them to paw through to grass. I don't understand the phenomenon, but I do know the country well enough to be sure that those Indians kept Bonneville's men from losing their horses.

Bonneville remained near Fort Hall for fourteen days; then, leaving part of his men to trap, he started northward to his old camp on Salmon River with the rest. Here, luckily, he found his caches intact.

Bonneville reveals a little of inside Indian politics in his description of a battle in which twenty of his Nez Percé friends were attacked by 300 Blackfoot warriors. The battle, fought on the Snake River plains, was described to Bonneville by his Nez Percé friends who were in it.

With the Nez Percés was a renegade Blackfoot named Kosato. He was the first to be sighted but, thinking he would lead them to the Nez Percés, his old tribesmen didn't bother to kill him. The Nez Percés, who dug rifle pits inside their lodges and fought valiantly, suffered some casualties but no fatalities. The Blackfeet lost several warriors. A Nez Percé woman, seeing her husband badly wounded, did a Molly Pitcher by taking up his bow and arrows and fighting bravely by the side of the men. Thereafter she was permitted to take part in the war dances of the braves.

By coincidence, the Blackfeet were led by a renegade Nez Percé, who had no particular desire to kill his own people. It was not the most bitter battle in Indian history. Kosato sustained a head wound that was thought fatal and startled his "widow" by coming back to life and sitting up.

Bonneville was at and around the site of Fort Hall a

year before Wyeth unfurled his homemade United States flag there, but instead of starting a fort as the stolid Boston iceman was soon to do, he moved north to build an inconsequential cantonment on Salmon River. Wyeth was the one to see the strategic value of Fort Hall.

# 11

# THE EXPLORATIONS OF
# CAPTAIN BONNEVILLE

THE PAINSTAKING MR. WYETH
made notes of his journey from day to day, but they seem
colorless when compared to the tales related by Captain
Bonneville to Washington Irving. For accuracy Wyeth
has the better of it, but by virtue of his keen observation
and his curiosity about the unknown Bonneville did as
much as any man of his time to create interest in the West.

The preceding fall Bonneville had noted a stream which
seemed peculiarly adapted to trapping muskrats. Eager to
be back at his trapping, he hastened to his old cantonment
on the Salmon which he also called Fort Bonneville, and
arranged for a clerk named Hodgkiss to stay and conduct
trading at the post. Before leaving, Bonneville threw what
he called "a regular blow-out" for his men. He sent Cerré

on to contact the Nez Percés and invite them to join in the trapping and, no doubt, in the blow-out; then set out in high hopes of trapping the small but easily caught muskrat. In this, his maiden campaign, he offered white trappers and Indians alike an extra price for all the muskrats they could catch.

His ultimate destination, after leaving Godin's River, was the Malade River. There is some confusion regarding this stream. It is not to be confused with the Malade River that flows into Bear River, and was for many years a source of supply for Fort Hall. The better known Malade River is a short stream which bursts from the ground in a thousand springs on the breaks of Snake River. It is supposed to be fed from the three streams, the Big and Little Lost rivers and the almost equally large Birch Creek, that rise in the mountains and sink from sight in the lava beds. These sub-surface streams can sometimes be heard rumbling in the deepdown underground chasms. This Malade River has also been called Magic River, and Bonneville and many others have confused it with Wood River, well known to the play people who vacation at the famous Sun Valley resort.

When Bonneville reached the muskrat swamps, says Irving, "All now set to work for the next day's sport. The utmost gayety and animation prevailed throughout the camp." The optimism was premature. Scarcely were the traps set than a hunter came galloping into camp yelling, "A trail! A trail!—lodge poles! lodge poles!"

The work was suspended and all hands turned out to see whether the travois trail was made by friend or foe. It turned out to be not quite either. The invaders were a party of Rocky Mountain trappers led by two of the partners in the company, Milton Sublette and Gervois.

Bonneville knew them both but he didn't wait to visit; he broke camp and headed west. Let them have the musk-rats; there were more, and beaver besides, on Malade River. He must get there first. As Irving points out, there are few more difficult regions in the West to cross than the lava beds between Godin's River and the Malade. Sublette and his men pursued Bonneville in hot haste.

Jedediah Smith, it will be recalled, had made an agreement with Dr. McLoughlin that the Rocky Mountain men would stay on their own side of the Rockies, and Smith was a man of his word. His associates, however, did not feel themselves so bound. This region of the Snake, under the joint occupancy, was supposed to be a sort of no-man's land, but the nomadic Peter Skene Ogden had invaded their side of the mountains, and trapping expeditions like those of Bonneville and Wyeth had invaded Hudson's Bay territory. Men like the Sublettes were not going to stand back for either Hudson's Bay or these little one-horse outfits.

It was a bad season for Bonneville. The competition on Malade River was too stiff and he retraced his steps to the Salmon River camp, finding Hodgkiss on the 24th of June. Hodgkiss had another chapter to tell in the life of the ubiquitous Kosato.

Having persuaded some of the Nez Percé warriors to join him, Kosato had penetrated into Blackfoot territory at Horse Prairie. They soon made contact with the enemy and losses were heavy on both sides. Following Indian custom they suspended hostilities for a parley at which they could exchange mutual taunts.

"What need," said the Blackfoot chief, "have the Nez Percés to leave their homes and sally forth on war parties when they have danger enough at their own doors? If you want fighting return to your villages; you will have plenty of it there. The Blackfeet have hitherto made war on you as children. They are now coming as men. A great force is at hand; they are on their way to your towns, and are determined to wipe out the very name of the Nez Percés from the mountains. Return, I say, to your villages, and fight there, if you wish to live any longer as a people."

Knowing the Blackfeet well, Kosato realized that he had bitten off more than he could chew and he returned to the Nez Percé village to urge prompt and strenuous preparations for defense. Accustomed to the hot and braggart tongue of the turncoat Blackfoot, the Nez Percés received his warning indifferently. But this time Kosato was right, for a band of 300 Blackfoot warriors appeared. The Nez Percés were too badly outnumbered for a fight in the open and one of their strategists, a man called Blue John by the whites, conceived a plan to strike a secret blow at the enemy's horses.

Thirty men under Blue John headed for a certain defile, under an omen that if it did not rain they would be successful. There was a sudden shower, Blue John's men were cut off from front and rear, and all but one were killed. The lone survivor sprang onto the horse of a Blackfoot he had killed, and came back with the bad tidings.

Fortunately, the Blackfeet withdrew without following up their victory. The defeat of his friends was a blow to Bonneville and altered his plans somewhat. Hearing that several of the northern tribes, including the Nez Percés, were holding a rendezvous or regale to trade with a Hudson's Bay party that was short on goods, Bonneville hastened to the place of business. This was his first direct contact with the big company, and he was to feel its power; the Indians, fearing the displeasure of Hudson's Bay, would not trade with him.

At this time Bonneville appeared to be moving around aimlessly, achieving nothing. It was no reflection on his ability that he couldn't compete with the two powerful companies which had every natural advantage, including experience. He returned to his headquarters on the Salmon, divided his men into small parties and sent them eastward to rendezvous on Green River. On the way, a Nez Percé woman joined his camp, stating that she wished to join the whites; she was forthwith provided with a lodge and continued on as a member of the party.

July 13, 1833, found Bonneville back at Green River, where his men began to gather, each party with its own tale of hardship and danger. Here were gathered also trappers from the Rocky Mountain and American Fur companies and the independents. With no trapping between the middle of June and the middle of September, the trappers were on vacation and good fellowship prevailed.

This was Shoshone territory, and there was much rivalry for the favors of the tribe's beauties. New supplies had arrived and the young women knew how to take advantage of that situation. Both they and the trappers paraded in all the finery the mountains could provide. It was the season they all looked forward to, and mountain men forgot about home. By the time the rendezvous was over they were all heavily in debt, but no matter, the streams were still full of beaver. It was a life none of them would exchange for the comforts of civilization, which few of them had ever really enjoyed.

Most of the famous mountain men were there, including Jim Bridger, who was carrying an Indian arrowhead in his body from a recent encounter with Blackfeet. Jim had made the error of cocking his rifle when he should have talked. Bonneville talked with Bridger about the lake of salt to the south which Bridger had discovered seven years before. Learning that nobody had taken the trouble to go around the lake—there being no indications of beaver country to the west—Bonneville was seized by the urge to explore. He himself had other fish to fry so he despatched Joseph Reddeford Walker with forty men to circle the great body of water and then proceed westward. Walker duly fought his way around the dreary lake and headed out across the Great Basin, then known only as part of the Great American Desert, exploring more country than Bonneville ever did.

Walker, though an able leader, had a genius for getting into trouble, particularly with Indians. On his way across the Great Basin he had fights with the Piutes and "Digger" Indians which ultimately led to the deaths of many an American emigrant and many employees of the Pony Express.

On this trip Walker discovered Walker Lake and Walker River in Nevada and Walker Pass in California, and got into difficulties with the Mexican authorities. He was able to work his way back to the mountains, but some of his men were heard from later in connection with the troubles of Hall J. Kelley and Ewing Young.

In crossing the Great Basin, Walker passed over a great pleistocene lake, of which only the Great Salt Lake, which has no drainage, remains. That prehistoric inland sea now bears the name of Bonneville. A million years ago it burst its seams, poured its waters into the Portneuf, which emptied into the Snake a few miles below Fort Hall, and helped to deepen the gorges down the Snake and Columbia rivers to the Pacific Ocean.

Though Bonneville made some claim that Salt Lake should be named in his honor, it is doubtful if he ever saw much of it. He seems to locate fresh-water Utah Lake north of Salt Lake, when it is directly south of it—and in full view from my study window as I write.

Robert Campbell was going back to St. Louis with peltries, and Bonneville arranged to send his own furs with him under the direction of his lieutenant, Cerré. This business attended to, Bonneville prepared to go on a hunting trip into the Crow country of the Bighorns. One of the characters he encountered was Ed Rose, a renegade white man, whose loyalties were always with his adopted Crow people.

On July 25, Bonneville moved up the Wind River mountains, where finally he struck the Sweetwater, or Popo Agie, in the heart of the Crow country. This he descended until he made contact with Campbell's convoy. Two members of that party were Nathaniel Wyeth, returning from Fort Vancouver, and Captain William Drummond Stewart, the retired British-army officer. It is characteristic of Bonneville that he considered Stewart the more important man, though he and Wyeth were old friends. It did not occur to Bonneville that Wyeth's plans had been much better organized than had his own. Wyeth was then on his way back to Boston to organize the company which he would bring out the next year.

Bonneville's adventures in his Crow-country hunt impressed Washington Irving much more than they did the mountain men of his time, who had taken many trips equally, if not more, perilous. October 14 found Bonneville back at the rendezvous on Green River. It had been in Bonneville's mind right along to build a fort somewhere near the mouth of the Columbia. His trouble was that he always found so many interesting things to delay him along the way. It occurred to him now to go back to his cantonment on Salmon River, and from there proceed to the Columbia. On the way he passed Beer Springs, where for many years the mountain men got rollicking drunk on the natural mineral water and their imagination.

I have often drunk from these springs and never noticed any intoxicating effects, though the water is generally considered a good mix with more potent beverages. One story has it that two old cowhands who were diluting the soda water with whisky could scarcely believe their eyes when they saw a Mormon lady dip a cupful from the spring. "My God, Bill," said one, "she's drinkin' it *raw!*"

Proceeding down the Portneuf in the direction of Fort Hall, Bonneville joined a buffalo hunt held by the Bannack Indians from whom he purchased meat. Bonneville describes the Bannacks as great braggarts because they were always telling what they would do to their enemies, the Blackfeet. The worthy captain had had enough experience with the Blackfeet to make him think they were the greatest of warriors, but in the long struggle between the tribes the Bannacks always gave a good account of themselves.

Near the Fort Hall bottoms Bonneville perceived a skulking Indian whom he assumed to be a Blackfoot scout, and having no stomach for an encounter set off across the desert with all haste. Not finding the men he had left on the Salmon, he hurried on west and finally came upon them treed in the mountains. They had gone as far as the Boise, but were frightened back into the mountains by Bannacks they considered hostile.

Bonneville now retraced his steps toward the Portneuf, trying to gather his scattered trappers for a winter camp. Near the Snake he saw a band of Bannack warriors bluff out a larger party of Blackfeet. Instead of giving the Bannacks credit for bravery he attributed the victory to unusual cowardice on the part of the Blackfeet who, he thought, did not live up to their warlike tradition.

Bonneville had been pretty much going in circles, and the snow was two feet deep before he went into camp on the Portneuf, near where the city of Pocatello now stands. Restless as always, he set out again for the Columbia on Christmas day with three companions, keeping well to the left bank of the Snake, which he describes as 300 yards wide and running through an uncrossable gorge. Though he must have been aware that Wyeth had successfully negotiated the desert, crossed the Blue Mountains and gone down the Columbia in 1832, Bonneville apparently was thinking more of Wilson Price Hunt's 1811 expedition in describing the hardships of his journey, which were really not so bad.

On the way he encountered some of the poverty-stricken, rabbit-skin-clad Digger Indians living in crude wormwood (sagebrush) shelters. Much of the country Bonneville traversed is still nearly as wild and inaccessible as it was in his day, but it did include what has come to be known as Magic Valley, which, thanks to the miracle of irrigation, is one of the most fertile areas of the Northwest.

On January 12, 1834, Bonneville found himself near the mouth of Powder River which he declared much the largest stream he had seen since leaving the Portneuf, a fact which indicates that he had stuck to the left bank of the Snake all the way. On Powder River, three miles from its confluence with the Snake, Bonneville saw more Digger Indians; their condition he thought was deplorable. He continued on to the beautiful Grand Ronde Valley, where he found Nez Percés encamped, and paid some of them a visit. Here he found the rightful owner of a horse he had purchased from an Indian back on the "Wyer" (Owyhee) River. The owner proved to Bonneville's satisfaction that the horse had been stolen from him, but the considerate "savage" said, "You got him in fair trade—you are more in need of horses than I am; keep him, he is yours—he is a good horse; use him well."

Guided by friendly Nez Percés, Bonneville crossed the Blue Mountains to Fort Walla Walla and found a garrison of six or eight men under command of Pambrun, the Hudson's Bay factor. The allegedly predatory company received Bonneville as kindly and hospitably as it had Wyeth.

The object of this Western trip was to establish a trading post on the lower Columbia. After many tribulations the way was open, but Bonneville did not go down the Columbia. The reason he assigned was that he had promised his men to be back on the Portneuf by the first of March. Had he been driven by indomitable purpose, he surely would have gone on a little farther instead of wasting time visiting with the friendly Nez Percés. He finally followed the Immaha back to the Grand Ronde and soon was headed for the Portneuf again.

The trip was so rough and supplies so short that it was necessary to detour by the caches on Salmon River. The wolves had dug up the caches, the feared Blackfeet were in the country and Bonneville lost no time making tracks for the Portneuf. A buffalo hunt was necessary to get food, and he made camp a short distance above American Falls. He was blissfully unaware that his friend Wyeth was even then on his way to build Fort Hall, within seeing distance of where Bonneville himself was then camped.

Seeing four men on the opposite side of the river, Bonneville attracted their attention by gunfire. They turned out to be some of his own men, and they told him the others were camped on Blackfoot River, not too far away. There was a great reunion on the Blackfoot, characterized by something of a saturnalia—enjoyed with a happy holiday spirit that smacked of the gamy flavor of the wilderness.

Bonneville now set out for the rendezvous on Green River, meeting more of his men on the way. He says he amused himself by hunting buffalo. It is impossible to follow the writhing snake tracks of his travels. We find him at Beer Springs, Bear River, Bear Lake, and again on one of those doubtful explorations of Great Salt Lake. Yet somehow the various groups of Bonneville's party finally assembled at the rendezvous. Cerré arrived with supplies from the States. He and Joe Walker, returned from his California venture, were to return to St. Louis, while Captain Bonneville once more headed for his original destination, the lower Columbia.

He knew now that Wyeth was also on the way to the same place, but he didn't wait for him. Later, however, Bonneville was delayed by meeting a party of Hudson's Bay men. Relations, at first friendly, grew strained but Bonneville restored peace by filling up a half-emptied keg of honey with alcohol, which led to a long nap on the part of the Hudson's Bay leader. When the hungover Hudson's Bay men finally took their departure Bonneville paused to make a cache, and while he was so engaged Wyeth, riding in advance of his party, arrived to pay his respects.

The two groups joined in a buffalo hunt on the Blackfoot and they were always on friendly terms, though essentially trade rivals. Both leaders hoped to establish their main base on the Columbia, but while Wyeth lingered to set up Fort Hall Bonneville pressed ahead and on August 26 reached the headwaters of the Walla Walla, in the land of the horse-rich Cayuse Indians. He sent men to explore a possible route down the Columbia while he went on to buy supplies from Hudson's Bay at Fort Walla Walla, but there was refused by the HBC.

This and similar incidents have been used to condemn Hudson's Bay Company, but they were in the fur business and could hardly be expected to supply a rival company from a nation which was far from being on friendly terms with their own. They fought with every legitimate means to preserve their monopoly, even though at times their methods seemed a bit rough. Their business was with the Indians, whom they taught to hate and fear the "Bostons" so that they would not trade with them, but it would be slander to say that the Indians were deliberately incited to violence.

In the end, Bonneville for the second time gave up going down the Columbia to establish a trading post, and turned back to spend the winter on the Portneuf. The spring of 1835 found him attending the annual rendezvous on Horse Creek. He had overstayed his three-year leave and was dismissed from the army; later he was reinstated, and lived out a long and honorable career. Years afterward, when things were peaceful, he served a short time as commander of Vancouver Barracks.

There was one time when Wyeth and Bonneville contemplated joining forces in a venture south of the Columbia. Wyeth had arrived there in 1832. About all we know of their pact is contained in a letter Wyeth wrote to Bonneville, dated at Salmon Falls, June 22, 1833:

"The following proposition for mutual hunt in the country south of the Columbia river which I visited last autumn and winter. As prospects for beaver there I can only say I have no doubt of taking 300 skins fall and spring, as much sign given this as I have seen. I have little doubt much more might be found, but in that part of the country you cannot hunt with horses alone. Boats must be used.

"I have obtained some maps of the country beside my own observations. I have little doubt that I can make my way through it without guides, which cannot be procured. As this country is distant an immediate answer is required.

"As regards the mules, horses would do but are by no means so good for grass, which in places is very bad. The number required is a great objection. Nine would do, but goods enough to buy three more must be given an estimate.

The men who are wanted must be good, peaceful and industrious. I would prefer men who have not been more than one year in the country.

"In case of agreement you are to engage to deliver letters I wish to send home, a boy about 13 years old, and about 25 pounds of sundries and the expenses of the boy. My brother in New York will pay for him when he is to be delivered. The boy will have a mule to carry him.

"So many animals as I have and so few men I cannot come to the forks, and these Indians will come no farther than where in your route to Green River you strike the three buttes."

Wyeth discusses a meeting for the next year, and goes on with terms of the agreement: "The furs to be equally divided between us and I to have the right to take mine at any time during the year. Yourself to have the right to send a man to see to your interest.

"To be furnished by Mr. Bonneville nine men armed, clothes for the year, with saddles, mules, skins dressed for making boots, forty good traps, two dozen files, one dozen knives, 20 pounds tobacco, 200 pounds grease if possible, 3 bales Indian meat, a few small tools, 3 axes, 12 pr horseshoes if you have them, 4 packsaddles & harness, 6 pr lashes, $25 for cost of sundries, 25 pounds powder and lead to go with it.

"To be furnished by Mr. Wyeth: 19 horses, 3 mules, 20 traps, three men with myself, 1 dozen knives, 1 lodge, 1 cooking apparatus, vermilion, fishhooks, a few sundries, 10 pounds powder and lead, 14 pair horseshoes, 4 packsaddles and harness. Said men to do duty the same as other men with no other control, and to assure your interest in the division of the skin.

"In case you are ready to make this arrangement you may have no doubt of my being ready to enter in one, except that in the meantime I lose my animals. You have the liberty to send a load of goods to pay off the men you furnish. All property at the risk of its owner. Neither to be responsible for the debts of the other. Yours, etc."

The letter bore no signature, so we may assume that it was never sent, and it gives rise to speculation. It was written while Wyeth was on his way home to Boston, and since there was assuredly no mail service it is likely that he planned to leave it with someone at the Green River rendezvous, who would pass it on to Bonneville. In case he met Bonneville personally it would serve as an agreement to the partnership. There is a possibility that Wyeth changed his mind before the letter could be sent. At any rate, the venture was never carried out.

A comparison between Bonneville and Wyeth is inevitable. The steady, thoughtful Wyeth could have had little in common with the mercurial Bald-Headed Chief who took life so much less seriously than most of his peers that he does appear to be the playboy of the mountains. Bonneville underwent hardship and danger, but he was not a man of steadfast purpose. He was never concerned about Oregon for the sake of the country. Wyeth hoped to see it an American state. He and Dr. McLoughlin held many long talks on the subject.

"If Oregon is ever settled," said the doctor, "it will be by sea from England." Wyeth believed that if he could hold his outpost at Fort Hall it would be a jumping-off place for American settlers who would come by wagon. Fort Hall was to play its part, but not under Wyeth.

It is hard to assess Bonneville's contribution to the West. During the three years he was in the country immediately around Fort Hall he knew it far better than the other Americans. He controlled more men, and trapped more beaver. He did much less for Oregon and the Northwest than did Wyeth or Kelley, but his name is still remembered while theirs are almost forgotten. Bonneville, or Washington Irving, brought a certain amount of glamour into the West, and convinced many that there were no obstacles that could not be overcome. Bonneville, too, helped to open the gateway to Oregon.

If the wandering captain's explorations were empty of results, they are comparable to the mighty pleistocene lake to which his name has been given. Once it covered an area one-third the size of the states of Nevada and Utah; now only the Great Salt Lake remains. Two of its long-ago beaches may still be plainly seen for a hundred and fifty miles through Utah's great central valley. The farm on which I live is on the lower one of these beaches. Every time I step outside my door I have cause to remember Captain Bonneville.

Nathaniel J.
Wyeth

Dr. John
McLoughlin

Hall J. Kelley

Peter Skene Ogden

Jason Lee
(*Idaho Historical Society*)

Francis
Ermatinger

Captain B. L. E.
Bonneville

Jack Edmo, prominent Fort Hall Indian

Indian tepee, Fort Hall bottoms

Tes Pokebro, well known Fort Hall
Indian

Old Fort Hall (*Idaho Historical Society*)

Fort Hall, government trading post, 1878

Eagle Rock Bridge, Snake River; Utah & Northern locomotive
(*Idaho Historical Society*)

Overland Stage (*Idaho Historical Society*)

Ezra Meeker, "Father of the Oregon Trail" (*Idaho Historical Society*)

Discovery of old Fort Hall site, 1916. Ezra Meeker, Dr. W. Howard and Dr. Minnie Howard in foreground (*Agnes Just Reid*)

Dutch John townsite, near Flaming Gorge Dam, Green River
(*U.S. Bureau of Reclamation*)

# 12

# THE SURRENDER OF FORT HALL

History cannot overlook the good judgment displayed by Nathaniel Wyeth in choosing the location of Fort Hall. Circumstances had forced him to start one somewhere to get rid of the goods Sublette had refused to take. There were other places he might have located just as favorable to the fur trade, but none that could have had quite the influence on the destiny of the Northwest.

It had certain natural advantages, such as beaver and buffalo that were sparse in many other sections, and it had reasonably friendly Indians. Most important, it was still to a large extent neutral ground between the two big fur companies, though both were viewing the Snake River country with covetous eyes.

Wyeth owed something to Hudson's Bay for the good

will he was to find among the Indians. Its explorers had been in the country long before and they had made friends with most of the tribesmen.

Gigantic (302-pound) Donald McKenzie had operated around the Snake in 1818–19 for the Northwest Company. One of his assistants was Alexander Ross, whose book, *The Fur Hunters of the Far West*, is a classic. Ross describes the difficulties McKenzie had in fighting bureaucracy in the company while trying to win over the Indians. Old Perpetual Motion, as McKenzie was called, would not write a letter unless he had to, and it is fortunate that he had such a chronicler as Ross.

Heretofore, the bourgeois of the Northwest Company had lived an easy, luxurious life, which Ross describes with considerable contempt, but the fur trade in Oregon was not paying the dividends its owners wanted, and McKenzie was sent out to instill new life in the moribund organization. They could not have chosen a better man.

The old policy had been to establish posts and let the Indians come to them if they wanted to trade. Spokane House was the easternmost one, but it was out of touch with the Indians. McKenzie established Fort Nez Percé, later to be called Fort Walla Walla. Around here dwelt the Nez Percés, Cayuses, Palouses, Yakimas and Umatillas. Down around the Dalles were other tribes which caught and sold fish and exacted tribute from travelers on the river.

McKenzie and Ross had their troubles with these Indians as well as the horse tribes, but they soon won them over. McKenzie wanted to extend the trade with the Shoshones who dominated the little known Snake River country. They were at war with the Nez Percés, who McKenzie, after considerable difficulty, got to agree to peace, and, armed with this offer of truce, he moved among the Shoshones. He was the first real explorer of the country.

Just where he traveled it is impossible to know, but he was in sight of the Three Tetons, and he gave names to most of the streams. Since the headquarters of the Bannacks and Shoshones he had come to trade with were on and around the Fort Hall bottoms, it is a safe assumption that McKenzie was familiar with the section where the fort would someday stand. He was a past master at making friends with the Indians and establishing peace among the tribes themselves. For this Wyeth and many others were in his debt.

In 1821 the Northwest Company was absorbed by Hudson's Bay and Alexander Ross became an HBC employee until he terminated his services in 1824. We are indebted to Ross for many shrewd observations on the people of his time. He learned the value of patience in dealing with Indians. The usual proceedure seemed to be that they first would demand presents for themselves and all their friends. When this was refused, they would go into a sulk for a week, while their chiefs harangued them about the iniquities of the white men. Finally a peace pipe would be smoked, and after another week of speechmaking the traders would get a chance to present their views. In the course of a month some kind of agreement could be reached.

The whites assumed that the Indians would steal anything they could lay hands on, so the trading was conducted where the goods could be watched at all times. The red men always protested with oratory, but accepted the facts of life. Ross learned that gratitude was no part of their nature. He tells of a young Nez Percé warrior called Prince who tried to kill himself because his sweetheart had been stolen by the Shoshones. The bullet was not fatal to the youthful Nez Percé, and Ross dressed the wound and nursed him back to health. At the end of six months Prince demanded presents, particularly a rifle. When Ross told him he would have to pay for it, Prince became his avowed enemy.

McKenzie's party was a conglomeration of French-Canadians, British, half-breeds and Iroquois imported from the East. These latter, though capable hunters and trappers when they cared to be, were the source of many of McKenzie's worries. Whenever they were left alone they traded everything they owned, including their traps, for the favors of the local women, and some of them decided to live with the Shoshones, who had little use for them after their wealth was gone. So the story of the Iroquois was one of constant desertions and pleas for reinstatement.

The Bannacks were the ones with whom the whites had the most trouble; although they were blood-brothers of the Shoshones their proclivity for trouble made them pariahs of the plains. McKenzie learned that it was Bannacks who had massacred the Reid party that had been sent out from Astoria in 1814. Here was the beginning of the last chapter on the Dorion woman, who, finding herself left alone after the supposed murder of the men of Reid's party, made her way back to the Nez Percé country with her children after suffering near-starvation and incredible hardship. This heroic Sioux woman was an alien among whites and Indians alike.

McKenzie had broken the ice in the Snake River country and got the Indians in the habit of talking and barter-
ing with the whites, but there was no extensive trade until
McLoughlin took over at Fort Vancouver in 1824. The
valley of the Snake was the easternmost, and still most unknown, part of his domain. There was no post there, but
since McKenzie's time the company gradually had been
adopting the tactics of the Americans and trading with the
Indians where they found them.

Greatest of all the free-roving Hudson's Bay traders
was short, stubby Peter Skene Ogden, who was familiar
with the fur country from the eastern slopes of the Rockies
to the Pacific Coast. In 1825 he established his headquarters
where Ogden, Utah, now stands, and sent his men out in
all directions. Etienne Provost was the first trapper to explore Utah Lake, and he was the second, if not the first,
white man to see Great Salt Lake. The city of Provo, Utah,
was named in his honor.

Ogden's men were brushing shoulders with the suc-
cessors to General Ashley around Bear Lake, and both sides
were familiar with Cache Valley, a favorite place for the
storing of furs. In 1825 Ogden is known to have been around
Ferry Butte and the mouth of the Portneuf, nine years
ahead of Nathaniel Wyeth. From there he drifted south
to the Humboldt or Mary's River (it was first known as
Ogden's River, being changed to the Humboldt twenty
years later by John C. Frémont, who named it in honor of
a German scientist who probably never knew of the river's
existence).

At any rate, Hudson's Bay was familiar with the Snake
River country long before Wyeth crossed it in 1832. Mc-

Loughlin liked the American but felt he would bear watching, so when Wyeth left Independence in the spring of 1834 he had as a fellow traveler McLoughlin's stepson, Thomas McKay, one of the ablest of the Hudson's Bay men. From the rendezvous on Horse Creek, McKay accompanied Wyeth's party as far as Fort Hall, the only good reason for his presence being to keep an eye on the New Englander. Beyond a doubt, McKay's advice was often valuable to Wyeth and there is no indication that he ever tried to discourage him. Good fellowship seemingly existed while the fort was being built; McKay's men, who had come out from the Columbia to meet him, joined in the celebration.

McKay left Fort Hall with the missionaries and some others ahead of Wyeth, who could hardly have been surprised to learn that McKay had detoured to build a rival fort near the mouth of the Boise just above its junction with the Snake. It was never a very prosperous venture, but after all its real purpose was to insure that Fort Hall should not succeed. McLoughlin and McKay liked the young New Englander, but they meant to see that he failed in business.

The no-man's land that had existed so long was no-man's land no longer. McKay and Ermatinger were there with the "'Ere Before Christ," Hudson's Bay banner. Bonneville was there, busy as a bee and soon to have his hopes dampened by the veteran Rocky Mountain Company men, who were determined to have their share of the last good beaver country left in the mountains.

Wyeth hurried on to Vancouver to get Fort William started on Wappatoo Island. He was of course received cordially by Dr. McLoughlin, and his ship the *May Dacre* arrived at almost the same time. Now he would have plenty of trade goods to send back to Fort Hall, though he would have to transport them a couple hundred miles farther than Hudson's Bay had to in order to reach Fort Boise. Also, Wyeth found his old mentor, Hall J. Kelley, practically under house arrest at Fort Vancouver, but could do nothing for him.

Never was man busier than Captain Wyeth these days. He got Fort William going, and his salmon-packing plant started, but the Indians blandly refused to trade with the Bostons. Some of his trade goods were destroyed by rain, and the salmon run that year was light. The *May Dacre* had but half a cargo to take back to Boston.

Even in modern times a man might have difficulty managing two projects so far apart, but that was the task Wyeth set himself. He made several trips back and forth, each time having to stop at Fort Boise, where, we may be sure, he was royally entertained and regaled with tales of the business Fort Boise was doing, which, human nature being what it is, was surely exaggerated.

The pressure was building up. Wyeth had two good men, Captain Thing at Fort Hall, and I. R. Walker at Fort William, but instead of the steady growth he had anticipated he was faced with the inexorable law of diminishing returns.

In 1836 Wyeth gave up on Fort Hall, and made a deal with Tom McKay for its sale. Jovial Francis Ermatinger was put in charge; the Stars and Stripes were hauled down and replaced by the arrogant HBC flag of Hudson's Bay. With

Ermatinger at Fort Hall and equally genial Francis Payette at Fort Boise, the British had their feet firmly planted on the threshhold to Oregon.

Wyeth returned to Wappatoo to concentrate his energies there, but that, too, was a losing struggle. The next year he offered Fort William to McLoughlin for whatever the big company was willing to pay and, thanks to that good man, received a fair price. Disheartened, he wrote to his parents, disclaiming that he had undergone any unusual hardships but saying that he would be glad to be home.

His friends in the Willamette valley, the missionaries, Jason and Daniel Lee, had met with success. McLoughlin had given them provisions and transportation to their field of labor, and helped them build their mission. The company had even made Jason Lee a loan that put him forever in its debt, but the motive was not as selfish and mercenary as was afterward claimed. McLoughlin could afford to be generous with the missionaries—they were not in competition with Hudson's Bay. He sincerely wanted the Indians civilized and taught, particularly the half-breed children, which included his own.

Wyeth made another trip to Oregon in 1837 to finish closing out his affairs, after which he returned to Boston to engage again in the ice business, in which he made a conspicuous success. His failure in Oregon was no discredit to his ability, and there was no such tragedy in his life as there was in that of Hall J. Kelley, but with his bowing-out came the end of the first epoch in the history of Fort Hall.

# 13

# THE SOCIAL CHASM

THE AGREEMENT FOR JOINT
occupancy of 1818, which was renewed in 1828, automatically created a rivalry for ultimate possession. It was largely
a question of which nation took better advantage of its
opportunities. Each at times seemed determined to muff
its chances. It might almost be said that Scottish conservatism lost Oregon for the British. They had a good thing
in the fur business and they were reluctant to change the
status quo.

For a while it appeared that Sir George Simpson had
been converted to the idea of settlement, and he made
promises to the Canadians of Red River, but his conversion
was short-lived, and the promises were not kept. The settlers returned to Red River, and when Sir George showed
up there he left in a hurry for fear of his life. The threatened

rebellion was ended when Simpson offered the leader, James Sinclair, a chief factorship on the Columbia.

While Simpson was accusing McLoughlin of losing the country south of the Columbia he did nothing to further McLoughlin's hope of importing settlers from England by sea. The good doctor had his own brand of conservatism. He was doing all he could to discourage American immigration, short of violence, but once the Americans were there he would not see them suffer. When they began to seep in he followed about the same course he had adopted with Jedediah Smith and Captain Wyeth. He had treated both men hospitably, but he had exacted a promise from Smith not to trap west of the Rockies and had set about quietly and efficiently to break Wyeth.

With Ewing Young it had not been quite the same. He would not deal with a man accused of being a horse thief, but once he found out Young was innocent he had apologized handsomely, though still refusing to sell him goods. He had sent the things Young needed as a gift, but the proud Tennesseean had refused.

In 1841 two Americans, Joseph Gale, described as a renegade sea captain, and a man named Hathaway, said to have been a deserter from the *Convoy*, arrived at Fort Vancouver and tried to buy cattle and sheep, which McLoughlin would not sell them. They proceeded to build their own ship, painted black with a white ribbon around it, which they named *The Star of Oregon* and then took to Yerba Buena and sold. The next year they returned to Oregon with forty-two American settlers, 600 horses, 1250 cattle and 3000 sheep, thus breaking the monopoly which McLoughlin had previously enjoyed.

McLoughlin could have kept Gale and Hathaway from building their ship, and he doubtless could have prevented their return had he used the weapons at his command. He also could have incited the Indians against them. Perhaps Simpson was right in accusing him of lack of aggressiveness, for McLoughlin placed his Christian duty as a man ahead of even his loyalty to Hudson's Bay.

For the Americans, rather primitive people at best, it was easy to turn against McLoughlin when he began to have troubles. His ways were not their ways, and they knew that his men always tried to turn potential immigrants away at Fort Hall. They were frontiersmen and farmers, poorly educated, and their ancestors had fought the hated redcoats of the nation McLoughlin represented.

Once they would have been the peasants and the people at Fort Vancouver the aristocrats, but the War of the Revolution had changed all that, proving that one man was as good as another, and perhaps a little better, since there were too many people around the fort with the taint of Indian blood. To the Americans McLoughlin's wife was a half-breed squaw; it meant nothing that she was a woman of culture and education.

The prejudice was not confined to those times. Writing years later the historian Bancroft opined that it would have been a waste of time to try to teach "McLoughlin's mongrels." It is not to be wondered at that the poor settlers from the States were envious of the wealth and power they saw at Fort Vancouver. There it stood, a great parallelogram 700 by 450 feet, a walled city to which the average uncouth American was denied entrance, unless he had specific business; never was he able to enter as a guest.

The largest building was the Roman Catholic Chapel, which most of the natives attended, and this added religious prejudice and bigotry. The smaller congregation of Episcopalians held religious services in the large dining room of the governor's mansion, but few of the sturdy Americans cared to go there to worship.

One of Hall J. Kelley's grievances was that he had never been admitted to Bachelor Hall where the single men of prescribed station lived, and where guests like Nat Wyeth were entertained. This was also a museum of Indian relics and other curiosities, but since Kelley was refused entrance his imagination was left to ferment over the orgies he thought must be taking place there.

The dances and parties, anything but orgies, were models of decorum, but it was a world denied to the rough American farmers. There were beautiful women there with olive skin and coal-black hair. There were McLoughlin's two daughters: Eliza, who married Captain Epps, an officer of the British Army; and Eloise, the real princess of the Oregon Territory, a beautiful and gracious young woman who married William Glen Rae, who became a factor at Stickeen, and later was in charge of the Hudson's Bay post at Yerba Buena—now San Francisco.

Besides Eliza and Eloise, there were Nelia Douglas and Victorie, daughter of La Bonte, from the valley. From time to time other beauties came down from Walla Walla, to celebrate Christmas and other holidays. Among them were Maria Pambrun, who had inherited her father's light hair and complexion, and the Birnie girls. There was Catherine, the beautiful girl who was to marry Ermatinger after

Dr. Barclay had cut him out with Maria Pambrun. They all had Indian blood but they were educated young ladies, and the balls given by Governor McLoughlin were equal to the best in any society.

There was Governor McLoughlin himself, the White-headed Eagle, six feet four, with his long white hair flowing over his shoulders, resplendent in broadcloth and knee breeches and with silver buckles on his shoes, the symbol of wealth and power. No wonder the independent and far from humble American settlers regarded the fort with envy and distrust.

The Hudson's Bay trappers had taken Indian women, but unlike the Americans, who considered such unions temporary, the HBC men were legally married and accepted the responsibility of raising families. McLoughlin himself set the example and brought his children up as if they had been all white. Most of the children of mixed blood acquitted themselves well. An example was "Billy Boy" McKay, Tom's son, who was sent east to school and became a doctor. Of more practical import was the fact that the Indian wives helped to maintain good relations within the various tribes, prevented wars and promoted trade.

There were, of course, frustrated romances. One such was that of David McLoughlin and Trottie Dring, daughter of Captain Dring, commander of the barque *Janet*, the finest ship in the coast trade. Trottie was called the queen of the sea. At one of Governor McLoughlin's balls she danced with David and they fell in love. Captain Dring was violently opposed to the marriage and unexpectedly raised sail. David rushed down to the river, but the *Janet* was gone and he was never to see Trottie again. After that David is said to have lost interest in business and he married the daughter of an Indian chief.

Among the women guests at Fort Vancouver for a winter were Narcissa Whitman and Eliza Spalding, wives of the Waiilatpu missionaries—the first white women ever to cross the continent. They got along splendidly with the McLoughlin girls, and they had much to teach each other. Eloise and Eliza were avid for learning, and the girls taught the visitors much about furs and sables and Indian customs which would serve the missionary ladies well in their chosen work.

The missionaries were always around. Jason and Daniel Lee were welcome guests, and the governor loaned them money and helped them build their missions. Only occasionally was there trouble.

As more new missionaries arrived they avoided the fort as much as possible and were influenced greatly by the McLoughlin-hating settlers. It did not take them long to realize how much they and their church would be enriched if they could seize McLoughlin's property, and in the end they stripped him of most of it on the pretext that as a British subject he had no right to hold land in Oregon. They sent lobbyists to Washington to promote one of the most indefensible land grabs in the history of our country.

They complained of noble Jason Lee, who had done more to build up their mission than anyone, and in the end they got him recalled by the Missionary Board under which he worked. Lee had undergone many troubles and privations since he had preached that first sermon at Fort Hall.

He had sent east for a wife, Anna Maria Putnam, and the union was a happy one until her untimely death.

No one had worked harder than Jason Lee to get a provisional government, but against him was the charge that he had been born in Canada and was a friend of Dr. McLoughlin, and had accepted a loan from him. Lee had begun his work in a twenty-by-thirty-foot cabin, and though a Protestant it was largely the Canadian Catholics who attended his services. Once Lee had gone east to plead for more missionaries and means and he got them, including a $40,000 grant. He had besought the government to guarantee land to the settlers.

Had all the missionaries possessed his stature and tolerance there would have been no need to apologize for what they did. Few of them were bad men but many of them were narrow, and the Missionary Boards in the East which directed them had little conception of actual conditions. In the field too many of them directed their energies to fighting other churches rather than helping the people they were supposed to save, and to gain their ends it was sometimes easy to ignore truth.

Too much honor cannot be paid such missionaries as Jason and Daniel Lee, Marcus Whitman, H. H. Spalding, and Fathers De Smet and Blanchett. It was the Johnny-come-latelys like Gary, the man who succeeded Jason Lee and engineered the conspiracy against McLoughlin, whose eyes were blinded by ambition. With Jason Lee it was never a one-way street, and it didn't matter to him whether McLoughlin was a Catholic or not. The later missionaries loudly proclaimed that McLoughlin had to be an enemy because he was an Englishman and a Catholic—neither of which was true.

The Hudson's Bay Company was thought of by the settlers who got past Fort Hall as an octopus drawing everything it could into its greedy tentacles and McLoughlin was accused of all manner of crimes, the chief charges being that he refused to sell supplies to starving people and incited the Indians against them. The only truth in the accusations was that he had tried to keep American emigrants out of Oregon, and even this he had modified to an attempt to keep them south of the Columbia. When they did arrive anyway he succored them, and he tried to protect them from the Indians. There were no Indian wars under his regime until after the Whitman massacre, and by that time he was no longer with the company. He had made it clear to the Indians that they would be punished as readily for killing or robbing a Boston man as a Hudson's Bay man.

His accusers were the missionaries. Of them Holman has said, "To them the fortress of Vancouver was Mecca . . . and its commander was a prophet of Allah." Why then the change?

From the first McLoughlin had been interested in agriculture. As early as 1829 he encouraged the Canadians and half-breeds to start farming the wonderfully fertile prairies. Lucier was only one among many, and that was before there was an American farmer in Oregon. He encouraged them to build schools and churches, and rear their half-breed children the way white children were raised.

Under the joint occupancy no legal title could be acquired, and the best any settler could get was squatter's rights. When it became apparent that the United States would take the land south of the Columbia McLoughlin assured his people that the Americans were honest and would protect all honest men. He had hoped that Great Britain could hold the country but he became convinced that they could not long before the owners of Hudson's Bay, back in England, realized the situation.

The first Americans to arrive in important numbers did so in 1842, when about 125 came, fifty-five of them being men more than eighteen years of age, but half of them went to California the next year. McLoughlin employed as many of them as he could at fair wages, and he furnished those going to California with supplies upon their promise to pay the company's agent at Yerba Buena. Few of them paid, and McLoughlin assumed the debt personally.

Foreseeing the day of his retirement, McLoughlin as early as 1829 had laid out a claim for himself where Oregon City was to stand, holding it privately as he must until a government was established. Part of this claim was a small island suitable only for the location of mills; he proceeded to build them in 1832 and continued to improve the property until 1838. Since, under the joint occupancy, British and American citizens were to have equal rights McLoughlin was surely entitled to first claim as soon as formal filings could be made. He did everything he could to protect and perfect his claims, including becoming a naturalized American citizen.

In 1841 old Ewing Young, Oregon's first stockman, died wealthy on his French Prairie ranch, and there being no established law to distribute his estate the Willamette settlers were inspired to form a provisional government at Champoeg. In the first election the opposing groups were evenly divided until two Canadians joined the Americans.

As soon as the Americans, which meant the missionary party, were in control, efforts were made to wrest McLoughlin's property at Oregon City from him, and in the main they were successful. The old man had accumulated his property there in anticipation of the time when he would retire from the service of Hudson's Bay, and his claims were just. He had donated land for the building of three churches and had sold lots for little or nothing, but a campaign of slander was begun against him which was to reach Congress.

In 1850, Congress passed a General Land Law, called the Donation Act, giving settlers title to the land they occupied, but the statute contained an exception deliberately designed to rob McLoughlin and a few others of their holdings. His millsite was awarded to the Willamette Milling Company—an association of missionaries. He was not allowed to confirm title to the lots he had sold, and the remainder of his claim was placed at the disposal of the legislature for the endowment of a university.

It was unjust, and came to be so recognized too late to do Dr. McLoughlin any good, except to do honor to his memory. One can understand the enmity toward him, but it is hard to forgive the ingratitude of those for whom he had done so much.

He was the symbol of the Hudson's Bay Company, so national patriotism was aroused against him. The settlers had come overland by way of Fort Hall, and the Hudson's Bay men there had tried to discourage them from coming to Oregon, and actually had succeeded in turning many aside. They had been compelled to pay what they considered exorbitant prices for the supplies they had to have. They were resentful because McLoughlin was claiming the best of the land, and they were skeptical of his sincerity in becoming an American citizen. They were ready to believe all the propaganda being circulated against him by the missionaries and the politicians. That that propaganda was inspired by greed and malice was not known to the Congress, or to President Fillmore when he signed the Donation Act of 1850.

The chief lobbyist against McLoughlin was Oregon's Territorial Delegate to Congress, Samuel R. Thurston, an able man with a gift for oratory, whose career was cut short by an early death on the high seas.

Thurston and the missionaries succeeded in breaking McLoughlin financially, but that not all of McLoughlin's former friends deserted him is proven by the following exchange of letters between Delegate Thurston and Nathaniel J. Wyeth.

Chicoppee, Mass.
Nov. 16, 1850.

Capt. Nath J. Wyeth:
My dear Sir:

You will excuse me, I am sure, when I assure you that I am from Oregon and her delegate to the Congress of the United States, for addressing you for a purpose of interest to the country to which I belong.

I desire you to give me as correct a description as you can at this late period, of the manner in which you and your party, and your enterprise were treated by Dr. John McLoughlin, then its Chief Factor. This Dr. McLoughlin, since you left the country, rendered his name odious among the people of Oregon, by his endeavors to prevent the settlement of the country, and to cripple its growth.

Now that he wants a few favors of our government, he pretends that he has long been a friend of Americans and American enterprise west of the mountains. Your early reply will be highly appreciated both for its information, and your relation to my country.

I am, sir, yours very truly,

S. R. THURSTON.

To which Wyeth replied:

Cambridge,
Nov. 21, 1850.

Hon. Sam'l R. Thurston:
Dear Sir;—

Your favor of the 16th. inst., was received on the 19th. The first I visited the Columbia, in the autumn of 1832, I reached Vancouver with a disorganized party of ten persons, the remnant of twenty-four who left the states. Wholly worn out and disheartened, we were received cordially and liberally supplied, and there the party broke up. I returned to the States in the spring of 1833 with one man. One of the party, Mr. John Ball, remained and planted wheat on the Willamette, a little above Camp du Sable, having been supplied with seed and implements from Vancouver, then under the charge of John McLoughlin, Esq., and this gentleman I believe to have been the first American who planted wheat in Oregon. I returned to the country in the autumn of 1834, with a large party and more means, having on the way built Fort Hall, and there met a brig I had sent around the Horn. In the winter and spring of 1835 I planted wheat on the Willamette and on Wappatoo Island.

The suffering and distressed of the early American visitors and settlers on the Columbia were always treated by Hudson's Bay Company's agents, and particularly so by John McLoughlin, Esq., with consideration and kindness, more particularly the Methodist missionaries whom I brought out in the autumn of 1834. He supplied them with the means of transportation, seeds, implements of agriculture and building, cattle and food for a long time.

I sincerely regret that this gentleman, as you state, has become odious to his neighbors in his old age.

I am your ob't serv't, NATH J. WYETH.

Wyeth immediately wrote Robert C. Winthrop of Massachusetts, Speaker of the House, protesting against Thurston's charges, and also wrote a kindly letter to Dr. McLoughlin himself.

Nothing more would seem to be needed to prove that McLoughlin was the victim of a scandalous and vicious campaign of slander. A lesser man than Wyeth might have taken advantage of the opportunity for revenge upon the man who had caused the failure of his enterprise, or if not having directly caused it, who could have made it successful and would not. But Wyeth understood that McLoughlin's integrity toward his employers made it impossible for him to have acted other than in the way he did. Both honorable men, they liked and respected each other. Dr. McLoughlin had to be pretty much of a man to command the respect and loyalty of Nat Wyeth and Jason Lee.

# 14

# "THE RIDDLINGS OF CREATION"

If hall j. kelley had done nothing more, he had opened a Pandora's box of oratory relating to Oregon. After Thomas Jefferson there were few American statesmen who evinced any interest in the Northwest, but Kelley had kicked up too much of a furore for the region to be completely ignored.

The only people who took Kelley seriously were a handful of missionaries and the land-poor farmers of New England, always ready to listen to the siren call of free land. Most statesmen took their cue from President Andrew Jackson, who proclaimed that the future of the nation depended on a compact population within easily defended boundaries.

Thomas Hart Benton set the tone when he said in a speech in 1825, "The ridge of the Rocky Mountains may be named as a convenient, natural and everlasting boundary. Along this ridge the western limits of the Republic should be drawn, and the statue of the fabled God Terminus should be erected on its highest peak, never to be thrown down." In after years Benton was to recant, thanks to his colleague, Senator Linn, who for a time stood as the only influential champion of Oregon, and to his explorer son-in-law, John C. Frémont.

Senator McDuffie, typical of the spokesmen for the opposing group, said in the debate on the Ashburton-Webster Treaty: "What is the character of this country? As I understand it there are seven hundred miles this side of the Rocky Mountains that is uninhabitable; where rain never falls; mountains wholly impassable, except through gaps and depressions, to be reached only by going hundreds of miles out of the direct course. Well, now, what are we going to do in such a case? How are you going to apply steam? Have you made an estimate of the cost of a railroad to the mouth of the Columbia? Why, the wealth of the Indies would be insufficient. Of what use would it be for agricultural purposes? I would not for that purpose, give a pinch of snuff for the whole territory. I wish the Rocky Mountains were an impassable barrier. If there was an embankment of even five feet to be removed I would not consent to spend five dollars to remove it and allow our population to get there. I thank God for His mercy in placing the Rocky Mountains there."

Others joined in the torrent of abuse of Oregon with such statements as ". . . the whole country is as irre-claimable as the Desert of Sahara" and "Of all countries upon the face of the earth Oregon is one of the least fa-

vored by heaven. It is the mere riddlings of creation. . . .
Russia has her Siberia and England has her Botany Bay,
and if the United States should ever have need of such a
country in which to banish her rogues and scoundrels, the
utility of such a region as Oregon would be demonstrated.
Until then, we are perfectly willing to leave this magnificent country to the Indians, trappers and buffalo hunters
that roam over its sandy banks."

There were many more such expressions, in Congress
and out. A few spoke for Oregon. Floyd of Virginia had
made a plea for the occupation of Oregon back in 1820, and
such a bill was actually passed by the House in 1824 but
was killed in the Senate. In February 1838 Senator Linn of
Missouri introduced a bill along the same lines, and again
it was defeated. Benton, who now favored the bill, had his
own words quoted against him by Senator Winthrop of
Massachusetts. The idea of Oregon as future American territory was being talked to death, while England, through
Hudson's Bay, sat quietly in possession.

Kelley, Bonneville and Wyeth had failed. Only the missionaries and old Ewing Young, steadily building up his
herds of cattle and horses on the Willamette, called themselves Americans. Oregon was sliding from our grasp.

The British held four aces, but they were only playing
one. McLoughlin alone could see beyond fur. His pleas to
the British fell upon deaf ears. His superior, Sir George
Simpson, accused him of neglecting business to promote
farming.

The British were looking forward to compromise, and
were prepared to give up the country between the south
bank of the Columbia and the north boundary of California.

As has been noted, they were abandoning their settled policy of conservation to trap out all the beaver in the country they expected to give up, Ogden and McLeod having been sent there with that purpose. Except for the small settlement on the Willamette, the British intended the Americans to get nothing of value.

Unless somebody brought American settlers over the Rockies the fate of Oregon was the same as settled. Said Senator McDuffie scornfully, "Do you think your honest farmers in Pennsylvania, New York, or even Ohio and Missouri, would abandon their farms and go upon any such enterprise as this?"

One man who thought they would was Marcus Whitman. When he finished one of the most historic rides in our history in 1842 from Oregon to Washington, D.C., to plead for help he was told, "There cannot be a wagon road over the mountains; Sir George Simpson has said so."

Whitman's reply deserves to be commemorated: "There *is* a road, for I have made it."

It wasn't much of a road then, and it still wasn't as late as 1900 when I came over it from Walla Walla to the Grand Ronde Valley in a covered wagon. There was mud up to the hubs, but over that road passed the thousands of American farmers who were to save the Northwest for the United States.

Some historians maintain that Whitman's part in the saving of Oregon has been overrated, but his efforts cannot be discounted. It was Whitman who made the road from Fort Hall and across the Blue Mountains, and that road opened Oregon. It is beside the point to argue that other men might have done it if he hadn't.

We must go back to Hall J. Kelley and Nathaniel J. Wyeth. If Kelley hadn't interested Wyeth in Oregon, and if Wyeth hadn't brought Baptiste and the Nez Percé lad back to Boston on his first return the American Missionary Board might not have thought of sending a mission to the Indians in Oregon.

First among these were Jason Lee and his four companions, who accompanied Wyeth back to Fort Hall and Fort Vancouver in 1834. The next year the Board sent Marcus Whitman and Reverend Samuel Parker out on a voyage of exploration to ascertain the real conditions.

At Green River they thought they had seen enough to acquaint them with the possibilities. There was too much godlessness among the trappers, Indians and half-breeds to let go on unchecked. It was decided that Reverend Parker should go on, while Dr. Whitman, who was not technically a missionary, should return with a report.

Parker seems to have been a devout and devoted missionary, but hardly the type to promote good will. One incident related about him is somewhat indicative of his character. Coming upon the grave of a child that had just died and finding a cross at its head, he broke the cross into small pieces and replaced it with a marker that was more to his liking, untainted by Papacy.

Dr. Whitman took two Indian boys, Richard and John, back with him, and his report to the American Board was so impressive that he was called to start the mission. He planned to begin the journey the next year; not, however, before his marriage to Narcissa Prentice, a woman of good family whom he had won from his friend, Reverend H. H. Spalding. Meantime, Spalding himself had married, and he and his wife, Eliza, a rather frail woman, were called to accompany the Whitmans. Both ladies, the first women pioneers of the Oregon Trail, proved themselves real heroines.

The party set out down the Ohio, accompanied by H. H. Gray, a layman, two teamsters and the two Indian boys. They went up the Mississippi and Missouri rivers, then overland to Green River, Dr. Whitman taking his wagon over the ruts made by Captain Bonneville. At Green River they met Jim Bridger, and the doctor removed from Bridger's back the Blackfoot arrowhead that had bothered "Old Gabe" so long.

Gratitude and genuine liking caused Bridger to implore Whitman to leave his wagon, telling him it was impossible to go on with it. Whitman nevertheless went on with the wagon as far as Fort Hall, which at that time belonged to Wyeth, but the men in charge there were equally insistent that Whitman could not take the vehicle any further. Marcus Whitman made one compromise: he made a cart of the wagon, but carried along the other wheels and gear so that it could be put together later.

Things were getting difficult. Their flour was gone, and Mrs. Spalding sickened on the steady meat diet. Reverend Spalding was not exactly a congenial traveling companion, being full of doubts and complaints. The entire trip had been one of the most arduous ones in the history of the West. Neither of the two women complained, though Narcissa Whitman worried about the trouble the wagon caused her husband.

Even before reaching Fort Hall she wrote: "Husband has had a tedious time with the wagon today. It got stuck in the creek, and on the mountain side, so steep that the horses could scarcely climb, it was upset twice. It was a wonder that it was not turning somersaults continually. It is not grateful to my feelings to see him wearing himself out with excessive fatigue. All the more difficult portions of the way he walked, in a laborious attempt to take the wagon."

Surely it was not for the sake of luxury that Whitman insisted on taking it along. We might credit him with the purpose of showing that people could get to Oregon by wagon.

Narcissa's account of the stay at Fort Hall reveals that Wyeth's post was not nearly so well stocked as the fort on the Boise. They succeeded in buying a little rice, which was a welcome change from their steady diet of game. She described the crossing of Snake River at Fort Hall: "We put the packs on the tallest horses, the highest being selected for Mrs. Spalding and myself. The river where we crossed is divided into three branches by islands. The last branch is half a mile wide and so deep as to come up the horses' sides, and is a very strong current. The wagon turned upside down in the current, and the mules were entangled in the harness. I once thought of the terrors of the rivers, but now I cross the most difficult streams without fear."

Narcissa describes the way some of the Indian women crossed on a homemade ferry composed of a dried elk hide with two ropes attached. The party to be ferried lay flat down on the hide while the two Indian women doing the ferrying swam across, towing the elk-hide craft and its human cargo by the ropes they held in their mouths.

Knowing something of the Indians around Fort Hall,

I am almost certain that this ferrying was done for sport and not from necessity. I think they were merely putting on a show, and I can almost hear the giggles of the girl being ferried.

The Whitman party had a well deserved rest at Fort Boise, and Narcissa in her journal speaks gratefully of the fine food, and perhaps of more importance to the women, the fine linen and chinaware, provided by Mr. Payette, the factor. This genial gentleman always liked to have company, and he must have given them sound advice about the road that lay ahead. He was well aware that it was too late for them to turn back.

Since Whitman claimed to have made a wagon road across the Blue Mountains at this time, and the remains of his wagon were on view at Fort Boise for some years, the only explanation is that he took the front wheels, which he had made into a cart, on across the mountains and left the remainder, which he had been hauling on the cart ever since leaving Fort Hall, at Fort Boise. The important thing is that he had taken wagon wheels across the mountains to the Pacific slope.

In September the Whitman party arrived at Fort Walla Walla, and were definitely in Hudson's Bay territory. The factor, Mr. Pambrun, was friendly enough, but it was thought best to have an understanding with Dr. McLoughlin, though this would entail a 300-mile trip by boat, with Indian oarsmen.

They were, of course, welcomed cordially by Dr. McLoughlin, who could not have helped admiring the two courageous missionary ladies. McLoughlin was as favorably impressed by the Whitmans as he had been by the Lees.

Missionaries were not settlers, and he would give them all the aid possible.

There is some question as to McLoughlin's religious affiliation, but though he had been reared for some years as a Catholic by his maternal grandmother, a member of the aristocratic Fraser family, he seems to have belonged to the Established Church of England. He was friendly to all sects and helped build their churches and missions.

McLoughlin advised the Whitmans to return to Walla Walla and build one mission there, and another 125 miles to the north among the Nez Percés. The horse Indians were more intelligent and less treacherous than the river Indians and, besides, they had been clamoring to be taught. However, McLoughlin suggested, it would be wise for the two ladies to remain at Fort Vancouver while the men returned and built a shelter for them. This was done, and Narcissa Whitman instructed McLoughlin's daughters in classroom and music. The ladies remained there for six weeks until Spalding came for them.

Dr. Whitman had located his mission at a place he called Waiilatpu, about twenty-five miles from Fort Walla Walla. The ladies arrived there December 10, and were delighted by what they saw, crude though Narcissa admitted it to be. Here the Whitmans were to do much good for the Indians, and here they were to become the first Christian martyrs of Oregon. The Spaldings moved to Fort Lapwai to establish their own mission, and what Reverend Spalding lacked in tact and understanding was more than made up for by those qualities in his wife.

What would seem to be the ideal Indian mission was soon under way at Waiilatpu. Many of the Indians consented to work on Dr. Whitman's farm and in his mills. Their children came to Narcissa's school, and its fame spread. Relations with Hudson's Bay were pleasant, for the missionaries were not suspected of empire building by anyone, except possibly Sir George Simpson. Pierre Pambrun was friendly, and his daughter Maria was having a romance with one of Whitman's helpers, a young man named Rodgers.

Back at Fort Hall the factors were being quite successful at discouraging emigration, yet a few wagons did get past Ermatinger in spite of his jovial trickiness, such as selling the Americans blooded cattle which turned out to be Spanish longhorns.

Joe Meek and Doc Newell took wagons over the Blue Mountains in the later 1830s. Meek brought along his daughter Helen Mar to attend Narcissa Whitman's school, and with her also was a daughter of Jim Bridger. There were a few others but it was only a trickle, nothing to get alarmed about. Even the famed Peoria Party of 1839, of which more later, broke up in too many fragments to be a threat.

Then in 1842 a former Willamette missionary named Elijah White, who had had difficulties with his fellows, returned from the East with an appointment as Indian Agent for the United States government in the Northwest. When he arrived at Waiilatpu he had with him a company of 120 American settlers, among them Amos L. Lovejoy. It was time for England and Hudson's Bay to take a second and longer look. This immigration must be stopped.

Down in California Captain John Sutter occupied a land grant on the Sacramento River which he called New

Helvetia. He had become a Mexican citizen and held a commission which he boasted gave him the power of life or death over the Indians, and the whites, too, if need be. Still, he would feel safer if there were American settlers in California. American farmers could raise produce which Sutter could trade to his friends, the Russians.

Sutter wanted the Americans; McLoughlin did not. So, on a jaunt to Sitka, Sutter stopped over at Fort Vancouver to visit McLoughlin. The genial Sutter made a hit wherever he visited, and he was warmly welcomed on the Columbia. There is no record that he made a deal with McLoughlin to divert the Americans who were headed for Oregon to California, but there is considerable circumstantial evidence that such a deal was made, for both men stood to gain by it.

Ermatinger at Fort Hall, and his successor, Captain Johnnie Grant, became wildly enthusiastic about the opportunities in California and correspondingly eloquent in their assertions that travel to Oregon was well nigh impossible. Old Caleb Greenwood and his three half-breed sons, in the service of Captain Sutter, took up headquarters at Fort Hall, and expatiated not only on the easy road, but on how much help they could expect in the way of men, mules and supplies to get them over the Sierras, and also the fine farms that would be given them when they reached New Helvetia.

To the weary travelers who reached Fort Hall and listened to the tales of the unparalleled hardships they would have to endure if they went on to Oregon and the easy road to the land of milk and honey in California, the choice must have seemed as simple as between heaven and hell—but, surprisingly, most of them persisted in going on to Oregon.

The emigrants were hard-headed farmers, inclined to look dubiously on every statement where there was a possibility of exaggeration. Like most mountain men, Caleb Greenwood was given to hyperbole, and there was strong suspicion that Sutter's promises would not be fulfilled. As a matter of fact, Sutter kept nearly every promise he made, but his case was probably oversold at Fort Hall.

The chief reason why the early Oregon immigration was not stopped lay in the simple fact that people who had been reading, talking and dreaming about Oregon for perhaps years could not be persuaded to change their plans at the last minute. An influential factor was the belief that Oregon would soon belong to the United States, but California belonged to Mexico. Few of the migrants were disposed to give up their American citizenship.

Captain Sutter certainly had no intention of getting mixed up in the Indian troubles at Waiilatpu which resulted in the Whitman Massacre and the Cayuse War; that he did so was entirely accidental, and with no culpable intent on his part. To have done with that matter now, there was a Cayuse chief called Yellow Serpent, or Pio-pio-mox-mox—there are various spellings of the name—whose bright young son attended the school at Waiilatpu and was baptized under the Christian name of Elijah. To the missionaries he was a model young Indian with great possibilities; Sutter called him a braggart and a brawler.

Elijah and some other young men went down to Sutter's Fort for horse-trading purposes and while there Elijah killed a white man in a quarrel, and was himself killed. That was a grievous blow to Pio-pio-mox-mox, who rode down to Sutter's with forty warriors demanding justice. Rebuffed, and with hatred in his soul, he stopped long enough on his way home to kill some men who were not party to the quarrel. It was the opening wedge that turned the Cayuses against Dr. Whitman. By no means the only one, it was a very real threat to American emigration.

Amos Lovejoy gave Dr. Whitman the information that the Ashburton Treaty fixing the boundary between the United States and Canada might soon be ratified, and Whitman felt that unless the Congress was alerted to the situation of the settlers in Oregon they would be left at the mercy of the British. He was well aware of the general ignorance about Oregon in the East, and felt that they must be enlightened—and he was the man to do it.

He could not leave his post without permission of the American Board, but there was no time. According to Dr. Ells, a fellow missionary, he said, "I am not expatriated by becoming a missionary."

Reverend Spalding says: "Dr. Whitman's last remarks were as he mounted his horse for the long journey: 'If the Board dismisses me, I will do what I can to save Oregon for my country. My life is but of little worth if I can save this country to the American people.'"

So began the famous ride to save Oregon, and Amos Lovejoy volunteered to go with Dr. Whitman. They started on the third of October, 1842, with a guide and three mules. It was to be a trip of incredible hardship.

They were well received at Fort Walla Walla, but the Englishmen there were confident that England would now get all Oregon. While they were there a messenger arrived from Fort Colville with the news that a colony of 140 Englishmen and Canadians was on the way. A young priest threw his cap in the air and shouted, "Hurrah for Oregon —America is too late, we have got the country."

Whitman and Lovejoy arrived at Fort Hall after eleven days of hard riding. Captain Johnnie Grant, says Nixon in his book, *How Marcus Whitman Saved Oregon,* "seems to have been placed at this point solely to discourage and defeat immigration, set about his task in the usual way. . . . He had before had many a talk with Whitman, and knew something of his determination. It was Grant who had almost compelled every incoming settler to forsake his wagon at Fort Hall, sacrifice his goods, and force women and children to ride on horseback or go on foot the balance of the journey.

"Six years before he had pled with Whitman to do this, and had failed, and Whitman had taken the first wagon into Oregon that had ever crossed the Rockies. Now he set about to defeat his journey to the States."

Hudson's Bay was making a valiant effort to hold Oregon for the British, and Fort Hall was the doorstep to the country. We cannot doubt that the future of the Northwest Coast was decided there.

Captain Grant persuaded Whitman that he would find the Rockies under twenty feet of snow, and the plains Indians on the warpath. It was enough to dismay the most stout-hearted, but instead of turning back Whitman and Lovejoy turned southeast by way of Salt Lake and Fort Uintah in an attempt to reach Taos. Turned back by storm before they reached there, and without a guide, they separated but eventually made Bent's Fort, Whitman having the harder time. They arrived finally in Washington—only to learn that a treaty had been signed before they left Oregon.

Some details remained to be ironed out, and it was being proposed to trade Oregon for fishing rights in Newfoundland. Whitman got a hearing before both President Tyler and Secretary of State Webster, the president giving him a much warmer reception than did Mr. Webster.

Just how much good the famous ride did is still a moot question, but that it was not without its effect is indicated by the simple fact that the tide soon began to turn in favor of the Americans. More important than Whitman's words was the fact that he started back to Oregon in the spring of 1843 with a party of 300 emigrants and sixty wagons. The fate of Oregon rode with that party, and it got through despite the efforts of Johnnie Grant to stop or detour it at Fort Hall.

Among the emigrants was Jesse Applegate, a most capable leader, and it is usually referred to as the Applegate wagon train. That train broke the dam, though Johnnie Grant and Caleb Greenwood were by no means finished with their business of trying to divert the migrants to California.

Whitman's reward was a severe reprimand from his missionary board for absence without leave. He was told that it was a Protestant, not a national, issue.

# 15

# OREGON OR THE GRAVE

AMONG THE EARLY OREGON
emigrants few have been more widely discussed than the
turbulent and strife-torn Peoria party of 1839. It added
materially to the knowledge of the country, and an unusually large percentage of its members later became leading citizens of Oregon. A number of them kept journals,
and the leader, Thomas Jefferson Farnham, became a writer
of books on the West and was considered to be something
of an authority.

There were originally fifteen men in the Peoria party,
captained by Farnham, a Vermont lawyer, and they called
themselves "The Oregon Dragoons." So determined were
they to go to Oregon and help wrest the country from the
British that they carried a flag on which Farnham's wife
had painted the words, *Oregon or the Grave.*

The genesis of their journey could be traced back through Jason Lee, Nathaniel J. Wyeth and, of course, Hall J. Kelley. It was Kelley who had inspired Wyeth; Wyeth and his two Indian lads had inspired Jason Lee; and when Lee returned to the States on a lecture tour in 1838 to raise funds for the Methodist Mission he inspired the Peoria party.

Jason Lee attended the Illinois Conference of the Methodist Church at Alton. "He entered the conference accompanied by five Indians of that region, on his way to New York," says C. J. Brosnan in *Jason Lee, Prophet of the New Oregon.* "While at Peoria, Thomas Adams, one of the Indian boys, took sick and had to be left behind. He remained at the town through the winter, and as he learned English became a great booster for Oregon. His stories of the abundance of salmon and other resources of the Northwest . . . . thrilled a group of young Peorians, and they decided to organize an emigration party." Thomas J. Farnham, the Vermont lawyer who had moved to Illinois to farm, was the natural leader. "He fathered the project and stirred patriotic fervor with his plea to take possession of disputed Oregon Territory and resist the hold of the powerful Hudson's Bay Company."

Of the fifteen men who started several dropped out, but others were recruited to replace them. A list of the supplies each man was to have as directed by Captain Farnham is of interest.

| | |
|---|---:|
| A good riding horse, say— | $75.00 |
| A rifle, carrying ball from 13 to 42 lb. | 15.00 |
| Brace of pistols, | 10.00 |
| Hunting knife, | 1.00 |

| 8½ lbs. powder, with lead in proportion, | 5.00 |
|---|---|
| 2 woolen blankets, | 5.00 |
| A pack pony to be purchased on frontier, | 25.00 |
| Contingencies, | 25.00 |
| | $161.00 |

Newspaper reports of the time indicate that many other people were talking about forming emigration societies, but the movement had not yet gained momentum, and the Farnham party was one of the few that actually got under way. They were all relatively young men with a taste for adventure—a taste that for some of them was soon satisfied.

Farnham, who was college trained, had attended lectures in Paris and traveled throughout Europe. As a man of the world, he was the natural choice for leader; yet leadership talent was a thing he seems not to have possessed. Still, he dreamed of taking Oregon Territory by force, to end the British fur-trade monopoly.

By the time they reached Independence, Missouri, the party numbered eighteen, and they set out on the well known Santa Fe Trail. At 110 Mile Creek three of the Peoria men, Owen Garrett, Thomas Picket and John L. Moore, turned back with an eastbound wagon train. At the Santa Fe crossing of the Arkansas three other members, Chauncey Wood, Quincey Jordon and John Pritchard, joined a caravan going to Santa Fe, while one W. Blair joined the Farnham party.

By the time they reached Bent's Fort there occurred what Farnham termed a mutiny, and the party split up. Four men—Smith, Oakley, Blair and Joseph Wood—remained with Farnham, while eight mutineers under Robert Shortess took another direction.

Shortess appears to have been an able man; he became a prominent citizen of Oregon, playing a big part in the organization of the Provisional Government, and was one of the leaders in dispossessing Dr. John McLoughlin of his property. Farnham seems to have been justified in calling him a troublemaker.

Tempers had been at a raw edge before the combined party reached Bent's Fort. They had faced no large dangers, but a thousand petty annoyances. Those who think traveling in constant rain and knee-deep mud was trivial simply have not undergone such conditions. The ground was so soft that often their horses pulled up their picket-pins and headed back along the trail, each time necessitating a delay until they were found. The owners of the missing horses had to find them, while the others chafed at the delay.

Captain Farnham at first had tried to introduce a military order of march which didn't appeal to the farmers and mechanics of the party. Chauncey Wood, a New York farmer, thirty years of age, was elected lieutenant, and a general order was read:

"Oregon dragoons, attention: The order of march for the first day is: The first platoon (four men to a platoon) will march in front, the second platoon in rear of first, the third platoon in rear of second, which will take charge of the public mules, and the fourth platoon in rear. Take your places. [Trumpet sounds.] Forward! March! Close order."

So the company at that point consisted of two officers and sixteen men. They fell in with Captain Kelly's wagon train bound for Santa Fe. They were in a storm of wind, rain, thunder and lightning, "such as is seldom witnessed," Shortess says, and they were glad to take shelter under the lee of Kelly's wagons. It is hard to picture them holding military formations under such conditions.

The Kaw Indians had just hunted the country and buffalo were hard to find. The bitter feeling among the men grew and was further aggravated by an accident to Sidney Smith. There are two widely varying accounts of how it happened. According to Obediah Oakley, Smith, in drawing his gun toward him, muzzle forward, permitted the trigger to come in contact with some part of his saddle and the gun went off, striking Smith in the lower part of his chest, the ball penetrating the flesh, severing two of his ribs and lodging near the spine. Oakley caught him while he was falling.

There was a surgeon with the Santa Fe party ahead who returned and dressed the wound, and put Smith in a carriage. When the time came for separation from Kelly's company, it was necessary to make a litter to carry Smith. At this time, Oakley says, Shortess and another man proposed to abandon Smith and let him perish. "This diabolical suggestion originated with Shortess and one other, who swore that unless it was complied with they would leave the company; and—shameful and humiliating truth must be spoken—*all* but five, consisting now of thirteen, joined the miscreants in this scheme of wickedness! One of them carried his inhumanity so far as to refuse Smith a draught of water from his can!"

Robert Shortess gives another version of the accident, saying he was absent at the time, but got the story from eyewitnesses. "A wordy war broke out between the men while packing in the morning. One of them seized his rifle by the muzzle and drew it toward him with a jerk: the hammer being entangled with his saddle was drawn back and the rifle discharged. . . ."

Psychologists might make something of an incident Oakley relates when the buffalo were so thick along the road that the wagons could not get through them. They would stand about thirty feet away staring at the men around the campfire. Shortess slipped up and cut the tail off one of the animals, having the effect on it of "a galvanic battery." It makes it easier to understand why Shortess would have been willing to ride on and leave a wounded man to die—especially if he didn't like the man.

Not even the Donner party members developed as much hatred for one another as did those of this Peoria party. Shortess accuses Farnham of intemperance and neglect of duty, incompetence and waste of funds placed in his hands. Farnham, Shortess claimed, resigned, and with two others narrowly escaped expulsion because they had become obnoxious to the party. After they arrived at Bent's Fort Farnham, Oakley and Smith were voted out, and Blair and Joseph Wood chose to go with them. Here the property was divided, and Farnham's group set out for Fort Davy Crockett on Green River. The others headed toward the South Platte, where Denver now stands.

Shortess, in speaking of the time at the crossing where they parted from the Santa Fe men, says, "After spending a day trying to make a litter for our invalid, and failing from lack of skill and proper material, we placed him on our gentlest mule, detailed three men to attend him, and resumed our journey, toiling slowly under a burning sun over sandy plains. We reached Bent's Fort, a distance of 150 miles, in about ten days. We remained at Bent's Fort about one week, during which the division of property was effected, as was also the stores and property held in common."

The division probably prevented actual violence, for Shortess never tried to conceal his dislike for Farnham, Smith and Oakley. One cannot help but wonder how Shortess and Smith got along after they reached the Willamette, for both became prominent leaders of the community. Shortess, as already noted, helped spearhead the drive against Dr. McLoughlin, and Sidney Smith became the owner of Ewing Young's ranch when the problem of probating Young's estate led to the formation of the provisional government. Shortess tells with some delight of the arrival of some strangers who addressed Smith as "Mr. Carroll," letting him conclude that Smith was an alias.

The two parties made various detours but both eventually wound up at Fort Davy Crockett in Brown's Hole on Green River. Brown's Hole in those days was the most used station on the overland route between Bent's Fort and Fort Hall. It had certain natural advantages which the mountain men appreciated—good winter climate and inaccessibility. General Ashley had been there, as had most of the other traders of the day. It was a natural bastion, isolated and surrounded by the high Uintah Mountains, but the snow seldom got very deep in the valley along Green River, and livestock could live well there all winter. There are still very few places to get in or out of the Hole, now known to the fastidious as Brown's Park. Famed Lodore Canyon, where the Green cuts through the mountains, is still a challenge which only the most daring boatmen with modern equipment will accept.

After the mountain men had gone Brown's Hole was the main hangout for the outlaw gang known as Butch Cassidy's Wild Bunch. They could winter their stolen stock there in perfect safety, and if a sheriff showed up, which seldom happened, it was easy to get over the line into another state. Even in this century an old Negro called Speck, who had been a member of the Wild Bunch, was found living on a bar of the river where he had existed alone for years, his clothing made from old mailbags taken in some forgotten stage or train robbery. At the present time one of the biggest dams in the West is being built there. It is called Flaming Gorge, and the town surrounding the dam is called Dutch John. It will soon be a recreation area, but in its early history it was a testing ground for men.

The place got its name from one Baptiste Brown, who had lived there for some time with the Indians. Fort Davy Crockett, sometimes referred to as Fort Misery, was owned by a trio named Thompson, Craig and Sinclair. Such mountain men as Kit Carson and Joe Walker were well known there, and two of the fraternity's more famous members, who were to pioneer Oregon, Joe Meek and "Doc" Newell, made their headquarters there; both of them had contact with our heroes from Peoria.

The Shortess party reached the area where Denver now stands, then went back to Fort St. Vrain, named after a partner of the Bents. They waited here for six weeks for a trading party bound for Green River. They hunted with the men of the fort and were successful in getting meat. Shortess tells of two worn-out Sioux warriors who limped in on foot telling of a great victory over the Pawnees and Omahas, in which they killed ninety Pawnees and forty Omahas. The two Sioux rested a day and a night and then were seen ten or twelve miles from the fort traveling north. The next morning seven horses were missing and were never recovered, though the two Sioux were seen with them by another party.

The expected party did not arrive so Shortess and his men spent the time hunting and berrying, and visiting the three forts within ten miles of each other on the South Platte, and in visiting the Cheyenne, Arapaho, and renegade Sioux villages close by. As a result of the civilizing influence of commerce, Shortess comments, "The Indians were drunken and debauched, and the whites ditto, but more so."

The bunch of traders finally showed up and Shortess and his companions traveled with them across the Black Hills to Fort Laramie, eventually struck Little Bear River, went down it a short distance, then headed across the barren desert to Brown's Hole. They were with two trading parties led by T. Biggs and Warfield, but underwent no such hardships as were to be endured by the other branch of the Peoria party.

At Fort Crockett they encountered Joe Meek and Doc Newell, who, in spite of a storm that left ten inches of snow in the valley and three feet in the mountains, were about to start to Fort Hall with their furs and lay in a supply of goods for the winter. Shortess alone of his party accompanied Meek and Newell.

Shortess gives the distance as 300 miles; that is greatly exaggerated but it gives an idea of the distances fur was brought in for sale at Fort Hall. It was no easy road to travel in the winter time, which is true even to this day. They started out with enough jerked meat to last them three days. They sent out two hunters who returned empty-handed, ate supper and breakfast, and disappeared to be seen no more.

They proceeded up Green River through mountains covered with snow to the mouth of Henry's Fork, where they shot a wolf which was taken along as a last resource against starvation. Later they met a small party of trappers who gave them meat to last a few days. They traveled northwest to Black's Fork, where Fort Bridger is now located. They went on to Bear River, followed it down to Soda Springs, then across to the Portneuf and down to Fort Hall, where they were well received by Francis Ermatinger, the factor. For two days they had lived on a few crumbs of dried meat and a cup of coffee per man a day.

Shortess, who was later to inveigh against Hudson's Bay, was full of praise for Mr. Ermatinger, who fed and entertained him until he was rested up. There were few trappers at Fort Hall, and Ermatinger thought a journey across the desert and the Blue Mountains was ill-advised but finally agreed to send what furs he had to Fort Vancouver by Shortess and a Canadian named Sylvertry. Two Indians and a half-breed boy, who was returning to his father at Fort Nez Percé, were to accompany them.

Encountering a severe snowstorm, the Indians deserted, taking the boy with them, and the party was reduced to two men and fourteen horses. Since Sylvertry could speak no English and Shortess no French there was little communication between them. It took them two weeks to reach

Fort Boise, where they rested a day or so before pressing on.

The conditions as Shortess described them were bad enough. "The hills were covered with snow, the ground bare and frozen, and thick ice was on the waters; and although only the latter part of November, winter reigned on the Blue Mountains. We travelled two days in snow from one to three feet deep; our animals were so weak from hunger and fatigue as to be hardly able to make their way through the snowdrifts, and sometimes fell under their loads or became restive and could hardly be moved by the severest blows."

Eventually they made it across to the mild climate of the Umatilla Valley, and after resting their horses continued on to Fort Nez Percé, which the Americans called Fort Walla Walla, where they were well treated by Pierre Pambrun. Shortess was told, however, that it was too late in the season to cross the Cascades to Fort Vancouver, so he went to Dr. Whitman's mission at Waiilatpu and worked there until spring.

There were few Indians there, but two white married couples: Dr. Asahel Munger and his wife, independent missionaries from Ohio; and Edwin O. Hall and his wife, from the Hawaiian Mission. The Mungers had also recently enjoyed the hospitality of Ermatinger at Fort Hall.

Shortess praises Whitman for his success in raising food enough to supply the missions and in his efforts to civilize the Indians, but adds gratituously that he would have continued successful if his benevolent, self-sacrificing labors had not been thwarted by Jesuit and Popish intolerances. Unlike Farnham, who carried a large book on his back in which he painstakingly wrote down the events of each day, Shortess's notes were written after he had become involved in Oregon politics and had acquired quite a few intolerances of his own.

Shortess set out alone for the Willamette on March 12, 1840, and overtook an Indian chief of the Deschutes village with whom he continued his journey to The Dalles. There, Shortess was welcomed by Reverend H. K. W. Perkins, the missionary in charge. He also found at the mission a Mr. Ben Wright, who wanted Shortess to promise to fight the Indians in case they made trouble over some horses they claimed to have sold but for which they had not received payment.

Ben Wright had been an itinerant missionary but, tiring of the profession, had gone to Texas to engage in trade and there had just naturally branched out into the business of selling liquor to Indians and Negroes. He had left Texas in some haste and in Oregon had received saving grace and gone back to his old profession of saving souls. He had played a part in a recent revival at The Dalles, where a thousand Indians were said to have been converted. Wright and his partner, Dutton, had gone into the business of buying horses from the Indians and driving them to the Willamette for sale. Shortess decided to work around The Dalles until Wright and Dutton were ready to leave. It was then that Wright asked him if he would fight if the Indians made trouble about their horses. Shortess says the Indians were satisfied with a few shirts and other trifles, and the peace was kept.

The party proceeded on to Fort Vancouver, the commercial and political center of Oregon, where they replenished their stock of goods and provisions and made their way to the settlement along the Willamette. The one-man advance guard of the Peoria party that was going to conquer Oregon by force of arms if need be had finally arrived. The beauty of the country threw Shortess into rhapsody: "And, I said, is there peace to be found in the world, a heart that is humble might hope to find it here."

He stayed for a time with Thomas Jefferson Hubbard, one of Wyeth's men who had elected to remain in Oregon, along with three others, Thornburg, Richardson and Courtney. Thornburg and Hubbard had trouble and when one night Hubbard invaded the other's cabin Thornburg killed him, successfully claiming self-defense.

Shortess went to work for A. O'Neil for a dollar a day and board. He says there were remaining in the country six men who came there in the employ of the American Fur Company in 1812, one American and five French-Canadians, all thriving, well-to-do farmers. Shortess neglects to mention that all of these men worked for Hudson's Bay and that Dr. McLoughlin was the man who supplied them with the things necessary to start their farms. A few years later Shortess was sending petitions to Washington claiming that McLoughlin and the Hudson's Bay Company were trying to keep the Americans out of Oregon and were harassing the settlers at every turn. In fact, Shortess received kindly treatment at Fort Hall, Fort Boise, Fort Walla Walla, and at Fort Vancouver—Hudson's Bay posts, every one.

Shortess was one of those who supplied Territorial Delegate Thurston with propaganda to be used against Governor McLoughlin. One of Thurston's "infamous lies," for which Shortess must have been at least partially responsible was that "This company has been warring against our government these forty years. Dr. McLoughlin has been their chief fugelman, first to cheat our government out of the whole country, and next to prevent its settlement, has driven men from claims and from the country to stifle the efforts of settlement. In 1845 he sent an express to Fort Hall to warn the American emigrants that if they attempted to come to the Willamette they would be cut off. They went and none were cut off. This, sir, I consider fully bears me out that our public lands will not be thrown into the hands of foreigners who will not become citizens and sympathize with those crocodile tears. . . . Dr. McLoughlin refuses to file his intention to become an American citizen . . ."

The truth was—and Shortess and Thurston must have known it—that McLoughlin had already applied for United States citizenship.

# 16

# BROWN'S HOLE

THE PEORIA PARTY CRUMBLED
to pieces almost before it got under way and it cut little
ice in history, yet it shed more light on the Oregon emigration than most of the larger parties that succeeded it. Its
young men were typical of the adventurous spirit of the
pioneers. They worked, brawled and fought, and they became a legend. Some of them became leaders in the settlement of a great state. They were the men who were separated from the boys. And whether they had education or
not, a high percentage of them wrote or kept journals of
inestimable value to historians. They were almost the only
ones who left a record of the important stretch of road
between Brown's Hole and Fort Hall. Modern traffic has
taken a different route, but the old abandoned road more
than served its purpose when the fate of the Northwest
hung in the balance.

After the separation at Bent's Fort both branches of the Peoria party headed for Brown's Hole; both suffered while getting there, the Farnham party much more than the Shortess group. Of the five in the Farnham party only two, Farnham and Smith, ever reached Oregon, and they became bitter enemies. Oakley and the other two turned back at Brown's Hole when a party from the Willamette led by Paul Richardson, who had been Wyeth's guide and hunter, stopped by and told them the Oregon country wasn't as good for farming as the land they had left at home. Home looked even better to them after spending a winter in Brown's Hole.

They had starved and sizzled crossing the desert from Steamboat Springs, or its vicinity, to Brown's Hole. They were not exceptional hunters and game was scarce, so they learned to eat dog or horse meat when they could get it. They met Joe Meek, who had just had a brush with Indians and was on his way to Brown's Hole, where his Indian wife was staying. None of them could have foreseen that a statue of Joe Meek fighting a grizzly bear would be seen by countless thousands in a Missouri museum, or that this ragged old squawman would before long be a Territorial Marshal, sit in the Oregon Legislature and, following the Whitman Massacre, ride to Washington, D.C., and hobnob with statesmen while he pleaded for help for Oregon.

Just after they had cooked their last meat, the Farnham men encountered three trappers, one of whom was William Craig, one of the owners of Fort Crockett. They divided their scanty meal with the visitors, on their way to the South Fork of the Platte to meet Thompson, who had gone to St. Louis with Sublette for supplies. Craig and seven more men camped a few miles away and then proceeded on their way, but two of the men, Ward and Burns, and a squaw turned back and joined our pilgrims.

They now had guides, but were no better off in the way of provisions, having nothing for supper, Oakley writes, but nettles and briars; the trappers being as badly off as they were. After going without food for three days they lay by to hunt, and fortunately killed an elk, shot several ducks, caught some fish, and at night one of the trappers caught two beavers. These, Oakley says, were especially delicious.

They soon parted with the trappers and continued alone down Bear River along a path so rough the horses could scarcely keep their footing. They soon met four French trappers who had left Brown's Hole fourteen days before, and had been attacked by a party of Sac Indians—who probably were from some tribe further west. The attack had been made on Little Snake River (a branch of the Yampa) and here Smith effected a horse trade.

Coming into a better game country, they saw a number of grizzly bears and shot two of them, only to find they were so fat they were not fit for food. They soon were out of food again. They saw many antelope but couldn't get close enough to them to shoot; then they managed to kill a couple of bear cubs which saved them from starvation.

They traveled over twenty-two miles of sandy, parched desert before they found water. Ten miles farther, on the evening of August 12 they reached Fort Crockett in Brown's Hole. Having been told that the way ahead was worse than the one they already had traversed, it is small wonder that three of the Peoria pilgrims decided to turn back as soon as the opportunity presented itself.

The post was large enough to afford protection for thirty men and their families, but on Farnham's arrival there were but two white men there: Prewitt Sinclair, one of the owners, and a trader named John Robertson, generally known in the mountains as Jack Robinson. There were, however, a number of Indian women and their children in near-by lodges awaiting the return of their white lords and masters.

Among the families were those of Joe Meek and Doc Newell, who had already located farms along the Willamette. Kit Carson is also known to have been in Brown's Hole that fall of 1839. In the winter of 1837–38, Carson had been engaged as hunter for the fort and had kept the score of men who wintered there supplied with meat.

Of Jack Robinson, Farnham writes: "He usually stations himself here to traffic with the Indians and white trappers. His skin lodge was his warehouse; and buffalo robes spread upon the ground his counter, on which he displayed his butcher knives, hatchets, powder, lead, fish-hooks, and whiskey. In exchange for these articles he receives beaver skins from travellers, and horses from the Indians. Thus as one would believe Mr. Robinson drives a very snug little business. And indeed, when all the independent trappers are driven by approaching winter into this delightful retreat, and the whole Snake village, two or three thousand strong, impelled by the same necessity, pitch their lodges around the fort, and the dances and merry making of a long winter are thoroughly commenced, there is no want of customers."

Two people can contemplate the same scene at the same time and get quite different impressions. Farnham, having reached Fort Crockett August 12, writes: "The bluff opened before us the beautiful plain of Brown's Hole. As we entered it we crossed two cool streams that tumbled down from the stratified cliffs near at hand on the right; and a few rods beyond, the whole area became visible. The Fort as it is called, peered up in the center upon the winding banks of the Sheetskadee. The dark mountains around it rose sublimely, and the green fields swept away into the deep precipitous gorges more beautiful than I can describe. . . .

"The fort is a hollow square of one-story log cabins, with roofs and floors of mud. . . . Around these we found the conical skin lodges of a few Snake Indians who had preceeded their tribe into this their winter haunt. . . ."

A different view is that of German-born Dr. F. A. Wislizenus, a distinguished gentleman—later the United States Minister to Turkey—who arrived in Brown's Hole August 17, just five days after Farnham and his party. He had been with a trapping party to Fort Hall, and was returning to the States. In his book, *A Journey to the Rocky Mountains in the Year 1839*, he wrote:

"On August 15 we crossed the Green River which winds its way among precipitous mountains, and at this point can be easily forded, going slantingly downstream for two more days. The road was generally steep, and led through forests of pine and cedar. The river valley at first was narrow but widens further on. . . . On August 17 we reached Fort Crockett. It is situated close by the Green River on its left bank. The river here is broad and has good pasturage and sufficient wood. The fort itself is the worst thing of its kind we have seen on our journey. It is a low, one-story building, constructed of logs and clay, with three connecting wings, and no enclosure. Instead of cows the fort had only some goats. In short the whole establishment appeared somewhat poverty stricken, for which reason it is also known to the trappers by the name of Fort Misery. The fort belongs to three Americans, Thompson, Gray and Sinclair. [It was Craig, not Gray.] The latter was at the fort and received us very kindly, but regretted his inability to offer us any supplies. For our store of meat was exhausted, and we had hoped to supply ourselves here with new provisions. But the people at the fort seemed worse off than we were. The day before they had bought a lean dog from the Indians for five dollars, and considered its meat a delicacy. I, too, tried some of it and found its taste not so bad. In addition to some trappers and Indians, we found five Americans here who had started in the spring with a larger party from Peoria, Illinois, to make a settlement on the Columbia River. . . . On August 18th. we started from Fort Crockett. Our next objective was the North Fork of the Platte."

Oakley states that the party bought enough meat for three meals, and were then compelled to purchase three dogs for $15 apiece. After commenting bitterly on the monopoly, he adjures: "But, gentle reader, do not elevate thy nose at it [dog meat]; for, to hungry men, even dog's flesh is exceedingly palatable. The Indians consider it a great luxury, and fatten large numbers of them. Thus we lived the five or six days we remained there."

On the 17th they proposed to start to Fort Hall, some 200 miles distant, though Kelly, their guide, had never been there. Their only provisions consisted of one of the three dogs, though they were able to obtain horses, four of them for pack duty. Sinclair had told them that they would have to spend the winter at Fort Hall, and because of the scarcity of game there would doubtless have to kill their horses and live on them until spring. The prospect ahead "looked rather gloomy."

As they were mounting their horses they saw a party of five men approaching and waited for them. Under the leadership of Paul Richardson, the five were just returning from Fort Hall, to which they had escorted Reverends Munger and Griffiths and their wives. Richardson's report of Oregon, where he had spent two years, was so discouraging that Oakley and Joseph Wood decided to accompany him on his eastward journey. Dr. Wislizenus was another member of the party. Of this trip Oakley says that nothing of importance occurred except that they were captured by Sioux Indians.

With the prospects ahead being what they were it is unfair to disparage them for turning back when they did. Many others went on to Fort Hall and then turned back. Farnham, Smith and Blair were lucky enough to fall in there with a company going to Fort Walla Walla.

Here they apparently parted company. Farnham and Smith had fallen out. Blair, who had quit the Santa Fe wagon train to join them, was an old man and had been hard put to it to reach Walla Walla. Farnham showed genuine concern for the old man, and was able to find him a job at Spalding's mission at Lapwai. Blair went through the dangerous days after the Whitman Massacre and the Cayuse War, and eventually died in California.

Before going on to the Willamette, Farnham spent considerable time at Waiilatpu with the Whitmans, and gives one of the best accounts of that mission anyone has ever written. There was no hint of Indian trouble at that time, and all was peace and industry. The mission farm was worked largely by Indian help, and everyone seemed happy.

Farnham was greatly impressed by Narcissa Whitman's school—as was everyone who visited it. At both the Whitman and Spalding missions the children were taught to read, to sing hymns and to pray. Farnham also admired the doctor's practicality in raising what the mission needed, unaware that that very practicality was to have much to do with the doctor's death a few years later. While Delaware Tom's charges that Whitman was really giving the Indians poison instead of medicine may have been the direct cause the underlying one was the Indian's fear that the white men would take their land after it had been demonstrated how productive it was.

As a good Protestant, Farnham got in a few little digs at the Jesuits, telling with considerable enjoyment how an Indian chief defeated a priest in argument. According to the story, the priest was urging the Indians to leave the Americans, who would lead them to hell. The chief told him how much the Americans had given the Indians, and how much he had given, closing with the crushing inquiry, "Did Jesus Christ wear a long black robe like you do?"

Farnham went on to Fort Vancouver and visited Dr. McLoughlin. Like Hall J. Kelley, he had demanded the ouster of the Hudson's Bay Company and the settlement of Oregon by Americans; indeed, that had been the sole purpose of the Peoria party when it left home. It is improbable that he informed McLoughlin of the military character of his expedition at its beginning; it is also doubtful that McLoughlin had ever heard of Peoria, or of Farnham. A leader without a single follower and anxious to be on his way, Farnham accepted a gift of a suit of clothes from Dr. McLoughlin and a free ticket to the Sandwich Islands, and sailed away from Oregon.

Four other young men who were members of the Peoria Party and spent that winter in the vicinity of Brown's Hole and Fort Hall, were later to make their marks as pioneers of Oregon. They were Joseph Holman, Amos Cook and Francis Fletcher, all of whom wrote accounts of their adventures, and R. L. Kilbourne. Holman, from England, had been a manufacturer of fanning mills; Kilbourne, a restaurant keeper; Fletcher, a butcher; and Cook, a farmer. At least, that is the way Shortess described them, although they were all only about twenty-two years of age when they left Peoria.

Joe Meek and Doc Newell, who were holing up at Fort Crockett with their families, told them it would be impossible to make it through to Oregon that season, so instead of going on to Fort Hall the four young men backtracked to the Yampa and built a log cabin with a big fireplace. They chose a sheltered canyon where their horses could find protection, which should entitle them to some sort of an accolade. Game was plentiful and they shot deer, mountain sheep and rabbits for their present needs, but much of their time was occupied in killing buffalo and jerking the meat for future needs. For a while Holman, the mechanic, worked for the Shoshones, making saddle trees and repairing their old guns, which service they paid for with beaver skins.

At the first sign of spring they returned to Brown's Hole and found Doc Newell about to start to Fort Hall, from where he proposed to go to Oregon. He had been over the trail many times and was confident the trip would not be too hard. Usually, he made the journey to Fort Hall in ten days, but the snow was deeper than he thought, and it was forty-five harrowing days before they reached Fort Hall.

The creeks were frozen over, but the horses would break through. At times the men had to spread their blankets on the snow for the horses to walk on. Men and animals were worn out, and once they were four days without food and finally had to kill and eat Newell's dog. They still had the horses as insurance against starvation, but were reluctant to resort to this last extremity.

They had almost ceased to feel hunger when they came to an Indian camp and bought two dogs for a piece of scarlet cloth. There were enough young cottonwood branches along the creek banks to keep their horses alive, and they plodded on. In a narrow valley they came upon a wildcat living high on the half-starved, defenseless rabbits. They killed some rabbits and the wildcat, the latter furnishing strong and disagreeable meat. When they reached the Portneuf, three days' journey from Fort Hall, they came upon a poor wandering derelict buffalo bull which provided enough meat for them to reach the fort, where they traded their furs for corn and dried salmon, and were again able to subsist.

They probably were not too welcome at Fort Hall, where times were a little tough and Ermatinger had little reason to love anyone from Brown's Hole. The preceding fall Ermatinger had let men from Brown's Hole have some horses to use, since they had lost their own. This kindness had been repaid when men from the same place raided Fort Hall horses. One of the thieves was said to be Thompson, one of the owners of Fort Crockett; another, Bill New, an old associate of Doc Newell. Several others had been with Joe Walker in California and were responsible for the troubles of Hall J. Kelley and Ewing Young when they were accused of being horse thieves. It was Joe Walker, however, who followed the thieves and forced them to return the stolen animals.

The four Peoria men found feed for their horses very scarce at Fort Hall, so they went out on the foothills a few miles from the fort and found excellent grass. They built themselves a sod shanty, intending to remain several weeks until their animals regained their strength. There was a band of friendly Shoshones close by with whom they got along very well.

Then they got word that another party was about to leave for Fort Boise, and the safety-in-numbers urge made them hurry back to Fort Hall and join the group for an uneventful journey. When they reached Fort Boise they were told that Sioux hostiles had carried out a raid against Fort Hall, killed some of the settlers and also the band of friendly Indians who had moved into their abandoned sod shanty as soon as they had moved out of it. "So you see we came just that close to losing our scalps," Amos Cook wrote.

It may be doubted that it was a Sioux raiding party. I know of no other instance when the Sioux raided that far west. Fort Hall was on the main Indian highway long before there was any Oregon Trail, and the tribes passed over it on their way to visit one another. They traveled from the Columbia as far east as Green and Wind rivers, and the region around Fort Hall was supposed to be neutral territory to all tribes except the Blackfeet.

Once as a boy I came across the Blue Mountains in a covered wagon. As we were coming down into the Grand Ronde Valley we passed a large bunch of Umatilla Indians. I shall never forget their horse herd grazing upon a hillside. There must have been a thousand, and they were all colors; white, pintos, roans, sorrels, blacks, bays and buckskins. My father made inquiries, and they told him they were just returning from a trading visit to the Shoshones of Wind River, Wyoming, and those on the Fort Hall Reservation. Indian habits are hard to change. I once knew a half-breed who was said to do a thriving business stealing horses from one reservation and selling them on another, and he seldom returned from a trip empty-handed.

An incident that occurred in Wyeth's day had to do with the Blackfeet. One day a party of Blackfeet appeared near the fort and asked for a parley, and to smoke the pipe of peace. A number of men went out from the fort to smoke with them, including that Godin whose hasty action had precipitated the battle of Pierre's Hole in which Wyeth had participated on his first trip to the mountains.

Perhaps they felt some degree of safety since the leader
of the Blackfeet appeared to be a white man, a fellow called
Bird, sometimes referred to as Jemmy Jock. He had once
worked for Hudson's Bay, had been taken prisoner by the
Blackfeet and become one of them. He had pledged himself
to avenge the death of the Blackfoot chief who had been
killed under a flag of truce at Pierre's Hole on Godin's orders.

As the men sat smoking Bird gave a signal and several
Indians fired a volley into Godin's back. Bird was said to
have been a man of some education, and he proved his
literacy by calmly removing Godin's scalp and then carving
Wyeth's initials, N J W, on the dead man's forehead with
his knife. The Blackfeet were gone before the men at the
fort could rally for a counter attack.

The last four members of the Peoria Party who had
started out so bravely under their banner of OREGON OR
DEATH, having finally arrived at their promised land, became pioneers and rightfully earned their places as founders
of Oregon. Cook, the last survivor, and Fletcher took up a
claim together in Yamhill County, but since there was only
work enough for one Fletcher went to work for wages at
the Lee Mission, while Cook remained alone on the farm.
He has reported that during the summer he saw only two
white men, and did not get to speak to them since they
were passing along the road while he was working in the
field. His only visitors were Indians, who, he says, "would
often come and surround a huge kettle of boiled wheat
which I had prepared for the hogs and, peacefully dipping
it up with their fingers, would eat with evident satisfaction
and relish."

Holman settled in Salem and eventually became a leading citizen of the state, while Kilbourne later went to California, which concludes the odd little odyssey of the Peoria party. Of itself it accomplished little, but some of its members did prove that it was possible to get past Fort Hall. T. J. Farnham helped to make the West better known by his writings and undoubtedly the others helped to encourage more emigrants to come to the Northwest. Oregon simply had to have more Yankee settlers if it was to be held by the United States.

# 17

# THE FORKS OF THE TRAIL

IT WAS NO EASIER GETTING TO California than it was Oregon. Trappers and traders knew the trails but getting there with wagons was a different thing. Joe Walker and Jed Smith and their men had been over the trail across the Great Basin. So had Peter Skene Ogden and so had Caleb Greenwood. In 1841 the Bidwell-Bartleson party made an attempt to get wagons through, cutting a little south of Fort Hall. They had to abandon the vehicles before they made it across the Sierras. Joe Walker, who knew the country as well as anyone, attempted to guide a similar train across the Great Basin, but again the wagons had to be left behind.

Captain Sutter was getting desperate. The Mexican government in California was undergoing an upheaval, and

Sutter had guessed wrong. His safety and that of his colony could only be insured by more American emigrants. The failure of the Bidwell-Bartleson party did not discourage others. In 1843 one that has usually been known as the Stevens-Townsend-Murphy party was being organized, but didn't leave Council Bluffs until the spring of 1844. After a conflict, leadership seems to have fallen on Elisha Stevens, a bachelor traveling alone who had no favor to curry with anyone. It was a successful expedition, arriving in California with its wagons and with two more people than were started with—babies born on the trail.

The first wagon train to reach California over the northern route, the Stevens party numbered only twenty-six men, eight women and seventeen children in eleven wagons. Stevens was a capable leader but he was fortunate to have in his party one of the great mountain men of his time— old Caleb Greenwood, who had been in California as early as 1826 and was undoubtedly the guide on the expedition.

Greenwood, who was to play an important part in the history of Fort Hall, is worthy of considerable attention. When he was eighteen Greenwood killed a sheriff in defense of a Negro slave woman. His father gave him all the money he had and started him out West to begin one of the most fantastic careers among the frontiersmen. He was in St. Louis in 1787, and he says that he first went into the Indian country in 1807. He is believed to have been a member of Manuel Lisa's expedition of that year, and from that time on he was one of the most active of them all.

In 1810 he signed up with Wilson Price Hunt's party, but remained with Hunt no more than two months when he was officially termed a deserter. He signed up with Lisa again and was around the headwaters of the Missouri. During the years 1812–13 he was in the Crow Indian country at Wind River; while there he married a Crow girl named Batchicka and old Greenwood was always proud to claim that "My wife was a Crow." He seems to have been adopted into the tribe, and always maintained that the Crows were the bravest of all Indians. "They don't shoot and run like the skulkin', thievin' Blackfeet varmints. They stand up and fight like men," he maintained.

The life of Caleb and Batchicka is one of the great romances in the annals of the West. They raised a family of five sons and two daughters. Sometime in the mid-1830s, Greenwood found himself going blind. Batchicka believed that he might be cured in St. Louis, and against the advice of her husband she started out with him and all her children except Joseph, her eldest son, on a perilous journey of more than a thousand miles through hostile Sioux and Arickara country. Greenwood, the White Chief of the Crows, was nearing seventy and half blind and so the burden of the trip fell on Batchicka.

They traveled as much as possible in early morning and late evening but finally they were spotted by a Sioux war party, who pulled their boat in to shore. Greenwood could do nothing except tell his wife to let them have everything, which she did except for a kettle of meat she had hidden under her skirt to stave off the hunger of her younger children. The hostiles were about to leave when a brave saw the kettle of meat and grabbed for it with a yell. Determined not to lose that which might save the lives of her children, Batchicka grabbed an oar and knocked the brave overboard. When he recovered his senses he said she was a "heap brave squaw." In admiration of her pluck the Sioux returned everything they had stolen.

The Greenwoods made their way to St. Louis and Caleb eventually got his sight back. They hung around St. Louis for a while, but Batchicka sickened and died and Greenwood was left with six children, including a seven-month-old daughter, Sarah Mojave. When Caleb signed on with the Stevens party at the age of eighty, he had his family with him, including six-year-old Sarah Mojave.

Caleb Greenwood's age had never seemed to bother him. Historians speak of the Ashley party as being composed of young men who could endure the hardships, but old Greenwood was with them and he held up his end; indeed, he may have been one of the most valuable members of the party, for on the frontier experience counted.

He was still Old Greenwood when he helped take the first wagon train into California. Looking for "a nigher route" from South Pass to Fort Hall, he led the wagons over a cut-off which has since been known as the Sublette Cut-off, though some call it by its rightful name, Greenwood's Cut-off.

When the Stevens-Townsend-Murphy party arrived at Fort Hall, not enough wagons had gone on to Oregon to make a clearly defined road. Hudson's Bay had by no means given up trying to discourage emigration there, but there was no wagon road from there to California so their efforts had to be directed at persuading the emigrants to turn back, or to leave their wagons at Fort Hall, which many of them did.

The one thing Old Greenwood never lacked was confidence. He told the emigrants he had been over the country eighteen years before and knew a safe, easy route. That route ran from Fort Hall to Raft River, passed through the City of Rocks, went down Goose Creek, crossed to Bishop Creek and down that stream to the Humboldt and to Humboldt Sink, and over the Sierras to Sutter's Fort.

"Just when and under what circumstances Greenwood first traveled that route will never be known; the important fact to remember is that he led his wagon train over the only safe and logical route between Fort Hall and Fort Sutter, and that road—the Greenwood Road—was followed by all subsequent travelers, with few exceptions, until the coming of the Iron Horse," says Charles Kelly in his book, *Old Greenwood.*

Greenwood's contract as pilot had expired at Fort Hall, but he and his family went along and there would be no reason to believe that his knowledge and experience went unheeded. He was particularly useful in communicating with the Indians along the way—the despised Piutes and Diggers, who had hated the whites ever since the passage of Joe Walker. In later years emigrants amused themselves by shooting Indians the way some people shot rabbits.

Stevens's party had its share of hardship and trouble. Greenwood naturally knew of no wagon road, since there was none, but it was he who talked with Chief Truckee, father of Chief Winnemucca and grandfather of Sarah Winnemucca Hopkins, the educated Indian girl whose writings furnish much information about the time and the place. Truckee's name, incidentally, was bestowed upon him by members of this wagon train because he was a friendly old man who answered "Truckee" to questions which required an answer equivalent to "All right," or "Okay."

It was Truckee who advised them to follow up Truckee River to where a pass over the mountains might be found. So it was that the party arrived at the foot of what later has been called Donner's Pass two full years before the ill-fated Donner party arrived there.

The story of the Donner party is too well known to be related here, but the Stevens party experienced practically the same dangers and difficulties. The difference was that, in Elisha Stevens, a man with a big hooked nose and a peaked head, they had a capable leader—and that they had Old Greenwood.

One has only to drive along the modern highway over Donner's Pass today to realize how impassable it must have looked to those early emigrants. Stevens divided his party. Some of them took a longer route without wagons to try to reach Sutter's Fort and get help. Five wagons were left at Donner's Lake, and the other six were dismantled and drawn to the top of the pass with ropes. They became snow-bound on the Yuba, but managed to tough it out. Here Elizabeth Yuba Murphy was born, and she survived, just as did Helen Independence Miller, who had been born back at Independence Rock. Not a single person on the train was lost, though it was a near thing with young Moses Schallenberger.

Three young men had been left to guard the five wagons back at the lake. Here they built a cabin which was later used by some members of the Donner party. When the snow got up over the roof the young men decided to try to make it through on foot. When they reached the pass Moses Schallenberger, sick and given out, decided to go back to the cabin; and he was soon on the verge of starvation. The snow was ten feet deep, but he found some traps and managed to catch a coyote which he lived on for three days. Then he had better luck and caught a couple of foxes. From then on he caught both coyotes and foxes, eating the foxes, but hanging up the carcasses of the coyotes for an emergency.

His cabin was buried under snow, but he had two of Dr. Townsend's books to read: Byron's *Poems* and *The Letters of Lord Chesterfield*. Years later he wrote: "My life was more miserable than I can describe."

Dennis Martin, a member of the main party who had learned the use of snowshoes in Canada, had been caught in a revolution and gone on to Los Angeles. When he returned and learned that young Schallenberger had been left behind he courageously set out to rescue him, and so not a single life was lost. The six who had gone on ahead were the first white people ever to see Lake Tahoe.

It was an heroic venture, but had it not been for Caleb Greenwood and Johnnie Grant, the Hudson's Bay factor at Fort Hall, it is safe to say the party would have gone on to Oregon and had a much more comfortable journey.

Captain Sutter decided that Old Greenwood was just the man he was looking for and the next year Greenwood and his three sons returned to Fort Hall to pick up more wagon trains. There is no proof that Greenwood was in Sutter's employ, and he may have counted on getting his pay by guiding the wagon trains, yet Sutter authorized him to tell the emigrants that the Captain's men would meet them on the east side of the Sierras with men, mules and supplies. We have proof of this in the history of the Bonney party, which we will get to later.

Though Greenwood was well into his eighties he remained active. The old man established himself at Fort Hall in the summer while he was not guiding wagon trains, and in the winter he took to the mountains. That the Greenwood Road was traveled by thousands of emigrants during the next few years is beyond question. In 1850, the peak year after the gold rush, more than 50,000 people passed over this road. In fact, thousands of emigrants continued to use it until the completion of the railroad in 1869.

Among others who hoped to divert emigration at Fort Hall was Lansford W. Hastings, who is best remembered as the man who directed the Donner party to by-pass Fort Hall and go around the south end of Salt Lake over the murderous Hastings Cut-off which led to the tragedy of that party.

Another old mountaineer, James Clyman, had guided a party to California in 1844, and the spring of 1846 saw Old Greenwood, Hastings and Clyman all crossing the Sierras on their way to Fort Hall, two of them with the expressed purpose of diverting emigration from Oregon to California. Clyman was taking a party of disillusioned emigrants out of California, but no doubt his services were available to take emigrants in the other direction if the pay was right. Old Greenwood was by far the most active. He and Johnnie Grant at Fort Hall had much in common. Both were real mountain men; they were holdovers from the fur era, and both were married to Indian women.

The Bonney party seems to have been the next group that Greenwood guided after the Stevens train. Benjamin F. Bonney was born November 28, 1838, in Fulton County, Illinois. There was so much fever and ague there that his family decided to move to Oregon in 1845. The elder Bonney was influenced to go to the Willamette Valley because he was an inveterate fisherman and he had heard that the fishing there was mighty good. The family, which included Bonney and his wife and their eight children, seven-year-old Benjamin among them, started for the Willamette Valley April 2, 1845. This party also included Benjamin's uncle, Truman Bonney and his family.

At Independence they joined Barlow's wagon train of 300 people, headed for the same destination under command of Samuel K. Barlow, one of the leaders of the 1845 migration. Barlow was the man who built the Barlow Cutoff around Mt. Hood that same year, and was a leader in the development of Oregon.

Although only a child of seven, Benjamin Bonney seems to have retained a vivid recollection of Old Greenwood. He says: "At Fort Hall we were met by an old man named Caleb Greenwood and his three sons, John was 22, Britain 18, and Sam 16. Caleb Greenwood, who originally hailed from Nova Scotia, was an old mountain man and was said to be over eighty years old. He had been a scout and a trapper and had married a squaw, his sons being half-breeds. *He was employed by Captain Sutter to come to Fort Hall to divert the Oregon bound emigrants to California.* [Italics added.] Greenwood was a very picturesque old man. He was dressed in buckskin and had a long heavy beard and used very picturesque language.

"He called the Oregon emigrants together the first evening they were in Fort Hall and made a talk. He said the road to Oregon was dangerous because of the Indians. He told us that while no emigrants had as yet gone to Cali-

fornia there was an easy grade, and crossing the mountains
would not be difficult."

Greenwood had been with the Stevens party two years
before, so why did he say that no emigrants had crossed?
There are two possible reasons. One is that Benjamin Bonney's memory was defective. The other is that had Greenwood told of being with the Stevens party he might have
had to answer embarrassing questions when the Bonney
party reached Donner's Pass.

Continuing, Benjamin Bonney says: "He said that
Captain Sutter would have ten Californians to meet the
emigrants who would go, and that Sutter would supply
them with plenty of potatoes, coffee and dried beef. He
also said he would help the emigrants over the mountains
with their wagons, and that to every head of a family who
would settle near Sutter's Fort Captain Sutter would give
six sections of land of his Spanish land grant.

"After Greenwood had spoken the men of our party
held a pow-wow which lasted nearly all night. Some wanted
to go to California while others were against it. Barlow,
who had charge of the train, said that he forbid any man
from leaving the train and going to California. He told us
we did not know what we were going into, and that there
was great uncertainty about the land titles in California,
and that we were Americans and should not go to a country under another flag. The meeting nearly broke up in a
mutiny. Barlow finally appealed to the men to go to Oregon and make Oregon an American territory, and not waste
their time going to California to help promote Sutter's land
schemes.

"Next morning old Caleb Greenwood with his boys

stepped to one side and said, 'All you who want to go to California drive out from the main train and follow me. You will find that there are no Indians to kill you, the roads are better, and you will be allowed to take up more land than in Oregon. The climate is better, there is plenty of hunting and fishing.'

"My father, Jarvis Bonney, was the first one of the Oregon party to pull out of the Oregon train and head south with Caleb Greenwood. My uncle, Truman Bonney, followed my father, then came the Sam Kinneys of Texas, then came Dodson and then a widow woman named Tetters, and many others. There were eight wagons in all that rolled out from the main train to go to California with Caleb Greenwood.

"After driving southward for three days with Caleb Greenwood, he left us to go back to Fort Hall to get other emigrants to change their route to California. He left his three boys with us to guide us to Sutter's Fort. Sam, the youngest of the three, was the best pilot, though all three of them knew the country as well as a city man knows his own back yard."

Bonney digresses at this point to tell some of the adventures of the trail, most of which have been corroborated from other sources. Although this was on the fringe of the buffalo country he tells of the men corralling their oxen to keep them from stampeding with the buffalo.

Other adventures were far less pleasant. "One day when John Greenwood was acting as pilot an Indian suddenly raised up from the sagebrush, frightening John's horse. . . . It nearly unseated him. Some of the young men laughed. This made John Greenwood furious. . . . John took his gun from in front of his saddle and pointed it at the Indian. The Indian threw up his hands. The young men with John remonstrated with him and told him the Indian had meant no harm and not to shoot. One of the young men called to the Indian to run. The Indian obeyed and started to run at full speed. This was too much for John, who drew a quick bead and fired, shooting him through the back. . . .

"The men on horseback waited there until the others rode up, but John rode on as fast as he could go. My uncle, Truman Bonney, who was a doctor, examined the Indian, and said he had been shot through the lungs and that it was a fatal wound.

"My mother took a quilt from our wagon and laid the dying Indian on it; she also brought him a drink of water but he shook his head and refused to drink. We drove on a mile or so and just about dusk Caleb Greenwood and his son Sam who were escorting some other emigrants rode into our camp. They had come across the Indian who was still living. Caleb told his son Sam to shoot the Indian through the head to put him out of his misery, which he did, and they dug a hole in the sand and buried him. When Caleb Greenwood came into our camp he said, 'The man who killed that Indian must die.' He thought Kinney had killed him. My father said, 'Your son John shot him.' Greenwood told the men of the party to meet and state the full facts. When he found that John had not shot in self-defense but had shot the Indian wantonly, he said: 'I will act as judge of this trial. I order that the murderer of the Indian be killed.' He told the men of the party to shoot John on sight as they would a wild animal."

Old Greenwood's reaction was perfectly natural. He had already had trouble restraining his son who, as a Crow warrior, was anxious to take as many scalps as he could, and Old Greenwood wanted his trail to be as safe from Indian trouble as possible.

Knowing better than to face his father, John kept on going, but by the time they reached California tempers had cooled, and we read of John being with his father again, and participating in a war against Indians in California. John was later killed by a Mexican in a card game in southern California.

Greenwood had reason to suspect the Texan, Sam Kinney, who had large ideas of capturing as many Indians as he could and taking them back to Texas to sell as slaves. He did indeed capture one and made a slave of the poor fellow until some others of the train managed to help the Indian escape.

"At the foot of the Sierras," writes Benjamin Bonney, "we were met by ten Mexicans with a pack train consisting of flour, potatoes, dried beef and other provisions. We camped at the foot of the mountains for several days, waiting for other emigrants who had turned off at Fort Hall."

When they reached Donner's Pass, a full year ahead of the Donner party, they took their wagons apart and hoisted them up to the rim by ropes. It required four days. Bonney relates that while going down the other side some of the children came back with little gold nuggets varying in size from a grain of wheat to that of a pea. If true, this discovery of gold was three years ahead of Marshall's at Sutter's Fort. The men of the party recognized it for what it was, and warned the children not to tell anybody.

To get on with the narrative: "When we arrived at the fort Captain Sutter made us heartily welcome. He told my father the fort would accommodate twelve families, and the first twelve families joining his colony would be furnished quarters there. He furnished us quarters in the fort and also gave us plenty of fresh beef, potatoes, onions, coffee and sugar. He gave work to all men who cared to work. So many emigrants were crowded into the fort that winter that there was a good deal of sickness. In those days it was called mountain fever; now it is called typhoid. A large number of the natives died of this, and some of the emigrants, mostly children. Among those who died was Dr. Gilden. He was the one who was going back the next spring with my father to get rich picking up gold nuggets at our old camping place."

Bonney devoted some pages to trouble with the ever-changing Mexican authorities who questioned the legality of foreigners coming to California without passports. Castro and Castillero came north to question the emigrants as to their intentions. The emigrants promised that if allowed to stay until spring they would go away peacefully.

Bonney speaks of Sutter's plan to get the American settlers to grow wheat for him to sell to the Russian government at Sitka and other parts of Alaska to be paid for with fur. "By this time the Russian government had given up their settlements in California; the Hudson's Bay Company was retiring from Oregon to British Columbia. Sutter's plan would probably have worked if gold had not been found in California. Those Americans who were not willing to renounce their native country were required to move in the spring. Among the Americans were some single men who were unwilling to take the oath of allegiance to Mexico and wanted to stay in California; so they took to the hills and stayed anyway."

Jarvis Bonney and his family were among those who left, driving, Benjamin says, 250 miles to where General Frémont was camped. Captain Sutter furnished each departing family with a fat beef animal, and sent along ten Mexicans to drive their loose stock. They arrived in Oregon City, June 16, 1846. Theirs had been quite a detour.

Old Greenwood and his boys made the trip back to Fort Hall, the Forks of the Trail, a number of times. Britain played a prominent part in the rescue of the Donner party. Caleb's youngest son was named Governor Boggs; another son was called Crockett. After his trail days were over Caleb fought Indians in California for a while and finally settled down, as much as such a man could settle down, near Coloma. "Eighty-three years is a long time to live," Old Greenwood said once, but he lived to be past ninety. He died near a cabin near Oroville, attended only by his sixteen-year-old son James. He refused to stay in the cabin and died in the open. His coffin was made from two sections of the bark of a tree.

Old Greenwood did everything he could to divert emigration from Oregon at Fort Hall, and during the few years he was around there he probably was the most effective of them all in turning the emigrants aside. One of the myths about the mountain men is that they were silent and taciturn. Some of them may have been but others, like Old Greenwood and Jim Bridger, had the gift of gab. This, combined with their great knowledge, made them effective propagandists.

For years Hudson's Bay had tried valiantly to keep Americans out of Oregon. Fort Hall was the place to stop or slow down the flood, but the only years in which the campaign was really effective were in Old Greenwood's time, from 1843 to 1847, and even as many emigrants went on to Oregon as turned aside. Fort Hall was where the pilgrims stopped to take the long look. Dr. John McLoughlin and Captain John Sutter were alike in that they were two of the greatest, yet most tragic figures of the Old West. Could they have halted emigration to Oregon at Fort Hall, as they both tried to do, their destinies and that of the American West would have been changed considerably.

That most California traffic was by way of Fort Hall is attested by Henry William Bigler, a veteran of the Mormon Battalion which marched from Council Bluffs, Iowa, to San Diego in 1846–47, while serving in the Mexican War. Bigler was present at Marshall's discovery of gold on the south fork of American River, January 24, 1848, and left the most authentic account of that historic event (see *Bigler's Chronicle of the West*, by Erwin G. Gudde, published in 1962).

After being mustered out of the Mormon Battalion, Bigler and other Saints went to work for Captain Sutter. Bigler, a modest and thoroughly reliable man who kept a journal, prospected for gold a short time with some success, but he and his companions were ordered to return to Salt Lake City, which the main body of the church had reached the previous year. They set out from Pleasant Valley, eight miles southeast of Placerville, July 3, 1848, and were the first to build a wagon road over the Sierras from Placerville to Carson Valley, a most difficult feat, the more so in that they were constantly being bothered by Indians.

August 27, while laying by for rest and prayer after having crossed the divide and the sink of the Humboldt, they met Captain Samuel P. Hensley and a company of ten. Captain Hensley, in Sutter's employ, was returning from Washington, D.C. Hensley had been unsuccessful in trying to follow the Hastings Cut-off, but claimed to have found a shorter route to Salt Lake without going by Fort Hall, the route Bigler and his party had intended to take.

On August 30 they met a larger train of forty-eight wagons under Captain Joseph B. Chiles which had come by way of Fort Hall, though Bigler did not know this and wasted considerable time trying to follow his tracks, thinking he had a shorter route. They finally found Hensley's trail south and west of Fort Hall, and followed it to Salt Lake City by way of Malade River.

Captain Chiles had gone to California with the Bidwell-Bartleson party in 1841, and was thoroughly familiar with the country. He had gone east with Commodore Stockton in 1847, and was returning with this party of emigrants. That he came by Fort Hall is evidence enough that it was still on the most important highway to California.

# 18

# INDIAN TROUBLE

THE FUTURE OF OREGON
might have been far different had Johnnie Grant won his
argument with Marcus Whitman at Fort Hall in 1843.
Grant knew that if Whitman came back with a big wagon
train others would follow, and the country would be held
by that nation which could bring in the most settlers. Whitman refused to be discouraged, and the wagons came
through.

Joe Meek, Doc Newell and Elijah White had brought
a few wagons over the Blue Mountains, but Whitman's
was the first really important movement. Great Britain had
long since reconciled itself to losing the country south of
the Columbia, but now Whitman was taking his people
north of the boundary England hoped to hold. Johnnie
Grant, undoubtedly acting on orders from Fort Vancouver,

went on trying to send the settlers to California but he never was able to stem the main tide. The British were sending in a few settlers to Spokane and some to Puget Sound, but such efforts were dwarfed by the Walla Walla invasion.

Marcus Whitman knew what he was doing. He made friends with Indians and put them to work. He built mills and proved that farming could be successful. Most of the emigrants were going on to the Willamette, but some of them were crossing the Columbia.

Hudson's Bay did as it always had done: it waited. Sooner or later Dr. Whitman would stub his toe. If he lost control of the Indians he was finished. Meanwhile, it was Whitman, not Pierre Pambrun, who was selling goods to the emigrants.

The doctor was practicing his profession and healing the Indians, but some of them were bound to die and it was redskin nature to blame the medicine man. Word began to go around that Dr. Whitman was there to kill the Indians rather than to help them. A personal tragedy began to undermine the Indians' faith. The Whitmans had a little three-year-old daughter who was the pride and pet of Waiilatpu, Indians as well as whites. When she was accidentally drowned Whitman's influence began to wane. The killing of Yellow Serpent's son, Elijah, at Sutter's Fort had already angered some of the Cayuses.

Up in the Blue Mountains lived Tom Hill, a Delaware Indian who was a graduate of Dartmouth. We do not know the reason for his implacable hatred of the Americans but it was he, more than any other, who was spreading the stories that Dr. Whitman was poisoning the Indians.

Among the workers at Waiilatpu was a Montreal half-breed named Joe Lewis, who had once been an employee of Hudson's Bay. Lewis added his voice to that of Delaware Tom Hill. In the tragedy of 1847 that resulted in the massacre of Marcus and Narcissa Whitman and many others, Joe Lewis was an active participant.

Was this a last dying gasp of Hudson's Bay's attempt to hold Oregon, or was the massacre the result of other causes?

It seems clear now that Hudson's Bay must be acquitted. The issue had been settled the year before, so the company had nothing to gain, but the accusation was common for many years to come. It was, say the traducers, the result of previous years of company policy, and they lay the blame on Dr. John McLoughlin, that kindly man who had never turned an American away in distress, and who before the massacre had made application for United States citizenship.

The accusers were the missionaries who had long raged against Hudson's Bay and against the Catholic missionaries whom they claimed were in the service of the company, although they later denied that religious jealousies had anything to do with the massacre. In his book, *How Marcus Whitman Saved Oregon*, Oliver W. Nixon, a strong partisan of the Protestant missionaries, says:

"For nearly half a century, as we have seen in the history of Oregon, the Indians and the Hudson's Bay Company had been working harmoniously together. It was a case in which civilization had accommodated itself to the desires of savage life. The Company plainly showed the Indians that they did not wish their lands, or to deprive them of their homes. It only wanted their labor, and in return it would pay the Indians in many luxuries and comforts. The Indians were averse to manual labor, and the great Company had not seen fit to encourage it. They did not desire to see them plant or sow, raise cattle, or build houses for themselves and their families. That would directly interfere with their work as fur gatherers, and break in upon the source of wealth to the Company. To keep them at the steel trap and in the chase was the aim of the Hudson Bay policy, and such was congenial to the Indian, and just what he desired.

"The Jesuit Priests who were attached to the Hudson Bay Company, seconded the interest of the Company and attempted to teach religion to the Indian and still leave him a savage. Upon the coming of the Protestant Missionaries, the Indians welcomed them and expressed great delight at the prospect of being taught. They gave their choice locations to the Missions, and most solemn promise to co-operate in the work. But neither they nor their fathers had used the hoe or the plow, or built permanent homes in which to live. They were by nature opposed to manual labor. Squaws were made to do all the work, while the men hunted and did the fighting. The missionaries could see little hope of Christianizing them unless they could induce them to adopt civilized customs. . . .

"It was right there that the breach began to widen. They were willing to accept a religion which did not interfere with savage customs, which had become a part of their lives. It was the custom of the Hudson Bay Company, by giving modest bribes, to win over any unruly chief. It was the best way to hold power; but the missionaries held the tribes which they served up to a higher standard of morals."

Dr. Nixon goes on to relate that the Cayuse Indians, the strongest tribe around Waiilatpu, had made a foray upon a weaker tribe and levied on their stock in payment for some imaginary debt and were reprimanded by Dr. Whitman. "The Indians grew very angry in being thus reminded of their sins. . . . It was the boast of English authors that 'The English got along with Indians much better than Americans.' This seems to be true, and it comes from the fact that they did not antagonize savage customs. As long as their savage subjects filled the treasury of the Hudson Bay Company they cared little for aught else. As a matter of policy and self defense, they treated them honestly and fairly in all business transactions. They were in full sympathy with the Indians in their demand to keep out white immigration, and keep the entire land for fur-bearing animals and savage life."

With a few notable exceptions, such as Marcus Whitman, Henry Spalding and Jason and Daniel Lee, the attitude of the Protestant missionaries was one of arrogance and self-righteousness. Hudson's Bay treated the Indians as people; the missionaries treated them as savages. One group got along with them, the other did not. The evidence indicates that the Americans were more interested in taking the Indians' land than they were in saving their souls. It can even be questioned that the Missionary Boards back in Boston, which had reprimanded Dr. Whitman and broken Jason Lee's heart by dismissing him after years of devoted service, knew better what was good for the Indians than did John McLoughlin, who had married an Indian woman and lived among Indians most of his life. Even at the time of the Whitman Massacre, the so-called Missionary Party of the Willamette was striving by every devious means at its command to deprive McLoughlin of the lands that were honestly his.

It was McLoughlin who warned Whitman of the treachery of the Cayuses at the beginning, and who just before the massacre pleaded with him to leave before it was too late. And it was a Hudson's Bay man, Peter Skene Ogden, who at the risk of his own life went among the Indians after the massacre, and purchased the freedom of the captive women and children with $500 of company money. Only a pretty biased mind could claim that this was the act of a guilty conscience.

It took real courage for Ogden to undertake his mission of mercy, for thirteen white people, men, women and children, including beautiful Narcissa Whitman, still lay unburied at Waiilatpu, and the excited Indians were still fearful of reprisals. On his side, Ogden had little except a record of fair dealing and the fact that his wife was an Indian woman. No Protestant missionary from the Willamette volunteered to go with him.

The short, chunky trader could not dominate the tall, straight warriors by his mere presence. One of the captives he proposed to liberate was a young white woman who had become the wife of Five Crows, son of the chief who had led the massacre, and Five Crows was good to the woman. Even the factor at Walla Walla was afraid to move. Ogden's speech to the Indians has been reported thus:

"Friends and relations, I regret that all the chiefs are not here. Repeat to them what I say. We have been among you for thirty years without shedding blood. We are traders, and of a different nation from the Americans. But recollect: we do not supply you with ammunition to kill the Americans. They are the same color as ourselves, speak the same language, are children under the same God. Their cruel fate causes our hearts to bleed. Besides this wholesale butchery, have you not robbed the Americans passing peacefully through your country and insulted their women? You tell me your young men did this without your knowledge. Why do we make you chiefs if you have no control over your young men? You are unworthy of the name of chief. Do not deceive yourselves. If the Americans begin war, war will not end until every one of you is cut off from the face of the earth. Your people have died. So have others. Dr. Whitman did not poison them. It is merely advice that I give you. I promise you nothing. We have nothing to do with your quarrels. On my return, if you wish it, I will see what can be done for you. I do not promise to prevent war. Deliver me the captives. I will pay a ransom. That is all."

In answer, Tiloukaikt, the alleged leader, said, "They are our brothers. They bury their dead along with ours. Chief, your words are weighty, your hairs are gray. We have known you for a long time. I cannot keep the families back. I make them over to you, which I would not do to another man younger than yourself."

The captives there were ransomed, but Ogden still had to wait for some who had taken refuge with the Nez Percés at Lapwai. On New Year's morning of 1848 Cayuse warriors who had heard, rightly, that the whites were marching from Fort Vancouver, appeared on the other side of the river. Ogden took to his boats through hostile territory, and met the advance guard of the Oregon volunteers at The Dalles.

He continued on to Fort Vancouver and James Douglas sent this message to the settlement at Willamette Falls: "Mr. Ogden has this moment arrived with three boats from Walla Walla, and I rejoice to say he has brought down all the women and children from Waiilatpu, and Mr. and Mrs. Spalding. Mr. Ogden will visit the Falls on Monday [the next day]."

Ogden, the veteran of Fort Hall and a hundred other trading posts, had done his job well, and none too soon, for the Cayuse War was already beginning, and the captives would surely have been killed had Ogden not been able to rescue them. Governor Abernathy was marching from the provisional capital at Champoeg with nearly a thousand men. Old Joe Meek, whose daughter had perished at Waiilatpu, was already on his way to Washington to demand help.

On the other side, the tribes were gathering. Even "Old Joseph," father of the Nez Percé chief American generals were one day to call "the Indian Napoleon," was gathering his warriors. The worst Indian war in the history of the Northwest was in the making.

We still are not sure of its precise causes. It could have been primarily the fear of the Indians that the Americans intended to take their lands. They were horse-rich and in the Palouse country they owned some of the finest grazing land in the world. Whitman was showing that it could be broken up and farmed successfully, introducing an entirely new and different kind of life from that the Indians had known. More and more settlers were getting past Fort Hall. This meant more to them than preaching.

No doubt many of those Indians were like an old Shoshone named Shinite I once knew who grew tired of endless donations. Said he, "Me Jesus man. But whatta matta that man Jesus—him all time broke?"

More emigrants had come in 1844–45–46, and they found the going as rough as Johnnie Grant had told them it would be. Dr. Whitman posted Indians in the hills to light fires to guide them in. The end of October, 1844, found some 500 people still in the mountains. Hearing of their distress, Dr. McLoughlin, who the Americans believed was hell-bent to keep them out of Oregon, sent provisions and clothing and boats to help them down the Columbia. Ragged and weary and, we may presume, grateful men piled their household goods on the Hudson's Bay *bateaux* and were safely landed on the Willamette. The good governor knew they were only the vanguard of what would be thousands.

One fatherless and motherless family of seven children had been left with the Whitmans, including a baby only five months old. They were taken in, although Marcus and Narcissa already had four adopted children. No more than McLoughlin could the Whitmans refuse aid to the needy.

We may be getting down to the nub of our question. People of the frontier were in the habit of helping those in distress. To Sir George Simpson and the directors of Hudson's Bay in London, and to the American Missionary Board back in Boston, it was an abstract matter and the sufferings of people they never saw meant little compared to the busi-

nesses in which they were engaged. The people of influence
on both sides were mostly absentees, and had no idea how
to get along with either Indians or the independent American farmers.

The Missionary Board wanted Whitman to save more
souls than the Jesuits. As for Sir George, he had never wholly
approved of the way Governor McLoughlin catered to the
Americans. He had never liked the man, and he felt that
McLoughlin's humanitarianism was weakening the company.

Sir George believed in the system which so aroused
the sarcasm of Alexander Ross, who told how the employees
of the company were seated at table: the bourgeois at the
top, the clerks in the center, and the ordinary citizens at
the bottom. Strict protocol was observed and none dared
sit until the head man himself was seated. At his signal,
the lower orders left the table, and only people of importance remained.

Seeing England threatened with the loss of Oregon,
Simpson blamed McLoughlin. He sent out Lieutenants
Warre and Vavasout of the Royal Engineers, ostensibly to
strengthen the defenses of Fort Vancouver, but privately
he told them, "Watch the Doctor." Unknown to Mc-
Loughlin a secret report unfavorable to him was sent to
London, and again he was called back to explain his con-
duct.

The pressure became so great that in 1846 McLoughlin
severed his connection with Hudson's Bay, giving up a $12,-
000 annual salary, repaired to his home at Oregon City on
the Willamette and announced his intention to become
an American citizen. The only thing his missionary-dom-

inated American neighbors asked was that he give up all his property.

From this it might be deduced that Hudson's Bay could have inspired the Indians against the American settlers, but the deduction would be wrong. Hudson's Bay lived according to tradition, and part of that tradition was to keep the Indians peaceable. They were not so dull that they didn't know an Indian uprising could harm them as much, or more, than anyone else. They never hesitated to use their economic strength or their power of persuasion—even McLoughlin did that—but it was too much their rigid policy to keep the Indians under control for them ever to have incited them against either the emigrants or the missionaries.

Alexander Ross relates that on one of his expeditions he had a group of troublesome Iroquois. They were, he says, great ones to sing hymns, and when they sang loudest he knew they were up to mischief. The American missionaries, on the other hand, were accustomed to take piety at face value. Dr. Whitman himself may have been deceived in this way, for among his murderers were some of his most ardent disciples.

Whitman was the recognized leader of the people who threatened to take the land from the Indians, or at least in Indian eyes he was. They were superstitious and suspicious, and when their head men began to charge that the doctor was poisoning them the massacre was the inevitable result. But the people who hated Dr. McLoughlin and Hudson's Bay were quick to lay responsibilities for the crime on their doorstep.

In 1846 the issue of sovereignty over Oregon was settled, and on August 14, 1848, Oregon became a United

States Territory. It embraced all the country from the Pacific Ocean to the Rocky Mountains, and from the 42nd to the 49th parallels. In 1853 it was reduced to the present boundaries of the State of Oregon when the rest of the original area was organized as the Territory of Washington. From this latter was created the Territory of Idaho, in 1863.

First to take office in Oregon were General Joseph Lane of Indiana as Governor and Joseph L. Meek as United States Marshal. They arrived in Oregon City by boat and proclaimed the territorial government March 3, 1849, the day before President Polk went out of office. Joe Meek, the old mountain man, had gone to Washington after the Whitman Massacre to serve as self-styled "Envoy extraordinary and minister plenipotentiary from the Republic of Oregon to the Court of the United States."

The question of sovereignty had been resolved with comparative ease after the long struggle, but the discovery of gold in California in 1848 altered things. Within a few months two-thirds of the population of Oregon had stampeded to join the gold rush, but it was still a boon to the new territory. Many returned with fortunes in gold that was badly needed in the new country, but more importantly it opened up a market for Oregon's lumber, wheat and flour and other food supplies. The prosperity of Oregon seemed almost assured.

# 19

# HUDSON'S BAY IN RETREAT

THE CAYUSE WAR HAD NOT
ended the Indian trouble. Rather, it had started a smolder-
ing fire all through the Northwest, ready at any moment to
break out in a blaze. Few Indians were so dull as not to
realize that the white men intended to take their lands and
put an end to their way of life.

The Bannacks had always been a warlike people, though
they operated more in small bands than as a tribe, but now
even the peaceful Shoshones were getting stirred up enough
for them to join the Bannacks in occasional forays. The
Plains Indians were in revolt, and the tribes in the Snake
River Valley seethed.

Wagon trains continued to roll to Oregon amid increasing dangers. Some of them still used the old road south
of the river, but others crossed the Snake at Ferry Butte,

some ten miles from Fort Hall, and struck out across the lava beds where there was less danger from Indian attacks. Old Greenwood and Johnnie Grant had not lied about the dangers the emigrants would encounter between Fort Hall and the foot of the Blue Mountains. Increasing Indian attacks caused more and more of the emigrants to turn south over the California Trail. At Winnemucca on the Humboldt, many of them swung northwest again to reach Oregon, but it was a long and tedious detour.

In 1849 General Harney sent a Rifle Regiment under Colonel Howe to Fort Hall. The soldiers camped a few miles away at Cantonment Loring, and for a number of years it became more of a military post than a trading one. Camp Reed was established at Salmon Falls; Camp Wallace, on Camas Prairie. Lieutenant C. H. Walker guarded the territory east of the Three Buttes. It was not a hurry-up war but a guerrilla campaign that lasted for years.

As Hudson's Bay found itself under an alien and somewhat unfriendly government it began to lose its influence over the Indians. Its first really serious trouble with them was the Umatilla War of 1855. Living on the Columbia, this tribe had always been troublesome in demanding tribute. Of the old-timers who knew how to get along with the Indians, only Peter Skene Ogden was left. McLoughlin was in retirement, Tom McKay was dead of consumption, and McTavish, the new factor at Fort Vancouver, was inexperienced.

In October of 1855 Indian Agent Olney ordered Sinclair, the company's agent at Fort Walla Walla, to abandon the post. Sinclair threw a large amount of powder and ball into the river, for which Olney gave him a receipt.

Two Hudson's Bay men, Boisclere and Desjardins, were killed between Walla Walla and Fort Hall and McTavish threw in the towel. Fort Boise was the next to be closed, and the Indians were angry because of the friendship between the company's agents and Major Haller and his American troops.

Fort Hall was left alone, unprotected, and the fur business could no longer be conducted on the former grand plan, so Peter Skene Ogden was ordered to go back there and close it down. Thirty years before, the old man had trapped around Fort Hall in complete safety; now when he did not return on schedule his friends feared for his life. Colonel Shaw had just defeated the Shoshones in the Grande Rond Valley, and it was feared Ogden had encountered the hostiles on their retreat. Had he done so, it is probable that he would have talked his way out of it, but he didn't meet them.

It must have been a tough assignment for the old field marshal of the Hudson's Bay Company to close the post. He had been there nearly ten years before the fort was built, and he had known all the mountain men who had been associated with it. They numbered such as Donald McKenzie, Tom McKay, Francis Ermatinger, Johnnie Grant, Nathaniel Wyeth, Captain Bonneville, and all his great trade rivals, the Sublettes, Bridger, Kit Carson, Joe Meek, Doc Newell and the rest. For him it was the end of an era, a glorious and adventurous one, and he must have felt that he had outlived his time.

Some of the stuff from Fort Hall had been removed to the Flathead post, north of Missoula, Montana, in 1855.

Now in 1856 Ogden sent as much of the remainder as he could to the same place, but it was estimated that $37,000 worth of goods was left behind, abandoned.

It was not yet the end of the old fort. Young Johnnie Grant and Joseph Pattee continued to operate there for some years as agents for the American Fur Company: there were still a great many beaver in the streams, though the trading was mostly local. The great days of the fur business were gone but it was hard for the old-timers to give it up. Even Nathaniel Wyeth, according to David Lavender in his great book, *Bent's Fort*, made overtures to the Bent brothers to go into partnership with them east of the Rockies. They treated him well, set him down at a table with fine linen, but his offer was refused.

A one-time resident of Fort Hall, Miles Goodyear, must not be overlooked. As a sixteen-year-old boy he had started to Oregon with Marcus Whitman, but had left Whitman at Fort Hall to raise vegetables for the fort. The first man to farm in what is now Idaho, later he moved to where Ogden, Utah, now stands, and became the first man to farm and raise a crop of vegetables in Utah. He was farming there when the Mormons came and bought him out.

Despite the Indian trouble, wagon emigration to Oregon continued, and 1860 was perhaps the big year. Few of them escaped unscathed; some were wiped out entirely and others suffered casualties. A woman driving a herd of a hundred horses lost the animals and she and her fourteen-year-old daughter were taken prisoner.

Some of the adventures had their light side, though they seemed serious enough at the time. A man named

Morris attempted to cross Snake River during high water. A box of household goods on top of the wagon floated away with Morris on top of it, and after a wild ride down the river the man was rescued. A woman and her baby had a similar experience and floated two miles down the river before being rescued by a white man and an Indian.

The tactic commonly employed by the Indians was to follow a wagon train to a tight place and then demand tribute. Most were willing to settle for an ox but sometimes the Indians were not satisfied, and it was too bad for a weak or isolated party. At one time the Territory of Idaho offered a bounty for Indian scalps, which did not improve relations at all.

One train which suffered most consisted of eight wagons and fifty-four people. They left Fort Hall September 13, 1860, with an escort of twenty-two soldiers which traveled with them for six days but turned back when no Indians were seen. A hundred Indians who had been following them, unknown to the soldiers, made the usual demands for supplies, then fired on the emigrants and continued a general harassment. The emigrants abandoned four of their wagons, hoping to satisfy the Indians, but they were still followed. With the train were four well-armed discharged soldiers who were sent ahead as scouts, but the men kept on going, nor did they stop until one of them encountered Captain Dent on the Columbia and told him of the wagon train's plight.

Meantime, the emigrants, fighting a losing battle, abandoned the remainder of their wagons and cattle and tried to reach Snake River under cover of darkness. Without supplies, they fled along the bank of the river at night, living only on their dogs, what fish they were able to catch, and a few roots.

Finally reaching the Owyhee—Captain Bonneville's "Wyer" river—they stopped running. They had lost their guns and blankets. In this pitiful condition they existed for forty-five days, eating the bodies of four children who had died. They were living skeletons when Captain Dent found them. Of the party of fifty-four, there were only twelve survivors.

Other wagon trains were attacked and some of them nearly wiped out. For a time Oregon emigration was practically halted while the soldiers pursued the Indians from Fort Hall. The transition from fur to farms had not been a bloodless one.

In 1863 the Oregon Volunteers who reached Fort Hall by way of Lost River met with Chief Pocatello and made a treaty of peace which accomplished very little. When he died a few years later, Chief Pocatello's body and his horse and personal effects were buried in an allegedly bottomless spring within a few miles of the old fort.

A new factor was introduced with the discovery of gold on Salmon River; a small group of prospectors was easier prey than a wagon train. The Grimes party in Boise Basin and the Smith party on Salmon River were two which suffered.

It had never been a full-fledged war, just a continuing state of hostilities. The Indians still came to Fort Hall to trade, then went out to see whom they could shoot. Even the Mormons, who had a knack for getting along with Indians, were driven from Fort Lemhi, a few miles above where Bonneville had his old camp, after Brigham Young had tried to found a colony there in 1855. Like many others, they lived to regret that they had ever gone north or west of Fort Hall.

There were no Indian writers and so the Indians' side of the trouble has never been told. In the spring of 1962 I made some effort to find out what it was. My brother-in-law, Ted Faulkner, who is part Indian and has lived all his life on the Fort Hall Indian Reservation and knows most of the 1400 Indians who still live there, guided me over the bottoms, around Ferry Butte and as close to the site of the old fort as it was possible to get because of the high water. After that we visited some of the older Indians who talked freely because I had Ted along to vouch for me.

First, we called on Lizzie Edmo, who at 109 believes herself to be the oldest Indian on the reservation. Although blind and bedfast her recollection was remarkably clear. She remembered a great deal about the old fort. Then we visited Ted's friends, Birdie and Leon Calico, a very interesting couple who are both about seventy. They are full-blooded Indians and speak excellent English.

Birdie was careful to say that she was not drawing on her own personal knowledge, but she had vivid recollection of the tales told by "the old ones." According to them, the trouble on the bottoms began when some hungry Indians killed a cow belonging to an emigrant, and they thought little about it since the emigrants never hesitated to kill any game they encountered. The next the Indians knew the soldiers came and marched them all to the fort, not giving them time to gather up any of their personal belongings. Some of the young men went on the warpath as soon as they could get away.

Our conversation turned upon a notorious Indian renegade called Bigfoot who terrorized the Oregon Trail for
some years. Many tales are told of Bigfoot, whose Indian
name was Nampuh, and after whom the city of Nampa,
Idaho, was named. He was of mixed blood, probably a
Cherokee, and a man of tremendous physical proportions
with the ability to outrun a horse in his native element, and
who also could go into the settlements and pose as a white
man, since he was a college graduate. To the whites he was
an outlaw to be hunted down and killed, as he eventually
was, but to the Calicos and the other Indians he was a red
Robin Hood who only avenged the wrongs of the Indians.

So great was the fear and distrust of the soldiers that
when World War One broke out and the soldiers came
to register the young Indians for the draft, most of them
took to the hills, climbing the high slopes of Mt. Putnam.
The Indians thought the army was moving against them,
and some whites thought the Indians were in revolt.

Birdie Calico remembers having gone with her family
to the headwaters of Lincoln Creek. Leon Calico, however,
was working at the Fort Hall Agency and did not go. Some
of the Indians came to the Agency to ask for an explanation. The frightened Agent came to the door, but would
go no further until the Indians assured him there was no
threat to his safety.

Misunderstandings finally were cleared up, the young
men came down to register for the draft, and many of them
served their country with great credit to themselves.

It is apparent that fear and misunderstanding were at
the bottom of most of the trouble. Too many instances are
on record of Indians having been shot down without provo-

cation and otherwise mistreated for us to believe that the red men were always at fault. They were proud, and they reacted according to their code; nor should it be forgotten that the early-day traders and trappers were able to get along with them.

The early trouble culminated with the massacre of the Bannacks by General Pat Connor at Battle Creek, a small tributary of the Bear River, January 29, 1863. General Connor was determined to end the trouble once and for all. On January 23, Captain C. H. Hoyt left the post at Fort Douglas; and on the 24th, General Connor and Majors Edward McGarry and M. F. Gallager left with 2333 men and two howitzers. Three hundred Bannacks had gone into winter camp on Battle Creek, and the attack was a complete surprise. It was almost another Sand Creek.

The fight lasted four hours. Nineteen of General Connor's men were killed and thirty-eight wounded; some of the wounded dying later. There were 224 Indian casualties, 175 horses were captured and the lodges and provisions were destroyed. The power of the Bannacks was broken forever, and Connor was promoted to Brigadier General as a result of this successful campaign. A mining man named Rose, on his way from Virginia City, Montana, to Salt Lake happened along after the battle and found an abandoned Indian girl baby, whom he took with him to Tintic, Utah, and raised to womanhood. It would appear that General Connor spared neither women nor children, but another military reputation had been made.

On July 6, from six to eight hundred Shoshones made peace with General Connor and Governor Doty of Utah. The Shoshones blamed the Bannacks, and surrendered 150 stolen horses and mules. Fifty warriors refused to give up and General Connor sent 108 men to round them up. That same summer Connor, in command of 1500 men at four posts, made peace with the Ute chiefs Blackhawk and Sanpitch near Springville, Utah.

There was peace around Fort Hall until 1877 when two young Bannack chiefs, Buffalo Horn and Bearskin, raised a war party and attempted to march through Oregon to join Chief Joseph of the Nez Percés in his amazing but finally futile dash for Canada. Both Buffalo Horn and Bearskin were killed in the Owyhee country and that settled the Indian trouble around Fort Hall.

The emigration of 1865 is said to have been immense, and the soldiers were still in control. Lieutenant C. H. Walker, who had been at Gibson's Ferry, was sent into winter quarters at Fort Hall and Lieutenant Palmer's entire company was already there. Soon, however, the old fort was falling to pieces. Bancroft describes it thus: "The old fort was found to be a heap of ruins, but out of the adobes and some abandoned buildings of the Overland Stage Company a shelter was erected at the junction of the Salt Lake-Virginia City and Boise roads. This post and Camp Reed were maintained during the winter by the Oregon infantry, the latter having only tents for shelter. . . ."

Bad flood conditions of 1862–63 washed over the site, and Snake River and the Portneuf were continually cutting new channels. The soldiers had moved to a new site, carrying away most of the materials of the old fort. J. N. Ireland had erected a station for Ben Holladay's Overland Stage near by on a crossing of Spring Creek, but flood conditions caused it to be moved to higher ground at the Spring

Creek bridge. It was then known as Holladay's Adobes. Holladay probably used some of the adobes from the old fort, which would account for the confusion as to the original site.

Lizzie Edmo is sure that the old fort was never moved but it is probable that what she remembers is the old adobe ruins of Holladay's stage station. To make confusion worse confounded, Captain Putnam established a new Fort Hall on Lincoln Creek. This fort was nine miles southeast of Blackfoot and about forty miles northeast of the old fort. It never had any particular military history.

Near the beginning of the present century the Lincoln Creek post was abandoned, and the Agency was removed to its present site, some twelve miles from the old original fort, as located by Ezra Meeker and Jim Broncho.

# 20

# THE ROARING SIXTIES

CAPTAIN E. D. PIERCE'S DIS-
covery of gold in Canal Gulch, on Orofino Creek, indirectly
gave Fort Hall a new lease on life. With the great years
of the California rush passed, the eager argonauts moved
north into Oregon and Idaho. Captain Pierce, who had
prospected in California and British Columbia, made his
find in 1860 on the Clearwater's tributary, in northern
Idaho. It led directly to the organization of Idaho Territory.

During the winter of 1860–61 the men located claims,
and whipsawed lumber for the sluice-boxes. Brosnan, in
his *History of Idaho*, says that in the spring forty-one of
these claims had yielded twenty-seven cents to the pan. One
prospector returned to civilization with $800 worth of gold
dust. The Civil War was just beginning and as in other
boom camps the men were about evenly divided between

Northern and Southern sympathizers, but the gold that was to be taken out of Idaho diggings would play its part in financing the Union.

New towns now were dominating the Oregon country. Portland had superseded Vancouver in importance, and in northern Idaho Lewiston, at the junction of the Snake and Clearwater, vied with Walla Walla. Pierce City and Orofino had sprung up at the scene of the first gold rush, but far richer strikes were soon to be made.

Prospectors pushed up the Clearwater and the Salmon. A rich strike was made at Elk City on the south bank of the Clearwater in 1861, but that same year the richest ground to the inch was found at Florence, north of the Salmon, and southwest of Elk City. Here a pan of dirt yielded dollars rather than cents. One pan from Baboon Gulch, named after Peter Bablaine, netted $800. Bablaine himself left the district with seventy-five pounds of dust.

Florence was so high that there was frost nearly every night in the year. On July 3, 1861 a blinding snowstorm raged there all day. It was in a basin surrounded by high, snow-capped mountains, and one observer stated that at twilight its thousands of campfires, dispersed over six or eight square miles of gravel, reminded him of an army in camp.

In 1862 James Warren made a strike of less spectacular but more permanent proportions a few miles south of the Salmon, and this was called Warren's Diggings. A small party led by George Grimes and Moses Splawn wandered to the southwest, and discovered gold in Boise Basin, the richest strike Idaho was ever to know.

They were attacked by Indians and Grimes was killed.

Splawn and the others made their way back to Walla Walla, recruited more men and returned to the spot from which eleven million dollars' worth of gold was to be taken. By 1864 more than 16,000 people were in Boise Basin. Idaho City, at first known as Bannock, was to become for a time the largest city in the territory. Other towns were known as Placerville, Centerville and Hog'em—which later changed its name to Pioneer.

When I was in the basin in 1942 they were still dredging for gold in the creek beds, but Idaho City was close to being a ghost town. Some of the old buildings like the Masonic Hall were still standing. Among them was the jail, with its inner planks covered by the heads of spikes that made a break-out impossible. It was a heavily timbered country and I saw pine trees fifty feet high and eighteen inches in diameter growing out of some of the old graves.

Idaho Basin ran the whole gamut of a bonanza mining camp. Some of the area's greatest fortunes were started there, and it had some of the West's best known killers and outlaws. Like Virginia City, Montana, it had to be cleaned up by vigilantes, but thanks to William J. McConnell the process was a little less violent.

McConnell, who located at a place called Jerusalem in the Payette Valley, instead of looking for gold began to raise vegetables, which he took over the mountains by pack train and sold at inflated prices, making himself rich. Finding the good citizens and the rough element lined up against each other for battle, McConnell took charge of the law-and-order group, and as leader of the vigilantes established order with a minimum of hangings: he preferred giving tickets of leave to using the rope.

Horse-stealing was a major industry, and those around Horseshoe Bend of the Payette were particularly active under the leadership of a Boise sheriff named Updike. McConnell's vigilantes took over and Sheriff Updike, like Henry Plummer of Virginia City, was hanged, and the outlaw gang broken up.

Later, McConnell became governor of Idaho, 1893–97, and the father-in-law of Idaho's most famous statesman, Senator William E. Borah. As a small boy, I recall seeing the white-whiskered old gentleman sitting on his porch in Moscow, Idaho, peacefully smoking his pipe.

Bill McConnell had a larger influence than came merely from taming the outlaws. His success in raising vegetables made some men consider the advantages of farming over trapping or searching for mineral wealth, and many of the pioneers gave up the will-of-the-wisp of gold to settle down in the valleys and become permanent and substantial citizens.

The colonizing Mormons were pushing up from the south. In 1855 Brigham Young sent out a party to settle on the Lemhi and a fort by that name was constructed, but it was built on a flat and the Indians could shoot into it from the surrounding hills, and after a short time it was abandoned. They had better luck founding the town of Franklin, just on the Idaho side of the Idaho-Utah boundary. They had their troubles until General Pat Connor defeated the Bannacks at Battle Creek, just a few miles north of their settlement.

Near Ogden, Utah, a dissident Mormon Prophet named Joseph Morris began to have visions and revelations not recognized by the hierarchy. The Utah militia was called out to arrest Morris and disperse his followers, and the resulting trouble was known as the Morrisite War. Morris and some others were killed, and the survivors were conducted safely to Soda Springs by United States soldiers. The Morrisite group gradually disintegrated, with some remnants moving north to introduce irrigation in the Upper Snake River valley where once the men of Henry, Wyeth and Bonneville had trapped beaver in the early part of the century.

The story of the Morrisites has been well told in a book titled *Letters of Long Ago,* by Agnes Just Reid, who lives near Firth, Idaho, on Wolverine Creek, near the mouth of the Blackfoot River and only some thirty miles from Fort Hall. Her mother was a child during the Morrisite War, and was one of those taken to Soda Springs, where she married a soldier named Bennett. Her second husband, James Just, dug the first canal near the now booming atomic-energy city of Idaho Falls, formerly known as Eagle Rock. This was the beginning of the transformation of the region around Fort Hall from frontier post to the home of the Idaho potato.

Back in the sixties some of the miners had pushed their way across the Bitter Roots to Alder Gulch and unlocked Montana's mineral treasures at Bannack and Virginia City. The Bitter Roots had stood as a barrier to explorers and mountain men since the days of Lewis and Clark, and they now stood as a barrier between the Montana gold fields and the Pacific Ocean. The only practicable way out was via Fort Hall, Corinne and Salt Lake City. Some freight was being laboriously hauled from Fort Benton on the Missouri, but Salt Lake City was closer and cheaper. It gave new importance to Fort Hall in the middle of the route.

Near Promontory, where the railroad lines were to meet, was Corinne, the Gentile capital of Utah. Corinne was the outfitting point for the trip north, and its streets were full of heavy freight wagons, horses, mules, oxen, and blustering teamsters and bullwhackers. It was a tough town, with twenty-six saloons and numerous houses of prostitution. It was one of the original "hell on wheels" towns along the railroad right of way, but it took much longer than most fading into oblivion. Today it is a quiet Mormon hamlet.

The road went up Malade River, over a divide near Malade, down Marsh Creek, into which prehistoric Lake Bonneville had once broken out of its confines to pour its surplus waters en route to the Pacific. Marsh Creek emptied into the Portneuf, and the road followed the Portneuf to Fort Hall.

Heretofore, most travel had been west to Walla Walla by way of Fort Boise, but now there was much more traffic north and south. The first need of any mining district was mail and passenger service, and the Jehus of the frontier were always ready. First among them were Oliver & Connover, who established a stage line between Salt Lake City and Virginia City in 1863. Ben Holladay, the stagecoach king, was running lines out of Omaha all over the west, and in 1864 he was in competition with Oliver & Connover.

Holladay's first step was to get a government contract to carry the mail between Fort Hall and Virginia City for three years at $13,271 a year. By lowering passenger fares to twenty-five dollars, Holladay drove Oliver & Connover out of business on that line, though they started an express route between Virginia City and Blackfoot, and between Virginia City and Helena. About the same time Holladay secured two contracts from the government for carrying mail to the Northwest, a tri-weekly service from Salt Lake to The Dalles for $156,000 a year. A second contract brought it up to $186,000 a year. In addition, he was carrying express and passengers.

It will be noted that Fort Hall was the division point, and the only strange part about it was that Holladay, who seldom missed a bet, didn't collect double revenue from Salt Lake to Fort Hall on the Virginia City line. This made Fort Hall, at the junction of the two routes, his most important way-point, and Holladay built a commodious station a short distance from the old fort.

Holladay sent his superintendent, Spotswood, back to Kansas to bring back thirty coaches, ten lumber wagons and 290 mules. They traveled overland and reached Salt Lake City June 29, 1864. One of Holladay's agents came out from Salt Lake City to locate the new road, and on August 11 the first stage reached Boise City. The Dalles *Weekly Mountaineer* published a letter from Senator Benjamin F. Harding of Oregon giving details:

"The mail from Salt Lake City to Walla Walla is already secured. We have by dint of persevering boring succeeded in getting the postmaster to let the contract for a tri-weekly four-horse coach service at $156,000 per year. Time, ten days for eight months, and fourteen days for the balance of the year."

It doesn't seem very fast now, but it would have looked like lightning to those early-day emigrants whom Johnnie Grant had told the trip would be impossible.

It was still hardly a road one would want to travel for pleasure, but Ben Holladay made it as comfortable as possible. The entire length of the route was about a thousand miles, with six-horse stages used between Salt Lake and Fort Hall. The fare between Salt Lake and Walla Walla was $240 in gold. Each passenger was allowed twenty-five pounds of baggage free, but express cost a dollar and a half per pound.

Holladay received around $360,000 the first two years, and he sub-contracted the mail from Boise to The Dalles to Thomas & Company, who turned it over to Haley & Greathouse, who purchased the equipment and completed the agreement. A published schedule was adhered to probably as well as those of the common carriers of today. However, during the winter months of 1864–65 heavy snows interrupted the schedule between Salt Lake and Boise for several days.

A newspaper report of the time states that the bad weather would have stopped the route entirely had it not been for the determination of the Holladay agents and drivers. One mail was carried on pack horses through snow fifteen to twenty feet deep across the Bannock Mountains. Anyone who has experienced an Idaho winter will realize the difficulty of such a trip.

Ben Holladay, one of the West's legendary figures, provided a service that enabled the country to develop much faster than it otherwise would have done. His drivers, as lusty a breed of men as the fur trappers who had preceded them, were a swaggering, cursing lot, but they knew their job. Holladay provided the best equipment it was possible to get, and when the passengers reached a station they could relax in frontier comfort.

Fort Hall was one of the most extensively used, and one of the best outfitted. The drivers liked their work, and few of them quit their jobs to leave for the gold fields, though no other work could have been more hazardous. During the sixties the Indians were angry and resentful, and the drivers had no trade goods with which to placate them as the early traders had. Wagon trains were being attacked, and while the stages got through there were some harrowing chases. The horses of the six- and four-horse stages had been selected for speed and endurance, and could usually outrun the Indian cayuses. If the drivers had to make a fight they could do that, too.

Possibly the worst hazard was the road agents who plied their trade south of Virginia City. The Plummer gang, which was to be routed eventually by the vigilantes of Montana, made it difficult for the miners to leave with their wealth, and if they did get out there were other outlaws, such as the Lockart gang, lurking further down the line.

One of the worst was Boone Helm, who was hanged in Virginia City, and whose grave is still carefully preserved there. Helm was a heartless killer. He spent part of one winter near Fort Hall subsisting by the simple expedient of killing and eating his companion. Later, he trekked across the mountains to Soda Springs, carrying one leg of his victim in a sack as emergency rations.

The most dangerous part of the road was along the Portneuf, south of Fort Hall. The road had to follow the river between reefs of lava rock and basalt which provided perfect hiding places for the highwaymen. That section, called Robber's Roost, was one of several by the same name throughout the West.

There were many holdups, and occasionally drivers and passengers were killed, though in the long run most of the outlaws were caught and hanged. The late State Senator George Fisher, whose father had been a pioneer sheriff of Oneida County, once showed me some rope that had been used to hang road agents at Malade. Only a couple of years ago some interest was aroused by the finding of an old rusted leg iron a few miles out of Malade. After a few old-timers had scratched their heads it was recalled that there had been a jail-break many years ago and some prisoners had escaped; one of them had been wearing leg irons.

For many years people hunted along the banks of the Portneuf for a supposedly hidden cache of some $60,000 taken in a stage robbery. It was never found. Whether the doomed man who told about it was only playing for time will never be known. If it really was buried there, most natives agree, the rampaging flood waters eating away at the banks of the Portneuf over the years would have washed it out.

When I was a lad some cowboys came upon a freshly dug hole on Grave Creek, and the evidence indicated that a square box had been taken out of it. Another tale that used to stir our imagination had to do with one of the wagon trains using a cut-off between the Blackfoot and the Portneuf over what was called the Trail Creek Pass. One of the wagons was said to have been loaded with barrels of whisky. Pursued by Indians, they are supposed to have buried whisky, wagon-box and all, built a fire over it to keep the Indians from finding it, and proceeded on to Oregon. Thirsty but hopeful cowpunchers chasing dogies over the trail kept a lookout for some telltale mark which might indicate an old excavation, but their hopes were never realized.

Those were the hectic days with all the ingredients that combined to make the Wild West. Eastern farmers still plodded over the old emigrant roads and buried their dead along the way. Indians chased them, and soldiers chased the Indians. Miners broke their backs digging gold from the earth and road agents lay in wait to take it from them. Vigilantes and peace officers were handy with both rope and gun. Those who had money spent it freely, and those who lost it went back to try for another stake. Fort Hall was without mines, without industry, without farms, but it was so geographically located that it was the center of the activity.

Ben Holladay did a much larger business on his line from Fort Hall to Virginia City than he did on the one from Fort Hall to The Dalles. There was a considerable stretch across the Snake River desert where drivers and passengers could still lose their hair, and little time was lost crossing it. Along the way were the stage stations and many of the tenders cultivated gardens on little plots of ground to vary the monotony of beef, bacon, saleratus biscuits and chicory coffee. These vegetables were always welcomed by the passengers who stopped there.

Meat was the main staple for many years, but the game that was so plentiful in Wyeth's and Bonneville's day was fast disappearing. An old gentleman named Stuart Dixon once told me as he sat on our woodpile spinning yarns of the past that he had killed the last deer on Haystack Mountain between Pocatello and Chesterfield. There were no deer in the country during my boyhood, but now, thanks to game-preservation laws, there are hundreds of them. I frequently used to see wolves near my home, but they have vanished, and even the coyotes are nearly gone.

In the sixties there was a tri-weekly stage schedule between Fort Hall and Virginia City during eight months of the year; the trip took four days and ten hours. For the other four months, there was a weekly schedule with a trip of five days and ten hours. The six-horse Concord coaches cost $1500 each and would accommodate seventeen passengers when the top seats were used. In 1864 only 500 passengers were carried from Boise to Virginia City, but with the end of the Indian scares and the addition of new stages business picked up considerably. The fare from Boise to Virginia City was $140, and it was about the same from Salt Lake City.

Most of the gold from the Montana mines went by stage to Salt Lake City, but the ticket specified that the holder waived all claim on the proprietor for the loss of any bullion, gold dust, bank or treasury notes carried on the stage. This was not classed as baggage under the free twenty-five-pound clause, and had to be paid for at regular express rates. All of this had to pass through Fort Hall.

There were other stage lines around the terminals. A. J. Oliver, Holladay's old competitor, ran a line from Virginia City to Helena, as did Al Guitwitz and Ben Stafford, but in 1866 Holladay started a competing line and soon put those two rivals out of business. Holladay cut the time from sixteen to ten hours and dropped the fare to

$2.50, which was soon raised to $25 in bankable gold, or $35 in "Lincoln skins," or greenbacks, when "Old Ben" gained his monopoly. A schedule of other rates of the times shows: Virginia City to Boise City—$125; Boise City to Salt Lake City—$100; Boise City to Missouri River—$400. Passengers could ride Holladay stages from Fort Hall to points along the Pacific Coast, or by way of Salt Lake City could go to Denver, Omaha or Atcheson.

In some ways the life at Fort Hall during the stage-coach era of the sixties was more exciting, though perhaps less dangerous, than at any other time in its history. The teamsters, stage drivers and bullwhackers were about as self-reliant as any men on the frontier, and also to be found around the fort were some of the old trappers, the miners and the soldiers, and of course the Indians. The people of the wagon trains still rolling westward to Oregon must have been impressed if not alarmed by the assortment of uncurried types on display there. But Fort Hall was one of the most important places they would ever see, for here they could replenish their depleted supplies, could even trade their worn-out wagons and weary animals for others, and they knew that now they were on the very doorstep to Oregon.

For the well-heeled traveler there was a good bed and meals if he cared to wait over a day or two, and those travelers arrived by five different roads. Here they had a choice: they could go to Salt Lake City, to Virginia City, to Soda Springs and eastward, to Boise or to California.

The last important stage line was operated by J. N. Ireland. Wires, rails and concrete finally deprived the old stages of any further use. There is even argument today as to the exact location of the old stage station. Perhaps 109-year-old Lizzie Edmo is the only living person who remembers what it was like around the old fort and the old stage station, and the things that went on there were beyond the comprehension of the bright-eyed little Indian girl. When I talked with her our interpreter was her seventy-year-old son, Gene Edmo, once a champion rodeo performer. One of her daughters helped to make the famous movie, *The Covered Wagon*. Lizzie Edmo has seen a lot of changes. She graciously got out of her bed to have her picture taken and she talked freely. Gene was something else again: when I was introduced to him he said, "Why bother? No writer has ever yet told the truth about the Indians."

The sixties were the darkest time of all for the Indians, and I think I know how they were able to endure it. It was their sense of humor; their ability to laugh at themselves. As we sat in the kitchen of the Calicos, Leon Calico told us of being accidentally dragged into a vat in which cattle were being dipped. It was a harrowing experience, and for a time it was thought that he was dead. His body was so badly burned that today, many years afterward, he can wear nothing but silk next to his skin. He laughed heartily as he told us of the episode, blaming his own awkwardness. "It's hard to kill an Indian," he finished.

# 21

# THE LAST OF THE FUR TRADE

DURING THE GOLD RUSH OF the sixties Fort Hall was in somewhat the same fortuitous position in which the Mormons of Salt Lake City found themselves after the California gold rush, when the gold seekers reached Salt Lake City ready to make any sacrifice in order to continue their journey. In the forties old Johnnie Grant had been able to drive a hard bargain with the emigrants who reached Fort Hall, whether their destination was Oregon or California. In the sixties young Johnnie Grant was doing the same thing and even more profitably, since there were more emigrants as well as prospectors.

Oddly enough, the region around Fort Hall lasted longer as beaver country than almost any other place in the West. In the sixties young Johnnie Grant was still sending out trapping parties along the Portneuf and Blackfoot rivers, and as far away as the Salmon. The pelts they took were taken to Vancouver by pack trains, which returned laden with trade goods that were in great demand at Fort Hall.

The emigrants who reached Fort Hall had always taken a good, hard look. They were ignorant of the country, and their view of the Snake River desert was intimidating. Ahead of them lay 200 miles of hellish sagebrush and lava. Maybe they could reach water, and maybe they could not. There were few places they could reach the Snake even if they chose to follow the stream. They would have to cross it a couple of times, and it would not be easy.

There were lava reefs and gorges to be traversed, and there was no benevolent government to build roads and bridges. When they detoured around them they had no idea how many extra miles they would have to travel, nor what difficulties they would encounter. There was always danger of Indian attack; the red men had been friendly at first, but cheating and plundering by the greedy had made them hostile. Rather than risk their wagons, many of them in the early days left them at Fort Hall, that "graveyard of wagons," and went on by pack train. That was profitable for Ermatinger, Grant, and the others.

If the Hudson's Bay people had not treated the Indians fairly, there would have been many more Massacre Rocks to mark places where emigrants had been murdered and despoiled. Indian violence could be measured by the way their women were treated. Hudson's Bay men married them and provided for their families. The American mountain men made casual alliances, but while the women were with them they were treated kindly. The miners were a different breed. Their "wooing" usually consisted of rape, often terminating with murder.

The emigrants desired only to be let alone. They wanted the Indians' land when it looked good to them, but tried to avoid personal contact with them. They had other problems. One of those emigrants was my great-uncle, Harvey Matthews, some of whose letters to my grandfather, written more than a hundred and ten years ago, I still have. He went on to make his farm on the north side of the Columbia, directly opposite the mouth of the Willamette. His letters bubble with enthusiasm for the fruits and vegetables he could raise, and he was constantly imploring my grandfather, Reverend T. Q. Matthews, of Keokuk, Iowa, to join him. On the debit side, he tells of Indian scares and of trouble with the United States military. The settlers objected to the soldiers voting, and on one occasion my great-uncle and two of his sons were badly beaten up by army men, Uncle Harvey being bedridden for several weeks as a result. A minor thorn in his side was that he had left his property back in Iowa in the hands of a brother-in-law he had trusted, but who consistently refused to make an accounting, or send him any money. There were no courts to which he could appeal. It was an experience common to many early Oregon immigrants.

That those early-day settlers owed much to the factors of the various Hudson's Bay posts there can be no doubt. A little description of the life that went on at Fort Boise from the trenchant pen of T. J. Farnham, who visited the post in 1839, is apropos. At that time it was in charge of Francis Payette, for whom were named the Payette River and the city of Payette, Idaho.

"Mr. Payette received us with every mark of kindness; gave our horses to the care of his servants, and introduced us immediately to the chairs, table, and edibles of his apartment. He is a merry, fat old gentleman of fifty, who, although in the wilderness all the best years of his life, has retained that manner of benevolence in trifles, of seating and serving you at table, of directing your attention continually to some little matter of interest, so strikingly agreeable in that [French-Canadian] people.

"The 14th and 15th [of September, 1839] were spent pleasantly with this gentleman. During that time he feasted us with excellent bread, and butter made from an American cow, obtained from some of the missionaries; with baked, boiled, fried, and broiled salmon—and, at my request, with some of his adventures in the wilderness. On the 16th . . . with a 'bon jour' having been returned by Mons. Payette, with an additional kind wish of a 'bon voyage' to use over the mountains, we left the old gentleman to his solitary domain."

This was the same kind of hospitality dispensed at Fort Hall, Fort Walla Walla and Fort Vancouver. There was method in everything Hudson's Bay did, but it didn't hurt them that their head men were gentlemen rather than boors and roughnecks.

What Mr. Payette was to Fort Boise, such as Francis Ermatinger, the Grants and Mr. Pattee were to Fort Hall. They and their half-breed children constituted a sort of aristocracy of the mountains. Many of their descendants are prosperous landowners whose Indian blood has been long forgotten, but the happy-go-lucky French-Canadians accepted life as it came to them, and were more adaptable to the country than the stiff-necked and puritanical New Englanders.

After Peter Skene Ogden closed out the interests of Hudson's Bay at Fort Hall in 1856, affairs there were in the hands of young Johnnie Grant and Joseph Pattee and life went on much the same. They were the new aristocracy. Most of the women had been East to school, and they were hostesses to the prominent visitors who were entertained there. Among the military visitors were Generals Albert Sydney Johnston, and those old Indian fighters, Generals William Tecumseh Sherman, Phil Sheridan and Pat Connor. Most of the children of the forts spoke English, French and Shoshone, which gave them a decided advantage.

These families scattered all over the basin from Soda Springs on the east to Fort Boise on the west, and despite the vast distances they visited back and forth regularly. It was nothing for a Fort Hall girl to get on her pony and, leading a pack horse, strike out for the Payette or the Salmon to visit her cousins.

The best account of life at Fort Hall in the sixties is by George Goodhart, who came to Fort Hall as a boy in 1860 to work for Johnnie Grant. He married first a Pattee girl from Fort Hall and, after her death by drowning in Snake River, a Payette girl from Fort Boise. She was accidentally shot by some unknown person, and Mr. Goodhart later married a white woman and for many years lived on a ranch on Slug Creek, near Soda Springs.

It was my good fortune to see George Goodhart when he was an old man. By that time the gay young blade of the sixties had snow-white hair, mustache and goatee, but he was still a frontier dandy. At the time I was living in the

barn of A. J. Knollin, the sheep king, for whom I was working, and I used often to see Mr. Goodhart, by that time
known affectionately as "Pop," riding down the main street
of Soda Springs on a fine roan horse with a liberally stamped
and embroidered saddle and bridle. He was a friend of my
older brother, who was foreman of a cattle outfit in the
country, and I got some of his stories from that source.

Later, when George Goodhart was living in the Old
Soldiers Home at Boise, he dictated the story of part of his
life to his friend Abraham C. Anderson. Published in 1940,
it gives an excellent picture of the last days of the fur trade
and the social life around Fort Hall.

Johnnie Grant, Junior, picked Goodhart up in Omaha
when he was a boy of sixteen and brought him west to serve
as a messenger to the various camps of the trappers. It was
then the practice for a couple of the men to make camp
on some creek and trap there until Johnnie Grant sent
them word to bring their furs to some designated spot where
he would pick them up. A few like Bob Dempsey, a squawman, had permanent camps. His was on Dempsey Creek,
a tributary of the Portneuf, near the present town of Lava
Hot Springs, which was long known as Dempsey.

Goodhart met the first of his many Indian girl friends
at Bob Dempsey's camp. Sally Martin was a young widow,
her American husband having been killed by a bear. Sally
was looking for another American husband, but George
considered himself too young for matrimony and Sally a
little too old for him, but he introduced her to several white
trappers, among them a man named Osborn, whom Sally
later married. Some of their descendants are still respected
citizens on the Fort Hall Indian Reservation. George and
Sally remained firm friends, George being particularly well

pleased with her because she made such fine dumplings; once he made a trip to Utah for flour just so he could have more of his favorite delicacy.

One winter Goodhart and three girls—Sally, Lizzie Pattee and Julia Payette, daughter of "Three-fingered" Louis Pattee and granddaughter of Francis Payette, one-time factor at Fort Boise—spent a winter on an island in the middle of Snake River. In time Goodhart married each of the younger girls, both of whom were to meet tragic deaths.

At Soda Springs Goodhart got his first introduction to Indian social life when the trappers learned that an Indian village was near by and proposed to have them over for a dance. George and some of the trappers suggested clearing away a place for the dance, but young Johnnie Grant advised against it: wait until the squaws arrive and let them do it, said he. Goodhart thoroughly enjoyed the dance.

George Goodhart was just one of the venturesome young Americans who knew how to adapt himself to circumstances. He was lucky to spend his best years in an era of relative peace, and it is doubtful that he ever drew a gun on an Indian, though with white outlaws it was a different story. He was loyal to young Johnnie Grant, for whom he worked for a number of years, though sometimes not too sure of him. With the Pattees it was different. They took the young fellow in as if he was their own son—which he was indeed to become. Mrs. Pattee offered to make him a fine buckskin suit if he would provide the hides, and among them he and the girls secured the best available. It is not unreasonable to suppose that the fringed and beaded suit Mrs. Pattee made him was the one in which George was married, or that Lizzie was arrayed in just as fine apparel.

It may have been the most gala occasion old Fort Hall had known since the christening of Nathaniel Wyeth's flag.

The young couple, in spite of their comradeship, had to be pushed into matrimony. George still didn't feel he was quite ready for it, and Lizzie had a sweetheart she had gone to school with in St. Louis. It was probably a good thing for them both, for it stopped George from rambling, and Lizzie had hated the East and would have been unhappy there.

The Pattee family, however, was doomed to tragedy. While Lizzie was drowning in a freak accident at a ford which she had often crossed, Mrs. Pattee lay dying in a cabin on Rock Creek not far away, and the two bereaved widowers buried their wives on the same day. George, Pattee said, was all he had left, and Fort Hall had too many memories, so he moved his cattle north to the valley of the Lemhi. The Pattees are an old and respected family, but it is probable that few of their neighbors realize that they were once part of an aristocracy that dominated the southern part of Idaho in the early days of the territory.

Fort Hall was approaching the end of its fur-trapping days when George Goodhart became suspicious of Johnnie Grant. Goodhart had been engaged to help take a pack train of fur to Vancouver, but when he learned that Grant intended to take the furs to Texas without consulting Joe Pattee, Goodhart declined to make the trip. This was probably the last sizeable shipment of furs from the Portneuf. Goodhart remarks with casual exaggeration that 100 beaver and mink pelts were worth about as much as one plug of tobacco.

Once while herding sheep on Three Mile Knoll, out

of Soda Springs, I came upon four old graves. I was told that three of them contained the bodies of three outlaws who had been followed and killed there after they robbed a saloon in Soda Springs. The fourth one was undoubtedly the body of a well known trapper named Charley Robinson, whom Goodhart often mentions in his memoirs. The two were close friends. One day as the two were riding along together near the Three Mile Knoll, Goodhart became alarmed at the careless manner in which Robinson was carrying his rifle and rode on ahead. A few minutes later he heard a shot and, going back, discovered that Robinson had accidentally and fatally shot himself. As was customary at the time, Robinson was buried where he fell.

The beaver are not all gone. I can remember when there was a stiff fine if one killed a beaver without a government permit, even when they were doing damage to irrigation ditches. Now they have become so numerous in certain places that the government sends out trappers to get rid of them. Beaver skins are not worth much, but the mountain men who trapped them when fortunes could be made in fur were the forerunners of the prosperous and civilized West we know today.

Life was hazardous for the mountain men and most of them were fatalists who didn't look too far into the future. For the Indians, says George Goodhart, it was mostly a case of *Navashi kucheem* (After while we cook it) and *Tehe anitch kahinen* (Deer meat all gone). Life was dangerous, but good.

# 22

# THE THUNDERING HERDS

LIKE MOST OF THE WESTERN states, Idaho became a great cattle range after the passing of the beaver and the buffalo. Following the Civil War the great unbranded herds of Texas were being rounded up and driven north to the Plains states. On better feed and away from the ticks, they were able to add considerable poundage by the time they were ready for market. Dodge City, Abilene and the rest had their days of transient glory as trail towns. My own father was one of the cowboys who trailed cattle from Texas to Kansas in the early seventies. The tide swept north to the Canadian border, and beyond. Soon the cattle were being trailed to Utah, Idaho, Nevada and even farther west.

Oregon had its own cattle industry, and there was another lesser known cattle trail from Oregon to Wyoming and Montana. The herds crossed Snake River west of Boise, but the owners had no stomach for retracing the old Oregon Trail across the desert. Instead of bending south they struck out eastward, skirting the northern edge of the desert over the country once so well known to Captain Bonneville. They crossed the Wood and Lost rivers and Birch Creek and went on to the upper reaches of the Snake. One of the early-day cattle towns on the Snake was a place called Lorenzo, only a few miles from where Andrew Henry had started his fort in 1810. Some found valleys where they could stop and put down roots; others continued over the Lander Trail to Wyoming.

Oregon knew such cattle emperors as Miller and Lux, and Pete French. The McIntyre brothers from Texas drove their herds into the Tintic district of Utah when the grass was belly-deep to a horse and ran thousands of cattle profitably. Some of their profits they invested in the Mammoth mine near Eureka, and a town called Mammoth grew up around the famous mine. It was one of the richest glory holes in the world: the McIntyres became millionaires.

About the same time a Frenchman named Alex Toponce got into the cattle business at Fort Hall in a unique way. He was a shrewd trader and freighter who started his fortune freighting between Corinne and Virginia City. His headquarters was usually on a ranch near Corinne at a place called Call's Fort.

When the army sold out all its supplies at Camp Floyd, forty miles south of Salt Lake City, Toponce, who was herding mules in the near-by hills, attended the sale. He noticed that mules were being bought by Ben Holladay for $40 a span. The ones being auctioned were small ones—and as fast as they were sold numbers were placed on them. Soon Toponce noticed that the numbers were being taken from the small mules and placed on larger animals which never went under the hammer. So he bought twelve of the small ones, and then followed Holladay's example of exchanging the numbers to big, fine mules, some of which he later sold for as much as $500 each. Nobody complained.

"I knew too much," he said simply.

Like Bonneville, Toponce was loquacious, and a friend helped him write his memoirs. He had adventures galore as he freighted out of Corinne to Montana and Nevada, and had the knack of making money out of most of them. He could size up men quickly, and his observations on some of the prominent people of the day were most penetrating. He found Brigham Young to be as sharp a trader as he was, but a man whose word could be absolutely depended upon. At the opposite pole was Senator Sharon, of Nevada, whom Toponce delighted to get the better of. Once he sent Sharon a bill for $50 for "horse dentistry," and collected.

Toponce became a merchant in Salt Lake City just before Brigham Young started his boycott against Gentile merchants. Though a friend of Brigham's, Toponce thought he had better get out. He traded his boots and shoes for wild cattle, and trailed the animals north to Fort Hall, a country he knew well. Here he made a deal with the government to lease a portion of the Fort Hall Indian Reservation seventy miles long and forty miles wide. This took in the best part of the Fort Hall bottoms, but he built his corrals near Chesterfield on the upper Portneuf. The large creek which empties into the Portneuf there has since been known as Toponce Creek. It is only four or five miles from where

Bonneville's men spent the winter of 1834–35. Toponce gave up the lease when the Indians themselves began to raise cattle.

Toponce was a prominent figure at Corinne, by some called "the Gentile Capital of Utah" and, by others, "the Burg on the Bear." He was one of the few Gentiles—as all non-Mormons were called—who was able to keep on good terms with the Mormons. He was present at the completion of the transcontinental railroad at Promontory, which event eventually led to the downfall of Fort Hall as well as Corinne, though for a time it instilled new life into both places. Corinne became the head of the line of the freighting business to Virginia City and the booming mining business of Montana. Fort Hall, while Toponce was there, was the most important way-station. For the first time Fort Hall saw more wagons going north and south than there were going west and east.

Alex Toponce and his wagonmaster, Calensus Hawkins, made many trips over the road to Virginia City, and to the almost equally booming Salmon River country of Idaho. Toponce was one of the few men able to participate in three great eras of the West: the fur trade, the mining boom, and the day of the cattle kings. It would be hard to imagine a better cattle range than he enjoyed in the very heart of the Fort Hall Indian Reservation.

Another large Texas outfit called the Warbonnet drifted into Fort Hall and remained for some twenty years. The bottoms were as good winter pasture as could be found anywhere, and if it was not enough there was the whole Snake River desert with bunch grass growing around the roots of the sagebrush, and enough snow in the winter to protect from thirst but not deep enough to cover the grass.

For summer range there was the whole country lying between Snake River and the Bear. In the spring they moved their herds up to the headwaters of the Portneuf and the Blackfoot. The summer headquarters of the Warbonnet was on Corral Creek, just over the Chesterfield, or Aspen, Hills. Because the bulls were kept there during the summer the place was known as "The Bull Pens." Since my wife was raised on an isolated ranch within three miles of the Bull Pens, and I have ridden, or herded sheep, over every acre of the country we are quite familiar with the locale and its traditions.

There was another summer camp on Crane's Flat, a few miles from Gray's Lake, one of the great beaver and muskrat districts of the early days. Their summer town was Soda Springs; in the winter Blackfoot got most of the cowmen's trade.

I once worked with a former Warbonnet cowhand named Joe Graham, who told me of an episode when nearly the entire outfit went to Blackfoot to celebrate the Fourth of July. A train carrying a brass band had stopped for water, and the band good-naturedly gave a free concert, which appealed to the cowhands so much that they drew their guns and kept the train, including mail cars, waiting until sundown. The next day they saw a buggy coming toward Crane's Flat and, surmising that it was the sheriff, which it was, rode off to the high croppings in as many directions as there were men. Nothing more came of it.

The Warbonnets, whose foreman was a rock-hard character known as Cheyenne Bill, came to Fort Hall in the seventies, and sold out just before 1900. The story is told that the cattle were trailed past and around a knoll in such a manner that many of them were counted several times.

A story I can vouch for—it was told me by several Chesterfield men who rode for them—indicates that the Warbonnet didn't always come out on top. An outfit had sold a herd of cattle to the Warbonnet to be paid for at a later date, and sent along a Mexican called Carmen to look after their rights. He appears to have been the one man Cheyenne Bill could not bluff, and not only did Carmen protect his employer's interest, but he put an end at gun point to the Warbonnet's claiming calves that belonged to the Mormon settlers in Chesterfield. I know of a few other instances where the Warbonnet men had to admit regretfully that the good old days were gone.

Range monopoly could not last. Other cattle outfits and later the sheep horned in, and the government belatedly decided that the Fort Hall bottoms belonged to the Indians. One of the outfits I remember was called the Keogh outfit, and its foreman's monicker, which didn't fit him at all, was Bilious. I could name a dozen others who ran cattle in the vicinity of Fort Hall.

For some years the Chesterfield and Portneuf cattlemen were permitted to use the bottoms as a winter range. There was some trouble when the Indian police and cowboys took to tying down all the stray cattle they found on the reservation, and many were in bad shape when discovered by the white cowhands. Some of the cowhands themselves were arrested and taken to the agency and fined, but there was no bloodshed.

In general the white and red cowboys got along very well. My brother Chauncey counted many of the Indians among his best friends. They ran horses on Mt. Putnam in those days and they also permitted the Portneuf ranchers to run horses there; the annual roundup, in which both whites and Indians participated, was the most colorful and exciting event of the year. Once my brother Obe, who also rode on the reservation, bought a little white Indian cayuse named Pompey for me for five dollars, and on that day I thought I had achieved manhood. No celebration at Chesterfield in my youth was complete without horse races and wrestling matches and foot races between white men and Indians. I do not believe that life was ever better around Fort Hall than in those days.

There was some complaint by the Indians when the government decided to stock the reservation for them. The cattle were branded USID, standing for the U.S. Indian Department, and the Indians maintained the white men thought it stood for U Steal and I Divide. There were several near-scandals. Sometimes the Indians claimed the count was short. Occasionally yearlings were substituted for three-year-old cows, or calves which were supposed to be counted with their mothers were counted separately and charged to the Indians as a cow.

I knew some of the Indian cowboys. They were skillful in their work, and fine, upstanding men. It was a sad day for them when a paternalistic government decided that the Indian cattle were to be in charge of white foremen; from that day, the Indian cattle business began to dwindle, and the Indian riders were soon put afoot, with nothing to do.

The crowning insult came, I think, when most of the reservation was leased to sheepmen. It spelled the end of the Indian cattle business, and the end of another era. True, there are still Indian cattlemen. The late Ralph Dixie of Blackfoot was one; he was respected by white men and Indians alike. For many years he made trips to Washington to represent his people. But the Indian who used to own a few cattle and a band of horses has largely disappeared. Many of them own farms between Blackfoot and Pocatello, but the Indian seldom takes kindly to farming, and most of them lease their farms to white men and have nothing to do themselves.

There are always the exceptions. An Indian named Captain Willie, with whom my brother used to ride, was one. One time while he was living in Teton Basin, Chauncey stopped off at Fort Hall to visit his old friend and found Captain Willie and his wife Minnie operating a small dairy farm. Captain was as proud of his herd of pure-bred Jerseys as he had once been of the fact that he was the Reservation's champion roper and bronco rider.

The Indians once owned the entire country there without question, and they lived a good life. The government took it away from them and gave each one a head right to 160 acres of land. Thus have we done our duty to the Indian. It may be argued that his lot might have been worse had he been neglected entirely. He was a proud man at the beginning, and self-sufficient, but when the flood of emigration began he was bewildered and lost.

In some ways, I think the Indians have done very well, for it is not like it was years ago when one traveler described ration day on the reservation:

"It was ration day and 400 or 500 bucks in blankets and feathers, and squaws with papooses were present to receive their weekly ration of beef, flour, coffee, salt, baking powder, etc., and they fought and wrangled for the best places in line like boys scrambling for advantage at a circus ticket wagon. Everything was goodnatured and everybody was finally served to his satisfaction.

"The bucks were dirty and without dignity, and the squaws homely and even repulsive. Most of them wore blankets, but some wore discarded, ragged citizen's clothes, ill-fitting and awkwardly worn.

"Occasionally among them was seen a well-dressed, self-possessed man who except for his copper skin could have passed for a businessman. An occasional squaw, mostly a half-breed, carried her baby in her arms instead of on a board on her back."

The situation was not too pleasing to the Indians themselves. Pocatello Jim of the Bannack Creek Shoshones is quoted as saying, "Don't know what to do. Coat was once new, now old. Once red men spoke in parallel lines—now they cross."

An item from the *Pocatello Tribune* under dateline, April 11, 1897, reads: "Indian Tom's squaw died Tuesday in Happy Hollow district. She was a progressive woman and a short time ago decided she wanted to live in a house. She was no sooner dead than he took it down and went back to his tepee."

The same year a ghost dance was held on Camas Prairie in which there were 300 to 400 "unwelcome" visitors from Ross Fork. Presumably the people who "unwelcomed" them were the white settlers. Yet the Indians from Fort Hall had been digging camas roots there for centuries.

I have been told that the Warbonnet Cattle Company

used old Fort Hall for a winter headquarters, and there are men I know like Tom West and Ted Faulkner and many of the Indian riders who have punched cows on the Fort Hall bottoms. Perhaps some of them still do but of course it is not like the old days. I cannot write about them without a feeling of nostalgia, since I knew and rode with many of them, but all things change, the Indians perhaps most of all. I can remember many times seeing an Indian coming into town in his dilapidated wagon, he and the boys of his family, unless they were a pony escort, sitting in the spring seat, while his wife and daughters were sitting flat down in the bottom of the wagon-box. You seldom see a wagon any more.

Recently I visited Ezra and James Corneilison and their families at present Fort Hall, where they have been in business more than forty years. We grew up together on the upper Portneuf, and like me they are friends of the Indians. They refuse to think Indians are different from other people. "Some of them pay their debts promptly, and some will beat you if they can—just like white folks," Jim Corneilison told me.

But where you used to see Indian ponies standing in front of the stores and blanketed women sitting placidly on the steps waiting for their men to finish their loafing, you now see automobiles—everything from Cadillacs to jalopies held together with barbed wire. The colorful blankets and beaded moccasins are gone, although some of the older women still make beautifully beaded buckskin gloves for the menfolks. The women dress as do their white sisters, and you have to look at their complexion to tell Indian teen-agers from white ones. More often than not, the women are seen driving the automobiles while the men are in the back seats.

I stopped for a second look when I saw an Indian man walking along a Pocatello street with his wife walking a respectful twenty feet behind him. Nobody calls them bucks or squaws any more except Easterners. But there is a sad side. The tall, straight young Indian riders of my youth are seldom seen, and most of them run to fat, with pronounced beer-bellies. Too often young Indians are found dead beside the highway as a result of drinking anti-freeze from the radiators of their cars. Where once they would have been out on the range, you now find them loafing around the beer parlors and pool halls.

It is true that many of them are becoming educated and hold responsible positions, but I think it was a better life when the Fort Hall Indian Reservation was one vast cattle range. I also think it was still better in the days when it was known as the land of plenty game, and the Indian was free to live his own life.

The days of the roundup are over. The cow camp of the Chesterfield Cattle Association is the log cabin where my wife grew to womanhood and was scared stiff when she saw anyone except a cowboy, a sheepherder or an Indian. Now the roundups are conducted by farmers who bring along their wives and children for a vacation. It is not like the old days when on a cold, frosty morning you might see fifty cowhands scratching out their broncos with a fair proportion of them hitting the dirt. Even the cattle are purebred and gentle and nothing could possibly stampede them. I think the cattle era ended when the cattlemen changed the headquarters of the roundup from the old chuck-wagon to a log cabin.

The new freeway leaves Fort Hall a little west of the main stream of traffic, and you could easily overlook it. There are a couple of stores and gas stations patronized by white farmers as well as Indians, but the stores sell little except soda pop and notions. Automobiles take the customers to the cities of Blackfoot and Pocatello where most of them do their trading.

There is a good school at Fort Hall, as well as a modern hospital where the Indian children are born—a far cry from the old days when the Indian mother went out in the sagebrush alone to have her baby and hurried back to the tepee to cook supper for her family. Civilization has helped the Indians in some ways but has been bad for them in others. The hope for the future lies in the children who are beginning to think of themselves as Americans rather than Indians. If their parents ever call them papooses it is usually with a grin and some slightly profane adjective.

I was in the store of my friend Jim Corneilson when half a dozen little Indian girls aged from four to eight came in. They were as clean and happy youngsters as can be seen anywhere. I bought them each a bottle of pop which they accepted with a polite "Thank you" and wide smiles that warmed my heart.

Mr. Corneilson operates a portable merry-go-round, but there is no calliope, and instead of mechanical ponies the Indian kids ride the string of burros which plod round and round the wagon. He moves it from place to place on the reservation, and those burros are about the only link with the past those children will ever have. Once a year they may get to accompany their parents out to watch the Sun Dance on Bannack Creek, but they will probably no more understand its significance, which is associated with religion and prayer, than will the white people who come out from the cities to watch it.

In one way the Indians have been fortunate. Their country never experienced a real mining boom. There were a few small mines, but not enough for anyone to get excited about. In the old files of the *Pocatello Tribune* I read about a dispute over a rock quarry; if the white men quarreled with the Indians about the royalty rights to some building stone what would have happened if it had been gold? It would have been thrown open to the whites just as the best of the farm land was thrown open to homesteaders soon after the turn of the century.

Irrigation has changed the face of the Snake River desert, and the results cannot be quarreled with. While we were talking with Gene Edmo and his mother a white farmer was waiting patiently outside to buy hay from Mr. Edmo. Indians can at last do business with white men on equal terms. Most of the old cattle range has been taken up by dry-farm homesteaders, but comparatively little of it is on the reservation. Indian riders give good accounts of themselves in the rodeo competition and I have known several part-Indian girls who have been chosen as beauty queens. Many Indians have become educated, and a good share of them are devoting their lives to the service of their people.

Few places have seen more dynamic changes than the region around Fort Hall, culminating in the many defense plants which dot the Snake River valley; yet immediately around the old Fort Hall the physical aspects of the country has not changed much since Paul Richardson shot a buffalo bull and Nathaniel J. Wyeth decided it would be a good place to build a trading post.

At Ferry Butte there is now an old wooden bridge across the river with a sign at either end warning that you must cross at your own risk. That was what the emigrants had to do, and they were well warned that the risk would continue all the way to Oregon if they persisted.

It is hard to realize now that issues were determined there on which the fate of the nation depended. We can be glad that the emigrants had the fortitude to go on, and looking back at the kaleidoscope of history we must do honor to the men and women who refused to deviate from the stern line of purpose. We must also pay tribute to the gallant men of Hudson's Bay, their Indian wives and their descendants.

Fort Hall was the center of a great spider web, carelessly at first, and then carefully, woven to catch the great fly of emigration. The web extended from Alaska to New England, and it grew tighter as it neared the center—Fort Hall, the most important point on the old Oregon Trail. It had to be torn away before anyone knew who would be victor in the fight for the entire Northwest Coast. As with real spider webs, all that remained at the core was the dried-up spider.

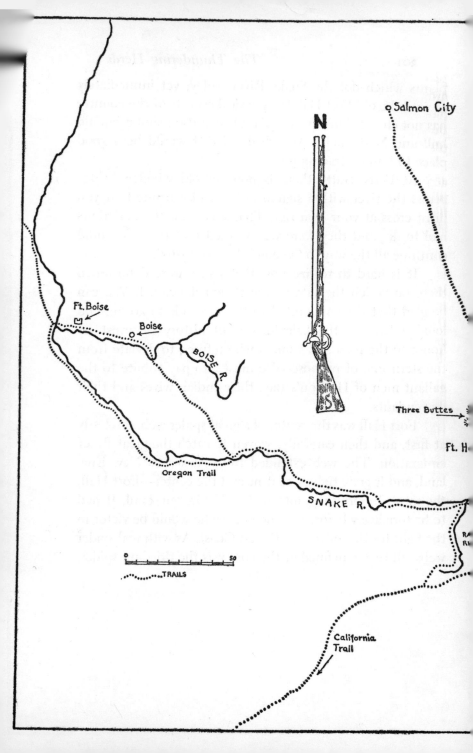

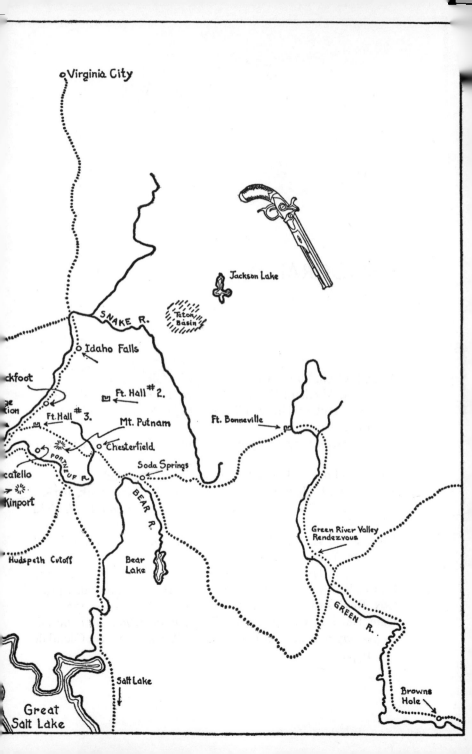

# BIBLIOGRAPHY

Alter, J. Cecil. *James Bridger*, Salt Lake City, 1925.
Anderson, Abraham C. *Trails of Early Idaho*, Caldwell, 1940.
Bancroft, Hubert Howe. *History of the Northwest Coast*, San
    Francisco, 1884.
———. *History of Oregon*, 2 volumes, San Francisco, 1886–
    1888.
Benton, Thomas H. *Thirty Years' View*, New York, 1856.
Brosnan, C. J. *History of the State of Idaho*, New York, 1918.
Brown, Jessie Broughten. *Fort Hall on the Oregon Trail*, Cald-
    well, 1934.
Chittenden, H. M. *The American Fur Trade of the Far West*,
    New York, 1902.
Clark, R. C. *History of the Willamette Valley*, Chicago, 1927.
Clarke, S. S. *Pioneer Days of Oregon History*, Portland, 1905.
Cox, Ross. *Adventures on the Columbia*, New York, 1832.
Dale, Harrison C. *The Ashley-Smith Explorations and the Dis-
    covery of a Central Route to the Pacific, 1822–29*, Glendale,
    1942.

Dana, Julien. *Sutter of California*, San Francisco, 1934.

De Voto, Bernard. *Across the Wide Missouri*, Boston, 1947.

Dunham, Dick and Vivian. *Our Strip of Land, History of Daggett County, Utah*, Manila (Utah), 1947.

Dye, Eva Emery. *McLoughlin and Old Oregon*, Chicago, 1900.

Farnham, T. J. *Travels in the Great Western Prairies in 1839*, London, 1841.

Frederick, J. V. *Ben Holladay, the Stagecoach King*, Glendale, 1940.

Fuller, George W. *History of the Pacific Northwest*, New York, 1931.

Gray, W. H. *History of Oregon, 1742–1849*, Portland, 1870.

Gude, Erwin G. *Bigler's Chronicle of the West*, Berkeley, 1962.

Hafen, LeRoy R. and Ann W. *To the Rockies and Oregon, 1839–42*. Vol. III. *To the Rockies and Oregon*, Vols. IV & V: including *Russell B. Sage's Correspondence and Papers*, and *Scenes in the Rocky Mountains*, Glendale, 1955.

Harris, Beth Kay. *The Towns of Tintic*, Denver, 1960.

Holman, Dr. F. V. *John McLoughlin, the Father of Oregon*, Cleveland, 1907.

*Idaho, A Guide to the State*. Federal Works Project, New York, 1942.

*Idaho, Yesterday and Today*. Souvenir Handbook, Fort Hall Centennial, Pocatello, 1934.

Irving, Washington. *Astoria* and *Adventures of Captain Bonneville*, reprints of both works in one volume, Chicago, 1900.

Jackson, W. Turrentine. *Wagon Roads West*, Berkeley, 1952.

Kelly, Charles. *Old Greenwood*, Salt Lake City, 1936.

———. *Outlaw Trail*, Salt Lake City, 1938.

Lavender, David. *Bent's Fort*, Garden City, 1954.

Lockley, Fred. *Oregon Trail Blazers*, New York, 1929.

Lucia, Ellis, *The Saga of Ben Holladay*, New York, 1959.

Mackey, Douglas. *The Honorable Company*, New York, 1936.

McConnell and Driggs. *Frontier Law*, Chicago, 1926.

McLean, John. *Twenty-five Years Service in the Hudson's Bay Territory*, 2 Volumes, London, 1845.

Morgan, Dale. *Jedediah Smith and the Opening of the West,* New York, 1953.

Nixon, Oliver W. *How Marcus Whitman Saved Oregon,* Chicago, 1895.

Paden, Irene D. *In the Wake of the Prairie Schooner,* New York, 1953.

Parkman, Francis. *The Oregon Trail,* New York, 1933.

Powell, F. W. *Hall J. Kelley, Prophet of Oregon,* Portland, 1917.

Ross, Alexander. *Fur Hunters of the Far West,* London, 1855.

Schoolcraft, H. R. *Journal of a Tour into the Interior of Missouri and Arkansas,* London, 1821.

Scott, Harvey W. *History of the Oregon Country,* Cambridge, 1924.

Simpson, Sir George. *Fur Trade and Empire,* Cambridge, 1931.

Thwaites, Reuben Gold. *Early Western Travels, 1748–1846,* Cleveland, 1904–1906.

Toponce, Alexander. *Reminiscences,* Ogden, 1923.

Townsend, John K. *A Narrative of a Journey Across the Rocky Mountains in 1834,* Philadelphia, 1839.

Victor, Frances Fuller. *River of the West,* Hartford, 1870.

Wagner, Henry R. *Spanish Voyages to the Northwest Coast of America in the 16th Century,* San Francisco, 1929.

Wislizenus, F. A. *A Journey to the Rocky Mountains in the Year 1839,* St. Louis, 1840. Originally in German.

Writers' Work Project. *Oregon, End of the Trail,* Portland, 1940.

Wyeth, John B. *A Short History of a Long Journey,* Cambridge, 1833.

Young, S. G. *Sources of Oregon History,* Berkeley, 1899. (Contains *Correspondence and Journals of Nathaniel J. Wyeth, 1831–1836.*)

## MAGAZINES & MANUSCRIPTS

*British Columbia Historical Quarterly*. Victoria, B.C., 1938.
Young, F. G. *The Oregon Trail Report for the Year 1902, of the Public Archives Commission*. Washington, D.C., 1902.

## NEWSPAPERS

*American Farmer*, Baltimore, Maryland.
*Boise Statesman*, Boise, Idaho.
*Deseret News*, Salt Lake City.
*Double Standard*, Moscow, Idaho.
*Idaho State Journal*, Pocatello, Idaho.
*Pocatello Tribune*, Pocatello, Idaho.
*St. Louis Inquirer*, St. Louis, Missouri.
*Weekly Mountaineer*, The Dalles, Oregon.

# Index

Abernathy, Governor, 249
Abilene, 288
Adams, Thomas, 198
Alaska, 301
Alder Gulch, 269
American Board, 186, 194, 250
American Falls, 16
American Falls Reservoir, 109
American Fur Company, 55, 73, 134, 139, 149, 209, 257
Anderson, Abraham C., 284
Applegate, Jesse, 61, 196
Arapaho, 205
Arco, 18
Ashburton-Webster Treaty, 183, 194
Ashley, William H., 66, 72, 73, 134–135, 203
Astor, John Jacob, 24, 28, 30, 35, 39, 41, 67
Astoria, 27–30, 33, 35–36, 39–41, 65

Bablaine, Peter, 266
Baboon Gulch, 266
Bachelor Hall, 172
Bactrian camels, 64
Baker's Bay, 26, 40
Bald Headed Chief (Bonneville), 135
Ball, John, 59, 71, 99, 180
Bancroft, Herbert Howe, 27-28, 54, 68, 124, 171

Bannack Indians, 152, 153, 254, 262, 269
Bannack Creek, 81, 299
Bannack Mountains, 272
Baptiste (Indian boy), 102, 119, 186
Batchicka (Crow woman), 227, 228
Battle Creek, 262
Bear Lake, 155, 165
Bear River, 139, 142, 146, 155, 213, 262, 292
Beaver (vessel), 35–36
Beaver, Reverend, 48
Beer Springs, 142, 152, 155 (see Soda Springs)
Bent brothers, 73, 257
Benton, Thomas Hart, 64, 182, 184
Bent's Fort, 195, 199, 200, 203, 204, 212, 257
Bering, Vitus, 21
Biddle, Captain James, 41
Bidwell-Bartleson party, 225–226, 241
Big Butte, 18, 114
Bighorn, 100, 101
Bigler, Henry William, 240, 241
Birch Creek, 18, 146, 289
Birnie Girls, 172
Bishop Creek, 229
Bitter Roots, 269
Bird (renegade white man), 222
Black, Captain, 40

Blackfeet Indians, 14, 135, 142, 143, 148, 150, 222, 223, 271, 274, 292
Blackfoot, Idaho, 109, 155–156, 264, 271, 274, 292, 295, 299
Blackfoot River, 81, 106, 109, 110, 155–156, 264, 269, 279, 295, 299
Blackhawk, Chief, 263
Black's Fort, 206
Blair, W., 199, 217–218
Blanchett, Father, 175
Blue John (Nez Percé), 148
Blue Mountains, 153, 255
Boisclere (Hudson's Bay man), 256
Boise Basin, 259, 266, 267
Boise City, 272, 277, 284
Bonneville, Benjamin Louis Eulalie de, 12, 48–49, 54, 61, 63, 70, 72, 75, 124, 133–143, 145–150, 152–154, 158–159, 184, 187, 256, 259, 269, 289, 290
Bonney, Benjamin, 232–235, 237–239
Bonney, Jarvis, 235, 239
Bonney Party, 232
Bonney, Truman, 233, 235
Book of Mormon, The, 103
Borah, Senator William E., 268
Boston, 22
"Bostons," 56, 116, 156
Bridger, Jim, 66, 72, 104, 134–135, 150, 187, 191, 239, 256, 257
Broncho, Jim, 17, 108, 264
Brosnan, C. J., 198
Broughten, Lt. William, 24, 85
Brown, Baptiste, 204
Brown's Hole, 203–204, 211, 215, 219, 221
Buenaventura (Columbia) River, 20
"Burg on the Bear" (Corinne, Utah), 291

Bullfinch, Charles, 22
Butch Cassidy's Wild Bunch, 204

Cabrillo, Juan, 21
Cache Valley, 165
Caldron, Linn, 32
Calico, Birdie, 260
Calico, Leon, 260, 278
California, 265, 279
Call's Fort, 289
Camas Prairie, 255, 296
Cambridge, Mass., 101
Camp Floyd, 289
Camp Reed, 255, 263
Camp Wallace, 255
Campbell, Robert, 66, 73
Canal Gulch, 265
Cantonment Loring, 255
Carson, Kit, 123, 204, 214, 256
Carson Valley, 241
Carver's Travels, 20
Catherine the Great, 23, 172
Cayuse War, 193, 218
Cerre, M.S., 137, 139, 141, 145, 151, 155
Champoeg, Ore., 118, 177, 249
Chappine, Antoine, 32
Charbonneau, Touissant, 30
Chesterfield, Idaho, 16, 142, 290, 294
Chesterfield Cattle Association, 298
Cheyenne Bill, 292, 293
Chiles, Captain Joseph B., 241
Civil War, 288
Clarke, John, 35, 40
Clark, William, 24, 30, 31, 118, 140
Clayoquot Sound, 27
Clearwater River, 266
Clyman, James, 232
Columbia (vessel), 22, 23
Columbia River, 20, 21, 23, 26, 29,

43, 44, 129, 151, 176, 177, 183,
    184, 216, 222, 242, 243, 250, 281
Columbia River Valley, 56, 58
Comcomly, Chief, 27, 29, 35, 39,
    40
Connor, General Pat, 262, 263, 268,
    283
Cook, Amos, 219, 222, 223
Cook, Captain James B., 21, 22, 26
Corinne, Utah, 269, 270, 289, 291
Corneilison, Ezra, 297
Corneilison, James, 297, 299
Corral Creek, 292
*Cowlitz* (vessel), 95
Craig, William, 204
Crane's Flat, 292
Craters of the Moon National
    Monument, 18
Crooks, Ramsey, 32, 33, 134
Cushing, Caleb, 131


Dalles, The, 162, 208, 271, 272,
    275
Day, John, 30
De Fuca Straits, 56
Dempsey, Bob, 284
Dempsey Creek, 284
Dempsey (see Lava Hot Springs),
    284
Dent, Captain, 259
Denver, 204
Desjardins (Hudson's Bay man),
    256
DeSmet, Father, 61, 175
"Digger" Indians, 153
*Discovery* (vessel), 22
Dixie, Ralph, 295
Dixon, Stuart, 275
"Dobies," The, 110
*Dolly* (vessel), 30
Donation Act, 178, 179
Donner's Lake, 230

Donner Party, 202, 232, 237
Donner's Pass, 230, 234, 237
Dorion, Pierre, 30, 33
Dorion Woman, 33, 164
Doty, Governor, 262
Douglas, Sir James, 91, 98
Drake, Sir Francis, 20–21
Dring, Captain, 173
Dring, Trottie, 173, 174
*Dryad* (vessel), 129
Dutch John, Idaho, 204
Dye, Eva Emery, 119


Eagle Rock (see Idaho Falls), 269
Edmo, Gene, 278, 300
Edmo, Lizzie, 260, 264, 278
Elk City, 266
Ells, Dr., 194
Epps, Captain, 172
Ermatinger, Francis, 95, 96, 99, 114,
    115, 166, 168, 172, 192, 206,
    207, 221, 256, 280, 282
Eureka, Utah, 289


Farnham Party, 212
Farnham, Thomas Jefferson, 67,
    197, 199, 200, 202, 207, 214,
    215, 217, 218, 224
Faulkner, Ted, 142, 260, 297
Ferry Butte, 17, 107, 165, 260, 301
Figueroa, Governor, 123, 125, 126
Fillmore, President, 179
Fisher, Senator George, 274
Fitzpatrick, Thomas, 66, 72, 104
Five Crows (Cayuse Indian), 247
Flaming Gorge, 204
Flathead House, 99
Flathead Indians, 103, 118
Fletcher, Francis, 219, 223
Florence (mining town), 266
Floyd, Congressman, of Virginia,
    55, 56, 184

Fontenelle, Lucien, 138
Fort Benton, 269
Fort Boise, 67, 107, 114, 116, 168, 169, 189, 207, 209, 221, 256, 270, 281, 282, 283, 285
Fort Bonneville, 76, 137, 145
Fort Bridger, 206
Fort Cass, 100
Fort Colville, 99
Fort Davey Crockett, 202, 203, 204, 212, 213, 215, 216, 221
Fort Douglas, 262
Fort Hall, 12, 14, 16–19, 29–31, 39, 42, 44, 46, 59, 60, 65, 70, 81, 96, 99, 107, 108, 111, 114–117, 120, 127, 133, 137, 141–144, 146, 151, 152, 160, 166–168, 174, 176, 178, 185–189, 192, 193, 195, 196, 206, 207, 209, 211, 215, 217, 219–222, 224, 226, 228, 229, 231, 232, 233, 235, 237, 239, 240–242, 255, 260, 264, 265, 269–273, 275, 279, 280, 282, 283, 284, 286, 290, 291, 293, 295, 296, 297, 299–301
Fort Hall Agency, 261
Fort Hall Bottoms, 107, 108, 153
Fort Hall Indian Reservation, 260, 291, 298
Fort Henry, 32
Fort Lapwai, 190
Fort Laramie, 205
Fort Lemhi, 259
Fort Misery (see Fort Davey Crockett), 204, 205, 216
Fort Nez Percé (see Fort Walla-Walla)
Fort Nonsense (see Fort Bonneville), 76
Fort Ross, 42
Fort St. Vrain, 204
Fort Uintah, 195
Fort Union, 101

Fort Walla-Walla, 82, 99, 154, 156, 162, 194, 207, 209, 217, 218, 242, 248, 249, 251, 255, 256, 266, 267, 270, 272, 282
Fort William, 37, 86, 115, 119, 120, 126, 166–168
Franklin, Idaho, 268
Frémont, John C., 109, 183, 239
French, Pete, 289
French Prairie, 99, 126
Fuca, Juan de, 21

Gale, Joseph, 170–171
Gallager, Major M. F., 262
General Land Law (see Donation Act)
"Gentile Capital of Utah" (Corinne, Utah), 291
Gervois (Sublette partner), 147
Ghent, Treaty of, 41
Gibson's Ferry, 263
Gilden, Dr., 238
Godin, Antoine, 77, 222, 223
Godin's River, 114
Goodhart, George, 283, 284–285, 287
Goodyear, Miles, 257
Goose Creek, 229
Gore, Lt. John, 22
Graham, Joe, 292
Grande Ronde Valley, 16, 154, 155, 185, 222, 256
Grant, Captain Johnnie, 96, 194, 196, 231, 232, 242, 256, 257, 271, 279, 280, 282, 283, 284, 285, 286
Grant, Johnnie, Jr., 255, 284
Grave Creek, 274
Gray, H. H., 187
Gray, Robert, 22–24, 52, 85
Gray's Bay, 57
Gray's Lake, 292

Great Salt Lake, 135, 142, 155, 165
Green River, 72, 100, 104, 152
Greenwood, Britain, 233
Greenwood, Caleb, 192, 193, 196, 225–228, 230, 231, 237, 239, 247
Greenwood, Crockett, 239
Greenwood, James, 239
Greenwood, John, 232, 235, 236, 237
Greenwood, Sam, 233, 235, 236
Greenwood's Cut-off, 228
Grey, Earl, 94
Griffiths, Reverend, 216

Hall, Edwin O., 207
Hall, Henry, 107
Haley and Greathouse, 272
Haller, Major, 256
Ham's Fork, 135
Harding, Senator Benjamin F., 271
Harney, General, 255
Hastings Cut-off, 232, 241
Hastings, Lansford W., 232
Hathaway (Joseph Gale's partner), 170, 171
Hawkins, Calensus, 291
Hecata, Bruno, 21
Helena, 271, 276
Hell's Canyon, 33
Helm, Boone, 273
Henry, Andrew, 30, 269
Henry's Fork, 206
Hensley, Captain Samuel P., 241
Hill, Tom, 243
Hoback, John, 30, 31
Hodgkiss (Bonneville's clerk), 145, 147
Holladay's Adobes (stage station), 264
Holladay, Ben, 270–272, 275, 276, 289, 290
Holman, Joseph, 219, 220, 224

Hopkins, Sarah Winnemucca, 229
Horse Creek, 135, 139, 157
Horse Prairie, 140, 147
Houston, General Sam, 55
Howard, Dr. Minnie, 17, 108
Howe, Colonel, 255
Hoyt, Captain C. H., 262
Hubbard, Thomas Jefferson, 209
Hudson's Bay Company, 54, 55, 63, 65, 67, 70, 74, 75, 81, 85, 95, 96, 99, 114, 116, 122, 156, 255, 256, 280, 283
Humboldt River, 165
Hunt, Wilson Price, 14, 25, 30–34, 39, 40, 134, 153, 226

Independence Rock, 230
Ireland, J. N., 263, 277
Iroquois Indians, 164
Irving, Washington, 12, 27, 28, 133, 135–137, 145–147, 152

Jackson, Andrew, 182
Jackson, David E., 66, 72, 134, 135
Jackson's Hole, 139
*Janet* (vessel), 173
Jefferson, Thomas, 22, 23, 182
Jemmy Jock (see Bird), 222
Jones, John Paul, 22
Joseph, Chief, 100, 263
Julia (wife of Peter Skene Ogden), 39

Kelley, Benjamin, 50
Kelley, Charles, 229
Kelley, Hall Jackson, 12, 22, 23, 48, 125–131, 133, 150, 182, 184, 186, 198, 217, 218, 221
Kelley, John, 50
Kelley, Samuel, 50

Kendrick, Captain, 52
Kilbourne, R. L., 219, 224
Kinney, Sam, 235, 237
Kosato (renegade Blackfoot), 143, 147, 148
Kullyspell House, 36

Ladore Canyon, 203
Lady Washington (vessel), 22
Lafayette, Marquis de, 23, 133
La Framboise (Hudson's Bay trapper), 125
Lake Bonneville, 270
Lake Tahoe, 231
Lamazee (Indian), 27–28
Lancaster, Joseph, 123
Lander Trail, 289
Lane, Joseph, 253
Lavender, David, 257
Ledyard, John, 22–23
Lee, Daniel, 102, 124, 168, 174–175, 246
Lee, Jason, 92, 102, 103, 110–112, 118–119, 126, 168, 174–175, 181, 186, 198, 246
Lewis, Joe, 243
Lewis, Meriwether, 23, 24, 30–31, 140
Lewis River (see Snake River), 81, 106
Lewiston, Idaho, 266
Lincoln Creek, 81, 106, 261, 264
Linn, Senator, 183–184
Lisa, Manuel, 30–31, 226
Little Bear River, 205
Little Lost River, 142, 146
Little Snake River, 213
Livermore, Thomas, 71–72
Lockart Gang, 273
Lorenzo (cattle town), 289
Louisiana Purchase, 61
Lovejoy, Amos L., 191, 194–195

Lowell, James Russell, 67
Lucier, Etienne, 86, 176
Lupton, P. Lancaster, 73

Mackenzie, Sir Alexander, 24, 36
Magic Valley, 154
Malade River, 146–147, 241, 270
Mammoth (mining town), 289
Manifest Destiny, 61
Mar, Helen, 191
Marie Julia (Ogden), 39
Martin, Dennis, 231
Martinez, Estavan Jose, 21
Massacre Rocks, 280
Mathieu, 139, 142
Matthews, Reverend T. Q., 281
May Dacre (vessel), 102, 115, 116, 117, 119, 166–167
McConnell, William J., 267–268
McDougal, Duncan, 25–26, 29–30, 34–35, 39–40
McDuffie, Senator, 183
McGarry, Major Edward, 262
McIntyre Brothers, 289
McKay, Alexander, 25–29, 43, 90
McKay, "Billy Boy," 173
McKay, Thomas, 106–107, 112, 113, 114, 155, 166, 256
McKenzie, Donald, 25, 40
McLean, John, 89
McLeod (Hudson's Bay man), 96
McLoughlin, David, 173
McLoughlin, Dr. John, 12, 29, 41–48, 63, 82, 83, 85–87, 90, 96, 98–99, 115, 117, 118, 125–129, 147, 167, 173, 174–181, 184, 190, 192, 200, 203, 209–210, 218–219, 240, 244, 246, 247, 250–252, 255
Meares, Captain John, 21, 85
Meek, Joe, 191, 204–205, 212, 214, 219, 242, 249, 253, 256

Meeker, Ezra, 17, 108–109, 264
Miller, Helen Independence, 230
Mills, Robert, 64
Missionary Board, 174–175, 246, 251
Montana, 273, 289–291
Morris, Joseph, 268
Morrisite War, 269
Mormons, 257, 259, 268, 279, 291, 293
Mt. Hood, 24
Mt. Kinport, 17
Mt. Putnam, 17, 106, 261, 294
Multnomah (Willamette) River, 57–58
Munger, Dr. Asahel, 207, 217
Murphy, Elizabeth Yuba, 230

Nampuh (see Bigfoot), 261
"Natwyethium," amphibious vehicle, 71–73
New Albion, 21
New, Bill, 221
New England, 301
New Helvetia, 191, 192
Newell, Doc, 191, 204–205, 212, 214, 219, 242, 249, 253
Newell, Don, 256
Nez Percé Indians, 15, 32, 77–78, 100, 102, 119, 139, 140–141, 143, 146, 147–149, 154–155, 162–164, 186, 190, 206, 248, 263
Nookamis (Indian chief), 27
Nootka Convention, 62
Nootka Sound, 21, 23, 34, 62
Northwest Coast, 24–25, 52, 64, 130, 301
Northwest Company, 24–25, 29, 35–37, 63, 65, 85, 116, 162–163
Northwest Passage, 21
Nuttall, Thomas, 103, 110, 112

Oakley, Obediah, 212, 216–217
Ogden, Peter Skene, 38, 39, 46, 81, 95, 105, 135, 147, 165, 185, 225, 247, 255, 256, 283
Old Soldiers Home, 284
Oliver, A. J., 276
Oliver & Conover stagecoach line, 270
Olney (Indian Agent), 255
O'Neil, A., 209
*Ontario* (vessel), 41
Oregon, 26, 29, 41–42, 45, 49, 52, 63, 95, 96, 110, 111, 114, 116, 119, 120, 122, 124–126, 129–133, 168, 170, 174, 176, 178, 183–185, 188, 192, 193, 200, 220, 254, 257, 259, 263, 266, 275, 281, 288, 289, 301
Oregon City, 177, 178, 239, 251, 253
"Oregon Dragoons," 197
Oregon Short Line Railroad, 14
Oregon Trail, 16, 60, 109, 137, 222, 261, 289, 301
Orofino (mining town), 266
Orofino Creek, 265
Overland Stage, 263

Pacific Fur Company, 24, 26, 29, 40, 41
Palmer, Lieutenant, 263
Palmerston, Viscount, 94
Palouse Indians, 162
Pambrum, Pierre, 82, 154, 189, 191, 207, 243
Pambrum, Maria, 172, 173, 175, 191
Parker, Reverend Samuel, 186
Pattee, George, 286
Pattee, Joseph, 257, 283, 286
Pattee, Lizzie, 285

Payette, Francis, 168, 189, 281, 282, 285
Payette, Julia, 285
Payette River, 281
Pelly, Sir John, 94, 95
Pend' Oreilles, 141
Peoria, Illinois, 204, 216
Peoria Party, 191, 197, 204, 209, 211, 219, 223, 224
Perkins, Reverend H. K. W., 208
Pierce, Captain E. D., 265
Pierre's Hole, 75–77, 79, 81, 100, 135, 139, 141–142, 222, 223
Pio-pio-mox-mox (Cayuse chief), 193, 194
Piutes, 150, 229
Placerville, 240
Pleasant Valley, 240
Plummer Gang, 273
Plummer, Henry, 268
Pocatello, Chief, 259
Pocatello, Idaho, 17, 153, 295
Pocatello, Jim, 269
Pocatello Tribune, 296, 300
Portneuf, 16, 17, 142, 151, 206, 220
Powell, F. W., 49
Pratt, Parley P., 103
Promontory, Utah, 270, 291
Provost, Etienne, 165
Puget Sound, 21, 243
Putnam, Captain, 264

Quadra, Bodega Y., 21
Quincey, Josiah, 52

Raccoon (vessel), 40
Rae, William Glen, 172
Raft River, 81
Red River, 169
Reid, Agnes Just, 269
Resolution (vessel), 22

Rezner, Jacob, 30, 31
Richardson, Paul, 107, 110, 209, 212, 217, 301
Robbers Roost, 274
Robertson, John (see Jack Robinson), 214
Robinson, Edward, 30, 31
Robinson, Charley, 387
Robinson, Jack, 214
Rock Creek, 286
Rocky Mountain Fur Company, 45–47, 66–70, 73, 101, 103, 104, 135, 149
Rose, Ed., 151
Ross, Alexander, 162, 163
Ross Fork, 296
Ross Fork Creek, 81, 106
Russell, Osborne, 107
Russian River, 42

Sacajawea, 30, 140
Salmon River, 99, 139, 140, 143, 144, 147, 149, 155, 259, 266, 280, 283, 291
Salt Lake City, 45, 57, 195, 240, 241, 262, 269, 270, 272, 276, 277, 279
Sandwich Islands, 21, 26, 35, 40, 116, 129, 130
Sanpitch, Chief (Ute), 263
Sante Fe Trail, 199
Saptian (see Lewis River), 81
Sarah Mojave, 228
Schallenberger, Moses, 230, 231
Scott, Harvey W., 132
Sharon, Senator, of Nevada, 290
Shaw, Colonel, 256
Sheep Rock, 142
Sheridan, General Phil, 283
Sherman, General William Tecumseh, 283

Shortess, Robert, 200, 206, 208, 209, 210, 212

Shoshones, 14, 30, 141, 142, 149, 162, 164, 220, 222

Simpson, Alexander, 90, 95

Simpson, Sir George, 36, 43, 44, 74, 86, 88, 95, 169, 184, 185, 191, 250, 251

Sinclair, James, 170, 204, 255

Sinclair, Prewitt, 214, 216, 217

Sioux, 205

Smith, Jedediah S., 45–47, 66, 72, 90, 105, 124, 125, 128, 134, 147, 170, 212, 217, 225

Smith, Joseph, 103

Smith Party, 259

Smith, Sidney, 201, 202, 203

Smith, Solomon, 99, 118

Snake River, 17, 31, 32, 49, 107, 109, 114, 141, 151, 153, 154, 160, 162, 165, 188, 258, 280, 285, 291, 292

Snelling, W. J., 59

Soda Springs, 142, 206, 269, 270, 272, 276, 277, 279

Sowle, Captain, 35

Spalding, Eliza, 174, 187–188, 190

Spalding, Reverend H. H., 61, 92, 175, 186, 190, 194, 207, 246

Splawn, Moses, 266

Springville, Utah, 263

St. Anthony, Idaho, 31

Stafford, Ben, 276

Steamboat Springs, 212

Stevens, Elisha, 226, 230

Stevens, Townsend (Murphy Party), 226, 228–230, 234

Stewart, Captain William Drummond, 110, 151

Stickeen (Hudson's Bay post), 172

St. Louis, 55, 58, 73, 101, 103, 155, 286

Stone, Elizabeth Jarvis, 68

Stuart, David, 26–27, 39–40

Stuart, Robert, 26

Sublette Cut-off, 228

Sublette, Milton, 66, 77, 78, 80, 81–82, 100–101, 103–104, 134, 147

Sublette, William L., 66, 72, 74, 78, 80, 101, 103, 104–105, 121, 134–136, 139, 212

*Sultana* (vessel), 67, 83, 102

Sutter, Captain John, 62, 191–193, 225–226, 231, 234, 238, 240

Sutter's Fort, 229–230, 235, 237, 243

Taos, 195

Territory of Idaho, 253

Teton Basin, 295

Teton Pass, 31

Teton Peaks, 17, 142

Thomas and Company, 272

Thompson, David, 24, 36

Thing, Captain Joseph, 115, 117, 167

Thorn, Jonathan, 25–28, 39

Three Mile Knoll, 286, 287

Three Teton Peaks, 31, 163

Thurston, Samuel R., 179–180, 209

Tiloukaikt (Cayuse chief), 248

Tintic (district), 289

*Tonquin* (vessel), 25, 27, 28–29, 39, 90

Toponce, Alex, 289–291

Toponce Creek, 290

Townsend, John K., 79, 103, 106–107, 112–113

Trail Creek Pass, 274

Truckee, Chief, 229–230

Tudor, Frederick, 68

Twenty-four Mile Creek, 142

Twin Buttes, 18, 114

Tyler, President, 196

Umatilla Indians, 162, 222
Umatilla Valley, 207
Umatilla War, 1855, 255
Umpqua River, 46–47, 125
Updike, Sheriff, 268
Utah, 257, 270, 285, 288
Utah Lake, 165

Valerianos, Apostolus, 21
Vancouver Island, 21, 27
Virginia City, Mont., 267, 269, 271, 273, 275–277, 289, 291
Vivasout, Lieutenant, 251

Waiilatpu, 193, 207, 218, 244, 246
Walker, J. R., 124, 125, 137, 140, 150, 151, 155, 167, 204, 221, 225, 229
Walker Lake, 150
Walker River, 150
Walla Walla, 33, 184, 189, 190
Wappatoo, or Suave, Island, 116, 166
Warbonnet Cattle Company, 291, 292, 293
Warre, Lieutenant, 251
Warren, James, 266
Warren's Diggings, 266
Washington, D.C., 57
Waterhouse, James, 80
Webster-Ashburton Treaty, 61
Webster, Daniel, 61, 196
West, Thomas Payne, 108, 297
White, Elijah, 191, 242
Whitman, Dr. Marcus, 61, 92, 96, 175, 185–191, 194–196, 242–244, 246, 247, 250, 252

Whitman Massacre, 193, 212, 218, 247, 253
Whitman, Narcissa, 174, 187–191, 218, 244, 247, 250
Williamette Milling Company, 178
Williamette River, 57, 125, 209, 210, 243, 247, 250, 251, 281
Williamette Valley, 98, 119, 168
Willie, Captain, 295
Winnemucca, Chief, 229
Winthrop, Robert C., 181, 184
Wislizenus, Dr. F. A., 215–216
Wood, Blair, 202
Wood, Chauncey, 200
Wood, Joseph, 202
Wright, Ben, 208
Wyeth, Jacob, 66, 68, 70, 71, 80
Wyeth, John B., 71–72, 80
Wyeth, Nathaniel J., 11, 12, 14, 17, 48–49, 54, 59, 61, 63, 68, 70, 74–75, 77–79, 81–83, 90, 97, 98–100, 103, 110, 112, 114, 115–118, 126, 128, 134, 136–137, 139–140, 144–145, 147, 151, 160, 165, 172, 179–181, 184, 186–187, 198, 209, 222, 223, 256–257, 269, 286, 301

Yakima (Indians), 162
Yamhill County, 223
Yellow Serpent, see Pio-pio-mox-mox
Yerba Buena, 95, 170, 172
Young, Brigham, 57, 259, 268, 290
Young, Ewing, 61, 90, 123–124, 170, 203
Young, Frederick G., 60

# Praise for *Awakening Joy*

"In our pursuit of happiness, this moving book should be a dog-eared, worn-out companion. . . . As you work through this elegant material, you will find yourself laughing a little longer, dancing a little more, and awakening to the beauty of what lies inside you and in those nearby."
—DACHER KELTNER, professor of psychology, UC Berkeley,
and author of *Born to Be Good: The Science of a Meaningful Life*

"This book is an inspiring gift that will open your heart to the presence of love and joy in everyday life."
—FRANCES VAUGHAN, PH.D., psychologist, and author of
*Shadows of the Sacred: Seeing Through Spiritual Illusions*

"This book should be read by every person who cares about making this a better world. It can enhance the joys of working to develop a wiser and more compassionate society, and help make us both happier and more effective in challenging times."
—DANIEL ELLSBERG, author of
*Secrets: A Memoir of Vietnam and the Pentagon Papers*

"Faith, hope, and love have long been considered the essential virtues of the religious life. James Baraz has done us all a great service by elevating joy to its rightful place alongside the trinity of sacred emotions."
—PATRICIA E. DE JONG, senior minister,
First Congregational Church of Berkeley

"This is an inspirational and practical resource that helps us identify where we are or are not experiencing joy in our lives. This original book addresses the primary obstacles or beliefs that hinder our access to joy, and includes timeless practices and ways in which we can expand, cultivate, express, and experience more joy in our lives and within our own nature. Well-written, informative, and a significant contribution to everyone's well-being."
—ANGELES ARRIEN, PH.D., cultural anthropologist, and author of
*The Second Half of Life: Opening the Eight Gates of Wisdom*

"I have been deeply touched and inspired by James Baraz's accessible, practical wisdom. His genuine caring for people and enthusiasm for life generously pours forth and permeates everything that he teaches—now in the pages of this book."
—RABBI MARGIE JACOBS, Institute for Jewish Spirituality

"*Awakening Joy* is a wise treasure house of valuable information, anecdotes, potent quotes, and creative suggestions to step into one's power and live life to the max. This book is a rich, inspiring resource I'm excited to share with my yoga students."
—GABRIEL HALPERN, founder and director of the Yoga Circle (Chicago)

"To awaken joy in oneself and others is one of life's great skills, a skill taught by sages across the centuries, and now distilled in this book."
—ROGER WALSH, M.D., PH.D., University of California Medical School,
author of *Essential Spirituality: The Seven Central Practices
to Awaken Heart and Mind*

"Grounded in brain science and positive psychology, and illuminated by the practical wisdom of Buddhism, this book shows you many effective ways to have more happiness, love, and inner peace. Honest, powerful, and profound, each page comes alive with James's warm and friendly voice, sharing his own hard lessons and the stories of others, and guiding you toward an unshakeable joy of your own. A gem."
—RICK HANSON, PH.D., founder, Wellspring Institute for Neuroscience
and Contemplative Wisdom, and author of
*Buddha's Brain: The Practical Neuroscience of Happiness, Love and Wisdom*

# Awakening Joy

# Awakening Joy

10 STEPS THAT WILL PUT
YOU ON THE ROAD TO
REAL HAPPINESS

*JAMES BARAZ*
*&*
*Shoshana Alexander*

BANTAM BOOKS

NEW YORK

Published in the United States by Bantam Books, an imprint of
The Random House Publishing Group, a division of Random House, Inc., New York.

BANTAM BOOKS and the rooster colophon are registered trademarks of Random House, Inc.

ISBN 978-0-553-80703-5

Printed in the United States of America

Book design by Ellen Cipriano

*To:*

*Arnold Baraz, who taught me how to love,*

*Neem Karoli Baba, who showed me that love and goodness are all around if you look for them,*

*H.W.L. Poonja, who helped me reclaim my natural joy, and*

*Jane Baraz, my life partner, who teaches me to keep letting in the love and sending it out, no matter what.*
*—James Baraz*


*To my son, Elias, and the late Buddy-gi, my fountains of joy, and to an emerging world where love and compassion make all the Earth beautiful again.*
*—Shoshana Alexander*

# CONTENTS

FOREWORD *Jack Kornfield*     xi

PREFACE     *Ram Dass*     xiii

INTRODUCTION     xv

STEP 1:     Inclining the Mind Toward Joy     3

STEP 2:     Mindfulness: Being Present for Your Life     29

STEP 3:     Grateful Heart, Joyful Heart     60

STEP 4:     Finding Joy in Difficult Times     86

STEP 5:     The Bliss of Blamelessness     123

STEP 6:     The Joy of Letting Go     152

STEP 7:     The Sweetness of Loving Ourselves     180

STEP 8:     The Joy of Loving Others     206

STEP 9:     Compassion: The Natural Expression of
            a Joyful Heart     240

STEP 10:    The Joy of Simply Being     274

ACKNOWLEDGMENTS     295

BIBLIOGRAPHY     301

RECOMMENDED READING LIST     304

# FOREWORD

### by JACK KORNFIELD

You hold in your hands a book that can change your life—filled with inspiration and practical wisdom on how to live with more joy and well-being. James Baraz, my longtime colleague and dear friend, has always delighted in sharing teachings that inspire the mind and open the heart. This book is James at his finest. It draws on his wonderfully successful Awakening Joy course, which has shepherded thousands of students, even die-hard "unbelievers" and cynics, into a more joyful and happier life.

Without understanding the importance of happiness, spiritual life can feel like a grim duty or be confused with an endless self-improvement project. James, and Shoshana Alexander, who was one of my students in my early years of teaching, skillfully build on principles and practices from the Buddhist tradition to offer a pathway to true happiness.

As human beings, we all participate in the eternal dance of pleasure and pain, gain and loss, praise and blame, and birth and death that make up our lives, what Oscar Wilde called the "tainted glory" of worldly incarnation. In *Awakening Joy,* you will learn how to find and live with joy in the midst of all life's changes. To be joyful does not mean ignoring the great measure of suffering in the world, nor avoiding responsibility for alleviating as much suffering as we can. James and Shoshana show us how joy enables us to be a part of the solution to suffering, as it enables us to uplift all those we touch.

Joy is our birthright. All young children (if they are not traumatized) have it; it is innate to our consciousness. Joy is a reflection of our true nature—a pure, timeless, inviolable spirit found in each of us. In these pages, which include modern neuroscientific research as well as inspiration from exemplars like the Dalai Lama, you will discover how the transformative practices of *Awakening Joy* can lead each of us to live with dignity, compassion, and gracious freedom.

Read these words slowly. Savor them and practice the exercises in this book. Use them to open your heart and transform your life. Your days on Earth will be full of blessings.

May it be so.

JACK KORNFIELD
*Spirit Rock Meditation Center*
*Woodacre, CA*
*May 9, 2009*

# PREFACE

by RAM DASS

Joy gives life color, and it counteracts the negative around us in people and in society. I am finding that old age can be joyful. There's wisdom in it; it's unhurried. Even the absence of memory has its good points. By connecting to the joy in myself, I find the joy in everybody else. Our own joy becomes something we share, and that helps awaken it in others.

Real joy is deeper inside us than the happiness we get from external circumstances. Knowing that you're going for true happiness is a very joyful thing. My guru, Neem Karoli Baba, would become joyful just knowing that his devotees were all aiming for the purest place in their heart. He said that if you love everyone, serve everyone, and remember God—that will naturally bring you joy.

Love and contentment bring me very close to joy. Contentment leads you deeper into the moment, and there you find joy because you see that everything—the grass and the trees and the clouds—is a manifestation of the Divine. Everything becomes radiant. If you're a good lover of life, you will be tapping into joy.

I've known James Baraz for a long time, and he is skilled at present-ing teachings on happiness in an accessible way. *Awakening Joy* is fun to read. The stories are marvelous and the information is to the point. It's a very friendly book, appealing to all readers. And if you happen to be a practitioner of Buddhism, you will find that it's a deliciously Buddhist book—with the accent on *delicious.* This book shows that the celebration and love of life can go together with deep wisdom. This is a beautiful, beautiful book. Enjoy it.

RAM DASS
*Maui, Hawaii*
*July 15, 2009*

# INTRODUCTION

By his own admission, Warren was a pessimist. "You're looking at someone who tends to see the downside of things," he warned me when he
started coming to my classes. He had some reasons for feeling this way.
Life had thrown him a few curveballs, among them an accident in his
youth that had left him with chronic pain. Despite being pretty well
committed to "the downside," when he heard that I was creating a course
called Awakening Joy, and would be teaching it in Berkeley where he
lived, he was intrigued. He actually told me he wondered if changing his
way of seeing things could make him happier. I wondered that myself, especially as the class got under way. Although I could see that the strategies and techniques were helping the other participants find more joy in
their lives, after each session Warren would express his skepticism. I just
figured, "Well, you can't win 'em all."

Then one evening he arrived at class with a noticeably different expression on his face. I was curious to hear what had happened. We started
the class with each person reporting how the practices I gave as homework had been going since our previous meeting. To my surprise and
delight, when Warren's turn came he told us that something quite unexpected seemed to be happening to him. "As I was driving into the city,"
he started, "there was a whole lot of really slow traffic. I tend to get frus-

trated when I'm caught in that, and I started, as I often do, thinking about everything that's wrong in our society. I was really getting on a roll."

We all nodded our heads, easily identifying with the scene. Warren continued, slowly speaking the words, as if amazed that they were coming out of his mouth. "Suddenly I stopped and said to myself, 'Now wait a minute. Is there any joy here?' I saw that I could just switch the channels. I looked out and I saw the water in the San Francisco Bay. I looked up and it was a clear day. I opened my sunroof and I said to myself, 'You know, it's not so bad.' I realized there is a switch that I'm starting to find that I didn't know was there before." He looked at us and smiled as if to say, "Go figure." At that moment I knew that the tools in the Awakening Joy course had undeniable potential to unlock joy.

> *My life has taken a positive turn I'd have never believed possible. I truly believe my new focus is what made it possible to let go of a collapsed marriage, foreclosure on a home, and a bankruptcy. I now wake up and go to sleep with a conscious feeling of happiness."*
>
> —A COURSE PARTICIPANT

Joy and happiness are more than just good ideas. They can be the baseline on which we live our lives. The purpose of this book is to show how to access that switch inside and live life with greater joy. It's based on the program I've been teaching since the first course in my living room in 2003. Within a couple of years, it became an online course with people enrolled from around the world. Repeatedly I've seen that by cultivating certain behaviors and attitudes, participants can indeed bring greater well-being into their lives.

## THE MANY FLAVORS OF JOY

Awakening Joy is based on a key principle: Our joy and happiness is up to us. Our suffering or well-being is not solely determined by what's happening in our present circumstance but to a large degree by our *relationship* to what is happening. As happiness experts Rick Foster and Greg Hicks say in their book *How We Choose to Be Happy,* happiness is a choice, and over time we can learn how to make it a habit.

This book will not create joy for you. Joy is already there inside you.

It is inherent in every one of us, an innate capacity, like the ability to learn a language or to love. As innocent babies we came into this world with a natural joy, and we can discover it again.

The feeling of well-being I'm calling joy comes in many different flavors. And it can look very different from person to person, from a quiet sense of contentment to bubbly enthusiasm. For some people it's an energetic radiance; for others it's a quiet feeling of connection. Joy can arise as a belly laugh, or as a serenely contented smile that accepts life just as it is. We experience a profound joy when we let ourselves be touched by beauty and nature. We can feel an energetic lightness when we let ourselves be silly and playful. Acting with generosity or compassion uplifts our heart, as does the feeling that comes from living with integrity. We delight in seeing others happy, and we can be moved when we behold goodness and truth. We each have our own unique ways of experiencing and expressing joy based on our individual temperaments. Your happiness may not look like someone else's, but you can find the expression that is uniquely yours. One of your discoveries as you follow this program will be the many flavors of joy you can find in yourself.

## "WHAT IF I'M NOT A JOYFUL PERSON?"

Is there a limit to how happy any one of us can be? Yes . . . and no. The idea of a "happiness set point" became popular for a while among psychologists and the general public. Early studies suggested that no matter what events or experiences happen to us—good or bad—we return to our typical level of happiness. However, recent research has painted a more complex picture, showing that in general, people have a changing happiness level that rises and falls over time. This means we have the opportunity to improve our own level of well-being.

For example, Dr. Richard Davidson's research at the University of Wisconsin has been demonstrating the brain's ability to change and develop, even in adults. In her book *Train Your Mind, Change Your Brain,* Sharon Begley writes extensively about the results of Davidson's experiments. She concludes: " . . . the basic finding that cognitive activity can alter activity in one of the brain's emotion regions supports the hope that mental training can shift the happiness set point." Davidson's intention is to demonstrate how such training can transform "the emotional mind." Whether you consider yourself a joyful person or not, you have a brain that is capable of changing.

Some people are uncomfortable with the word "joy." Perhaps the thought of "being happy" makes your eyes roll as if you're being asked to wear a permanent smiley face. Maybe it brings to mind syrupy TV ads of couples skipping through meadows of daisies. Don't worry. Truly happy people are not happy all the time. This is what Rick Foster and Greg Hicks found in their research, identifying and interviewing over three hundred individuals who live genuinely happy lives. Being sad and angry and feeling the whole range of human emotions is part of being alive. I'm not talking about adopting a Pollyanna attitude or living in denial. What I'm calling joy is a general feeling of aliveness and well-being that is characterized by meeting the ups and downs of life with authenticity and perspective.

> *This course has been superb! The fog of depression in which I began the year has almost entirely lifted. I am unspeakably grateful."*
> —A COURSE PARTICIPANT

If "joy" and "happiness" bring up resistance, see if there's another word that resonates better with you—well-being, contentment, delight, ease, aliveness—and substitute it as you participate in this program. You might use a variety of words to describe these uplifting states as I will do throughout this book.

## What Is Joy?

Take a few moments to reflect on what the word "joy" evokes in you. What images come to mind? How is joy most naturally expressed through you? Notice any resistance you may have to the word and, if you need to, find the words that most closely express a state of well-being you value. Begin to pay attention to this state whenever you experience it in your life.

## FINDING JOY IN DIFFICULT TIMES

The thought of finding joy may seem out of touch with reality, especially during times of great challenge in your own life and in the lives of others. Every day we read stories in the news that make our hearts ache—from global climate change, to ideological wars, to mass foreclosures and company layoffs. Or we see in our neighborhoods and among our friends the fear that comes with economic uncertainty or health problems. Perhaps closer to home, we feel that fear ourselves. Awakening joy might seem like a frivolous endeavor.

*I know the course has had a positive impact on me—but it is amazing to see how it can benefit others in my life. This stuff is absolutely contagious."*
—A COURSE PARTICIPANT

For those of us who tend to carry the world on our shoulders, being joyful in a world of suffering can feel self-centered or like sticking our heads in the sand. Someone with this perspective stood up to speak at the opening session of an Awakening Joy course, his voice both thoughtful and troubled. "I'm having a big reaction here," he confessed. "All this talk of well-being and joy seems so disconnected from what's going on in the world. It's like we're all sitting around, safe and comfortable, singing, 'Someone's crying, Lord, Kumbaya.'" There were lots of nodding heads in the group.

Together we ended up dubbing this roadblock the "Kumbaya Factor," and it is one of the most convincing reasons to stop looking for joy before we start. While this critical issue will be considered more fully in Step Four, something was said in the discussion with this young man that made sense to him. Focusing only on the terrible things in the world, and overlooking the beauty and goodness, can lead us to pull back from life and fall into despair. Staying in touch with the well of joy enables us to be part of the solution, rather than part of the problem. It can motivate and support us in making a positive difference in our lives and in the world, not only through actions we might choose but also through the uplifting effect we can have on those we're in contact with.

In 2004, historian Howard Zinn published an inspiring article in *The Nation* magazine, entitled "The Optimism of Uncertainty." In it he wrote:

> An optimist isn't necessarily a blithe, slightly sappy whistler in the dark of our time. To be hopeful in bad times is not just foolishly romantic. It is based on the fact that human history is a history not only of cruelty, but also of compassion, sacrifice, courage, kindness. What we choose to emphasize in this complex history will determine our lives. If we see only the worst, it destroys our capacity to do something. If we remember those times and places—and there are so many—where people have behaved magnificently, this gives us energy to act, and at least the possibility of sending this spinning top of a world in a different direction.

In Taoism it's said that life is made up of ten thousand joys and ten thousand sorrows. If we only focus on the sorrows, we're not seeing the full picture. When we open up to the joys—the beauty and goodness around us—we can view our suffering with a wider perspective. This course is not about denying the hard stuff. In fact, dealing with sorrow wisely when it comes is one of the essential practice themes of the Awakening Joy course.

The ten thousand joys and ten thousand sorrows are part of the full tapestry of life. Life is often hard; to awaken our joy does not mean to deny that. Those who discover the secret of well-being are capable and centered, able to be authentically engaged with whatever circumstances life presents. Although they feel the full range of emotions, they also know that anger, sadness, and fear are temporary visitors.

*Trying hard* to be joyful or happy will just be frustrating and work against you. When you're feeling sad or worried or angry or having other difficult feelings, don't pretend they're not there. Allow your experience to be just as it is while opening to the possibility of joy.

As we awaken to all that is good in ourselves and in others around us, we are reminded of how much we love life and care about this planet. Cultivating our goodness, aliveness, and joy not only feels good, it also helps us express our love more and awaken it in others. Our own joy becomes a gift to everyone we meet.

## WHAT RELIGION IS A JOYFUL HEART?

Because I've been a teacher of Buddhist meditation for more than thirty years, many of the basic principles and time-tested practices in the Awakening Joy program come from that body of teachings. The Dalai Lama, a Tibetan Buddhist, says in *The Art of Happiness,* "The purpose of life is to be happy." The Buddha himself was known as The Happy One. He encouraged each person to discover where true happiness is found, saying if we aim for the highest happiness—a mind free of all negativity and confusion—every other kind of happiness will follow.

However, this is not a Buddhist course on happiness. There is no "Buddhist" happiness or Christian, Jewish, Muslim, or Hindu happiness. Our natural state of well-being is not exclusive to any particular spiritual tradition. Ministers, rabbis, and people from every faith—as well as those who follow no religion—have found this course beneficial. In fact, many people, including myself, consider Buddhism to be more a philosophy than a religion, a way to live a harmonious life. Because of its emphasis on discovering the truth for oneself rather than living by a set of doctrines, its basic principles can be put into practice by anyone.

> *If you look at all the ancient teachings—Hinduism, Buddhism, the teachings of Jesus—you'll see they have two things in common. . . . First, they all saw that there was something not right with the human condition. . . . And second, they all realized that there is a way beyond that, and that way is the spiritual path."*
> —ECKHART TOLLE, FROM AN INTERVIEW WITH STEVE DONOSO IN *THE SUN* MAGAZINE, JULY, 2002

## CAN A BUDDHIST HAVE A GOOD TIME?

I was first drawn to the teachings and practices of Buddhism when I saw they could help with the insecurity and anxiety that had been my longtime companions. It was a great relief to hear what is known as the First Noble Truth: There is suffering in life. Finally someone was telling it like it is, rather than saying I should cheer up, count my blessings, and go shopping.

But it made me wonder if there was any room for enjoyment. I couldn't help noticing that dancing and singing didn't seem to be an integral part of the practice. I could see that the Buddha was smiling in most depictions of him, yet as I sat silently in meditation practice, sometimes in pain, there didn't seem to be the potential for a lot of what I was used to defining as "fun." In fact, we were being taught that seeking pleasure could lead us into the trap of unhealthy attachment—a kind of addiction to pleasure that causes us to suffer.

Soon after my introduction to these teachings, I hit a real snag about what this was supposed to mean for my life. In 1974, I was at Naropa Institute in Boulder, Colorado, taking a class from Joseph Goldstein on Essential Buddhism, and we were learning how to meditate. Trying my best to focus on my breath and be in the present moment, suddenly I remembered that I had put on my New York Knicks T-shirt that morning. I was not only a passionate fan, but a season ticket holder as well. Some of the most ecstatic moments in my life had occurred in Madison Square Garden as I wildly cheered for my beloved team. My mind wandered off, reliving those peak highs until, with a bit of a start, I woke up to the fact that I was supposed to be seeking a stillness and calm that would bring me peace. Unnerved, I wondered, *What effect would full-on commitment to meditation have on my enthusiasm?* The dissonance between exhilarating passion for the game and the calm of meditation was so unsettling that at the end of the class I mustered up the courage to speak with Joseph for the first time.

I approached him and, with some embarrassment, explained my quandary. After becoming proficient at meditation, would I end up at a game in Madison Square Garden, head turning serenely as I followed my team from one side of the court to the other, equanimously acknowledging, *Nice shot, Frazier. Very good move, Havlicek.* "If that's where this is heading," I confessed, "I'm not sure it's for me."

Joseph smiled. "Don't worry," he assured me. "I think you'll still be able to enjoy the games just as much. If anything changes, it will probably be that you'll be able to get over a loss sooner with less devastation." He couldn't have given me a more satisfying answer. And he was right. Learning to live with a mind at ease doesn't mean giving up our enthusiasm for life.

Some of us were taught in our religious upbringing that rejecting the world would make us holy—the "vale of tears/hairshirt" approach to religion. This same attitude can be found in Buddhism, with students mistakenly believing that if they enjoy and appreciate life, they risk getting caught up in imprisoning attachment. But closing yourself off to the life that's here before you is simply another form of aversion, a belief that says, "It's dangerous to enjoy positive experiences." Buddhist monk Ajahn Sumedho has a different perspective. He was born in the United States and, after serving in the Navy and the Peace Corps, became a monk in Thailand. Sumedho has been able to interpret the ancient teachings in a way that is applicable to our contemporary lives. In his book *The Way It Is,* he writes:

> *Joy is not incidental to the spiritual experience. It is vital."*
> —RABBI NACHMAN OF
> BRESLOV (1772–1810)

> Sometimes in Buddhism one gets the impression that you shouldn't enjoy beauty. If you see a beautiful flower, for instance, you should contemplate its decay. . . . This has a certain value on one level, but it's not a fixed position to take. . . . Once you have insight, then you find you enjoy and delight in the beauty, and the goodness of things. Truth, beauty, and goodness delight us; in them we find joy.

It's important to remember that a major goal of Buddhist teachings is to find happiness in the here and now, and that includes appreciating all the beautiful gifts of life that are right in front of us.

## THE AWAKENING JOY COURSE

In recent times, the subject of happiness has become increasingly popular. Many wonderful books have been written pointing people in that direction. *Awakening Joy* is joining that effort by offering a slightly different approach. This course introduces practices that have been used through centuries as methods of training the mind to learn new ways of thinking. What makes the Awakening Joy course so effective is that it presents these ancient teachings in an accessible form and combines them with strategies to change habits and behaviors that are informed by contemporary psychology and science.

This book is based on the ten-month Awakening Joy course, building on the same themes offered there and in the same sequence of steps. While using this book can allow you to move through these steps at your own pace, it is the process of cultivating new habits over time that will bring about a sustained quality of well-being. You might read the book straight through and then go back and focus on the exercises and topics that are particularly relevant to you. Or you may want to go through it chapter by chapter, spending as much time as you need on each step.

I refer to each chapter here as a "step," but the journey of Awakening Joy is not a linear process. All of the practices interact with each other— a kind of hologram to open you to more joy. And it's based on a systematic program that has been tested over several years by a large population and proven to be effective.

Throughout the book you will see quotes from those who have benefited from this course. Some of them are from participants who responded to online surveys, some from personal communications or from interviews done specifically for this book. Many of the moving stories in these chapters are drawn from the experiences of students attending the silent mindfulness meditation retreats I lead.★ Many of the personal stories I tell about my own life, as well as those from Shoshana, are drawn from experiences we've had on retreats ourselves. Silent retreats are a kind of crucible that reveal the workings of the mind in a unique and illuminating way. However, these stories are not intended to suggest that training your mind or learning how to be happy can happen only on retreats. These insights about human experience can be realized in many different ways, as you will also see in these pages.

People can participate in the Awakening Joy course either over the Internet through video and audio recordings, or in live classes. All include presentations from various happiness experts, neuroscientists, and spiritual

---

★ Most of the stories are conveyed as they actually happened, but some stories or quotes are composites of different people's experiences. Unless permission was specifically granted, all names have been changed.

teachers. Words of wisdom from those who spoke at the course held in Berkeley in 2008 are included throughout this book.

There are many sophisticated theories and intricacies of how the mind works. I combine three particular Buddhist teachings to form the cornerstone of the Awakening Joy course. The effectiveness of applying these principles to developing happiness has been corroborated by neuroscience research, some of which will be referred to in the book. The three principles at the heart of the program are:

> *I have been quite amazed by how powerful it is to pay attention to things that make me happy instead of overlooking them. As you say, when the mind is inclined this way, my brain seems to change gears and look at everything more positively."*
> —A COURSE PARTICIPANT

- **Inclining the Mind toward Joy.** As the Buddha clearly stated, "Whatever the practitioner frequently thinks and ponders upon, that will become the inclination of the mind." But our minds can be trained. A central aim of the course is to incline the mind toward states that give rise to joy.
- **Developing and Increasing Wholesome States.** When we are kind or generous, at ease or calm, we experience genuine happiness and well-being. These are called wholesome states in Buddhist teachings. Once we understand what healthy activities help support these wholesome states, we can intentionally invite and cultivate them.
- **Focusing on the Gladness that Arises with Wholesome States.** While engaged in a healthy activity, we experience an actual positive uplift of energy. The teachings speak of the value of strengthening this "gladness connected with the wholesome" and the delight that "gladdens the heart." Increasing that gladness is what I've come to mean by awakening joy.

In creating the course I reasoned that if over several months participants "frequently think and ponder upon" as well as deliberately focus on these wholesome states and the "gladness" that accompanies them, that would become "the inclination of their minds." Over time your mind and heart have become accustomed to certain habits that may be limiting your full potential for happiness. With practice you can change your default setting so you can consistently access your natural joy.

# BUILDING UP A STOREHOUSE OF POSITIVE EXPERIENCES

"To help us survive, the brain has evolved to register negative experiences more readily than positive ones. A single bad event with a dog stands out more vividly than a thousand good ones. In other words, the brain is like Velcro for negative experiences and like Teflon for positive ones. The amygdala, a little almond-shaped bunch of neurons in the center of the brain, plays a big role in storing emotional memories, and it's primed to look for bad news.

"Because we're set up in this way, we can go through life doing the things that confirm our worst fears. We look for what's negative in a situation, just in case it's a survival threat. Because our brain is set up to be wary, we have to help ourselves toward happiness by inclining our attention to positive experiences by consciously intending to do so. Through conscious attention you can gradually build up a storehouse of positive experiences to neutralize the negative ones. The most powerful method I know is to deliberately look for positive experiences and take them in by being present with them. This helps the brain register the positive experiences long enough for those neurons that are firing together positively to start wiring together."

—RICK HANSON, PH.D., AUTHOR OF *BUDDHA'S BRAIN: THE PRACTICAL NEUROSCIENCE OF HAPPINESS, LOVE AND WISDOM* AT AWAKENING JOY COURSE, BERKELEY, 2008

## SUPPORT PRACTICES

Besides the principles and practices presented in each step of this Awakening Joy program, there are a set of activities I encourage you to bring into your life to support your journey. Use these suggestions in any way that works for you, without making them a burden or one more thing you *have* to do. Don't worry about what you haven't done. Feel good whenever you do *any* of them:

*If you can walk, you can dance. If you can talk, you can sing."*
—ZIMBABWEAN SAYING

- **Move your body.** Walk, exercise, dance, or do yoga regularly. Develop a healthy relationship with your body. Stretch it. Walk it. Exercise it. Move it around vigorously if you can. This will clear the cobwebs, get you out of your head, help you live longer, and make you feel more alive. Your body tries to serve you as best it can. Be nice to it. All with the intention of awakening more joy.
- **Regularly engage in some kind of creative expression,** like singing, writing, drawing, playing an instrument, or dancing. I especially suggest singing, since it opens up the throat and tunes you to a vibration of well-being, and many participants have found it to be a key to increased happiness. Even if you feel silly singing, try it anyway! Studies have shown that exposing ourselves to music helps boost our immune system. You could also experiment with listening to music that uplifts your spirit. I've put together my own compilation of music that brings me joy, and every time I play it (and sing along), it works. Any form of creative expression, however, will help lift your state of mind and keep the joy juices flowing.
- **Create a Nourishment List.** One of the supports to greater well-being is recognizing ways you can nourish your spirit and then regularly fitting them into your routine. Creating a Nourishment List will help you make that come about. Take time to

write down everything that brings you joy. It can be a simple thing like eating a peach, or something exotic like windsurfing, or anything in between (walking the dog, having tea with a friend, etc.). Which ones could you actually see doing to bring more joy into your life?

- **Do something nourishing** for yourself three or four times a week, daily if possible, no judgments if less. Your ability to access joy is greatly enhanced by nourishing your spirit. This does not necessarily mean maximizing pleasure. You can eat three helpings of ice cream and, although there might be lots of quick pleasure, your spirit will probably not be nourished. In fact, you'll get indigestion! Nourishing your spirit is usually connected with engaging in healthy activities and experiences. Sink into a hot bath. Go for a walk in nature. Meet a friend for lunch. Do any of the support practices mentioned here. You might do these as a reward or just because you deserve it. Instead of leaving joy up to chance, recognize what evokes it and then prioritize that in your schedule. Let yourself have fun and play.

> *Each species has its own habitat, that place where the species can flower forth. If a species cannot find its proper habitat, its true powers of life cannot be evoked. A species denied its habitat perishes; we see it all around us. What is the true habitat of the human? Adventurous play."*
>
> —BRIAN SWIMME,
> FROM *THE UNIVERSE IS A GREEN DRAGON*

- **Meditate or take some time by yourself regularly,** every day if possible. Even if you don't meditate, try sitting with a cup of tea for five to ten minutes as you look out the window. See what it's like to be quiet without doing anything else. Getting in touch with your internal life helps access the goodness and joy that is there. Course participants find that doing this has a major impact on their well-being. Neuroscience confirms that meditation actually creates positive changes in brain structure that support greater happiness.

- **Keep a Joy Journal** to keep track of your experiences as you do the practices suggested throughout the book. At the end of each day, you might write down what brought you joy, well-being, and happiness that day. It doesn't have to be volumes. No judgments if you can't think of anything. But remember that even the smallest things count, such as nuzzling with your dog, hearing a favorite song, or talking to a friend. Writing them down allows you to reflect back on those moments and bring them to life.

• **Find a Joy Buddy or Joy Group.** Having a buddy, especially someone who is also reading the book or taking the course, to check in with regularly can be a tremendous support for this process. This is like having an exercise buddy—someone to keep you on track. Stay in touch with your buddy by email, phone, or face-to-face. You'll want to agree on how to do this in a way that serves both of you (time, frequency, mode of communication). Even a five-minute check-in will help keep you both inspired. The purpose is to support each other in discovering the effects of the practices and to share insights. It's also okay if you choose not to have a buddy.

> *What I've noticed is how often I actually feel well-being already! I've always thought of myself as moody and anxious, but as I've been paying more attention, I'm realizing that I actually feel joy way more than I thought I did. This isn't going to be as hard as I thought."*
>
> —A COURSE PARTICIPANT

The online Awakening Joy course helps set participants up with a buddy. All over the world, groups (including e-groups) have formed for people to work on the materials together, which is a very supportive way to do it.

## USER-FRIENDLY EXPERIENCE

I want to make clear at the outset that there should be no guilt as you do this program. Guilt is counterproductive to cultivating joy! No failing, no pressure. Take this as a nourishing experience. Whatever you do as part of this experiment, please feel good about it. You may decide that simply reading this book is all you want to do. One course participant told me that reading the program materials was the only thing she did but that it reminded her that there's another way to be in the world, and she felt a significantly positive impact.

*I have seen the most miraculous changes in my life since beginning this course. It is as if there is now a light on my path where before all I had was feeling around in the darkness. I understand how to be happy and that it is my choice. What an amazing feeling!*

—A COURSE PARTICIPANT

Thousands of people from all over the world have gone through this program and experienced its benefits. It gives me great pleasure to share it with you through this book. My sincere hope is that it will help you change habits that don't serve you and strengthen those that lead to more well-being and aliveness. Beyond the personal benefits, I believe finding more joy in your life will also have rippling effects that can touch everyone you know and make a real difference in the world. And it begins with making the choice to be happy.

# Awakening Joy

# 1

## INCLINING THE MIND
## TOWARD JOY

---

With our thoughts we make the world.

—The Buddha

*O*ne *evening after* hearing me give a talk on real happiness, a student approached me. "I have something to show you," he said, opening a slick magazine to a two-page advertisement. There, in shimmering glory, was a beautiful woman draped in gold jewelry, looking satisfied and happy. Across the pages in bold lettering were the words: "The Gold Shivers." I felt both amused and appalled as I read the pitch:

*From the First Small Shiver*
*when a Shimmering Necklace of Gold Beads Catches a Woman's Eye.*
*To the Great Shivers of Delight*
*when the Coveted Object Actually Becomes Hers . . .*

*Among Life's Pleasures, Count this Deeply Held Euphoria as Unique.*
*The Only Way to Get the Gold Shivers is by Getting the Gold.*

Because we're bombarded with thousands of marketing messages like this every day, it's easy to think that gratifying our desires is the way to find happiness. We might even know, as one bumper sticker says, "The best things in life are not things," but we can still believe that something else out there will make us happy. *When I find my soul mate, or when I write the great American novel, or when I retire . . .*

*If I had known what it would be like to have it all, I might have been willing to settle for less."*
—LILY TOMLIN

There's no denying the hit of pleasure we feel when we fulfill a desire for a particular experience or object or goal. But how long does the satisfaction last once we receive the "coveted object"? Perhaps until we notice there's something else we want. When we equate true happiness with getting something (or someone), we can end up like hamsters in an exercise wheel—running but never arriving.

If genuine happiness is not based on objects or experience, where can it be found? And how? Like following a road map, once you know where you're going, it's easier to figure out how to get there.

## TAKING THE FIRST STEP

The journey of awakening joy begins with setting a clear intention. Although we all want to be happy, most of us don't place an explicit wish for that at the center of our lives. We think if we are successful, rich, or liked by others, happiness will come. We tend to hope that achieving certain goals in the future will make us happy. But these are roundabout ways to get to happiness, and they don't necessarily work. What *does* get you there is starting where you are and discovering what you are looking for in the midst of your current life.

You might think that the circumstances of your life will have to change a lot before you can find happiness in the midst of them. While it's true that our well-being is affected by how we live, we also know that even in the best of circumstances we can be unhappy. And sometimes in very challenging situations, we can feel surprisingly at ease. While this book will encourage you to bring experiences and circumstances into your life that contribute to your well-being, the key factor is deciding to change your mind. As my colleague Sylvia Boorstein puts it, "Happiness is an inside job." When we consciously *intend* to be happy, actually saying that intention aloud or to ourselves, we set in motion a radical transformation. Profound changes begin to take place inside us, in our body and our mind. The momentum of positive change grows as we learn to choose actions and situations that align us with our intention.

*I tend to ask myself what I have to be joyful about? I'm still out of work, I'm overweight, and the relationship and life I was hoping for didn't happen. But slowly, with just this one question and being present in the moment, I've begun to realize, my answer is: EVERYTHING! I'm alive, I'm facing my difficulties, I'm actually living my life and not hiding from my pain. I realize I'm just happy to be here. I can feel my breath, the sun on my face, the movement in my limbs as I go walking, the pleasure of smiling, laughing, and singing. It's not delusion or hiding or shutting down in denial: It's being present and taking things one moment at a time!"*

—A COURSE PARTICIPANT

## Go Ahead, Say It: "I Want To Be Happy."

What happens when you let yourself say, simply and clearly, that you want to be happy, that you want joy to become part of your daily experience? Do you feel like you need to look over your shoulder to see if anyone is watching as you dare to consider such a thing? Maybe you wonder if it could really be possible. Or perhaps you feel a sense of relief at finally letting yourself say it. Whatever your response, this is how you take your first step toward awakening joy.

## THE GOLD OF TRUE HAPPINESS

I was a gloomy existentialist in college until one day it struck me that I actually wanted to be happy. I believed the only way to achieve that was to get and to do what I wanted. My personal strategy to ensure happiness was trying to string together enough moments of pleasure and gratification that the underlying unease couldn't get through. Getting the latest album of cool music felt good—for a little while. Having fun at a wild party was exhilarating—at the time. But no matter how many happy moments I had, I still didn't feel any closer to being a "happy person." I felt like I was on a roller coaster, and the ride down seemed to last a lot longer than the occasional trip up. There had to be another way.

That was what led me in 1974 to Naropa Institute, a kind of spiritual summer camp, in Boulder, Colorado. I'd read some books on Eastern philosophy that made me question a lot of my assumptions, and I wanted to check things out for myself. When I walked into meditation class that first day, I was excited about the promise of an exotic new teaching. There in the front of the room a man was sitting cross-legged—but he didn't at all fit my image of the great spiritual guru I was expecting to see. In fact, he didn't seem very different from me. He was Jewish and sounded like he was from New York, and I wondered if this guy could really tell me something new. But after spending the first ten minutes of the lecture judging the package, I decided to start listening to what he was saying.

Within moments it was clear that Joseph Goldstein understood something about genuine freedom and happiness and how to get there. I saw for the first time the possibility of not being a slave to my neurotic thoughts and fears. By the end of the class, I knew I had found a sure road to happiness, and I was determined to follow it.

Joseph talked a lot about one of the basic teachings of the Buddha— the recognition that everything we experience in life is impermanent. No matter how good things are, they will change. *Well, that's for sure,* I thought. *That's the story of my life.* We don't get what we want and feel frustrated. We get what we don't want and feel upset. Or we get what we want and then find out it doesn't quite satisfy us in the way we thought it would. We find that the pleasure of the gold shivers lasts for a few moments, then fades away. As those famous "philosophers," the Rolling Stones, so profoundly put it: "I can't get no satisfaction."

Because everything changes, no circumstance, experience, or object can give us lasting happiness. Our bodies change, our minds change, the seasons change. Yet we try to hold on to pleasure, youth, summertime, happiness. As Joseph puts it, trying to hold on to anything in an ever-changing reality is like holding tight to a rope you're sliding down. All you get is rope burn. And the more you hold on, the more you suffer.

What is the way out of this predicament? Awakening joy isn't about fulfilling goals or changing particular circumstances. It's about training the mind and heart to live in a way that allows us to be truly happy with our life as it is right now. Not that we stop aspiring to grow and change in positive ways, or that we remain in harmful situations, but we begin to find the joy inside us right where we are. As you work with the practices offered here, you will discover that happiness is not a place you arrive at but rather the result of training your mind to ride with ease and flexibility the roller coaster of life.

> *The point cannot be overstated: Every desirable experience— passionate love, a spiritual high, the pleasure of a new possession, the exhilaration of success—is transitory."*
> —DAVID MYERS, PH.D., FROM *THE PURSUIT OF HAPPINESS*

## DECIDING TO BE HAPPY

Vickie was hoping for a miracle. For five years she had been living with chronic pain, unrelieved by anything doctors and healers had been able to offer. By the time we spoke, her disappointment had spiraled down into severe bouts of depression. "Often I break down and cry just from trying to get through the day," she told me. Vickie had come to talk about whether or not she should enroll in an Awakening Joy course. "But I just can't believe it's possible for me to be happy," she said.

Recently her situation had gotten even harder. Friends who had been trying to help for years had begun to drift away, afraid of being pulled into the black hole of Vickie's despair. "And my boyfriend has real doubts about our future," she said through tears. "I know he loves me and feels a lot of compassion for me, but he says he wonders if I haven't given up on life."

"You're going through so much, Vickie," I said softly. "But I've seen other people going through really hard times make major changes when they decide to. I think you can do it."

Despite her doubts, Vickie decided to enroll in the course. The very first meeting of the group proved to be a critical turning point for her. As usual I opened the course by asking participants to get in touch with their intention to bring more happiness into their lives. The evening was spent exploring this uplifting prospect, and by the time the class ended, the room was filled with enthusiasm and promise. Some participants lingered to talk with friends, and others came up to ask questions or make comments. I noticed Vickie sitting quietly at the side of the room, and when the others had left, I went over to see if she was okay.

"I just don't see how this will work for me, given my physical condition," she began. "I can't even conceive of what it would be like to be joyful."

"I understand how you can feel that way," I said, taking a seat next to her. "And don't try to be any different from how you are at this moment. But I think the most important ingredient in changing your situation is letting yourself open to the *possibility* of finding joy in your life. That needs to happen before you can get clear on your intention."

I knew there had to be a way to help her realize she had the capacity to enjoy her life. I had seen so many people, including myself, turn their lives around once they had embraced that possibility.

"Vickie, are there ever any moments in your life when you're enjoying something?" I asked her.

She replied, a little hesitantly, "Yes . . . when I play with my three-year-old niece."

"Can you right now bring to mind an image of playing with your niece?"

Vickie settled into her chair and closed her eyes. Almost immediately a tiny smile appeared.

"Now just stay with that image and those feelings for a few moments," I suggested. I could see a subtle change pass over her face as she sat there in silence. When I asked her to describe what she was feeling, it took her a while to find the words.

"I feel a kind of tingling throughout my body . . . a lightness in my mind . . . my heart feels warm . . ."

"Okay, good. Now let yourself breathe in that feeling, allowing it to deepen with each breath," I suggested, knowing that letting the experience fully register in her body and mind was a key to making the shift she wanted.

---

## IMAGINING A CHANGE

Doing an activity repetitively changes the structure of the brain. However, even just *imagining* the same activity has an impact on neural structure. Researchers at Harvard Medical School demonstrated this with an interesting experiment. They asked one group of volunteers to play a five-finger exercise on the piano over the course of a week. A comparison group was asked to merely imagine moving their fingers to play the same exercise. Though actually doing the action had a greater impact on brain structure than simply imagining it, by the end of the week, the same region of the brain in *both* groups had been significantly affected.

By actively imagining feelings of happiness or recalling happy experiences, you can help to make those changes in your brain that can bring more joy into your life.

---

"Now project your mind forward in time and imagine that you've practiced accessing this feeling of well-being regularly during the next ten months of the course. Can you tell me what your life would look like then?"

I could see Vickie's body relax as she reflected.

"I have less stress . . . I enjoy being with my friends again . . . I see myself taking more walks in nature, and letting myself have more fun."

"Great. If this feels worth going for," I said softly, "take your time to get in touch with your intention to make it happen. See if you can decide that you'll do your part to bring it about."

As she silently contemplated that suggestion, it looked to me as if Vickie's body actually grew lighter. When she finally opened her eyes, the smile she gave me was genuine and bright. "That was amazing," she offered. "Something in me said not only *can* I do this but I'm *going* to do this." That decision began a process within her that would eventually look like the miracle she had longed for. As the saying goes, "God helps those who help themselves," and Vickie's "miracle" was actually set in motion when she was willing to open to the possibility of joy.

## FINDING THE "MAGIC" WORDS FOR YOUR INTENTION

As Vickie found, setting the intention to awaken joy works best once you've recalled your capacity to be happy. Trusting that knowledge, you can make the heartfelt decision to do your part to make that happen. This is the heart of setting your intention to be happy—your determination to do what you can to fulfill your vision.

Finding a phrase that encapsulates your intention is a useful way to remind yourself of your direction. You might say something like "I intend to allow more joy into my life," or "I want to experience more happiness

---

### Inviting Happiness into Your Life

Think of a time when you felt real joy. Maybe skiing down a fresh powder slope; watching your dog bound across a field; being with a close friend; receiving an award for a job well done. As you imagine this experience vividly and in detail, paying attention to colors, sounds, smells, notice what you are feeling in your body. Where does the joy register? Maybe a slight swelling in your chest or tingling throughout your body. You may find that you are smiling. What is your *state of mind* as you experience this memory? Maybe a sense of being uplifted or feeling open and alive.

Now let those feelings of well-being register deeply. Breathe them in, feeling them pervade your body and mind. How would your life change if this kind of joy were increasingly part of each day?

each day," or "May I live with a greater sense of well-being." The exact way you phrase your intention doesn't matter, and the wording may change over time. What's most important is to begin.

Joan wrote from Canada about the struggle she got into when she tried to find the perfect way to state her intention. She had joined the Awakening Joy course in order to find more joy in her relationships with her husband and two children. "I keep falling into knee-jerk reactions such as irritation and negativity with them," she wrote. Because the change she was looking for felt so important, Joan wanted the phrase she used to state her intention to be exactly right.

After several frustrating days of trying out various possibilities, she decided to just sit quietly and see what came. The words that arose were "I'm going to give joy a shot." Not at all the profound phrase she was looking for! "I felt almost repulsed by the words and dismissed them," she wrote. But the phrase kept coming back. At some point Joan realized, "I can just be silly with the intention and stop worrying about the 'right' words. Instead I can try to stay connected with the raw energy behind these 'silly' words and go for it!"

## A GAME OF REMINDERS

The more you do something, the easier it gets. The more often you re-mind yourself that you are actually intending to bring more feelings of

### Meaning What You Say

Are you ready to bring more joy into your life? If you are, take whatever time you need right now to make the heartfelt decision to do so. Allow a phrase or a statement to arise that can remind you of your intention. Whenever you say that phrase, rather than just repeating empty words, let it remind you of your capacity for joy. Be willing to be open and receive the feelings of well-being you are inviting.

joy and well-being into your life, the more you will be open to them when they arise. And when you remain aware of your intention to grow in happiness, you're more likely to make choices to support it.

Shirah came to an Awakening Joy course highly motivated to get herself out of a rut. At the end of the second week, she reported to the group that she had discovered a successful strategy. On her computer at work, she set a timer to chime every twenty minutes. Each time she heard that little musical signal, she reminded herself of her intention. "The first week I would say, 'May I be open to more joy and well-being in each moment.'"

As she continually worked with that statement, she began to recognize that fulfilling her intention depended upon making choices in what she was doing or thinking. By the second week, each time the chime sounded, Shirah had begun asking herself, "What would make me happy right now?" Would it make her happy to complete the task she was working on? To take a needed stretch-break? To offer encouragement to a co-worker? "I really like the question," she added, "because it engages me in an exploration and makes it more difficult to go on automatic. And it works."

One person's magic trick doesn't necessarily work for another, however. You may feel that having a chime go off when you are trying to concentrate would drive you crazy. Be creative and find what works for you. A playful spirit can help deepen your commitment to well-being.

My friend Ina developed a unique way to remind herself of her intention. A New Yorker with a sarcastic bent, she found the word "joy" to be just too sugary for her. Each time she thought about "joy," instead of opening up, she found her body and mind recoiling in aversion. A sure way *not* to fulfill her intention! Ina devised an ingenious alternative:

I love the color green. It lifts my spirits. So I decided that instead of "awakening joy," I'd start telling myself "I'm awakening green." That was something I could relate to. I could never have guessed the effect that little device would have. I started noticing green all around me, and each time I did, it made me happier. Now I look for the green, and it seems to trigger that response automatically. Who would have guessed this cynic would become so joyful!

One online participant made up a set of cards using inspiring quotes from the course materials and sent them to the website for others to download. Other participants' suggestions have included:

- I put little signs that say "BREATHE" on my refrigerator and on my bathroom mirror. Every time I see them and take a conscious breath, I remind myself to incline my mind toward more joy.
- I posted cards all around my kitchen: Sing! Meditate! Laugh!
- My two young boys and I start out each morning saying to each other: "Let's make this a happy day." One day when we were *not* having a happy morning, my son reminded me we'd forgotten to say our happiness chant. We said it together, took a deep breath, and started the day again. Things worked out much better the second time around.
- Before I fall asleep at night, I bring my awareness to my whole body, feeling the sheets surrounding me and the comfort of the bed. I say to myself silently and inwardly the following words: "I open my heart to the universe to accept love and peace." This often brings a wonderful feeling of well-being and contentment into my heart. I let this feeling permeate my entire being as I fall asleep.

As you remain aware of your intention, lots of surprising transformations can come about. Katy wrote from Ireland to say that keeping her intention in mind made her aware of how much she was afraid of going into new situations. Whether at work or at parties or traveling, she had always been asking herself, "What will happen to me in this situation?" She realized that what she'd really meant was "What can go wrong here?" As Katy continued to remind herself of her intention to bring more happiness into her life, she found a new question instead: "What is the *best* thing that could happen in this situation?" And of course, as her expectations changed, new situations were no longer so frightening.

## WHAT GETS IN THE WAY?

You've set your intention, come up with a phrase and some ways of reminding yourself, and suddenly you find yourself doubting the whole process. It's not unusual during the first few sessions of the Awakening Joy course to hear protests and resistance from some people. I've noticed, in fact, that the course seems to be a magnet for skeptics who want to be happier. Michael came up to me after the second class and told me that he just didn't think this "awakening joy business" was for him. He had been practicing seeing the glass half empty his whole life. "That's just the way I am," he told me, the resignation in his voice betraying a certain frustration.

As we continued talking, Michael relaxed and joked about being such a cynic: "I think I'm going to be one tough nut for you to crack." As we laughed together, I suddenly asked, "With that big smile all over your face, what are you feeling right now?"

"Light . . . playful," he confessed.

"There it is," I said. "Let yourself feel that fully."

After a pause, Michael admitted that he felt pretty good, although he was a little surprised to think that those feelings had anything to do with happiness. I assigned him the task to have his radar out for moments of well-being and to slow down and feel them fully. He somewhat reluctantly agreed to "give it a try." Over the next few months, Michael began to see that those moments arose more often than he might have expected. After the last session of the course, he sent me a note:

> Being happy had always seemed like luck or some sort of accident, and when I wasn't happy, I felt like I was a victim of life's circumstances. But I realize now that I have a lot more to do with experiencing joy than I thought. I can choose to be happy—and I can choose to be unhappy, even miserable.

## "THE COMMITTEE"

Like Michael, many of us go through our days on the lookout for what can go wrong. We carry around a lot of voices in our heads that tell us all of the bad things that have happened, or could happen, to us in our life. One colleague refers to these voices as "The Committee." Each voice in that group is trying to get us to follow its own particular direction, with the result of not only confusing us but limiting what we believe is possible. You might want to be happy, but subtle thoughts may be lurking not far from the surface: *Who am I fooling? I know I'll only be disappointed again. How can I bring more joy into my life when* . . . You can probably fill in any number of reasons. Even if we believe we can create more happiness for ourselves, negative voices can undermine our intention.

Max wrote from Australia to say that he'd begun doing the practices with great enthusiasm and was actually seeing progress. But soon he encountered a major obstacle:

> When I notice myself feeling happy or joyful in the midst of some activity, almost simultaneously there arise memories and feelings of failure and worthlessness, which send the message "You don't deserve happiness/success in awakening joy." It takes real effort to disregard these nagging negative thoughts, which form an almost constant, day-long backdrop to my ongoing efforts to awaken joy. I need to get on my own side totally in this endeavor! But how? Why do these voices want me to fail? And how can I silence them?

Max isn't to blame for those voices that "want [him] to fail." They are probably not so different from thoughts he had when he was a little boy and doubted he could hit a baseball or make friends in a new school. When we're learning new and healthier ways of being, all our old self-sabotaging patterns of thought can become more evident. The contrast between how we want to be and the way we have been is painfully obvious, and the voices of doubt and fear are often loud and clear. This is not a bad thing. Becoming more aware of them is actually very good, because then we can see what gets in the way and understand the conditioning that we're deal-ing with. When we don't recognize these negative voices, we're under their spell with little idea of how powerful and persuasive they are.

Sometimes course participants get waylaid by believing that awaken-ing joy means they must have only positive thoughts. I'd like to make it clear that you don't have to get rid of all negative thoughts. In fact, that's nearly impossible, and trying to do so has the opposite effect. Right now, try to get the thought of a pink elephant out of your mind. Now try harder! Is it gone? Our attention gives life to thoughts, and the more we try to push them away, the more persistent they become.

Other chapters in this book will offer ways to work with negative or unwelcome thoughts, whether they are in the form of undermining voices, critical perspectives, or pink elephants that won't leave the room. For now the key is to stay in touch with your intention and be patient and compassionate with whatever gets in the way.

### Hearing a New Voice

What are some of those inner voices that try to keep you from being happy? Each time you notice them come up, rather than believing them or giving them energy through reacting, just let them pass. Restate your intention, recalling if possible the positive feelings that accompany joyful experiences. As you incline your mind toward well-being and happiness, those negative voices inside will begin to diminish.

## THE COMFORT OF THE FAMILIAR

Although you may want to be happier and more at ease in life, changing habits you've grown used to usually requires moving out of your comfort zone. Many years ago during a workshop I was participating in, I wit-nessed a conversation between a teacher and a student that made clear to me how caught up we can get in resistance to change. At the end of one of the movement sessions, a number of us had gathered around the teacher with our questions. One of the students had been experiencing some pain in her hip joints during the session, and it was distracting her from quieting her mind. What might the teacher recommend? After making sure she didn't have a medical problem, he suggested an exercise to gently stretch her tight muscles. She responded with a sigh saying she feared the stretch might put some pressure on her knee, which sometimes acted up. Could he suggest something else?

The teacher then recommended a different exercise, which avoided flexing the knee. "Oh no, I couldn't do that," she shook her head, explaining there was a chance her back would then flare up. Was there another alternative? He patiently gave her a third option, which she once again deftly parried, saying it might cause another problem. After a few intense moments of silence, the teacher said, in a kind and compas-

> *I have found having the intention of being joyful can have an amazing effect on my mood. When I'd wake in the morning on weekends, I used to think of depressing things until I didn't want to get up. The more I lay in bed the more down I would get. Now, as long as I remember to do it, I can completely switch off those feelings which sapped my energy. I can just say to myself 'Get up now, the sun is shining and it's going to be a good day full of new things.' And I end up full of energy."*
>
> —A COURSE PARTICIPANT

---

### Stretching Beyond the Familiar

When you join a gym and begin working out, those first few days of exercise can leave your muscles really sore. But if you keep going, using those muscles over and over, you arrive at a new level of fitness. Be willing to go through the natural discomfort that comes from letting go of the familiar as you move to a new level of well-being. Be patient. Don't put pressure on yourself. Keep reminding yourself of your intention, knowing that little by little you're bringing about greater well-being in your life. There will be ups and downs, but each time you try the new way, notice how good it feels.

sionate tone, "I think your intention to stay the same is greater than your intention to change. When you're ready to change you will."

You may think that bringing more joy into your life is a good idea, but until you're willing to stretch yourself and alter the patterns that have maintained the status quo, change won't happen. It's all too easy to fall back on the safety of the familiar and avoid putting yourself in potentially uncharted territory. In doing so, you stay stuck in a prison of predictability. It may feel comfortable, but is that what you want to settle for? Stretching beyond your comfort zone will lead to the happiness you're looking for.

## DOING YOUR PART

Once you consciously set out on your pathway with a clear intention to be happy, it might look like something magical or mysterious is happening as you actually find more well-being in your life. It's like when you learn a new word, you suddenly notice it everywhere. Neuroscience tells us that setting an intention "primes" our nervous system to be on the lookout for whatever will support what we intend to create for ourselves. In his book *The Mindful Brain,* Daniel Siegel talks about the effect paying "attention to intention" has on our brain and thus our experience of our surroundings. He writes: "Intentions create an integrated state of priming, a gearing up of our neural system to be in the mode of that specific intention: we can be readying to receive, to sense, to focus, to behave in a certain manner." This suggests that when we pay attention to the intention to bring more happiness into our lives, we are more likely to notice the actions, opportunities, people, and things that can bring that about for us. It's sort of like recognizing which piece of a jigsaw puzzle will fit the picture.

Life is always presenting us with unexpected circumstances—obstacles as well as opportunities. Remaining aware of your intention helps you to more readily recognize, from the multitude of options life offers, those that support your vision.

Setting your intention for joy doesn't mean that you're going to *make* joy happen, but rather that you will *allow* it to happen. When you plant seeds in your garden, you can't will the vegetables to grow. You can only do your part by tending and caring for them, seeing what they need in order to develop as fully as possible. Likewise, you support your intention by keeping it in your consciousness and doing your part to help it manifest.

## BUILDING ON SMALL SUCCESSES

Establishing your intention is not the same as setting a goal with a fixed timeline, such as, "I'm going to be happier in two months." Although goal-setting can be a very skillful motivator in certain circumstances, it can be counterproductive in this program. If you're trying to "get joyful" on a schedule, or in a particular way, you're likely to end up assessing whether you are succeeding or failing. *Am I there yet? What do I need to do now to meet my goal?* This creates a tightness in the mind rather than the spaciousness that allows your natural joy to arise. To open to more well-being, let go of timetables and scorecards and just do your part by staying connected to your intention, and see how things unfold.

When asked by a reporter how it felt to fail so many times before successfully inventing the lightbulb, Thomas Edison replied, "My good man, I did not fail. I invented the lightbulb. And it was a 2,000 step process." We might say something similar about awakening the joy inside us. It's a process that not only requires commitment but patience as well. The conditioned patterns of a lifetime don't shift overnight. It would be wonderful if we could just declare, "From here on out, I'm going to be happier," but unfortunately it doesn't work that way. The path may not always be as simple and smooth as we would like, but if we're facing in the right direction, in time we'll find what we're looking for.

During the 1980s, the San Francisco 49ers, my local team, were the

> *Rather than wishing friends would ask me to visit, go to the movies, or have a meal together, I approached three different acquaintances and asked if they would like to go out to a movie. I know it's so simple, but I've been afraid of 'no.' I'm now sharing enjoyable outings, like walks, movies, meals, and coffee chats, and I have three new friends."*
>
> —A COURSE PARTICIPANT

best team in all of football. (Well, everything changes . . . ) They didn't try to go for the long touchdown every play, or even much of the time. The secret to their success was chipping away five to ten yards at a time, getting into a rhythm and building on their success as they slowly marched down the field. I learned a lot from watching them. Keep building on your small successes and feel good about what you've done.

When you're on the lookout for it, you will find joy right where you are, even in those places where you might least expect it. Edith, who was taking the course online in Germany, had a revelation when she stopped looking for something special and simply opened up to the feeling of well-being.

I had been looking for some kind of "spiritual joy," some other-world joy (that I'd failed to find), and totally overlooked how much "ordinary joy" was already present in my life. As a matter of fact, I sometimes find myself in very ordinary situations—noticing the beauty and radiance of one of my children, for example—and experiencing a kind of ecstatic joy. Isn't it amazing how believing that there is some kind of "worthier joy" elsewhere can keep one from seeing and experiencing all the joy that is already there?

Most of the things that bring us joy are not elaborate or costly. Charlie, another course participant, reported that after checking in with his Joy Buddy one night, he got inspired to write to several friends he had been out of touch with for a long time. That simple act brought him immeasurable joy. Florence had been worried about the prospect of taking

### Focus on Success

When you check in with your Joy Buddy, don't dwell on what you haven't done. Focus on what you *have* done. Share how that feels, and inspire each other with your successes, even if they seem small.

care of her four-month-old granddaughter for a couple of weeks, but she remembered her intention "to live this life fully, with joy and gratitude always."

As a result I missed not a moment of this wonderful experience with my granddaughter and was completely joyful, mindful, very alive and conscious, even with a sometimes not-totally-happy baby. I feel my own peace, love, gratitude, and joy were a wonderful influence on her as well. I did lots of singing to her and much walking to help her be happy, soothed, peaceful. I learned so much, am continuing to learn so much—about myself and about fully enjoying this short, beautiful experience called life.

Michelle found that setting the intention to be joyful before doing activities such as washing dishes, folding laundry, and walking the dog made these routine activities so much more pleasant. "These days," she writes, "I sing and dance while cleaning and end up getting much more done than I used to."

As you allow joy to be part of your daily life, you will find that, little by little, it builds on itself until it becomes a natural way to live.

Despite the chronic pain she had told me about after her first Awak-

---

### Frame It with Joy

What routine chores or other activities do you usually feel resistance to doing? Bills? Cleaning the house? Laundry? Commuting to work? Before you begin, set an intention to let that activity bring more happiness into your life. You might try: *Paying bills contributes to my well-being,* and then see if something new can happen. Or your intention might be: *I enjoy traveling in my car,* and then notice if any ideas arise that help make that happen. You might begin listening to recorded novels or singing along with favorite music during your commute. Let yourself be surprised by the possibilities.

ening Joy session, Vickie did continue with the course. Accepting that it was possible to be happy helped her let go of some conclusions she had made about her own life and about life in general. Over the following months as the course continued, rather than focusing her attention day after day on how hard things were, Vickie increasingly paid attention to what she loved in life and to her vision of well-being. And life began to unfold in a way that supported major changes for her. At the end of the course, she sent me a note:

> The changes I've experienced in myself over these months have been amazing. Setting the intention to be more alive and to experience joy has been incredibly powerful. I find that I am less afraid of my constant physical pain. My friends are noticing also that I am having fewer episodes of extreme despair. And my boyfriend recently proposed marriage. I was very surprised, and he explained that he had seen so much progress in the stability of my moods and my ability to live life that he no longer doubted my commitment to "getting better." I'm so very grateful.

## LIKE A TENDER SAPLING

When we get clear on our intention to change, we set in motion a process that ripples out, like a pebble dropped in still water, affecting everyone and everything around us. A shift occurs in how we are perceived, not only through our own eyes but through the eyes of those who know us. As the positive results of the practices begin to make a difference in your life, some friends will be cheering you on. "It's wonderful to see you so happy!" Others may be threatened. "Don't you think that going out for a drink after work is a lot more fun than a yoga class?" Or, "You're not like you used to be, and I'm not sure I like this new you." In the early stages of this program, your own belief in fulfilling your intention may be

*Keep away from people who try to belittle your ambitions . . . the really great people make you feel that you too can become great."*

—MARK TWAIN

fragile, so it's important to minimize the influence of those who do not want to change the status quo.

The Buddha likened the needs of someone in the process of change to those of a newly planted sapling. In order to establish itself, a young tree first needs proper placement, with enough sun to be nourished yet enough shade to keep it from being overexposed. It needs the right amount of watering. And it needs a fence around it to protect it from hungry animals eyeing the luscious green shoots. In short, it needs tender loving care so that the roots can take hold and it can develop into a healthy, vital tree that can offer shade and protection.

*Companionship, even if only imagined, activates the brain's attachment and social group circuitry. Physical and emotional closeness to caregivers and other members of the band was a necessity for survival during our evolutionary history. Consequently, activating a felt sense of closeness will probably help you feel safer."*

RICK HANSON, PH.D., FROM
*BUDDHA'S BRAIN: THE
PRACTICAL NEUROSCIENCE
OF HAPPINESS, LOVE
AND WISDOM*

Once the seed of your intention takes root and grows, it will bloom and provide refuge and support for everyone you meet, including those who may have initially questioned your attempts to be happy.

## Nourish Your Intention

Your intention to awaken joy is at first vulnerable and needs to be protected from negative outside influences. Spend time with those who support you in bringing more joy and well-being into your life. Nourish your intention through choosing activities that keep reinforcing it. Stay in touch with your Joy Buddy. Spend time with good friends, good books, and nature. As best you can, do the supportive practices suggested for this program. No guilt for what you don't do. Feel good about *any* practices that you do. And avoid the negativity of those who doubt your efforts. Instead of getting into debates with anyone about the value of what you're doing, simply try to maintain boundaries that respect and support your needs.

## WIDENING YOUR INTENTION

Whatever motivates you to grow in happiness becomes the wind in the sails of your intention. It might seem pretty obvious *why* you would want to be happy, but if you take a close look at your motives, you might find a few other reasons. Maybe you believe that if you have more joy, you'll make more money, or you'll get the right guy or gal. Those are not necessarily bad reasons for intending to be happy, but you might also consider opening up to other options. The more inspiring your motivation, the more energy you can bring to fulfilling your intention.

In 1994, I was invited to a conference for Western Buddhist teachers to be held in Dharamsala, India, with the Dalai Lama. When I mentioned to a friend that my flight called for a stop in Frankfurt, Germany, she immediately said, "Oh, you should visit Mother Meera. That's where she lives." I'd heard about this holy woman before and said I'd consider it. My friend looked directly at me and, as if channeling instructions from on high, she repeated, "You should meet her. She's known to grant one's deepest wish." That was hard to resist, and I set about arranging a visit to the Mother's Center.

There was a buzz that evening as I waited in line with a crowd of about one hundred fifty others. We all were shepherded into a softly lit room with an empty chair in the front for the master. After about thirty minutes of silence, there was a rustle of excitement as a beautiful young Indian woman entered. The purity and serenity Mother Meera radiated was palpable. For a while I watched as, one by one, people would bow at her feet in respect, look into her eyes for a few moments, and leave with a blissful smile. Then I turned to the question that had been at the back of my mind for days. If this holy person could actually fulfill my deepest desire, what would I ask for? Over the next hour as I waited my turn, I dropped deeper and deeper into my heart, moving past layers of desire, dismissing the luxurious vacations, new cars, and houses that crossed my mind. What really mattered to me?

By the time my turn came, I knew clearly what I would wish for. I knew what my deepest intentions were for my life—to live with a pure heart and embody my highest ideals as I serve others. I kneeled before her, silently repeating the simple phrases I had arrived at, each one feeling both authentic and humbling. At one point I looked up into Mother Meera's eyes, and it was like gazing into a vast ocean of eternity. As I continued to fervently repeat my intentions, I felt as if they were being seared into my heart.

I don't know what powers Mother Meera might possess, but I do know that getting clear on my deepest intentions that evening set in motion a process that has increasingly aligned the elements of my life to fulfill them. Getting clear on our highest intention establishes our most authentic connection to our heart and is a powerful part of awakening the joy within us.

## SINCERE MOTIVATION

The intention in our minds at the moment of any action determines whether we are planting seeds of future happiness or future suffering. If we want the seeds we plant to produce huge beautiful blossoms, our intention for greater well-being must be motivated by a big beautiful desire. So don't hold back. Let your intention be about fulfilling your highest potential, or letting your actions come from love, or bringing more happiness into the world.

I came to understand the power of that kind of motivation through something the Dalai Lama said at that 1994 meeting in Dharamsala. He

### Following Your Heart's Desire

What do you hold as the purpose of your life? What are your ideals? If a holy person or a magic genie could grant you your heart's deepest desire, what would it be? Take a few moments to contemplate those questions. Can you align your intention to be happy with those deeper desires? The more encompassing your vision of happiness, the greater the potential for joy.

sat before us, beaming ease and joy and compassion, yet he had in his life faced a number of life-threatening situations, and he had listened to thousands of fellow Tibetans pour out the stories of abuse and torture they had undergone when their homeland was invaded. One participant asked him how he had managed not to be overwhelmed when faced with so much tragedy and suffering. He answered: "My sincere motivation is my protection." Later when I asked him how it is possible to remain calm and balanced in threatening situations, he gave the same answer: "My sincere motivation is my protection."

I'd heard him use that phrase before, but the meaning of it sank in this time. Aligning our intention with the goodness of our heart keeps us from getting swept up in fear, confusion, or negativity. When our intention to be happy is based on our highest values, we can rely upon it to lead us in the right direction. Even when we are caught up in the challenges of life, we know we can choose to be kind or to act with compassion. This in itself opens us up to well-being and contentment.

A verse in the *Dhammapada,* a collection of sayings of the Buddha, sums up this promise:

> *Speak or act with an impure [confused] mind*
> *And trouble will follow you*
> *As the wheel follows the ox that draws the cart.*
>
> . . .
>
> *Speak or act with a pure [clear] mind*
> *And happiness will follow you*
> *As your shadow, unshakable.*

## WHAT IS "WHOLESOME"?

In Buddhist practice the actions and attitudes associated with well-being are called "wholesome," because they help us feel healthy and whole, and they contribute to the well-being of everyone and everything around us.

There are many levels of pleasure and happiness, but the joy I am talking about here is what the Buddha called "the gladness connected with the wholesome." This gladness arises naturally from the goodness that is within every one of us. We know the warm and uplifting feeling we have when we are kind or generous. Contrast this with the unpleasant feeling that accompanies something hurtful or insensitive—telling a lie, putting someone down, putting ourselves down. There is a direct connection between true happiness and thinking and acting with a clear mind and kind heart. If you want to be truly happy, causing harm to others won't get you there. The more you are motivated by kindness and the desire to act from the goodness of your heart, the greater the possibility of awakening joy.

---

## Empowering Your Intention to Awaken Joy

You may want to write the answers to these questions in your Awakening Joy journal, and refer to them from time to time in order to remember what you are envisioning for yourself.

- What do you want to experience as a result of doing this program? Find a phrase that best expresses this—perhaps something like: "May I be open to experiencing more joy (happiness, well-being) in my life." This is your intention.
- Imagine what your life might look like six months from now if you stay connected with this intention. A year from now? Two years?
- Get in touch with a heartfelt decision to do your part, to the greatest extent possible, to bring about the joyful life you want to live.
- Repeat your intention to yourself as you start each day, and then throughout your day remind yourself of your intention to develop more joy. You might also repeat your intention whenever you begin a new activity at work or at home.
- Spend a few moments at the beginning or end of your meditation or quiet time focusing on your intention and imagining how you feel and what your life looks like as you fulfill it.
- If you have a Joy Buddy, discuss your intention with him or her. That way you can support each other in realizing your visions.

Noticing when you're acting with mixed motivations can help you sort out which ones you want to cultivate. For instance, you may feel motivated to do a kind act for a friend because you know it will make both of you feel good. However, you may also have a slight hope that perhaps that friend will do you a favor back. If you become aware of that kind of mixed motive, instead of dwelling on the less noble intention, turn your attention to that more wholesome impulse. We might have 90 percent pure motivation to help and 10 percent ego-based hope for acknowledgment. If we focus on the 10 percent, we might get down on ourselves for being phony and end up dismissing the value of the 90 percent. The real magic is that even if we initially have only 10 percent selfless motivation, the more we stay connected to that, the more it grows.

*Last night I had a restless sleep. My husband woke me at 5:00 AM with a cup of coffee; how lovely of him to do so. Instead of staying in bed, I got up with the intention of enjoying my day, tired or not. He was listening to a radio show and the song 'Soul Man' came on. I was suddenly hit with the inclination to move to the song. As I began dancing, I was struck with the thought, 'Don't do this, it's silly.' Remembering my intention for the day and my intention for taking the course, I just let go and started dancing. It felt great. After a few minutes I looked up and saw my husband, who was across the room, dancing too. I realized then that my joy was rubbing off on him. I now intend to dance more often."*

—A COURSE PARTICIPANT

To live with joy and well-being is possible for all of us, and it is a gift we can pass on to others. Setting our intention launches us on the journey.

## MINDFULNESS:
## BEING PRESENT FOR YOUR LIFE

There is a most wonderful way to help living beings overcome grief
and sorrow, end pain and anxiety, and realize the highest happiness.
That way is the establishment of mindfulness.

—The Buddha

*It was a warm* April afternoon in Yucca Valley where I was leading
a meditation retreat. During a break from teaching, I was in the staff room
with my son Adam, then two years old. On the table was a huge bowl of
luscious ripe strawberries, which happened to be his favorite food. I lifted
Adam to a chair so he could take one. He started stuffing one strawberry
after another into his mouth, the red juice streaming down his shirt. As I
watched him, the naive notion occurred to me that I could teach him the
value of enjoying the moment. I would show him, as I do with adults
through "eating meditation," how to slow down enough to fully taste the
strawberry in his mouth before taking another. I moved the bowl out of
his reach and coaxed him to finish what he already had. Adam would have

none of it. He began howling. His mouth filled with juicy red fruit, he lunged for the bowl, imploring at the top of his lungs, "Strawberry!"

That image has stuck with me over the years as a symbol of our human predicament: We often don't enjoy the experience at hand because we're so caught up with reaching out for the next one. The way Jane, my wife, once put it: "Sometimes I think there's something more out there that will make me happier when really the best thing to do is to settle back and enjoy the moment I'm in." The secret to awakening joy is being present with whatever part of life we're tasting right now. The key to this secret is the practice of mindfulness, and it is the underpinning of all the other practices in this Awakening Joy program.

With mindfulness we live in the present moment. This is not, however, where most of us spend a lot of time. We topple forward into the future and worry about the next day or month or year. We think about what happened yesterday or last week or five years ago. We plan a vacation for months, then when we're finally lounging on the beach, our mind drifts off to the problems we left at home. The habit of being a little (or a lot) ahead of ourselves, living in the past, or lost in fantasy, exacts an enormous price: We miss out on our life.

Of course, there's a place for conscious planning or holding an inspiring vision of the future. And we can learn valuable lessons from our past or recall with fondness moments that connect us with joy. But if you spend most of your time in the past or future, you're lost in your thoughts instead of experiencing the actual moments of your life. As meditation teacher and psychologist Jack Kornfield likes to point out, the signs in Las Vegas casinos have it right: "You must be present to win."

The power of mindfulness to affect our well-being is widely recognized and is increasingly integrated into healthcare systems. Mindfulness-Based Stress Reduction, a program developed by Dr. Jon Kabat-Zinn at the University of Massachusetts in the late 1970s, is used throughout the United States to help people with chronic pain, fear, panic, anxiety, and other health problems. The value of mindfulness meditation in bringing about positive changes in the mind and body has been verified by numerous research studies. In one such study, Kabat-Zinn paired up with Dr. Richard Davidson, head of the Laboratory for Affective Neuroscience at the University of Wisconsin, which is known for the groundbreaking research on the brain wave patterns of Tibetan lamas in deep meditation.

Davidson and Kabat-Zinn studied the effects of mindfulness training on a group of employees in a high-pressured biotech industry. During a period of two months, participants learned mindfulness meditation in one class a week, and they attended a one-day retreat. They were also asked to practice mindfulness meditation at home for forty-five minutes each day. At the end of the study, not only did they report that their "negative emotions went down and their positive emotions went up," but in comparison to the control group—those who did not practice mindfulness—the meditators also showed increased immune function.

Training your mind to enhance your well-being can happen in a number of ways. In this program I emphasize mindfulness, because I have seen and experienced its undeniable efficacy over the course of many years. If you're not drawn to meditation, you don't have to jump right into that in order to learn mindfulness. As you will see in this chapter, there are ways in which you can gradually bring mindfulness into your daily life. However, as with learning anything, the more you focus on developing a new capacity, the more you will get out of it.

Mindfulness has many benefits, but for our purposes the most important is that it can help you live a happier life. You can't *make* joy or well-being happen, but you can help create the conditions in which those states more naturally arise. This starts with allowing yourself to be right where you are. Mindfulness is a tool that helps you learn to do that.

## WHAT IS MINDFULNESS?

Mindfulness is commonly described as "nonjudgmental awareness" and refers to a specific practice of consciously paying attention to what is happening in the mind and body in the moment without judging it, without getting tangled up in a commentary about the experience, without wishing it were different. The ability to pay mindful attention depends upon awareness or consciousness. As long as we're alive, awareness is happening. It's an automatic process, but as mindfulness reveals, we can also direct it. This is the essence of the practice of training your mind.

Stopping for a moment to just listen is a simple way to experience what awareness is. Right now, take a few deep breaths, relax your body, and focus on listening. You may hear sounds nearby, other sounds far away. You might even notice the sound of silence. Notice too that you are not trying to hear. Hearing happens naturally because *awareness* is functioning. As you listen, tune into the experience of *knowing* that hearing is happening. This knowing is the faculty of your mind that is engaged when you are being mindful.

Here's an example of how this works in the midst of daily life. As I sit here in my backyard, I can feel the soft breeze on my arms. I hear my wife Jane through the open door putting things away in our kitchen. I also hear a bird cawing and traffic in the distance. With mindfulness I know that right now I am hearing. Looking at the dance of leaves in the sunlight, the patches of blue sky peeking through, the Buddha statue at the base of the tree, and the books piled on the table next to me, I mindfully know that seeing is happening. I am also aware of the continually changing itches, throbbings, and vibrations inside my body. With mindfulness, I am aware of being a creature with five senses constantly interacting with my environment.

Likewise, I can also notice what is going on in my mind, which Buddhism considers to be a sixth sense. I am aware of my current mental state, knowing that I'm both relaxed and interested as I wonder what words will come next from my pen onto the paper. I notice the succession of thoughts coming and going—my mind commenting on how much I love soft breezes; the thought that says, along with a tinge of guilt, *You should be helping Jane wash the dishes!* But instead of diving into the guilt, I notice the uncomfortable feelings it creates in my body and the way my thoughts suddenly begin to weave a story about what I'm doing wrong, what I should be doing, how I always do this, and on and on. Fortunately, being mindful, I recognize this familiar pattern, label it as "guilt," and notice when those thoughts are replaced by the next experience that catches my attention.

Mindfulness focuses on the *process* of our experience—the fact that we're seeing, hearing, sensing, feeling an emotion, or thinking a thought.

This keeps us from getting lost in the "stories," or the content of our thoughts, or our reactions to what we're experiencing.

Most of the time, we carry on a running commentary about our experience: *This is the way it should be.* Or, *If I were in charge of the Universe, I would certainly do a much better job than this!* When we add that kind of report card to what's happening, we continually set up a test for life to pass or fail. In a sixth-century text, "Verses on the Faith Mind," Sengtsan, the Third Zen Patriarch of China wrote: "To set up what you like against what you dislike is the disease of the mind." This disease disconnects us from the truth of our experience.

Sergeant Friday's signature line from the old TV series *Dragnet* would be a good slogan for mindfulness: "The facts, Ma'am. Just the facts." This is not a cold, disconnected assessment but rather a simple, clear acknowledgment: "Oh, this is what is happening." Mindfulness calls it like it is, without embellishing our experience—not making it more dramatic or intense, nor pretending it's easier than it is. If we're sad, we're sad. If we're peaceful, we're peaceful. When we are clear about our actual experience, we can be completely authentic. This authenticity is a basic component of a joyful life.

### Just As It Is

Pause for a moment and notice right now how you're feeling, physically and mentally. You may be seated comfortably somewhere as you read this or on a crowded subway train in New York. Wherever you are, check to see if your body feels tired or energetic. Notice the sounds coming and going. Rather than just looking around you, become aware of the fact that you're seeing. Notice any tension in your shoulders, neck, hands. Observe the thoughts going through your mind: *I love sitting here reading.* Or, *I can't wait to get off this train and get home.* Your experience might be pleasant or unpleasant, but allow it to be just as it is without wishing anything were different. You might notice how restful it is to simply be aware of what is happening in you, instead of getting caught up in making an assessment of it.

## WALK SLOWLY

It only takes a reminder to breathe,
a moment to be still, and just like that,
something in me settles, softens, makes
space for imperfection. The harsh voice
of judgment drops to a whisper and I
remember again that life isn't a relay
race; that we will all cross the finish
line; that waking up to life is what we
were born for. As many times as I
forget, catch myself charging forward
without even knowing where I'm going,
that many times I can make the choice
to stop, to breathe, and be, and walk
slowly into the mystery.

—DANNA FAULDS,
from *Go In and In*

Although mindfulness is non-judgmental awareness, this doesn't mean that we abandon the faculty of discrimination. In fact, when we are aware of what we're actually thinking and feeling, we can clearly discern the difference between those thoughts and actions that are harmful and those that are beneficial. When we're blind to our thoughts and impulses, they run our lives. Becoming aware of our habits and the automatic ways we react when we're confused or upset is the first step to freeing ourselves from their power. Mindfulness helps us untangle the tangle, as some Buddhist scriptures put it, and then we can act with greater clarity.

## BRINGING THE WORLD ALIVE

In *The Little Prince,* the simple but profound book by Antoine de Saint-Exupery, the Prince is puzzled by the way grown-ups get so caught up in what they consider such grand "matters of consequence." Often we are those grown-ups, so busy with important things that we have no time for what the mathematician in the story calls "loafing or balderdash." But what in our lives are the *real* matters of consequence? Our child presents us with a drawing for our birthday, our partner prepares a delicious meal,

*Mindfulness is knowing what is happening in this moment and what is happening in me in response to it.*"
—SYLVIA BOORSTEIN
AT AWAKENING JOY COURSE,
BERKELEY, 2008

we wake up in the morning to find the first snowfall of the season has transformed the world. Too often we can barely pause to notice, because we've got to get to our next appointment, check our email, finish a project. Such "matters of consequence" can distract us from recognizing the blessings that life is offering us over and over each day.

There's magic all around us if we just take the time to notice. With mindful presence we activate the natural curiosity we all came into the world with as innocent children. Look closely at the mystery of a spider web. Or stop to think for a moment how amazing it is that you can read the word "blue" and see a color in your mind, or hear the word "pizza" and taste a slice. When we are mindful, even the most ordinary experiences become wondrous. In his book *Peace Is Every Step,* the great Vietnamese meditation master and poet Thich Nhat Hanh writes:

*I was dealing with a really hard situation at work and came home feeling bone-tired and despondent. I went out to dinner with my partner and had this epiphany as I looked across the table at him. I realized that my life is incredibly full and that I'm so thankful for having a loving partner and for our life together. A switch went off in my mind, my problems at work were reframed, and I was flooded with gratitude for the gifts I have in my life."*

—A COURSE PARTICIPANT

> To my mind, the idea that doing the dishes is unpleasant can occur only when you are not doing them. Once you are standing in front of the sink with your sleeves rolled up and your hands in warm water, it really is quite pleasant. I enjoy taking my time with each dish, being fully aware of the dish, the water, and each movement of my hands. I know that if I hurry in order to eat dessert sooner, the time will be unpleasant and not worth living. That would be a pity, for each minute, each second of life is a miracle. The dishes themselves and the fact that I am here washing them are miracles!

We don't always have time to move at such a pace or to be so attentive, but when we can bring a wholehearted presence to what is right before us, life becomes more fulfilling. For the Little Prince, paying attention to a single flower gave him great pleasure. The wise Fox tells him, "It's the time you spent on your rose that makes your rose important." While taking the Awakening Joy course, Art shared this insight about being mindful:

> I once considered my life to be relatively bland and uneventful. It was even hard for me to remember what had happened during the day, since it was almost by definition "unimportant." But I now think this is more a matter of perception than fact. Seeing the wonder in what is, rather than looking for something wonderful and disregarding the rest, has been a big discovery.

When you slow down and pay careful attention to what is happening inside you and around you, a new world opens up. Everything comes alive. In fact, you *may* notice that surges of joy arise in you spontaneously, even when nothing special is happening, and even in the midst of difficult times. When my coauthor Shoshana was going through a particularly trying period in her life, her only relief was remaining in the present moment. Thinking about the future brought up too much anxiety. "To my surprise, I'd be walking down the street, for instance, and suddenly I'd be feeling inexplicably joyful, even though the circumstances I was in looked so dire. I began to recognize that little instances of joy arise on their own from time to time, simply as part of life."

*Look at everything as though you were seeing it either for the first or last time. Then your time on earth will be filled with glory."*
—BETTY SMITH, FROM *A TREE GROWS IN BROOKLYN*

With mindfulness we can appreciate that every moment of life, whatever our experience, is precious. When we live in this way, a certain kind of vitality comes into our lives.

## KALEIDOSCOPE OF CHANGES

As we live more mindfully, something we saw in Step One becomes increasingly clear: The present moment is constantly changing. This might seem obvious, but most people do not live as if this is the case. Mindfulness directly reveals this truth of impermanence. All the tinglings, pulsations, tightenings in your body—even the discomforts—come and go. Look at your mind and you'll see how quickly your thoughts and feelings change.

When we see this truth of change for ourselves, our relationship to experience dramatically shifts. We learn to enjoy pleasant experiences without holding on to them when they pass (which they will), and we are able to remain present with unpleasant experiences without fearing they will always be this way (which they won't). When times are hard, instead of thinking *I'm never going to get out of this mess,* remembering that things will change allows you to be with your experience without fighting or pushing it away. Without this struggle, you can respond wisely to the situation rather than reacting from confusion. One of the participants in the Awakening Joy course wrote:

> *I am noticing, with a much keener sense, how often my state of mind changes in any given hour, no less any given day. It brings me hope to realize that everything is always changing. I embrace CHANGE! Whoa, that's pretty amazing."*
> —A COURSE PARTICIPANT

> Combining mindfulness with the intention to be happy, I have found the surprising result of being more present with unwelcome experiences. With mindfulness I can say to myself, "This is an unpleasant experience I am having, and I am unhappy," and yet I can feel it completely and let it move through me with the confidence that I can be happy again soon, that happiness is nearby, not so hard to find. So this negative experience need not overwhelm me or cause panic and aversion. This has been a great relief.

The same truth of impermanence holds when life is good to us. If we forget that everything changes, we may start thinking, *Wow! I finally have gotten my life together! I've worked really hard to get to this point and now I have arrived.* Then when things change, we wonder, *What happened? How did I blow it?* Knowing that change is an inherent part of life allows us to fully appreciate the good times when they come, without thinking that life has been unfair to us when they go.

Mindfulness develops our capacity to see the ups and downs of life not

*A nail is driven out by another nail, a habit is overcome by habit."*
—DESIDERIUS ERASMUS,
FIFTEENTH-CENTURY
HUMANIST AND CHRISTIAN
THEOLOGIAN

as an obstacle course but as an adventure. Being mindful of the ongoing kaleidoscope of changes gives you the opportunity to transform your life. Your mind and body become your laboratory for understanding how to awaken joy and well-being.

## THE PAUSE THAT MAKES THE DIFFERENCE

We are creatures of habit. Like rats in a maze, given a particular stimulus we will predictably react the way we have practiced over time. For example, you're walking down the street on a hot day and pass someone eating an ice-cream cone. For many of us, that sets up the desire for a pleasant experience that starts us looking for the next store to get something cold and sweet to eat, even if it's not on our diet. As the thought of the ice-cream cone makes you salivate, a surge of desire says, "Go for it.

## THE EMOTION TRAP

In his book *Emotional Awareness*, coauthored with the Dalai Lama, psychologist Paul Ekman talks about how we can be blinded by emotions like desire or anger once they are triggered. "Once the emotional behavior is set off, a refractory period begins in which . . . we cannot perceive anything in the external world that is inconsistent with the emotion we are feeling. We cannot access the knowledge that would disconfirm the emotion." When we're caught up in anger, for instance, we tend to interpret anything that is said or done as more fuel for the fire. We can be lost in these emotions for hours. The good news, Ekman says, is that mindfulness seems to reduce the length of the refractory period to help you more wisely assess the situation.

It'll feel good." When you don't pay attention, the voice of desire easily wins out. But when you pause long enough to listen, and notice what is happening inside, instead of reacting in ways that don't serve you, you might choose a different response.

The practice of mindfulness interrupts the habits that put your mind on automatic. For instance, when you get to the ice-cream shop and see that there is a special on the double-cream vanilla, you might think, "Well, 320 calories won't matter, just this once." But when you pause for a moment of mindfulness, your image in the mirror that morning might pop into your mind, and suddenly you remember the promise you made to yourself to get in shape. Now you can either choose the double-cream vanilla, decide to get a nondairy sherbet, or let go of the impulse altogether. You're no longer the rat driven by habit.

Likewise, a negative stimulus can set us off in a very unpleasant direction. A coworker says something critical to you. When you hear the words and feel the anger begin to rise, pausing to be mindful allows you to notice what is happening inside. Your face may feel hot, your throat tight, your heartbeat rapid. You might be thinking, *How dare she say that to me? After all I've done!*

Instead of launching into defense and attack, if you pay attention to the sensations in your body and to your state of mind, you might make a wiser choice. Perhaps in that pause you recall how venting your anger in the past only made things worse. So you decide to say, "Could we talk about this later, please? I need some time to think." This doesn't mean

*Last week two much-loved family members did something that made me unhappy. Instead of my typical pattern of getting more and more upset, going over and over in my mind how and why I'd been wronged, I was able to ask myself: Do I really want to feel bad? Do I really want to prolong and deepen my suffering? Will it help me or the others involved for me to assign blame and feel self-righteous? Or do I want to create a more positive path—one that accepts that something didn't go the way I wanted—and choose to let go and move on. I diffused my anger, went on with my day, and then later talked with them, without blame or anger, about my hurt feelings over what really was an unintentional action on their part. This saved all of us from what could have escalated into a lot of anger and chaos."*

—A COURSE PARTICIPANT

that you roll over and let yourself be mistreated, but at least you can choose to respond in ways that don't leave you later regretting what you say or do. With mindfulness you begin to develop the freedom to make choices that lead to greater happiness and well-being instead of suffering and regret.

## "YOU BREATHE OUT AND IN"

Kate has been teaching mindfulness to children at inner-city elementary schools as part of a program called Mindful Schools in Oakland, California. Many of the students are from poor families who live in neighborhoods plagued by violence. In a survey of a fourth-grade class, 40 percent of the children knew someone who had been shot, and 70 percent knew somebody who had gone to jail. The challenges these students experience daily became clear when Kate asked her first-grade group to practice being mindful of sounds at home. Some of them came back reporting gunshots, people screaming, the police at the neighbor's door. "They're experiencing mini-traumas all the time," Kate says. "But these kids have so much potential. They're very smart, and I can see that the right tools bring out all the love and wisdom that's right inside of them."

Kate uses mindfulness exercises to help the children become aware of their thoughts and feelings. "They're like sponges," she says. "When they start to realize how their minds work—that instead of being present, they're sometimes in the past, sometimes in the future—it gets really exciting. I've had kids run up to me saying things like, 'Miss Kate! Miss Kate! I've just had a future thought!' They're building a new muscle in the brain to pay attention to themselves."

*When I am mad or sad, I practice mindfulness. First you have to close your eyes. Then you breathe out and in.*
—STUDENT IN THE MINDFUL SCHOOLS PROGRAM

Kate's young students have also been using mindfulness in their interactions with others. "Many of these kids understandably are dealing with anger," Kate reports, "and often they believe that showing they're strong, or even hurting people, will feel good or help them survive. By learning mindfulness, they can see the difference between *feeling* an emotion and *acting* on it. We talk about how mindfulness can squeeze in between the two and create a space. I tell them, 'When you feel the sensations of the emotion in your body, it's a cue to create that space.' " They talk about ways to do that, whether it's breathing, walking away, or telling someone to stop and give them a minute. "As we've practiced together, they've become willing to stop when they're angry, take a breath, and say, 'Okay, maybe there's another way.' "

In fact, one child shared how he used mindfulness during his summer break to make a better choice. He told one of the mindfulness teachers that he'd gotten really angry at his brother and decided to go get a weapon. On his way, he remembered what he had learned during that previous year at school, and he actually decided to stop and pay attention to his breath and his emotions. He never did pick up the weapon. Without his ability to let go of that impulse, things might have turned out very differently.

Just as the tool of mindfulness is helping these children get perspective on fear and destructive anger, it can do the same for us when we are trapped in negative thoughts. Whether you're holding on to the belief that the world is dangerous, as many of these inner-city kids have learned, or the expectation that life should always be pleasant and something's wrong if it isn't, using the tools of mindfulness will "create the space" that frees your mind. Like the child who let go of his desire to harm his brother, letting go of blind reactions by being mindful of them lets you make choices you won't later regret.

## RELEASED FROM THE PRISON
## OF THE MIND

One of my favorite examples of the power of mindfulness to influence positive choices was told to me by my friend Mary Reinard, who teaches mindfulness meditation in maximum-security prisons. One of her students, Matt, seemed an unlikely candidate for meditation. Matt was big and buff and had a temper to match. Before being imprisoned for a violent crime, he had been a Green Beret in the U.S. military, trained to react quickly and forcefully. One day in class Matt suddenly asked, "Can you teach me to control myself?"

During that session Mary talked about mindfulness as a way to harness the power of the mind. Rather than being at the mercy of every whim, she explained, the more conscious we are, the more choice we have. She ended the class with a challenge: "Before acting, pay attention to your thoughts and the feelings in your body, and choose the way that will serve you best." A few weeks later Matt arrived at the class excited to report his success.

"You won't believe what happened this week," he began. One day at lunch someone at Matt's table had started "razzing" him. Inmates are assigned seats in the huge cafeteria, and sitting elsewhere can get them in trouble. Stuck at his table, Matt tried to ignore the man but found himself feeling more and more annoyed. Then he remembered what Mary had talked about in class.

"I noticed what the anger was doing to my body. It was tight all over. It was really uncomfortable. I was thinking that if I punched this guy out, there'd be some release. At least it would shut him up. But then I thought, 'Hey, the challenge was to choose a different way.'" Even though Matt knew he could get in trouble, he picked up his plate and moved to another table. "I decided to just suck it up and move," he told the class. "And get this, as soon as I sat down at another table, I saw all the tension in my body just disappear, like magic! Lunch tasted great!"

The positive result of Matt's action didn't end there. "The best part of the story is that this guy came up to me after the meal and apologized! No one ever apologizes in prison, and here was this guy saying he was sorry. You know, I think we both left feeling satisfied. Imagine that."

If Matt had reacted in his usual way, this scene would likely have ended in a fistfight, maybe a brawl in the cafeteria. He, and perhaps others, could have been put into solitary, people might have been hurt. But being mindful of what was going on inside him—the tension in his body and the angry thoughts in his mind—enabled Matt to make a different more positive choice.

Matt wasn't an evil or bad person. As a Green Beret he had received highly effective training to react to aggression with aggression. By learning mindfulness, he was able to start changing a pattern that was not appropriate to his circumstances. If Matt can do it, I believe we all can.

## BEING PRESENT FOR YOUR LIFE

Because we're so used to not being present, being mindful takes practice. You can begin right in the midst of your daily life. Setting aside even five minutes a day to do nothing but sit still and notice what is happening inside you can begin to teach your mind to be more focused and present. Or you might choose something you do each day, such as relaxing with a hot cup of tea or coffee. But rather than reading the newspaper at the same time, or talking on the phone, just be there

*When I'm fully present, everything becomes more interesting. I feel complete and whole. Nothing needs to be added or taken away to make it a better moment. When I'm fully here, it feels so good I wonder why I'd want to be anywhere else."*

—A COURSE PARTICIPANT

with your experience. Notice the taste, the warmth of the cup in your hands, the liquid moving down your throat as you swallow.

Also notice when your thoughts move out of the moment. You may be smelling the fragrance of the coffee one instant and five minutes later realize you drank the entire cup without noticing. Instead of being present with your actual experience, you were caught up in thoughts about what you were going to do later in the day, or you were going over last night's conversation with your partner. Don't be discouraged. You're just learning how the mind works. Keep a sense of humor, and gently turn your awareness back to the moment. The very act of inclining the mind to be present is potent and will soon begin to bear fruit.

I like to make a game of being mindful during my daily activities. That makes the practice less "work" and more fun. Here are a few of the ways I remind myself. Experiment with what works for you.

- When the phone rings, take a few mindful breaths before answering.
- When you're waiting in line—at a store, at the movies, in

traffic—especially if you are feeling agitated or frustrated, notice those feelings. Then turn your attention to what you're experiencing in your body. Notice how you are standing or sitting. Take a slow deep breath and feel that you are alive in this moment.

- Take a mindful walk around your neighborhood. Feel your feet on the ground with each step. Just walk and know that you are walking. When your mind wanders, bring it back to your steps.
- I know this one is radical: Instead of multitasking, try *unitasking*. That is, try doing one thing at a time. It's much easier to be present for your experience when you do.

The more often you practice paying attention, the easier it gets to steady your mind and remain present. You will notice that being present in itself awakens a feeling of well-being.

## THE MINDFUL MOMENT

*"Several times a day I take sixty seconds or less to be mindful. Often it's before a meal. I reflect on the actual physical nature of the food I'm eating. Where did this chicken come from? Where did this corn come from? I think about the people driving the trucks, and the gasoline that propelled those trucks. The sunlight, the DNA in domesticated corn. I feel all that going into my body, which gives me a sense of being part of that whole process in a very direct way. That's a moment of mindfulness."*

—RICK HANSON, PH.D., AUTHOR OF *BUDDHA'S BRAIN:*
*THE PRACTICAL NEUROSCIENCE OF HAPPINESS, LOVE AND WISDOM*
AT AWAKENING JOY COURSE, BERKELEY, 2008

## THE PRACTICE OF
## MINDFULNESS MEDITATION

As you will readily discover, the mind is hard to rope into the moment. For this reason, a very effective way to train yourself in mindfulness is by practicing it in a structured period of formal meditation, as in a class or on a retreat. In these environments, free of the usual distractions that keep you from noticing your inner experience, you sit in silence for periods of time long enough to let you see how the mind works. Mindfulness meditation is traditionally called "insight" meditation or *vipassana,* which means "to see things clearly." In contrast to other forms of meditation, in which you might focus on an object or a mantra or an inner image to bring about a certain state of mind, mindfulness is about simply being present for your experience, whatever it is. Mindfulness meditation prac-

### How Do You Do It?

Sit in a posture that allows you to be comfortable and relatively still but not so relaxed that you fall asleep. You want to be both alert and at ease. Now, begin with paying attention to your breath. How do you know you're breathing? Where in your body do you feel it most clearly? You might notice the breath coming into your nostrils and passing out again. You might instead feel the rising and falling of your abdomen. Or you might simply be aware of your whole body sitting and breathing. Each time your mind wanders, gently return to the breath. Paying attention to breathing helps focus and calm your mind so that it can more easily stay present in the moment.

In addition to the breath, you can be mindful of other experiences inside you as they call your attention—various sensations in your body, your moods, your thoughts as they come and go. One moment you might notice a breath, the next you're aware of an itching in your back or arm, then a sound, then a thought, then the breath again. The key to being mindful is remaining aware of any of these experiences as they arise, without getting lost in the story or thoughts connected with any of them.

tice does typically begin with focusing on the breath, but then the attention is turned to whatever else is happening in the body and mind.

Whether doing formal meditation practice or just taking a few minutes to quiet the mind, most people find that soon after they begin to pay attention to their breath or to some sensation in their body, without even knowing it, they're gone, lost in their thoughts. This is not bad. It's just the way it is. The eye sees. The ear hears. The mind thinks. Thoughts are not the enemy, and the mind can be trained.

How we respond when we realize the mind has been wandering is critical to the process of developing mindfulness. If you get lost in a thought, patiently bring your attention back to the moment, remembering that you're sitting and breathing. It's important to do this with kindness, because reacting with frustration or annoyance only strengthens those qualities. You're in the process of training your mind, and just like training a puppy, it's patient repetition rather than punishment that works best. Rather than feeling aggravated because you've been lost, you can appreciate that you've woken up from the dream. Each time you return your attention

## THE FLICKERING OF THOUGHT

*"Consider this for instance: In your lifetime how many thoughts have passed through your mind? Billions perhaps, and not one of them has stuck. You might say, 'Oh, I have repetitive thoughts,' but if you examine, you'll see each so-called repetitive thought is actually a new thought. They're not a constant hum, but rather tiny ephemeral electrical pulses we call thought.*

*"Once at Omega Institute in New York, I took the group I was leading in a silent retreat for a walk out in the countryside at night. At one point along the road, we stopped by an open field where thousands of fireflies were winking on and off in the expanse of dark space. We all stood in silence, smiling at each other and giggling, understanding the metaphor together. It was very much like the flickering of thought in the open space of awareness."*

—CATHERINE INGRAM
AT AWAKENING JOY COURSE,
BERKELEY, 2008

with patience and kindness to the moment, you strengthen those qualities as well as your ability to remain present. Over time you will find negative patterns naturally unwinding and wholesome attitudes increasing.

## HOW DOES MINDFULNESS WORK?

How can mindfulness help free us of negative habits? A method that uses observing the mind in order to change our actions may seem pretty mysterious. However, the Buddha tracked the process with a precision that some psychologists and neuroscientists are beginning to recognize the validity of today. Changing negative habits depends upon paying mindful attention to what is happening inside us when they arise. As I've been emphasizing in this chapter, the key to success is in *not reacting* to what is going on in our thoughts, our feelings, and in our body.

The mind and body are interconnected, each affecting the other. We take in information through our five senses, and that's where the process begins. The first thing that happens in any situation in which we might react is that one of our senses is stimulated. For instance, we hear someone say something to us. If we were hearing only the sound, with no evaluation of it, we would have no reaction. But that's not the way we're set up as humans.

When we hear that sound, our brain immediately evaluates it, primarily based on our past experiences. If the sound is soft and warm, it is equated with loving experiences we've had, and it's called a "good" sound. If it's harsh and explosive, it's most likely connected with painful experiences in the past (unless you're a heavy metal fan), and it's evaluated as a "bad" sound.

Simultaneously, whether we are aware of it or not, the sound registers in our body. If it's a pleasant sound, we may feel little ripples of delight; our muscles may relax. If the sound is unpleasant, we may feel prickles of fear, and suddenly we're tense.

Finally, depending upon whether the sound is pleasant or unpleasant, we react. We like it or we dislike it. We want more of it, or we want none of it.

In releasing old habits, the trick is not to get caught up in that last part—the reaction. There is no way to interrupt the first three steps in this process. They all happen automatically. You can't *not* hear a sound if your ears are open. But if your attention is engaged elsewhere, you might not register it consciously. This happens all the time and can lead to typical

misunderstandings. "I called you to dinner three times!" "But I was reading and didn't hear you."

The step in this process where you have a choice to change your life
and create more happiness is at that point of wanting or aversion. This
process can also take place entirely in your mind, that "sixth sense." You
might remember something someone said to you, and all those same
inner responses can take place. Whether you are interacting with someone, or you are alone and recalling something that happened to you, if
you simply remain present and aware of the experience in your mind
and body, you are no longer feeding the habit through reaction, and it
begins to diminish. As neuroscience would explain it, the synaptic connections that are not strengthened through repetition begin to weaken.

This effect of mindfulness is known as freeing or purifying the mind.
As negative patterns are released, they are no longer obscuring the beneficial mind states. Therefore, your natural joy and goodness can express
themselves.

## CHANGING YOUR MIND

As neuroscience expert and psychologist Dr. Rick Hanson says, the mind
and the brain are a unified system. As the brain changes, the mind changes.
As the mind changes, the brain changes. This means you can use your conscious mind to make lasting changes in your brain to bring about more well-
being and happiness in your life.

Each time you repeat a particular thought or action, you strengthen the
connection between a set of brain cells, or neurons. The phrase neuroscientists use to describe this phenomenon is: "Neurons that fire together wire
together." This means that the more often you repeat a thought or action,
the stronger the related neural pathways become, and the more easily that
thought or action can recur. That's bad news if you're caught up in some
negative habits. But the good news is that you can interrupt old patterns
and put new ones in their place. Over time, the brain actually changes structure by strengthening the new, more frequently used circuits, and the un-
used ones fall away.

## CHOOSING THOUGHTS THAT
## LEAD TO JOY

The Buddha was a preeminent mind researcher 2,500 years ago. Before his enlightenment, he wandered the countryside of northern India for six years, trying many methods in order to understand the nature of life and where true happiness can be found. As he investigated his mind in meditation, he noticed two different categories of thoughts: those that led to suffering and those that led to happiness. The first group included thoughts connected with blind desire, ill will, and cruelty which led, as he put it, "to my own affliction and the affliction of others." The other set of thoughts—those of contentment, kindness, and compassion—had just the opposite effect. Not only were they harmless to himself and others, but they actually led to happiness.

*When we're in the car, my husband and I often quibble about which route is the fastest. The other night I was about to yell at him when he was driving, but I stopped myself and took some deep breaths. I said to myself,* I don't have to act on these thoughts. I don't have to say what I'm thinking right now. *Then I started noticing the way my breath felt going through my body. I ended up feeling more relaxed and didn't care which street we drove on or how much traffic there was."*
—A COURSE PARTICIPANT

We have little control over what thoughts arise in any particular moment. If we did, we would probably have only thoughts of love and goodwill toward all of humanity. But a few others seem to slip through. We have profound thoughts, bizarre thoughts, and ugly thoughts. Seeing some of what goes on in our mind—the fears, the pettiness, the judgments—can be humbling. I once heard a Tibetan Buddhist teacher playfully refer to looking at what's going on in our minds as "one insult after another." Or, as a common saying goes, "Self-knowledge is usually bad news."

But actually it's very good news. While what arises in our mind is somewhat random and out of our control, we do have control over which thoughts we choose to dwell on. By training ourselves to pay attention to what is happening in our mind and body in any situation, we make it more likely that we will empower those thoughts that support our well-being.

At one Awakening Joy class, meditation teacher Sylvia Boorstein told a story about how becoming aware of what she was thinking helped reframe an experience. One evening when she was staying in New York City, she had arranged to meet a friend for a theater performance and decided to take a bus to get there. As the bus crept along through the heavy traffic, Sylvia started worrying: *I'm going to be late. I'll miss the curtain. My friend will worry about what happened to me. I shouldn't have taken the bus. The subway would have been so much faster.* Figuring she could walk faster than the bus was going, Sylvia got off, "and of course as I'm walking, the bus passes me by . . . and now I'm thinking, *I should have taken a cab.*"

Sylvia has been meditating for years, but she has also, by her own admission, been fretting for years, so it was an easy reaction to fall into. Continuing her story, she describes running down Broadway—in high heels with a cold wind whipping around her. And then:

> All of a sudden I have the thought: *What am I doing? I'm grumbling.* That's a moment of mindfulness. Up until then, I was caught up in a habit-driven narrative, an editorial comment about what was happening. The moment at which the mind says, *Sylvia, you're grumbling,* the lens switches, and suddenly the truth of that moment is: *I'm a seventy-one-year-old woman running down Broadway in the middle of winter in high heels. That is far out! That is an extremely fortunate thing to be able to do.* It changed everything. I felt proud, and I actually hoped a lot of people saw me.

When we are mindful, we can let go of thoughts that undermine our well-being and thereby frame our experience in a way that invites more ease. As Sylvia puts it, "A moment of mindfulness is always a moment of freedom. We can have the courage to make choices that result in a positive difference for ourselves and others."

After recounting to his followers his experience of seeing the two kinds of thoughts and their outcomes, the Buddha shared with them the secret of training the mind in states of well-being: "Whatever a practitioner frequently thinks and ponders upon, that will become the inclina-

## THREE LEVELS OF MINDFULNESS

*"I see mindfulness as distinctly connected to joy on three levels: the physical, the personal or psychological, and the universal.*

*One: Mindfulness is thrilling on the physical level. Something happens neurologically in the body when the attention is brought in from all the ways it gets scattered. To feel your hands touching each other, or to simply put your foot down and know that you're putting your foot down, is tremendously pleasurable. Being present in that very action sends a thrill of rapture through the body. When the mind is focused on one thing, it's not caught up in the inner narrative of fear or yearning.*

*Two: Each of us has our own idiosyncratic set of memories, views, and opinions based on our personal experience. These play over and over like a tape loop. Mindfulness illuminates the habits of our mind and sets us free from being held captive by them. These moments of clarity can happen at any time simply by inclining the mind toward being present. Over time the mind becomes used to being clearer, and we learn how to live wisely.*

*Three: Mindfulness illuminates truths that are universal. Things pass. Everything—you and I and everyone and everything—has a life span. This moment is all there is, and to the degree we can remember that, we can actually experience the joy of living, even in situations that are quite difficult.*

*We often imagine or plan that when this or that happens, we'll have a good time. But who knows if this or that will ever happen? A million things can happen on the way there. There's only now. So mindfulness is about being in this moment. It's the only one in which joy is available."*

—SYLVIA BOORSTEIN, AUTHOR OF *HAPPINESS IS AN INSIDE JOB*
AT AWAKENING JOY COURSE, BERKELEY, 2008

tion of his mind." We strengthen habits of thought through repetition. If you often think unkind, negative, or depressing thoughts, you'll tend to continue thinking in that way. If you choose thoughts that uplift, nourish, and bring kindness to yourself and others, your mind will increasingly lean in that direction.

Mindfulness teaches us to incline our mind toward joy by helping us wisely choose our thoughts and actions. And the more we do this, the more readily it happens. Research psychologist Sonja Lyubomirsky says in her book *The How of Happiness* that "an unhappy person spends more than twice as much time thinking about unpleasant events in their lives, while happy people tend to seek and rely upon information that brightens their personal outlook."

## FINDING REFUGE IN THE PRESENT

It started out as an almost imperceptible phenomenon. I was preparing for a talk I was going to give at a retreat in Southern California, and as I looked over my notes, I had the sense that a shade was ever so slightly being drawn over my upper right field of vision. I dismissed it as just my imagination. Although I'd had no vision in my left eye since childhood, my right eye had been serving me well enough. The next day, however, that mysterious little pull-down screen happened again, and I thought I should probably check it out. Little did I know what lay in store.

The doctor at the clinic was friendly, and I felt at ease as she dilated my eyes and began the exam. But a few minutes later I felt her demeanor change. She turned the lights back on, and I could see in her face this was not good news. "I'm afraid you have a giant retinal tear," she said with concern. "Since this is your one good eye, it's particularly serious. You could end up completely blind. Either we perform an operation immediately and you stay here for the next five or six weeks to fully heal, or you get on the next plane back to the Bay Area and hope for the best."

I was stunned. When I could finally think, I told her I'd rather be at home with family and friends for the procedure. She warned me against any sudden movements or lifting, told me to be very careful, and wished me luck. During the forty-five-minute drive back to the retreat center, I would experience firsthand the benefits of mindfulness practice.

I made my way to the parking lot. I don't know if it was the time of day, but as I turned on the car ignition, everything suddenly seemed darker both outside and inside. Hands gripping the steering wheel a bit more tightly than usual, I took the familiar route through the stark landscape of the desert hills. Although I wasn't driving fast, my mind was racing. *I could be blind next week. What will my life be like? Will I be totally dependent on Jane?* Then something curious happened. It was like a voice reminding me from a distance, "You don't know about next week. Just be here now."

My attention turned to my hands on the wheel, and I realized I could relax my white-knuckle grip. I began noticing my breath move in and out of my nostrils. My mind calmed down . . . for about a minute or so before the next swirl of disturbing thoughts arose. *Adam is just eleven years old. What will his teenage years be like if I can't be there for him the way I want to?* Once again the words inside gently and firmly reminded me, "You don't know what the future will be like. Just come back to this moment."

This process of my mind spinning out with fearful images, followed by a return to the breath and a calming down, took place at least another twenty-five times as I made my way back to the retreat center. What was so illuminating was not that my mind was filled with worry, but that it didn't kick into outright panic. My years of meditation practice proved to be my greatest ally. I was experiencing the power of mindfulness. Each time the nightmare fantasies were starting to take over, they were inter-rupted by a return to the present moment and a recentering on my breath. Remaining mindful carried me safely back home and even helped me get through the operation a few days later with a level of calm and acceptance.

This refuge from our fears—the present moment—is always available to us. And with practice we learn to more easily return to it, even in the midst of confusion. As we do this over and over, we begin to understand how the mind works and what choices incline it toward well-being and joy. In time our experience shows us that mindfulness can indeed, as the Buddha said, help us "overcome grief and sorrow, end pain and anxiety, and realize the highest happiness."

## HOW CAN I TELL IF I'M HAPPY?

Knowing whether or not we're happy might seem like a no-brainer. You might feel on top of the world, but if it's because you're jacked up on a double-cappuccino and your heart is racing, are you really happy? A colleague who works in a high-powered industry told me she had been wondering about this very thing. "I can think I am 'happy' about something happening at work, but when I notice that I'm speedy and breathless and my stomach is tight, I'm not so sure." If we don't know how to recognize when we're actually happy, we can end up choosing states of mind and body that lead us in an entirely different direction. As you might know from experience, that caffeine high can suddenly subside yet keep you wired for hours. So how can you recognize the kind of happiness that is connected to genuine well-being?

*I struggle with being the best mom I can be to my two kids. Being at home all day with my four-year-old daughter and seventeen-month-old son can try my patience. Recently I yelled at my daughter. Before learning mindfulness, I would have told myself I was a bad mother, that I was stupid, useless, and so on. But instead I just said to myself, 'I yelled at Sasha' and moved on. That actually let me be a better mom, because I wasn't being so hard on myself. This freed up more time to have fun with her and be happy."*

—A COURSE PARTICIPANT

In the early 1970s, a remarkable little book came out—*The Lazy Man's Guide to Enlightenment* by Thaddeus Golas. One of the many points that rang true for me was Golas's idea of "expansion and contraction" in describing various states of mind. He said: "We experience expansion as awareness, comprehension, understanding." In contrast, "contraction is felt as fear, pain, unconsciousness, ignorance, hatred." Recalling this distinction helped me define something basic to happiness. Genuine happiness goes along with a feeling of openness and ease in the mind and body. Even when your focus is acute, as in mountain climbing or playing a musical instrument, the mind is not rigid.

Being mindful of your internal state is a great aid in helping you discover what will bring you more happiness. By noticing if your body is feeling contracted or open, you will realize whether or not you are in the midst of an experience you want to strengthen and repeat or one you want to let go of. Likewise, you can check if the mind is tense or at ease to know if you're moving toward or away from joy. As you do so, you'll begin to discover that certain ways of thinking and acting lead to a deep satisfaction and well-being.

At first it might be a bit tricky to discern the distinction between the two states. Contracted states can disguise themselves as uplifting. The adrenaline rush that comes with anger can make us feel powerful and in charge. The excitement that comes with desire may feel like bliss. But how does your body actually feel when you are angry or filled with desire? What state of mind are you in? That rush of anger can make you feel great, but watch out if someone dares to disagree with you! And that driving desire to get what we want, from window shopping to lust, can feel exciting and invigorating, but rarely peaceful and open-hearted. When we burn with anger or desire, our body is tight, our mind is in turmoil, and joy is nowhere in sight.

## Noticing Contraction and Expansion

When you find yourself in a contracted state, what do you notice in your body and mind? Course participants responded:

- Like it's hard to breathe.
- I want to go away and curl up somewhere.
- Like I hate everything.
- A little sick to my stomach.

When you're feeling expansive, what do you notice in your body and mind?

- Every one of my cells feels like it's smiling.
- I feel unafraid and open.
- I feel connected to the people around me.
- I feel warm and happy and also like crying, which surprises me.

States of well-being are the opposite of stress and agitation. How does your body feel when you're giving a gift to someone you love, delighting in the antics of a cute toddler, or reveling in the satisfaction of a job well-done? When my wife Jane walks through the door of my office and gives me a hug, I notice that my heart instantly feels warm. The smile on my face tells the rest of my body to relax. My breath gets slow and easy. My mind, too, feels spacious and at ease. This is the quality of expansion that accompanies happiness.

*We have invented myriad shortcuts to good feelings: drugs, chocolate, loveless sex, shopping . . . television are all examples. . . . Positive emotions alienated from the exercise of character lead to emptiness, to inauthenticity, to depression. . . . The positive feeling that arises from the exercise of strengths and virtues rather than shortcuts is authentic. Strengths and virtues are characteristics that bring about good feelings and gratification."*
—MARTIN SELIGMAN, FROM
*AUTHENTIC HAPPINESS*

This difference between expansion and contraction is directly linked to the Buddha's distinction between wholesome and unwholesome thoughts and actions. When we're kind and compassionate, we feel open and happy; when we're angry or fearful, we feel contracted and dissatisfied. The trick here is not to resist whatever you're experiencing. It's all part of being human. Instead of tightening up in reaction, be mindful of what is happening, noticing without judgment how and what you're feeling. Then choose thoughts and actions that expand your heart and your understanding.

As you will see throughout this program, the wholesome states presented in the following chapters are invariably connected with what is beneficial to yourself and others. This not only brings us genuine happiness but also develops, as the Buddha said, "a mind that is without hostility or ill will"—in other words, a mind at peace.

## AMPLIFYING YOUR JOY

Mindfulness did help me get through that critical eye operation, and over the course of the following year it would offer another and unexpected gift. While my eye had been saved, the operation had left me with a complication—the world looked like a Jacques Cousteau underwater documentary filmed on a cloudy day. I carried around a magnifying glass to read with; my notes for teaching were written in big letters with brightly colored felt pens; students' faces were a blur. By the end of that challenging year, my joy in life was subtly dimming along with my vision. When the options were presented to me—going slowly but surely blind or undergoing another high-risk surgery—I took my chances.

Once again I found myself facing the unknown and, moment by moment, trying to remain present to avoid sliding into fear. And then came that unforgettable experience after the operation when the bandages were removed. I could actually see! Not only notice what was around me but *see*, clearly and sharply. I remember the words to Johnny Nash's song ringing in my mind: "I can see clearly now the rain is gone. . . ." Every chorus of that song lifted me to a higher level of gratitude. "It's gonna be a bright, bright sunshiny day. . . ."

Far from subsiding, the gratitude I felt at my good fortune became a continuous backdrop to everything else in my life. I could see Jane smile. I could see the sparkle in Adam's eye when he did something that made me proud. I could read books and newspapers, I could see the joy of understanding on the faces of students, I could watch a sunset, I could travel alone. Whatever pain and travail that arose was short-lived whenever I'd remember *I can see.*

I had trained for years to examine my experience carefully, not only for my own spiritual growth but also to share my findings with students. Clearly the topic now up for investigation was this tremendous

*I was waiting in my car, with barely enough time for lunch, as a group of elderly individuals, whose car occupied the only available parking space, slowly maneuvered a walker into their trunk. I began to realize that I didn't need to define this situation as being about me and my desire for a parking space but could instead see the situation as an opportunity to recognize our human connection. By the time I called out the window to ask if they wanted any assistance, my offer was not primarily about getting into the parking space faster but mostly about seeing whether I could help make their lives easier at that moment. They didn't need help, and as I continued waiting, I allowed myself to notice some beautiful, red, sunlit leaves on a plant right outside my car window. I realize how much choice I have in defining the moment."*

—A COURSE PARTICIPANT

feeling of gratitude. I became fascinated with the question, "What is gratitude?" Bringing all my attention to the experience in my body and mind, I became an explorer of the landscape of the grateful heart. I became intimate with the expansive feeling in my chest, with the lightness that seemed to course through every cell.

As I paid close attention to the feeling of gratitude, I began to notice that being mindful of this state actually seemed to increase it. I had always taught the principle that when we pay attention to wholesome states, they increase. Now it wasn't just theory. In a very real way, I was experiencing in my body and mind a profound truth—simply paying mindful attention to the experience of gratitude was intensifying the feeling of gratitude in the moment. And besides that, it was also giving rise to a sustained sense of happiness.

Mindfulness has a unique power. It weakens all mind states that lead to suffering, such as anger, greed, and fear, while awakening and strengthening within us all the mind states that lead to happiness such as kindness, love, and clarity. As you bring the practice of mindfulness into your life,

## Building Your Happiness Muscle

You can actually strengthen the happiness circuits in your brain. Whenever you are experiencing a moment of joy or contentment—walking, listening to music, watching a sunset, being kind, feeling grateful—DON'T MISS IT! Pause to notice the feelings in your body and the state of your mind. Do you feel warmth in your chest? Tingling through your body? Does your mind feel light, open? Now consciously intensify that feeling. Some psychologists call this "memorizing" the feeling. Either way, you are causing the same neural circuits to fire repeatedly, thereby strengthening them. Dr. Rick Hanson, author of *Buddha's Brain*, calls this "taking in the good" and suggests first intensifying the experience in your body, then letting it calm down, and then intensifying it again. He says, "As with any positive state of mind, see if you can develop a strong 'sense memory' of the experience so you can reactivate it deliberately when you want to."

take note of how your life changes. Besides enhancing your positive states of mind, when you pause to notice what you usually overlook, a new world opens to you. Instead of worrying about the future, regretting the past, or being lost in fantasies of what you long for or fear, when you are mindful, you're brought into the immediacy of *now.* Whatever your experience is, you can hold it as a sacred moment of life worthy of your attention.

# GRATEFUL HEART, JOYFUL HEART

Be grateful for your life, every detail of it, and your face
will come to shine like a sun, and everyone who sees it
will be made glad and peaceful. Persist in gratitude, and
you will slowly become one with the Sun of Love, and
Love will shine through you its all-healing joy.

—Andrew Harvey
*Light Upon Light: Inspirations from Rumi*

*A student once complained* to Nisargadatta, a great twentieth-century spiritual teacher from India, that daily life seemed so tedious to him. "You've done the most amazing thing," the sage replied. "You've made life boring!" In this culture of thirty-second sound bites and block-buster action movies, we can easily get into the habit of looking for a never-ending diet of peak experiences. When only highly stimulating events and fantastically wonderful things are worthy of our appreciation, we easily end up disappointed and feeling that life is mostly dull and un-interesting. In the midst of abundance, we find life lacking.

The founder of Gestalt psychology, Fritz Perls, used to say, "Boredom is simply lack of attention." As we've seen with mindfulness, when we pay attention, anything can be interesting. My friend Joe Kupfer discovered this in college, and it set his life in a new direction. Joe and I attended the same rigorous high school in New York City, and we came out with an almost identical grade point average—decent but not stellar. Neither of us had been that interested in going for top academic honors. Four years later we both graduated

*There are two ways to live your life: One is as though nothing is a miracle, the other is as though everything is a miracle."*

—ALBERT EINSTEIN

from Queens College, and while I had continued my casual scholastic attitude, Joe had achieved magna cum laude and went on to become a professor of philosophy. What was his secret? (Unfortunately for me, I didn't ask him until my senior year!)

When he started college, Joe told me, he'd made the decision to excel. I remember him saying he figured that the more interested he was in the course material, the easier it would be for him to learn the subject. So he devised a game: At the start of each semester, no matter how boring a class might appear to be, he would ask himself, "Why has the professor devoted his whole life to specializing in this subject? Why does he find it so interesting?" In searching for the answer, he invariably found something valuable and even fascinating in the material. Joe had interrupted a pattern of not appreciating what was before him and supplanted it with an eager openness that enabled him to shine.

As Joe discovered, you don't have to wait for appreciation and gratitude to spontaneously arise. You can consciously cultivate this powerful ally to a joyful heart. Each day of your life, you have many opportunities to develop a grateful heart by paying attention to the blessings,

*I'm allowing myself more time to appreciate what I see, be it the clouds in the sky, a fallen leaf, the trees changing, or my friends and loved ones. As I do this, I find myself loving life more and feeling the joy that's inside me."*

—A COURSE PARTICIPANT

big and small, that are all around you. Even if things are uncomfortable, or not as you might wish, it is still possible to find something you can be grateful for.

You can miss those blessings when your mind is contracted with stress or filled with negativity. There's no room for them to enter. But the moment you pause and let yourself notice something to be grateful for, even in the midst of a challenge, it is virtually impossible to continue being lost in worry about the future, or regret about the past. Negative states like anger, bitterness, and resentment dissolve in the presence of gratitude.

*I've been thrilled to watch my daughter flourish, and feel free when I allow myself to relax and feel the love and openness that gratitude rewards me with. It's almost like watching myself in a mirror."*

—A COURSE PARTICIPANT

One Tibetan lama says gratitude is like a satellite dish. When we feel grateful, our receptors are wide open to receive the abundance available to us. The very act of appreciating someone or something instantly calls forth joy. You can try it right now for yourself. Think of someone or something you feel grateful for, and notice what happens. It is impossible to feel genuinely grateful and not have a little rise of joy.

What does gratitude feel like, in your body and mind? Course participants offered these reflections:

- I breathe more deeply.
- I feel a glow in my chest, a tingling in my fingers, and a half-smile appears on my face.
- It feels like a blanket of goodness descending upon me.
- It brings me energy and peace at the same time.
- It makes me feel loved by God.
- I like myself and my muscles relax.
- I feel like my body is resting on the perfect pillow created to hold all of me.

As you notice all you have to be grateful for, pay close attention to the many different ways the experience of gratitude manifests inside you. Developing gratitude is for some people a turning point in their practice of awakening joy. It becomes immediately apparent how available joy really is. With practice, the grateful heart increasingly sees the goodness and wonder around us. As you explore this new step, notice the effect cultivating gratitude has on your life and the lives of those around you.

## THE GLASS HALF EMPTY

What gets in the way of feeling gratitude? Most participants in the Awakening Joy course name the culprit as the frenetic pace of their lives. They write comments like these:

*"Scatter joy."*
—RALPH WALDO EMERSON

- Rushing through the moment, I often get fatigued and then tend to take things for granted.
- In my usual goal- and achievement-oriented attitude toward life, every moment has to be spent productively.
- I have the belief that I must complete a list of "to dos" before stopping to enjoy anything.

Many of us probably can relate to those statements. We can get so focused on what we're doing (or on the next thing we have to do) that we overlook how much we have to be grateful for. There just doesn't seem to be enough time to smell the roses. While there's a place and time for not being distracted from our goals, we can become so habituated to a

---

### *Feeling* Gratitude

Take a few minutes to think of some of the people and things you feel gratitude for in your life. You might begin with being grateful that you can read these words. As each person or quality or thing comes up in your imagination, say silently to yourself, "I am grateful to . . . or for. . . ." Pause with each to feel the experience of gratitude that arises in your body and mind.

Before you finish with this exercise, stop and take in the fullness of the feeling of gratitude itself. Breathe it in deeply, and let it pervade your body and mind.

fast pace that even when we don't have to get somewhere or get something done, we just keep going.

When Laurinda broke some bones in her foot, she was forced to slow way down. As she hobbled around the house with a supportive brace, she began to notice that even though she couldn't move quickly, inside herself the rushing pace she was used to was still driving her. It was as if she would miss something if she wasn't fast enough. As Laurinda made the effort to pull back and literally take it just one step at a time, she began to see how much she really had been missing.

> Every night I brush my hair, but suddenly I saw that I had been going at it like it was a chore. Instead of a wonderful pleasure that I could relax and appreciate, it was just something to get done. Rather than quickly counting off the one hundred brushstrokes, I started feeling each one and noticing how good it felt to lift my arm and draw the brush through my hair. I found I could actually slow down inside and give myself this simple joy. I felt so grateful, not just to change this small habit, but to begin to release the tension that has been a lifetime habit.

## GRATITUDE SQUELCHERS

Gratitude grounds us in the present. When we're lost in galling regret about something in the past or overwhelming concerns about the future, we can forget what we have to be grateful for right now. Before I met my wife, I spent many a painful moment feeling sorry for myself and fantasizing about how good it would be when I found the love of my life. Caught up in longing, I overlooked the fact that I had many wonderful friends, but they didn't really count, because I was so focused on what I didn't have. When we get lost in fantasies of "My life could (or should) be better," we're missing the only life we actually have. Having a positive vision of the future is healthy, but in order to get there, it helps to appreciate and build on what's good in our life right now.

One thought away from "It could be better" is "*I* could be better"— a sure gratitude squelcher. When we think we're not good enough, we can spend our energy trying to prove the opposite to ourselves and to the world. We can get caught up in a kind of perfectionism that keeps us from appreciating ourselves as we are.

We can also be retroactive perfectionists, living in regret that things could have or should have been better. While we certainly can learn from past mistakes, playing over and over in our minds what might have been is guaranteed to keep us unaware of anything we can be grateful for, then or now. For example, you might go out for dinner and a movie with a new friend, and although you both obviously had a good time, you end up later replaying in your mind the one sentence that didn't come out the way you meant it to. *I'm such a dummy,* you berate yourself. *I guess that's the end of that friendship.* The next thing you know, that friend tells you how great it was to spend time together. And there you'd been, lost in regret rather than remembering the joys of that evening. What a waste. The same kind of thing can happen with months or even years of our lives when we focus on what went wrong rather than on what went right.

*It sounds almost simplistic or meaningless, and yet there is a deep truth in it: that life and Now are one."*
—ECKHART TOLLE, FROM AN INTERVIEW WITH STEVE DONOSO IN *THE SUN* MAGAZINE, JULY, 2002

Another equally useless version of regret is wishing things were like they used to be in "the good ol' days." When we look at people or events through a rearview mirror, they often seem better than they really were. An argument with your partner might leave you feeling nostalgic for the single life, forgetting how excruciating the dating scene had been. When we're attentive and grateful for our lives right now, we can make sure that our present moments, soon to be our "good ol' days," are fully lived and appreciated.

## RIGHT UNDER OUR NOSES

In one of my favorite stories about Mulla Nasruddin, an eccentric wise man/fool from the Sufi tradition, Mulla and his donkey have been frequently crossing the border between Persia and Turkey. As time goes on, the customs officials on both sides of the border notice that Nasruddin seems to be getting increasingly richer. His clothes are finer and he is wearing elegant perfumes. The officers are sure he is smuggling contraband. They thoroughly search him, his donkey, and the donkey's straw, but each time they can find nothing. For several months the situation continues in this way. Nasruddin looks richer and richer, yet despite careful inspections of both him and his donkey, nothing is found.

Many months later, one of the customs officials sees Nasruddin shopping in the bazaar. He approaches him and says, "Mulla, I have retired from my post as a customs official. I now have a generous pension and want nothing from you except one thing. We all know you were smuggling something across the border but could never find anything on you or the donkey. I swear I won't tell a soul if you share your secret with me. What was it you were smuggling?"

Nasruddin looks at him with a mischievous grin and replies, "Donkeys."

Often the precious riches we are looking for are right under our noses but we miss them. We can find valuable gifts in the most unexpected places if we get in the habit of being grateful for whatever is before us. Sometimes they are even hidden right inside the challenges we face.

My friend Abby developed cancer of the throat. During an eight-month ordeal of chemotherapy, radiation, and receiving nourishment through a feeding tube, she chose to focus not on the pain and discomfort but on how fortunate she was to have access to good medical care and the fact that the doctors caught the tumor in time. Her recovery was extraordinary and, of course, she was a true inspiration to everyone who knew her.

*You can complain because roses have thorns, or you can rejoice because thorns have roses."*
—ZIGGY, CHARACTER IN A COMIC STRIP BY TOM WILSON

About three months later, however, Abby received the startling news that there were signs of malignant cells in her lung. The specialists gave her two choices—the less invasive procedure would remove some tissue in the lung, but there was some chance that this would not completely remove the problem. The more dramatic choice, while the surer solution, would entail removing the entire upper lobe of the lung. On the advice of her doctor, Abby chose the second option.

"When the surgery was over, my doctor informed me that they hadn't found cancer in the lung after all. It had been a false read," she told me. I think most people in the same situation would have understandably been very upset. But Abby was determined to incline her mind toward appreciation rather than regret or anger. Even though she might have seen little to be grateful for in this situation, she chose to look at this as another opportunity to open to what life was giving her. "My prayer going into the operation was that I would come out of it with no cancer in the lung. And in the end, that's what I got!" she says. "My prayer was answered." Rather than being brought down by bitterness, Abby's ordeal deepened her capacity for gratitude, and she was invigorated by the joy she felt from focusing on what there was to appreciate.

Abby's ability to respond to her ordeal with gratitude was grounded in years of spiritual practice. She knew that anger and frustration, though justified, wouldn't change what had happened and would only lead to more emotional upset. While it usually takes time and practice to develop this kind of wisdom, it

## SAYING YES! TO LIFE

*"We often think if only life were a little different—better, easier, more comfortable, more in my favor—then I could feel joy. We hold our joy out there like a carrot on a stick, saying, 'When I get through this conflict with my boss or my mother, then maybe I'll have a moment of joy, or when I get past my depression, my despair, my loneliness . . .' But the potential for joy is always present, and the key to accessing it is saying 'Yes' to whatever is true in this moment, whether or not we like what's going on or expected it.*

*"Think of something in your life that you're not too happy about—perhaps a conflict, a health issue, something you wish hadn't appeared at all. Without any judgment, notice your first reaction. Then try saying 'Yes' to this situation. Notice what happens inside you as you do this. What you're experiencing may not be what you wanted or expected, but saying yes can empower you and give you the courage to handle whatever rests on your plate."*

—CAROLYN HOBBS, LMFT, AUTHOR
OF *JOY, NO MATTER WHAT*
AT AWAKENING JOY COURSE,
BERKELEY, 2008

begins with realizing you have a choice. The shift toward responding with gratitude in the midst of difficult circumstances can be a gradual process or it can happen in an instant. As you keep in mind the fact that what you really want is happiness and peace, you learn to act in ways that are more likely to bring that about.

It took years for me to realize
that the very twists and turns
and shadows I labeled "problems"
were really sacred ground,
grace disguised as obstacles,
the whole path a pilgrimage,
mysteries baring themselves
before me all along the way.

—DANNA FAULDS,
excerpted from "Every Step Is Holy"
in *From Root to Bloom*

Author Carolyn Hobbs suggests that we try saying yes to whatever we're experiencing. This means we're not fighting our circumstances. Any situation, even the most disappointing, may have a hidden gift we can be grateful for. Sometimes we see that better in retrospect, but by then we may have spent many unhappy moments bound up in anger or depression. When we remain open to whatever is happening to us, we are far more likely to find the valuable gifts hidden in our challenging times.

## "GRACE DISGUISED AS OBSTACLES"

For decades Ram Dass, a much-loved spiritual teacher and author, mesmerized audiences with his fascinating lectures. Then in 1997 his life radically changed when he suffered a major stroke. He went from being able to cast a magic spell with words to struggling through long silences just to construct a simple sentence. In his book *Still Here,* Ram Dass describes how painful this process initially was as he tried to hold on to his old identity, remembering how things used to be.

One of his first public events after the stroke was held at Spirit Rock Meditation Center in California, on a day dedicated to celebrating him. The talk he gave was short and halting. Although everyone was moved by his presence, when I saw him afterward, he expressed sadness that he would never be able to do what he had done before.

Besides losing his eloquence, Ram Dass could no longer do most of the activities that had given him great joy. Of course he had to go through a period of grieving. But eventually he was able to say yes to this new version of himself and transform his frustration into a profound gratitude. He writes in *Still Here:*

> I used to say, "I'm a golfer and a sports car driver" . . . But now I'm someone telling that story. I can't golf or drive anymore. If I cling to that identity, I suffer. . . . The stroke was like a samurai sword, cutting apart the two halves of my life. It was a demarcation between two stages. Before I had the stroke, I was full of fears about aging. . . . The stroke took me through one of my deep fears, and I'm here to report that "the only thing we have to fear is fear itself" . . . The stroke cleaned out some of the pockets of fear. It's happened, and here I am.

The result of this change, Ram Dass says, is that he has grown closer to God than ever before. "What more could I ask?" he writes, acknowledging the gift deeply hidden in his suffering.

Over time Ram Dass has not only adjusted to his new identity, he has become even more of an inspiration than before. He invites his adoring audiences to use the pauses in his speech to enter into a meditative silence. In allowing his stroke to be a teaching, he now conveys, in an even more profound way, the wisdom he's been communicating for decades.

Gratitude in our darkest times is more than a matter of remembering our blessings so we can hold the hard stuff in a bigger perspective. With understanding, we see that often it is the suffering itself that deepens us, maturing our perspective on life, making us more compassionate and wiser than we would have been without it. How many times have we been inspired by those who embody a wisdom that could only come from dealing with adversity? And how many valuable lessons have we ourselves learned because life has given us unwanted challenges? With a grateful heart, we're not only willing to face our difficulties, we can realize while we're going through them that they are part of our ripening into wisdom and nobility.

*It took years for me to realize that the very twists and turns and shadows I labeled "problems" were really sacred ground, grace disguised as obstacles, the whole path a pilgrimage, mysteries baring themselves before me all along the way.*
—DANNA FAULDS, EXCERPTED FROM "EVERY STEP IS HOLY" IN *FROM ROOT TO BLOOM*

## GLASS HALF FULL

Lisa came to a retreat at Spirit Rock eager to get away from all the distractions of her busy life. Instead, what was revealed in the silence was the continual complaining taking place in her mind. When she came in for her interview, the fifteen-minute check-in with the teacher scheduled during silent retreats, the look on her face was a combination of frustration and humor. With a sigh she began, "I can't believe the way I talk to myself all day. No wonder everything seems so heavy. I'm constantly whining! And I'm so tired of it."

"What kinds of things is that internal voice saying?" I asked.

"It's always the same refrain," Lisa answered. "No matter what I'm about to do, my mind grumbles, 'Oh now I *have to* do this. Now I *have to* do that.' When I'm in the meditation hall and the bell rings at the end of the sitting, the thought comes, 'Oh, now I *have to* do walking meditation.' Then when the bell ends that period, my mind says, 'Oh now I *have to* do sitting meditation.' Even when the bell for lunch sounds, my response is 'Oh now I *have to* go to lunch.' And I know that's what I always do in my daily life as well. I wish I could stop it," she went on. "But I don't know how to break the habit. Now I see why I often feel that life is a drag. I make it a drag!"

Lisa had actually pinpointed the problem herself. "What if you just change one word in there?" I asked. She looked at me quizzically. I continued, "I wonder what it would be like if, whenever you hear yourself complaining about what you *have to* do, you try saying instead, 'Now I *get to* do this' and 'Now I *get to* do that.' That way each activity would feel less like a chore and more like a change of scenery for you to appreciate." She agreed to give it a try.

A few days later Lisa came in for her next interview, beaming. "What a difference that one little word makes!" she began. "I haven't minded the bell ringing these last few days at all. I've even been looking forward to my work meditation folding the laundry. I'm taking each activity as a new adventure, and so I notice all kinds of things I used to miss. I don't want to jinx myself by saying it, but I'm actually having fun!"

I'd been delighted to learn that Lisa had discovered on the retreat a new way to relate to her life, but even more impressive was that she sustained it. Several months later in Berkeley, I ran into her by chance. She said that keeping up her "Now I *get to*" practice was having a profound effect. "I'm so much lighter now," Lisa smiled. "Changing that one little word has changed my life."

The habit of seeing what's wrong in our lives is like reading only the depressing articles in the newspaper. Taking in a steady diet of bad news, we can forget about the cartoons or the inspiring feature stories. Gratitude helps us shift the perspective so we can see what is filling our cup rather than what might be missing.

*After a week of overwhelming generosity bestowed upon me, instead of enjoying it, I started to feel fear and caution about becoming too joyous, as this might mean I'd let my guard slip and get sideswiped when I least expected it. This revealed my tendency to limit joy or feel like I somehow have to "pay back" for the joy I receive. I wonder how often I have limited joy in my life. Funny, as I don't seem to put limits on the pain."*

—A COURSE PARTICIPANT

## From "Have to" to "Get to"

Choose a particular task or situation in your life that feels like a burden. Try changing "have to" to "get to" and see if you get a different perspective. "Now I get to take out the garbage" just might make you feel grateful to the people who come and take it away. The more you notice what there is to be grateful for, the sooner your half-empty glass begins to look at least half-full.

## FRAME IT WITH GRATITUDE

One year I was in Los Angeles visiting my then eighty-nine-year-old mother. I brought with me a copy of *Greater Good* magazine, a magazine published by a couple of brilliant minds at the University of California at Berkeley. Their focus is on reporting the breaking research on altruism and well-being. The topic of the particular issue I had with me was the beneficial effects of gratitude. As we sat at the dining room table eating the special eggplant dish my mother always makes for me, I told her about some of the findings. She said she was impressed by the reports, but admitted she had a lifetime habit of looking at the glass half empty. "I know I'm very fortunate and have so many things to be thankful for, but little

---

### THE BENEFITS OF GRATITUDE

- Martin Seligman, the father of Positive Psychology, asked people who considered themselves severely depressed to write down three good things that happened to them each day for fifteen days. At the end of the experiment, 94 percent of these subjects had a decrease in depression and 92 percent actually said their happiness had increased.
- Leading gratitude researchers, UC Davis psychologists Robert Emmons and Michael McCullough, divided volunteers for a study on the benefits of gratitude into three groups. Once a week for ten weeks the "Gratitude Group" wrote down five things they were grateful for. The "Hassle Group" wrote down five things that displeased them. And the "Neutral Group" listed five things that affected them but without emphasizing the positive or negative aspects of their experience. The results? On a scale used to calculate well-being, the Gratitude Group registered 25 percent happier than either the Hassle or the Neutral Group. They also felt better about life, were more optimistic, had fewer health complaints and symptoms of illness, did more physical exercise than the Neutral Group and *significantly* more exercise than the Hassle Group.

things just set me off." She said she wished she could change the habit but had doubts whether that was possible. "I'm just more used to seeing what's going wrong," she concluded.

After dinner my mom and I broke out the Scrabble set, as we often do. (She's a terrific player and derives great joy from trouncing her poor son!) Our conversation continued as the lines of tiles filled the board.

"You know, Mom, the key to gratitude is really in the way we frame a situation," I began. "For instance, suppose all of a sudden your television isn't getting good reception."

"That's a scenario I can relate to," she agreed, with a knowing smile.

"One way to describe your experience would be to say, 'This is so annoying I could scream!' Or you could say, 'This is so annoying . . . *and* my life is really very blessed.'" She agreed that could make a big difference.

*During my first bike ride of the season, I encountered a very steep hill and watched my mind fret and body tighten. In that moment I also realized how grateful and lucky I am to have a healthy body and to be alive on this beautiful spring night. I smiled at my fretting mind and took one pedal at a time. I slowed down, turned the gears down (literally and figuratively), and got present. I did not focus on the top of the hill. I focused on the foot on the pedal, the movement of the body, and the beauty, freedom, and immediacy of the practice of gratitude."*
—A COURSE PARTICIPANT

"But I don't think I can remember to do that," she sighed.

So together we made up a gratitude game to remind her. Each time she complained about something, I would simply say "*and . . .*" to which she would respond "*and* my life is very blessed." I was elated to see that she was willing to try it out. Over the next few days, as the complaints rolled off her tongue, we had many chances to play our little game. We'd both chuckle each time she dutifully gave her agreed-upon reply. Although it had started out as just a fun game, after a while the exercise began to have some real impact. Her mood grew brighter as our week became filled with gratitude and a genuine good time.

After I got home I called my mother a lot during the first few days to support her in keeping her gratitude practice alive. Miraculously she kept at it, and the new habit took hold. My sister, who had been out of town, called me when she got back. "What did you do to Mom?!" she asked.

To my delight and amazement, my mother has continued doing the practice, and the change has been revolutionary. Seven months after my visit, she sent a card for my birthday. As is our family tradition, it contained a poem she wrote for the occasion. This one I especially cherish. Even though she started losing her sight during those months, the effects of her gratitude practice are evident in this poignant excerpt. And it goes to show you that you *can* teach an elder human new tricks!

*Ninety is just fine with me, I no longer rant and rave*
*About where the world is heading and my exclusive job to save.*
*I wallow in contentment and know that I am blessed*
*Awakening to the joy of living at its best.*
*I'm happier than I've ever been and truly mean each word.*
*The thoughts that caused the worries now all seem so absurd.*
*Though my eyesight has been dimmed I see clearer than before,*
*The glass is not half empty, it's overflowing to be sure.*

The choice is ours. We can go through life focusing on the burdens or letting our challenges serve as reminders of the blessings that also surround us. Maybe the story of my ninety-year-old mother can inspire you to remember in the midst of life's hassles that your life too is really very blessed.

---

### . . . and my life is really very blessed.

Each time you find yourself worrying or complaining, try adding on that little phrase. Even if it seems false at first, let yourself play with it and see what happens. You might find it helpful to enroll an ally to keep you on track—your partner, child, or Joy Buddy. Remember you're in a learning process, and be patient with yourself. Every time you succeed in shifting your outlook to a more relaxed sense of gratitude, tune in to how good you feel, and pause to anchor that in your body and mind.

## STRENGTHENING YOUR
## GRATITUDE MUSCLE

If appreciation and gratitude feel so good and lead directly to joy, why aren't we going around all of the time counting our blessings? Because, as with other wholesome states, it takes practice to get in the gratitude habit. But even putting a little time into it can have a significant impact on your level of well-being.

For a number of years, Jane, my wife, has been doing a daily gratitude practice. It started with her taking five minutes each night to exchange emails with a friend, reporting on what they were grateful for that day. The results have been dramatic, but in the beginning she remembers that it took focused effort.

"When we first started the gratitude practice, it was a stretch for me," she recalls. Raised in a family where it was considered smart to be cynical, she had become an expert in scanning the horizon for problems instead of for what was going well. "I would sometimes struggle to think of something to write if it hadn't been a particularly positive day. If I'd been hassling with my teenager, working on taxes, or getting stuck in traffic, it was sometimes pretty hard to feel grateful." But Jane stayed with her commitment, and as she kept her radar out, she began to notice things she had taken for granted.

> I began to see how much I have to be grateful for. I have clean drinking water and food on my table. I've had the opportunity to get an education, I have a loving family, and I like my job as an ESL teacher. I also learned that I could choose what to focus on. When my car needed repair, I could get grumpy, or I could feel grateful that the mechanic caught the problem before the car broke down on the freeway, grateful that I could afford to have it repaired, and grateful that I have a car at all.

Knowing she would be reporting each night on what she was grateful for gave Jane the extra impetus to notice people, things, and events that she appreciated. Before long, her gratitude emails flowed with an abundance of appreciations. As we cultivate the habit of being grateful, the mind naturally comes to rest on the goodness in our lives. As Jane found, if you have the intention to awaken gratitude, over time it will gradually become the natural rhythm of your heart, strong enough to hold even suffering.

## THE GRATITUDE PERSPECTIVE

Several years after starting the nightly emails, Jane's partner in the gratitude emails, Bonnie, was diagnosed with breast cancer. Bonnie would find that her years of gratitude practice were a major support as she went through the intense treatments. In one of her emails, she wrote:

> The second round of chemo has been difficult, but I don't add to the difficulty. What I feel most is gratitude. I cry now just feeling this. I'm perhaps more aware than ever of the suffering in the world. Yet when I woke up the other day and looked at the full moon through the skylights—clouds surrounding it, then moving to cover it—aahhhhhh, life.

Gratitude for the small wonders continued to carry Bonnie through her healing. Her messages would say, "I can't walk hills, but this week I can walk . . . I'm very grateful for the beautiful spring days . . . Wishing you mindfulness of the preciousness of this life."

When we're faced with challenges, gratitude opens us to a larger perspective that helps us more effectively address them. When we're unhappy—depressed, angry, in pain—we contract. The simple practice of gratitude actually begins to relax the mind. Instead of seeing things from only one perspective, we become "open-minded." The causes of suffering don't go away, but the context in which they're happening gets bigger.

*It used to seem wrong to feel any joy when I was filled with sorrow. But I realize now that I need joy for myself and for those around me especially during a time of sorrow."*
—A COURSE PARTICIPANT

Mary is a social worker at an elementary school in a large urban center. Many of the students she works with live with their grandparents or in single-parent families; some come from large families in which the parents struggle to make ends meet. "The children who come to me are, for the most part, experiencing grief and loss," Mary told me. "There is much poverty, death, incarceration, divorce, domestic violence, and violence in general in their young lives." Doing the gratitude step in the Awakening Joy program, she began to remember times in her life when being actively grateful had made such a difference in how she felt. "I decided to try bringing some balance into their days by doing 'gratitude rounds' with the children. We'd sit in a big circle, and one by one they'd say what they were grateful for that day. They are such amazing teachers, and with little prodding they thought of and were eager to share their deep and heartfelt gratitude."

Seeing the positive effect on the children at school, Mary gave them the assignment to interview each of their family members about what he

## Deepen Your Happiness Groove

- Spend five minutes at the end of each day writing down what you are grateful for. In addition to the more obvious blessings, be sure to include simple things, such as seeing a sunset or your child's smile. You can do this in your private journal or set up an email exchange with a friend or Joy Buddy.
- Each time you eat, pause to say some version of a "grace before meals," remembering the many elements that have made your meal possible.
- A course participant said she has started saying thank you to her family members when they do even routine things around the house. Try this and see what happens.

Whenever you feel that open and delightful experience of gratitude, deepen your "happiness groove" by pausing to consciously notice what's going on inside you. Just a few seconds is long enough to let the sensations in your body and the state of your mind register in your awareness. As you become familiar with the landscape of gratitude, you will more easily and naturally access it.

or she was grateful for. She encouraged them to come back with some specific examples from a sister, a grandparent, a mother or father. It turned out that their family members welcomed the chance to answer the question, and those reports brought another level of joy into the group. Even though the basic circumstances in the families of these children didn't change, some light shone through. "Every time we do our gratitude rounds," Mary reports, "there is extra cheer as we say our rousing good-byes."

A note of caution: You can't force gratitude, and if you try, you'll just feel frustrated and want to close down. If you are in the midst of great challenges and you don't feel grateful, just notice that and let the feeling be as it is. Bring a kind awareness to the resistance you're feeling, and know that there is one thing you can be grateful for—that you don't *have to* be grateful!

## SCATTERING GRATITUDE LIKE JOY

When I was in the sixth grade my teacher, Mrs. Oxman, taught us that the secret to adding a new word to your active vocabulary is to use it

Psychologist Martin Seligman is an expert on what makes people happy. In his book *Authentic Happiness,* he reports that of all the exercises he has developed for his Positive Psychology classes, one is particularly effective—writing a gratitude letter. He suggests that you pick someone you feel great gratitude for and write a one-page letter appreciating all the ways that person has enriched your life. Then slowly read it to him or her, face-to-face, and listen attentively to the response. I offer this exercise in my meditation classes and Awakening Joy course, and have found that mailing the letter or reading it over the phone can also be very meaningful for both appreciator and appreciated. Even if the recipient of gratitude has passed away, I suggest that people write a letter anyway. Just the action of expressing your gratitude has a major impact on your own well-being.

three times in conversation. "Then it becomes yours," she told us. Years later, a school teacher myself, I would try to have my students not only take in important information by reading or hearing, but also by discussing it, draw-ing it, and writing about it. The more senses that were involved, the deeper the material was absorbed.

In the same way, when we convert our thoughts, whether positive or nega-tive, into words and actions, we increase their impact. For example, you might be thinking fond thoughts about a friend or your partner, but what happens when you actually tell that person you love them? Even in a relationship of many years, speaking the words "I love you" makes something come alive. Our loved one

*Several years ago I had to decide what to give my dad for his sixty-fifth birthday. He has everything, wants nothing. So I wrote him a letter detailing why I'm grateful that he's my dad and that he is who he is. Then I went to a shop that makes handcrafted wooden boxes and found one that suited him and gave it to him as a 'Grat-itude Box.' It turned out to be a great gift."*

—A COURSE PARTICIPANT

lights up, and we light up back. Like completing an electrical circuit, the life force moves through and between us. The same thing happens when you express your appreciation to others. Scattering gratitude spreads a joy that encompasses us as well as those to whom we are grateful.

Our lives are filled with people whose presence helps us to live and thrive. If you think about it, your list might include the mail carrier, those who grow your food and transport it to market, the civil servants who help sustain the systems that support our towns and cities, your teachers and clergy, your coworkers . . . the list is nearly endless. If you really want to develop a grateful heart, in addition to thinking about how grateful you are for these people, express your gratitude to them when the oppor-tunity arises.

Besides opening your own heart, expressing appreciation to others makes them feel more comfortable around you. They're not on guard, fearing judgments. They can relax and feel your friendliness. Then they more easily appreciate you, which in turn allows you to feel more at ease. Expressing our appreciation and gratitude to others not only feels good, but it helps make the world a friendlier place.

## BUT I CAN'T FEEL GRATEFUL TO *THEM*

When my son Adam was little, I often read books aloud to him at bed-time. One of our favorite series was Lloyd Alexander's *Chronicles of Prydain*. In the wonderful volume *The Black Cauldron,* a main character ends up on the side of evil. At the end of the final battle when the heroes are honoring all the dead who helped their cause, this fallen character is included in the tribute. Taran, the young protagonist, is filled with disbelief at the gesture. A wise mentor and companion explains to him that although this man had betrayed the group, he was also instrumental in many ways in their ultimate victory, and so it was fitting to honor the good he contributed.

*After the assignment to express my appreciation, I decided at work to say thank-you and really mean it. It made a huge difference for me. I felt more connected to everyone with whom I shared thanks."*
—A COURSE PARTICIPANT

I vividly recall sitting in bed with Adam and, as I finished reading this to him, being moved to tears as I thought about all the people who had fallen off the pedestal I had put them on. Instead of appreciating them for how they had enriched my life at some point, a later disappointment had gotten in the way of fully opening my heart to them in a debt of gratitude. Tears flowed at the sorrow of having done that, as well as at the joy of allowing them back into my heart. This lesson has continued to help me remember that, in spite of difficulties, my heart can stay open to those who help me grow.

When we have a challenging relationship with someone, we can easily forget that we have reasons to feel grateful to them. My friend Rob came to this understanding during a meditation retreat. When he came in for his final interview, he had a big smile on his face.

"I just got in touch with something in the last twenty-four hours that I'd never really understood before," he began. He explained that he'd been blessed with a kind and supportive father with whom he shared a deep, loving relationship. His relationship with his mother, however, was not as easy for him. "She was often judgmental," he said, "and it felt like she was living from a place of fear and scarcity emotionally." In Rob's life story,

Dad held center stage as the hero in the limelight and Mom was often in the wings. "But something shifted for me yesterday," he said and went on:

> As I looked back on my life, I got in touch with all the ways my mom was there for me. She was the one who taught me to throw a baseball. She loved literature and taught me about writing, which is now my vocation. As I thought about the positive ways she impacted my life, I understood that despite all our mother-son challenges, she really cared about me. In fact, in her own way, she really loved me. In the last few hours I've had a feeling of gratitude for my mom that I never allowed myself to feel before. It's wonderful! I feel so much more open now. I don't have to hold back fully loving her. She can share center stage with my dad. She belongs there too.

Often those closest to us can be the most difficult to appreciate. As with Rob, your relationship with your parents might be a place where opening up to gratitude can be transforming. Or you might experience that release by remembering what you appreciate about a coworker, your child, or your partner. When you think of those who have been a challenge, can you also see how they might have helped bring out qualities in you, such as patience, determination, caring, or wisdom? Or perhaps there are positive qualities in that person that you have overlooked. When you can look beyond the difficulties to what you appreciate, you open another door to joy.

> *Practicing being thankful has made it possible to turn around my struggles with my teenage son, as I really am quite thankful he is in my life."*
> —A COURSE PARTICIPANT

## IT WOULD HAVE BEEN ENOUGH . . .

When I was a child, each year in springtime our family would celebrate the Jewish holiday of Passover. At the traditional meal called a Seder, we ate special foods that reminded us of the hard times before God led the Jews out of bondage in Egypt into freedom. The parsley dipped in salt

# OPEN IN GRATITUDE

*A guided meditation by Patricia Ellsberg*
*At Awakening Joy course, Berkeley, 2008*

Open in gratitude . . .

. . . for the breath that nourishes every cell in your body and has
sustained you from the moment you were born.

. . . for the miracle of your body that, despite whatever weaknesses or
limitations, serves you and allows you to sense the wonders of the
world.

. . . for your brain that coordinates all the functions of your body
without your even being aware of it.

. . . for consciousness that allows you to perceive, feel, and be amazed.

. . . for the eyes that allow you to see the abounding beauty that
surrounds you—colors and shapes, the face of a loved one.

. . . for the ears that enable you to hear birds singing, wind rustling in
leaves, words people say to you, and the laughter of children.

. . . for the sense of smell that allows you to enjoy the fragrance of
flowers, the scent of fresh air, your favorite food.

. . . for your mouth and tongue that enable you to taste the fruits of the
earth, to enjoy a ripe peach or chocolate melting in your mouth.

. . . for the skin that protects you and yet allows you to touch and sense
the world, feel warmth, coolness, softness, and the touch of a loved
one.

. . . for your heart that beats faithfully your whole life, from even before
you were born.

Open to a sense of wonder and gratitude for the amazing gift of being
awake and alive in this precious human form. The fact that we exist or that
anything exists at all is a wondrous mystery. We all live in the midst of a miracle.

water recalled all the tears we shed in slavery. The horseradish or bitter herbs helped us remember the bitterness of those times. We also ate lots of matzah crackers to remind us that there hadn't been enough time to let bread rise before fleeing Pharaoh's army. Throughout the long service, we prayed, sang songs, and heard the story of the Exodus.

*If the only prayer you ever said in your whole life was 'Thank you,' that would suffice."*
—MEISTER ECKHART
(1260–1328)

Then came the best part for me—not only could we finally dig into the sumptuous feast of "real food," but we got to sing the joyous song *Dayenu*. This Hebrew word means "It would have been enough." Following each of the fifteen verses recounting the many gifts God had given—freedom from slavery, miracles in the desert, closeness to the Divine—we would all break into that rousing refrain: *Dayenu!* This one thing would have been enough, but then You did this. . . . Just singing that song of gratitude would fill me up with joy. It still does.

Sometimes I realize I can look at life with that spirit of *dayenu*. To be given life would have been sufficient. But not only that, to have a healthy body, a kind heart, a good mind . . . thank you, Life. To be able to enjoy the taste of ripe peaches, delight in listening to Beethoven and the Beatles, take in the sweet smell of gardenias and bay trees, feel someone's caring through their hug. Thank you. What's more, this body with all its senses and intelligence comes with a mind that can think creative thoughts, crack jokes, reflect on philosophical questions, and be aware of itself. And in this mind-body process called "James" is the capacity to care for another's pain, delight in their joy, express my love, and be touched by the world around me.

Yet can I take credit for any of these things? Can any of us take credit for the life we have? We don't own any of it. It has all been given. There is something about life that is miraculously generous. Instead of the gardenia, there could have been only the cactus! This benevolent abundance evokes tremendous gratitude in me.

## THANKS TO LIFE

When I look back on my late teens and early twenties, I realize I did lots of crazy things. I was walking nonchalantly and unconsciously through a minefield of potential dangers. Yet, as many of us know, no matter how far

---

# THE BUDDHA'S DISCOURSE ON BLESSINGS

It is a great blessing:

—To spend time in the company of wise people and to honor those who are worthy.

—To live in a place that is good for you, to do good deeds, and to keep yourself going in the right direction.

—To be well-educated, to develop your skills, to train yourself in discipline, and to use words carefully and beautifully.

—To take good care of your mother and father, to cherish your partner and children, and to engage in a livelihood that is harmless.

—To give generously to others, to live with integrity, to care for everyone you consider your family.

—To avoid doing harm, to be careful with intoxicants, and to develop wholesome states of mind.

—To be respectful, humble, content, and grateful, and to regularly bring spiritual teachings into your life.

—To be patient, open to learning, to be in touch with people on a spiritual path, and to discuss spiritual teachings.

—To live simply and in a holy way, to understand the deepest truth, and to realize the highest freedom and happiness.

—To have a mind that is steady, unswayed by the ups and downs of life, free of sorrow and shame, and at peace.

Those who act in these ways cannot be dragged down. Everywhere they go, they find well-being.

—ADAPTATION BY SHOSHANA ALEXANDER
OF THE BUDDHA'S *MANGALAM SUTTA*

we go in the wrong direction, our lives can turn around. Some inner call gets us facing in the direction of goodness, truth, and happiness. Think back to the turning points in your life that got you to where you are now. Could you have written that mysterious script? How can we not be grateful for the amazing grace that keeps us heading in the direction of wholeness? As part of your gratitude practice, you might consider writing a thank-you letter to Life itself, not only for the endless blessings but also for giving you the lessons you needed in order to grow.

Once we start looking for blessings in our lives we see them everywhere. In her book *Attitudes of Gratitude,* M. J. Ryan writes:

> Gratitude is like a flashlight. It lights up what is already there. You don't necessarily have anything more or different, but suddenly you can actually see what is. And because you can see, you no longer take it for granted.

In a famous teaching, called the "Discourse on Blessings," the Buddha enumerates the many noble qualities and circumstances available to us in our daily lives. Among the qualities of the blessed person, he includes being grateful. To be grateful is in itself a blessing and an open door to joy. Each time you are grateful for something, stop to take in and fully experience that uplifting and joyful feeling. Gratitude can be an ongoing frame of reference from which to live your life. You might even, as Albert Einstein suggests, begin to see that everything around you is a miracle.

# 4

## *FINDING JOY*
## *IN DIFFICULT TIMES*

---

In the middle of winter, I at last discovered that there was
in me an invincible summer.

—Albert Camus, *The Myth of Sisyphus: And Other Essays*

*W*hen *things are* going well, it's easy to be joyful. "Isn't life wonderful!" you may say. "I'm so happy. Everything's on track." But as we all know, there's another side to life. How do we cultivate joy and well-being when we're in the midst of pain and suffering? Inclining your mind toward joy does not mean putting on a happy face, denying your feelings, or enduring pain with a stiff upper lip. But what *does* it mean when you're having a hard time?

The Buddha's teachings about life don't begin with: Be happy. Everything is cool. They start with the First Noble Truth: There is suffering in life. In *Pali,* the language of the Buddha, the word for suffering is *dukkha,* which also means stress, unsatisfactoriness, unreliability. Life is stressful, and it's often unsatisfactory and unreliable. We've all had some experience of that.

Circumstances beyond our control can turn our world upside down in an instant. Driving along, minding our own business, we get rear-ended. We go through our days taking our good health for granted, and suddenly, out of the blue, we get a diagnosis of illness. A dear friend dies. We lose a job, a house, a partner. Tragedies happen unexpectedly, as the newspapers remind us every day. As my teacher Joseph Goldstein puts it, "Anything can happen at any time."

Life was going well on all fronts for my friend Abhaya. She was teaching meditation, had completed a two-year training to get certified as a chaplain, and was working at a hospital with people facing life-threatening illnesses. Doing what she loved to do was greatly fulfilling. The last time I'd heard from her, she said she was very happy. Then one day I received an unexpected email from her, sent out to all her friends:

> *I have had an interesting week and have some news to share. A physical therapy appointment led to an ER visit which led to a CAT scan which a few days later led to an MRI, which yesterday brought me to a neurosurgeon who showed me the results, which reveal a rather large tumor in my brain. No matter how I say it, it sounds so dramatic! The neurosurgeon believes he can remove most of the tumor, but not all of it. He will not know the full ramifications until he knows what kind of tumor it is, which he will not know until he is in there.*

It's not a question of *if* the hard stuff comes but *when* it comes. Suffering and stress are part of the fabric of life. While some of us have easier lives than others, if each of us lives a normal life span, not one of us can escape old age, sickness, and death. These three facts of life shook Prince Siddhartha, the Buddha-to-be, out of his idyllic world at the age of twenty-nine and started him on the quest that was to transform him into the Enlightened One. Over the six years he spent as a wandering monk, he questioned how one could find true happiness in a world filled with so much suffering. His journey led him to the conclusion that the more we face the fact that suffering is a part of life, the greater the possibility of experiencing the happiness of a mind liberated from stress. In fact, when asked about the essence of his teaching, the Buddha's reply was simply, "I teach about suffering and the end of suffering."

Although everyone suffers, when things go badly we tend to think there must be some kind of mistake. My friend and teaching colleague, Rodney Smith, ran a hospice in Seattle for many years. He tells the story of a ninety-seven-year-old woman who, upon finding out that she had a terminal condition, began wailing, "Why me?!" My friend Abhaya, in contrast, was in her mid-forties when she found out about the brain tumor, and she responded by writing in the note that announced the news to her friends:

> My heart is very full today with all the love I am receiving. Know that I send this with love and gratefulness to all of you. Please be happy and feel some of the wonder of life.

What a difference in response between two people facing a similar challenge! Clearly one of them was happier, despite what she was experiencing. You have a choice as to how you deal with your suffering. You can try to avoid it and live in denial. You can resent it and grow bitter. You can simply endure it and resign yourself to your bad luck. Or you can discover that there's another way, one that opens you to wisdom and to life itself.

*"Some people walk in the rain. Others just get wet."*
—ROGER MILLER

Abhaya's operation was successful and, despite the inevitable challenges she faced during a long recovery, she consciously chose to keep her heart open and remember there is more to life than just the difficulty she was going through. Recently she sent out an email message to the circle of friends who had in various ways supported her healing. She wrote:

> I continue to be very grateful to each of you. On many levels you have helped me sort out and deal with things I was facing. There has been fear and confusion, yes, but there has also been a larger perspective, based in humor, gratitude, and being held by the mystery and joy.

Our life circumstances change all the time. To a great degree, how much joy we have in our lives is determined not by what is happening but by how we respond to it. Sometimes we're in the flow, other times we're stuck in the mud. In eighth-century India, the scholar and philosopher Shantideva wrote:

> *If there is a remedy when trouble strikes,*
> *What reason is there for despondency?*
> *And if there is no help for it,*
> *What use is there in being sad?*

This simple and practical advice is as useful now as it was over a thousand years ago, and it's a good platform for a healthy relationship with the challenges in our lives. Pema Chodron, a school teacher in California who became a Tibetan Buddhist nun and renowned meditation teacher, gives a modern context to this advice. She calls it "Shantideva's advice for stress reduction." In *No Time to Lose* she writes: "If we're caught in a traffic jam, for example, what's the point in fuming? If there's a remedy, like an off-ramp, there's no need to be upset. But if there are cars as far as the eye can see and no way out, then obsessing makes us unhappier." In any situation, instead of looking for reasons for our suffering, or worrying about what will happen in the future, we can just take it a step at a time, like Abhaya, and respond openly to what life puts before us.

This fourth step in Awakening Joy shows that by being open to the suffering that comes into your life, rather than resisting it, you can learn to let the pain of life's inevitable challenges move through you rather than get stuck in you. You also create the conditions that allow you to be open to more joy. In this chapter, mindfulness is the primary tool I am suggesting, because the resistance that intensifies our suffering is in our mind. Mindfulness can ease what we're going through in hard times, and it releases us from mental states that cause suffering. Other tools are also offered to help you when the going gets rough. Mindfulness, however, gets to the root of suffering and frees us from its power. As we stop trying to protect ourselves from our painful experiences and mindfully open to them, all those positive qualities within us—understanding, compassion, kindness—can also come to life.

Two of the most inspiring people I am aware of who remain open in this way are the Dalai Lama and Archbishop Desmond Tutu. Both have seen enormous suffering in their lives, yet somehow they radiate an infectious joy. How is that possible? I believe it is because both know deeply that suffering is part of life and, because of their dedication to spiritual practice, they are not afraid to be with it. I've seen the Dalai Lama get very serious, even cry, upon hearing about a tragedy and then, as the subject changes, laugh a few minutes later. His complete openness to the sorrows of the world lets him also be touched by delight, goodness, and joy when these arise.

*Before you know kindness as the deepest thing inside, you must know sorrow as the other deepest thing."*

—NAOMI SHIHAB NYE, FROM "KINDNESS" IN *THE WORDS UNDER THE WORDS: SELECTED POEMS*

As you explore this step, it's important to keep in mind that you don't need to go out and look for suffering in order to practice what you're learning here. On one of my first silent meditation retreats, many people around me appeared to be going through profound emotional release. Tears and tissues were everywhere. I, however, was basically following my breath and having almost no difficult feelings. I wondered if I was somehow missing out on something. I went to see my teacher, Joseph Goldstein:

"It seems like everyone else is going through stuff and having some kind of deep transformation. Should I be doing something different?"

"Don't go looking for trouble," Joseph smiled. "It will find you soon enough."

He was right. In subsequent retreats I would go through many a box of tissues myself and would realize that both ends of the spectrum have their gifts.

If you happen to be in a phase of your life that is easy and relatively unchallenged, you can just continue to incline your mind toward well-being and remain present for uplifting states as they come. When the difficult times inevitably come along, the tools in this chapter will prepare you to face your circumstances without being overwhelmed by fear or trapped in resistance. The willingness to be with any situation, no matter how challenging, trains the heart to stay open—an essential ingredient for a joyful life.

## BABY STEPS

When things are going well in your life, doing the Awakening Joy practices may be fun and easy. But it's when you're facing challenges that you need them most. I'm not suggesting that you pretend you're not hurting. But finding moments of well-being during a hard time will begin to make a big difference.

Paula had a high-paying professional job, was living in her own home, which she loved, and had achieved "all the things I thought I wanted to do that were going to change the world." A year later she was unemployed and living in a low-income complex where many of the residents were sick and elderly. Enrolled online in the Awakening Joy course, she wrote to say that while she was actually discovering some "great moments of joy," the daily challenges could still drag her down.

> Many of your stories have such happy resolutions, so I wanted to give you an honest reflection from the middle of the process, not just the euphoric result of a singular success, important as that may be. Being in the trenches daily is quite a roller coaster ride. For a few days there is the grace of happiness, and then suddenly someone says something that activates the voice of doubt in my head, and I'm back in a bad place again.

Instead of giving up in despair, Paula was learning how to keep going. "It's all about putting in the baby steps," she says. "That's really the key—repeating your intention, sitting through the hard stuff consciously when it happens, staying inside the good stuff for longer periods and really appreciating it, practicing lovingkindness for yourself, not becoming discouraged or impatient, and then getting up tomorrow and starting all over again."

Despite the challenging circumstances Paula was living through, she says she actually feels as if her "heart is fuller than it's been in some time, and I feel more mature and wiser." Putting in those baby steps, day after day, eventually pays off by awakening in us a deep trust in life and the ability to flow with it.

## LETTING IT ALL IN

When our dog Pal died last year, I was filled with sadness. He was a big, gentle labradoodle, and we loved him very much. Everyone who met him fell in love with his endearing sweetness. Pal had been my teacher of patience and unconditional love for twelve years. Though I'd been saying good-bye in my mind for the previous few months as he'd grown weaker and weaker, it still hurt. I missed him terribly. I missed burying my head in his belly and smothering him with kisses.

For a while after he passed, I had little energy for anything other than taking care of basic needs. I gave myself space to grieve and the time to absorb and digest everything I was feeling. Even when I wanted to distract myself from my feelings, I knew there were more tears that needed to come out. I found myself listening to a certain melancholy piece of music over and over. The cello tugged at my heart while the guitar gently en-

### Keeping Perspective

When you're going through a hard time, the suffering might feel relentless. But often there are moments when the sun peeks through the clouds. Keep in mind that everything is impermanent, including negative mind states, and notice any moments of well-being that arise—a smile when you see children playing, pleasure at tasting a favorite food, the warmth of sharing a hug with a friend, or the satisfaction in reading a good book. Don't miss these moments. You might also try gratitude practice to remind yourself of any blessings in your life. Whenever positive feelings arise in your body and mind, pause to notice and take them in.

couraged me to remember the beauty of my sweet dog. Even though Pal was gone, I would speak aloud to him in the same voice I'd used all those years, and the special love we shared would arise, along with the tears. I knew that denying all those feelings would not do justice to Pal and the rich bond we had shared.

One of the most painful sources of suffering is losing someone or something dear to us, a situation that is inevitable. We won't find happiness by trying to get around this unavoidable fact. There is a traditional Buddhist practice that, ironically, is intended to make us happy by directly focusing on the inevitability of change and loss. The Buddha advised his followers to contemplate these truths every day:

## THE UNBROKEN

There is a brokenness out of
which comes the unbroken,
A shatteredness out of
which blooms the unshatterable.

There is a sorrow beyond all grief which
leads to joy
And a fragility out of whose
depths emerges strength.

There is a hollow space too vast for
words Through which we pass with
each loss, Out of whose darkness we are
sanctioned into being.

There is a cry deeper than all sound
Whose serrated edges cut the heart
as we break open
To the place inside that is unbreakable
and whole

While learning to sing.

—RASHANI,
from *Beyond Brokenness*

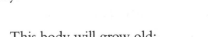

1. This body will grow old;
   I am not beyond aging.
2. This body will become sick; I am not beyond sickness.
3. This body will die; I am not beyond death.
4. Everything near and dear to me will become separated
   from me.

While regular reflection on these might look pretty depressing, one of its benefits is to get us used to the truth of how things really are. Instead of running away from life, you're setting yourself up to be here for the whole show, in all of its sorrow and glory.

I decided one year to share this practice with the weekly meditation group I lead in Berkeley. Each week we were to keep one of these reflections in our consciousness as much as possible and investigate the impact of that on our daily lives. At first, staying aware of such a bald statement of truth felt quite heavy to me. There was no running away, no distraction. I saw the ephemeral nature of everything that I valued. All my relationships would end. Jane would be gone. I would be separated from my family and network of friends. My good health and abilities were just a set of temporary circumstances. I saw myself in a nursing home with people who might not even know me. And perhaps I wouldn't know or even recognize them!

Continuing with the practice, however, was like putting on a new shoe that takes a while to break in. After the initial discomfort, these truths became familiar, and with them came not only the acceptance that "this is the way it is" but an awareness of the preciousness of each person and each thing in my life. I felt strangely liberated as I relaxed into the facts and let go of hoping that I could avoid the inevitable. As the Roman philosopher Seneca said, "You cease to be afraid when you cease to hope, because hope is accompanied by fear." Understanding that death and the ravages of time are unstoppable lessened my fear of their approach.

Because my mind was not filled with resistance when Pal was dying,

## ALLOW

There is no controlling life.
Try corralling a lightning bolt,
containing a tornado. Dam a
stream and it will create a new
channel. Resist, and the tide
will sweep you off your feet.
Allow, and grace will carry
you to higher ground. The only
safety lies in letting it all in—
the wild and the weak; fear,
fantasies, failures and success.
When loss rips off the doors of
the heart, or sadness veils your
vision with despair, practice
becomes simply bearing the truth.
In the choice to let go of your
known way of being, the whole
world is revealed to your new eyes.

—DANNA FAULDS,
from *Go In and In*

there was room to focus on appreciating all his wonderful qualities. I remember lying down next to his body, mainlining unconditional love. Love, sadness, acceptance, and appreciation were all in my heart and I could allow them to be there. No sorting, figuring out, wishing for a miracle. Just allowing all the feelings to be felt, to play themselves out, and move through me. In a peculiar way it felt good. My openness helped me connect to life instead of railing against it.

## JOY IN THE MIDST OF GRIEVING

The more willing we are to be present for the hard parts of life, the freer we are to be open to all of it. When Alice's grandparents died, she said, "We barely spoke about it. We didn't even have a ceremony." So a few years later when her father died suddenly and unexpectedly at the age of sixty-six, she decided to respond to the pain in a new way. "Every day I set the intention to experience my grief and let it flow—rather, rip—through me without fear." Something she heard Sylvia Boorstein say in her talk to the Awakening Joy course stuck with her: "The essential wisdom is to know what is happening when it is happening and not to be in contest with it."

That's what Alice knew she wanted to be able to do. But when the time came to pick up the ashes of her beloved father from the crematorium, Alice found herself in tears of anguish and regret.

### Having Known Them . . .

Recall an experience of losing a loved one. Allow yourself to feel the sorrow with tender awareness. Feel the love you have for this person (or pet) and the way he or she enriched your life. Open to the gratitude you feel for having known him or her, and focus on sending that beloved being your thoughts of love and appreciation.

I realized I was trying to push away what was happening. I was literally saying, "No!!" As I gently allowed the truth to sink in again, I could see that the "no" was an attempt to protect my heart, to control the experience. How could I protect my heart? It was already broken. How could I control anything? We die. I don't want to sugarcoat it. This hurts. The pain is powerful and often scary. But I am glad I'm here for it.

By being present with the truth of her pain, Alice was also able to flow with the full spectrum of feelings and experiences that were arising for her. She continues:

There have been many wonderful, joyful moments as well: connecting with my brothers and sister in a warm and open way, being washed over with powerful memories of my dad, feeling profound surges of love that erase all other difficulties, feeling connected to everyone else on earth who is grieving right now. Because I was able to talk about my feelings, everyone else in my family was free to do the same. In the end, we had the most beautiful, meaningful ceremony. I know the seed was planted by letting myself open to the pain.

When we fear that feeling our grief will be overwhelming, we may try to numb ourselves with alcohol or drugs, or lose ourselves in work or compulsive behavior. Or we get stuck, frozen in a state of sorrow or fear. As Alice found, remaining open and present with her feelings, without getting lost in them, allowed her to also be open to the joyful moments.

## MEETING PHYSICAL PAIN
## WITH MINDFULNESS

We all experience physical pain; there's no way around it. However, when our bodies are going through their aches and pains, we might remember that useful distinction encapsulated in the popular quote attributed to

M. Kathleen Casey: "Pain is inevitable, suffering is optional." This is not to minimize the plight of anyone in severe and relentless pain, but as a general guide it has value. We automatically contract from pain—it's a built-in response, warning us of something to avoid if we want to survive. But in the midst of pain we can't avoid, learning to respond with mindfulness can lessen our suffering. It is also a good training for remaining open and present with any kind of suffering in life.

Certainly you should reach out in various ways for relief and healing, but notice what happens when you try to just remain mindful of pain. (I say "try" because this is not always so easy, although practice helps.) Like all experience, pain arises and passes away. If you pause and pay attention to your stubbed toe, noticing the throbbing, the shooting pain, the heat, you may find that the sensations are not as solid as they first appear to be.

*When my ninety-five-year-old father was ill and dying, my grief was overwhelming. I felt exhausted, found it difficult to be with people and to keep my commitments. With mindfulness practice I came to see that the grief 'had me.' It had taken over my entire life. I saw that I could allow the grief and be fully with it whenever it came up, but that there were the other moments of the day when it wasn't there. This allowed me to 'have' the grief as well as be present in the moment with whatever else was there. I have since felt lighter, had more energy, and am once again engaged in my life."*

—A COURSE PARTICIPANT

There are moments of greater and lesser intensity. Eventually the pain in the toe subsides. Except in extreme situations, continuous pain is usually not our experience moment after moment.

The suffering, in contrast to the pain, comes in when your mind gets involved. As Stephen Levine, a spiritual teacher who has worked extensively with the process of death and dying, puts it, "The resistance to pain may be more painful than the pain itself." We can intensify our suffering by our reaction. If you stub your toe, the pain might be excruciating. Or a migraine headache might feel like an overwhelming wall of pain. Of course you want the pain to end, but getting caught up in stories of what terrible things might lie ahead only adds another layer to your suffering. *What I'm going through now is bad, but what if it gets worse? Maybe I broke something? What if this pain never stops?* Or we get caught in an emotional cul-de-sac: *Every time things are going well, something like this happens.* Long after the physical pain is gone, we can still be stuck in mental and emotional pain.

*I suffer from terrible chronic pain. Every joint in my body is an issue and my spine is breaking down. I've recently lost my job after thirty-four years, pretty much as a result of my illness. Yet I have so much to be joyful about. I have a wonderful and caring family and a beautiful home. I can read and type a little, but the most important thing for me is that I can be happy. I am not worried about tomorrow. It is amazing what a difference that makes. I am never going to be the hiking/camping grandma I always thought I would be, but I am still the grandma."*

—A COURSE PARTICIPANT

In a similar vein, the Dalai Lama offers a prescription: "To diminish the suffering of pain," says the Dalai Lama, "we need to make a crucial distinction between the pain of the pain and the pain we create by our thoughts about the pain. Fear, anger, guilt, loneliness, and hopelessness are all mental and emotional responses that can intensify pain." Especially with chronic pain, it's important to distinguish between the physical malady and the sense of helplessness that understandably can accompany it.

When physical pain is severe and constant, as for those suffering from cancer or other terminal diseases, to let down resistance and remain present with the sensations is nearly impossible. Yet mindfulness might still help to remind you that who you are is more than just the physical pain. In *Being Zen,* writer and Zen teacher Ezra Bayda says:

> We often think that being healed means the illness and pain will go away. But healing does not necessarily mean that the physical body will mend. . . . Healing is not just about physical symptoms. Many people heal and still remain physically sick or even die. Many who become physically well never really heal. Healing involves clearing the pathway to the open heart—the heart that knows only connectedness. . . . To heal, to become whole, means we no longer identify with ourselves as just this body, as just our suffering. We identify with a vaster sense of being.

## THE SECOND DART

Much of the suffering addressed in this chapter is the mental and emotional suffering that pulls us down and can be at least as painful as physical suffering, often more. When we are depressed, lonely, sad, angry, we often add to those states by talking to ourselves in ways that intensify the state: *What's wrong with me? I shouldn't be feeling this way.* Or we dig ourselves deeper into the emotion by feeding it with a story: *She did such and such to me. Of course I'm angry, and furthermore . . .* Or we try to deny the feeling: *Buck up. It's not that bad.* And the pain goes underground, only to express itself in other, sometimes even more painful ways.

*I have been having a somewhat minor yet painful illness, and I'm finding I am able to feel my underlying joy and aliveness in addition to the pain. It doesn't mean that I don't feel the pain, but it helps me to know that the pain is not all consuming. I am not the pain. It is a part of me, just as joy and love are."*

—A COURSE PARTICIPANT

To show how we multiply our suffering, the Buddha used a vivid analogy. If a person is struck with a dart, he feels intense pain. If he were to be struck immediately after with a second dart, the pain would be so much worse. That's what we're doing when we add negative thoughts to an already painful state. So how do you keep from launching that second dart?

As with physical pain, we take the experience one mindful moment at a time. Instead of compounding your suffering, with mindfulness you can learn to meet it with balance, clarity, and kindness. Chogyam Trungpa, the brilliant and iconoclastic Tibetan Buddhist master, used to say that every situation, no matter how challenging, is "workable." If you meet your difficult thoughts and feelings with nonjudgmental awareness—not getting lost in them, remembering that everything changes—you will find that you don't feel so overwhelmed. And in the process you also begin to deepen your understanding and open your heart.

## CAUGHT IN THE SPIN CYCLE

Fiona came to her first mindfulness meditation retreat knowing very little about what to expect. A young woman in her twenties with a high-powered job in New York City, she thought that meditating on a silent retreat would be the perfect counterpoint, a way to find relaxation, peace, and stillness within. She didn't realize that the road to inner peace usually entails facing all the demons and fears that obscure it. In the silence and simplicity of a retreat, there would be little to distract her from the habitual patterns of her mind. Instead of tranquility, Fiona was soon confronting an old companion—the anxiety that was just below the surface.

She came into her first interview with me in a very agitated state. "I want to be calm and peaceful," she told me in a frustrated voice, "but I can't stop my mind."

"Where does your mind go?" I asked.

"Everywhere!" she cried, exasperated. "What I need to do with my work situation when I leave. How to have a better relationship with my boyfriend. Why I get so nervous around people. You name it. I try to quiet it down, but it just won't quit." As she talked her voice became increasingly shrill. Her body fidgeted with restlessness.

The thoughts spinning around and around in our minds can be very convincing. We build elaborate scenarios of failure and chaos and believe them to be true. This may be very creative, but it's not conducive to happiness! Worry is a very real kind of mental suffering. I know because I come from a lineage of worriers myself. My mother used to joke that when she couldn't think of anything to worry about, she'd *really* get worried. "It was my way of making sure I was taking care of things," she says.

This approach reminds me of another story about the wise fool Mulla Nasruddin. Mulla's students find him one afternoon meticulously spreading bread crumbs around the perimeter of his house. After watching him for a while, one student finally asks him, "Mulla, why are you placing those crumbs like that?"

Mulla responds, "To keep away the tigers."

The confused student answers, "Tigers? There aren't any tigers for hundreds of miles!"

"Effective, isn't it?" Nasruddin replies.

Our minds can get stuck in worrying about phantom problems that we convince ourselves are real. As Mark Twain put it, "I have been through some terrible things in my life, some of which actually happened." Reasonable planning for the future can give us direction, but obsessing about what might go wrong puts us in a perpetual state of stress and rarely brings about positive results. Mindfulness interrupts the tape loop by bringing us back to the moment so we can respond to what is actually happening right now.

## STOPPING THE SPIN

During her interview, as Fiona talked about what it was like to be caught up in the turmoil of her thoughts, I could see how painful it was for her. She said the chaos in her mind was like being "stuck in a labyrinth with no way out." I asked if she was willing to stop talking for a few moments and just be present.

"Can you feel your feet on the floor right now?" She nodded yes. "Can you feel your body making contact with the chair?" Again she nodded. "How about your breath? Can you feel it as your belly rises and

---

### THE PROBLEM WITH WORRY

*"New solutions and fresh ways of seeing a problem do not typically come from worrying, especially chronic worry. Instead of coming up with solutions to these potential problems, worriers typically simply ruminate on the danger itself, immersing themselves in a low-key way in the dread associated with it while staying in the same rut of thought."*

—DANIEL GOLEMAN, FROM *EMOTIONAL INTELLIGENCE*

falls?" Yes, she could. "Don't do anything for the next few moments other than knowing you're sitting and breathing." As we sat there quietly, she started to relax.

"Everything you need for the peace you're looking for is right here in this moment, Fiona. Whenever you notice that you're going around in circles, here is your instruction: Simply stop trying. Let yourself relax and ask, 'What can I be aware of that is actually happening right now?' "

Toward the end of the retreat I could see that Fiona had a smile on her face as she walked gracefully around the meditation center. Before she left for home, she wrote me a note:

> The one thing that is indelibly fixed in my brain is finally getting, "You don't have to figure it out." That would never have registered as an option before. Just today when I was doing walking meditation, struggling as my thoughts were going 'round and 'round, those words came into my mind. I stopped and closed my eyes and asked myself, "What is true right now in this moment?" And what was true was the rising and falling of my breath, and various body sensations coming and going. "The rest of life will balance itself out in its own time," I thought to myself. And I resumed my walking. What a revelation!

When you're caught in the spin cycle, one of the most effective ways to return to the moment is being mindful of your breath and your body. The body is always in the present, and pausing to pay attention to it opens up the space to notice what is going on in the mind. You can step back and ask yourself what is really true in this moment. It's like pressing "Clear" on a calculator; no matter how complex the numbers have gotten, once you press that "C" button you have a fresh start. In the same way, coming back to feeling your body and breath helps you stop spinning your wheels. Instead of figuring things out, you can begin to trust that once you are in the present moment, your mind can settle you down enough to wisely deal with whatever is actually before you.

## RELEASED FROM FEAR

Sometimes the most overpowering illusion the mind can create is fear. This is not the kind of fear that keeps you alive when a tiger is coming your way. In that case, fear is a signal to get the heck out. I mean the kind of overwhelming fear in the mind that threatens to eat us whole. You probably could find valid psychological explanations for why particular fears arise, but rather than trying to figure out the cause, the Buddha suggests directly addressing the fear with mindfulness in order to free yourself of its power. In his parable of the poisoned arrow, he uses a metaphor to illustrate his point. If you are shot with an arrow, do you start asking, "Who shot this arrow? Who made it? What kind of poison did he use?" No, instead you ask that it be pulled out as soon as possible. In the same way, when you find yourself trapped in mental fear, instead of trying to figure out why it's there, or spinning around in it, a wise and effective way of freeing yourself of confusion is to bring your mind back to the present. Recognize that you are caught in *thoughts* that are giving rise to fear.

*I received some bad financial news, and found myself reacting with a familiar pattern of high anxiety. I went right into my bag lady fantasy and 'I'll-lose-everything-and-have-no-possibilities-in-life' pattern. But this time I was able to observe from a meta-level. I told myself that nothing bad was happening* now, *and that I didn't want to waste my life worrying. Amazingly I was able to shift into present time, which was actually quite lovely, and enjoy my daughter and the sunny day."*
—A COURSE PARTICIPANT

During one of her first meditation retreats, Shoshana understood what Joseph Goldstein was saying about facing fear with mindfulness, but the terror she felt inside seemed very real—as did its cause. "I know it sounds utterly irrational," she says, "but I had a tremendous fear of—of all things—vampires." Late at night alone in the room set aside for walking meditation, she would hear autumn leaves crackling outside the window and fear the footsteps of something monstrous. The fear was so strong that night after night, she fled from the room. After days of this, Shoshana decided to do something about it. If Joseph was right, facing the fear with mindfulness would free her from what she knew was an illusion—at least she hoped so.

One night, about two o'clock in the morning, she bundled up against the cold and stepped outside the meditation center, into the Massachusetts winter. She recalls:

> Either there were vampires and I would meet my fate, or I would at last free myself from this fear by facing it directly. There was a lake across the street, and I set out to walk the three-mile loop around it in the full-moon light. I was certain that a vampire lurked behind every tree. In the stillness, I listened for footsteps behind me. My heart felt like it would leap out of my chest, and the fear felt like electricity shooting through my body. But I managed to keep returning to awareness of my breath—which was really shaky—and to remain mindful of all those sensations. And I kept mindfully naming my experience, saying to myself, "This is fear. This is fear."

By the time she finished her long walk around the lake, Shoshana not only was freed of her fear of vampires, but she also had discovered the amazing power of mindfulness to cut through distress in the mind. And even now fear itself no longer seems as fearful. She says, "I don't think I've ever gotten so caught up in fear like that since, and when it comes up for any reason, I more readily remember 'This is fear,' and it doesn't carry me away."

A bumper sticker I see around a lot warns: "Don't believe everything you think." Whenever you find yourself lost in a swirl of thoughts, mindfulness of your breath and body can break the spell in the moment and even free you of mental patterns that don't contribute to your well-being.

## WHEN EMOTIONS ARE OVERWHELMING

Many legends have been passed down about the powers of Milarepa, the great eleventh-century Tibetan yogi, who spent years meditating in a cave to purify his mind. In one of these stories, Milarepa returns from an evening walk to find his cave filled with a dozen demons. Cherishing his solitude, he tries to get rid of them. First he offers them spiritual teachings, hoping they will be appeased and leave. No luck. Then he scolds them, hoping his anger will frighten them away. They just laugh. He decides to make peace with them, saying, "It's clear that you're not leaving, so we might as well learn to coexist and live together." Well, that's no fun for a demon, so all of them leave, except a particularly nasty and terrifying one. In an act of complete surrender, Milarepa places his head in the demon's mouth, saying, "You are much more powerful than I. I will not

## "STARING BACK" AT THOUGHTS

In March 2000, the Dalai Lama met with a small group of prominent neuroscientists, psychologists, philosophers, and Buddhist scholars to discuss the origins of negative emotions and the beneficial effects of spiritual practices. In his book *Destructive Emotions*, Daniel Goleman narrates the proceedings of this gathering, highlighting significant moments of dialogue. This excerpt is from Matthieu Ricard, who earned a doctorate in genetics in France and later became a Buddhist monk.

"At the beginning when a thought of anger, desire, or jealousy arises, we are not prepared for it. So within seconds, that thought has given rise to a second and a third thought, and soon our mental landscape becomes invaded by thoughts that solidify our anger or jealousy—and then it's too late. Just as when a spark of fire has set a whole forest on fire, we are in trouble.

"The basic way to intervene has been called 'staring back' at a thought. When a thought arises, we need to watch it and look back at its source. We need to investigate the nature of that thought that seems so solid. As we stare at it, its apparent solidity will melt away, and that thought will vanish without giving birth to a chain of thoughts. The point is not to try to block the arising of thoughts—this is not possible anyway—but not to let them invade our mind. We need to do this again and again because we are not used to dealing with thoughts in that way. . . . Finally a time will come when thoughts come and go like a bird passing through the sky, without leaving a trace."

resist you. Go ahead and devour me if that's what you want." In that instant the demon vanishes.

Overwhelming emotions, such as anger, grief, or sorrow, can feel like
terrifying demons, and our automatic response might be to run away or
resist them. But there's a problem with that. Trying to avoid or deny an
emotion locks it in, repressing it but not releasing it. Not resisting the
pain of negative states of mind is an act of bravery that allows them to dissolve. Like Milarepa, when we give up the struggle, when we stop trying
to avoid our pain or get rid of it and instead allow ourselves to just be
mindfully present with it, we begin to liberate ourselves from its hold on
us. We begin to clear our cave of its demons.

Mindfulness is a tool you can use at any time to help keep you from
getting lost in confusion. It can wake you up from the "bad movie" in
your mind. And with practice, you can train yourself to be mindful even
in the face of overwhelming emotions.

Fran has been a meditation student for many years, so she was well
prepared to remain mindful when, on a long retreat, some of her deepest
negative emotions arose. "A familiar heaviness of heart appeared almost as
soon as the retreat started," she told me. Over the next few weeks she explored what she called "that energy in my life that's the hardest thing I've
known—call it grief, contraction, depression."

In the silence and focus of a retreat, the deep mental patterns that
arise can pervade the body and mind and feel overwhelming. I encouraged Fran to take the process of releasing intense feelings in small doses.
"Start by allowing the feeling to just be there, and stay with it mindfully
for a minute or two. Then you can take a break and regroup until you're
ready to feel it again." By managing to remain present, even in small
doses, with a very difficult state of mind, Fran was able to come to a new
understanding.

This feeling is very powerful and sticky for me when it arises. So I
knew I needed to bring it into the light of awareness, to stay present
with it—with the piercing pain in the heart—to bring compassion
to it, to know the unstained awareness that can feel it and not be it,
to call on a kind of warrior courage in allowing it, and to see how I

habitually react to it. I don't know exactly what it will mean in my life to have done this work, but I know I had to do it.

Having the opportunity on a retreat to work so intensely released some of her negative mental patterns at a very deep level. But the basic process Fran was doing can be used to ease the mind, especially when emotions are overwhelming. Essentially she was recognizing what she was feeling without pushing it away, paying close attention to how the emotions registered in her body and mind, and realizing that the emotions were a passing phenomenon, part of being human. A convenient way to remember this process of working with difficult emotions is the acronym RAIN, a term first coined by meditation teacher Michele McDonald.

## RAIN: A MINDFUL APPROACH TO WORKING WITH DIFFICULT EMOTIONS

### *R is for Recognize*

In mythology a monster or demon has great power until its name is known. When the hero or heroine courageously names the demon to its face, the sinister force is broken, mastered now by the namer. Naming your emotions is the first step in weakening their power over you. For instance, in the midst of a heated discussion, you might recognize, "This is anger." Without condemning, resisting, or denying the feeling, this can keep you from getting lost in it. Or you might feel a kind of heaviness pulling you down and recognize, "Oh, this is sadness," and then do something to be gentle and nourishing to yourself. Even if you have no idea what you're feeling, you might simply realize, "I'm confused." At least this keeps you from doing a nosedive into chaos.

Ann, a participant in the Awakening Joy course, reported how honestly naming her feelings while in the midst of them helped her through a harrowing experience. One day her husband began complaining of chest pains. Not taking any chances, she drove him to the local hospital where he failed the stress test. Within minutes Ann found herself sitting in the waiting room while her husband was down the hall possibly having a heart attack. Remembering the instructions from the course helped Ann to remain present instead of spinning out in fear. She says:

> As I sat there waiting, I was able to simply notice my emotions and think, "Okay, this is what anxiety feels like." Doing that kept me from getting carried away by the whole situation. I was somehow able to just be present, trading "what if's" for being okay without knowing why or what the future would bring. I just kept telling myself that this was a moment of life for me to meet.

Someone I know uses a rather creative naming strategy when she's gotten stuck and feels agitated and overwhelmed. She gets a cup of tea, goes out on her porch, and lets herself be what she calls "Pissed-off Buddha" for a while. After a half hour or so the energy shifts and, the storm past, she returns to being just Sophia sitting on her porch drinking a cup of tea. Then she can address with more balance and clarity the situation that triggered her strong emotion.

## LABELING TO CALM THE MIND

Researchers in the Brain Mapping Center at the UCLA School of Medicine made a significant discovery about the value of using words to label fearful circumstances. When subjects in an experiment were shown faces with expressions of anger or fear, the fear centers in their brains showed increased blood flow, indicating that their own fight-flight responses were being stimulated. However, when the subjects were asked to choose a word to describe the facial expressions of anger or fear, the blood flow to the fear centers diminished. Additionally, parts of the prefrontal cortex—a brain area that regulates emotions—showed increased blood flow. The researchers conclude that the activity of labeling, which takes place in the higher regions of the brain, can regulate emotional responses, helping you to feel calmer.

## *A is For Allow and Accept*

Allowing and accepting what you're feeling means letting go of any agenda for the experience to change. As soon as you start hoping for a desired outcome—*Maybe if I'm mindful, the feeling will go away again, like it did last time*—you're resisting what you're feeling and creating aversion in your mind, even if it's subtle. As we've seen earlier, resistance locks a feeling in rather than allowing it to undergo the natural process of change.

But just remaining present for a painful emotion can be very hard. We're so used to resisting unpleasant feelings. We want to distract ourselves or figure out a quick solution. *I think I'll go out for a drink, or maybe a movie . . . and maybe I'll meet someone interesting.* Not that you shouldn't give yourself a nourishing break if you're having a hard time, but if you want the long-term reward of being freed from the pain of habitual negative feelings, distraction won't do it as readily as saying, "No matter what, I'm going to stay here with this feeling." You may feel certain painful sensations in your body. You may go through states of mind that are really uncomfortable. Allowing your feelings means you remain aware of them, without pushing them away if they're unpleasant, not holding on to them if they're pleasant, not getting lost in them. For a few moments at least, you give the experience permission to be just as it is.

## *I is for Investigate with Interest*

Once you Recognize an emotion and Allow it to be just as it is, you can then Investigate how it is expressing itself in your body and mind. Without trying to figure out or explain anything, notice what sensations accompany that emotion. What does sadness feel like? Heavy? Thick? Where do you feel it? In your chest? Your throat? How big an area is it? The size of a golf ball or softball or beach ball? Does it have a sharp outline or fade out at the edges? Notice if the sensations stay the same or change subtly, or dramatically, from moment to moment. They might diminish. They might get more intense. Your job is to Allow and Investigate with a kind, nonjudgmental awareness, moment by moment.

You might also shift your awareness for some time to include the mental atmosphere associated with the emotion. Is the mood dark, swirling, heavy, tight, light, expansive? In the same way, let the experience be just as it is, and touch it with a kind, interested awareness. Then, after some time, come back to your body. Are the sensations the same as before? Have they changed?

*I'm finding that when I'm open, compassionate, and curious about my suffering, it is greatly lessened. It's not a solid block of 'things always being wrong' but something that passes through. This has been opening up a lot of freedom and ease."*

—A COURSE PARTICIPANT

While the idea of allowing and exploring an intense emotion, like fear or rage, might sound overwhelming, you will find that your awareness itself can hold whatever emotion is arising in the moment. When you are afraid, for instance, the part of your mind that is *aware* of the fear is not afraid. It is simply aware of the thoughts and sensations that make up the experience of fear. The same is true if you're experiencing anger. The *awareness* of anger is different from the anger itself. You can rest in the awareness of those emotions, rather than getting lost in them. In this way, awareness becomes a refuge that lets you safely investigate your actual human experience.

## N is for Non-identification

When you identify with an emotion—*I am such an angry [sad, lonely] person*—you put yourself into a box. In actuality, a continual flow of thoughts and emotions passes through the mind. You can't point to any one of them and say, "That's me." Anger may come but you're not always angry. You may become frightened more than you'd like, but can you say you're a fearful person when you're laughing with a friend? Our emotions are all arising in the field of mindful awareness, doing their dance for a while, then changing into something else. Instead of thinking, *I'm such an angry person,* you can understand, *There is anger in this mind right now.* It does not define who you are.

Not identifying with an emotion is another way of saying, "Not taking it personally." From the perspective of Buddhist teachings, having a particular static identity is just not true. No emotion is you, nor is any emotion unique to you. Emotions are human experiences arising in response to certain conditions. Your anger or sadness isn't so different from my anger or sadness. Understanding the commonality of our experience leads to a profound shift in how we relate to our mental activity. Instead of thinking of our thoughts and feelings as *my* mind, we can begin to see them as *the* mind, a shared human experience.

Using the RAIN process when you are experiencing difficult emotions can have extraordinary results. When you don't push your feelings away nor get lost in them, after a while you see that, like everything else, they change. They have a beginning and an end. This can make a huge difference in your life. You're not as apt to believe you'll be stuck forever and start pushing the panic button. And you can trust that you have the capacity to work skillfully with strong emotions.

After thirty years of marriage, Robert found himself going through a painful divorce. Relating to his intense pain with mindfulness allowed him to get through some of the toughest times. He shared this reflection:

### RAIN

When you are in the midst of a strong emotion, take a few moments to try this approach:

**R**ecognize what you are feeling and name it. Anger, fear, sadness, confusion?

**A**llow the feelings to be present, without pushing them away and without getting lost in them.

**I**nvestigate the feelings in your body and mind. Explore the landscape of the emotion with curiosity and interest. Where in your body do you feel it? How does it feel in your mind—heavy, tight, open, agitated?

**N**on-identification is the key to freeing yourself from the emotion's grip. Don't take it personally. What you are feeling is a human emotion that arises and passes away. It does not define who you are.

Grief comes in waves. Sometimes I think I'm going to drown and can only chant "Help me, help me, help me." Using RAIN, I ride the waves. Each leads me to a variety of body and memory information. Paying respectful attention and not identifying, I ride the waves and they pass. My inner ship rights itself and sails on. I continue to feel awake and alert and radiant in the midst of this beautiful spring, and I have faith that I'm learning what I need to learn to go on in life. It's not fun, but on balance it feels like a rich adventure.

RAIN will help you move through emotions with more balance. What's more, the deep-seated tangles of stories and feelings will begin to diminish when you don't feed them.

## USING SKILLFUL MEANS

Sometimes emotions are just too powerful to work with using the RAIN method alone. We saw earlier that even someone like Fran, who had been meditating for years, had to be gentle with herself and take breaks from being mindful of intense feelings. Wisely opening to difficult feelings includes knowing when you've reached the point where you're no longer balanced in the process. If you're struggling or feeling overwhelmed, you need to back off. Otherwise, you will end up closing down or getting lost in your thoughts.

In situations like this it's wise to find ways to work with your emotions using what in Buddhism are known as "skillful means." These are basically any methods that work to diminish your confusion and develop your understanding of how to relate to challenging circumstances. My philosophy is "Get all the help you can get." Listen to your intuition. Whatever supports you in your ability to stay present with the hard stuff in a constructive way is a skillful means. Reaching out to wise friends, working with a good therapist, or taking medication if there's a chemical imbalance are all skillful means. One of the most important foundations for a healthy mind state is a healthy body. Besides working out or walking, holistic models of exercise, such a yoga or tai chi, can work wonders for the mind.

One of the primary values of mindfulness is that by directly feeling our difficult emotions, we begin to get to see and understand how they work. For instance, when we're in the midst of a strong emotion, it can seem like our suffering will go on forever. But just as physical pain is not a solid and unchanging experience, so too emotions, even very strong ones, have moments when the intensity shifts. Have you ever been sobbing in grief, and then suddenly everything inside you goes still, and you forget for a moment what you were crying about? Or have you been in the middle of being angry with someone, and suddenly you recall that you have something to take care of, and your entire focus shifts? Those pauses are like breaks in a storm.

Sylvia Boorstein says this is like a slight shaft of sunlight peeking through the clouds in the midst of pelting rain. That sliver of light can

## A WORD ON DEPRESSION

"It is important to recognize there are many helpful approaches to finding well-being, and you must find the ones that are best for you. This is particularly true for those suffering from clinical depression. While many of us can make choices that pull us out of negative emotions, the emotional exhaustion that seems to enervate physiologically depressed people makes that virtually impossible for them to do. However, Greg and I have seen a substantial group of people who report that they've chosen to pull themselves out of deep depressions. Their paths are torturous, but most of them talk about making mini-choices that start to build on themselves, like telling the truth, or appreciating some part of their lives, or giving to others. But we recognize that there can also be a value in using medications. In some cases, that seems to open up a door of opportunity for depressed people to walk through. They then can begin the make more happy and healthy choices."

—RICK FOSTER, CO-AUTHOR WITH GREG HICKS OF
*HOW WE CHOOSE TO BE HAPPY*
[FROM PERSONAL LETTER TO AWAKENING JOY PARTICIPANT]

give us the perspective to know all is not gloom and doom. In that moment we are reminded that everything—including very convincing feelings—will change. Even seemingly overwhelming emotions are not as solid or entrenched as we may believe. Your sorrow and suffering are not permanent, and no matter how bad things may seem, you will smile again, laugh again, and feel joy again.

If you need to, you can prevent intense emotions from snowballing by temporarily shifting your focus to something that distracts you. One of the skillful means suggested by the Buddha for dealing with disturbing thoughts and feelings is "forgetfulness and inattention." It may be surprising that one of the major advocates of being awake and attentive is telling us, "Just forget it." But the Buddha's methods are eminently practical, and when certain feelings are overwhelming, this is what works.

As a parent, I know the value of that method. Adam was a sensitive child and could be easily startled. One Saturday afternoon when he was four, his grandma and I took him to the Pickle Family Circus, an enchanting clown and magician show. In the middle of the performance, with no warning, a huge balloon suddenly exploded as part of the act. While the rest of the audience howled with laughter, that explosion launched Adam into a different kind of hysterics. His wailing wouldn't stop as I carried him out.

*My six-year old daughter, who has a very serious heart condition, was scheduled to see her cardiologist. The day before the appointment, I burned dinner and set off all the smoke alarms in the house, left the door of my car open which ran down the battery, and the battery in my cell phone died. The morning of the appointment, I burned breakfast, the car wouldn't start, and I completely flipped out. After seeing the cardiologist, however, as we were driving back home, a little voice in my head reminded me that everything changes, and even though at that moment things seemed really dire, this was not going to be the way it would always be."*

—A COURSE PARTICIPANT

When we got outside, I glanced over at the concession stand twenty feet away and happened to notice his favorite ice cream. "Oh look, Ad," I said to my howling son, "they have Ben and Jerry's." In an instant the screams stopped as he surveyed the field to locate the treasure. I calmly and gratefully carried him toward the ice-cream stand, slowly letting out each word: "Oh, we're in luck. They have Cherry Garcia!" (His favorite.) Adam forgot he was having a meltdown, and as soon as he had the cone in his hand, he was completely cooled off.

Sometimes when we're overwhelmed and thrown out of balance by an emotion, we're like little children. In fact, often what we're feeling is directly linked to our tender "child self," and we can use some skillful parenting means. Be gentle with yourself and consider using the Buddha's forgetfulness method. Take a walk in the park. Go get an ice-cream cone!

Whether you pause because you've taken a few mindful breaths, or you hear a baby cry in the next room, or you suddenly hear a song on the radio that changes your mood, use that opportunity as a way to consciously turn your attention away from a strong emotion. With this kind of "forgetfulness," you are remembering not to feed the negative feelings. Then they can begin to subside and you can consider more wholesome choices.

Another way to shift your focus and "change your mind" is to nurture yourself or do something to discharge the negative energy: exercise, do some yoga stretches, take a walk in nature, speak to a friend, or

---

### Overcoming Overwhelm

When you feel overwhelmed by an intense emotion:

- Look around you for something in the moment to appreciate.
- Engage one of your senses to return you to the moment. What do you see, hear, smell, or feel? You might listen to a favorite piece of uplifting music or take a relaxing hot bath. Let yourself sink into that experience.
- Imagine the frightened, sad, or confused part of you as a young child. How old is that child? Imagine holding him or her in a tender embrace. What would you want the child to know?

By shifting your focus from the intense emotion, you can wake up from the dream your mind is creating and wisely address what needs to be attended to.

give yourself a time-out in your room to let the feelings move through you.

What's most important in using skillful means is that you don't get lost in your suffering but instead use it to deepen your understanding of life, to act wisely, and to develop compassion. This openness will also most readily lead you back to joy and well-being. It creates the space to hear your inner wisdom, feel your kind heart, and get in touch with your aliveness.

## CALLING OUT TO SOMETHING GREATER

Often when our suffering is great we experience the pain of isolation—perhaps the most painful feeling of all. We feel like no one can understand or help us, even friends. If your feelings are too strong for you to be mindful of, and temporarily distracting yourself from them doesn't work, what do you do? You can reach out to something greater than yourself, you can call upon the forces of benevolence to help you. Whether you think of this as God, the Dharma, spirit guides, or some higher power beyond yourself, you can call out to that benevolence for the compassion and loving support you need.

We sometimes have to reach the depths of sorrow or pain before we finally turn to something greater than ourselves. This is a positive step, if for no other reason than it orients the mind away from fear, bitterness, and confusion and toward a healthy vision of possibilities. And there is a kind of innocence in this, like a child in prayer, as we get beyond our stories and dramas and humbly open our hearts in vulnerability.

*After a shocking diagnosis of cancer, I learned to sit with my fear, and when it felt too big, to use skillful means and do something else. I learned I could move from one thing to the next—from hearing test results, to doing my pre-op prep, to lying on the gurney waiting to go into the operating room. When it was just one thing at a time, it was not overwhelming. I felt embraced by love with the outpouring of prayers and calls and emails. I think I truly realized that I am not alone. I experienced compassion for others going through similar experiences in a way I couldn't quite understand before. So the gifts were endless, and it was not an 'all bad' experience. Life was filled with richness, presence and, weirdly, joy at times as I lived closer to the edge than ever before."*

—A COURSE PARTICIPANT

## SUFFERING IS GRACE

I once went to a talk by Julia Butterfly Hill, an environmental and social activist who spent two years living on a small platform in a two-hundred-foot redwood tree to protest logging of old growth forests. Her story was inspiring, and the power of her commitment to truth touched me deeply. During her first year, the powerful weather cycle known as "El Niño" brought in one of the wettest and stormiest winters on record. At times the wind was so fierce that Julia could do nothing but cling to the edges of the platform. Fearing for her life, she would pray for the strength to get through the ordeal. No sooner had she survived one storm than another even worse would come up. *Why isn't God listening?* she wondered. Then one day she realized that in fact she *was* getting what she was praying for. Precisely by going through those trials, Julia was discovering an inner strength and resilience that could meet any storm or challenge.

Neem Karoli Baba, a Hindu guru who has been one of my most beloved teachers, used to say, "Suffering is grace." When we're in the thick of it, suffering hardly seems like grace. Yet in my classes when I ask how many people have come to a spiritual path through suffering, almost

### Reaching Out to Be Held

Let yourself find that deep feeling of sincerity and innocence inside your heart, as if you are a child praying. Now from that place, call on the benevolence of life, however you conceive it, to guide and support you. Imagine a field of benevolent energy surrounding you and enveloping you, inside and out. Take that feeling in deeply and notice where you experience it in your body. Notice the state of mind it creates. If that benevolent field had a color, what would it be? Let yourself sink into and be infused by that soothing color. Allow yourself to be held by this field of benevolence. Relax into it. Feel its protection.

Return to this experience from time to time, and get to know it. This refuge is always available when you need it.

every hand goes up. I would say they have been graced. Suffering shakes us out of complacency and motivates us to look for a happiness not dependent on circumstances. If we look honestly, we can see that even very challenging times have bestowed on us invaluable gifts.

A great twentieth-century sage known as The Mother, who with Sri Aurobindo founded the international spiritual community of Auroville in southern India, talked about how our greatest difficulties can in fact reflect our greatest possibilities. She said: "You carry in yourself all the obstacles necessary to make your realization perfect. If you discover a very black hole, a thick shadow, [you can] be sure there is somewhere in you a great light. It is up to you to know how to use the one to realize the other." If you've come to this search for happiness because of great suffering, you can know that you have within you a great light. Don't feel discouraged at the enormity of the task. Rather, know that you are likely to be even more motivated to find the true gems hidden in the darkness.

*Two weeks ago my boyfriend broke up with me; I was devastated as I am deeply in love with this man. I was not able to see this as any kind of gift, but then I decided to try to cultivate an open heart, toward myself and toward him. This has been challenging and immensely rewarding, as I have found a deep well of love and caring that I thought was all about him. I've discovered instead it was all about who I am and who I can show up to be in the world."*

—A COURSE PARTICIPANT

By opening to our pain, rather than simply enduring it, we deepen our understanding and access those qualities in us that are most noble. Helen Keller, completely unable to see or hear, found the grace and insight to conclude: "Character cannot be developed in ease and quiet. Only through experience of trial and suffering can the soul be strengthened, ambition inspired, and success achieved. . . . All the world is full of suffering. It is also full of overcoming."

As you go through hardships, keep in mind that you are developing courage and strength you probably didn't realize you had. As Julia Butterfly Hill found, the strength to persevere in the face of relentless challenges doesn't develop overnight. Patience and perspective unfold over time as priceless gifts. One of the most profound aspects of suffering as grace is that we learn we have the capacity to meet whatever life brings us and respond with wisdom.

When my friend Don Flaxman found out that he had incurable cancer, all his years of spiritual practice bore fruit. He had learned how to face the hard stuff fearlessly and with balance. As he shared the news of his diagnosis with me, I was deeply moved not only by his acceptance of the situation but by how he had turned it into an opportunity to deepen his love of life. He told me:

> I'm now in the richest period of my life. Now that I have less time, I'm more open than I've ever been. I'm amazed at how much joy is available just by smelling a pretty flower, seeing a hummingbird, or hearing a friend's voice. I don't waste my time complaining. Expressing love and gratitude is the most important thing I can do now.

## A GIFT BEYOND WORDS

Nancy went through indescribable sorrow when her fourteen-year-old daughter, Julia, took her own life. I met Nancy on the first anniversary of that tragic event when she still felt she could barely find a reason to go on living. She had decided to come to a meditation retreat, seeking a way to cope with her pain. She found that meditation practice gave her a refuge and helped her remain sane in the midst of the swirl of emotions she was feeling. Each February she returned for another retreat, taking the time to sit with all the grief, anger, and confusion that were her constant companions. And each year she and I have shared a ceremony honoring the memory of her daughter.

Little by little, over the course of four or five years, Nancy learned to accept her daughter's tragic death and eventually to find the willingness to live again herself. During one of her retreats, Nancy shared with me an important realization. She understood that it wouldn't do her or anyone else any good to let that tragedy block all the love that was inside her. She knew that her daughter would much rather have her mother find happiness than freeze-frame her life. Nancy decided that being present for other parents facing the same tragedy would be the best way to honor her daughter. After that retreat she started volunteering as a support group leader for parents whose children have died—the same group she'd attended during her years of deepest grief.

## CHOOSING LIFE

The downward spiral starts.
Self-doubt and darkness
vie for center stage, while
I, the passive, drowning
one, wait for my demise.

Just as I sink beneath the
waves of my despair a
thought arises. Why go
there? I've made this
trip a thousand times,
and it leads nowhere.

I'm choosing life. The
darkness lifts just a little.
I'm choosing life. The
downward spiral slows,
then stops. I'm lifted up
and buoyant now, not
shrinking from the truth.

Okay, I'm not perfect,
and reality certainly
doesn't look like
what I'd choose. And
maybe that's the only
point—to ride the spirals
down and up, and make
the choice for life.

—DANNA FAULDS,
from One Soul

One day a beautiful card appeared in my mailbox, with a note from her:

I have received a gift that is beyond words. I've witnessed my deepest despair, the darkest, most wounded quarters of my heart, and learned not to flinch or back away. I rested in love and even tasted joy, all the while still knowing the sorrow of my loss. A few days ago I held a bereaved mother in my arms as she sobbed—she had lost her son to suicide. I held her to my heart as she held on for dear life. And as I rocked her it was as if I was rocking Julia, rocking myself, rocking the broken hearts of all beings. In that rocking, in that holding, we were all held in one heart. I have been so blessed.

Nancy had come full circle in that moment of being able to comfort someone who had gone through what she had gone through. Now several years later I see a radiance shining through this woman who has touched the depths of suffering and found something that sustains her and inspires anyone who meets her. She still has moments of sadness and grief, and she still misses Julia, but a joy and appreciation of life have emerged—a joy she thought at one point was no longer possible.

Psychiatrist R. D. Laing says that those who have traveled to the depths of despair are often the greatest healers. As Fran, the woman who chose on a retreat to face the pain and depression that had haunted her for years, puts it:

> What I can see already is that this ability to stay present with pain, with great awareness and kindness, is the heart of being able to be present in the same way with the pain of others—and that's a gift, for certain.

Nancy and Fran discovered one of the greatest gifts of suffering: the tender heart of compassion. When we open to our own pain with tenderness, we dissolve the armor that cuts us off from ourselves and life. When we relate to our pain like the mother who holds the child instead of scolding him, we develop the ability to offer a kind and caring refuge to others when they are in need. In Step Nine we'll further explore how remaining open to the suffering of others, and responding with compassion, leads to a profound sense of peace and well-being.

## STAYING OPEN TO THE WORLD

Although we don't have to search for suffering, hiding from it in order to be joyful doesn't work. For me an important part of awakening joy is staying aware of what is going on in the world, letting my heart remain open to the pain as well as the joy. For example, while reading the newspaper is not considered one of the most uplifting practices, I do it every day. It reminds me of our shared humanity, deepens my gratitude for the blessings in my life, and motivates me to express my caring in tangible ways.

When you don't close your eyes to sorrow and suffering, it's easy to feel weighed down. You may wonder, "How can I possibly be happy when there is so much pain in the world?" Poet Jack Gilbert encourages us to have "the stubbornness to accept our gladness in the ruthless furnace of this world." Although the Buddha's teaching starts out by focusing on suffering, the goal is happiness. Likewise, the crucified Christ is an image of intense suffering, but the true goal of a Christian's life is to live in the joy of the Resurrection. Despite our awareness of suffering, we can remember that happiness is also a gift of life.

By following the practices offered in this book, you've already taken several steps toward living a more joyful life. You've discovered that true happiness lies in wholesome ways of being. You've learned the power of setting your intention, and developed the tool of mindfulness to support wise choices. You've also explored how a grateful heart lets you see that life is full of blessings, along with the sorrows. And you've seen that fearlessly being with your sorrows keeps your heart open to all of life.

# 5

## *THE BLISS OF BLAMELESSNESS*

Speak or act with an impure mind
And trouble will follow you
As the wheel follows the ox that draws the cart.

. . .

Speak or act with a pure mind
And happiness will follow you
As your shadow, unshakable.

—The Buddha
*The Dhammapada*

*I remember the moment* as if it were yesterday, rather than a few decades ago. I picked the infant up and held him in front of me. Although I had doubted that he was actually mine, when our eyes met something in me knew it was true. It was like holding myself. As we looked at each other, his eyes innocent and filled with wonder, I could feel myself falling in love. My life with its new possibilities flashed before me. Since the age of fourteen, I had so many times imagined playing catch with my son. . . .

Suddenly my reverie was stopped short. I was twenty-two years old, it was the late 1960s, and I was just getting the hang of being on my own.

This wasn't the life I had envisioned. Terror struck. Thoughts flashed through my mind like a lightning storm as I tried to understand what had happened and how this scene came to be.

About a year before, my neighbor's sister, Bonnie, had started dropping by from time to time when she was in the neighborhood. Gradually our visits of friendly talk had slipped into singing together, making out, and eventually finding our way to my bed. "Free love" was the philosophy in those casual and permissive days, and "If it feels good, do it" was my credo. I didn't stop to think about the consequences, beyond making sure that we were using birth control. When she stopped coming around at some point, I just figured that was that and got on with my life. And now here I was, holding a baby.

A few days before this, I'd received a Christmas card with a photo of an infant boy and a simple note on the back: "Hi. My name is Anthony. I'm your son. If you want to see me, call . . . " Stunned and paralyzed with disbelief, I'd gone into a tailspin. For the next three days it had all seemed like a bad dream, a nightmare that I'd hoped would somehow just disappear.

But then the doorbell rang, and there was three-month-old Anthony in his mother's arms. I remember Bonnie saying, "Here, meet your son," and passing him to me. Dazed and flooded with a swirl of emotions, I'd told her I needed some time to be alone with him and carried him into my bedroom.

Those first moments of letting that beautiful baby into my heart were short-lived. Confused and immature as I was, barely able to take care of myself, the thought of taking care of someone else was overwhelming. Apprehension shot through my body as I imagined how my life would be turned upside down. And then there were my parents. Telling them I had a son seemed impossible, as did introducing them to his mom, who was African American. They were set on me marrying a "nice Jewish girl." I began to panic. If I held this baby, my son, for another thirty seconds, there would be no turning back.

I carried him back into the living room and thrust him into his mother's arms. "I can't do this!" I announced. "Why didn't you tell me sooner?" I remember her saying something about being afraid I'd pressure her to get an abortion. My bewilderment flared into anger, and as we began to shout at each other, the tender infant in our midst started to cry. The spell was broken. Bonnie bundled Anthony up and stormed out of the apartment, slamming the door behind her.

I collapsed onto the couch as a potent mixture of shock, relief, and shame engulfed me. Over the next few days, these emotions gave way to numbness and denial. It would be twenty-nine years before I would see my son again.

When fear and confusion drive our actions we cause suffering to others, often not realizing that we ourselves also suffer. Because I chose not to participate in his life, that beautiful innocent baby became the victim of my fear. His mother was denied my emotional and financial support as she faced the daunting task of being a single mom. I would not realize until years later the sadness and pain I myself carried for abandoning my son.

## LISTENING TO THE FRIENDLY GUIDES

Every choice we make has a consequence—this is the essence of what the Buddha referred to as natural law. Or as Jesus put it, "As you sow, so shall you reap." That's good news when we're sowing good seeds. It's the other

## REFRAMING GOOD AND BAD

Living with integrity is a practical strategy for awakening joy. It's also considered a "skillful" one, because it makes our lives work better. In Buddhist teachings, thoughts and actions are not categorized as good or bad but rather as "skillful" and "unskillful."

- To be skillful means to think and act in ways motivated by the desire to enhance the well-being of yourself and others.
- To be unskillful means to intentionally think or act in ways that harm you or others.

ones that worry us. You probably can think of times when you engaged in some kind of questionable behavior and later faced the consequences. It might have taken a while before your actions caught up with you and made you squirm. But you might also recall some of the immediate discomfort you felt when you first chose to do whatever you did—the turmoil in your gut, that sinking feeling, or the sense that someone was looking over your shoulder. That's an immediate and useful consequence. Becoming familiar with uncomfortable feelings like these and letting them inform wise choices are the underpinnings of a peaceful mind and joyful heart.

It's often said the body doesn't lie. No matter how cool we may want to appear, the blush of embarrassment on our face gives us away. Likewise, the knot in our stomach or constriction in our throat can tell us something's not right even as we think or say, "I'm fine" or "It's okay to do this." Marvin, a course participant, wrote about what happened as he paid attention to the actual experience of his body and mind when he was facing an ethical challenge at work:

> I was in a situation in which I was tempted to act in a way that was inconsistent with the best practices of my profession. For a while I thought I wasn't doing anything wrong, and most people would still agree. But whenever I thought about it, I felt uncomfortable, needing to hide my action. It was a gut-level discomfort that felt like a weight on me. Finally I decided, "Enough! This is not working for me, even if it feels legitimately okay for others. I need to stop doing it." I felt an immediate sense of physical release—my shoulders expanded, I took a deep breath and let it out with a big "Oof!" I felt physically light and mentally free of all that exhausting ethical juggling. Although many of my colleagues wouldn't understand what the big deal was, I know I got my integrity back in that moment of decision.

How do you feel when you've done an unskillful action? Responses from participants in the Awakening Joy course reveal in graphic terms the impact such choices can have on well-being:

- Sick to my stomach, haunted for days.
- Anxious, stressed, distracted, my blood seems to race.
- Tight in my chest, almost panicked.
- At first triumphant, then, shortly after, dark and remorseful.
- Chest collapsed, eyes downcast, body tense and defensive.
- Cringing, dead inside.

One answer in particular vividly captures the feeling: "My body slumped and my mind went gray with regret and sadness."

Not such happy feelings! In my experience as a teacher, these are not the feelings of a few neurotic individuals but rather what anyone might notice when paying mindful attention.

How do you feel after you've done a *skillful* action? Responses from participants in the course reveal quite a contrast to the feelings noted above:

- Content and peaceful.
- Light and joyful, playful.
- Like there is a glowing in my chest.
- Connected.
- Large of spirit.
- Like a smile is welling up from within.
- A desire to mentally replay the experience and enjoy it more than once.

Besides this friendly feedback system in our bodies, we also have what we often call "the voice of conscience." This one is a little trickier. I grew up with Jiminy Cricket singing, "Always let your conscience be your guide," and I knew without question what that meant. While moral codes vary with culture and history, once we've learned "right from wrong," it's pretty well wired into our internal program. However, it's important to know the difference between the encouraging proddings of a healthy conscience and the undermining voices of habitual self-judgment. The first leads you toward those expansive feelings of contentment and joy, the second toward fear and anxiety.

When you pay close attention, you will notice that the finger-wagging, critical voice that says *You're going to blow it again* is filled with

For one who leads a virtuous life,
it is a natural law that remorse
will not arise . . .
For one free of remorse,
it is a natural law that gladness
will arise . . .
For one who is glad at heart,
it is a natural law that joy will arise.

—THE BUDDHA

fear, and it pulls you down. The voices of wisdom that wish for your genuine happiness are, like the voice of a compassionate mentor, gentle reminders filled with patience, kindness, and love. They point you toward a new horizon. As you learn to listen to them, you will find the way to release yourself from negative conditioning and into a more easeful life.

The Buddha referred to the happiness of integrity as "the bliss of blamelessness," and he offered a set of guidelines to take us there. Once I truly began to follow these guidelines myself, I was on the path back to the deep and true connection I first felt with my infant son. It would lead me to finally give him the love and caring that was his birthright. And I would learn that it is never too late to set foot on the path of blamelessness.

## Remembering the Gladness of the Wholesome

Think of a time when you reached out and were kind to someone. Let yourself recall the pleasure you felt in your mind and body as you saw how happy they were. Or remember a time when you made a choice to be genuinely open and truthful. Even if it was hard to do, maybe you recall a sense of relief, clarity, and connection? Take these positive feelings in and let them motivate you to continue to choose skillful actions.

## THE DUBIOUS BLISS OF IGNORANCE

If we know that acting with kindness and integrity will bring us happiness, why do we choose to act in any other way? Growing up, we may have learned to think or act in ways that are less than wholesome, but even when we know better, we often continue to do what is easy and most familiar. We might spend years exploring the wounds in our past that lay the ground for our behavior, yet still continue doing things that hurt others and ourselves. Why? Because we make bad choices—even when we know we'll end up feeling unhappy—out of habits based in confusion.

While we might think that what we're saying or doing will get us what we want, when we look deeper, we often see that we're motivated by fear. Afraid of being caught in a compromising situation, we lie to cover up our part. Afraid of not getting enough of what we want, we take what's not rightfully ours. Afraid of being hurt by a loved one, we launch a preemptive strike. It might look like it's worth it at the time—that's the promise that keeps a habit in place—but inside us, our joy and aliveness are being compromised.

### GOING ON AUTOMATIC

When you have spoken or acted in ways you later regretted, what contributed to that choice? Participants in the Awakening Joy course answered:

- I was feeling tired or stressed.
- I wasn't taking care of myself.
- I was in a hurry.
- I was drinking alcohol.
- I was angry.
- I felt threatened or blamed.

When we're not taking care of ourselves, or we're lost in some strong emotion, we more easily act out of fear or get lost in blind desire. We go on automatic, and our unconscious habits take over.

That young man who turned his back on his son already had in place a history of habits based in fear that led up to that moment. While I wouldn't have considered myself an immoral person—I certainly didn't go out of my way to harm others—I knew how to conveniently disregard the effect my actions might have on another. I could feign helplessness or blame someone else when things spun out of my control. I could avoid responsibility by pretending to myself that I couldn't do a task at hand. I saw no problem in telling "white lies," concealing the truth from myself

## THE BOTTOM COMPARTMENT

"Even though we all desire integrity, we're hindered by unconscious factors that lie deep within each of us. When you turn awareness inward through meditation or relaxation, you find this dark recess of consciousness. I like to compare that to the lower compartment of the refrigerator. Imagine that you have a very nice clean house, a beautiful kitchen, a fancy refrigerator. But somehow a very bad odor is pervading the place. You wonder, 'What is going on? I cleaned under my toilet, I washed my dishes, I got new vegetables this morning. Where is this odor coming from?' But then when you open the refrigerator door, you realize you haven't looked into that bottom compartment for the last few months, and now there are lots of rotten vegetables in there.

"The unconscious realm is like that bottom compartment. It's in each of us. It's one reason why we practice meditation. Meditation is not about religious discipline but about becoming more and more aware of one's internal issues, so that nothing is hiding away from your awareness. We need to be courageous and honest enough to bring our awareness inward and see, 'Oh there is the psychological lower compartment of my refrigerator, and some rotten vegetables there smell pretty bad. But it's okay. This is who I am right now. But I must be fully aware of it.' Practicing awareness is the way to cultivate integrity."

—ANAM THUBTEN RINPOCHE
AT AWAKENING JOY COURSE, BERKELEY, 2008

or others to avoid being caught in unskillful actions. So although I found a spiritual path in my mid-twenties and committed myself to living a life of integrity, as the years went by, the momentum of habit supported my continuing choice not to find Anthony.

I rationalized I wouldn't know where to begin looking for him, but the truth is I was afraid—afraid of what he'd think of me, afraid of what kind of person he might have become, afraid of how my life might turn upside down if we actually found each other. Somewhere inside I knew my son was probably wondering about his father, and deep down there was a sense that my life wasn't whole. Each September around Anthony's birthday, a sense of shame and incompleteness would visit me. I'd wonder how he was, what kind of life he had, what sort of person he was becoming. And I'd wish him well in my heart wherever he was. Then I would conveniently forget about him until the next September.

"Ignorance is bliss" goes the familiar saying. Isn't it easier to just forget about the consequences of our actions, denying when our integrity might be slipping? But do we really forget? Do we really avoid suffering? From one September to another, I turned my attention to other things, convincing myself everything was fine. But inside I was unsettled by the dissonance between what I felt was true and what I didn't want to accept—between what I sensed was right and what I couldn't bring myself to do.

## FACING THE TOP TWENTY REALLY AWFUL DEEDS

There's a price we pay by becoming more conscious: We no longer can pretend we don't know any better. We more readily see the ways we fall short of our ideals. As meditation teacher Ruth Denison puts it, "Karma means you don't get away with nothing, darling!" Because karma is not an easy teacher in delivering to us the consequences of our actions, the humbling process of waking up requires genuine compassion and kindness for ourselves.

That begins with forgiveness, but it's not always easy to forgive ourselves. What do we do with the guilty feelings? How do we resolve, in our hearts and in our relationships, the pain we may have caused? I am some-what of an authority on guilt. Being Jew-ish, you might say it's part of my heritage. But I've learned that when we're stuck in guilt and self-condemnation, our capacity for joy is limited. To arrive at blamelessness requires facing the past honestly, doing what we can to reconcile with others, and forgiving ourselves by replacing guilt and self-judgment with compassionate under-standing.

*I am now at a place in my life where I can say with clarity and honesty that I act with integrity most days in most situations. I can also see areas for improve-ment every day. The fact that this is all a normal part of life (not a terrible shame, or secret, or crisis) brings me a lot of happiness."*

—A COURSE PARTICIPANT

I had a crash course in self-forgiveness on one memorable meditation retreat. Sitting in silence, with my own mind as my only company, I came face-to-face with a string of actions from my past that made me cringe. With all those hours of meditation each day, any mental states that got in the way of a loving heart came to the surface. Many of the memories from my days as a young man made me wince with shame. No matter how much immediate gratification I may have derived at the time of those actions, they were certainly not bringing me happiness now. My body would shudder with guilt and sad-ness.

I'm not trying to let myself off the hook, but in retrospect, some of my misdeeds may not have been all that terrible. Ram Dass points out in his book *Be Here Now* that as we become more conscious and aware, our "impurities will seem grosser and larger" because we're seeing them more clearly. I'd like to think that's what was happening.

Whether or not my misdeeds seemed bigger than they'd actually been didn't really matter as much as the fact that it was very painful to re-call them. This was a sign that I was a different person, no longer capable of hurting others the way I had in the past. But even though I was fast getting the lesson, the parade of unskillful actions continued replaying themselves. They eventually became so overwhelming I decided to make a list of the Top Twenty Really Awful Deeds I had ever done. I thought naming them might help me at least deal with them more consciously. To my immense relief, I was only able to come up with what I considered Seventeen Really Horrendous Actions. Nevertheless, my guilt and remorse felt as awful as if it were a bottomless pit of shameful acts.

Stanton Peele, a pioneer in the field of addiction treatment, talks about the "accumulated disgust" with our unwholesome behavior that crescendos into a moment of truth when we realize *This is not working for me anymore.* We become acutely aware in a new way of the horrible feeling inside when we lose our temper with our children yet again, overeat and overdrink, or exploit someone. When you see clearly that your choices lead to more misery, that's when you're ready to move in a new direction. However, you can't accomplish this by turning against yourself. You have to go gently, recognizing that you are in a process.

## FROM SUFFERING TO COMPASSION

A wise parent understands the confusion of an angry child. She knows that whether the behavior is due to frustration, fatigue, or hunger for attention, what the child really needs is to be held in love and for the pain to be understood with compassion. Then the child can begin to calm down. In the same way, by tenderly holding with kind awareness the pain and confusion that gave rise to our own hurtful behavior, we can begin to transform our suffering into compassion.

On my "Retreat of Awful Deeds," compassionate understanding for myself at first felt impossible. All I could do, hour after hour, was acknowledge and accept the truth of all those actions I had done. Then a curious thing started to happen. Because I wasn't pushing away or denying those images and feelings, I found that my guilt and shame and sadness were diminishing. In their place a tender understanding of my ignorance was arising. I could see how confused I had been to think that any of my deceptions or betrayals or denials could bring me happiness.

The Buddha didn't consider evil to be a disembodied force. Instead he said that all harmful and negative thoughts and actions come from ignorance—not understanding the way life works. We think we're doing what makes us happy, but because we don't understand, we make choices that lead in the direction opposite to where we're aiming. We miss the mark, which is in fact the root meaning of the word "sin."

The ways I had hurt or mistreated others had arisen from this kind of ignorance and confusion, and my choices also reflected how unkind I'd been to myself. Trying to avoid the pain of remorse by simply forgetting about or denying my harmful actions had disconnected me from being fully open to the love and compassion I yearned for.

During that intense inner process, my self-judgment was transforming into understanding, not only of myself but of others as well. I could clearly see that whatever anyone does makes sense to them at the time. We are all shaped by a multitude of circumstances, and some of them can give rise to a distorted perspective on reality. Sometimes our misdeeds are unintentional, but when we consciously hurt others, it is most likely because we ourselves were hurt, and that unprocessed pain is affecting our actions.

I once saw a poster that conveyed this point in heartbreaking terms. The picture of a sad-looking boy was the backdrop for this statistic: "A child raised in a home with domestic violence is seven hundred times more likely to become involved in domestic violence as an adult." When we recognize that every action has a cause, which is itself part of a long chain of cause and effect, a great compassion for ourselves and all others arises.

### Forgiving Yourself

Think of an incident from your past that you still regret or feel guilty about. Consider what conditions, inner and outer, might have motivated your words or actions. Was fear a part of what motivated your choices? Now imagine yourself as a wise and kind being who understands and forgives you. Notice if there is any change in your body or mind as you take in that forgiveness. Is there any way you might act differently if a similar situation presents itself in the future?

## WISE REFLECTION

Looking back at myself as a frightened, immature, self-absorbed twenty-two-year-old, I can see now why I was unable to accept responsibility for my son Tony. It doesn't change the fact that my actions created pain for him and added undue pressures to his mother's life. It doesn't change my sadness that he didn't have me as a loving dad as he grew into manhood. But insulating myself from ever feeling that pain would have prevented my heart from opening enough to feel my love for him, forgive myself, and eventually be open to reconnecting with him.

How you deal with your mistakes either compounds the problem or helps you grow. Rather than heaping on the guilt, you can reflect on what happened and learn from each situation. Recently I heard a Baptist minister, Reverend Welton Gaddy, define forgiveness in a fresh and insightful way. In a television interview he said, "Forgiveness is not about wiping away consequences. Forgiveness is about creating possibilities." That applies to both forgiving others and ourselves. The times when we fall out of integrity can serve as springboards to more skillful choices in the future. This process takes lots of patience and kindness. When you've practiced unwholesome habits for a long time, you need clear intention and

### WIRING UP THE POSITIVE

When you're trying to break a habit that doesn't serve you, instead of thinking about how poorly you've behaved, focus your attention on what you want to do and how you want to feel. Rather than getting caught up in self-judgment, recall the light and joyful way you feel when you *do* choose wisely, and let that feeling motivate you to continue. Research in neuroscience indicates that it can take several months for the neural circuits that would carry your new habit to consolidate fully. Sustaining a new way of being and acting over that period of time will help ensure that you've wired it into your brain.

real determination to wake up and change. Saints are few and far be-tween, but there are lots of people committed to waking up. As long as you're heading in the direction of more ease and peacefulness, that's what counts. In each moment, you are either deepening the ruts of sorrow or the grooves of joy based on what you choose to think or say or do. Why not choose joy?

## HABITS FOR HAPPINESS

As part of his direct path to happiness, the Buddha offered a set of guide-lines for building positive habits that get us in the right groove. These precepts, as they're called, recommend healthy and skillful choices in areas where we can easily go astray. The principle un-derlying all of them is the same—if you want to be happy, don't intentionally cause suffering to yourself or others. Every spir-itual tradition—whether a religion or a philosophy, such as humanism—has a code of ethics. Virtually all of these guidelines are based on not harming others and some version of the Golden Rule, to treat others as we would wish to be treated.

*Integrity feels good. When I act outside of integrity, there is a trace of pain that follows me around. When I act with integrity, I feel lighter in my body, and I can sim-ply go on to the next thought or ac-tion. There are no second thoughts about what I've said or done."*

—A COURSE PARTICIPANT

The basic Buddhist version, which will look familiar to anyone who knows the Ten Commandments, is made up of five precepts or promises: to refrain from killing, stealing, sexual misconduct, lying, and using intox-icants. However, rather than being strict directives, the precepts are viewed as guidelines, ways to support well-being and peace of mind.

For the path of Awakening Joy, I've reframed the five basic precepts as five habits you can actively develop to bring more happiness into your life. They are meant as inspiration, not as a measuring stick that ends up thrashing you with guilt. As you try these out and explore the layers of understanding in each one, you will learn more about yourself as well as the connection between acting consciously and inner peace.

## 1. Honor all life.

At the heart of all these guidelines is reverence for life, traditionally expressed in the first precept as refraining from killing or harming other living beings. The image of St. Francis of Assisi, with wild birds resting on his hands and the animals of the forest gathering around him, exemplifies the gentleness and purity of heart that is the essence of harmlessness.

The capacity to feel reverence for life is a natural part of us. Children, unless they've been harmed or taught to harm, often feel a deep caring for all living things and want to protect them. When I was about six years old, my uncle invited me for an exciting adventure—he was going to teach me how to fish. I was thrilled . . . until I pulled up a sunfish on the end of my line. At the sight of the poor creature struggling on the hook, I imagined having a hook in my own mouth. Feeling sick to my stomach, I begged my uncle to throw it back in. Only when I saw the fish free again did my discomfort go away.

We are faced daily with choices about how to honor life and yet stay alive ourselves. You're probably going to take antibiotics when the choice is between you and some bacteria. When you're barreling down the road at seventy miles per hour,

*As a child, I found myself drawn to tending to animals that were injured, animals that no one thought would live. I wanted to find the potential in something the whole world had given up on and then bring it back to life with my caring and love. I guess I'm doing the same thing as a nurse practitioner in a hospital emergency room. I love my work. It makes me feel that there's a deep river of life we're all connected to—the suffering in myself is no different from the suffering of others and the suffering in the world. When we realize that, we don't want to harm other beings."*

—FROM AN INTERVIEW
WITH JAMES

your windshield is a lethal weapon for flying insects. Although like many Buddhists I'm a vegetarian, some of my wisest, most respected friends are not. Tibetan Buddhists come from a high mountain terrain where fresh vegetables are scarce, so while they take the vow not to kill, they do eat animals. Eating meat does not preclude honoring living beings, as Native Americans and many hunters would attest. The intention with which we do any action is what has the most effect on our integrity.

We can develop the habit of honoring life in many ways in our daily lives. Respecting the ideas and feelings of others is a way of honoring the life within them. Protecting the environment, working for human rights, supporting organizations that serve those in need—all draw upon and awaken tenderness for life. Working at an occupation that contributes, directly or indirectly, to the health and well-being of others is a significant way to honor life. You might even see how it feels to help insects trapped in your house find their way outside. In this world filled with suffering, there are countless ways of reaching out to offer relief.

> *I've been having a very hard time at work. Something is really off. Every day I sit at my desk and do tasks I know must be hurting innocent people, and I'm reaching the point where I can't do it much longer. I don't know what I'll do for a job—I'm working for one of the few employers around here—but until I leave this place, I know I can't be happy."*
>
> —A COURSE PARTICIPANT

## 2. Share your time and resources.

The second precept is traditionally stated as not taking what is not given. Like the Commandment "Thou shalt not steal," on the most basic level this guideline refers to not taking the possessions of others. However, we can take what is not ours in other ways as well. If you push into line ahead of others, aren't you taking something from them? Or if you get so involved in your own fascinating story that you don't realize your busy friends are trying to get out the door, aren't you taking what is not given? This guideline encourages you to take care that your pursuit of happiness is not at the expense of others.

> *After a huge fire in our city, my husband and son and I decided to open our home to a family of three who had lost their own. It was pretty challenging for us—for weeks on end, we all had to keep stretching beyond our comfort zone. But what I recall most of all is the joy we felt in sharing with them as they struggled to deal with their displaced lives."*
>
> —A COURSE PARTICIPANT

Instead of just avoiding taking from others, you can increase your happiness by actively reaching out to be generous. As we saw in Step Three, sometimes that means consciously choosing to stretch beyond what you think you can offer. We are often bigger than we think, and when we stretch beyond our limits, we find our capacity for joy is also bigger.

Another level of this precept points to our relationship with the abundantly generous planet we live on. When we mindlessly take from her resources—depleting fossil fuels, harming delicate ecosystems, polluting air and water—aren't we stealing from the Earth? What is now known as the Deep Ecology movement goes beyond simply recycling or turning off a light. It holds that doing what we can to restore balance and health to the planet is an act of caring that deepens our connection to all of life and nourishes our spirit.

### 3. Take care with sexual energy, respecting boundaries and offering safety.

The common principle behind all five of the Buddhist precepts is a shift in perspective from "What's in it for me?" to "What can I offer another?" This shift in terms of sexuality can be life-changing. We move from regarding another as an object for our own pleasure to considering how we might bring greater happiness. Intimate partners can express their love by delighting in giving physical pleasure. In other relationships we can give the gift of safety in our presence by maintaining healthy boundaries. Traditionally stated as "refraining from sexual misconduct," this guideline ensures deep and true connection with another by advising us to offer the respect and safety that allows both of us to flourish.

*I recently almost had an affair with a married man, and while I felt intense desire, I also felt a profoundly awful churning in my gut which immediately told me that I couldn't do this. Because I tuned in to that churning feeling, I remembered again my commitment to try not to cause further harm in this troubled world, and I turned away."*
—A COURSE PARTICIPANT

Because sexual attraction is so powerful, it can easily lead to actions that can undermine our integrity and create a lot of suffering, for ourselves and others. Think of all the prominent public figures who have not only jeopardized their careers but deeply hurt their loved ones when they engaged in unethical sexual conduct. You might recall in your own life some moments of regret that followed certain choices. We might lead someone on for our own gratification. We might mistake sex for love. We might take advantage of another or cross a line that harms others. Sometimes we're not sensitive to our partner's needs and wants. Maybe we rationalize that it would be okay to do one thing and say another.

The potent force of sexual energy can bring great pain or deep intimacy. As a sexual being, you can move from seeing what you can *get* to what you can *give* through respect and nonexploitation. In this way, you create the conditions for well-being and joy, in yourself and others.

## 4. Speak kindly and carefully.

The fourth precept is about speaking what is true and useful in a kind way. Traditionally, it is stated as refraining from lying and false speech. Most of us are all too familiar with the guilt we feel or the pain of retaliation when we blurt out something hurtful to or about someone. We also know the sweetness of offering and receiving words that convey love and support. Because speech is so much a part of our lives, developing the habit of using words kindly and wisely can be one of the most significant ways to increase happiness for ourselves and others.

Sometimes being both honest and kind might seem like a difficult combination. But the next time you're in a conversation that could become confrontational, try practicing wise speech. Notice what your intention is. Is it to be right, to control? If the heart of your intention is deeper understanding and healthier communication, the other person will often sense that.

We communicate with more than our words when we speak. Psychologist Albert Mehrabian, a pioneer in the field of nonverbal communication, formulated what has come to be known as the 7%-38%-55% Rule. His research revealed that only 7 percent of our feelings and attitudes are carried by our words. The tone of our voice constitutes 38 percent of the communication while 55 percent is conveyed by body language. When our intention is to be kind, our words align with the sound of our voice and the way we are using our body, and we are more likely to receive a kind response.

Not lying also means being honest and accurate in communication. While we pretty well know when we're not speaking the truth, we can easily slip into another form of deception—speaking in superlatives. *This was the worst day of my life. That was the most boring talk I've ever been to. I could've just died. I'm absolutely starving.* Even though we're being casual and know we don't mean those things literally, a habit of using words loosely can easily slide into reporting facts loosely as well. When we exaggerate, we actually disconnect ourselves from the truth, from what's real.

The other half of wise communication is compassionate listening. However unskillful another's communication may be, if you listen wisely, you can hear the suffering, fear, or confusion beneath their words. Instead of getting upset and reacting, listening in this way can help you choose to respond with openness and kindness. You're also more likely to stay in touch with your own best intention, so that your focus can shift from "being right" to more deeply understanding.

Wise speech not only applies to your interactions with others but also to your relationship with yourself. Notice how you speak to yourself, the tone of thoughts in your mind. If they're harsh, see what it's like to change that to a kinder, more compassionate voice. Practice speaking to yourself as you would want others to speak to you, then consciously extend that same spirit of kindness and respect to your communication with others. Notice the effect on your level of happiness and ease.

*I'd get so frustrated during phone conversations with my father. He'd give me a minute-by-minute account of his day, and it was all I could do not to hang up out of impatience. During one call recently, I remembered that I was trying to bring more compassion and happiness into my life, and I said to myself, 'He's lonely. Just be here with him, for him.' I felt myself get so much bigger inside. I was more relaxed, and he sounded happier and more relaxed. I decided to try this out with other people and let go of grumbling to myself that I don't have time for them, or judging them for being so demanding. It has really made a difference in my relationships and in how I feel."*

—A COURSE PARTICIPANT

## 5. Develop a clear mind and healthy body.

The fifth precept is typically stated as: "Refrain from intoxicants that cloud the mind and lead to heedlessness." Because drugs and alcohol so obviously affect the mind and body, some choose to follow this guideline by complete abstinence. Others interpret it as using substances in moderation so that the line from clarity to poor judgment is not crossed. Beyond the obvious pain of substance abuse and addiction, intoxicants can compromise our faculty of awareness and our ability to assess a situation and make wise and skillful choices. When this precept wobbles, so do all the others, making it more likely for us to cause harm to others and ourselves.

As a child of the 1960s, I'm no prude. I understand very well the appeal of changing one's consciousness—the temporary good feeling that helps us forget our pain and feel "loose" or creative. Our brains are wired to pursue what is pleasant, but the paradox is that what we think will make us happy can sometimes perpetuate our suffering.

We all experience hurt and frustration in our lives, and a quick fix of immediate pleasure can look like a good way to deal with the pain. Getting high on drugs or alcohol, overeating, smoking cigarettes, shopping—all numb the pain but don't address it. As we saw in Step Four, the way out of our suffering is by facing it head on. The path to wholeness requires honestly feeling our pain. Though this may seem like the harder route, it is a surer path to abiding happiness than what temporary pleasure offers.

During a workshop I was teaching, one of the participants, David, told me about a time when he had to face head on what he was doing to himself. He said he'd been on a steady regimen of drugs and alcohol and was on the verge of losing everything dear to him—his wife, children, job, home. One night, shaken to the core when he realized where he was heading, he struck upon the words that turned his life around and have become his guiding principle for happiness ever since: "Act with integrity in the moment of choice." I was so struck by the power in these words that I pulled out my notebook and wrote them down. Years later I still refer to them. As you honor your body and mind in the "moment of choice," by being conscious of what you take in, you develop the clarity that helps you make wise choices in all areas of your life.

For those who meditate, clarity of mind has the added benefit of aiding the power of concentration. When the mind is concentrated and still, an inner happiness not dependent on external circumstances becomes available to us. Not only are these joyous mind states pleasant in themselves, the concentrated mind leads to deep purification and wisdom, cutting through and releasing old patterns that cause harm to ourselves and others.

Remember that these guidelines for behavior are not supposed to induce guilt but rather help wake us up to ways we can bring more happiness into our lives. If something "feels off," whether it's in your job or in how you are relating to others, keep in mind you have a choice. Take an honest look at what you can do differently. Sometimes the choice for integrity can be difficult, but knowing that you're making a choice for your own well-being can give you the courage to take a challenging step. No matter how far you've strayed from integrity, you always have the capacity to turn around and begin again. Aligning your life with your values is a process of development that requires patience, compassion, and continual commitment. But the reward is the bliss of blamelessness. What could be better than that?

## A COMPLEX AND REWARDING ADVENTURE

Living in our world with integrity can be a complex adventure, and sometimes there is no simple answer. Grappling with this led course participant Cindy to some wise reflections:

> In my experience, it's possible to get really entangled in choices that take multiple variables into account. *Should I buy food that is organic but non-local, which supports organic farming but has a big impact on the environment by requiring that produce be trucked long distances? Or should I buy local but non-organic, which might be supporting the pesticide indus-*

*try and compromising my health?* At some point, getting caught up in too many considerations makes virtue an intellectual exercise rather than a felt-sense in the body, and then it's no longer helpful. We cannot come up with a perfect answer! This is not easy. What is "right" is created afresh each moment.

The bliss of blamelessness depends upon listening carefully to the ring of truth inside. While choices in any given situation are not black and white, if you pay close enough attention, the feeling of tightness or ease in your body can pretty well guide you toward actions that are best aligned with your intention to live with integrity. As you refine your ability to hear the voice of wisdom, you increasingly choose behaviors that are healthy and make you feel genuinely alive, invigorated, and big-hearted.

## Cultivating Habits for Happiness

Choose one of the five habits or precepts that you would like to cultivate as a way to bring more joy and well-being into your life, and commit to doing it for one week. Brainstorm ways you might act in alignment with this guideline. Write them down and place the paper in a prominent location where you can readily see it every day.

Your old habits may rebel and struggle for dominance. Each time you are faced with the moment of choice, take a breath, and choose integrity. Whenever you do choose to think and act in alignment with integrity, notice how you feel. Is there a sense of relief or ease? What kind of response do you receive if others are involved? When you later recall your choice, how do you feel about it? These reflections will help anchor your new habit as it develops.

At the end of the week, notice if it has become easier to make positive choices. See if your level of well-being and happiness has increased.

## A SECOND CHANCE

For me, a major shift in my life began with a phone call that came one hot August day in 1999. A woman's voice asked if I had ever known someone named Bonnie with whom I might have fathered a child. After a silence, I quietly answered yes. *Who was this woman and what did this mean?* My breath caught, and I could feel the blood rushing to my head.

## HOLDING TO THE TRUTH

"In 1971, during the first year of our marriage, I helped my husband, Daniel Ellsberg, release to the press the top secret documents that came to be known as the Pentagon Papers, confirming that Congress and the American public had been misled into entering the war in Vietnam. Even though he faced going to prison for the rest of his life, Dan felt compelled to reveal the truth.

"We had both been inspired by the teachings of Gandhi, who lived with a deep respect for all life and a commitment to non-harming and non-violence, even toward those he would call enemies. He called the principle behind this *satyagraha*, 'holding to the truth.' The power that arises from this practice was known as Truth-Force or Soul-Force.

"I remember the day Dan and I stood in front of a bank of cameras and shouting reporters, and he took full responsibility for the release of the papers. We were holding hands in the middle of that chaos, and it was as if we were in an electrical current of great power. I believe this was an experience of Truth-Force.

"There is a dimension of integrity that comes from recognizing our oneness and interconnection with all life. Each of us can access the power of Truth-Force when we act with that kind of integrity. Wholesome states, such as kindness, compassion, and service, open us to that power."

—PATRICIA ELLSBERG
AT AWAKENING JOY COURSE, BERKELEY, 2008

"Yes," I replied again, "it's possible." My mind flooded with different thoughts and scenarios. *My son has found me! What is he like? He's in trouble and is turning to me for help. Maybe he's a drug dealer and wants to make sure I pay for my actions.* In the midst of my fears and concerns, I could almost feel the woman on the other end of the line begin to smile. "Oh, if that's so, you are very lucky," I heard her say. "I'm a friend of his, calling for him. Tony is one of the most wonderful human beings I've ever met."

A mix of emotions surged through me—gratitude, relief, curiosity, fear, guilt, excitement. "Have him call me as soon as he's ready," I heard myself say. When I got off the phone, I knew in the stillness of that August afternoon that my life was about to dramatically change. Shock intertwined with infinite possibility. I was being given a second chance.

Within a few hours, Tony's call came. During those first awkward moments our conversation was tentative, but by the end of the call we had made arrangements for him to fly up the following weekend for a visit. Over the next few days, I felt overwhelmed with both trepidation and excitement. *How would this work out? How would Adam feel about suddenly having a big brother? How would my own life change? What would Tony and I say to each other? Who was this "most wonderful person" and what would he think of me? Could he possibly forgive me?* Whatever was going to unfold from this opportunity, I was prepared to take full advantage of it. I had learned through years of practice that healing comes from directly facing the truth of whatever life presents me.

Over the course of that weekend, Tony and I both realized how fortunate we were that he had found me. I was struck by how much he reminded me of my father—the person who most taught me how to love. The sparkle in his eyes, the dimpled cheek, the infectious smile all radiated the same goodness I knew so well and had greatly missed since my dad had passed away fifteen years earlier. Tony's heart of gold dazzled me, and beholding this young man was like a rerun of that moment with him twenty-nine years earlier when I had mysteriously known him as my flesh and blood. Only this time I wasn't running away.

Tony too saw someone quite different from what he feared when his fiancée Leesa was first tracking me down, spending many hours on the Internet. Instead of encountering an uncaring and insensitive father who had betrayed him, he had found, despite what had happened, someone he could admire and feel an easy, natural connection with.

## NEVER TOO LATE

Four months after that first reunion, Tony came to my weekly meditation group in Berkeley. In the back of a room crowded with students, he sat quietly and anonymously. The stunned group listened as I recounted our story and the recent events of our reunion. It was a story that outlined my confusion, fear, and shame as well as the gratitude I felt for this second chance. I talked about the love I felt as I got to know this son of mine for the first time. I shared my awe and wonder at the mystery of life, and the joy I was feeling at both of us finding this missing piece of our lives. Finally, I expressed my hope that at some point Tony would truly forgive my confusion and let me completely into his heart.

Then, to the surprise of everyone in the room, I invited Tony to join me on the stage where I introduced him. As we sat there together in front of my silently marveling community, Tony reached out to me and whispered, "I forgive you, Dad," and suddenly burst into tears. The microphone picked up his voice, and the room filled with raw emotion and tenderness as everyone witnessed this amazing turning point between us. Words cannot describe the power of that moment for me as my heart took in his love.

Tony's reentry into my life has given me many lessons. He has conveyed the pain and hurt he experienced by my absence, and his anger over being abandoned. These deep wounds have certainly left their mark on him. Although I've forgiven myself, this is something I have to live with for the rest of my life. At times I consider that perhaps all of this is part of a bigger picture we just can't understand. It certainly has taught both of us a great deal about what is important in life. And because of what I've gone through with Tony, I have been able to help others choose wisely when faced with difficult decisions.

This story has continued with unimagined blessings. Adam has been thrilled, not only at having a big brother he feels close to, but one who is a musician to boot. Jane and Tony have an affectionate relationship, and she's happy he's in our lives. At Tony's wedding I walked down the aisle with my mom, who's crazy about Tony and is his greatest admirer. It's like they're long-lost friends who've found each other. I've met with Tony's mother, Bonnie, and expressed my sorrow for not being there for both of them when they needed me, as well as my deep gratitude for all the love and caring she gave Tony. Bonnie now considers my mother one of her friends, and she and I have a warm connection, occasionally spending time together at Tony's house when we're both visiting. Tony has taken my last name and has blessed me with three stunning granddaughters, Jordan, Sydney, and Taylor Baraz. He turns to me when he needs someone to talk to who will understand. As Tony has let me into his heart, and I've let him into mine, the hole created by all those missing years has filled with sweetness, laughter, and love. Like any family, we've had our challenges, but we also hold them in the context of all these blessings.

*I finished graduate school, took a job based on my course of study, and then realized that I didn't want to do it. As I work through the huge emotional response to this situation, I am aware that by leaving the job I didn't want, I acted with integrity toward myself. I did what was right for me, even if it was against what I had spent three years working toward. Now, as I try to figure out what to do next, I am trying to be more honest with both myself and my friends about the challenges, confusion, and sadness that are coming up, and I am working toward finding a wise livelihood that is in line with who I am, who I want to be, and what feels right.*

—A COURSE PARTICIPANT

## A North Star

If you're facing a decision that could compromise your integrity, imagine how you will feel five months or five years from now looking back on your choice.

Having deeply experienced the consequences of my actions informs how I live now. Rather than focusing on what the immediate effect of any decision might be, I imagine how it will feel six months or five years from now when I look back on the choice. This long-range view of well-being has been a great ally in wise decision-making. The Buddha's words about a life of integrity leading naturally to joy are not merely theoretical. I know the truth of that teaching from direct experience, and I use it as my North Star.

We can choose at any time to enter a life of integrity. It may be tempting to stay asleep, to continue sliding over all those little—or big—infringements we've gotten used to. But as my younger son, Adam, who spent a college semester in India studying Eastern philosophies, wrote in one of his essays for the program:

> When I mess up, I am again stuck with that altogether too familiar bad feeling. The voice in my mind chides, "And don't pretend you didn't know better!" When these moments start to feel truly excruciating, I pity myself and daydream about the peace I could have if I didn't know better. "How sweet it would be to go back to the bliss of ignorance!" But much farther down in my gut I know the truth. There is only one bliss. And in life, when given the choice between the short-lived pleasures—the Bliss of Ignorance—and the long-term fulfillment—the Bliss of Blamelessness—hopefully I'll choose the latter.

## BEING TRUE TO OURSELVES

Sometimes the hardest area of integrity is being truthful with ourselves. Are we telling ourselves the truth when we berate or put ourselves down? Is it true when we say "I don't have the capacity to handle this"? Are we acting with integrity when we betray ourselves by not developing our gifts and talents?

Integrity is not just about following guidelines for morality. On a deeper level, it's about being true to yourself. If you are in touch with your heart and your deepest impulses, you will make choices that do not harm yourself or others. It's not always easy to follow that "still, small voice inside," but it's worth listening carefully enough to hear it.

*You do not become good by trying to be good, but by finding the goodness that is already within you, and allowing that goodness to emerge."*

—ECKHART TOLLE, FROM *A NEW EARTH*

As part of your integrity practice, you might focus on being uncompromisingly honest with yourself. Not brutally honest, but honest in a kind and caring way that genuinely supports your intention for greater happiness. Try asking yourself, "What do I really need to do right now that would bring me greater well-being?" Then listen with care to your deepest wisdom—feeling it in your body, hearing the supportive and resonant voice of clarity in your mind.

## THE FRAGRANCE OF MORALITY

"In Buddhism we talk about the fragrance of morality. It means that when you practice integrity, it's almost like you have an extraordinary divine scent around you, and you magnetize everything you are searching for—all the goodness, virtue, joy, freedom, even enlightenment if that's what you're looking for. Integrity is the first step towards the highest goals you are trying to actualize in this human existence.

"When we practice maintaining integrity and demonstrate it through our actions, our speech, the way we treat other people, we become extraordinary examples to inspire others. It's like how one candle can light hundreds of candles, and those hundreds of candles can light thousands of candles. Can you imagine such an enlightened society? But we must start with ourselves. When you practice integrity, you will see the reward immediately. You'll discover that you're happy, that your friends and family members are happy, and even your dog is happy too. That is because of the fragrance of morality."

—ANAM THUBTEN RINPOCHE
AT AWAKENING JOY COURSE, BERKELEY, 2008

You can actively practice the "bliss of blamelessness" by paying attention to the uplifting feelings that arise in your body and mind when you choose to act with integrity. As you pay attention to the pleasant visceral sensations, you are training yourself to make the choice for happiness. Rather than looking to avoid suffering, you become motivated by the "gladness connected with the wholesome."

When we walk the path toward the bliss of blamelessness, our goodness overflows. The joy you're looking for starts with being aligned with your values. As you act with integrity, you become a clear vessel for goodness to move through you and touch others. That not only makes you happy in the moment, but the goodness that radiates out will come back to you many times over.

# 6

# THE JOY OF
# LETTING GO

He who binds to himself a joy

Does the winged life destroy;

But he who kisses the joy as it flies,

Lives in Eternity's sunrise.

—William Blake (1757–1827)
"Several Questions Answered"

$\mathcal{L}et$'s $say$ $you$'$ve$ been enthusiastically following the steps of the Awakening Joy course. Some old patterns that used to get in the way have lost their power, and some new practices have proven valuable in keeping the channels open to joy. "Great! I've finally figured out how to be happy," you declare. "This is the way life is supposed to be." Then one morning you wake up feeling lousy, or something happens that's not quite so pleasant, and you scramble to get back "your happiness." The more it fades away, the harder you try to hold on to it, and the very holding on squeezes out the joy.

We can't hold on to happiness any more than we can hold on to anything or anyone. As we've seen in previous steps, trying to hold on in a constantly changing world is futile, and it pulls us out of the moment. Yet we do it all the time. To begin with, we hold on to our material goods. There may be a lucky few of us who live simply and without a lot of things, but if you're at home, look around you. You've probably got a ton of reasons for hanging on to most of the objects you see.

That's just the external world. Our inner world is even more filled with stuff we hold on to—our ideas of what we think life is about, who we think is right (usually ourselves), how things are supposed to be. When any of these important things are threatened, our world can feel like it might crumble. *There's a scratch on my new car!* Or, *Why isn't it like it was when we first met?* Or, *Why did you do that?!*

It's natural and healthy to care about things or people or ideas. They are the stuff of life. Giving and receiving love and appreciating beauty and pleasure are some of the most fulfilling and joyful aspects of our lifetime. But caring too much can have a subtle, or not so subtle, quality of holding on. Relationships change, favorite things break, pets die. Trying to hold on to the way we want life to be only leads to frustration and disappointment.

The Buddha decided to teach when he realized that, although all human beings want to be happy, they continue to think and act in ways that create more suffering. He defined the cause of this suffering basically as hanging on to the way we want things to be. We want life to always be pleasant for us. And when it's not that way, we think something's wrong, and we struggle to set it right.

On my first meditation retreat, I learned an unforgettable lesson about this with the help of my teacher Joseph Goldstein. One afternoon I'd fallen into a most exquisite state of mind. A calm, easy presence and feeling of completeness had engulfed me. It was as if there were no separation between me and the rest of life. I was breathing in as the Universe was breathing out. The Universe was breathing in as I breathed out. I was so happy, and I didn't want that sweet state of mind to ever end. Of course it did. Over the next two days I tried everything I could think of to recreate the experience. *Maybe it was the way I was sitting on my meditation cushion. Maybe it had to do with what I'd eaten for lunch. Maybe I needed to more diligently pay attention to my breath.* But somehow the harder I tried, the more elusive that state was. In place of calm and presence were disappointment, agitation, and confusion.

Disheartened, I went to Joseph to tell him how frustrated I felt because I'd "had it" and then I "lost it." He smiled knowingly and told me a story. During his extended meditation practice in India, he had experienced a sustained period of bliss. For several weeks, every time he sat down to meditate, his mind was clear and his body was filled with light. When he had to return to the States to see his family and take care of some things, Joseph left this tremendously pleasurable experience behind, figuring that when he got back to India, he'd pick up with the bliss where he left off.

*Truly letting go doesn't come easy to a control freak like me. But what comes to mind when letting go is the memory of being a child again and sledding in a quiet place I discovered. It was a long, steep hill with many trees, and I felt the wonder and thrill of letting go and just flying down that long hill, steering around the trees, and landing safely at the very bottom. It was a feeling of utter peace."*

—A COURSE PARTICIPANT

But a couple of months later, back on the cushion in India, "instead of bliss, my mind was like mud and my body felt like twisted steel," he told me. Speaking slowly to let his words sink in, he went on. "I spent nearly two years trying to recapture that blissful state. Even though my teacher told me to let things be just as they are, I kept trying to make my experience different." Then Joseph leaned forward to drive home the point: "*I* was the dummy. Now *you* don't have to go through that. What you need to do is let go of the way things were and just be with what's happening now."

Circumstances change, we change, things change, and letting go of what we're holding on to can be a great relief. It is also the road to happiness. The Buddha taught that the end of suffering—the highest happiness—comes from developing "a mind that clings to naught." That's a tall order. But even loosening our grip just a little can bring about a lot of happiness. Letting go to any degree is not easy, and I don't want to sound flippant about it. Sometimes life asks us to let go of more than we think we can bear—our homes, our jobs, our loved ones. However, while we can't deny the suffering, holding on to what is already gone only adds to our pain.

I once saw the great Thai meditation master, Ajahn Chah, give a simple and profound teaching about letting go. One day a local villager, who was in the group gathered before the master, asked him if he could explain the teachings in a way that would be easy to remember every day. In response, Ajahn Chah reached for his ceramic cup and held it up. "You see this cup? It was given to me as a gift," he began. "It is pretty to look at. It holds my water. I enjoy it. If I can see this cup as already broken, I won't cry when that happens. In this way, I can fully appreciate it while it's here. Letting go like this is how I can truly be happy in a world where everything changes."

Letting go is about freeing ourselves from that which complicates and confuses our mind. That covers a very broad spectrum. When I ask Awakening Joy participants what they let go of during this step in the course, the answers have included:

- Ingrained ideas of having to say or do something perfectly.
- Love letters from my college boyfriend.
- My youth as I let go to the signs of aging.
- A certain kind of friendship with my children as they go off to college and don't want a lot of interaction with me.
- Independence and self-sufficiency due to a physical injury.
- Fear of being abandoned by my partner, who is actually very steady.
- The need to be right.

What are we really holding on to? Most fundamentally, it's the illusion that we have control in a world of change. This attempt to control keeps us bound in fear. And unless we let go as circumstances change, we end up suffering.

One of the secrets of happiness is learning to distinguish what we want from what we truly need. Wise letting go leads to joy when we realize we don't have to hold on to extra baggage, whether it's in our garage or the closet of our mind. We put down an unnecessary burden—the attachment that comes from grasping on to what we think will make us happy.

When you stop holding on so tight—to ideas, beliefs, objects or beings you cherish, and precious concepts of who you are—you begin to live in a way that lets you flow with life. You can meet what life brings you and respond creatively, in trust, and with generosity of heart. You discover that letting go is something you do *for* yourself, not *to* yourself. Happiness doesn't depend upon what you have or what you hold on to. Rather, by learning the art of letting go, paradoxically we get what we really want. You step into the contentment and ease of a relaxed mind.

> *If you let go a little, you will have a little peace. If you let go a lot, you will have a lot of peace. If you let go completely, you will have complete peace and freedom. Your struggles with the world will have come to an end."*
>
> —AJAHN CHAH, FROM *A STILL FOREST POOL*, COMPILED BY JACK KORNFIELD AND PAUL BREITER

## THE STORY OF STUFF

Friends have told me about the Dalai Lama laughing in one of his talks as he recalled a particular week he spent in Los Angeles. He has always loved scientific gadgets, and each day on his way to give teachings, he would stop to look at items on display at a nearby electronics store. He said that by the end of the week he wanted things he didn't even know the use for. He wanted them just because he'd seen them.

That's one of the ways the mind works—often what we see is what we want. This is fertile ground for the U.S. advertising industry. Annie Leonard's amazing short film, "The Story of Stuff," portrays how we in the United States are basically drowning in material goods.

Among a number of disturbing statistics, the film notes that:

- "The average U.S. person now consumes twice as much as they did fifty years ago."
- "We each see more advertisements in one year than people fifty years ago saw in a lifetime."
- "In the U.S., we spend three to four times as many hours shopping as our counterparts in Europe do."

In the film, economist Victor Lebow is quoted in order to explain how this glut of consumption came about. He was writing just after World War II had ended, and what he had to say was prophetic:

> Our enormously productive economy demands that we make consumption our way of life, that we convert the buying and use of goods into rituals, that we seek our spiritual satisfaction, our ego satisfaction, in consumption. . . . We need things consumed, burned up, replaced, and discarded at an ever-accelerating rate.

Of course desire is going to arise in response to clever advertising. "Bet you can't eat just one," the famous potato chip ad challenges us, summing up the strategy to get us to want more and more. We end up believing that the next new thing is going to make the difference in our life that will make us happy or healthy or lovable. We get a little thrill of excitement at the promise and again at the purchase. Fearing we might not have enough, we hold on to things we don't need, just in case . . . And where does this get us? Environmentalist Bill McKibben, in his book *Deep Economy,* writes: "In 1946, the United States was the happiest country among four advanced economies; thirty years later, it was eighth among eleven advanced countries; a decade after that it ranked tenth among twenty-three nations, many of them from the third world."

John D. Rockefeller, when asked how much money would be enough, replied, "Just a little more." When does "enough" become satisfying?

> It is an awareness of that optimum point where enhancement of true well-being coincides with the experience of satisfaction. Consumption . . . must be balanced to an amount appropriate with well-being rather than to the satisfaction of desires. In contrast to maximum consumption leading to more satisfaction, we have moderate, or wise consumption leading to well-being.

Getting and holding on to more and more stuff doesn't raise our level of happiness. In fact, quite the opposite. We can feel overwhelmed by all the papers, objects, toys, clothes, and other things that fill our closets, garages, storage rooms, and homes. When our goal changes from quelling desires to enhancing our well-being, we have a helpful guideline for choosing what we need over what we want.

When course participant Cynthia noticed she was doing "a little too much spontaneous buying," she decided to try an experiment.

I made a commitment for a period of time not to buy anything other than groceries and necessities. When the impulse would arise to buy something extra, whether that was Starbucks coffee or a spiritual book, I would just jot down the item in a little notebook, notice my feelings and reactions, and move on. Invariably I would discover that I had managed to survive and be happy without having made the purchase. It was quite liberating. I found that letting go is being at peace with what is and what one has—quite the opposite of "the more you get the better."

## SUSTAINABLE CONTENTMENT

"When you are living in contentment, you automatically start to have a lighter footprint, a lighter use of resources. You don't have to keep adding more and more to your life. In fact, it feels really good to want what you have, to take care of it, and to be aware that everything you're using is a representation of energy. You feel more and more as if you are a part of a family and that you don't want to gorge yourself at the table, taking ten times your share. Contentment chills out the desperation of accumulation, which the culture hammers you with. If you are saying, 'I'm quite content now, and adding on all of this stuff complicates my life,' then you are automatically moving toward being part of the solution. Your life is the expression of that."

—CATHERINE INGRAM
AT AWAKENING JOY COURSE, BERKELEY, 2008

Happiness comes from being engaged in life, not in acquiring more stuff. As you explore the revolutionary idea of having enough, you might try getting more involved in activities that don't have to do with buying or acquiring. Spend time just talking with a loved one or sitting down to listen to one of the CDs you already have in your collection. Go out for a bike ride or learn something new. An important key to greater well-being is spending time rather than money on what you love.

## LETTING GO INTO TIME

Shortly after Barack Obama was elected president, author Alice Walker wrote an open letter to him that has been posted on many sites on the Internet. One point in particular struck a chord in me.

> A primary responsibility that you do have . . . is to cultivate happiness in your own life. To make a schedule that permits sufficient time of rest and play with your gorgeous wife and lovely daughters. . . . From your happy, relaxed state, you can model real success, which is all that so many people in the world really want.

A schedule that "permits sufficient time of rest and play . . ." How many of us have that? Yet in the Bible, even God took a break after work, and commanded us to "remember the Sabbath and keep it holy." I don't mean to say that you can't be joyful when you're in the midst of lots of activity. I love being fully engaged, often in a number of projects. But when I get lost in the swirl, I get spun out of balance.

We live in a 24/7 culture, and if it *feels* to you like you're packing in more than you used to, you're right. In their essay "Consuming Time," professors David Loy and Linda Goodhew reported in the year 2000, "The husband and wife in an average U.S. household are now working five hundred more hours a year than they did in 1980." Add email, phone calls, the basics of life, the next exciting adventure, the latest movie, and lunch with a friend, and you're stressed out and far from joyful.

My colleague Patricia Ellsberg, who leads guided meditations at the

Awakening Joy course in Berkeley, likes to speak playfully to participants about a condition prevalent in our society—FOMS, Fear of Missing Something. Besides all those movies, concerts, lectures, meetings, friends, etc., we have sixty-plus television channels at home and endless amounts of important and fascinating information on the Internet. No wonder we're afraid of missing things—we have so many choices that we miss almost everything available to us every day! The Beatles movie *Yellow Submarine* that came out in the late 1960s was prophetic in featuring a character whose mantra was: "Ad hoc, ad loc, and quid pro quo! / So little time! So much to know!" He was called "The Nowhere Man." Being happy means recovering from FOMS and arriving at the *somewhere* in time that is this moment. It means being present for our lives in a balanced way and letting the rest go without regret.

Too much on our plate gives us indigestion. But sometimes the way we handle our overcrowded schedules is like trying to cure indigestion by eating even more. Course participant Beverly finds that her busy-ness feeds on itself. "If I get out of balance—too little sleep, no quiet time—the loop starts looping wildly, and I get busier, trying to make up for lost time." In written Chinese the characters for "busy" are "heart" plus "killing." Besides the physical diseases stress is known to cause—strokes, heart attacks, diabetes, and ulcers, among others—it also closes our heart spiritually and emotionally.

We might pack a lot into our schedules but, like eating a diet of junk food, we remain hungry because we lack real nourishment. When another course participant, Norma, looked at how she was spending her time, she realized she was involved in a lot of activities that, while seeming important, were actually unsatisfying and kept her from doing things that would contribute to her well-being.

> I realized that my favorite excuse for not doing things I would enjoy has been "I don't have time." Letting go of that belief has been really powerful for me. Whenever it comes up now, I look at what really matters, and I change those words in my mind to "I am making the time to enjoy life."

Just as we can be greedy for things, we can be greedy for experience and activities. Being interested in life is one of the ways to awaken joy, but you can do so without feeling compelled to do or have a multitude of experiences in order to be happy. Letting go means being right here with your life as it unfolds instead of continually reaching out for more. It is a shift towards simplicity, not complicating your life or your mind with a clutter of things to do. Peace Pilgrim, in her book by that title, shares the wisdom she developed during the twenty-eight years she spent walking across the country to deliver her message of peace. She writes:

> If your life is in harmony with your part in the Life Pattern, and if you are obedient to the laws which govern this universe, then your life is full and good but not overcrowded. If it is overcrowded, you are doing more than is right for you to do, more than is your job to do in the total scheme of things.

I once heard a decluttering expert advise being wary of the word *just,* as in "I'll *just* do this quick errand before my next appointment," or "I'll *just* check my email one more time before I go." *Just* is an unrealistic belief that things won't take time. Then we find ourselves rushing and hurrying to catch up. You will never get to the end of your "to do" list. As is sung in the celebratory song "Circle of Life" from *The Lion King,* "There's more to see than can ever be seen/More to do than can ever be done." What really needs your attention and is most important to your well-being? My motto regarding all the undone emails and tasks waiting for me is "*Behind* is just a state of mind." If you're too busy to enjoy your life, then perhaps you're too busy. What can you do with your time that will nourish you and make life

*Normally I race right through some of the things I have to do with my young son—picking up toys, getting him ready for bed. But the other day I discovered something that was delightful. I actually stopped to enjoy fully the happiness in his eyes and the smile on his face. I felt it with my whole body. I don't even remember exactly what we were doing, but I can instantly bring back the feeling of joy I had during that moment.*

—A COURSE PARTICIPANT

more worthwhile? Take a walk in nature. Play some music. Spend more time with your kids or loved ones.

Taking some quiet time for yourself is a good way to bring more joy into your days. Even a few minutes of down time can help you tune into what you really want to do in "your one wild and precious life," as poet Mary Oliver puts it. Trimming down your calendar may feel awkward at first, but eventually your time can be filled with quality rather than quantity.

Habits of busy-ness and the mindset of "more" are not easy to break. It takes a strong intention to change. Whenever you do "give yourself time," remember to pause and pay attention to how good it feels in your mind and body. This will help support your shift to a happier life.

## Letting Go of Busy-ness

What can you let go of in your schedule—or put into it—to have more ease and fulfillment in your life? What do you believe about yourself or about life that makes you do more than you are healthy or comfortable doing?

If you tend to overbook yourself, try this: For one week, if you add something to your schedule, see if you can delete something else. At the end of the week, notice if you have felt more spacious or balanced. What did you "do" with the extra time in your schedule?

Sometimes it's not possible to pare down a schedule. In that case, give yourself "mini-breaks." Take a brief moment, between dropping off one child at daycare and getting the other to soccer practice, to pause, close your eyes, take a deep breath, and feel what it's like to be "out of time." Even if you've just dashed down the hall at work from one meeting to another, stop for a few seconds before you open that next door, close your eyes, let your body relax, take a breath, and come back to yourself. Chances are you won't feel quite so *busy* after a mini-break.

## GETTING OUT OF THE MIND TRAP

Like any other skill, the ability to let go develops over time. When you first begin, you may find that instead of feeling freer, you're battling previous habits that don't want to give up. One course participant wrote to say: "The more I try to let go of habits that don't serve me, the more resistance I feel and the more I struggle."

*I am working with being more patient and open to empty slots of time in my schedule. I have found that I can really enjoy doing nothing when I allow myself that pleasure."*

—A COURSE PARTICIPANT

It helps to remember where that struggle is taking place. As we have seen in each Awakening Joy step so far, our *mind* is the main arena where our lives are happening. Life keeps changing around us, but the mind can dig in its heels. Another participant writes: "I find that my mind attaches itself to a particular problem or situation and keeps bringing me back to it." It can feel almost impossible to let go of fear, resentment, negativity, or compulsive behavior, especially if you've been practicing them for a long time.

In Asia there is a clever way of trapping monkeys that offers a helpful clue for getting out of a rut in the mind. A coconut, hollowed out and with a hole in one end, is filled with sweets and tied to a stake. The monkey comes along, smells the sweets, sticks its hand in and grabs a fistful. Though the hole is big enough for an open hand to get through, it's too small for a fist full of sweets to get out. Even as the monkey hears the humans coming and starts to panic, it holds on tightly to its prize. All that monkey has to do to be free is let go of the sweets and slip out its hand. As Joseph Goldstein likes to put it, "It's a very rare monkey who figures that out."

When you can't seem to get out of a difficult state, and negative thoughts play themselves over and over in your mind, the first step is to recognize them simply as thoughts. The reason they seem so convincing is because we believe that they are real. Often they have to do with who we believe ourselves to be. If you're trapped in resentment, for instance, it's most likely because you've identified with having been wronged.

Maybe you were, but as one course participant puts it: "So what? I realized I was storing resentment in my body and heart. When I let it go, I felt light, free, happy." Like the monkey in the trap, all you need to do to be free is relax your grip. Even if it's hard to let go of all that righteousness, if the choice is between hanging on or being happy, which do you choose?

## OPENING UP YOUR OPTIONS

When you let go of thinking that things should be a certain way, you open yourself up to the fact that there are usually a number of options that you hadn't considered. I've learned over time to pay more attention to that anxiety in my gut that's really trying to tell me: "Wake up. Something's off here. Get your bearings straight." When I slow down to acknowledge it, it usually helps me remember what my true aim is and how I might accomplish it. This recently happened when I set out for the airport one Friday afternoon, proud that I'd given myself plenty of time to park my car and board the plane. It would be a short flight to San Luis Obispo, about 250 miles south, where I was going to teach a retreat.

Two hours after leaving home, I was still creeping along in traffic that had turned the freeway into a parking lot. It would be a close call, but I was still confident I'd make the flight. I had my pre-printed boarding

### Lightening Up

Even a few minutes of mindfulness meditation each day carries over into your life, teaching you how to swim *with* rather than against the current of life. During meditation, each time you notice that you're thinking, no matter how interesting or important the content of the thought may seem, practice letting it go. Don't worry if the same thoughts keep coming back. That's common. Just keep letting go each time. Little by little you'll feel less rigidly attached to your thoughts in daily life. Try it and see.

pass, no baggage to check, and a good book to read. I was all set. When I finally got to the airport, thinking I'd made it just in the nick of time, the parking garage was full. The attendant directed me to a lot at some distant location, and anxiety kicked in. The signs were not marked clearly enough for my nervous eyes, and I ended up circling the airport three times, sure I'd stumbled upon the Bermuda Triangle of parking lots. I was getting more agitated by the moment. *They've been planning this retreat for a year. Fifty people will be very disappointed. I've got to get there.*

My pleasant little journey was turning into a real mess—until suddenly I realized I was simply not going to make the plane. The moment I let go of my idea of what should be happening and accepted the situation exactly as it was, the agitation and stress went away, making way for a new idea. *Wait a moment. This car I'm trying so desperately to park can actually take me there.* I felt waves of happiness as I turned out of the airport and onto the freeway, heading south. I spent the next five hours singing along with my favorite songs, enjoying my own company, with no email, chores, or tasks to be done. And I arrived at the retreat feeling happy and at ease.

*My husband and I have been working on letting go of taking offense when no offense was intended. Example: 'Why did you put that there? No offense. I'm not saying you are stupid for putting it there. I'm just curious.' Letting go of the need to be right is wonderfully freeing."*

—A COURSE PARTICIPANT

When you let go of how you think things should be, you can respond to challenging situations with openness and flexibility, imagining options and alternatives that can't arise in a contracted mind. We may have a tendency to see ourselves as the center of the world, but life manages to remind us that it's otherwise. Recognizing that you are just one part of an interacting system with others who have their own reality can be a great relief.

The ability to let go is critical in relationships because that's where we find ourselves continually coming up against the fact that things just aren't always the way we want them to be. Especially with those closest to us, it's easy to fall into habits of reaction when they don't conform to what we expect. Pamela was exploring what letting go meant as part of the Awakening Joy course when the perfect opportunity arose to try it out. One particular morning she woke up in a peaceful state, feeling full of gratitude. But when she went to the kitchen and opened the refrigerator, she saw that a bowl of chicken broth she was saving for soup had been tipped over and was dripping into the vegetable bins and onto the floor. "I knew my husband had done it while looking for a late-night snack," she wrote. "I felt the anger rise in me, along with the usual grumbling, as I went to get paper towels to clean up the mess." But then another possible response occurred to Pamela.

I realized I could let go of all of that and, in fact, that was what I wanted to do. I cleaned up the mess and didn't say a word to my husband. It was not a stifling or even an *effort*—those feelings were just gone. I was grateful for my husband, grateful for the abundance of food in my refrigerator, grateful to be able to get up in the morning, to be alive and well, to see how inconsequential the mess was. After that little bout of turbulence, my mind had returned to that clear and serene state I'd awoken in, just from choosing to let go of my usual reaction. Beautiful!

## Letting Go of Expectations

Having a plan is useful as a guide, but if it becomes a rigid expectation, you could be setting yourself up for disappointment. Choose a particular activity that you do regularly, such as a task at work, or cooking a meal, or having a conversation with a friend or one of your children. For one week, each time you are about to begin that activity, notice if you have an expectation of how it's "supposed to" turn out. Experiment with letting go and just being open to whatever happens. This doesn't mean letting go of accomplishing the task, getting the meal on the table, or bringing up certain topics in conversation, but rather being open instead of closed in your approach.

As you engage in the activity, notice how you feel in your body and mind when you let go of your expectations. Does letting go have any effect on your enjoyment of the experience?

Pamela could have responded in a number of other ways, but the point for her was letting go of a state of mind that would have left her, and likely her husband as well, feeling closed down and unhappy. If your intention is to be genuinely happy, you may find yourself shifting around some priorities. When you see yourself with the fisted hand in the coconut, you know how to get out of the trap.

## WHAT STORY AM I BELIEVING RIGHT NOW?

One evening during the break at an Awakening Joy class, I heard a cheerful voice which I soon connected to the middle-aged man buoyantly striding down the aisle to greet me. "James, I have to tell you something!" When he came closer, I could see it was Daniel, the accountant I had seen once for spiritual counseling, who was now taking the course. "It worked!" he beamed. "And I just want to say thank-you."

He must have known by the look on my face that I was sorting through my memory bank to find out *what* had "worked."

He reminded me of the time months ago when he had asked for my advice about reacting negatively to feedback from his wife. Whenever she'd suggest something, he'd take it as criticism. "I know she loves me and means well," he told me at the time, "but my mind says, 'There she goes again, trying to control me,' and I withdraw and get distant. I can see I'm being reactive, but I can't seem to do anything about it."

"What would you need to change inside so that you wouldn't react so quickly?" I'd asked him.

"If I didn't jump to those negative conclusions, I'd probably be much better off. But they're so deeply ingrained that I don't think it's possible to change."

I could see that Daniel had convinced himself of a particular way of looking at himself and his relationship. This was the story he told himself, over and over. Stories of some kind are happening all the time in our mind. They arise from our past experiences, and are reinforced through associations with present experiences. Mostly they go on outside our conscious control. A song from your teenage years comes on the radio, and there you are back at your first kiss. A bird chirping outside your window carries you to some idyllic place in your mind . . . or reminds you that you're stuck behind your desk all day. The reaction is automatic.

Even a single word can activate a stream of associations and emotional responses. Pause for a moment when you read this next word: *Trouble.* Notice if any particular images or memories associated with that word arise. Are there any particular feelings in your body? Maybe tightness or heaviness? Now take a few breaths to erase "trouble" from your mind, and pause when you read this next word: *Kindness.* Any images or associations? How does your body feel? Light or spacious?

If a single word can tangibly affect the mind and body, imagine the effect of the full-blown stories we carry around. Some of our stories are healthy and inspiring and contribute to our well-being. *I deserve to enjoy my life because I'm doing good things in the world, I'm kind to myself and others, and I'm learning to be open to the joy when it arises.* Or you might tell yourself: *Exercising regularly and eating well helps me live up to my full potential.* As we have seen, the more you feed these kinds of positive beliefs and conclusions, the more likely you are to be happy.

It's the negative stories that become a problem. You find yourself in a funk, and you feel compelled to explain why it's happening. There could be lots of reasons, but often the mind goes toward those based in fear or disaster. Patricia Ellsberg talks about how she sometimes wakes up in the night with feelings of free-floating anxiety or sadness. Immediately she wants to figure out why. She says:

> The stories may be different at different times, but they almost always make me feel worse, as I perseverate over why I feel this way or how I can get rid of the feelings. And the more I resist or try to escape from them, the more they persist. Most of the time the bad feelings just go away, especially if I just accept them with kindness. But if I had persisted with the story, I could have been caught in them all day.

The stories that limit you or free you are really all in your mind, and you can change them. I often give students a "prescription" to help in the process. Sometimes I write it down on a piece of paper and suggest they carry it in their wallet. "Whenever you find yourself getting reactive, withdrawn, or confused," I tell them, "remember that you have a prescription in your pocket that will relieve your pain." The prescription I write? "What thought or story am I believing right now?"

That was the prescription I'd given Daniel, all those months ago, when he'd come to see me for that counseling session. He had taken the medicine, and it had worked. "I still get caught," he said, "but when I remember to ask myself what story I'm believing, it makes all the difference in my relationship with Jean. We're getting along better than ever."

## LETTING GO OF STORIES THAT LIMIT US

Some of our most debilitating stories—those that limit our capacity to live full, rich lives—have their roots in our childhood. During our early experiences, we came to conclusions about ourselves and about life, and until we become conscious of these conclusions, they secretly control us. This was so clearly what Marian was caught up in when she came to talk to me during a meditation retreat I was teaching many years ago. I had known Marian for some time, and in all my interactions with her, she'd always seemed cheerful, and I'd sensed a genuine warmth. So I was a little surprised by what she started telling me when she came in for her scheduled interview.

"I know now why I don't feel love, for myself or anyone else," she began. "I've known why for years, and it's about time I just face the fact that that's the way it's going to be."

*Several times a day I've been asking myself that question: 'What story am I believing right now?' especially when my energy is low. For example, is this the story about how I have way too much to do and always feel tired and never get a break? Or is this the story about how I deserve to kick back and relax after a good day's work? Is this the story about how my body isn't perfect and my sister is thinner than I am? Or is this the story about how I've been working out consistently for two years now and actually feel pretty cute in those jeans I like?*

—A COURSE PARTICIPANT

"What do you think the reason is?" I asked, aware of how isolated and alone she must be feeling.

"It's because I was never loved as a child. My parents were not emotionally available, and there was no model for me to learn how to love. So, of course I'm incapable of giving or receiving love as an adult. I think at this point it's too late in my life to change the pattern. That's how I'm wired."

Although I could see Marian was convinced of her story, I didn't buy it. Obviously she wasn't seeing something in herself that others were. And I was sure she had been loved by someone.

*I grew up in a culture where women were supposed to get married and have children. Every morning, I would wake up with a voice in my head that told me I was a woman who had not been chosen. My mum and my sister have said some very indirect unkind things to me around that. This morning, I woke up and answered back. I said, 'That is a story I don't have to believe.' I realized that my mum and sister have been repeating the story that someone told them. I appreciate the freedom of naming it."*

—A COURSE PARTICIPANT

"Was there no one in your life when you were growing up who showed you love?" I asked.

"No one," she sadly replied.

"Marian, perhaps it's true that you've never been loved. If so, I'm terribly sorry. It seems that this belief about your childhood has had a big effect on you for some time." She nodded, sorrow written all over her face. "But before we assume that's so," I continued, "I want you to think back to see if there was *ever anyone* who loved you as a child. Close your eyes and take your time. Think of all the teachers, relatives, friends from your past. Was there anyone from whom you received kindness?"

After about a minute of holding fast to her position, Marian's face started to relax and then brightened into a smile. "Oh my! There was someone," she said sheepishly. "My brother. I never counted him, but he was really always there for me."

"Do you think he loved you?"

She paused; then, speaking slowly, she said, "Now that I think of it, he always stuck up for me and wanted me to be happy. I guess he really did love me."

"Well, I guess you'll have to change the story that you were never loved," I said softly.

With that, Marian began to sob, realizing she could let go of the limiting belief that had kept her from recognizing that she was capable of loving. Fifteen years later she still speaks of that moment as the beginning of seeing herself as the loving person she clearly is. It was also the beginning of a profound transformation toward real well-being and joy in her life.

Recognizing the stories you're caught in is the first and major step in freeing yourself of their power. Building on that insight is what supported Marian in making a real change in her life. You can't just say "abracadabra" and change such deep and long-abiding stories. Therapy, retreats, and other forms of self-exploration all help in changing beliefs and behaviors that undermine our happiness.

## TRYING OUT A NEW STORY

It's true that Marian didn't receive as much love as she deserved or would have liked, but that doesn't have to define who she is nor fuel the belief

---

### Letting Go of Your Story

The negative stories we tell ourselves are a major source of our suffering. Take some time to reflect on and write down responses to the following questions:

- What story do you believe about yourself or others that keeps you from experiencing well-being and joy?
- When you think of this story as being true, how do you experience it in your body and mind?
- Imagine for a moment what it would be like if you took it as just a story, didn't believe it, and could let it go. How does it feel in your body and mind when you do that?

Whenever you find yourself getting caught in an inner struggle, ask yourself, "What story am I believing right now?" You might even write that question on a piece of paper and carry it in your wallet. Pay attention to how you feel each time you let go of the story.

that she *never* received love. In paying attention to misleading beliefs, watch for the words *always* and *never.* Those non-provisional words keep us locked into one perspective. Like the proverbial blind men, each trying to say what an elephant is, based on the one small part they are in touch with, we take one part of our experience and proclaim it to be the whole truth.

While getting a broader perspective on your past doesn't change it, it does allow you to be less controlled by a story that no longer serves you. I discovered this in the midst of a dark time in my early twenties. Lying in my bed in the wee hours of a February morning, I was contemplating the sorry state of my life. Things never worked out for me, it seemed, and people didn't like me—well, certain people . . . namely, *girls.* (That's what we used to call women at that time.) I was listening to my favorite alternative FM radio station, and the soothing voice of deejay John Zacherley began to ease my troubled mind. He was telling me and the rest of his 2:00 AM audience to remember that, even though life is sometimes hard, we're all fortunate to be alive and why not make the best of it while we're here? Then, as if to underscore his point, he followed his words with a cut from the song "You Can All Join In" by the rock group Traffic. It was as if the lyrics were sent to me from above as a healing message:

Make your own life up if you want to
Any old life that you think will do.

Could I really make up "any old life" that I thought would do? What would that look like? And how could I get out of the life I was stuck in? Contemplating my predicament, I picked up a pad of paper and started doodling. I found myself drawing a circle, around and around, and suddenly realized that this was an image of exactly how I was stuck. I was putting out to others the message: *I'm a loser. I'm not likable. You don't want to waste your time with me.* What did I expect would come back to me from that line of thinking? Prom King?

What if I did make a different life? One where I believed things would work out, where girls would like me, where I was lovable and, as the Traffic song went on to say, could make a difference in the lives of others by just being myself? I watched as my hand drew a tangent off that endless circle, moved across the paper, and started an entirely new circle. I began to imagine what it would look and feel like to know I was lovable and that people actually enjoyed being around me. In my mind's eye there was an image of me radiating positive energy, and I could feel the experience completely filling my body. It was a landmark moment.

I made up my mind to try an experiment. For the next week I would project the image of that confident, lovable young man I had just met inside me. I would let go of the story that things wouldn't work out and try a new one. What did I have to lose?

During that week I discovered that exuding confidence and assuming the best would happen made me less preoccupied with wanting

---

## LETTING GO OF THE SOAP OPERA

"One area where we tend to hold on is that of our personal story, the running narrative that tells you who and what you are. We rehearse it and habituate to it as the character we know ourselves to be. We wake up in the morning, and here comes the story, like a long-running soap opera. One of the easy ways to begin letting go is to notice how debilitating it is to be carrying this story, to be obsessed with the wants and desires, the loves and the hates of this character. Simply notice how contracted that story feels, how old and tired it feels.

"One of the ways you let go is to stop paying so much attention to everything that is arising and passing in the mind. Then you start to become more and more interested in just being right here, in the freshness of now. And you start to feel more and more a mystery to yourself. As you stop giving yourself a narrative, you become more and more of a surprise to your own self. You experience yourself as a vibrancy, a floating awareness, sometimes as an emanation of love or curiosity or wonder. This becomes so delightful that it's very easy to become disinterested in all the neurotic material and extraneous thought."

—CATHERINE INGRAM
AT AWAKENING JOY COURSE, BERKELEY, 2008

validation from others; and what's more, I was able to actually be interested in who they were for themselves. This, of course, made them able to
feel more at ease with me and enjoy my presence. Although it would take
lots more work to fully embody this new way of perceiving my life, I had
opened the door of my self-imposed prison.

Once we let go of the limiting stories we've created about ourselves,
a whole new world of possibilities opens to us. The old stories may still
come up from time to time—those constellations of thoughts and beliefs
carry the momentum of years of practice. Even though the stories are
dysfunctional, because they're comfortable in their familiarity, we tend to
hold on to them. But with mindful attention, over time the healthier perspectives can get integrated and lead us in a new direction.

## THE JOY OF GENEROSITY

Generosity is an active form of letting go, and it is a sure avenue to happiness. You're not only giving away something, you're connecting lovingly with others through the act of sharing. The Buddha actually
recommended that when you are in the midst of a generous act, say to
yourself: "I am being generous." This is not to build your ego but rather
to "gladden the heart" as you reflect on the good feeling that accompanies a wholesome action.

Generosity not only releases the hold of the wanting mind, but also
recognizes our interconnectedness. What you share of yourself and your
resources deepens your connection with others. No matter what may
separate you in time and space, the wholesome bond of generosity en-
dures. If you take a look around your house, you are likely to see evidence
of that generosity everywhere. Every time I use the ceramic cups Jane and
I received as wedding gifts, I think of our friends Roger and Frances. And
there are doubtless a number of households where you are present
through what you've given.

One of the best ways to develop a generous heart is by stretching it a
little. Sheryl, a participant in the Awakening Joy course, said that most of
her life she'd thought of herself as stingy, holding back in situations where

she felt something was needed or asked of her. But as she became aware of how small and closed down this was making her feel, she decided to follow a suggestion from the course and see what it would be like to respond by giving when the situation arose.

The big breakthrough in her experiment happened during an appointment she had for a massage. Her massage therapist, Consuela, was supporting her two kids as a single mom and had just returned from Colombia where she was visiting her own mother who was dying of cancer. As she and Sheryl talked, Consuela said she hoped she might get back there in a few months to see her one more time. Sheryl asked if the airfare was expensive.

> Consuela said she wanted to do it anyway, even if she had to put it on a credit card. I thought of all the frequent flyer miles I'd accumulated and decided right in that moment that I wanted to use them to buy her a ticket. I felt so excited to be able to do this. When I told her my idea, she started to cry with gratitude. Doing this has filled me with so much joy. That day ranks up there with some of the best moments of my life. I still feel a fullness in my heart when I remember doing it. I'm seeing how good it feels to give. I love it!

When we give to others—whether a beautiful or useful object, our time, or a word of encouragement—we get at least as much as we give. Jesus said: "Give and it will be given to you; a good measure, pressed down, shaken together, and running over will be poured into your lap" (Luke 6:38). This is a beautiful image of abundance when you imagine the overflowing measure of grain he was talking about. When we give to others, we don't get back an equal amount, we get back in abundance. You may have to let go of certain expectations to receive back in kind— you may give someone beautiful objects, and they may give you back love in other forms. If you look for the joy inside yourself in the act of giving, your reward is already in good measure.

The value of giving is one of the underpinnings of Tibetan culture, in which generosity and happiness are seen as two sides of a single coin. Each winter thousands of Tibetans, in exile from their land, travel to the

village of Bodhgaya, India, to the site where the Buddha attained enlightenment. There they have the opportunity to hear their spiritual leader,
the Dalai Lama, speak specifically to them. Knowing how deeply ingrained the quality of generosity is in these pilgrims, the beggars in this
poorest area of India also converge on the village. I have seen even the
neediest Tibetans there happily stretch to share what they have, more
readily in fact than most of the well-heeled Westerners who visit. A common Buddhist teaching is that if you knew the value of giving, you would
not partake of even a small morsel of food without sharing some of it.
Deeply understanding this, these pilgrims see their generosity not as a
sacrifice but as a source of happiness.

We can consciously develop the quality of generosity. The Buddhist
scriptures speak of three kinds of giving. Step by step, they point the way
to increasing happiness through opening the heart. The first is known as
"beggarly giving." Perhaps you have something in your closet which has
been gathering dust for eons and, after some deliberation, you finally decide to pass it on. Even though it's clearing some space for new clothes,
you still feel a twinge of concern that you might need it some day yourself. The second kind of generosity is called "friendly giving." You have
enough of something you value, or it wouldn't really hurt to let go of
something you enjoy using, so you give it to someone. This giving is
rather fun and easy with no feeling of sacrifice. The most noble generos-

## Feeling Generous

For one week let yourself act on each generous impulse when it arises. Be
aware of the various sensations in your body and the thoughts in your
mind as you take action. When you walk your dog, let yourself feel what
you are giving. When you open the door for someone, feel the whole-
someness of the impulse. If any limiting thoughts arise, just mindfully notice them without judgment. Breathe into your heart and let go to the
spirit of generosity. Pay attention to the good feelings that accompany
contributing to the well-being of another. Feel the joy of generosity.

ity is called "kingly or queenly giving." You give what you prize highly, even if it's a sacrifice on your part. It's the kind of generosity I've seen in some cultures when I've traveled. I learned quickly not to admire objects or articles of clothing, because no matter how poor the owner, I was likely to be the immediate recipient.

In practicing generosity, the teachings suggest starting wherever you are on this continuum. If you're cleaning out your closet to give things to Goodwill, and you're berating yourself for being a "beggarly giver," you can instead tune in to the positive feeling of sharing something someone else might need. If you are obligated to volunteer time at your kids' school, even if it's a burden, perhaps you can discover the moments when you do feel good about what you're contributing. Little by little, as you focus on how good it feels to give, you reinforce and strengthen the power of generosity. Remember, however, to be kind to yourself and give in ways appropriate to your resources.

### Receiving Generously

Be sure to include yourself in your generosity practice. If you feel too depleted to be generous with others, take that as a cue to take time to nourish yourself. Whenever anyone is generous or thoughtful with you, receive their kindness fully and graciously. When you know yourself how good it feels to be generous, you can remember that by receiving you're allowing that other person to experience the joy of giving.

## GIVING TO LIFE

The Buddha had a number of wealthy patrons who were earnest spiritual seekers. One of them, Anathapindika, listened carefully as the great teacher taught his monks about the virtues of letting go of attachment to worldly goods. Moved by this idea yet puzzled, the rich man went to the

Buddha and asked if he should give up all his wealth, renounce the world, and become a monk. The Buddha replied, "A person who possesses riches and uses them wisely is a blessing to humanity," encouraging Anatha-pindika to honor his own destiny. You don't have to give away all your material wealth in order to be generous. You can use it in such a way that you become a channel for good. The Gates Foundation has done a tremendous amount of good, primarily by enhancing health and educa-tion around the world. If Bill and Melinda had decided to become monks, all that good might not have happened.

Whether we have great material wealth or very little, we all have per-sonal wealth beyond material goods. Psychologist Martin Seligman makes the point that true happiness comes from understanding our strengths and sharing them with the world. He refers to traits such as en-thusiasm, diligence, leadership as "signature strengths" we can offer.

Whatever talents or skills we have, sharing them is an important form of generosity—and one that requires letting go of the false stories that may hold us back. As Marianne Williamson so aptly puts it in her book *A Return to Love:*

> We ask ourselves, Who am I to be brilliant, gorgeous, talented, fab-ulous? Actually, who are you *not* to be? You are a child of God. Your playing small does not serve the world.

Sharing any of our gifts is a form of generosity that multiplies beyond what we might even imagine. Williamson sums it up: "As we are liberated from our own fear, our presence automatically liberates others."

When you let go of all the ifs, ands, and buts that keep you from doing what you're called to do, you can step into the joy of giving freely of what you have to offer from your own unique resources. In this way, as the Buddhist sage Shantideva says, you can be "lifted above poverty into the wealth of giving to life."

As we've seen, there are many dimensions of letting go that lead to a joyful heart. Letting go is a shift toward simplicity, uncomplicating our mental and physical environment—releasing what we don't truly need, like material stuff, crowded schedules, expectations, stories that don't serve us. Experiencing this letting go, this cleaning out, brings a great sense of well-being. We see how good it feels not only to put down the extra burden but to share what we have. Letting go is like weeding. When you get rid of the weeds, it makes room for more of the beauty to be seen and enjoyed. In the same way, when we let go of our extra stuff—whether material or mental clutter—it gives space for our creativity and full potential to flower.

## LET IT GO

Let go of the ways you thought life would unfold;
the holding of plans or dreams or expectations—Let it all go.
Save your strength to swim with the tide.
The choice to fight what is here before you now
will only result in struggle, fear, and desperate attempts to flee
from the very energy you long for. Let it go.

Let it all go and flow with the grace
that washes through your days
whether you receive it gently
or with all your quills raised to defend against invaders.
Take this on faith: The mind may never find
the explanations that it seeks,
but you will move forward nonetheless.

Let go, and the wave's crest
will carry you to unknown shores,
beyond your wildest dreams or destinations.
Let it all go and find the place of rest and peace,
and certain transformation.

—DANNA FAULDS,
from *Go In and In*

# THE SWEETNESS OF
# LOVING OURSELVES

*Searching all directions with one's awareness,*

*one finds no one dearer than oneself.*

—The Buddha
*The Raja Sutta*

*When I was a child,* a strange fantasy troubled me from time to time. I imagined myself before birth, along with countless souls on rows of shelves, waiting to be selected for life on Earth. A giant hand—of God or His right-hand assistant—was reaching out for the soul next to me but by mistake plucked me up instead. So I was the ultimate fraud, not meant to be here at all, making it only by accident. Each time this image arose, I was left haunted by the feeling that I would be found out and sent back.

Although I grew up in a loving home, inside I often felt lonely and afraid. Being the quiet one in a family of extroverts didn't help calm my fears. My sister was very pretty with a sparkling personality and wit that lit up a room. By contrast, I was chubby, wore glasses, and was shy and insecure. A familiar childhood memory is of watching my father, mother, and sister all boisterously engaged in witty repartee. Many a time, I would quietly mumble a contribution to the conversation, no one would seem to notice, and I would retreat into the bathroom in tears, wondering why no one listened to me.

As a teenager I had such a poor self-image that I actually winced when I looked in the mirror. Adults called me "cute," which was the last thing I wanted to hear. My sister kindly tried to assure me that I'd be fine and well-liked, but I wasn't convinced. No matter how much positive feedback I received from others, fear of being exposed as "not good enough" remained a familiar companion into my early adulthood. I felt like a loser with no chance of turning into the hip guy I dreamed of being. In short, I didn't like myself. If somebody had told me it was possible to truly love myself, I wouldn't have believed it.

In my experience of working with thousands of students and clients, rarely have I encountered those who easily love themselves. Most commonly I hear: "If only I were . . . " followed by some variation of "thinner, stronger, kinder, smarter, calmer, more successful." Our assessment of ourselves is usually in comparison to others or to some ideal or standard we've adopted. If we have curly hair, we want straight; blue eyes, we want brown. If we tend to be quiet, we wish we were the life of the party. If we have a short fuse, we're convinced we'd be lovable if only we were calm and patient. On top of assessing ourselves as falling short, we add yet another layer of suffering. We close our heart to ourselves. This is the predicament we're often stuck in: We resist accepting ourselves as we are, yet this is what we've got. We can't be somebody else, no matter how hard we try.

In my early years of teaching meditation, giving talks alongside some of the wisest and most gifted teachers left me wracked with painful comparisons. Joseph Goldstein would inspire the students with depth, wisdom, and clarity. Then Jack Kornfield would weave his magic spell, enchanting and moving them with poignant stories and stirring words. Sharon Salzberg would bring them to tears with her guided lovingkindness meditations. Then it would be my turn. I knew full well that if I was a student, I would be wishing this kid would get off the stage so that the senior teachers could speak again.

In desperation I tracked down my sometime-mentor Ram Dass to see if he had any advice. He did. "Don't try to be another Joseph Goldstein," he said. "There already is one. Just be the best Jamie Baraz you can be. There's only one of those, and you're it. What if you just let yourself be who you are and see what you have to offer those students? Who knows? You may even like what you see."

There's only one of *you,* and if you let yourself be the best one of yourself possible, you may also like what you see. In time you may even love yourself.

For many of us, the idea of loving ourselves may seem out of reach. But if you know how to love someone else, you have what it takes to love yourself. Think about what it's like to love someone. For instance, when I think of our son Adam my heart naturally begins to open. I become aware of that distinct combination of traits I sense as his essence—his insatiable curiosity about how the mind works, his mischievous spirit, the "edge" as he calls it that is a counterbalance to his tenderness, his charming personality, the genuine goodness that radiates from his heart. Even the quirky traits that sometimes drive me crazy can seem endearing when I hold them in the broader context of his goodness and potential. If I were to focus only on the negative, I would lose touch with all the amazingly good stuff. My love for him is there no matter what. The secret is to offer this same kind of love to ourselves—to love and accept the whole package.

The capacity to accept and love ourselves doesn't necessarily happen

## You're the One

Imagine meeting someone who laughs at all your jokes, has similar tastes, and really grasps your take on things. This person understands all your hopes and fears. In short, this is someone who really *gets you.* How would you feel? Probably ecstatic! There is only one person in this world who completely fits that description, and he or she is right inside your own skin. This is someone you can learn to love.

quickly or easily. Those negative voices from siblings, teachers, sixth-grade bullies, and disenchanted lovers still play in our mind. No matter how much positive reflection we've had, our brains are "like Velcro for negative experiences," as Rick Hanson puts it. Even seemingly insignificant events can leave deep impressions that color our self-concept and our ability to embrace who we are.

Learning to love yourself is a process that evolves over time. It begins with letting go of self-criticism and forgiving yourself for being who you are. In Step Five, we looked at forgiving ourselves for past actions and the confusion that produced them. Here we are forgiving ourselves for habits and behaviors we continue to get caught in that are less than wholesome. We forgive our bodies for how they look or for how they function; forgive our minds for being scattered or not being smart enough; forgive our personalities for not being witty or interesting enough.

As you stop focusing on what you don't appreciate and start seeing yourself as a unique, mysterious, changing being, you allow your best self to shine through. And the joy of that radiates out to the world.

## CATCHING LOVE

Meher Baba, the great Indian master, says, "Love is essentially self-communicative; those who do not have it catch it from those who have it." Our capacity to love is awakened in us through having received love from others. Even if we're convinced we've never known the experience of love, as Marian in the previous chapter believed, for very few of us is that true. Most of us—even those who had to build personal defenses in order to survive fearful circumstances in childhood—somewhere along the way received love from someone, whether that was a parent, a caring teacher, a kind relative, or a loyal pet. But until we are willing to recognize and accept that love, we block our capacity to give it to ourselves.

For me, a turning point in my ability to "catch love," and really take it in, happened during one of those "experiences" common in the sixties. I was in my apartment in Flushing, New York, and it was 1969, the height of the psychedelic revolution. Like so many in that era, I was seeking change, release from the pain of being me. I longed to belong to something bigger, something filled with love and joy, and the social-spiritual revolution of the counterculture gave me hope. In that era, before meditation and other more grounded ways to explore the mind had entered our culture, chemistry seemed to hold the key to what I was looking for. One evening, without a great deal of thought or preparation, I "dropped acid," eager to find out where it would take me. Unfortunately, that was to the brink of hell. While this experience was a turning point in my life, I would say it was a dicey strategy for transformation. Compared to others I know, I was very lucky. I managed to return from hell—but I didn't do it alone, and that opened me to an important revelation.

That night I wouldn't have been able to put my private nightmare into words, but looking back I remember that everything—inside and outside—was spinning around so fast that there was no ground anywhere. I was in uncharted territory with no guidance or wisdom to draw upon. I felt like I was teetering on the edge of the Void, about to be overwhelmed by something horrifying and incomprehensible. I knew I was about to lose my mind. When people talk about "abject terror," I can honestly say I know what that is like.

Not knowing if anyone could hear me, I started screaming for help, and my roommate and his girlfriend, who were in the next room, arrived as my saviors. Taking my hands, they sat on either side of me for what felt like an eternity.

"Don't leave me! Don't leave me!" I'd cry out from time to time.

"It's okay. We aren't going anywhere," they'd tell me again and again.

As they kept assuring me that they were present and would stay, something unfamiliar began to happen inside me: I let myself gradually open to their caring and attention. Instead of feeling awkward and unworthy, I let myself take in the warmth and support they were offering. At some point the thought occurred to me that here were two people I knew and respected, taking their time to be with me. At that, something switched inside me, the resistance stopped, and the love and connection began to feel natural. Even more remarkable, I stopped feeling like I didn't deserve it—a radical turnaround for me.

The next day, after the impact of the drug had worn off, I was faced with a sobering but delightful insight: For the first time in my life I directly questioned my belief that something was wrong with me and that I was unlovable. If that was true, then how could these friends have cared so much?

Taking in the love of my friends actually awakened a little love inside me for myself. Later that day when I passed by the hallway mirror, I stopped to take a look at the person reflected there. I still wasn't exactly thrilled at what I saw, but something was different in the way I was reacting to that image. A tiny smile seemed to hold the faint message that maybe I wasn't so bad after all. Maybe there was something there to at least *like* a little bit. That was the beginning.

## SHIFTING THE FOCUS

All of us can find something in ourselves to at least *like,* but it may be a long step from like to love. What's the difference and how do we take that step? Over the course of a few years I've watched a young woman, Alexa, gradually make that shift. I first met her when she came in for a scheduled interview during a meditation retreat. I was immediately struck by her vitality and sparkle. When Alexa told me she'd been in theater, I could easily imagine her feeling at home in the limelight. I had no idea, at the time, of the pain that accompanied her enjoyment of being on stage. As Alexa continued working with me as her meditation teacher and spiritual counselor, I came to understand how deeply self-judgment had penetrated her life.

Over the next few years, as part of her healing process, Alexa kept a journal and eventually wrote a thesis for her master's degree tracking her journey. There she reflected:

> I'm realizing that all my life I've compared myself to everyone else. Fatter, prettier, smarter, more creative, less intuitive, the list goes on and on. I have hated myself so much that I've clung to make-believe personas and addictive substances and behaviors. Anything to avoid the depths of my self-hatred. . . .

Alexa told me she hadn't always felt that way. Until she was seven years old, her childhood had been "silly and sacred." But when her parents divorced, she was left with "an emptiness I couldn't name. I began to do what most people in our culture do. I began to search for ways to fill the empty void." Part of that meant turning to food for comfort, which didn't really work.

"I began to view my body as my enemy," Alexa wrote in her journals, "and as the years leading up to high school went on, my self-loathing worsened." Unless she weighed one hundred pounds and looked like a Calvin Klein model, she hated her body. Unless she got top grades in classes, she concluded she wasn't smart enough. Less than the starring role in a play must mean she wasn't talented. By the end of her freshman year in high school, Alexa was so stressed and felt like such a failure that she began to binge and purge, and starve herself. Always a litany of self-judgment ran through her mind: *I hate my stomach, I'm too aggressive, I'm always depressed, I loathe myself.*

You might not feel as self-deprecating as Alexa, but perhaps you have your own litany of perceived shortcomings. Maybe you feel shame at how impatient you are with your partner or child. Or your face is covered with acne. Or the brilliance of a friend or colleague leaves you feeling worthless in comparison. From there you can easily build up a case against yourself and end up, like Alexa, focusing only on what's wrong.

The good news is: We don't have to like everything about ourselves in order to love ourselves. Ajahn Sumedho, the American who became a monk in Thailand, says that as you learn to love yourself, you don't have to "pretend to feel approval towards your faults." You just don't want to "dwell in aversion to them." Instead of getting caught up in judgment and self-hatred, which only feeds a negative state of mind, you can begin by shifting your focus to more positive ways of regarding yourself. For Alexa that kind of shift was the beginning of opening to let the love in.

As the retreat went on, one morning Alexa came in for an interview, looking dejected and hopeless. "I know I'm supposed to be practicing kindness toward myself," she began, "but I just can't pretend I love my body. I don't. I wish it were different. And I feel so stupid that I just can't get past that."

I knew that feeling very well myself and the prison she felt locked in.

"Alexa," I said softly, "you don't have to pretend anything, but if you focus only on what you don't like, you cut yourself off from seeing all the beauty and goodness that are also part of you."

I shared with her one of my favorite stories that my colleague Jack Kornfield likes to tell. The Babemba people in southern Africa have an approach to dealing with the personal shortcomings of tribal members. When someone acts recklessly, he or she is brought before all the villagers. Everyone stops working and gathers around for a ceremony that can typically go on for days. As Jack tells it in his book *The Art of Forgiveness:*

> Then each person in the tribe speaks to the accused, one at a time, each recalling the good things the person in the center of the circle has done in his lifetime. Every incident, every experience that can be recalled with any detail and accuracy, is recounted. All his positive attributes, good deeds, strengths, and kindnesses are recited carefully and at length.

When the ceremony has ended, everyone celebrates and embraces the person as once again part of the tribe.

When I finished with the story, Alexa remained silent and thoughtful. After a few moments, I said, "What if you were to do some version of that for yourself and shift the focus to all the good things there are to appreciate about yourself?"

I asked her to close her eyes and let an image come to mind of herself just as she is.

"Now let yourself be one of those villagers and tell Alexa all the good things she has done in her brief lifetime. And tell her about all the good qualities you see in her." After a few minutes I could see a tenderness come over Alexa's face. Tears flowed down her cheeks as she spoke.

"She's so sweet, and she just wants to see everyone happy. She's kind, and she's creative."

"Let yourself take in those good feelings, and when those thoughts of hating your body arise, see if you can shift the focus just a tiny bit. As you

## GIVING GENUINE AND EFFECTIVE APPRECIATION

"Saying to yourself, 'You're wonderful. You're great,' may not be the most effective way of loving yourself. A little voice inside says: 'Not always,' and underneath there's a gnawing feeling that you'll get found out. Effectively appreciating yourself is about acknowledging the specifics of *how* you are great. The more specific you can be about what you appreciate, the more you get in touch with the gifts you have to offer others and the resources you have to tackle challenges.

"In her book *Mindset*, Stanford University psychologist Carol Dweck talks about what she calls a 'growth mindset' in contrast to a 'fixed mindset.' When we say, 'I'm so great and wonderful,' we are encouraging a fixed mindset, which means we believe we're supposed to know it all already. Therefore we give up easily when faced with a challenge. We avoid negative criticism that might be helpful. We negatively compare ourselves to others. When we hear about amazing people doing amazing things, we feel worse. We end up looking at what's wrong with ourselves instead of what we appreciate.

"With a growth mindset, when you're faced with a challenge, you say to yourself, 'I'm still learning. I may not do this perfectly, but I'm learning how to do it.' When we hear criticism, we say, 'Thanks for letting me know, because I can get better based on what you're telling me.' We're inspired by people who are doing great things, 'because they're giving me something to go toward. I can try to do that too.' As a result, people with a growth mindset tend to reach more of their potential.

"If you want to appreciate yourself, or encourage others to appreciate themselves, this is what you can do: *Praise efforts, choices, and strategies,* and do it with specifics. When you do this, you're telling the brain: 'Do more of this. This is important, remember this in the future.' You're learning a lot of strategies in the Awakening Joy course. Whenever you use one of them, appreciate yourself, remind your brain, so you can continue to choose good strategies in the future."

—M. J. RYAN, AUTHOR OF *ATTITUDES OF GRATITUDE*
AT AWAKENING JOY COURSE, BERKELEY, 2008

practice this perspective, you might begin to see this person as worthy of your love."

Even the tiniest opening of seeing the goodness in ourselves can begin to break through a lifetime of self-judgment. By inclining our mind toward looking for what is good and wholesome in us, we stop feeding the negative and start bringing our positive qualities to life. As we do this, we cultivate a new way of regarding ourselves, so that over time the old voices inside that belittle us are replaced by others that are kind and supportive.

## PLANTING SEEDS OF LOVE
## FOR OURSELVES

One of the participants in the online Awakening Joy course wrote: "What I truly want to feel is the love of a holy person, like Dipa Ma, a love so vast it can forgive and embrace every storm everywhere." Dipa Ma was a simple and renowned meditator and spiritual teacher living in Calcutta. She radiated such a powerful field of compassion that in her presence one did feel loved without limit. But this great teacher herself would say that

### Seeing What You Like

Spend a little time in front of a mirror, looking deeply at the image you see reflected there. Notice any judgments or habitual reactions that may arise. Instead of believing or feeding them, just acknowledge them and let them go. In a heartfelt way, say aloud or to yourself at least three specific good qualities you know you have. For instance you might say, "You really care about others" or "You're a terrific dancer." Don't try too hard. Even a glimpse of self-appreciation is a good start. As you acknowledge your positive attributes, notice the feelings that arise in your body and mind. Be sure to pause and take them in.

we are all capable of such love. If we are to be the ones to give this kind of love to ourselves, rather than waiting for someone else to come along and do it, how do we begin?

As Dipa Ma taught, the capacity to love that is inherent in every one of us can be awakened and developed through the practice of lovingkindness or *metta,* which refers to a state of mind that radiates kindness, wishing well without wanting anything in return. It helps you awaken love when you're not feeling it, and deepen and amplify it when you are. We begin with ourselves and continue opening our hearts to eventually include all beings. Traditionally, the practice is done in meditation, directing loving thoughts to ourselves or others by silently repeating certain phrases. Typical phrases for sending lovingkindness to ourselves include: *May I be happy, May I be peaceful, May I live with ease.* Each time we say these words, we are planting seeds that will eventually blossom into love.

> *"[M]etta . . . is defined as the strong wish for the welfare and happiness of others. This isn't exclusively a Buddhist concept; in Christianity, the term for this kind of unconditional love is* agape. *In Judaism,* rachamim *is the love that motivates us to give to others and includes empathy and care. This same ideal of love is expressed in Islam with the word* mahabba, *which means spiritual love for others and the divine."*
> —MARCI SHIMOFF WITH CAROL KLINE, FROM *HAPPY FOR NO REASON*

When I first learned lovingkindness practice, I was taught that, in addition to repeating the phrases, it's helpful to engage the imagination in relevant ways. As you say a phrase such as *May I be happy,* you might visualize an image of yourself with a glowing heart. With *May I be peaceful,* you might imagine yourself on a hike in nature or relaxing on a sunny afternoon. As each image arises, I imagine that the thoughts and feelings linked with the words I'm saying are being splashed over that particular image of myself. Whenever a strong feeling of genuine well-being arises, let yourself sink into that feeling. Take in the love you are offering yourself.

The more fully we can embrace the meaning of these simple good wishes, the more effective they are. When we open and take in the good wishes we are offering to ourselves, the transformation can be profound. At Awakening Joy courses, I introduce participants to lovingkindness practice by gently speaking various phrases, encouraging them to repeat the words to themselves, and to feel and take in the meaning. After one class, Sandy sent me a note relating what had happened to her during that simple meditation:

> As the phrases were spoken, I let myself deeply feel each one. There was no analysis, no thinking about it, just a simple nurturing message I was giving to myself. A strong sense of compassion for myself arose, and then compassion for others. Since that time, whenever I say the words to myself, which I often do, I feel the same nurturing, compassionate, and happy feelings, like a warmth throughout my being. The experience that one night has changed my life.

## JUST BE AS YOU ARE

The practice of lovingkindness is often preceded by self-forgiveness. This helps clear anything that might block warm feelings we could have for ourselves. When I ask participants at a course what they need to forgive themselves for, I receive lots of responses. People seem to readily know their faults. Good thing this is asked in the context of learning to love themselves! Some of the responses include:

- Being unkind to myself in those moments when I most need kindness.
- Chickening out sometimes, giving up before I start.
- Being so opinionated.
- Blowing up at others.
- Stuffing my emotions with food.
- Making bad choices.
- Not being perfect or even good enough.

It's striking to see how often that last one comes up. The tendency to perfectionism is merciless, but forgiveness allows us to let go of any ideal standard we measure ourselves against. You can't be anyone other than who you are right at this moment, and that's where you have to start if you want to forgive and love yourself. On my Really Awful Deeds retreat, that realization that all of us are doing the best we can showed me what a huge misunderstanding this drive to perfection is. If any of us could have grown into different people, "more perfect" human beings, we would have.

Back in seventh-century China, the Third Zen Patriarch said that to live "without anxiety about non-perfection" is the key to genuine happiness. We don't have to get rid of our shortcomings before we love ourselves. Seeing non-perfection as part of our shared humanity, we don't have to take our flaws so personally, although we can take them as a gift to learn from. While granting ourselves forgiveness takes patience, as we practice lovingkindness, we plant the seeds that will flower in their own time.

Forgive yourself.
Now is the only time you have to be whole. Now is the sole moment that exists to live in the light of your true Self. Perfection is not a prerequisite for anything but pain. Please, oh please, don't continue to believe in your disbelief. This is the day of your awakening.

—DANNA FAULDS,
excerpt of "Awakening Now,"
from Go In and In

Embracing the totality of who we are means having compassion for our difficult-to-accept aspects. What we're doing is pulling out the second dart talked about in Step Four: When we're angry, not getting angry at our anger; when we're afraid, not being afraid of our fear; when we're jealous or petty, not getting caught up in condemning ourselves. Of course you'll make mistakes, but you don't have to throw out the baby with the bathwater. With understanding and compassion, let yourself be just as you are. Forgive yourself as you'd forgive someone else who is trying to do the best they can.

## THROUGH THE EYES OF LOVE

Although opening up to receive my friends' love many years before was a major milestone, its main effect had been to diminish my self-judgment. As important as that was, it was just the beginning. It's one thing to not beat yourself up; it's quite another to truly delight in who you are, and I still had a ways to go. The door to self-love had opened a crack, and eventually I would find the way to throw it open wide.

Once again the significant change happened on a silent retreat, this one focused specifically on the practice of lovingkindness. Hour after hour I sat in the stillness of my room earnestly following the instructions, beginning with sending caring wishes to myself: *May I be safe from harm. May I be happy. May I be healthy. May I have inner peace.* I knew that days later we would be moving on to sending thoughts of lovingkindness to others, and this would be the foundation.

After three days of continued repetition of the lovingkindness phrases, I had to admit that I was experiencing a kindly self-acceptance and friendly appreciation for myself . . . but nothing more. "Well," I thought, "as the Supremes sing, 'You can't hurry love.' " Though I noticed a slight frustration over the lack of juice, I trusted that with each phrase I was planting the seeds of lovingkindness for myself, and that they would eventually bloom. What I didn't know was that those days of mechanical repetition had led me to the doorway I was looking for—and it was right around the corner.

As I sat there, the fall sunlight making its way through the leaves into my room, I found myself musing about the fact that others often can find us lovable far more readily than we ourselves can. *If only we could see what others see,* I thought to myself, *it would be so much easier to love ourselves.* I decided to try an experiment: *What would I see if I tried looking at myself through someone else's eyes?*

*Who really loves me?* I asked myself. Immediately the image came to mind of a certain friend whose love for me was strong and never in doubt. I could see his smile of delight as he beheld me, and feel his open heart beam me with affection. As I took in that love, I began to experience a buoyancy and uplifting in my own heart.

Continuing the experiment, I asked: *Why does he feel that way about me? What exactly* does *he see?* I imagined being him and looking at myself from his perspective. Without any effort, I became aware of the kindness that so wants to be there for others, the playful spirit that loves to sing and have fun, the good heart that enjoys seeing others shine, the years of earnest and sincere spiritual practice. Without any squirming or pretending, I took some time to drink myself in, to really "get" what my friend was seeing.

*May you learn to see yourself with the same delight, pride, and expectation with which God sees you in every moment."*
—FATHER JOHN O'DONOHUE

Intellectually I knew those things about myself; the particulars were not surprising. But as I saw myself through my friend's eyes, there were none of the "yes . . . buts" that I would typically throw at myself. All at once I got the essence of *who I am.* The unique expression of "Jamesness" became apparent to me in a way that it never had before. I wasn't just a collection of good qualities and "yes . . . buts"; the whole was greater than the sum of its parts. And I began to understand and see for myself that James, this person my friend was looking at, was enough—more than enough just as I was. It was a moment of genuine and deep self-love, completing the circuit of an impulse that had been set in motion that fateful night twenty-seven years before when I'd finally opened up and let in the love of my friends.

I could also see and understand that loving myself in this way wasn't being on an ego trip. While I had made certain choices that allowed me to develop ways of being that I appreciated, I couldn't take credit for the raw material. Essentially "being James" was something that had happened as a natural unfolding of life. I had broken through self-assessment and understood the beauty and wonder of my true nature, the same true nature that is the essence of everyone. Each of us is a unique and beautiful expression of creation. Huang Po, a ninth-century Zen sage, said that "in a flash" it's possible to comprehend what and who you are, and it is so much bigger than what you might have expected.

Staying in contact with the qualities I had seen through my friend's eyes, I let my consciousness slowly move back inside me. Now those hours of planting seeds of love were bearing fruit, and a sweet loving energy fueled the phrases as I said them. I was sincerely sending myself kind thoughts of well-wishing, and at last feeling fully deserving of them.

Oliver Wendell Holmes wrote, "A mind stretched by a new idea does not shrink back to its original dimensions." Something shifted that day which has remained ever since. For years I had been looking for love and fulfillment outside myself—loving others, looking for love from others. I now understood that no matter how much love came to me from "out there," until I could truly love myself, I couldn't really take it in.

In the Awakening Joy courses, I invite participants to do the same exercise I did on the retreat. Just the process of recognizing a few of their good qualities is challenging for some people, but the real stretch happens when I then ask them to turn to one of their neighbors and share aloud those good things they saw. At first there is a lot of discomfort. Many people squirm at the thought of saying such positive things about themselves to another. After a few minutes, though, the room begins to light up with enthusiasm.

### Seeing Yourself with Love

Bring to mind someone who genuinely loves you. Imagine yourself as that person, and look at yourself through his or her eyes. What qualities do you see in yourself from that perspective? Pause a few moments to fully take in what you see.

Now shift your perspective back and feel what it is like for you to have those qualities. Appreciate them, delight in them. Write them down in your Joy Journal and share them with your Joy Buddy or with a trusted friend. For one week remind yourself each morning of the qualities you saw in yourself through loving eyes.

## THE TAPESTRY OF OUR LIFE

After that transformative experience, I had to reorient the way I thought of myself. Instead of my self-concept being "I am flawed and there's some good stuff in me," I knew instead that "I am good and there are some flaws." In time, this warm and tender love would also learn to hold, as we hold a suffering child, those aspects of myself that are harder to accept.

All those little blips of "what's wrong with us" can so easily get magnified into what seem like glaring faults. They suck all the oxygen out of the room of our psyche, and we come to believe that's who we are. By seeing yourself through the eyes of love, all the "buts" become like little clouds passing through a vast sky.

Embracing the totality of who we are is not about loving only our goodness and disregarding the rest. And it's not about being fond of just that part of us that is always sweet and kind. True love comes whole and unconditional. Loving the whole package means leaving nothing out. Unless we can do that, our love and joy are compromised. You might think, "I love 85 percent of myself, but if only I could somehow get rid of that other 15 percent." That thought keeps a lid on your joy. The love that embraces the whole package encompasses both compassion for the confused parts and love for the goodness.

An image from the brilliant PBS nature series *Planet Earth* sticks in my mind as an apt metaphor for the naturalness and perfection of all aspects of ourselves. The scene features a watering hole on a vast African plain. At various times we see the approach of giraffes, antelope, zebras, elephants, wildebeests, lions—some prey, some predators—all of them bound together by one simple fact, the need for water. Within each species are mothers and fathers, babies and the elderly. Watching them, I realized how it would make no sense to say, "Too bad that antelope is not a zebra," or "If only that giraffe were taller it would look better," or "That elephant is too old, it would be more beautiful if it were younger." Each animal comes to the watering hole with its own distinctive character and life.

Endless variation is part of the way life expresses itself. All of us, as human beings, are part of a vast and changing movement that is greater than any one of us. Just as sickness and death, volcanoes and earthquakes are part of what we might call the overall perfection of life, our confusion and ignorance are part of the totality of what it means to be alive. To feel wrong, bad, or not worthy of love because you're an elephant and not a giraffe is to see reality from a limited perspective. Even the tiger that attacks and eats the gazelle at the watering hole is not bad or wrong but simply part of the whole process, part of the way things are.

In the Eastern philosophy of Taoism, everything is part of the tapestry of life. And that includes you with all the unique qualities that make up who you are. Our tendency to believe that we, among all the other "elephants and giraffes," have something wrong with us and aren't good enough is—to borrow a phrase from Albert Einstein—"an optical delusion of consciousness."

## TAKING GOOD CARE

In saying good-bye to someone we love, we often use the phrase "Take good care." This phrase holds a clue to cultivating love for ourselves. Love is taking good care—of your body and your mind, nourishing them with healthy foods, kind and effective healing methods, enough exercise, adequate rest and quiet time, creative self-expression and play. But the key to awakening joy is *how* we do that.

Loving ourselves by taking care of ourselves doesn't necessarily mean we always feel a lot of love while we're doing what we have to do. A devoted parent isn't deliriously happy about working long hours, shopping, cooking, cleaning, driving, supporting, and helping in all the countless ways necessary to raise a family. If the actions are done with resentment, they can leave everyone feeling confused, closed down, and disconnected. Remembering, even for a moment, that you're doing all these things because you love that child opens the way for joy.

The same is true when caring for yourself. Doing it out of love instead of obligation has immediate benefits. Before I go to the gym to work out, a little voice inside sometimes (or often!) says: *Do you really want to do this? Why not kick back and take it easy?* At that point I can either force myself to go and get onto the weight machines because "it's good for me," or I can remember that I'm doing it because I love and appreciate my body. One way can make me feel a bit resentful, at least until the endorphins kick in. The other can open my heart to make room for even a little glimmer of joy. When you take care of yourself out of love, your love for yourself increases.

When I ask participants in the Awakening Joy course what it feels like to be kind to themselves, their answers include:

• Relaxed and contented.
• Spacious and light.
• Grounded.
• A welling up of joy in my chest, sometimes tears of joy.
• Like I'm in the key of C.
• Like I'm holding a baby in my arms—me!

You can bring this kind of tenderness and harmony into your own life by paying attention to what you need in order to really nourish yourself, and letting yourself have that—even if it means getting over that little hump of resistance and going down to the gym to work out. Pay attention to how good you feel when you're done, and acknowledge yourself for taking good care.

## SPEAKING KINDLY TO YOURSELF

Alexa's struggle to move from self-hatred to self-love went on for several years. One day she came to me to ask how it could be possible to treat yourself kindly when you see so much wrong. Where do you start?

"I'll share with you one of my practices, one I did for nearly two years," I answered, hoping to assure her that she wasn't the only one who felt that way. I asked her to close her eyes and let one of the negative thoughts she had about her body come to mind.

"Not hard to do," she answered with a wry smile.

"Now place your hand on your cheek and gently caress it as if that hand belonged to the kindest grandmother, or some other wise and compassionate being. Silently say to yourself in the most tender voice possible, 'That's okay, dear. It's just a judging thought.' "

Though Alexa was at first skeptical and resistant, after giving it a try, she began to let herself feel the kindness coming through her hand. As it melted her frustration, compassion arose, and with it tears filled her eyes.

We all long for kindness and care, and we are the ones who can give that to ourselves at any and every moment. Cathleen, a course participant, said she was learning to pay attention to herself in the same way she is used to paying attention to other people. "That means I let myself notice the little thoughts and feelings I might have about something I need and take them seriously rather than dismissing them," she wrote. As Cathleen recognized, being kind to ourselves includes not condemning ourselves for the feelings that arise. It doesn't make sense

*I'm finding myself naturally slowing down and seeing that I'm easily present, because I'm not on 'high alert.' My pace walking down the street to work is slower; I drive at a more relaxed pace, meaning with the flow of traffic and leaving plenty of distance between vehicles instead of rushing up on the car in front of me. Even my cardio workouts are done with an ease that is independent of the actual pace/speed I'm running. Now that I think about it, being kind to myself actually is a reduction of internal violence. Stress and tension are a form of self-inflicted harm."*

—A COURSE PARTICIPANT

to say, "I shouldn't be feeling what I'm feeling." Feelings arise in response to a complex of conditions. You don't say, "I could go for some fear right now" or, "How about a little self-hatred for a minute?" It's not like you have a choice about what pops into your mind. But you do have a choice as to how you *respond* to the fear or self-hatred when they're present. And that's where you can either deepen your suffering with self-criticism or hold the suffering kindly.

As discussed in the guideline for wise speech in Step Five, speaking kindly to yourself is one of the most important ways to bring more joy into your life. A dear friend of mine often exclaims, "Oh, I'm so stupid!" when she makes a mistake. Every time I hear it, I cringe at how painful that must be for her. Learning to recognize the harsh voice of judgment inside your head, and in its place cultivating the gentle voice of compassion and support, can help you stay in touch with what you need in order to love and care for yourself.

## LISTENING TO YOUR HEART

Jill said that when she began bringing a kind attention to herself as if she were a beloved child, her life began to change. One Saturday she awoke ready to do her normal routine: "a very full day of shopping and cleaning and working." As she was stretching out her breakfast with a final cup of tea, something inside called her to stop and take a bit more time that day to connect with herself. To her surprise when she just let herself relax and listen to her heart, a message came through loud and clear. Instead of doing a list of chores, she wanted to visit the Humane Society. For seven years Jill had been considering adopting a dog. That day she realized that being kind enough to herself to stop and listen opened her to a new, more joyous phase of her life.

> I needed that permission and "free" time to realize I could have something I wanted sooner rather than later. I could choose the happiness of living with a dog, instead of the more familiar belief that getting happiness takes a long time, and maybe I'm not ready enough or worthy enough to have it right now. Making that choice was a way of taking care of myself that has brought me tremendous joy.

An important way of caring for yourself that can get overlooked is developing your unique gifts and talents. Like a gardener lovingly tending a beautiful garden, we can delight in appreciating what we've been blessed with and bringing our potential to fruition. Whether your natural abilities lie in music, art, logic, intelligence, a sense of humor, kindness, connecting with people, or working with animals, great joy is found in identifying these gifts and sharing them with the world. This is not a matter of inflating your ego or falling into the trap of grandiosity. It's about honestly recognizing your particular gifts and abilities and expressing them. This is what leading a fulfilling human life is about.

Having doubts about our abilities doesn't mean we don't have gifts or skills. Nor does trying to get over our doubts mean that we're deceiving ourselves. Everyone has some special abilities, and allowing them to blossom is the true expression of self-love. In her book *The Life and Work of Martha Graham,* choreographer and dancer Agnes de Mille relates a conversation she had with Graham, the renowned pioneer of modern dance. De Mille, who as a child had been told she wasn't pretty enough to be an actress and didn't have the right body to be a dancer, was questioning her own talents, despite a recent success in choreographing a show. In response Graham offered her this wisdom and advice:

> There is a vitality, a life force, an energy, a quickening that is translated through you into action, and because there is only one of you in all time, this expression is unique. And if you block it, it will never exist through any other medium and it will be lost. The world will not have it. It is not your business to determine how good it is nor how valuable nor how it compares to other expressions. It is your business to keep it yours clearly and directly, to keep the channel open.

There are many ways to take good care of ourselves, and we can offer them to ourselves as we would to someone we are deeply in love with. This begins with shifting our focus away from what we think is wrong with us and toward a genuine appreciation of our very existence. It was this shift that led Alexa to a major turning point. One day, after all her efforts to let go of her self-criticism, something inside shifted, and Alexa saw herself at last.

> I just sat there, silently weeping. I wept for the sadness I've carried, the shame, the unworthiness, and I wept in painful joy and visceral gratitude. . . . I am grateful to my body and my muscles and my lungs, my beating heart . . . I am falling head over heels in love with myself. . . .

## WHO'S DOING THE LOVING?

How can our little fragmented and conditioned self manage to get big enough to offer ourselves unconditional love? In truth, it can't. Einstein wisely said that a problem can't be solved on the level at which it was created, and to embrace ourselves fully requires realizing we are bigger than who we think we are.

Howie Cohn, a fellow teacher of mindfulness meditation, tells a tender personal story about how he came to know who is really doing the loving. During one of the many retreats he attended before he became a teacher, Howie found himself feeling unusually restless. He sensed that the pervasive feeling of discontent meant some deep discomfort was rising to the surface of consciousness and would have to be faced. As the days went by, a great feeling of isolation and loneliness came over him. The more intense the feeling, the more restless he became, wanting to do anything other than sit and be present with the pain.

One afternoon in his room as he was finishing a session of silent meditation, Howie opened his eyes and looked around. Neatly folded in one area was a large pile of his fashionable sweaters. His first impulse was to admire the collection and pride himself on his good taste, but he found himself instead wondering, *Why do I have all of these sweaters?* Then he began to notice all the stuff he had brought along to the retreat— handsome shirts and trousers hung in the open closet, several upscale toiletries lined the shelf above the sink, and a few gadgets he'd brought along that had seemed so essential covered the bedside table.

As he recalled the hours and hours he had spent searching for that "thing" that was just right, he began to understand. All around him was inescapable evidence of his futile attempts to run away from the feeling of emptiness that always lingered somewhere in the background—and was now filling every moment. This time he couldn't go out shopping to escape the great void. Added to that was the pain of self-judgment: *Why is comfort such a big deal for me? Why do I need so much stuff?* Now, here in the safe container and silence of a retreat, he knew there was only one way to respond to that emptiness, and that was to go into rather than away from it.

As Howie stayed present with the loneliness, he could feel the deepening ache in his heart, the bottomless hollow in the pit of his stomach. When the pain crept through his entire body and loneliness turned to fear, Howie found himself curling up on the floor and sobbing. "I felt like a desperate child," he recalls. "I put my arms around my body and started rocking myself." Surprisingly soothed by the loving energy of this caring action, Howie began to notice a curious shift taking place inside him. Now he was no longer the small frightened child needing to be held but rather the compassionate and wise one doing the holding. He was literally embracing the part of himself he had been so afraid to face. And he knew that what he felt wasn't "Howie's love," it was unconditional love itself, able to accept and hold with compassion every part of who he was in that moment.

As we've seen before in this course, running away from difficult feelings doesn't make them go away. When Howie let himself stay in touch with the painful loneliness, he found himself carried through it to a new perspective. While Howie had the supportive atmosphere of a retreat, the transformation he went through in loving himself unconditionally can happen in other ways as well. Psychotherapist Linda Graham points out that if you've never felt loved, the presence of an "empathic other" can serve to awaken the loving presence inside you.

In whatever way you begin this process, you will come to understand that what you experience as "negative emotions," when addressed with wisdom and support, unfold into a broader knowing of who you are. You are not just the loneliness, anger, fear, or envy that might be overwhelming you. You also have within you the benevolent presence that can tenderly hold your confusion like a mother holds a child.

I think of this presence as our basic nature, as goodness itself. We all get glimpses of it in a moment of gratitude or generosity, or in the joy we feel when we hear about or witness a noble action, or behold an object of beauty. When we quiet down enough and listen carefully, we find it is there all the time, beneath the confusion and static in our minds. The way

I see it, this pure force is the impulse inside us that wishes for our happiness, that roots for our well-being. The process of learning to love ourselves means accessing and then empowering this force, so that it directs our choices and our life.

## LOVE FINDING ITSELF

Your ability to love yourself evolves as you evolve, but when you finally love yourself, you have passed a watershed point in your spiritual practice. You no longer are trapped in looking to others to prove that you are okay. When you are unhooked from that need, you can simply open to the love coming your way from others without feeling unworthy or deflecting it. You can just let it join the love inside you.

In *Awakening Through Love,* writer and teacher John Makransky suggests a practice of being present for all the acts of kindness that come your way each day. When your partner gives you an affectionate hug, really take in the love. When a co-worker expresses appreciation, she is sincerely sending positive energy your way. Be there for it. When a dear friend greets you with genuine delight, he's communicating his love for you. Don't miss it. A stranger holds a door for you or smiles as you pass on the street. That is a communication filled with warmth and friendliness. Let yourself feel it. As Makransky puts it, if you're looking for all the small and large expressions of goodwill, you'll see that life is letting you know how deserving of love you are. If you're really present for all this kindness, you

### On the Lookout for Goodness

Be on the lookout for those moments when something good expresses itself through you—a spontaneous urge to call a distressed friend, an impulse to give a donation to a charity. Be sure to pause and let those thoughts, feelings, and sensations register in your awareness.

will be continually nourished by the benevolence around you. The more you open to receive all that love, the more you attract it to you. And you'll find that you become both a beacon and a magnet for love.

Following my own path has led me a long way from the adolescent wincing at seeing himself in the mirror. Over time the glimpses I've had of loving myself have become more of a consistent outlook. It's true that if the right button is pressed, I can still find myself back in the third grade, a mass of insecurity. But those thoughts don't last very long anymore, nor do they run my life, and I'm not so dependent upon the feedback of others to prop up my self-love. Even when stressed and confused, before long I can find my way back to that sense of compassion for my own humanity.

Loving ourselves means not only remembering who we are, but appreciating our particular way of being as one of life's infinite expressions. It means understanding that all the confusion and pain and shortcomings are part of the process of waking up. Alexa, who had been so deeply caught in self-hatred that she thought there was no way out, beautifully articulated this realization:

> On some days I am so full of love for myself and everything around me that it is all I can do to stop my heart from exploding with joy. I honor my pain, I bow to my capacity for change and growth that has manifested by pushing through the difficult times, and I rise in pure joy for the gift and blessing that is my life. As I rise in love for myself, I open to the myriad blessings in the universe and on Earth.

# STEP

## 8

## THE JOY OF
## LOVING OTHERS

---

It is important to understand how much your own happiness is linked to that of
others. There is no individual happiness totally independent of others.

—The Dalai Lama

*When I was twenty-five,* I fell in love for the first time. Margarita was my nurse in the hospital where I'd landed with a bad back. While being stuck in traction could have been depressing, I felt like I'd died and gone to heaven. Margarita was the woman of my dreams. I'd never felt more at home with myself or so open and connected with another human being. And what was even more amazing, she felt the same. After so many years of wondering what love really felt like and whether I'd ever experience it, it had finally happened. Unfortunately, the relationship didn't last. The pain of separation was excruciating for me, but I had tasted something I would never forget—the joy of love.

Our most prized possessions don't compare in value to loving and being loved. Whether the juicy romantic love I felt for Margarita, the natural and unquestioned love between a parent and child, the deep bond that forms between good friends, or the unconditional love we can have for life when we feel connected to everything around us, the essence of the experience is the same: to be held in a powerful, mysterious force, a living presence that allows us to be part of something greater than ourselves. We humans long for love, pray for it, die for it, live for it, and feel deep happiness or deep pain over it. Central to our lives is this capacity of the heart to know another, to feel understood and accepted, relaxed and connected, to be cared for and to care, to be delighted by and to delight.

Would anyone doubt that when our hearts are full of love we're happy? When we've got it, it feels like "this is what life is about!" Yet while we yearn for connection, relationships are often a source of hurt and disappointment. Friends can let us down. Our beloved children behave in ways that give us pain. Marriages begin with such promise, but nearly half end up in divorce court. From epic films and novels to country and western music, the *pain* of romantic love is almost a truism. How does that happen? How can something as beautiful as love be a source of so much bitterness and pain? In the face of such challenges, how can loving others become a reliable avenue to joy?

Relationships can bring us so much joy, yet can so easily occasion anger, disappointment, sorrow, and unhappiness. But as we've seen throughout this course, what is happening *inside us* is far more important than what is happening "out there." We can't control circumstances or other people, but we can train our minds to see clearly and our hearts to remain open, even in the face of pain. All the tools previously presented in the Awakening Joy course are brought to bear in Step Eight. The intention to be happy can be a guide and touchstone for how we relate to others. Mindfulness is the tool that helps us be truly present for and with others, as well as for the love that flows between us. Gratitude allows us to appreciate the lovely qualities in others that touch us. We learn to work with our pain and sorrow when things don't go our way or people disappoint us. Integrity is the basis of trust and respect so vital to the foundation of any relationship. Letting go of the stories and the expectations

we place on others allows us to see them for who they are. Loving ourselves is the prerequisite for loving others and remembering that they too
want to be happy.

Relationships of any kind can be challenging, but marriage and intimate partnership often seem like the ultimate test. When Jane and I decided to get married, my friend Sylvia
Boorstein (who recently celebrated her
fiftieth wedding anniversary) gave me
some sage advice. I confided in her, as my
first (and only) wedding day approached,
that along with my excitement was some
nervousness. I knew I'd found the right
partner, but I wasn't sure how good I'd be
at the institution of marriage. She looked at me with a twinkle in her eye
and said with great compassion, "Don't worry, dear, you'll be fine. It's the
first fifteen years that are the hardest. After that it gets easier." We both
cracked up.

*The most important criterion for females and males alike in their search for love, an overwhelming universal across the thirty-seven countries surveyed, is kindness."*
—DACHER KELTNER,
FROM *BORN TO BE GOOD*

Jane and I have been married for almost thirty years now. She's my
best friend, life partner, and the most important person in my life. There's
no one I enjoy laughing with, playing with, creating with, loving with,
and sharing life with more than her. She tells me the same is true for her.
And there's no one with whom I more often lose my patience, feel frustrated, get angry, or feel disappointed and hurt by. When you feel such
an intense connection with someone, what he or she says or does really
matters.

From the beginning, Jane and I agreed that we're together to help
each other wake up and to realize our full potential. Our wedding vows
explicitly stated that we'll use our relationship as a vehicle to deepen our
trust, respect, understanding, and love. When things get sticky or there's a
messy situation, we have an agreement to use our marriage as a catalyst to
deepen our love and connection. Of course this isn't always easy to remember when we're in the thick of it. But that commitment to help each
other grow is the container that helps hold those difficulties. They become like a grain of sand that irritates the oyster into producing a beautiful pearl.

In his Hierarchy of Needs, noted psychologist Abraham Maslow posited that after our survival and biological needs are met, the "need to belong" is our highest priority. This is true whether you're a spiritual seeker who wants to feel "at one with everything" or an inner-city gang member who will do almost anything to be accepted by his homies. This connection with others is one of the most important sources of joy. The Buddha recognized this as well. When his attendant, Ananda, speculated that it seemed that having good friends was half of the holy life, the Buddha replied, "Not so, Ananda. Having good friends is the *whole* of the holy life."

For most of us, that means connection with other humans, although some people find the company of animals far more delightful, and some find their deepest relationship with a divine being. In our society, however, isolation and disconnection are all too common. The truth is, the world is filled with potential relationships of all kinds. If you put all your eggs in one kind of love-basket and think that love can only be found in romance, you undercut your own happiness. And as so many know, you can feel just as lonely and isolated in a marriage as in being single. If you feel too alone and on your own, this chapter may inspire you to develop new ways of connecting with others and awakening love.

Keira got divorced ten years ago and hasn't found a new partner, yet her life is full of connections through friends, service organizations, and work. She went through an initial period of feeling lonely and disconnected, and eventually realized she could choose to reach out and make connections. As a result she has discovered a life that's very rich. She now says, "If a special relationship comes along, I'm not going to turn it down, but having or not having one is not going to define whether or not I'm happy." Love is love, wherever it's found, and it starts inside each of us as we let the barriers to connection dissolve. Rather than expecting relationships to make you happy, if you focus on getting in touch with the joy inside, you will create happier and healthier relationships of all kinds.

Just as we saw with gratitude, we don't have to wait for love to strike. We can develop the capacity to awaken the love inside us by practicing loving. In this context, all those difficulties that arise can be seen as opportunities to grow in our ability to love. In Step Six, Ajahn Chah was quoted as saying, "Let go a little and you will have a little freedom. Let go a lot and you will have a lot of freedom." For this chapter we might paraphrase that quote to read: "Love a little and you will have a little joy. Love a lot and you will have a lot of joy." Step Eight explores many flavors of love and how we block their expression, and it offers various practices to help cultivate the joy of a loving heart. When it comes to the joy of connecting with others, I think the Beatles got it right: All you need is love.

## LOVE LOST—AND FOUND

The summer after my relationship with Margarita ended, I traveled to Boulder to study at Naropa Institute. There I sought out my hero, Ram Dass, for advice. As I sat in his office, surrounded by pictures of various spiritual beings smiling their beneficent smiles, I told him my sad tale. I had somehow lost the love that was meant for me, and my world had fallen apart. We talked for a while about how Margarita and I might have fulfilled our part in each others' lives and that we were ready to go on. Maybe that was so, but it didn't stop the pain I felt. Margarita had awakened a feeling of love in me that I'd never known before. And now it was gone.

"What am I supposed to do about that?" I asked, still distraught.

"Perhaps her gift to you is showing you that you had the capacity for love," Ram Dass offered.

"Yeah. Loved and lost."

Ram Dass looked at me with compassionate eyes. "Did you really lose it? As long as we think someone else is the cause of our feeling love, then when they go, we think we've lost that love. But I don't believe that's how it works."

"What do you mean?"

"While it's true that someone can awaken that love," I remember him saying, "it can never be lost, since it's been right inside us all along waiting to be activated." He went on to explain that our beloved is merely the catalyst that allows love to come alive. The experience of love is so wonderful that when we think that other person is the cause, we want to hold on to them. We get afraid to lose them, we resent them if they do something that "makes us stop loving them" for the moment, or we get possessive and jealous at the thought of their possibly awakening love in someone else. What we call the pain of love arises from mistaking unhealthy attachment for love. It looks like love but it's very different. Love is a movement of the heart that opens and radiates out. Attachment is contraction of the heart as it closes in fear. "Love is not painful," Ram Dass said with a wise smile, "and now that you know the experience of it, you know what your heart aspires to. That's what Margarita gave you."

While it would take a while longer for the wound to heal, Ram Dass's words managed to start unwinding the knot in my heart and opened me up to understanding what love was about on a deeper level. The personal love between two people was a taste of a universal love that exists in everyone, and it shines on everything without conditions. I've seen this kind of continuous unconditional love in a few holy men and women. To develop that in myself is an aspiration I'm still working on. This kind of pure love is pure joy.

## RELEASING THE AGENDA

Most of our "love" comes with some level of the kind of attachment that's painful. We want the people we love to think and act in ways we think are best for them. We want them to do and say things we like. When my son

### Feeling the Love

Think of someone you love dearly. (Pets are fine too.) As you imagine that person or being here with you, notice what happens in your body. Maybe your chest feels warm. Maybe a smile comes to your face. Let your attention rest on the feeling of that loving energy. Where did it come from? Does it belong to that person? A beloved one may awaken that experience of love, but the love is *inside you*. You can cultivate a loving heart by strengthening that feeling through mindful attention.

Adam was a teenager, I could see our relationship was changing. He didn't always agree with what I thought was for his own good, and he wasn't shy about letting me know it. And I certainly had an agenda for his behavior—getting homework in on time, contributing around the house, getting home by midnight on weekends. I found a great book, *Uncommon Sense for Parents with Teenagers,* by "teen-expert" and psychologist Michael Riera. He advises parents to move from the role of manager to consultant as their children mature—and he admits that it's easier said than done.

Once I was sure that Adam wasn't self-destructive, I tried to let go of thinking he needed to be a certain way and stepped back a bit to the consultant role. This meant I picked my battles. And most importantly, I focused on letting him know I respected his judgment. I noticed that the

## WHAT'S THE DIFFERENCE BETWEEN ATTACHMENTS?

In Western psychology, "attachment" has a positive connotation and refers to the theory that a secure connection with primary caregivers in early childhood is the basis of healthy social and emotional development. If we experienced adequate love and nourishment early on, we are likely to be resilient, have healthy relationships, and feel worthy of love. If we did not, we tend to be anxious or withdrawn, have difficulty in relationships, and feel uneasy in the world. Secure attachment is a solid basis on which to build a happy life.

Attachment in Buddhism, on the other hand, is defined as the cause of suffering. It is the futile attempt of the mind to hold on to or cling to anything or anyone in this ever-changing world. When we want things or people or ideas to be a certain way, we are *attached* to them, and when they're not the way we want, which is often the case, we suffer. It is the holding on that leads to "the pain of love."

To playfully sum up the difference between the two types of attachments: In general, a baby is supposed to be attached to its mother; an adult is not.

more he felt my respect and confidence in him, the more he sought my advice. When he tripped up, rather than judging him by how he was or wasn't matching up to my expectations, I had to remember first and foremost that I loved and respected him. That helped loosen up *my* agenda for *his* happiness.

When we love someone, we want that person to be happy. It requires a lot of surrender to trust that they will find their way there by a different route than the one we think is best. This kind of letting go is needed in all relationships but is especially true with our children. We fear something might go wrong, and in the process, sometimes we forget that the reason we're so concerned is because we love them. Not that we shouldn't look out for their safety, but being overly attached to what we think is best for them can turn our love into worry instead of joy.

Edith was concerned about her eldest daughter, who was six years old. She often found herself wondering if the girl was happy, watching to see if she was okay. Sometimes she felt helpless and unsure what to do to protect her from suffering. Although Edith knew her worrying wasn't helping, she didn't know how to stop or what else to do. Taking the Awakening Joy course inspired her to try a different approach. She decided to start focusing on the joy she could see in her daughter rather than on what might be wrong, and she sent an email relating what happened: "We have since had some beautiful moments together when I've shared her joy and aliveness. I let that resonate with me and felt happy, and I got the impression that my happiness in turn was resonating with her. I feel this is strengthening and nurturing her, much more than the worrying mode was doing."

What we think of as love can sometimes end up being a strategy to get our loved ones to behave in ways we think are "right," or to give us what we think we need. In doing so, we're seeing them only through our own filter, and it can cut off a genuinely loving connection.

I'd known Phyllis for a number of years as a meditation student, and I could see she had a deep commitment to getting through the ways in which her heart was closed. When she came in for an interview during a retreat I was leading, she felt open and trusting enough to share a profound insight she'd just had about herself.

"I realize that with people in my life I really care about, like my children, my husband, and close friends, I try to anticipate their needs, then do things for them to help them out and show them I care. I realize I'm trying to *make* them love me. And I'm seeing now how draining that is. It just doesn't work."

"How do you know it doesn't work?" I asked.

"Because they often tell me that I'm trying too hard. And they're right. But I don't know what else I can do. I really want them to love me."

I asked her to imagine putting herself in their place. "How would you feel about someone who was trying to make you love them?"

"Awful," she said. "I'd want some space."

"And how would you want that person to relate to you?"

Phyllis thought for a few moments. "I'd just want them to let me be who I am. I'd want to feel their love and support without them wanting anything in return."

"There's your answer. Just let them be who they are. Get in touch with what you love about them, and stay focused on that rather than what you want to get from them."

A key element in sharing a loving connection with others is shifting the focus off ourselves. If we're preoccupied with ourselves, we can't truly be present for others. We're too busy wondering how we're doing or what we can get from the interaction. *Do they like me? Am I boring? Do they notice how (intelligent, attractive, anxious, depressed, etc.) I am?* When you see yourself as the center of the world, you assess everything and everyone around you based on your likes and dislikes, wants and needs.

Say, for instance, Jane, my wife, walks into the living room. Without stopping to find out how she is or what might be on her mind, I launch into some item on my list—our plans for the weekend, whether Adam or Tony called, the latest news about a friend . . . It might take a few moments to realize that she could have her own reasons for coming to see me, or maybe she was coming in just to say hi and I missed it. Of course we need to communicate with others about the ten thousand things that make up our lives. But once in a while, if we can pause and simply recognize a beloved friend or family member not as a satellite to our world but as someone we love, we can feel our connection with them in a fresh way.

Without a self-centered agenda, we're curious and want to understand and know what another person's reality is like. To relate to others in this way—allowing them to be who they are and to be at ease with themselves in our presence—invites true intimacy. This is the basis of the joy of love and connection. Rather than assessing how others can satisfy our needs, we can appreciate their unique expression of life as it relates to our own.

## OPENING A CLOSED HEART

During the course of the retreat, Phyllis came to see that wanting to be loved and doing everything she could to get that from her family was based in a pattern that began in her childhood. "Will it ever end?" she asked one day.

Feeling compassion for her pain, I asked softly, "Do you want it to end?" She nodded. We were at Spirit Rock, which is located on four hundred acres of rolling hills dotted with forests of oak and bay trees. I suggested that she find some place outside where she felt safe and comfortable and do a little ceremony to consciously let go of that pattern.

"There's a particular tree I feel really good sitting under," she said with a spark of hope.

"Good. Go there and let that tree be your witness. Let go of the thoughts that keep you focused on what you believe is missing in your life. Turn your attention to all the love that's there. You're starting on the next chapter of your life. Let go of the past and let yourself discover the joy of loving—your own self as well as others. And be open to receiving their love."

On the last day of the retreat, Phyllis came in to see me. She was beaming as she gave her report on what had happened when she did her ritual at the tree. "As I sat there, it occurred to me that we've all meant well and done the best we could. In that moment, I was able to let go of all the blame and what-if's I've been carrying around. I think I'm ready to learn a different way of relating to my family now. I'm looking forward to seeing what it's like to express my love for them without trying to figure out what I can get back."

My exchange with Phyllis had a profound effect on me as well. That afternoon I found myself reflecting on her story and looking at my own life and the subtle expectations I was bringing to some of my close relationships. I decided to practice what I was preaching and focus on the love I felt rather than what I was hoping to get or what I was expecting from the other person. Each time I've managed to do that since, I've noticed an immediate release as the pain of wanting turns into the joy of loving.

## FORGIVENESS FLOWS FROM
## A HAPPY HEART

As the saying goes, "Forgiveness is giving up all hope of a better past." The past is gone, and even though we may legitimately know we were

### From Agenda to Love

Bring to mind someone you love—a friend, a child, or perhaps a pet. Focus on how much you care about his or her well-being and happiness. Notice how good it feels to simply love that being.

Now turn your attention to something you *want* from him or her—attention, reassurance, affection, a certain behavior. Notice if the feelings in your body and your state of mind shift from openness to contraction, from a sense of fullness and connection to pulling back and closing down. Before you finish this exercise, let your thoughts return to the love and positive feelings you have for that individual.

When you notice that you're closing down to someone you love, stop for a moment and ask yourself whether you are attached to a particular agenda for that person. You may have reasonable expectations of others, and you might be annoyed if they don't fulfill them, but even through the disappointment, stay in touch with the love.

wronged, we are the ones who end up suffering when our hearts are closed in anger. The Buddha likened holding on to anger and ill will to picking up a hot coal to throw at someone, and ending up getting burned ourselves. When we're holding on to resentment, we feel closed down, disconnected, isolated. We might be right, but are we happy? As discussed in Step Seven, the way back to ease and openness, which is really what we're looking for, begins with forgiving others. According to the Dalai Lama, an essential component of compassion and forgiveness is realizing that the other person's words and actions are not about *you*, but about *their internal reality*, which has intersected with yours.

> *Forgiveness does not change the past, but it changes the present. Forgiveness means that even though you are wounded, you choose to hurt and suffer less. Forgiveness is for you and no one else. You can forgive and rejoin a relationship or forgive and never speak to the person again."*
>
> —DR. FRED LUSKIN, AUTHOR OF *FORGIVE FOR GOOD*

Karen's marriage got off to a very rocky start. Bob's addiction to pain killers, successfully hidden during their courtship, had soon become apparent. But it took a couple of years before Bob was willing to face the problem and enter a recovery program. Although she supported him through the process, the shock and disappointment had left Karen feeling very ambivalent about the marriage and filled with resentment. "I did lots of therapy and meditation and workshops, but honestly, when I look back, I see I was holding on tight to my hurt and anger, and I didn't want to let go of them." It was a distant marriage. "It reminded me of a dry and barren desert," she said.

A real change began when Karen signed up for the Awakening Joy course. After the first few sessions, she wrote me a note: "I'm guessing that all of the work I've done over the years created some of the conditions for joy to enter my being, but without this course, I'm not sure what would have happened. Within a month of following the guidelines, I was experiencing a joy and a freedom that I never thought possible for myself. It was the singing that first really opened up the 'joy channels.' But the other practices have kept them open."

By giving herself permission to experience joy, Karen was entering an expansive new life, and as her heart softened, her feelings for Bob began to shift. "I began to feel a love towards him that I simply had not thought I was capable of." But it was almost too late. Bob was still operating on the momentum of "the marriage in the desert," and one night he announced that he'd spoken to a mediator about a possible separation. "The course had tenderized me enough by then that I cried and cried all night long," Karen remembers. "Bob was a bit confused by my vulnerability, which I'd rarely shown him, and he lay next to me holding the space as best he could." Karen describes that evening as a "dark night of the soul" that led her to "a profound cellular experience of *knowing*

*When my husband is angry and in a bad mood, it is really helpful for me to recognize that he is confused and suffering, and that he doesn't realize this is not the way to happiness. This completely changes my state of mind from blaming and criticism (and from becoming just as angry as he is) into compassion and acceptance. I have also found that I can just let him be mad and still be happy myself."*
—A COURSE PARTICIPANT

## THE BENEFITS OF FORGIVENESS

Learning to forgive is good for both your mental and physical well-being as well as your relationships. In his book *Forgive for Good*, Dr. Fred Luskin includes the following research results:

- People who are more forgiving report fewer health problems.
- Forgiveness leads to less stress.
- Failure to forgive may be more important than hostility as a risk factor for heart disease.
- People who blame other people for their troubles have higher incidences of illnesses such as cardiovascular disease and cancers.
- People who imagine forgiving their offenders note immediate improvement in their cardiovascular, muscular, and nervous systems.

that I *did* want this marriage and our life together." Looking back now, she says:

It has been different ever since! I sometimes pinch myself and wonder if it's all a dream. Bob, understandably, is sometimes baffled by
the profound shift in my openness and love. I am not so naive as to
think that the rough times will never come, as they always do. But
my hard core anger and resentment has dissolved into compassion
and love, and the joy that I feel with my husband and with myself is
unmistakable. Needless to say, it has transformed our household as
well, and our two beautiful children feel the shift, though they don't
talk about it. The change is palpable in our home.

However closed or wounded your heart may be, it wants to open.
When you forgive, you're not just doing it for the other person but for
your own healing. As Archbishop Desmond Tutu, who chaired the Truth
and Reconciliation process in South Africa, puts it: "To forgive is the
highest form of self-interest. I need to forgive so that my anger and resentment and lust for revenge don't corrode my own being."

True forgiveness is based on understanding what might cause someone to act in ways that hurt us. Whether it's someone close to us or politicians we read about in newspapers, we are all products of forces beyond

---

### Asking Forgiveness

Bring to mind someone you have harmed in some way. Imagine that person right here with you. Allow any feelings of remorse to arise. Reflect on
the confusion or ignorance that may have caused you to act in that way,
not to excuse yourself for your behavior but to awaken compassionate
understanding. You might silently say, "I'm truly sorry for any harm I might
have caused you. I ask your forgiveness." Imagine that person hearing
your sincerity, taking in your words, and forgiving you. Notice how that
feels in your body and mind.

our control—genetic makeup, upbringing, influences of people we spend time with, and life circumstances. Although someone's actions may seem bizarre from our perspective, they make sense to that person. The forgiveness we talked about offering ourselves in the last chapter we are offering to others in this step toward happiness. When you can see the truth of what Jesus said on the cross, "Forgive them, for they know not what they do," you can forgive the confusion that leads someone to do a harmful action. You might think, "They know very well what they're doing." But Jesus, like the Buddha, was conveying that ignorance—the misunderstanding of where happiness lies—is behind that behavior. Realizing this, we can replace our anger with compassion. As the Dalai Lama says, "If you want to be happy, practice compassion. If you want others to be happy, practice compassion."

If you're not yet ready to forgive someone, then forgive yourself for being just where you are, particularly if you judge yourself for feeling the way you do. We can't hurry up the process. Sometimes hurts take a while to heal. But know that you're the one who benefits most from forgiving another, so be open to the possibility of forgiving sometime in the future.

## Offering Forgiveness

Bring someone to mind who has harmed you in some way. Imagine that person in front of you. Reflect on the confusion or ignorance that may have caused him or her to harm you—again, not to overlook the actions but to open your heart to compassion. Offer forgiveness by silently saying, "For any harm you may have caused me, intentionally or unintentionally, I forgive you. I forgive your confusion." Imagine that person taking in your words and feeling your forgiveness. Notice how that feels.

When you find yourself feeling resentful or angry with someone, and you want to find your way back to connection, it can help to imagine that person as a small child, afraid and confused. Let your heart soften, and feel the relief as you let go of the tight feelings.

## DEVELOPING A LOVING HEART

Developing a kind and loving heart may be the most important thing we do in life if we want to be happy. The Dalai Lama, who is one of the best examples I know of a happy person, says, "My religion is kindness." One of Jesus' main instructions to his followers was to "love one another." But how do we do that? How do we make kindness our religion? Some may think the ability to love is like a special talent—you either have it or you don't. Sometimes we look at someone and say, "She—or he—is a very loving person," and we might believe we can't be the same. But the capacity to love is inherent, we all have it, and it can be developed. The practice of lovingkindness, introduced in the last chapter as a way to love yourself, is also a way to cultivate your ability to love others, well beyond what you might think you're capable of. By repeatedly evoking the spirit of love within you, you strengthen it, and become an even more loving person.

The same phrases we use to send thoughts of lovingkindness to ourselves are here turned toward others to wish them well: *May you be safe from harm. May you be happy. May you live with ease.* You can also use any other words that feel natural and genuine. There are several categories of people to whom you can send benevolent thoughts, starting with those who are easiest for you to love, then those who are challenging, and then those you don't know. Ultimately you practice sending love to all beings everywhere.

Since lovingkindness practice is typically done while sitting quietly in meditation, you might wonder if there is some kind of magical energy that leaps across time and space and into the hearts of those you are thinking of. Some say yes, others no. I tend to think our thoughts do have an effect. Have you ever been thinking of someone you care about, and suddenly they call or email you "out of the blue"? Perhaps there's more than meets the eye in how we are interconnected. What I do know for sure is that sending kind and loving thoughts to others definitely has a beneficial effect on *you*. And as your love grows, you and everyone around you becomes a beneficiary.

This practice doesn't have to be limited to times of quiet meditation. During any encounter you have in your day, you can practice lovingkindness by silently wishing others well. You'll find that as you send thoughts of well-being to others, your own well-being increases.

## LOVING THOSE YOU LOVE

You begin getting in touch with your capacity to love by starting with those who are easiest to love. The first group of people you send lovingkindness to includes those you feel grateful to for enriching your life in some way. They might be parents, relatives, teachers, clergy, friends, or mentors—those who have been kind to you, shared their knowledge, helped you get through a hard time, or believed in and supported you in some way that has made you a better person. This doesn't necessarily have to be someone you know personally. Mahatma Gandhi was my childhood hero. When I read his biography, something about him moved me to want a good heart, wisdom, and courage like his, and thinking of him opens my heart. For some, other saints or holy people might do the same. Or you might open your heart in gratitude and send lovingkindness to public figures, past and present, who have inspired many to develop their skills and talents for the benefit of others.

Your good friends and others you easily and readily love are in the next circle of lovingkindness practice. This is a nearly guaranteed way to awaken love in your heart. Just thinking of certain people can bring a smile to your face. The people in this group probably love us, as we love them. As you feel their love for you, complete the loop by sending love back their way.

When you first start this practice, what is most important is that you choose those who awaken your love, so that you can get to know that experience in your body and mind, and learn how to strengthen it by offering that energy of lovingkindness to others. As you dwell in your open heart, you are deepening your capacity to love.

As part of your practice of lovingkindness-in-action, take time to be present for the people around you whom you are closest to. Try seeing them with fresh eyes, perhaps as if they were new friends you're just getting to know. Ask them what's really going on with them these days, and then really listen. Tell them what you like about them. Tell them you love them. And express your appreciation. All of you will benefit from the field of love you create.

---

### Radiating Love

Bring to mind someone you love or feel deeply grateful to. Notice where in your body you register these feelings. Many people experience a warmth and swelling in their chest. You might also explore what happens if a smile arises. What is your state of mind as you tune in to your love for that person? Let these feelings amplify as you radiate out gratitude and loving energy: *May you be happy. May you be healthy. May you feel my love for you.*

---

## SCATTER LOVE

Think of how many people you pass in an average day for whom you have little or no personal feeling at all. Probably most of them. These are the people in the next ring of the expanding circle of lovingkindness, the "neutral" category, those we don't know and may never get to know. As you send them lovingkindness, it becomes evident that you have the capacity to develop a warm connection with almost anyone.

On my first lovingkindness retreat many years ago, I decided to choose my new neighbor, Richard, as the neutral person I would send lovingkindness to. Jane and I had recently moved to the neighborhood, and I'd had very little contact with the family across the street other than a wave and a hi. I

*I've been practicing lovingkindness by noting tiny positive things in strangers, like saying to myself, 'He has good posture,' 'She looks good in that color,' 'He's using his turn signal.' This minuscule adjustment in where I place my attention has big results. I'm happier overall!"*

—A COURSE PARTICIPANT

started my practice by picturing Richard coming out of his house and giving me a smile and a pleasant hello as he got into his car for work. Then I imagined him in tender moments with his daughters and wife. Next I saw him in my mind's eye playing with his dog. I reflected that, just like me, he had his sorrows and joys, disappointments and successes. And just like me, he wanted to be happy and safe and open to all the love in his life. It seemed to me that he was basically a decent human being, and I figured if he was happy, everyone around him would benefit as well. As I held those images in my mind, I wished him well: *May you be safe from harm. May your life be filled with ease and joy.* I did this continuously for the next two days. I had no idea the effect it would have on me when I met him again.

*I have made an effort to be more consciously present with all of the 'service' people I encounter every day: the checkout guy, the bus driver, the security guard in the lobby of the office building where I work. I make sure to engage them in some way, thank them for their efforts (and mean it), and sincerely wish them a good day when I leave. It takes me out of my head, and I leave feeling more connected to the community of people I come in contact with."*
—A COURSE PARTICIPANT

The first time I saw Richard after the retreat, I suddenly felt so happy. Here was the object of my well-wishing right in front of me! I immediately went over to him, gave him a warm hello, and struck up a conversation. From that moment on we've shared a sweet connection. Only years later, one day when we were appreciating our friendship, did I mention the lovingkindness retreat to him. How surprised he was to find out that our warm relationship had started with two days of me silently wishing him well.

There are endless opportunities to open your heart to the many "strangers" around you. Here are a few suggestions. As you try any of these, be sure to pay attention to how you feel in your body and mind as you reach out toward others with the spirit of good will. That is what anchors the feeling of lovingkindness more deeply in your being.

- Choose a "Person of the Week," someone you see regularly but don't really know, to receive lovingkindness from you, in thoughts and actions.

- When you're waiting in line at the grocery store or caught in traffic, send thoughts of kindness to those around you.
- Smile or say hello to people you pass as you walk around town.
- As you hold open the door for someone in a public place, silently wish that person happiness and well-being.
- Stop and talk with a homeless person on the street. Your act of kindness might mean even more than a few coins.

## SEEING GOODNESS

Most of the people we get to know in life started out as strangers. This gives us a wide and fertile field for scattering love. In just about any situation we enter, we can have a positive impact by connecting with others in a kind and loving way. Doing this with a genuine intention to enhance the well-being of others, and not just to "win friends and influence people," means we are drawing upon our goodness and meeting their goodness. Nelson Mandela, imprisoned for twenty-seven years, was much loved by his guards because he made a point of doing exactly that.

Seeing goodness is something I have tried to do in my life. Forty years ago when I first read about Neem Karoli Baba, an Indian guru who influenced many Westerners, I was struck by something he said: "The best form to worship God is every form." To me that teaching was an instruction to see the good in everyone. I've found that the more I look for what is good and beautiful in others, the more I see of it. And when I do this, it seems to draw the best out of them.

How do you feel inside when you sense someone is judging you, looking for all your flaws? Probably self-conscious, if not downright flawed. But when you're with someone who, even if aware of your flaws, is seeing your inner beauty, don't you feel beautiful? It's as if shining a light on those parts of you gives them more life.

I discovered the transformative power of this perspective as a young elementary school teacher at P.S. 122 in New York. At the beginning of each year, I gave myself a personal challenge: Could I find the secret to each child's heart so they could all come out from their hiding places inside? If they could take that leap—a huge jump over a giant abyss for some—I knew I had a good chance of opening their hearts. When you know your teacher loves you and believes in you, especially when you're eleven or twelve years old, you start to maybe love and believe in yourself.

Seeing the goodness in most of those kids was easy. My heart was melted by their joy and enthusiasm, their wit or cuteness or sweetness. But there were almost always three or four who became my special projects for the year, often the kids with mean streaks, perhaps because they were abused or were so used to getting attention by being yelled at for doing something stupid that they didn't know another way. So I tried to get to them little by little with my love. I'd spend time alone with them at recess, or give them some kind of responsibility in the classroom to show I respected and trusted them. In quiet moments, one on one, I'd ask what they loved to do and listen with genuine interest. Most of the time it worked, and by the end of the year the feeling in the class was usually pretty magical.

Love can work wonders, building bridges across the greatest chasms.

---

### Looking for the Good

Seeing the goodness in someone brings something real, alive, and uplifting out of them. It allows trust to develop between people who scarcely know each other.

For one week, take on the practice of looking for the good in everyone you come in contact with. See in each person the desire to be safe, accepted, and loved. Even if you know someone's shortcomings, keep looking for the positive qualities—creativity, playfulness, a caring heart, intelligence, loyalty—any and all positive qualities you might admire. Notice what effect this has on how you feel toward other people and on your interactions with them. Notice the effect it has on your own state of mind.

I had another experience of this at P.S. 122. The school was located in Astoria, at the time a predominantly conservative neighborhood in Queens, New York. In fact, that area was chosen as the home site for *All in the Family,* a TV sitcom featuring Archie Bunker, the outrageous stereotype of a narrow-minded and opinionated American. Into that setting in 1969 came Mr. Baraz with long hair and a beard. The first time I walked through the halls, I left behind a trail of gasps and laughter from the stunned students and faculty. The principal called me aside, said the

*"CJ had been very depressed. She'd had lupus for fifteen years, was in a lot of pain, and often used a walker or wheelchair. When she heard that a Buddhist lama was coming to town, she hoped he might help. The day of her appointment, she hobbled up the pathway with her walker, sat down in front of the lama and proceeded to tell him about her suffering. Instead of the compassionate gaze she'd expected, he looked directly at her and rather brusquely said, 'Stop feeling sorry for yourself and start focusing on bringing happiness to others.'*

*CJ was utterly shocked. Dejected, she went home and brooded for a few days. Still miserable and rather desperate, she began thinking about the lama's suggestion. But in her state, what could she do to make others happy? Remembering a certain meditation practice, she made a commitment to try it for one year. The practice was lovingkindness.*

*Every day she sent wishes of happiness, compassion, and peace to herself, to everyone who came to mind, and to everyone she met. By the time the year was up, CJ's happiness levels were soaring. She is now out of the wheelchair, is exercising three times a week, and is completely symptom free. The doctors call it a medical miracle. The only thing CJ had done differently was sending herself and others wishes to be happy and healthy."*

—MARCI SHIMOFF, AUTHOR OF *HAPPY FOR NO REASON* AT AWAKENING JOY COURSE, BERKELEY, 2008

IN GRATITUDE FOR HER MIRACULOUS HEALING, CJ HAS STARTED THE KINDNESS CURE CAMPAIGN, AN ONLINE MOVEMENT ASKING PEOPLE TO JOIN HER IN COLLECTIVELY PERFORMING ONE MILLION ACTS OF KINDNESS IN ONE YEAR
(the kindnesscure.org).

school wasn't used to someone like me, and politely suggested that I get a cut and a shave.

But I liked the way I looked. It made me feel like I belonged to the hip counterculture movement that was afoot. And even more, maybe it would be good for people to get past their prejudices. I explained my thinking to the principal who, although impeccably dressed with his bow tie and suit, was not as rigid as I might have judged him to be. "Give me two weeks," I asked. "Maybe people can get used to someone different. If it doesn't work I'll shave off my beard and cut my hair."

During that time I intentionally "killed them with kindness." I opened doors for parents and students, greeted teachers in the hallway with a warm hello, and generally beamed everyone with love. The thing that made this work was that I really meant it. I could see how well-intentioned each of these people were, wanting the best for the kids. Although I started with an ulterior motive, in the process I genuinely opened my heart to them. And seeing their goodness established a real connection between us. In the end, I kept my hair, taught there for the next nine years, and ended up being a very popular teacher.

## LOVING THOSE YOU DON'T WANT TO LOVE

You might feel as if your heart is about as full as it can get, with appreciating people who've enriched your life, loving good friends, and opening up to include your mail carrier, co-workers, and the children you pass on your walk each morning. But lovingkindness practice knows that the heart has no limits. The next category of people to include in your heart are those you have a hard time with. Classically referred to as the "enemy" category, this group can include ex-lovers, bad neighbors, political figures whose actions anger us, and loved ones we're having a hard time with. Jesus taught, "Love your enemies, do good to those who hate you, bless those who curse you, pray for those who mistreat you." Here's your chance to try that out in the privacy of your own heart.

Why would you want to do this? What could be gained by sending good wishes to those who upset you? Why would you want to "turn the other cheek"? As with forgiveness, you are first of all practicing this for your own well-being. As long as you're holding on to the hot coal, you're the one getting burned.

Another reason for stretching to include those we don't really feel a lot of love for, at least not in the moment, is that anger and ill will don't really accomplish much. "Hatred never ceases by hatred," said the Buddha. "Hatred only ceases by love. This is an ancient and eternal law." While it's true that protesting against injustice, for instance, can arise from justified anger, ultimately what solves the problem is some degree of compassion and communication. This is not to deny painful feelings or pretend they're not there, in ourselves or others. But we can start where we are and honor our feelings with the intention of opening our hearts in understanding. In the end, when we do this, we are the ones who benefit, and in the spirit of lovingkindness our actions have more power.

Sending lovingkindness to our enemies is a kind of alchemy, transforming our bad feelings into good ones. One year on a lovingkindness retreat, I experienced exactly how that happens. My practice had progressed to the "difficult person" category, and I knew just who I'd pick. Sheila was someone who had temporarily moved into the large shared household where I'd lived for a number of years. Although she was impeccable in following the house guidelines, it seemed to me she was always complaining about something: Others in the household weren't pulling their weight. House meetings were too long. Someone was playing music too loud late at night, etc. Whenever we encountered each other, which was often enough living under the same roof, I imagined judgments cascading one after another from her mind. (Of course, one or two judgments arose in mine as well.) Every time I thought about her, my body would tense and I'd immediately feel a wave of dislike. There was no doubt about it. Sheila would be the perfect "difficult" person for me to send lovingkindness to.

In doing this stage of the practice, you bring to mind the positive qualities of the person—maybe he's good with children, or she's very generous with donations to good causes. This helps you soften your heart and makes you open to wishing them well. However, every time Sheila came to mind, all I could think of were those complaints and attacks. After a day or two of continually directing phrases of well-wishing toward her—*May you be safe from harm, May you be happy*—the negative images subsided a bit, but I felt nothing remotely close to what you would call warmth or an open heart. I was holding the hot coal, and I didn't really know how to put it down. Then on the third day there was a breakthrough.

While I was trying to send Sheila kind thoughts, the Dalai Lama came into my consciousness. It occurred to me that he'd probably have no trouble at all doing this task that was so challenging for me. His love and compassion are so tangible that you can't be around him without having your heart touched, and you end up feeling full of good will. I'd seen him a few times in a setting small enough to watch him interact with people personally. He always welcomed each one with complete openness and love. An image came to mind of a time when I'd seen him greeting a line of people coming for a blessing. As I watched the scene in my mind's eye, to my surprise, Sheila appeared, awaiting her turn. Compassion was emanating from the Dalai Lama toward the two people ahead of her, and then she stood before him.

*What if I were to see Sheila through the Dalai Lama's eyes?* I wondered. The scene unfolded in slow motion. First I noticed her openness and vulnerability. Then I became aware of all the pain and sorrow she'd gone through in her life that shaped who she was. I could see her good heart and how she so wanted to be loved. Suddenly Sheila became a radiant being, beautiful to behold.

The wishes for the health and happiness of my "difficult person" now came more easily and sincerely. Something that was tight inside me began to relax, and it felt like all the energy I'd been putting into keeping my heart closed to Sheila was releasing itself into caring and joy. In the teachings of several Eastern religions, the peacock is an important symbol of the ability to transform negative feelings into positive ones. This is based on the belief that this magnificent bird can eat poison and turn it into its splendid plumage. I felt like all that poison of ill will inside me had been turned into something beautiful.

## Loving Even *Them* (Yes, Even Them)

Bring to mind someone with whom you have a difficult relationship. Think of some positive qualities he or she might have. Try to remember some kind action he did that might soften your heart, or perhaps imagine her as a young child who's had a hard time. Now silently say these phrases as you think of that person: *May you find happiness in your life. May you be at peace.* Notice how this feels in your body and mind. If you feel any expansion or warmth, take those feelings in and let them grow.

It's important not to try to force any particular feeling. If you're not able to feel kindness toward this other person, be kind with yourself by allowing your feelings to be as they are, without attachment or aversion.

## DISARMING HOSTILITY

Sheila was basically a good person from the start. But what about difficult people who are mean or cruel? One might wonder about practicing lovingkindness toward those who intentionally cause harm to others. Why should we wish for their happiness? The poet Longfellow wrote, "If we could read the secret history of our enemies, we should find in each man's life sorrow and suffering enough to disarm all hostility." When we look at the background of those who commit violent crimes, we usually find great suffering in their childhood. Those who seem to get pleasure from another's misfortune are themselves the unfortunate. Stuck in the prison of their contracted minds, they have little genuine love coming back to them. If your wish for their well-being were to come true, and they'd understand where happiness really can be found, they would no longer intentionally cause harm to anyone. So we send lovingkindness to them, not as a reward but as a prayer. And again, when you can wish for your enemy what you wish for your friend, another tight place in your heart will have softened into compassion.

When I did see Sheila again after that retreat, I felt a lot softer toward her. Somehow I could hear some of her remarks differently, not as complaints but as legitimate observations, and she and I have shared a warm connection since.

It's clear to me that the way we think of others certainly affects the way they relate to us. Hal has a difficult relationship with his mother, so he chose to direct his lovingkindness practice to her. He wrote:

> I noticed a marked difference in her responses. On days when she was just after me no matter what, I practiced lovingkindness toward myself and compassion for her situation, reminding myself of the good in her even if I couldn't see it in the present moment. Working through those times was difficult but enormously helpful. I hope to continue to heal this relationship and transform it, at least within myself.

## THE FULLY OPENED HEART

If you want to be happy, love everyone. This might sound pretty simplistic, but the happiest human beings I know are the spiritual teachers who make it their life's work to beam out love unconditionally. This is the kind of love we aspire to in the final category of lovingkindness recipients—all beings, human, animal, and beyond. When we cultivate lovingkindness for all beings, we replace the feeling of "other" with caring and connection. We include all without distinction: those who are suffering *and* those who in their ignorance cause suffering; those who are happy and those who cause happiness; people of all ages, ethnic groups, nations, and religious backgrounds, as well as all creatures and all forces seen and unseen. There is no limit to our love.

Buckminster Fuller came up with the phrase that famously defined our true situation: "We are all passengers on Spaceship Earth." And the fact that we're all on the same spaceship has become increasingly clear in recent times. What happens in Iraq influences what happens in Milwaukee. A downturn in the U.S. housing market has dramatic effects on the world economy. That in turn affects support for nonprofits doing charitable work which has consequences for the poor in Bangladesh or kids wanting to participate in the Special Olympics. Burning fossil fuel with little regard for consequences can throw our climate system completely out of balance, melting polar ice caps, increasing the fury of hurricanes and other storm systems, and hastening the extinction of many species. In short, we are part of a vast, interconnected web of life. By realizing we're all in this together, it becomes clear that it's in our own interest to practice lovingkindness for the Earth and all of our shipmates.

## A FREE JOY RIDE

We see a baby squeal with delight and we feel delighted. We watch a movie and feel satisfied when the good guy finally gets the gal. Someone we love succeeds at a project they were nervous about, and we feel happy for him or her. There is a Sanskrit word used in Buddhist practice for the feeling of happiness at the joy and good fortune of others: *mudita*. Mudita, translated as sympathetic joy, means resonating with the happiness of another. It's the joyful feeling we have when we're cheering for others or celebrating their success. Just as with loving-

## SURELY THIS IS LOVE

I am intimately connected with all that is. When you water your roots, my heart blossoms. When I see you smile, that's when I know I'm fully alive. As you are able to live in truth, I raise the roof on this house I am exploring. I throw the doors wide, let the breeze blow in the windows. When you grow, I know it as my own opening. You stretch, I breathe. I give, and you receive. Just beneath the fabric of our lives, coiled, ready to spring or budding like a rose, reaching out to embrace, or sitting, bathed in grace and stillness—this singing, circling, radiant, one with everything—surely this is love.

—DANNA FAULDS,
from *Go In and In*

ingkindness practice, we can do "mudita practice" to develop and expand the natural uplifting we feel when others thrive.

When we focus on the good fortune and happiness of others, we are entertaining positive images in our mind, which makes us happy. The moment we think, *Oh, but I don't have that,* we drop into negative comparison, the mind tightens, and we're unhappy. If you're honest with yourself, you might have to admit that sometimes you do feel a little twinge of glee upon hearing of someone's misfortune. The French philosopher Montaigne wrote, "There is something altogether not too displeasing in the misfortune of our friends." The German language even has a term for this: *schadenfreude,* feeling happiness at the misery of others.

What is this feeling about? We probably can find the roots of this tendency in the way competition for survival is programmed into our brain. To me it suggests that we believe we are competing for happiness, as if there is a quota on the amount of happiness in the world. *If they have it, there's less for me.* But this is not true. For instance, it doesn't work that way with anger. Ever notice what happens when someone comes into a room who's very angry? Do you relax and think: *Oh, good. They're angry, so there's less for me!?* Probably not. We all know how being around a negative person rubs off on us. Fortunately the same happens with joy when we get our comparing mind out of the way and let ourselves rejoice in the happiness of others.

Jim knew how easily he could fall into envy and judgment with cer-

## Lovingkindness for All Beings

Begin by sending wishes for well-being to everyone in your home and immediate family. Gradually expand outward in your mind to include your neighborhood, your city, state, country, continent, and the entire planet. The traditional practice even includes beings beyond that. If you believe in angels, saints, nature spirits, and extraterrestrials, this is the point to include them in your lovingkindness practice. You might say: *As I want to be happy, so may all beings be happy. As I want to be peaceful, so may all beings have peace in their lives.* Notice how it feels in your body and mind to wish well to all without omitting anyone from your heart.

tain people in his life, especially those who loved their jobs and enjoyed their lives—quite a contrast to his own situation. He wrote me an email about this after the Awakening Joy session in which sympathetic joy was introduced.

"It's really hard to wish successful people even greater success. If they become happier, I'll feel even worse."

"Why don't you try it a few times," I wrote back. "See what happens, and let me know how it goes."

Much to his surprise, Jim found that the practice had the opposite effect. In his next email he said:

> Whenever I find myself being critical in my mind toward someone, I've started changing the thought to: *May your joy and happiness continue, and may good fortune follow you everywhere.* Once I've wished it for them, I find I really want them to have it.

I remember hitting a snag once when working on sympathetic joy. The practice traditionally begins with thinking of someone in a moment of triumph. For a while my mind was blank. I knew a lot of people who were pretty happy, but I wanted to root for someone who was in a moment of intense celebration. And then in a flash it came to me—Steve Young, the quarterback for the San Francisco 49ers, my all-time favorite

---

### Joy in the Joy of Another

Imagine someone you are fond of smiling or laughing in happiness. What happens to you? Notice if a smile automatically arises. Take in those good feelings and send them out to that person: *May your happiness continue. May your happiness grow.* Think of others you would like to send this energy to, and notice how your own good feelings increase.

Now imagine all those people in a cheering section rooting for you. Direct the phrases of well-wishing toward yourself, taking in the feeling of support from them.

athlete. For years, every time I'd thought about him, I would feel joy. So I imagined him right after winning the Superbowl, running around the stadium deliriously happy, going into the stands to high-five fans with a beautiful, goofy grin on his face. Bringing that image to mind was like opening the faucet of joy in my heart. My eyes welled up with tears. Once the valve opened, I was able to turn that thought toward other people in my life, sending them heartfelt wishes: *May your happiness grow.* Mine certainly did.

Keep your radar out for happiness around you. When you see or hear about others who are experiencing happiness in their lives, know that their joy is contributing a little more happiness to the world. Tune in to their reality and let their happiness rub off on you. Silently send them wishes that their happiness may continue and grow. Notice how you feel in your body and mind as you do this. If any thoughts of jealousy or envy arise, notice them without judgment, and return to your wishes for their continued happiness. As the Dalai Lama says, if we derive happiness from the happiness of others, we have at least six billion more opportunities to be happy.

## PLAY IS LOVE

Play is one of the most immediate ways to access the joy of loving others. But we all too often turn down the opportunity because we must attend to those "matters of consequence" that the Little Prince lamented. Bruce was taking the course online from Connecticut and wrote to say that one snowy day he was outside with his two young boys building a snowman and fort. "I wasn't particularly enjoying the activity," he reported. "It was cold, I had stuff to do, and I was ready to go in." But his eight-year-old and four-year-old weren't. "In the Awakening Joy course we were talking about feeling joy at the joy of others, and I couldn't help but see how much fun they were having. I thought, 'This is a special moment. I need to let this soak in, not just get it over with.' " Instead of calling it quits, Bruce proposed huddling inside the fort and having hot cocoa. "We sat down together and shared a simple, precious cup of cocoa," he recalls. "The memory of that time of just being together still brings tears to my eyes, even a year later."

Playfulness and humor are actually ways of loving others, and they are a direct link to joy. Here are some of the ways course participants said they have let the love flow through playing:

- Laughing at unexpected situations instead of getting mad.
- Engaging in "time-wasting" activities such as Four-Square or Scrabble.
- Adopting a pet. "I named my dog 'Happy,' and she's really good at playing."
- Taking tango lessons and laughing instead of apologizing for all my mistakes.
- Skipping down the street with my kids.
- Singing conversations with my family, as if we were in an opera.
- Making music with friends.

Notice what happens inside you when you are engaged in play. The feeling is a lot like love, isn't it? Whatever we call it, this is the energy of life, endlessly changing, infinitely creative, and it is one of the easiest ways to love others. Play is not just an "extra" in our lives but essential for our well-being. David Elkind, Professor Emeritus of Child Development at Tufts University, says in his book *The Power of Play:* "Decades of research have shown that play is crucial to physical, intellectual, and social-emotional development at all ages." Play opens our heart and connects us with others in a joyful way. Instead of seeing it as a luxury, give yourself some playtime, not only for the fun of it, but as a way to open your heart.

## LOVE IS ALL AROUND US

When Adam was a little boy, he would often have tantrums—usually meltdowns from being too wound up or overtired. When he quieted down enough to be able to hear me, we'd sometimes go through a little ritual. "Would you like me to tell you the people who love you?" I'd softly ask. He would quietly nod yes, and I would take him into my lap and wrap my arms lovingly around him. "Mommy loves you and Daddy loves you. Grandma loves you and Aunt Susan loves you. Gigi loves you and Linda loves you. Michelle loves you and Rose loves you. . . . " As I'd continue, I could feel Adam's body relax as he calmed down. Love is perhaps the best medicine around. When you're feeling down, recalling those who love you can be a comforting and healing balm. You can relax into that connection.

The more we allow our hearts to open, the more we see the truth that love is all around us. This is not just a pretty idea but a reality any of us can experience if we give ourselves a chance to let go into it. Kate, the young woman who teaches mindfulness to inner-city children, says she knows that "When all of the fear and sadness and feeling of separation falls away, the only thing left is love. That's the undercurrent." This unshakeable knowledge arose from something that happened to her one day quite spontaneously.

> I was sitting on the porch one beautiful sunny afternoon, feeling very happy. I'd closed my eyes for a moment, and when I opened them, the tree about ten yards in front of me had colors so vibrant it looked like it was glowing. I felt such a strong connection with it. I was part of that tree. Even the space between us was part of the connection. With no boundaries, I became part of the chair I was sitting in, part of the deck I was sitting on. The physical boundaries were still there in my mind, but on a deeper level there was no identifying *That's a tree, and this is me*. And I knew that the thing connecting us all was an energy of love.

Similar descriptions have occurred in cultures around the world and through millennia. Modern physics corroborates the fact that on the level of energy there are no boundaries. While science might not recognize the glue as "love," it's the word mystics most often use. Kate talks about her experience as "a feeling of coming home," and it has had a profound impact on her life.

I'd been horribly shy, with no confidence. That feeling of connection completely changed my life. I can feel connected with anybody now. All I have to do is love them. We're all part of this undercurrent. Though we all share suffering, we're also all linked by this love.

That underlying energy is love loving itself through you. Love moves in a circle. You take it in and send it out; you send it out and it comes back to you. You might notice that letting love flow through you happens quite naturally. And you can amplify its effect by engaging in the process consciously. Without resistance, receive the love that comes to you. The more you take it in, the more you can give it out. You are an instrument of love, and as your relationship to others becomes an expression of that, your capacity for joy grows. If your love rests on wishing happiness for everyone you meet and everyone you share this life with, your joy will be boundless.

> *If one completes the journey to one's own heart, one will find oneself in the heart of everyone else."*
> —FATHER THOMAS KEATING

# 9

## COMPASSION: THE NATURAL
## EXPRESSION OF A JOYFUL HEART

---

*The only ones among you who will be truly happy are those who have sought
and found how to serve.*

—Albert Schweitzer
Commencement Address, 1957

*By the time* I reached my junior year in college, I was deeply disillusioned by the world I saw around me. I had grown up believing in Superman, in "truth, justice, and the American Way," but this was the 1960s. The assassination of President Kennedy three years earlier had put an end to Camelot, for me and for many in my generation. The deaths of innocent people in Vietnam had shattered my belief in the benevolence of U.S. foreign policy. And here in the Land of the Free, thousands were struggling for basic civil rights.

Majoring in psychology, which I thought would be an exploration of what makes humans tick, turned out to mean listening to dry academic lectures about the behavior of rats in mazes. I wondered what learning

standard deviations in statistics had to do with anything in my life. In philosophy, Camus and Sartre began to make a lot of sense and were swiftly
leading me toward my very own existential crisis. I ended up deciding
that life had no meaning at all and must be the bad joke of some Higher
Intelligence with a bizarre sense of humor.

I became more and more depressed. For several months I steered
every conversation toward my gloomy perspective. Friends began to keep
their distance, not wanting to be brought down by their brooding philosophical companion. The counterculture was increasingly attractive and
offered some hope—peace, love, and the Beatles—but inside I still
couldn't find anything that made life seem worth living.

Then one day while eating my lunch in the Queens College cafeteria, something happened that steered me in a new direction. As I sat there
alone, under my dark cloud, I started looking around at the crowd of people in the room, some talking earnestly together, some wandering around
looking a bit lost. Instead of falling into my usual habits of comparing
myself to them, or thinking about how isolated I felt from everyone, I
began to just look at them as they were going about their business. Suddenly they all seemed to me to be basically decent human beings simply
trying their best to find their way in the world. It was like the shifting of
a kaleidoscope into a whole different configuration, and from that perspective, I understood that all they wanted was to be happy—and it
seemed to me they all had that right. I don't know why, but in that instant
a philosophical insight occurred to me. The one thing that could give life
meaning for anyone would be to bring happiness to others. That would
be a noble endeavor in an ignoble world.

As I contemplated the simplicity of my new theory, it gradually
dawned on me that helping others in this way might be reason enough
for *me* to be here and to live life fully. *Could that be? Might there be something that would make life worthwhile? What if I thought of myself and my own
life in this way—about bringing happiness to others?* I felt a momentary rise of
something inside as that little beam of light broke through my perpetual
cloud. I left the cafeteria with a bounce in my step that had been missing
for a long time.

Those thoughts followed me around over the next few weeks, and the rightness of them kept growing. Somewhere inside I think I knew that if I could help others find happiness, I would actually be happier myself—that would be a big leap for the cynic I'd become. It would take a while before I was living this new way of looking at myself and the world, but something changed that day that set me on the road to finding real happiness.

In a commencement speech he delivered in 1957, Albert Schweitzer said, "I don't know what your destiny will be, but one thing I do know: The only ones among you who will be truly happy are those who have sought and found how to serve." Over the years I began to discover this myself, first as a schoolteacher, then later as I came into contact with various spiritual practices. Throughout my search for my own happiness, the recognition I had in the college cafeteria—that everyone wants to be happy—has stayed with me. While we may find happiness and contentment for ourselves, we don't have to look very hard to see there's suffering in the world all around us. Rather than shielding ourselves from this all-pervasive reality, I've learned that responding to it with compassion and caring action leads to an even deeper level of well-being and a joyful, fulfilled life.

When we're motivated by a true spirit of generosity, we benefit as much as those on the receiving end. Jesuit priest Anthony de Mello says it this way: "Charity is really self-interest masquerading under the form of altruism . . . I give myself the pleasure of pleasing others." In the same vein, the Dalai Lama playfully speaks of working to benefit others as "selfish altruism." Step Nine focuses on this path to happiness: relieving the suffering of others and helping them find happiness.

The altruistic urge to serve others has been held up as an ideal throughout human history. We call those who act on it "heroes," "saints," "paragons of virtue," "humanitarians." We say they are courageous, greathearted, compassionate, and noble. I saw these qualities in my childhood heroes, Fiorello LaGuardia, Lou Gehrig, and Gandhi. LaGuardia was a mayor of New York in the early 1940s, when I wasn't yet born, but I learned about him when I was a kid. One of my favorite stories was of a time when he was officiating in misdemeanor court in New York City. A man who had stolen bread to feed his family came before him charged as a thief. LaGuardia fined the man ten dollars, then turned to the courtroom and said, "I'm fining everyone in this courtroom fifty cents for living in a city where a man has to steal bread in order to eat." The defendant left with $47.50 in his pocket. LaGuardia's spirit so inspired me I knew *that's* the kind of person I wanted to be.

We have seen this same spirit in heroes like Martin Luther King, Jr., Nelson Mandela, and Mother Teresa. We saw it in the firefighters at the Twin Towers of the World Trade Center on 9/11. The acts of such individuals can move us to tears and also inspire us to act on behalf of others. In Buddhist teachings I was introduced to a term that encompasses all these qualities and folds them into a spiritual aspiration I find deeply meaningful—*Bodhisattva*.

> *A hundred times every day, I remind myself that my inner and outer life depends on the labors of other men, living and dead, and that I must exert myself in order to give in the measure as I have received and am still receiving."*
> —ALBERT EINSTEIN

This word in ancient Sanskrit means a being who is headed for enlightenment, and specifically refers to those who aspire to that lofty goal for the purpose of liberating all beings from suffering. The term is now commonly used to describe one who selflessly works to relieve suffering whenever possible. Although this term may be unfamiliar to some readers, I am going to introduce it here since it so well names the ideal and the qualities that are the point of this chapter.

The idea of liberating all beings from suffering sounds like a stretch. But working to benefit others is something any of us can do. So I like to call those of us who are inspired by this vision of relieving suffering and increasing happiness "Bodhisattvas-in-Training." We do the best we can and in the process learn how rewarding and beneficial it is to express our caring heart.

For centuries students of Buddhism have affirmed their aspiration to serve others by formally taking Bodhisattva vows. Thirty years after my existential crisis and epiphany in college, I had the opportunity to do this in a ceremony led by His Holiness, the Dalai Lama. In an auditorium surrounded by thousands of others, I repeated these words, formulated in the eighth century, that would induct me into this high caliber club:

> For boundless multitudes of living beings, may I be their ground and sustenance. For everything that lives, as far as are the limits of the sky, may I provide their livelihood and nourishment until they pass beyond the bonds of suffering.

Most Buddhist vows, like this one, typically push the envelope of possibility. I assume it is a way to keep us aspiring to our highest abilities. But as I spoke those words, meaning them as fully as I could, I realized that I had taken my own version of this vow years before in that college cafeteria when I had that insight about helping others find happiness. Since then I had come to know the vow not as a heavy burden but as a reminder of what gives meaning and fulfillment to life.

Making a conscious pledge to yourself in this way can focus your aspiration to serve others. It is not necessary to be a Buddhist or get involved in formal ceremonies. You can do it your own way and create your own vows. However you may decide to do it, taking this step is a powerful prescription for an ever-deepening joy.

---

### Creating Your Own Bodhisattva Vow

You can make up your own version of a vow to relieve suffering in the world. The basic principle is seeing your own happiness in the context of how it can benefit others. Take a few moments to ask yourself what words would sincerely convey that wish in a way that uplifts your heart. For instance you might say something along the lines of *May my happiness lead to the happiness of others*. When you've found the phrase that resonates with you, silently state those words as a promise to yourself, connecting with the sincerity of intention they express. Notice how your body and mind feel as you do this.

## THE HEART OF COMPASSION

The quality of heart that moves and supports the Bodhisattva is compassion. In English the word means "to suffer with," but a beautiful and perhaps more meaningful definition of compassion in Buddhist teachings is "the quivering of the heart in response to suffering." It is the sincere wish that others be free of suffering. At its core, compassion is a recognition that we are all interconnected, that your suffering is my suffering, that when I see you in pain, my heart trembles.

Compassion is not the same as pity, although they are sometimes spoken of interchangeably. Pity carries a subtle quality of distancing and aversion: *Too bad about you. (I'm glad it's not me!)* Though pity may lead us to respond to another's suffering with a good intention to help, the heart is holding back, not opening to the joy that is potential in the response. Compassion is a profound softening of the heart when it encounters suffering. When our hearts are moved this way, the wall of protection that might separate us from another dissolves. Tibetan lama Chogyam Trungpa

## THE MIRROR OF COMPASSION

Neuroscience is revealing that we literally "feel with" others through what are called "mirror neurons" in our brain. In his book *Field Notes on the Compassionate Life*, Marc Barasch describes this process:

"Mirror neurons . . . [are a kind of] brain mechanism dedicated to empathy's motto: *I feel you in me* . . . One study showed that the same cells that light up when a person's finger is jabbed with a pin also light up when someone *else's* finger is pricked. We wince when we see someone stub her toe and hop painfully on one foot. We know how it feels . . . Just as our brain is said to have a 'grammar nugget' that enables us to acquire complexities of language, perhaps we have a 'Golden Rule nugget' containing the neurological ground rules for compassion itself."

says that with compassion, it is as if "your heart is completely exposed. There is no skin or tissue covering it. . . ." There is something sweet in the tenderness we feel when we reach out in compassion. To feel that tender is to feel alive.

When asked what compassion feels like, some participants in the Awakening Joy course responded:

- I feel uplifted and fulfilled as I give, a peaceful warmth.
- I feel very present and softer in my mind.
- I feel "soft" and a bit teary.
- My heart hurts in a good way, and I am pleased to be feeling that connection to another.

The deep caring that suffering evokes in us, the greatness of heart, is actually an uplifting state. It feels good to care. This capacity to care about others and about life is the essence of the compassionate heart.

## CULTIVATING COMPASSION

Keeping our hearts open in the face of suffering takes patience and practice. The Dalai Lama himself had to learn how to develop compassion. In *Worlds in Harmony: Compassionate Action for a Better World,* he says:

Whenever I speak about the importance of compassion and love, people ask me: What is the method for developing them? This is not easy . . . You cannot just press a button and wait for them to appear . . . When I was fifteen or twenty, I was quite short-tempered, but through Buddhist training and through difficult experiences, I have been able to improve my mental stability. Difficult experiences are very good training for the mind. They help us develop a kind of inner determination. . . . Through training, we can change.

The Buddha, who so profoundly understood suffering, was known as The Compassionate One, and one of the main aspects of his teachings is how to develop our caring heart. While our own suffering can open us to empathize with the suffering of others, we can also systematically deepen our compassion through formal practices. As with other practices you've learned in this Awakening Joy program, an effective way to begin is by training the mind through meditation.

Modern neuroscience corroborates the fact that focused meditation is one of the most direct ways to activate and strengthen those areas in the brain that increase empathy. In his laboratory at the University of Wisconsin, Richard Davidson did extensive research on the effect of compassion meditation on the brains of student volunteers who had done the practice for one week, as well as Buddhist monks who had done thousands of hours of such meditation. In this particular kind of practice, the meditator becomes completely focused on experiencing lovingkindness and compassion for all beings. In her book *Train Your Mind, Change Your Brain,* Sharon Begley reports the results of the functional MRI scans Davidson took of participants in one of his investigations:

> *When asked what unites the ethics of the world's religions, scholar Karen Armstrong responded with the simplest of answers: 'compassion.' If faced with their own version of the question— What is the central moral adaptation produced in the evolution of human sociality?—evolutionists would converge on a similar answer: 'compassion.' On this, the religiously inclined and evolutionists would agree."*
>
> —DACHER KELTNER, PH.D., FROM *BORN TO BE GOOD*

During the generation of pure compassion, the brains of all the subjects, both adept meditators and novices, showed activity in regions responsible for monitoring one's emotions, planning movements, and positive emotions such as happiness. Regions that keep track of what is "self" and what is "other" became quieter, as if, during compassion meditation, the subjects . . . opened their minds and hearts to others.

Stephanie has been studying a particular Tibetan Buddhist practice that teaches how to tune in to another person's experience. Even after a short time, she has begun to see the difference in her daily life. The meditation, she says, has begun to change her perspective, like switching the figure-to-ground focus.

> Instead of getting so caught up in *What about me?* you do a little more of *What about you?* and that changes everything. You can tune in to another person's pain and find out what might be needed. We all share the human condition. When you practice shifting your focus to others, you're able to get outside yourself enough to really be there when you're with them.

As has been pointed out throughout this book, this doesn't mean forgetting to pay attention to your own needs or collapsing into another's pain. As Stephanie has discovered:

> When you tune in to another's suffering and send out compassionate thoughts to them, rather than draining you, it actually fills you

---

### Developing the Compassionate Heart

While you are sitting quietly, bring to mind someone you care about who is perhaps going through a hard time. Feel the connection you share and your love for that person. Then, staying in touch with the meaning of the words, silently direct these phrases toward him or her: *May you be free of suffering.* Or, *I care about your suffering.*

You might also direct these phrases toward yourself, as well as toward those categories of others discussed in lovingkindness practice—those close to you, those you have difficulty with, those you may never know. Ultimately you might include in compassion all the people and creatures on the planet.

As you do this practice, pay attention to what happens in your body and mind. You might notice a softening of your heart or perhaps a feeling of expansion in your chest. Let yourself fully welcome these feelings. By being present with them, you are deepening your capacity for empathy and developing your compassionate heart.

up with more energy. You seem to clear out the confusion of your small mind and replace it with something much more vast and vibrant. Under all the chatter in your mind, there's a basic goodness you touch that's deeper and more profound. When you let down the fear, you get filled up with that basic goodness and sweetness of your caring heart.

Compassion practice does not have to be limited to formal meditation. Throughout your day whenever you see someone having a hard time, you can tap in to that place of caring inside you and send out thoughts of compassion.

## AWAKENING THE COMPASSIONATE HEART

By the time she was thirteen, Spring was well on her way to trouble. With her father out of the picture, things were hard at home and school wasn't much better. One day she was caught stealing. It was her good fortune that she was only ordered to do community service. Her mother sent her to volunteer at a local church that is well-known for its generous and successful social service programs. There Spring found herself in a new world, in more ways than one. She was serving meals to the homeless, side by side with former addicts and prostitutes who were now clean and sober. To her surprise, she says, "I felt all this love, and it was beautiful." The very first lunch she served to the destitute and homeless turned out to be a transformative experience for her.

> I went to the refrigerator and saw packs and packs of hot dogs, stacks and stacks of bread that looked really old, and these giant cans of pork and beans. I remember thinking, *This is lunch?*

It was a cold day and Spring started wondering if anyone would show up. In fact, when it came time to serve, she looked out the door and there were hundreds of people in a line that seemed endless. As they came through the line, "I noticed that everyone looked so sad," Spring said.

"They all had their heads down." At first the cook told her to give each person two hot dogs, two pieces of bread, and two scoops of beans. After a while as people kept arriving and the line still went on as far as could be seen, the cook announced, "One hot dog, one piece of bread, one scoop of beans."

> I started to feel a sense of desperation as people kept coming through, holding their kids, with tattered clothes, hair uncombed, and hoping for some food. Before long the cook came out again and said, "Half a hot dog, half a piece of bread." And then we ran out of food, and there were still more people in line.

Spring watched for a long time as people drifted away, still hungry. Later, after she'd helped clean up, she went outside and sat down on the curb in front of the church.

> I started sobbing, thinking *This is not right.* What struck me most of all was how much I cared. I cared about all these people I didn't even know. I cared about the kids. I cared that they didn't get food, that it was cold, and where would they would go? I just sobbed and sobbed. I'd never felt like that before.

Even though she was used to seeing homeless people in her neighborhood, being face-to-face with so many in such need had a profound effect. Spring says she was changed after that. "Something deep within me was affected by it all."

What Spring went through was a deep encounter with suffering that is a kind of initiation onto the path of compassionate action. Keeping your heart open in the face of suffering is not easy. We often want to run away from such pain. I think even that impulse proves the point that we care. We feel the suffering of others, and it is often painful because we don't know what to do. Sometimes what we encounter can be so overwhelming that remaining present with it can seem impossible. But when you can't close your eyes anymore to the pain, and you recognize how deeply you care, that is the awakening of the compassionate heart.

Spring, now in her twenties, is considered a pioneer in bringing mindfulness-based meditation practices to youth and communities of color at the East Bay Meditation Center in Oakland, California, which she cofounded and where she teaches. She has also taught yoga and meditation to young people in juvenile hall. Having once been a troubled teen herself, she understands the experiences of those who end up there, and she can respond without judgment and without distancing herself from their suffering. The need and pain she saw that day serving lunch to the homeless and destitute opened her to the rich rewards of compassionate action.

## COMPASSION IS A VERB

Thich Nhat Hahn, Buddhist teacher and activist, makes the point that compassion does not stop with letting our hearts feel the suffering of others. "Compassion is a verb," he stresses. Compassion and action go hand in hand. In those same MRI scans of monks meditating on compassion, neuroscience researcher Richard Davidson discovered that the areas of the brain responsible for planning action also lit up. In *Train Your Mind, Change Your Brain,* Sharon Begley quotes Davidson conveying his report to the Dalai Lama:

> This was a novel and unexpected finding . . . There's no physical activity; they're [the meditating monks] sitting still. One interpretation of this is that it may reflect the generation of a disposition to act in the face of suffering. It gives real meaning to the phrase "moved by compassion."

Not only are we wired for compassion, we appear to be wired for compassionate *action*. When we see suffering and feel compassion, it is natural to want to do something in response.

In his book *Field Notes on the Compassionate Life,* Marc Barasch quotes a young boy who understands exactly how this works. This eight-year-old was asked, "If you knew how someone else felt, would you be more likely to help them than if you didn't?" He replied, "Oh yes. What you do is, you forget everything else that's in your head, and then you make your mind into their mind. Then you know how they're feeling, so you know how to help them." From the mouth of babes . . .

When we remain present with our own aching heart at the suffering of another, we "make our mind into their mind," and that helps us know what to do. While Nyla was taking the Awakening Joy course, a friend of hers gave birth to a baby who lived for only three days. "I wanted to do something for her," Nyla wrote, "but I noticed that my first instinct was to run away from the hard feelings and uncertainty, and my fear that I might do something wrong." Learning about the practice of pausing to sit with her feelings, she decided to try it. What happened gave both Nyla and her friend deep comfort.

> I got in touch with my heart and realized I wanted to send my friend something to remember her baby with. I sent her a journal, a candle, and a tree to plant. The email she sent me in thanks still gives me goose bumps. She said the gift was exactly what she needed. Sitting with those difficult feelings allowed me to get to the other side of my fear and make a real connection with someone having such a hard time. And when I saw her again, I also had the courage to ask to see a picture and talk about her baby. She was so grateful and said it was hard when people pretended like nothing had happened. Without the tools to face my own fear, I could have been one of those people.

## COMPASSIONATE PRESENCE

When we don't know what to say in response to the suffering of another, sometimes just being present is enough. A story submitted for Canfield and Hansen's *A 3rd Serving of Chicken Soup for the Soul* has since become a popular example of the value of this response. The writer Leo Buscaglia was asked to be a judge for a "most compassionate child" contest. The winner was a four-year-old boy whose mother told the following story.

Her son noticed that his next-door neighbor—an elderly man whose wife had just died—was sitting outside in his yard crying. The boy went over and climbed into the man's lap. When he returned home, the mother asked, "What did you say to him?" Her child replied, "Nothing. I just helped him cry."

Offering our compassionate presence not only helps another but deeply nourishes us as we do it. And we don't need to know how to do anything other than be present. Jennifer is a hospice volunteer in Canada. One day she was asked to spend some time with a frail woman in her mid-eighties. "She tends to speak mostly in Dutch," Jennifer was told. When she found Louisa, she was talking to herself quietly and picking at the belt holding her into her chair. Jennifer introduced herself, and Louisa looked up and began speaking to her in Dutch. It didn't matter to Jennifer that she couldn't understand. Instead, she says:

> I just let go into her big beautiful eyes and rested fully in whatever feeling or emotion she was communicating. It was an astonishing experience. At times I'd be sharing in a quiet happiness, and at other times I'd be awash in deep sadness. Sometimes both our eyes were full of tears, and sometimes we smiled and laughed together. For almost two hours, there was a sense of open-hearted connectedness that I found intensely nourishing.

## In the Field of Compassion

When others you know are going through a difficult time, instead of rushing into action, pause for a moment to imagine what it would be like to be in their situation. From a wise and centered place, sense what kind of action would be appropriate. Perhaps it is to simply sit with them, or listen without trying to take away their pain. If it seems that they want to open up but can't, you might ask a question that helps reveal their feelings. Stay connected to your heart, both the ache and the sweetness of your caring response, and hold their suffering in that field of compassion.

When Jennifer was leaving, Louisa pulled her toward her and gently kissed the top of her head. Jennifer says:

On reflection, joy seemed to be the absolutely appropriate word to apply. While on one level I experienced a whole myriad of emotions, behind that shifting panoply was this steady sense of connection, of wholeness, of joy.


## FROM RIPPLES INTO WAVES


Sometimes our compassion ripples out into the world in ways we can't even imagine. The ripple my sister Susan created when she lost a dear friend would unexpectedly become a great wave that now alleviates the suffering of thousands around the world. Susan is a gifted artist who was trained in fashion design. At school she studied alongside a brilliant Puerto Rican student, Antonio Lopez, whose creative genius set a new standard in the fashion industry.

Susan and Antonio had immediately recognized something in each other. In class they would work side by side, and Antonio would tease her: "I don't know why you're bothering to draw when you're going to be my model." Susan says, "I used to laugh when he'd say it, but secretly I knew I would have been glad to be his pencil sharpener. He exuded a positive energy that was just magical."

Susan did become Antonio's model—his first and favorite. And over the next two decades she would be his confidant as well as a close friend to both Antonio and his partner, Juan. In 1987, struggling with complications from AIDS, Antonio moved into Susan's Los Angeles home to spend his final few months. With no health insurance or money left to pay his medical bills, Antonio was essentially wasting away with no treatment to ease his suffering. Moved to take action, Susan decided to put on a show of Antonio's work as a fund-raiser. "In those days people were scared to even mention the word 'AIDS,' " she says, but Susan managed to convince a friend who owned an art gallery to host the event. To his amazement, 2,500 people came to Antonio's show.

Having watched helplessly as her friend died, Susan turned her personal sorrow at losing him into compassionate action to benefit all those who suffered from this epidemic. "I was devastated," she says, "but putting my energy into that idea provided an outlet." As a memorial tribute to Antonio, she and a couple of friends asked photographers they knew to donate their work for a silent auction and benefit to raise awareness of AIDS. Now, two decades later, the organization she and Hossein Farmani started and still run—Focus on AIDS—regularly presents a benefit auction of works donated by world-class photographers. It has raised over $3 million for AIDS projects, including establishing the first children's AIDS hospital in India, which treats four thousand children each month, an orphanage and women's organization in Cambodia, and various AIDS projects in Africa.

*Action absorbs anxiety."*
—ANGELES ARRIEN,
ANTHROPOLOGIST AND
AUTHOR

Acting from her heart for the sake of others actually helped Susan discover not only her life's calling but also her career. Because of Focus on AIDS, she now plays an extensive role in the world of professional photography. And year after year her sorrow for the suffering of others continues to turn into the abundant joy of working to do something to help. Reflecting on what has happened, Susan says:

> It's funny, I was doing something to honor Antonio from my heart, and it not only made a big difference in others' lives, but it completely changed my life too. It's the most meaningful thing I do. And what's interesting is that I could never have imagined it would lead me to who I am now.

Whether what you do to alleviate suffering is small or large, compassionate action is one of the most fulfilling ways you can live your life. Angelina Jolie, who could choose to live in the lap of ease and luxury, has instead become a UN ambassador, traveling the world to speak about the poverty of children around the globe. Her dedication began when she was filming on location in Cambodia and saw the plight of children there. I saw a television program with Jolie in which the interviewer remarked on how generous she was to devote so much time to humanitarian activities when she could be more fully enjoying the life of a Hollywood celebrity. I remember Jolie looking at the woman and replying, "You don't understand. This is what really brings me joy, and my celebrity status is what allows me to do it."

Although it is wholesome and virtuous in itself to feel compassion, acting on it is what leads to your greatest happiness and hopefully to the greater well-being of those you seek to help. When you feel compassion rise in your heart, listen to hear what it motivates you to do. Julia Butterfly Hill is known for her work saving the old-growth redwoods in California. At a lecture I heard her say that people often come up to her after a talk or presentation saying, "Oh, Julia, you've really inspired me!" Her response: "That's wonderful . . . inspired you *to do what?*"

## THIS IS THE WAY IT IS

Rose, a physician and a meditation teacher, volunteered to go to Tibet for a month as part of a medical team setting up clinics in monasteries, schools, and orphanages. There she witnessed extreme poverty—people living without access to clean water, women with crippling arthritis whose job was repairing roads because their nomadic life was gone, or-

### Caring for the World

The next time you read or hear a news story that reveals yet more suffering in the world, pause and notice how you feel. It may be outrage or helplessness. Go beneath those feelings and get in touch with how much you care. How might you respond? Whatever action you take—volunteering, writing a letter, sending funds—do it as a conscious compassion practice. You might speak the phrases silently as you carry out your action: *May you be free of suffering* or *I care about your suffering.*

phans whose parents had died of tuberculosis and who'd had little food and care since. As she encountered such suffering, Rose felt increasingly helpless. As she watched the women faithfully spinning their prayer wheels in hopes of improving their lot in life, their ritual looked so hopeless.

Her despair and dismay only intensified back at home when she was faced with all the luxuries and excesses of our culture. The great disparity between the two worlds was just too much to bear. In a crisis of faith, Rose went on a personal retreat to try to sort things out in her mind.

In the presence of a wise teacher, she allowed all the feelings of anguish to pour through her. Looking back, she says she felt like a child who was having a tantrum and screaming, "I don't want it to be this way, and it *is* this way. It has to stop! Somebody has to stop it! Why doesn't somebody stop it?!" Day after day, Rose's body and mind tightened with her futile desire for the terrible suffering in the world to end. On the other side of this debilitating anguish would be a profound and unexpected gift, but Rose would get there only when she accepted the truth of the suffering in the world and balanced her compassionate heart with a deep understanding.

Vowing to keep your heart open to suffering doesn't mean that you add to it by getting overwhelmed or burning yourself out. The point of the teachings is to create balance and well-being in your life, not overwhelm and chaos. You are one of the most important recipients of your compassion. This can be hard to remember, but it is essential.

What helps with this is the practice of equanimity, the ability to remain composed and balanced, even in the face of challenges. Equanimity means neither getting caught up in the desire for circumstances to be a certain way nor pulling away from them in disgust or annoyance. While it can sometimes look like indifference, equanimity is actually based in a deep and compassionate understanding of the nature of life—that all things change, and that reacting from frustration or anger rather than responding with wisdom only creates more suffering. President Obama is sometimes criticized for his equanimous disposition, especially by some who want more bluster and bravado in his reactions. But in my eyes he is a good example of equanimity in action.

Like the tool of mindfulness, equanimity is a quality of mind that lets us simply acknowledge, as American monk Ajahn Sumedho puts it, this is "the way it is." In fact, so essential is this teaching in developing a balanced state of mind that that phrase became the title of one of his books. Energy spent feeling distressed and wishing things were different diminishes our capacity to respond. Suffering exists. Now what can effectively be done about it?

*Equanimity is more profound than calm. When we are calm, we are not upset. When we are in a state of equanimity, even if our mind has gotten reactivated, we are not upset about the disturbance of mind.*

—RICK HANSON, PH.D., IN *WISE BRAIN BULLETIN*, VOLUME 2, NUMBER 4

Compassion doesn't mean rescuing everyone we see from suffering. It means doing what we can, while also honoring our own limits. As the Serenity Prayer, used in the twelve-step program of Alcoholics Anonymous, says: "Grant me the courage to change the things I can, the serenity to accept the things I cannot change, and the wisdom to know the difference." Equanimity teaches us to care deeply but not be overwhelmed by our caring.

---

### Inviting Equanimity

Take a few deep and mindful breaths. Now let your awareness move slowly through your body, inviting each area to relax. Silently say to yourself: *May I have balance and equanimity in this moment* or *May I be centered in this moment.* Imagine what you would look like, what you would do and feel, if you were in easeful balance, and let yourself step into that.

This is especially useful if you notice that you are in a situation that is upsetting. As you do this practice, notice when thoughts arise wishing for things to be different from how they are at the moment. Allow even the confusion and agitation in your mind to just be, instead of trying to overcome it or push it away. Breathe, and let yourself relax into equanimity, leaning neither into desire nor aversion.

Thich Nhat Hanh, who was deeply involved in trying to alleviate the suffering in his country during the Vietnam war, often talks about the importance of equanimity for acting effectively in the face of danger. As an example, he refers to the boat people, refugees who risked the high seas and other dangers as they attempted to escape the war. Many were lost. Those boats that made it to safety, he reports, were the ones that had at least one calm person aboard. Their energy was enough to inspire others to find that place of courage, determination, and calm within themselves.

## YOU NEVER KNOW . . .

Reading or hearing about suffering and cruelty, or about the destruction of the planet, awakens compassion and the desire to take action. But once you actually take that step, the task can seem so enormous that anything you do may seem to make little difference. Equanimity also allows us to not be rigidly attached to the outcome of our actions. Once we've done what we can, we don't really have control over what happens, nor can we ever accomplish everything that needs to be done.

Oren is a young activist who, like a lot of young people, has many different irons in the fire. Besides teaching meditation and Marshall Rosenberg's Nonviolent Communication skills, he works with people to heal trauma, is involved in sustainability efforts, participates in a nonprofit peace organization, and is a singer and musician. Engaged in so many ways, he has come to understand the value of equanimity. In a conversation about compassionate action, he told me:

> *[B]ehind every human being who cries out for help there may be a million or more equally entitled to attention. . . . How to determine which of one million sounds surrounding you is more deserving than the rest? Do not concern yourself in such speculations. You will never know, you will never need to know. Reach out and take hold of the one who happens to be nearest."*
>
> —NORMAN COUSINS

Thomas Merton says that an activist has to come to terms with the fact that what is done may ultimately be fruitless but that you're not doing it solely for the "hope of results." He says that as "you get used to this idea, you start more and more to concentrate . . . on the value, the rightness, the truth of what you do for itself." A Talmudic story similarly says that if the world were ending and you knew that nothing would make a difference, you'd still do what's most aligned with the heart's deepest values. Beyond the effect any action may have, living with integrity and responding to the circumstances in the best way I know brings the possibility of joy.

Aline is another dedicated young person who has learned to live and work with equanimity. She has been engaged in environmental protection and community development in countries like Senegal, Peru, Romania, and Ukraine. Yet despite all her work, she still witnesses heartbreaking destruction. "In Siberia, 60 percent of the logging in the formerly pristine region where I lived is illegal. I would see trucks and trucks of logs going to China. It was really painful."

We might think it could actually be too painful for her to continue doing the work. Aline could quit in disappointment and with a sense of failure. Instead, her response is a model of equanimity.

I think it's important to take the long-range view. It's not about getting immediate results. It's like planting seeds. If you plant a seed and come the next day and think, "Oh nothing's come yet," you can get really frustrated. But if you plant the seed and think, "Okay, now is the time to water it and nourish it and be patient," it will grow. There's something about trusting when you don't necessarily know what the results will be that comes back twofold. You may not see something concrete but there's a feeling of belonging to the world, being part of the larger community. Something good comes back that you never would have expected.

As Joseph Goldstein likes to say, "You never know." When taking action comes from your heart rather than from the desire to see results, you can continue working without getting depleted, and you can derive joy rather than disappointment from the part you are playing. Gandhi said,

"Whatever you do may seem insignificant to you, but it is most important that you do it." Why? Because as we do even the smallest compassionate action, we ourselves grow and unfold as noble beings.

## DEVELOPING EQUANIMITY

Some of us may be temperamentally more equanimous than others, but like any other quality, equanimity can be developed. Each moment of mindfulness, nonjudgmental awareness, strengthens equanimity. As with lovingkindness, there is also a practice to develop this facility. The phrase traditionally used is: "Your happiness or unhappiness depends on your actions, not only on my wishes for you." Once again, this practice is intended to help us accept the way things are. But when I first heard that phrase, it felt to me rather cool and detached and seemed to be lacking in compassion. Even the variations I tried felt like they had an edge of not caring. But over time I began to understand that I can't prevent people from suffering, even those I love most deeply.

*We ourselves feel that what we are doing is just a drop in the ocean. But the ocean would be less because of that missing drop."*
—MOTHER TERESA

The first time I participated in a retreat dedicated to developing equanimity, I collided with that truth. I'd begun doing the practice by imagining various friends and saying the equanimity phrase. Suddenly my son Adam, then ten years old, came to mind. As I tried to direct those words toward him, something in me snagged. It was much harder to accept someone's suffering with equanimity when the someone was my own son. Could I really do that?

What followed for the next hour I refer to as my "Clockwork Orange" meditation. In the famously wrenching film by that name, there is a scene in which the protagonist is being programmed through forcibly viewing a string of ugly and horrifying scenes. As I sat in the meditation hall trying to practice equanimity, one scene after another of every parent's nightmare passed through my mind—drug addiction, car accidents, terminal diseases, self-destructive habits. As each horrible thing that could happen to Adam came into my mind, I would try to say that traditional phrase. Over and over I found myself recoiling in horror, silently crying out *No, No!* After some time I began to realize that as my son grew older, there would be little I could do to protect him from whatever suffering he was to meet in his life.

At some point the horror gave way to acceptance and finally relief in giving up the idea that my vigilance could protect my son. Of course he would face challenges, and the equanimity phrase I was using eventually morphed into *I honor your life's journey*. The entire process was tremendously freeing and has since allowed me to trust Adam's wisdom to find his own way. I'm happy to say, he's an amazing young man who is now in his twenties. None of my worst fears have come to pass, and although I have little control over how his life unfolds, I'm confident that he is going in the right direction.

### Equanimity Practice for a Loved One

Bring to mind someone you care about, preferably someone you love deeply. Hold an image of that person in your mind's eye and repeat these words as if they were a blessing: *Your happiness or unhappiness depends upon your actions, not only on my wishes for you.* Or you might want to say: *I care for you but I cannot keep you from suffering.* Just notice any feelings that arise and continue to repeat the phrase while taking in the meaning. When you can see and accept that the actions of that loved one have more affect on his or her life than whatever you might want, take in that feeling. Find where the sense of balance and release is expressed in your body and mind. You may at this point want to change your phrase to: *I honor your life's journey.*

## BREAKING OPEN TO LOVE

Tibetan Buddhism teaches that equanimity allows for compassion without limits. It is the ability to feel compassion for the good and the bad, your allies and your enemies, the environmental activists and the polluters. Even if this is understandable as a concept, it might be hard to truly feel this. Perhaps the only way to really allow ourselves this degree of equanimity is to fully acknowledge and accept the depth of suffering in the world.

Rose knew that being on a retreat would not protect her from the overwhelming feelings she had in response to the suffering she'd seen in Tibet. In fact, it was the opposite; there would be no way to avoid that pain. So when she came face-to-face with its deepest expression, she didn't pull away. One day as she was meditating, all the feelings came to the surface, and letting go into them entirely, she found what was on the other side.

> I was crying and sobbing, "My heart is breaking. My heart is breaking." And I just kept allowing that experience. All of a sudden it became, "Ah, my heart is broken. My heart is broken open!" It felt as though something I was holding on to had shattered inside. I'd broken completely wide open. And all of this love began pouring through. It was like I broke open into universal compassion.

The grief and the pain continued, but Rose now felt like she was in the depths of a vast and caring Universe.

> There was no one to hold and no one being held. Just the deep recognition: This is how it is in the world. There *is* this much pain. Beings *are* doing this to each other. It's true *and* there's this much compassion and care, this much love.

What arose then was that profound understanding that arises when equanimity and compassion are in balance.

I felt a deep love for all beings—all beings without exception. I saw behind the suffering to the beauty of each being. I could see the divinity in all the people I'd seen in suffering—the shining of who they were was untouched by the suffering. And the beings who were causing the suffering had that same shining.

"Do not be daunted by the enormity of the world's grief.
Do justly, now.
Love mercy, now.
Walk humbly, now.
You are not obligated to complete the work,
But neither are you free to abandon it."
—The Talmud

For Rose this was an utterly transforming insight. She adds, "I know the potential for any one of us to cause harm through our suffering, and I felt great compassion for that." That experience lifted the despair that had paralyzed Rose. Now when her work leads her into the midst of so much suffering, she is able to respond with an open heart, yet hold the clear and balanced perspective that is the basis of effective action.

## NURTURING THE SEEDS OF A NEW GENERATION

In 1975, when I was a young man still searching for my place in life, I was fortunate to get to know Robert Hall, a well-known and inspiring Gestalt therapist who was teaching at Naropa Institute. One day he asked me what I thought my destiny was. I replied I didn't know, but I thought I was supposed to do something that would contribute to other people's lives. He looked at me directly and said with great kindness and conviction, "I think you will. I think you'll touch people and make a difference in the world." His words had a huge impact on me. I sensed that perhaps he saw something that I didn't quite know. And I started to believe he could be right.

We don't have to be famous or charismatic leaders to have a similar effect. Each of us can empower others to find and fulfill their destiny. Every young person is a good candidate to invest in, even those who might be confused or seem to be lost. In fact, these are the very ones who need us, but it takes courage to respond when the challenge is great. Jan was on the verge of surrendering to failure when she came to a weekend workshop I was leading. While there, she found the inspiration to go on and ended up learning the value of never giving up.

Jan told me she had been teaching elementary school for fifteen years, and loving it—until a child appeared in her third-grade class who actually caused her to consider leaving her job. I'll call the girl Teresa, but her real name, aptly enough, translates into English as "Warrior Princess." Teresa was loud, disruptive, pushy, and she fought—with the other children, with the rules, with everything. Nothing Jan tried had affected that behavior.

When she asked if I had any advice, I told her I was a former school-teacher and shared with her my practice of looking for the key to each child's heart. I suggested that she give herself the same challenge by spending some private time discovering who this girl really was. When the workshop was over, Jan returned home eager to give this idea a try.

A few weeks later I heard from her. When Jan arrived at school on the Monday after the workshop, Teresa was peeking around the corner waiting for her. "I felt a certain sadness at the sight of her darting eyes—like an animal that doesn't know if she's going to be punished or welcomed with open arms," Jan wrote. "In that moment I realized what a large stick we wield as adults over the mental state of children. I had been so focused on punishing and making her as miserable as she was making me that I had almost lost her, this strong, strange, feisty girl."

To the child's surprise, Jan gave her a hug and told her they were going to work at understanding each other and find ways to make their day joyful. Even more surprising to Teresa, Jan invited her to have lunch, just the two of them, each day that week. Usually a student had to earn that privilege through good behavior. Teresa showed up for lunch that day and each day after, eagerly offering Jan "a week's worth of eye- and mind-opening conversations." She learned that there was a lot of trouble at home, and she began to understand some of what her Warrior Princess was dealing with every day.

By the end of the week, the two were laughing together, "looking for the joy in each other," as Jan put it. There were a few relapses into noisy and loud, pushy behavior, but the change in the child seemed hopeful. Then, on the first day when Jan didn't have lunch with her, Teresa didn't show up for class that afternoon. "The other children told me a boy had hurt her on the playground, and she got in a fight with him." When Jan saw her Warrior Princess in the school office, she says, "I wanted to cry with her. We had made such progress, but the scars in this child's life run deep." Jan's final words in that note held some promise. "I won't give up . . . and at least I now see her as a fellow human being who is trying to find a path that makes some sense in this confusing world."

*Serving is different from help-ing. Helping is based on inequal-ity. . . . When we help we may inadvertently take away from peo-ple more than we could ever give them. . . . [When we serve], we serve with ourselves. . . . The wholeness in us serves the whole-ness in others . . . Service is a re-lationship between equals."*
—RACHEL NAOMI REMEN, IN *NOETIC SCIENCES REVIEW,* SPRING, 1996

Jan had found a balance of compassion and equanimity in her relationship with Teresa that was helping her ride the waves and continue trying, even when things looked hopeless. Being willing to be pres-ent for a young person, and to remain loyal when the rewards are not immediate, is true compassionate action. The same power that Jan recognized as "the large stick we wield as adults," can be transformed into a having a tremendously positive impact when we be-lieve in children and see their potential.

Four months after that first message, Jan sent me an update on her Warrior Princess. Recently the principal had to adjust class sizes, which meant moving one of Jan's students to another teacher. Teresa might have been the logical choice. But Jan wrote:

> I realized then that I didn't want to lose this amazing person who had been a thorn but is becoming something else in our evolution together. That's when it hit me—she would be the last student I would want to part with!

Jan may never know what her caring has meant for Teresa's life. As a schoolteacher myself, rarely have I found out the results of my efforts to support young people in discovering their true beauty. But a few years ago, I received an email that said: "Are you the Mr. Baraz who was my teacher and changed my life?" There at the end of the message was the name of Suzanna who had been in one of my sixth-grade classes decades before.

I remembered that she was always trying to be helpful and make others happy. But there was a sadness about her that used to make me wonder what else was happening in her life. Although I would not learn the inner landscape of her world until years later, the intensity of her pain revealed itself one dramatic afternoon. During lunch Suzanna tried to put an end to her life by swallowing a bottle of aspirin. She returned to class, but when she began feeling sick, she started having second thoughts. She says, "I remember thinking, 'No, I do not want to die. Not like this.' " Suzanna passed a note to one of her friends. Terrified, the girl showed it to me. Within minutes an ambulance had arrived. After the school day ended, I spent the next few hours at the hospital until I could see that Suzanna was out of danger.

*Recent scientific studies are identifying the kinds of environments that cultivate compassion. This moral emotion is cultivated in environments where parents are responsive, and play, and touch their children. So does an empathic style that prompts the child to reason about harm. So do chores, as well as the presence of grandparents. Making compassion a motif in dinnertime conversations and bedtime stories cultivates this all-important emotion."*

—DACHER KELTNER, IN
*BORN TO BE GOOD*

For the rest of the year I made sure that she received all the love and attention I could give her. At the end of the school year, I signed her autograph book with a sincere message that said, in part: "The sooner you become aware of the <u>real</u> you, like I have, the sooner you'll be able to appreciate yourself as I do."

In these last years since reconnecting, we've become friends. Suzanna's good heart is as radiant as ever, and what's more, she's at peace with herself. In a letter she wrote to me recently, I was surprised to find out that our year together and the words I wrote in her book were major factors in contributing to her shift toward well-being. Suzanna wrote:

Though it took some time and, of course, life experiences, you gave me strength in believing that there must be more to me. . . . You helped open me up to a different perspective, and for that I thank you more than you could ever know. Every time I looked at your page in my autograph book, I felt happy. It was those very words that helped make me aware of the "real me." Not only did I begin to like myself, but I found that I love and respect myself.

You will find that there is hardly a better way to awaken joy than helping young people blossom. If your work doesn't put you in direct touch with young people, there are many volunteer mentoring opportunities available in your community, in your nation, in the world. In the process of responding to the call, you may find you have many opportunities to experience compassion—and equanimity! You may never know, but you can be sure that the good you've awakened will ripple out and make the world just that little bit better.

### Being a Mentor

If you don't know how to begin offering your time to work with young people, contact a social service organization, such as the United Way or the Big Brother/Big Sister organizations or refer to serve.gov. If you belong to a church or other spiritual group, you will likely find there are many places you are needed and valued. The young people you have the opportunity to spend time with will teach you what works for them. Be present. Be absolutely trustworthy. Be genuinely encouraging. Help them fulfill their dreams. Let your connection be a practice of compassion and equanimity. And don't miss the joy.

## CALLING ALL BODHISATTVAS

When we become Bodhisattvas-in-Training, we set ourselves on a path toward a life that is meaningful and fulfilling. Expressing your caring by lessening the suffering around you is deeply rewarding. No matter how many challenges my young friend Aline has faced in her work around the world, she knows she'll continue doing this kind of service for the rest of her life.

> *The place God calls you to is the place where your deep gladness and the world's hunger meet."*
> —REVEREND FREDERICK BUECHNER, PRESBYTERIAN MINISTER

> I think it's a very human thing to want to serve. It feeds something in the soul. If people look honestly, living their values counts more than money. If you're not aligned with your values it eats at you. When you are, something in you grows and comes alive. Each one of us has our own hidden purpose inside, and needs to uncover it and give it wings. Service is one of the things that gets us in touch with that most natural and true part of ourselves.

According to Buddhist teachings, when the mind is clear and not preoccupied with *what's in it for me,* our inherent compassion is revealed. As Richard Davidson's neuroscientific research on compassion meditation has suggested, the natural response to seeing someone in distress is the impulse to help. We care about the suffering of others. And we feel good when that suffering is relieved. Whether we're involved in compassionate action ourselves, witnessing heroic actions in a movie, or reading about noble actions, a caring response to the suffering of others lifts us up. As Aline puts it, knowing that she's making a positive difference in people's lives is "one of the best feelings I've ever known."

Oren, the multitalented young activist, agrees that making a positive difference in the world has given him "some of the most deeply satisfying and meaningful moments in life." He continues:

When I'm engaged in my work, at its best I'm stepping out of the way and life is moving through me. Whether teaching someone about Nonviolent Communication or working with someone in trauma or performing a song in front of an audience, the sense of self is not in the foreground. Life is moving through this mind and body and expressing what needs to happen in the moment, and that is a joyful experience. I am a part of life, not separate from it. That's what we're here for.

*"[T]he vagus nerve . . . resides in the chest and, when activated, produces a feeling of spreading, liquid warmth in the chest and a lump in the throat. . . . [P]hysiological psychologist Steve Porges has made the case that the vagus nerve is the nerve of compassion, the body's caretaking organ."*

—DACHER KELTNER,
IN *BORN TO BE GOOD*

These young people love what they're doing, and they're doing what they love. As they demonstrate, sharing their talents and abilities for the well-being of others is the key to happiness.

You may think, "Yes, but those young people are doing things that are exciting and interesting, and I have to be stuck here in this little cubicle all day, or waiting on all these impatient people, or doing the same thing every day." Of course if you hate your job or are getting burned out, it's harder to access the joy of service. If your current livelihood or daily activities don't in themselves allow you that opening to joy of service, you could do compassionate action through simple acts of kindness—offering a sincere smile to coworkers, or taking an interest in the well-being of customers, or imagining how your job benefits people you'll never see.

Finding ways to lift up your heart changes your own life, which undoubtedly makes a difference for others. Shoshana's son Elias discovered this when he came home from college for the summer and found a job as a checkout clerk at a grocery store. Very soon he came up against the challenge it can be "to serve the public." Elias realized he could either spend the next couple of months gritting his teeth and getting through his shift, or he could reframe what he was doing in his job. He says:

As a cashier it's really easy to get frustrated. Often people who come through the line are disrespectful or rude. You've been standing up all day, and you just want to be rude right back. I decided to make it a meditation practice to remember the human goodness of each person coming through, and to let that remembrance, and my love for humanity, shine out in the way I interacted with them—a kind of spiritual *namaste,* or bow to their spirit. It turned the job into a practice that made a visible difference in my life.

And it probably also did in the lives of those who came through Elias's checkout line. I certainly know how much a kind greeting did

## GIVING IS GOOD FOR YOU

Numerous studies have shown that giving in various ways has a beneficial effect on the giver.

- According to the measures of a Social Capital Community Benchmark survey, those who gave contributions of time or money were "42 percent more likely to be happy" than those who didn't give.
- Psychologists have identified a typical state of euphoria reported by those engaged in charitable activity. They call it "helper's high," and it's based on the theory that giving produces endorphins in the brain that provide a mild version of a morphine high.
- Research at the National Institutes of Health showed that the same area of the brain that is activated in response to food or sex (namely, pleasure) lit up when the participants in the study thought about giving money to a charity.
- At Emory University a study revealed that helping others lit up the same part of the brain as receiving rewards or experiencing pleasure.

for me in a similar situation. I regularly cross a toll bridge on my way to the Spirit Rock Center where I teach. Several years ago there was a toll-taker whose presence was so uplifting that I'd try to guess which lane he was in, just so I could receive his "blessing." As I'd hand over my fee, he'd give me a radiant smile and a heartfelt "I hope you have a great day!" I'm sure he did that with every single person crossing the bridge.

*I think if you're only thinking about yourself, your life becomes diminished. The way to live a full life is to think about: What can I do for others? How can I be a part of this larger project of making a better world?*

—BARACK OBAMA, RESPONDING TO A QUESTION AT STRASBOURG, FRANCE TOWN HALL MEETING, APRIL 3, 2009

It's easy to imagine the sense of satisfaction that he'd go home with each night. Years later I still remember him for how he brightened my day with his joyful spirit. We can't all be Albert Schweitzers, but we can be ourselves, doing whatever we do and recognizing the tremendous power we have to bring a little more happiness into the world.

If your job can't be transformed in some way, consider getting involved in volunteer activities outside of work—helping out in a senior center or at a food bank, reading to children in library programs, assisting those with special needs. You never know what kind of change might come about in your life as you get you in touch with your spirit of compassion and make a difference in the lives of others.

Perhaps you have been moved and experienced a warm and uplifting feeling as you read some of the stories of kindness and compassion in this chapter. Maybe you've been inspired to reach out to help others yourself in some way. If so, you know the feeling psychology professor Jonathan Haidt has called the "elevation" response, the feeling of uplift and inspiration we experience on witnessing selfless acts and good deeds. Haidt writes: "Elevation is elicited by acts of virtue or moral beauty; it causes warm, open feelings . . . in the chest; and it motivates people to behave more virtuously themselves." Those "warm, open feelings" sound a lot like the way participants in the Awakening Joy course describe happiness.

Awakening joy in ourselves is also a way to serve others. By remaining in touch with your own aliveness and appreciation for life, you remind those around you of their own capacity to do the same. Rather than being self-indulgent or frivolous, to be joyful is a gift we give to those we meet and to the world. Joy awakens our love for life, and it's contagious. This is what the planet needs in order to heal and thrive. This is what we all need in order to blossom and to live fulfilling lives. For the sake of all of us, be happy.

# 10

## *THE JOY OF*
## *SIMPLY BEING*

Happiness cannot be found through great effort and willpower
but is already there in relaxation and letting go.

—Lama Gendun Rinpoche

*I was lying* on the white sands of a spectacular beach on the Greek island of Sifnos. The Mediterranean Sea was a deep blue. The delicious smell of spanikopita from the nearby taverna filled the air. I was surrounded by a group of wonderful friends I had recently met while we were all gazing at the wonder of the Acropolis. And to top it off, we all loved singing together. I was in Paradise. Or could have been.

It was my annual European holiday, something I treated myself to each summer after a year of teaching elementary school in New York. I was right where I'd planned and hoped to be. But instead of really being there, immersed in that idyllic setting, I was caught up in my usual worries: *What am I going to do next? Something feels missing in my life. Will I ever really be happy?* I'd carried into Paradise the same agitated thoughts that ran my mind at home. They'd followed me as I drove to school in the morning. They'd been with me as I tried to fall asleep at night. And they made it so that I was everywhere but *here.*

On that island of Sifnos, if I had just let myself settle into where I was at that moment, I would have found exactly what I was looking for—the joy of simply being. It would take a few weeks in the magic of Greece, but eventually I did experience what it was like to stop looking for the next thing and just let myself *be.* I have to admit that being in Paradise definitely helped in the process, but the point is still the same. When I finally allowed myself to relax, let go of all my concerns about the past and the future, and just settled back into the moment, I discovered that the happiness I longed for was right under my nose. And for the first time in my life, it occurred to me that it might be there anytime, anywhere.

> *When you are not hungry or threatened or in pain, your brain's natural state has these characteristics: It is conscious, calm, contented, caring, and creative."*
> —RICK HANSON, AUTHOR OF *BUDDHA'S BRAIN*

As I've been saying throughout this book, the joy we're looking for is inside us. Each step in the Awakening Joy program has focused on cultivating positive mind-states, such as gratitude or compassion, that allow our inherent capacity for joy and well-being to arise. But there is another way to access joy—letting go of trying to make any particular state of mind happen, and connecting with your innate joy and aliveness.

The key to this deeper level of joy is learning how to relax, body *and* mind. As you do, your natural capacity for well-being and happiness emerges. I once heard a great Tibetan master say that the whole of spiritual practice could be summed up in two words: Be spacious. That is what the joy of being is about—entering into a spacious relationship with the moment. You let go of agendas and let your mind settle into a sense of presence. This state of ease and openness—this place inside I like to call our true home—is waiting for you all the time.

Allowing yourself to just relax and simply *be* might be so foreign that it takes a little time to get used to, as I found that first week or two I spent in Greece. We *think* we want more intensity, perhaps because it seems to make us feel more alive. But when we take a break from the adrenaline rush of stimulating activities and learn to rest in the moment, we meet a dimension of well-being that is full of vitality and renewal.

If you've ever undertaken a cleansing fast, you know that there's an initial period when all the food you can't have looks so good and you feel deprived. But as your body starts to detoxify, you begin to feel light and energized, and you don't miss all the potato chips, pizza, and fudge brownies. When you return to eating, you're attuned to the subtleties of taste and texture, and everything seems more flavorful. In the same way, there's a period of adjustment as you slow down or take a break from the momentum of a busy life. When you've learned how to take a time-out for *non-doing*, everything in your "doing" life becomes more alive and fulfilling.

*Our culture invariably supposes that action and accomplishment are better than rest, that doing something—anything—is better than doing nothing. Because of our desire to succeed, to meet these ever-growing expectations, we do not rest. Because we do not rest, we lose our way. We miss the compass points that would show us where to go, we bypass the nourishment that would give us succor. We miss the quiet that would give us wisdom. We miss the joy and love born of effortless delight."*
—WAYNE MULLER, FROM *SABBATH· FINDING REST, RENEWAL, AND DELIGHT IN OUR BUSY LIVES*

Such moments of renewal can happen even when you're involved in daily activities. A martial arts student begins by slowly practicing movements of defense, and after a while he or she has the ability to fend off three attackers at once. In the same way, as you become more familiar with this quality of non-doing in quiet times, you can also find it in the midst of a busy life.

What I'm primarily encouraging, however, is consciously taking regular time-outs to be right here, right now. Eckhart Tolle says, "[L]ife is inseparable from the Now; it can unfold only Now." Most of our "Nows" are filled up with planning, fixing, producing, and all the other necessary actions of daily life, but there is a great joy in getting out of the fast lane to simply *be*. You can do this for an instant or for a day. Whatever length of time you find, it will renew your spirit and connect you with life in a profound way. Relaxing is the healthy complement to doing. Even God rested on the seventh day of creation.

You might think, "Great! This is the kind of road to happiness I like. I'm going to flop down on the couch and just *be* there in front of the TV for a while." Sorry, but *being* is not the same as spacing out and doing nothing. Although it might look like kicking back or vegging out, in the state of being I'm referring to, you are alert and relaxed at the same time. So turn off the TV, put down the remote, and see what happens when you discover *this* moment.

All of the other steps in this program support this final step. You started with setting the intention to awaken joy, deciding to do your part to find where true happiness lies. Mindfulness is what gets you here in the present and helps you wake up to life. Gratitude expands the heart so that you can meet the moment with appreciation and wonder. The capacity to work with difficulties as they arise gives you confidence to know that you can be present for whatever hand life deals you. Living with integrity aligns you with your highest values and frees you of remorse, creating the conditions for inner peace. Developing the ability to let go allows you to flow with the changes of life, rather than trying to hang on to something you think will make you happy. Learning to love yourself helps you stop the self-judgment, access the goodness inside, and settle into being who you are. Connecting with others is about letting your love shine through naturally. Compassion arises as your heart meets suffering and responds. All these qualities and actions are ingredients in our recipe for happiness, and they continue to support you, functioning like a hologram in which they interactively strengthen each other. In this step you rest on what you have derived from them and enter into a connection with life that is effortless and joyful.

## WHAT IS *BEING*?

Most of you reading this book in some way or another know the experience of *being* I'm talking about. You may recall moments as a child when you sank into a deliciously relaxed state of ease and happiness. You may find yourself accessing this state in a yoga class, during moments of quiet reflection, or while out running. It can happen when you're dancing, playing an instrument, or looking at microorganisms in a biology lab. There are different "flavors" of being and different ways of accessing them.

Being "in the zone" is an experience common among athletes or performers when they are so engaged with the game, the music, or the drama that they forget themselves. Time slows down, and they often find themselves executing brilliant moves. Karlene Sugarman, a sports psychology consultant, lists a number of qualities that characterize the zone: relaxed, confident, focused, effortless, automatic (the thinking mind is not in the way), and fun (deeply enjoyable). These qualities also define the state that I'm talking about. However, there is another quality Sugarman includes to describe the zone for performers and those engaged in a certain task—being in control. This is different from the state of *being* addressed in this chapter. The only task here is to let go of effort and settle into a state of relaxed presence.

In describing the state of *being,* course participants most commonly use words such as: aware, spacious, peaceful, smooth, restful, and light. They say that during the experience:

• A calmness falls over me, I "quiet" and feel my physical body loosen.

---

### *Being* Aware

In the midst of any activity in your day, stop for a moment of being. Become mindfully aware of your experience. Notice that you are thinking, that thoughts come and go. Notice whatever emotions that might be arising. Feel the sensations in various parts of your body. Feel your breath coming in and going out. Notice that you are not making awareness happen. It happens by itself effortlessly. You are simply aware. Feel the spaciousness and peace.

- I feel open and ready, no thought.
- I feel a fullness in my chest and a feeling in my throat as if I'm about to sing or cry out in joy, and sometimes there are tears of joy.
- My mind becomes more available to a deeper sense of order. My body posture comes more into alignment.
- I feel whole and at ease, unjudged, unjudging, loving and able to love myself as I am and circumstances as they are.

## BOREDOM AND BREAKTHROUGH

You might wonder: If you're not busy doing something, where's the joy in that? We're so used to stimulation and entertainment that the idea of quieting down enough to tune in to stillness and silence can sound pretty boring. It might even seem scary. When I was younger, the thought of not having something planned in my calendar for a Friday night was terrifying. "What will I do with myself?" I'd wonder. A weekend with nothing going on can feel to us like a terrible emptiness. So we persist in perpetual motion. But what exactly are we afraid of?

There are some good reasons for being afraid to stop filling up your life with action. When you're not distracted, you're alone with your mind. Having nothing to immediately chew on, it can dredge up a little frightening "entertainment" from the past, or create a horror movie of the future. This is where meditation or some other reflective or introspective practice is such a valuable support. In seeing how the mind works and learning to be at ease with all of its contents, you develop the faculty of equanimity. As Rick Hanson pointed out in Step Nine, equanimity is deeper than calm, because even when our thoughts are bouncing off the walls, with equanimity we can remain balanced and aware, not collapsing into the chaos. We can abide in the awareness of the swirl, rather than in the swirl itself.

There is a huge reward in learning to make friends with your mind: You discover the exquisite experience of just being present. Drawing upon the practices you have learned throughout this book, you build the foundation for a mind that needs no entertainment to enjoy the moment. This allows it to relax into a state of ease. I once attended a lecture by a Tibetan master who started his talk with the enticing line, "Tonight I will talk about the real breakthrough in spiritual practice." The huge crowd in the auditorium was abuzz with excitement, thinking that they would be the fortunate ones to receive these special teachings. The master then proceeded to ramble on for the next two hours in a rather uninspired manner. As the crowd grew increasingly disappointed and restless, he suddenly stopped mid-sentence, leaned forward, and whispered, "The real breakthrough is boredom!"

Smiling, he sat back to explain to his puzzled audience what he meant. As long as we're looking for the next experience to delight or entertain us, we miss the big secret: When we learn to disconnect from constant stimulation and distraction, we begin the work of freeing our mind from the restlessness of wanting and not wanting. And we also arrive at the doorway to the peace and well-being that come with completely resting in this moment. The flip side of boredom turns out to be peace.

## DOORWAYS TO *BEING*

When I was a child, I was enthralled by astronomy. But growing up in New York City, I couldn't see many stars in the sky, so I would beg my parents to take me to my favorite spot in the world: the Hayden Planetarium. When the day would arrive for the new monthly show, I could hardly contain my excitement. Gazing up at that magic star-filled sky dome, all I could say, over and over, was "Wow!" The vast expanse seemed limitless. The Earth, and everything on it including me, was just a tiny speck. I somehow felt both infinitely small and mysteriously connected with something infinitely great. Those moments in the darkness of the planetarium, with my parents on either side of me, I was led by wonder into the present moment. Nowhere else existed.

We're all born with the capacity for wonder and awe, and these are doorways for us into being. Jesus said, "Truly I tell you, unless you change

and become like children, you will never enter the kingdom of heaven"
(Matthew 18:3). When we pause in childlike wonder and appreciation,
we enter the kingdom of heaven, for in those moments we are profoundly connected to life.

As a child I regularly fell into this state of wonder by experiencing
what I came to call the Big Giggle. I'd ask myself certain questions that
would stop my mind and turn me inside out: *What does it mean to be alive?*
*How did I get into this body and end up being this person other people call*
*"Jamie" and I call "me"?* Then I'd wait as the questions carried me deep
into a place where I could no longer tell who was asking the question.
The boundaries between me and the rest of life would dissolve. In that
moment there was just presence, with no distracting thoughts or feelings.
It was an experience of life moving through me, and it was profoundly
joyful. This could happen to me anywhere—in the middle of school,
walking down the street, or lying in my bed at night. When I let myself
go into it, I would often start to laugh to myself—sometimes right out
loud. It was like a button I could press at any time, and the Big Giggle
would follow.

In the right frame of mind, we can be in awe of just about anything
and be transported through our attention into the moment of being. This
is essentially an attitude of deep appreciation. We might find it in viewing
a painting, washing dishes, or watching a superb actor at work. While there
are endless things to appreciate, poets and scientists would agree that being
in the natural world rivets us to the moment in a special way, and we find
ourselves in a profound state of being. Sally Clough Armstrong, one of my
teaching colleagues at Spirit Rock, puts it this way:

When I let my mind really appreciate what is right in front of me—
the clouds or a rainbow or a bird flying by—there is a sense of wonder and amazement at the richness of life. To truly open to that, the
mind has to be still. There's a sense of aliveness relating to the outside, but the internal experience is one of stillness, of stopping and
connecting with life. It's just stillness and aliveness without a lot of
mental content to it.

Nature has no agenda for us. When we're present with the sights and sounds in any natural setting, we are free to not-do. We can be simply present for the soft breeze touching our face. We can open our senses to receive the images of trees and flowers, and take in the sounds of crickets and the rustle of wind in the leaves. And we enter the "stillness and aliveness" Sally describes.

*When I stop to appreciate a flower, the weight drops from my shoulders. I settle and get quiet, and I feel spacious and expanded inside."*

—A COURSE PARTICIPANT

Wonder and appreciation are in themselves relaxed and receptive states, a receiving rather than reaching out. We are awake and attentive, and the door opens to a delightful state of being. This is the way Guy Armstrong, another of my teaching colleagues, puts it:

It's not that we have to do anything special, but rather when we stop striving, natural happiness is there to be touched. Our basic nature is peaceful, and that peace brings a kind of joy. All we have to do to find it is to stop disturbing it. When the body calms down and the mind can just relax and rest, there's a joy and delight in that experience which is very pleasurable in itself and very renewing. There's a feeling of the batteries being recharged: aliveness refreshing itself.

You can drop into this relaxed, effortless presence at any time—while listening to music, soaking in a hot bath, meditating, or sipping a cup of tea. It can also happen in the midst of energetic activities, like swimming, or hiking, or singing. It happens when we invite it and stand in awe at the miracle of being alive. It happens when we set aside the judging mind that separates us from the moment. And it arises when we realize we have nowhere to go but here.

## WEEDING THE MIND

The state of being is not only delightful and renewing, it has a very practical benefit as well. Deeper than conflicting thoughts, it is the source of wisdom. When we find ourselves confused or pulled apart by indecision, tapping in to what some call our "peaceful center" can align us with what will bring our life into harmony.

For my wife, Jane, gardening is a way to drop into that feeling of wholeness and experience its benefits. She says:

> Gardening helps me relax and connect with an inner peace. I love taking a break from the emails, phone calls, and never-ending to-do lists to step outside into the world of dogs, birds, and squirrels, into the changing weather patterns, and feel the anchoring of big trees, which have been around longer than I have. The interesting thing is that even though I'm not trying to solve any problems, clarity comes and things just seem to fall into place. While I'm weeding the garden, it's like I'm weeding my mind as well.

When we give ourselves the time to relax and let our minds be "weeded," we can better listen to those inner promptings that keep us on track with our deeper life purpose. We're all familiar with what happens when we don't listen or can't hear because the chaotic thoughts in our mind are taking the driver's seat. We're likely to plunge over a cliff. That's what happened to Allison when, in confusion, she gave up the love of her life.

I met Allison on her first meditation retreat at Spirit Rock and, although it was clear she had some major struggles going on in her life, I was struck by her sincerity and deep longing for peace. She'd come to the retreat looking for a lifeline, she said, and told me about how she'd been through several destructive relationships, and in and out of substance abuse, often occasioned by or in response to bouts of depression. Finding a way to pay the bills was one of her main preoccupations. Now she was ready for a change, a big change, and she was ready to do whatever would help.

Over the next two years, Allison regularly attended my weekly meditation group in Berkeley, and I got to know more of her story. A couple of decades before, when she was in her twenties, Allison met David. She had been leading a wild life, many boyfriends, lots of partying. "I was out of control," she told me. In hope of finding some balance, she'd made an appointment with an acupuncturist—David. Right from the start there was a special chemistry between them. When the strong attraction became apparent to both of them, David stopped seeing her professionally, and they began a loving relationship. "I had been living a lie with many of my friends until then. David said to me, 'You have to tell the truth.' And somehow that stuck."

Allison did start telling the truth—to everyone but herself. The voice of fear told her that what she and David shared couldn't possibly last. After a few months, Allison broke off the relationship. Although something within her was begging to stay with David, doubt and fear, disguised as the lure of fun and adventure, had won out. "I knew he was a healthy partner who would love me, but I didn't love myself," Allison recently reflected. "I felt awkward being in a 'wholesome' relationship. It was too foreign for someone with my background. And I just wasn't mature enough to listen to what I really needed. He was like a saint and I wanted excitement. I ended my relationship with him because I was not done 'being bad.' "

David was devastated, and his grief led him further into the spiritual practice he'd been doing for a couple of years with a Kriya Yoga teacher from India. He soon found himself managing his guru's ashram in the United States. A few years later David became a monk himself and took a vow of celibacy. The title of swami, a master of yoga and Hindu philosophy, was conferred upon him. David brought his big heart, his guitar, and his storytelling ability to his work as a spiritual teacher, and in time he became known as the Storytelling Monk. As the number of his followers increased, he was able to establish a network of orphanages, schools, and shelters throughout India and South America, dedicated to providing refuge and support to street children and the poor in the villages he visited. He never forgot Allison and would often explain, when people asked how he became a swami, that a woman in Berkeley had unwittingly pushed him into the arms of the Divine by breaking his heart at the perfect time.

Meanwhile Allison floundered. For the next seventeen years, she was led down dead-end alleys by those confusing voices inside saying: "This way to happiness; no, that way." The unexpected catalyst that began to turn her life around was a class in physiology taught by an inspiring teacher at a community collge. "Wow, we are just amazing beings," Allison remembers thinking. "I was learning that there are over a trillion cells in the human body, and each little cell's only job is to work for my well-being. I began to wonder how could I do anything to harm this body that is nothing less than a miracle."

That was the beginning. Allison stopped drinking, started letting go of unhealthy relationships, and soon found her way to Spirit Rock and that meditation retreat I was leading. "I felt like I'd found everything I'd been looking for my whole life," she told me. "Part of me literally woke up." It would take her a while to climb out of the disorder in her life, but Allison knew she was on the right track and steadily moved in a new and positive direction.

## THE STILL, SMALL VOICE WITHIN

The voice of wisdom, that inner guide, is hard to hear when the mind is filled with distractions, conflicting desires, and self-doubts. Throughout this book we've seen many instances of people's lives descending into chaos when they believed a particular "story" they were telling themselves. And we've also seen that although these stories are programmed into us, they are not our only guide. A deeper wisdom is always available. It might be covered by a lot of static, but it's there, and we hear it when we drop into being present, when we get past all the noise, relax our grip, and tune in to the clarity that arises from the stillness within.

Each of us has our own way of accessing this wisdom. We might call it intuition or guidance or the "still, small voice within." The Third Zen Patriarch says: "Stop talking and thinking and there is nothing you'll not be able to know." For many, prayer is the way to contact this deeper level of truth. Mother Teresa said, "Prayer is putting oneself in the hands of God . . . and listening to His voice in the depth of our hearts." Buddhist monk Ajahn Chah spoke about "listening to the One Who Knows." In letting go of agendas and being at ease with this moment, the "figuring out mind" gets out of the way and we can hear the wisdom inside.

It's hard to connect with the receptivity of *being* and hear the truth inside when you're anxious or stirred up. How do we sort out the various voices when we must make a decision or choice in life? I sometimes find that taking a break from my mind and getting into my body—going for a walk or taking a bike ride—helps discharge agitated energy, gets me grounded, and clears my mind enough to discern the answer that feels right.

How do we know when an answer "feels right"? For me, the voice of wisdom usually has a tone of kindness, clarity, compassion, and understanding. I sense it won't steer me wrong. There's usually a feeling of relaxation in my body, a softening in my heart, a release in my gut, a drop in my shoulders.

When I ask course participants how they know when they've arrived at a good decision, responses have included these:

- I feel like everything in my body and mind is in alignment.
- There is a great feeling of calm and readiness to accept what is happening now and what may happen in the future.
- I feel solid, like I'm standing in my truth.
- The muscles in my body feel soft and released, as opposed to tense and holding on, and my monkey mind quiets down.
- I live inside my skin with greater ease.
- I feel a clarity in my mind and a sense of kindness in my heart.

It was challenging for Allison to break the habits that were driving her, and the voice of wisdom inside was still distant. But David had helped awaken something in her those many years before by seeing what was true and real, and now she was watering that seed by taking care of her body, meditating, and paying attention to what she really wanted. "I started reading a lot and spending time by myself. I had wanted inner peace, but I never thought it was possible before. I just hadn't known how to get there." Allison was finding her way toward happiness.

And then she slipped. Longing for love and connection, she struck up a friendship with a married man. Although she knew it would cause pain to everyone involved, the attraction was strong, and the confusion of voices inside drowned out the voice of wisdom she was just getting to know. Desperate, she talked to friend after friend. "When I contemplated having an affair, I told at least four people what I was planning to do, and not one of them said 'Don't do it.' " Allison sought out an old boyfriend who surprisingly provided exactly what she needed. "He said, 'Don't do it. It's not you. You aren't that person anymore.' There was this huge 'Thank-You' that arose inside me and a tremendous sense of relief when I heard the truth. It rang like a siren inside my soul and *woke me up.*" We know the ring of truth when we hear it.

Allison heard another clear message as well: Contact David. This time when she searched for him on the Internet, she found him—as the Story-telling Monk. "I was looking for my anchor of truth to keep me on the path I had worked so damn hard to stay on." Allison mustered up her courage and sent the swami an email. Within minutes he replied. "He wrote me that he was just telling his students the week before that I was one of his first gurus, because when his life went into crisis after we parted, he found his true self. He said he'd been sending me blessings and prayers for the last twenty years."

Over the course of the next two months, they stayed in daily touch by email. It soon became obvious to both of them that their old love story was not finished. David invited Allison to join him in India for a medita-

### Setting Up a New Ring Tone

The more we practice quieting down and listening to the truth inside, the more easily we access our wisdom. Think back to a good decision you've made in your life. Try to remember the moment when your course of action became clear to you. How did you know it was the right thing to do? What was the feeling in your body? What was the tone of voice in your mind? Each time you make a good decision, pay attention to your experience, that sense of rightness and ease in your heart. Get to know how it feels. Whenever you are facing a decision, see if you can quiet down enough to access it and listen to what it is trying to tell you.

tion program and a pilgrimage to various holy places he had organized for a group of his students. This time when Allison met David, she was able to hear what she had known to be true all along—he was the perfect partner for her.

With the blessings of his fellow swamis in the order, David has made the decision to forego being a monk, marry Allison, and continue doing his spiritual work as a lay person. As Allison looks back on her life and the lessons she's learned, one of the most important among them is knowing how to listen carefully to her deepest self and act on that. Now she knows the signs that point the way. She says:

> When I stay grounded in my truth, my heart feels light and open and expansive. When I am living outside the truth and out of alignment with my integrity, I feel a weight on my chest, on my heart. This pressure disconnects me from others. And it doesn't leave until I make peace with whatever the problem is.

## TRUSTING LIFE

When you know how to listen to that voice inside, you begin to live in a way that aligns you with life. You find yourself increasingly in the right place at the right time. You can call it listening to your intuition or to the voice of God in your heart, but it lets you live in trust instead of fear.

Part of trusting life is knowing that what you need in order to live in harmony with yourself and with life is always available. As Ram Dass says in *Be Here Now,* "Whenever you're ready, you'll hear the next message." You might not always hear it inside you. Sometimes the message we recognize as the truth comes from someone else. Your best friend or your grandmother offers some sage advice, or you get an astrology reading, or you open up a fortune cookie, and you immediately have a sense that what you are hearing is just for you. You are brought back from a confusion of thoughts and into the moment. Once again you realize that you can trust in life.

This became clear to me one memorable time long before I'd learned how to listen for the wisdom inside me. At a major turning point in my life, I consulted a psychic, and the message I received still remains a guide. Reverend Miller looked a lot like Colonel Sanders, but instead of dispensing Kentucky Fried, he served up his own brand of wise guidance. Overwhelmed by indecision, and a little desperate for some good advice, I made an appointment. At five dollars a reading, what was there to lose?

I made my way past the clutter of books in his living room and sat down before him to lay out my problem. There were several directions I could go in my life, and I didn't know which one to choose. Every one of them seemed good, I told him, but what if I blew it by choosing the wrong way?

Reverend Miller listened intently as I poured out my confusion, then closed his eyes and sat there for what felt like an eternity. I imagined he was consulting with the spirit guides he often spoke about. Finally, he opened his eyes and looked straight at me.

"Well, I'm not going to tell you what to do," he pronounced. My disappointment must have been obvious as I sighed. Just as I began wondering if this was worth the five dollars after all, he spoke again: "But I will tell you one thing."

"Yes?" I replied eagerly. Reverend Miller looked at me with great kindness and a clarity that came from years of being a keen student of life. "It doesn't matter," he said.

"What do you mean it doesn't matter? That's my life you're talking about," I shot back, incredulous and somewhat annoyed. At that, the Reverend proceeded to give me my money's worth.

"Fear blocks any movement on your journey," he began. "But once you get past that and take the first step, life opens up and shows you what to do next." He went on to say that we might find that a choice clearly leads us to the goal we wanted, or we may discover after a while that another option is better. But either way we learn valuable lessons. Or we might start out thinking we know where a certain choice is leading us, and in the process, other possibilities and opportunities we never could have imagined turn up. "Any way you choose, it doesn't matter," he said. "If you listen carefully and you're patient, life will lead you where you need to go as you continue on your journey."

It was the best five dollars I ever spent. And over time I saw that Reverend Miller was right. When I listen to fear, things only get more confusing. But if I let go of the fear and just move forward, the way becomes clear.

Einstein is reported to have said that the most important question we can ask ourselves is: "Is the Universe friendly?" That's a question that comes up when we talk about trusting life. One could make a good a case for the Universe being unfriendly. Life is filled with suffering and the good times don't last. We lose people we love and at any moment something thing terrible could happen. Maybe the only answer to the question is: It depends upon how we choose to look at it. And that choice affects our experience of life.

*Pessimists are up to eight times more likely to become depressed (than optimists) when bad events happen; they do worse in school, sports and most jobs than their talents augur; they have worse physical health, shorter lives and rockier interpersonal relations. Teaching ten-year-old children the skills of optimistic thinking and action cuts their rate of depression in half when they go through puberty.*

—MARTIN SELIGMAN, IN
AUTHENTIC HAPPINESS

I choose to answer Einstein's question with a resounding *Yes!* When life is hard, we learn to deepen our compassion and understanding. When it's wonderful, we can enjoy our good fortune gratefully. The more I see that each moment of my life, good or bad, is a gift, the more I trust that I can let go into life.

Learning to trust life is a lot like learning to swim. The first time you're on your own in the water, you flail around, sure you're going to drown. Then as you relax a bit, you see that treading water is possible. Finally, when you let go completely and just relax, you find that you are magically held up by the water. It was ready to support you all the time. You just needed to trust enough to relax and let it do that.

When you stop flailing around and let yourself relax in trust, you begin to see that life is not out to get you but is instead a beautiful ocean in which you are swimming. The more you tune in to your peaceful center, the more confidence you develop in your ability to "stay afloat" no matter what is happening. The more you rest in being, the more you trust life. And the more you trust life, the more you can let yourself be guided by the wisdom available to you in that profound relaxation.

I had a glimpse of knowing what it would be like to so profoundly trust life that I would have no fear. It has been a guiding aspiration ever since. On one of my trips to India, I traveled to Lucknow to spend some time with a remarkable teacher, H. W. L. Poonja, called Poonjaji or Papaji by his students. Earlier in life he had been in the British Army, and he and his wife had raised a family. By the time I met him he was eighty years old, yet one of the most vital human beings I'd ever encountered. His electric smile alone made me feel more alive.

As a student of Ramana Maharshi, a great Indian sage who taught the philosophy of nondualism, Poonjaji was committed to getting his students beyond simply developing a meditation practice. He wanted them to have the direct realization that their true nature is much vaster than the limited idea they had of themselves. The route to his goal was simply relaxing the mind and letting go deeply into their *beingness*. By that time I had been a teacher of mindfulness meditation for a dozen years. In my experience, training the mind took a lot of effort, which seemed necessary in order to reap the many benefits I'd seen in myself and countless others. And here he was telling me to stop all effort and let go of any doing as the method to free the mind. I was intrigued by Poonjaji's approach but skeptical. Yet little by little I found myself putting aside my thoughts and questions and simply melting into the incredibly delicious and powerful energy of Poonjaji's presence and love.

At one point he asked me a question, and as I searched inside for the answer, I went deeper and deeper, as if being pulled into a vortex. I'm not sure exactly what happened next, but it seemed that my mind short-circuited and stopped. When I came back, it was like I'd taken a trip into Eternity. I found myself looking at Poonjaji with deep love and appreciation. As our eyes met I sensed a strong energy flowing between us, along with the feeling that both of us were connected to one big ocean of *being*—the same ocean of being that I sensed as the source of all life. Whether it's called love, awareness, God, Self, or the Divine, I knew I was always held by it, that I could trust it, and that the way to knowing it was through simply relaxing into being.

## WITHIN YOU AND WITHOUT YOU

We are part of life. How could we not be? We breathe in what the trees and plants breathe out and vice versa. We live in an entirely interconnected Universe. Thich Nhat Hanh talks about seeing that the paper you are reading these words on contains "the cloud, the forest, the logger." The fact that all things are connected in this way he calls "interbeing." In this complex web of interdependence, every living being is part of and affects everything else. The "butterfly effect" in chaos theory holds that a butterfly flapping its wings in Asia contributes to conditions that can result in a tornado in Oklahoma. A mutating virus in one part of the world causes ripples of fear across the entire globe. Just as we are not separate from our environment, we are also continually "interbeing" with all the other humans who make up our lives, from our ancestors to musicians on the other side of the ocean. A scruffy band from Liverpool, writing songs about love, can transform a global culture. As John Lennon put it: "I am he as you are he as you are me and we are all together."

> *When you know you're the ocean, the waves don't scare you."*
> —JENNIFER WELWOOD, POET AND PSYCHOLOGIST

We can understand interconnectedness as a concept, but knowing it through experience is what helps us to live in accordance with this reality. Alexa, the young woman who did her masters thesis on her journey from self-hatred to self-love, wrote:

I can listen to myriad eco-psychologists tell me that I need to envision a world in which I know that I am a bit of the walking skin of the Earth. I can listen to the story of the Universe and be intellectually inspired, but it is not until I can integrate the concept of interconnection into a whole body, mind, heart experience that I truly know I am connected to all else.

For Alexa that experience comes through her spiritual practice, and through connecting with others through their personal stories. She says, "Through various spiritual paths, we begin to see our interdependence throughout the Earth community. Through sharing our stories, we can begin to *feel* connection." Through the many stories in this book you may have identified with, you have experienced interbeing with others. You have found yourself in them.

Knowing our interconnection changes our sense of who we are. Biologist Lewis Thomas reveals in a fascinating way how the cells of our body are "ecosystems more complex than Jamaica Bay." In *Lives of a Cell* he writes:

> A good case can be made for our non-existence as entities . . . We are shared, rented, occupied. At the interior of our own cells, driving them, providing the oxidative energy that sends us out for the improvement of each shining day, are mitochondria, and in a strict sense they are not ours. They turn out to be little separate creatures . . . replicating in their own fashion, privately, with their own DNA and RNA quite different from ours. Without them, we would not move a muscle, drum a finger, think a thought . . .

Thomas's recognition of "our non-existence as entities" is echoed in modern psychology, neuroscience, and Buddhist philosophy, all of which say we do not have a self separate from the complex process that sustains our existence. Buckminster Fuller said we are not nouns, we are verbs—fields of activity happening with thoughts and moods coming and going, countless sensations happening simultaneously, blood flowing, nervous system firing, hormones shooting through. We are a mind-body process that gives rise to a sense of a continuous, cohesive identity.

In an interview with Steve Donoso in *The Sun* magazine, Eckhart Tolle said:

> [I]f I am not who I think I am; and I am not who everybody I know has been telling me I am; and I am not the story in my head; and I am not the beliefs, the accumulated experiences, the memory

traces—then who am I? Every answer to that question is dangerous, because every word that one might use will create another concept. The reality of who you are can never be expressed in words. Words are only signposts that point the way.

Tolle's words point toward that aware presence that observes and knows that we are thinking, feeling, loving, living. When we go beyond the illusion of separation, we see that on a deeper level we are connected to everything else in a way that sounds like what mystics throughout the ages have talked about. It's that ocean of being I felt with Poonjaji. From that awake and aware presence arises the love that consciously links us to all creation, from the mitochondria to the stars.

*My sister was only a very tiny child then, and she was drinking her milk, and all of a sudden I saw that she was God and the milk was God. I mean, all she was doing was pouring God into God, if you know what I mean."*
—J.D. SALINGER, FROM "TEDDY," IN *NINE STORIES*

As you become increasingly familiar with the stillness and contentment of being, you lay the ground for a deep, abiding happiness. The last time I saw Ram Dass, he told me he was writing a book on contentment. When I asked him if he could sum up the secret of contentment, he looked at me with a smile and slowly said, "Plumb the depths of this moment." When you do that, you may find not only a new aliveness and wakefulness but an avenue to "the peace that surpasses all understanding."

In doing this program, you've developed various states of well-being and probably taken some significant steps in your life. You've seen that there are many ways to find happiness. This is a lifelong process, and as you continue this journey, you will deepen your connection to joy and allow it more and more to shine through. The great Sufi poet Rumi said, "Keep knocking, and the joy inside will eventually open a window and look out to see who's there."

May you be happy.

# ACKNOWLEDGMENTS

We are both deeply grateful to Toni Burbank, our acquiring editor at Bantam and one of the publishing industry's all-time greats, who welcomed this book with her hallmark enthusiasm and warmth. Beyond offering feedback on our initial drafts that significantly strengthened the material, she was a friend who offered heartfelt support. Danielle Perez carried the manuscript onward to completion, asking intelligent and insightful questions with a perspective that opened the door to a broad readership. She went beyond the norm in including us in the process, willingly responding to our ongoing requests and suggestions. Her vision and careful attention to detail at every point allowed the book to become all we had hoped it might be. We also appreciate and share Danielle's love of canine companions. Stephanie Tade, our agent, had unwavering faith in our proposal and landed it swiftly and expertly in the hands of our dream publisher. She embodies what this book is about—joy, compassion, caring, and integrity.

We are deeply grateful to Danna Faulds, who graced this book with her beautiful and profound poetry. Wise and heartful, her poems capture the essence of the teachings and elucidate the steps that awaken joy. We also thank Dr. Rick Hanson for his brilliant intellect and kind heart. Even in the midst of his own book deadlines, he offered careful feedback on our neuroscience references and was always forthcoming with an impressive mental index of resources. Jack Kornfield read an early draft of the manuscript and offered feedback that steered the book in the right direction. Joseph Goldstein answered some critical questions as we grappled with fine points about the nature of reality that ultimately went the way of non-being in the text. Fred Goldsmith and Ed Gerstenhaber did meticulous readings of the manuscript and offered insightful comments from welcome and needed perspectives. Jane Baraz read every chapter, sometimes in several drafts, always making useful suggestions, even at the eleventh hour.

James:

It gives me great happiness to express my appreciation to everyone who made this book possible. I want to begin by saying that from the start this book has been a collaborative effort—a fruition of thirty-three years of friendship and ongoing conversation into the nature of true happiness. I first met Shoshana on my second meditation retreat in 1976. Overwhelmed and feeling not a little self-pity with a mountain of lunch pots to clean, this fellow retreatant came up to me whispering in an angelic voice, "Would you like some help?" I gratefully said yes and I've been benefiting from her help and support ever since. It was Shoshana who first encouraged me to write this book. In working together, she not only skillfully helped me clarify my ideas every step of the way, but also contributed her decades of spiritual wisdom and writing expertise. Although writing a book is not easy, the process for me included many moments of true joy and deep gratitude for our co-creation.

The Awakening Joy course, which the book is based on, has come about through the amazing grace and dedication of an extraordinary team, starting with Gretchen Thomas, whose technical know-how and incredible generosity helped take it from a small group of participants to an online course that has reached thousands. "Thank you" doesn't begin to cover it. Deep bows to Mary Helen Fein, who created a fabulous website that's both engaging and easy to navigate. Jane Baraz's wisdom, judgment, and hard work have consistently steered the course in the right direction. Kate Janke, course coordinator, has brought dedication and her natural radiance to make the participants feel welcome and part of something special. Gratitude to all the other behind-the-scenes people who've made the course a success: Deborah Todd, Andy McGuire, Nathan Friedkin, Jill Goodfriend, Deborah Henry, and Shoshana Cole. Northbrae Community Church and especially Bob Davis gave us our home.

A big thank you to my special Joy Buddy Patricia Ellsberg, whose Big Love comes through her guided meditations, inviting participants to directly experience the various course themes. Musicians Eve Decker, Betsy Rose, Jennifer Berezan, and Melanie DeMore bring wisdom and inspiration to their music and allow everyone to experience the joy of song. I'm grateful to the stellar lineup of speakers—happiness experts, neuroscientists, and wisdom teachers—who bring to life the points I'm trying to convey. Special thanks to Rick Foster and Greg Hicks whose book *How We Choose to Be Happy* originally inspired me to create the course and was a valuable resource for the earlier courses. Deep appreciation to Rick and Greg, as well as all the other presenters at the Awakening Joy course in Berkeley, many of whose words are included in this book: Sylvia Boorstein, Rick Hanson, M. J. Ryan, Dacher Keltner, Marci Shimoff, Catherine Ingram, Anam Thubten Rinpoche, Jack Kornfield, Paul Ekman, Carolyn Hobbs, Guy Armstrong, and Dan Clurman.

I feel tremendous appreciation to all the people who have participated in the Awakening Joy course these last six years, and a special debt of gratitude to those who so generously shared their words and stories.

I am so blessed to have the friendship, wisdom, encouragement, and support of my teaching colleagues at Spirit Rock Meditation Center and am grateful to Spirit Rock, including the staff and Board, for being the beacon of consciousness that it is.

My main spiritual teachers and benefactors, Joseph Goldstein and Ram Dass, put me on the road to real happiness and have inspired and guided me since 1974. I pay homage to the Buddha for showing a way to end suffering and to the highest happiness. My undying gratitude to Neem Karoli Baba, who has guided this project from the beginning.

The sincerity and support of the Insight Meditation Community of Berkeley inspires me to find something useful to say every Thursday night. Special appreciation to Giedra Gershman, Joyce Rybandt, Nancy Benson-Smith, Ross Smith, Gay Gale, Joyce Kelley, Suzy Sloka, Jim French, Ernie Isaacs, Janet Keyes, Jennifer Braun, John Porter, Jenya Zellerbach, Isabella

Wilk, Mac Lingo, Dave Seabury, and Hime Levine for their incredible support. Also, great thanks to the Berkeley Buddhist Monastery and Rev. Heng Sure, for their gracious hospitality all these years.

I'm so grateful to the Dedicated Practitioner Program groups I lead for their ongoing wisdom, encouragement, and support as well as to all the Community Dharma Leaders who help me feel a part of a large network of people who have taught so many to discover deep peace and freedom for themselves. A big thank you to the group of young dharma mentors I have the privilege to guide—Alexa Ouellett, Anthony Rodgers, Kate Janke, Erin Hill, Oren Sofer, Aline Prentice, and Will Henry—part of the next generation who will share these principles so skillfully and touch so many people in the coming years.

Thanks to Daveen and Alan Fox and Lynn and Henry Moody, who generously provided me space to write. Sylvia Bell-Tull spent many hours transcribing and Janet Keyes organized my earlier writings, which were the foundation for much of this book and the Awakening Joy course. Thanks to Adi Bemak, Steven Newmark, and Toni Burbank for encouraging me to find my own voice. Special thanks to Catherine Ingram, Tara Brach, and Anna Grete Mazziotta for being there during some hard times.

Selma Baraz, Susan Baraz, Tony Baraz, Adam Baraz, and my beloved Pal gave me all the support and love I could want. And finally, to the love of my life, Jane Baraz, who, through thick and thin, has been with me every step of the way: Thank you, thank you, thank you.

Shoshana:

I am deeply grateful to James for the joys and challenges we have shared in creating this book, which has been a rite of passage for both of us. Through thousands of hours on the phone, hundreds of emails, and dozens of hours side by side, we have shared not only the work but the ongoing story of our lives. Thank you for climbing the mountain together and for your sincere dedication to living with an open heart, and inspiring me to do the same. It has been an honor and a gift to help make the Awakening Joy course available as a book, and to discover that it absolutely works. During the course of this work, James's "other half," Jane Baraz, has in so many ways offered her understanding, wisdom, and insight. I am grateful for her mind and heart, and for our deepening friendship.

The love of friends and family has been my support and fall-net throughout this process. Elias Alexander willingly shared his mother with yet another book as he passed through his final years of childhood and emerged as an amazing young man. I am deeply grateful to Laurinda Gilmore Graves for her steady friendship, fierce support, and for always returning my calls. Sypko Andreae and Carolyn Shaffer conspired to feed me nutritious meals at critical times and in so many ways were there, including mini-celebrations along the way. If not for Carolyn, our dear dog would have spent many more endless hours lying in my office while I worked, only dreaming of running through meadows. My heart is filled with gratitude for the joy and constant love of that beautiful creature, Buddy-gi, and for her profound teaching as she graciously let go into death. Stephanie Phillips and AvYitz supported us both with such care during her long passage out of life.

Deedie and David Runkel rescued me and the book by putting us up in one of Anne Hathaway's cottages during a very tricky time. Deedie's waffles at the finish line also helped a lot. Kay Lynne Sherman opened her home, her garden, and her heart, and has been a perfect Findhorn housemate. My "sister" Lolly Roy has, as always, understood at the most profound levels. A special thanks to all the rest of Elias's godparents, including my godbrother Jerry Roy, my godsister Amy Fates, Sypko and Carolyn, G. and R., Ted and Laurinda, Max Lan, and Barbara and Arnie Meyer, for carrying my son while I carried this book. Enduring thanks to Janet King for her enormous wisdom and constancy, right up to the end, and to Norma Burton who walked me through the valley to the light. And to my mother, Carol Susan Berry, who is an inspiration and guide.

Special thanks to the members of my fiction and nonfiction writing groups, who understood and supported all those cancellations, listened with such gentle care, and brought food and chocolate when most needed. My soul-sisters of the word: Susan DuMond, Lori Henriksen, Carol Hwoschinsky, Alissa Lukara, Maggie McLaughlin, Deedie Runkel, Carolyn Shaffer, and Jodine Turner. I am also grateful to the Rogue Valley

Peace Choir, the beloved Ensemble, and the late, great Dave Marston for the nourishment and remembrance of song. So many others deserve gratitude, including Nancy Bloom, Linda and Manny Cohen, Ted Graves, Connie Toth-Berindei, and special mention goes to Carly Newfeld's son Joss Mulligan who passed a sleepless night on the couch while the final chapter was being hammered out over the phone in the next room.

Finally, I owe a debt of gratitude to those who have offered the clarity and wisdom of Buddhist philosophy and practice, including that triple gem many years ago—Jack, Joseph, and Sharon—and especially S. N. Goenka, who untied the boat and set it moving. What a joyous gift to be alive.

# BIBLIOGRAPHY

Barasch, Marc Ian. *Field Notes on the Compassionate Life: A Search for the Soul of Kindness*. Emmaus, PA: Rodale Press, 2006.

Bayda, Ezra. *Being Zen: Bringing Meditation to Life*. Boston: Shambhala Publications, 2002.

Begley, Sharon. *Train Your Mind, Change Your Brain: How a New Science Reveals Our Extraordinary Potential to Transform Ourselves*. New York: Ballantine Books, 2007.

Ben-Shahar, Tal. *Happier*. New York: McGraw Hill, 2007.

Boorstein, Sylvia. *Happiness Is an Inside Job.* New York: Ballantine Books, 2007.

Byron, Thomas. *The Dhammapada*. New York: Alfred A. Knopf, 1976.

Camus, Albert. "Return to Tipasa" in *The Myth of Sisyphus: and Other Essays*. New York: Vintage Books, 1955.

Canfield, Jack and Mark Victor Hansen. *A 3rd Serving of Chicken Soup for the Soul*. Deerfield Beach, FL: HCI, 1996.

Chodron, Pema. *No Time to Lose: A Timely Guide to the Way of the Bodhisattva*. Boston: Shambhala Publications, 2007.

Dalai Lama and Howard Cutler. *The Art of Happiness*. New York: Riverhead Books, 1998.

Dalai Lama and Howard Cutler. *Worlds in Harmony: Compassionate Action for a Better World*. Berkeley: Parallax Press, 2008.

Elkind, David. *The Power of Play: Learning What Comes Naturally*, New York: Da Capo Lifelong Books, 2008.

Ekman, Paul and the Dalai Lama. *Emotional Awareness: Overcoming the Obstacles to Psychological Balance and Compassion*. New York: Times Books, 2008.

Emmons, Robert. *Thanks.* New York: Houghton Mifflin, 2007.

Faulds, Danna. *Go In and In: Poems from the Heart of Yoga*. Greenville, NC: Peaceable Kingdom Books, 2002.

Faulds, Danna. *One Soul: More Poems from the Heart of Yoga*. Greenville, NC: Peaceable Kingdom Books, 2003.

Faulds, Danna. *Prayers to the Infinite: New Yoga Poems*. Greenville, NC: Peaceable Kingdom Books, 2004.

Faulds, Danna. *From Root to Bloom: New Yoga Poems and Other Writings*. Greenville, NC: Peaceable Kingdom Books, 2006.

Foster, Rick and Greg Hicks. *How We Choose to Be Happy: The 9 Choices of Extremely Happy People—Their Secrets, Their Stories*. New York: G.P. Putnam's Sons, 1999.

Golas, Thaddeus. *The Lazy Man's Guide to Enlightenment*. New York: Bantam, 1980.

Goleman, Daniel. *Destructive Emotions: A Scientific Dialogue with the Dalai Lama*. New York: Bantam, 2003.

Haidt, Jonathan. "Elevation and the Positive Psychology of Morality" in *Flourishing: Positive Psychology and the Life Well-Lived*. Corey L. M. Keyes and Jonathan Haidt, Eds. Washington, DC: American Psychological Association, 2003.

Hanson, Rick. *Buddha's Brain: The Practical Neuroscience of Happiness, Love and Wisdom*. Oakland, California: New Harbinger Publications, Inc., 2009.

Harvey, Andrew. *Light Upon Light: Inspirations from Rumi*. Berkeley, CA: North Atlantic Books, 1996.

Hobbs, Carolyn. *Joy, No Matter What*. Boston: Conari Press, 2005.

Kabat-Zinn, Jon. *Full Catastrophe Living: Using the Wisdom of Your Body and Mind to Face Stress, Pain, and Illness*. New York: Delacorte Press, 1990.

Keltner, Dacher. *Born to Be Good: The Science of a Meaningful Life*. New York: W.W. Norton & Company, Inc., 2009.

Kornfield, Jack. *The Art of Forgiveness, Lovingkindness, and Peace*. New York: Bantam, 2002.

Kornfield, Jack and Paul Breiter. *A Still Forest Pool: The Insight Meditation of Achaan Cha*. Wheaton, Illinois: Quest Books, 1985.

Levine, Stephen. *Who Dies? An Investigation of Conscious Living and Conscious Dying*. New York: Anchor Books, 1982.

Luskin, Fred. *Forgive for Good: A Proven Prescription for Health and Happiness*. New York: HarperCollins, 2002.

Lyubomirsky, Sonja. *The How of Happiness: A Scientific Approach to Getting the Life You Want*. New York: Penguin Group, 2007.

Makransky, John. *Awakening Through Love*. Somerville, MA: Wisdom Publications, 2007.

Maslow, Abraham. *The Farther Reaches of Human Nature*. New York: Viking, 1971.

McKibben, Bill. *Deep Economy: The Wealth of Communities and the Durable Future*. New York: Henry Holt & Company, 2008.

Muller, Wayne. *Sabbath: Finding Rest, Renewal, and Delight in Our Busy Lives*. New York: Bantam Books, 2000.

Myers, David. *The Pursuit of Happiness: Who Is Happy and Why?* New York: Harper Paperbacks, 1993.

Nisargadatta, Maharaj. *I Am That*. Durham, NC: Acorn Press, 1990.

Peace Pilgrim. *Peace Pilgrim: Her Life and Work in Her Own Words*. Santa Fe, NM: Ocean Tree Books, 1992.

Ram Dass. *Be Here Now*. New York: Three Rivers Press (CA), 1971.

Ram Dass. *Still Here: Embracing Aging, Changing, and Dying*. New York: Riverhead Books, 2001.

Rea, Rashani. *Beyond Brokenness*. Xlibris Publishing, 2009.

Riera, Michael. *Uncommon Sense for Parents with Teenagers*. Berkeley: Celestial Arts, 2004.

Ryan, M.J. *Attitudes of Gratitude*. San Francisco: Conari Press, 2009.

de Saint-Exupery, Antoine. *The Little Prince*. Translated by Richard Howard. New York: Harcourt, Inc., 2000. [First published New York: Reynal & Hitchcock, 1943.]

Salinger, J.D. "Teddy" in *Nine Stories*. New York: Bantam Books, 1964.

Seligman, Martin. *Authentic Happiness: Using the New Positive Psychology to Realize Your Potential for Lasting Fulfillment*. New York: Free Press, 2002.

Sengtsan, Chien Chih (The Third Zen Patriarch of China). *Verses on the Faith Mind* (Hsin Hsin Ming). Translated by Richard B. Clarke. Toronto: Coach House Press, 1973.

Shah, Idries. *The Exploits of the Incomparable Mulla Nasrudin / The Subtleties of the Inimitable Mulla*. London: Octagon Press Ltd., 1983.

Shimoff, Marci with Carol Kline. *Happy for No Reason*. New York: Free Press, 2008.

Siegel, Daniel J. *The Mindful Brain: Reflection and Attunement in the Cultivation of Well-Being*. New York: W.W. Norton and Company, 2007.

Steindl-Rast, Brother David. *Gratefulness, the Heart of Prayer*. Ramsey, NJ: Paulist Press, 1984.

Swimme, Brian. *The Universe Is a Green Dragon: A Cosmic Creation Story*. Santa Fe, NM: Bear & Company, 1984.

Thomas, Lewis. *The Lives of a Cell*. New York: Penguin Books, 1978.

Thubten, Anam Rinpoche. *No Self, No Problem*. Ithaca, New York: Snow Lion Publications, 2009.

Tolle, Eckhart. *A New Earth: Awakening to Your Life's Purpose*. New York: Dutton, 2005.

Watts, Alan. *The Wisdom of Insecurity*. New York: Pantheon Books, 1951.

Williamson, Marianne. *A Return to Love*. New York: HarperCollins, 1992.

Wolcott, Harry F. *Sneaky Kid and Its Aftermath: Ethics and Intimacy in Fieldwork*. Walnut Creek, CA: Altamira Press, 2002.

# JAMES BARAZ'S ADDITIONAL RECOMMENDED READING LIST

Brach, Tara. *Radical Acceptance: Embracing Your Life with the Heart of a Buddha*. New York: Bantam Books, 2003.

Boorstein, Sylvia. *It's Easier Than You Think*. New York: HarperCollins, 1995.

Coleman, Mark. *Awake in the Wild: Mindfulness in Nature as a Path of Self-Discovery*. Maui, HI: Inner Ocean Publishing, 2006.

Das, Lama Surya. *Awakening the Buddha Within*. New York: Broadway Books, 1997.

Goldstein, Joseph. *The Experience of Insight*. Boston: Shambhala Publications, 1976.

Goldstein, Joseph. *One Dharma*. San Francisco: HarperSanFrancisco, 2002.

Goldstein, Joseph and Jack Kornfield. *Seeking the Heart of Wisdom*. Boston: Shambhala Publications, 1987.

Goleman, Daniel. *Emotional Intelligence*. New York: Bantam, 1995.

Kabat-Zinn, Jon. *Full Catastrophe Living: Using the Wisdom of Your Body and Mind to Face Stress, Pain and Illness*. New York: Delta, 1990.

Kornfield, Jack. *A Path with Heart*. New York: Bantam, 1993.

Kornfield, Jack. *The Wise Heart: A Guide to the Universal Teachings of Buddhist Psychology*. New York: Bantam Books, 2009.

Macy, Joanna. *World as Lover, World as Self*. Berkeley: Parallax Press, 1991.

Moffitt, Phillip. *Dancing with Life: Buddhist Insights for Finding Meaning and Joy in the Face of Suffering*. New York: Rodale Inc., 2008.

Ricard, Matthieu. *Happiness: A Guide to Developing Life's Most Important Skill*. New York: Little, Brown and Company, 2007.

Rothberg, Donald. *The Engaged Spiritual Life: The Buddhist Approach to Transforming Ourselves and the World*. Boston: Beacon Press, 2008.

Ryan, M.J. *The Happiness Makeover: How to Teach Yourself to Be Happy and Enjoy Every Day*. New York: Broadway Books, 2005.

Salzberg, Sharon. *Lovingkindness: The Revolutionary Art of Happiness*. Boston: Shambhala, 1995.

Salzberg, Sharon. *Faith: Trusting Your Deepest Experience*. New York: Riverhead Books, 2002.

Tolle, Eckhart. *The Power of Now*. Novato: New World Library, 1999.

Weisman, Arinna and Jean Smith. *The Beginner's Guide to Insight Meditation*. New York: Bell Tower, 2001.

Winston, Diana. *Wide Awake: A Buddhist Guide for Teens*. New York: Berkley Books, 2003.

## WEBSITES FOR JAMES BARAZ

**jamesbaraz.com.** For all of James Baraz's retreats, classes, workshops, and articles, and a link to his recorded talks.

**awakeningjoy.info.** For information and to sign up for the Awakening Joy course.

**insightberkeley.org.** For schedule and information on James Baraz's Berkeley meditation community, and an archive of recordings of all weekly lectures.

## ADDITIONAL RESOURCES

**accesstoinsight.org.** A comprehensive collection of the Buddha's translated discourses and commentaries by Buddhist teachers and scholars.

**authentichappiness.org.** The website of Positive Psychologist Martin Seligman. Includes questionnaires to measure your happiness level and archived copies of newletters on topics related to happiness.

**dharma.org.** For a schedule of retreats at the Insight Meditation Center in Barre, Massachusetts.

**dharmaseed.org.** For talks and lectures by well-known Western teachers of Theravada Buddhism.

**focusonaids.com.** For information on Focus on AIDS, its periodic fund-raisers, and to learn about its humanitarian projects around the world.

**greatergoodmag.org.** For cutting-edge research on the science of well-being, from the Greater Good Science Center at the University of California at Berkeley. Edited by Dacher Keltner, Ph.D., and Jason Marsh.

**mindfulschools.org.** For information and research on teaching mindfulness techniques to children in all education settings.

**PatriciaEllsberg.com.** For free downloads of Patricia Ellsberg's guided meditations for each step of the Awakening Joy course.

**ramdass.org.** For Ram Dass's teachings and schedule.

**spiritrock.org.** For the schedule of retreats and workshops at Spirit Rock Meditation Center in Woodacre, California.

**wisebrain.org.** The website of Rick Hanson, Ph.D., and Rick Mendius, M.D., focusing on the connections between psychology, neurology, and contemplative practices. Archived articles and copies of the Wise Brain Bulletin.

# ABOUT THE AUTHORS

JAMES BARAZ has been teaching meditation for more than thirty years and the Awakening Joy course, both on-site and online, since 2003. He is a cofounder of Spirit Rock Meditation Center in Woodacre, California, where he regularly teaches, and he leads retreats and workshops around the United States and abroad. He lives with his wife, Jane, in Berkeley, California. Learn more about the course at www.awakeningjoy.info and James's other activities at jamesbaraz.com.

SHOSHANA TEMBECK ALEXANDER has studied Buddhism since 1970 and is the author of *In Praise of Single Parents* and *Women's Ventures, Women's Visions,* and, with the Findhorn Community, *The Findhorn Garden.* She has guided various works of several prominent Buddhist authors, including Tara Brach, Sharon Salzberg, and Wes Nisker. She lives in Ashland, Oregon.